A Life of Service

THE MEMOIRS OF

MAURICE LUSH

1896 - 1990

Edited by A J M Lush

Published by A J M Lush, 97 Larkhall Rise, London SW4 6HR

Copyright © A J M Lush 1992

ISBN 0 9520687 0 2

Printed by Trinity Press, 37A Orlando Road, London SW4 0LD

Brigadier M. S. Lush CB, CBE, MC

23 Nov 1896 – 20 May 1990

CONTENTS

				Page
INTRODUCTION by Julian Lush				i
PREFACE – England in 1896				ii
Chapter				
	EARLY YEARS			
1	Childhood in Ryde, Brighton and Twickenham		1896-1905	1
2	School : Holland House and Tonbridge		1905-15	7
3	World War I		1915-19	13
	SUDAN POLITICAL SERVICE			
4	Secretary, British Legation, Addis Ababa	Abyssinia	1919-22	25
5	Intelligence Department, Sudan Government	Khartoum	1922-23	37
	Asst. District Commissioner, Kasala Province	Gedaref	1924-26	40
6	District Commissioner, Khartoum	Khartoum	1927-28	55
	Assistant Civil Secretary, Sudan Government	Khartoum	1928-29	58
	Private Secretary to Governor General	Khartoum	1929-30	65
7	Deputy Governor, White Nile Province	el Dueim	1930-32	75
	Deputy Governor, Upper Nile Province	Malakal	1932-34	79
8	Sudan Agent	Cairo	1935-38	87
9	Governor, Northern Province	Damer	1938-40	101
	WORLD WAR II – MILITARY ADMINISTRATION			
10	Chief Political Officer, OETA	ETHIOPIA	1941-42	119
11	CPO / Military Administrator, BMA	MADAGASCAR	1942	141
12	Chief Civil Affairs Officer, BMA	TRIPOLITANIA	1942-43	153
13	Chief of Staff & Vice President, Allied Commission	ITALY	1943-46	173
	POST WAR – INTERNATIONAL SERVICE			
14	Resident Representative for Germany/Austria, IGCR	GERMANY	1946-47	241
	Chief of Mission in Middle East/Africa, IRO	CAIRO	1947-49	249
	Special Representative for Middle East, IRO	GENEVA	1949-51	265
15	Representative, Anglo-Saxon Petroleum Company	LIBYA	1952-56	281
	Arab Adviser, Anglo-Saxon Petroleum Company	QATAR	1952	287
16	Managing Director, Pakistan Shell Oil Company	PAKISTAN	1956-59	299
POSTSCRIPT by Julian Lush				319
Appendix I – Decorations				321
Appendix II – Obituaries				322
Appendix III – Bidding Prayers				326

Introduction

It was during the course of the many occasions that the family foregathered at Brantridge Forest in the 1960-70s that the seeds of the notion that Maurice, our father, should write his memoirs were sown. It was a multiple seeding; the first casts struck stoney, reluctant ground but eventually they were to germinate and flourish into the huge tree - perhaps an arboretum - we now have.

Maurice and Diana spent 12 years at Brantridge Forest - by far the longest period together in any one place, and probably the happiest period of their joint lives. While here at Brantridge they saw all three of their offspring married and produce grandchildren; here they attracted an astonishing number of friends they had met over the previous years; above all, here was another garden of unsurpassed scale for them to tame and nurture. Over the table or after Maurice's piano playing and dinner, the talk would often turn to episodes from the past - mostly hilarious but some (e.g. wartime events) harrowing. To us of the younger generation it became quite clear that these episodes, and indeed the full background story, should be recorded for posterity - if Maurice could face the task. And so the seeds were sown.

But it was not until the transition from Brantridge Forest, because its upkeep had simply become too much for them to handle, to Kensington that the seeds took root. Then, mustering all his natural determination, towards the age of 85, Maurice sat down to write the story his life. As anyone can see, it was a monumental accomplishment: every word of the text - indeed, very many more in the drafting - was written in his longhand; it is a tribute to his classically trained hand that, for the several initial typists, his manuscript remained remarkably legible to the end. As time went on and he came to write or re-write the last sections, the time of day for this task was during the afternoon when Diana had her rest: sometimes the script bears the evidence - the track of his pen wandering dazedly over the page - that Maurice too needed and took some respite. For at 92, it had become a real labour on which he was working to the end.

When eventually Maurice had a stroke which rendered him devoid of coherent speech, I had seen enough of the draft to be able to assure him that his memoirs were virtually complete and to undertake to see them through to publication for his family and friends. I think this, as well as assurances about Diana, left him finally freed of his life's labours, for he died just a few days later.

The editing, in which Sylvia and Meriel have assisted, has been quite a task in itself. The work is, of course, too long: but then, his was a long and highly eventful life and there are important parts that have to be stated as he wrote them. Should it then, be cut down? Sylvia, Meriel and I decided against this and to leave the text virtually in its entirety, only eliminating repetitions, adding a few details and making adjustments where necessary. These are Maurice's own Memoirs.

A.J.M.L.
September 1992

Preface

England in 1896

The London Times of 24 November 1896 contained, no doubt, a variety of interesting news; to me the most significant item was the announcement, on the front page, of the birth, on 23 November, at "Navarino", Ryde, to the wife of Hubert S Lush, of a son.

In later years my mother asserted quite definitely (in a reply-paid telegram to my wife and me, who were staying with a horoscope-casting cousin in Switzerland) that I was born an hour before midnight. If her memory was correct, how did the admittedly important news reach Printing House Square in time for insertion in the issue of 24 November? There was surely no telephone between Ryde and London, and the Ryde telegraph office was as surely closed. The word telecommunications had hardly been invented - but they seemed to have excelled that night!

In this story of my life, however, I hope there will be few such mysteries: the purpose of autobiographies must be to pull back the curtains, not to draw them closer.

It may be interesting to recollect the conditions of the England into which I was born - some 90 years ago. The Old Queen, Victoria, was in the sixty-ninth year of her reign. The great majority of her subjects, including my parents, had never known any other monarch: had never seen any but Victoria's head on a penny coin nor on a half penny stamp (the tariff for a postcard). My Grandmother was six years of age when Victoria came to the Throne. Unofficially the reigning monarch was always referred to as the "Old Queen" and better known from the oleographs which adorned the walls of countless of her subjects' houses than from the commissioned works of art or the sketches in the newspapers of the Empress of India. She was an established institution but, when she died, her subjects felt that they had lost an aged friend rather than a Queen; and while the long funeral procession proclaimed the greatness of Britain, the coffin bore a Queen who had ceased, long since, to represent or even understand the attitudes of her people. They, her subjects, at home and abroad respectfully adored her memory.

She had always been intent on exercising an influence in politics, determined to be no cipher. Her influence in foreign affairs could never be discounted, for she was in close family relationships with most of the ruling families of Europe, and her correspondence with them was voluminous - all in manuscript.

I cannot remember ever having seen the Old Lady though my perambulator must often have been near Osborne, but I recollect vividly the minute guns of the Queen's Troop of the Royal Horse Artillery firing on the afternoon of her death in 1901, and causing the horse pulling the hansom cab, in which my aunt, my sister and I were travelling, to bolt around Hyde Park Corner. I was 4 then and I can claim this as my first, and very alarming memory. I cannot remember the wild and exaggerated scenes in which Britons celebrated the relief of Mafeking - a relief indeed to the endless stories of defeats in the disastrous Boer War which ended in victory; but the great soldier in South Africa "Bobs" (General Lord Roberts of Khandahar as he became) was a household name then and came into my life some years later.

Going back to 1896 one can read in the review of that year, compiled by The London Times, that "the peace of the world has been threatened in more quarters than one". The boundary dispute between Venezuela and British Guiana, over which the President of the USA was said to have shown "marked hostility to Great Britain" was deemed worthy of such a title: another was, prophetically, the Jameson raid into the Transvaal, the ill-fated venture carried out in the name of Rhodes and which led later to the annexation of the Rhodesias by the British South Africa Company. Also, with an eye to the future, it is worth recording that in 1896 General Sir Herbert Kitchener, Sirdar of the Egyptian Army, sent forward the Anglo Egyptian expedition against the Dervishes of the Sudan and occupied Dongola on the Nile. At the same time General Marchand left France to occupy Fashoda (higher up the Nile), the Italians were defeated by the Abyssinians at Adowa and France annexed Madagascar - all countries about which, if you persevere, you will read in the following pages. The increased militarism in Europe was demonstrated and countered by the British Navy, the most powerful and widely dispersed naval force in the world, mobilising a "Particular Service" consisting of two battleships, four cruisers and a flotilla of torpedo boats, "a task force ready to steam anywhere": an economical and successful way of ruling the waves.

Anglican orders had been declared invalid by the latest Papal Bull, a decree which The Times hoped would put an end to "much foolish talk about reunion". Meanwhile the universities were trembling with the controversy over degrees for women.

At the theatres, those older than I could attend performances of The Mikado, Charley's Aunt, The Prisoner of Zenda, or popular concerts at the Queen's Hall (Henry Wood did not start Promenade Concerts there until 1895). Alternatives to theatre-going included an advertisement by Thomas Cook for a "hundred miles of the Nile for one hundred pounds (with electric light in all the steamer cabins)"; or "65 days in the Barbados for £65". These passengers were more fortunate, presumably, than the "irate passenger" who wrote to The Times complaining about a dearth of foot warmers in the otherwise unheated carriages on the London and North Western Railway (it was November).

I was born into an England admiring, with affectionate pride, the presence of her aged sovereign, but admiring still more the great Empire which had been built before and during her reign, an Empire which brought dominance, wealth and pride to the British nation and, in many quarters, a belief that it was the mission and the duty of England to lead the world. The first fifty years of my life were to see the British nation sacrifice the flower of her population in two wars, fought with unflinching moral and physical courage, firstly to maintain that dominance and secondly to prevent its usurpation by forces which were rightly deemed evil; moreover, England herself was on the verge of a great social upheaval, for which it was ill prepared; the country had reached the end of Liberal England, of the rule of aristocratic and inherited leadership, of remarkable self reliance. History will decide, and it is too early in the 20th century to bring our nation to judgement, but coming from a middle class family with no wealth nor heritage of leadership among my forebears (indeed we were remarkably poor), I believe that my country fulfilled her task adequately as a dominant power, fought successfully with immense courage and self sacrifice to save the world from the dominance of evil, and still, having overcome her present weakness and weariness and apparent national sickness, still has a great part to play in the moral leadership of an apparently unhappy and fragmented world.

We can, I hold, look back to the past with great national pride and thanksgiving, to the present with prayer for perseverance and to the future with ever growing hope for fulfilment of our part.

Early Years

CHAPTER 1

Childhood in Ryde, Brighton and Twickenham 1896 - 1905

Ryde, Isle of Wight

I cannot remember the house where I was born - Navarino, Spencer Road, Ryde, though I have a blurred vision of an oak tree in the garden. The house exists to this day. There my parents had lived since their marriage in 1887 and my mother had produced three children - Josephine who died in infancy, Cecil born in 1890 (nearly called Gordon for he was born on the sixth anniversary of the death in Khartoum of General Charles George Gordon) and Christine, three years my elder. (Seventy-five years later she would introduce me as "my younger brother"!) We were all christened at All Saints' Church, Ryde, where my parents were regular worshippers. My mother, Florence Clark, was a devout but broad-minded Christian who taught us, at her knees, the true values of faith, hope and love.

My father, a solicitor, practised in Portsmouth, where my grandfather was a master brewer, living in Southsea and owner of a number of house properties in the neighbourhood, all mortgaged to the hilt! Father commuted daily by the Solent ferry. He adored that ferry to the end of his day.

Brighton

Then in 1899 we left Ryde and moved to Brighton. My first visual memory of my new home town is a clothes mangle in the yard of the apartment house where we stayed for a week or so in Springfield Road, Brighton, near the railway viaduct carrying the Lewes line, while my parents searched for an office and a house. Why we moved to Brighton I never knew. I suspect that my parents left Ryde because grandfather Joseph Lush wanted a higher rent for Navarino which was his property, and that Brighton's record of sunshine and educational facilities attracted my mother. It was she who found a very small six roomed house - diminutive compared with Navarino - at the top of Dyke Road Drive, a steep hill rising from Preston Park 300 feet below, and having a superb view of the Sussex Downs which were to play a most happy part in my boyhood and adolescent life.

26 Highcroft Terrace, Brighton

Here we lived, en pleine famille, for a very short time before my father left the family scene and emigrated alone to Canada. I was never told the reason, nor did I ever discuss it with my mother then, or with either parent in later years. The Victorian fog of "not before the children" descended over my father's life and movements, and even on his return fifteen years later, we all deferred to our parents' wishes and never discussed his absence -which covered the growing and formative years of his three children. I am practically certain that there was no matrimonial dispute between my parents and I am content to imagine that he went to Canada because he could not make the grade in the legal world in England and that he failed to do better in Canada. He wrote irregularly to my mother who told us of his existence - but he never wrote directly to any one of his children. He tended to fade from our memory. In any case he returned half a generation later as poor as when he departed, having proved himself as a man in the First World War, and he lived happily with my mother and in touch with his three children until he died (he came to my wedding) some score of years later in

1939. I cannot draw the curtain further on this episode - but it had a happy ending! Let us return to his family in Highcroft Terrace, in the early days of the century.

The move in 1899 from a sizeable house, with staff, in Ryde to a tiny terraced house in Brighton, with an interval in an apartment house in one of the cheaper quarters of Brighton far from the sea, with three children aged 9, 6 and 3, must have been a shock to my mother, who was about 40 years of age at the time. But there is no doubt that she then took hold of affairs so far as the Lush family was concerned. My father found himself a small office near the Lanes in Brighton where he set up as a solicitor for a short time. My mother, as I have written, found and rented the small house, moved thereto such furniture as we had brought from the island, hired a servant who could cook, and found a preparatory school for Cecil - Crescent House, near Montpelier Crescent. Mother entered Christine my sister, aged 8, for the junior side of Brighton and Hove High School for Girls. Maurice, aged 4, learnt to read and write at my mother's knee and right well she taught me. She had enjoyed no education herself and I remember, now, her avid reading of some of the books which Christine brought home from school and which appeared suitable for younger brother: her patience and endurance and faith when she taught me, while Chris did her homework unaided in the little dining room, until I was bundled up to bed in my mother's room! Chris, in Cecil's absence, went to the bedroom next door. On her elder brother's return she shared the third bedroom with the young servant. My mother was probably too busy to grieve for my father's departure!

As a fatherless youngest of three, it was natural that I should turn to my brother for leadership - and this I did. Cecil was my hero. He entered the Royal Navy at the age of 12 or 13 through Brighton College Junior School. I was 7 and I followed his career with pride and enthusiasm. I have his reports from school and Naval College to this day. At both Osborne and Dartmouth he was outstanding: he was Cadet Captain at both Naval establishments and everything seemed certain, at that time, for him to attain flag rank. He was devoted to his Naval career but no less to his mother, and as soon as he was commissioned, helped maintain her financially - teaching me to do the same. He never failed to give me good advice on work and career and general behaviour (though typically, for he was a shy boy, never on the "facts of life"): he sent me presents (including a real swordstick from Toledo) and stamps from all the countries he visited in training ships - HMS Cornwall, Hibernia and Dreadnought (his first battleship). Once, much later in life, he persuaded his Captain to allow me to sail round the British Isles in his ship HMS Royal Oak (in which as Navigator he had 2 cabins). He was a man of utter integrity and courage: but an early illness (typhoid) affected his heart and he died happily and suddenly in retirement after World War II as a Captain doing work for other people in his late fifties.

My sister Chris was a splendid protector of her small brother: she accompanied me when I first went to lessons near her school; she helped me with my prep at home. She was a figure of efficiency, devotion to duty and utter integrity which I strove to emulate. Later we read Plato's Republic together in the public library at Twickenham and stirred blackberry jam over the kitchen stove (coal heated) at home, conning Cicero. She helped me, by her own fine playing (she was an accomplished pianist) to play the piano; the din created in my grandmother's house in Twickenham (even more so in our own small home) by the Lush children rendering all the Overtures to the Gilbert and Sullivan Operas and Schubert's *Marches Militaires* etc, as piano duets or even trios was terrific: when younger brother was allowed to accompany on the side drum and triangle it must have been horrendous.

We were a very happy family, each having unspeakable love and admiration for our mother and a very healthy love and respect for each other.

It was sad that our mother who lived into a happy and healthy old age (97) did not live to see in 1963 her daughter join her two sons in receiving the present Queen's honour (the CBE) thereby making all three children Commanders of the British Empire.

My mother, for obvious reasons, was the dominant figure in my young life. Dominant however is not the correct attribute, for mother was the gentlest, the least domineering person that could be imagined. She taught us all that we knew but never by imposing her views; she was with us always, and sometimes, but by no means always, in advance: she educated her young family by love and example: (often when we were at first schools she would have to learn for herself the lesson - Latin, Arithmetic or History - before she tried to help us in our prep). She had no favourite: Cecil, intelligent, resourceful, musical, she loved as her firstborn son; Christine equally clever, and probably more intense (with a slight tendency to explosive anger at times) she loved as her only daughter; Maurice was her baby and, as such, a source of affection to her, but frequent ragging by his brother and sister who dubbed him "little lamb"! As we grew she must have been proud and not a little thankful at her early assistance to her children's learning, for Cecil was nominated for the Royal Navy at an early age and, as I have written, seldom scored lower than a 1st or 2nd in any class at the Royal Naval Colleges at Osborne or Dartmouth. Christine was head girl of the Brighton and Hove High School and won a music-cum-classical scholarship to Girton College, Cambridge. She was a fine hockey player (was not one of her grandsons Captain of Cambridge University Hockey XI in 1976 and of Oxford University Hockey XI in 1980?) and once invited her younger brother to play in her team: the Assyrians descending like wolves were nothing to those female hockey players and I never repeated the honour. Maurice, myself, won a Scholarship to Tonbridge School - to which I could not have gone had I not attained one, as my mother had assured me.

Thus we lived in this small house in Highcroft Terrace, Brighton. There was a diminutive garden in front of the house and a larger patch behind. In those two small areas my mother inspired in me the love of gardening - though the mowing of the grass was always more attractive than the weeding of the borders! It was from the front garden that I saw, and so well remember, the poverty of the Board (national) School children at the beginning of the century, running down the hill to school, shabbily and inadequately clothed, often bootless or shoeless. The poor, in those days, depended for help on private or public, but not state charity.

In that front garden there was planted by my mother, and grew to be a really bushy plant, a sprig of lavender of which my mother was alternately both proud, because it clearly loved and adored its surroundings, and ashamed, for she had brazenly stolen the original cutting from one of the flower beds in Hampton Court. In the back garden lay a plot of hallowed ground wherein Christine and I had solemnly, with the due rites of a Christian burial, interred our first white mice.

Mother engaged a living-in maid-of-all-work to help her for two or three years but had to give this up when school fees came on to the budget; we then had a French girl, as a paying guest. She, however, allowed the oil (heating) lamp to smoke one whole afternoon while she was out, and the subsequent redecoration of the room swamped all the income she provided, so we abandoned PGs! My mother performed all the household chores - cooking, cleaning, washing, gardening - now carried out by the modern housewife but without any of the modern aids to living. There were no electric nor gas stoves, no refrigerators nor mixing machines, no vacuum cleaners nor washing machines, no motor mowers. The hot water for baths and washing depended on a small boiler heated by the diminutive kitchen fire - coal fed.

We had our meals and did our prep in the tiny dining room, Christine wrestling with hers at a small Davenport desk, Mother aiding her occasionally but spending most of the evening with the family mending and teaching me reading, writing and arithmetic and also, culled from two books named *Near Home* and *Far Off*, elements of geography and a little history of Great Britain and abroad, the latter chiefly about the British Empire - after all we ruled a large part of the world and Cecil was already serving in the Royal Navy which defended many countries therein, making knowledge thereof very worthwhile - vide my stamp album of that period. Christine practised the piano every morning of her school life before breakfast. I started piano lessons from Miss Morgan at the age of 7.

We had the doctor (Bucknill was his name and he was kindness itself, due chiefly to his admiration for my mother) to the house only when we had chicken pox and mumps. We visited his surgery once and once only, when Christine had cut her hand dangerously after thrusting it through a glass panel door, chasing her younger brother. Nor did my mother "waste money on dental inspections". I visited my first dentist (in Cairo) at the age of 34, having broken a tooth on some metal object. I cannot claim, however, not to have lost a good many other teeth since then.

Cross Deep, Twickenham

One great respite my mother enjoyed (with all three of us). At first every summer and later every holidays my grandmother would invite our small family to stay with her at Cross Deep, Twickenham, a largish house at the top of King Street (the site later occupied by the Odeon Cinema). Here lived my grandmother, Emma Clark, her son, Dr William Marston Clark, my godfather, Medical Officer for Twickenham and District, a well-known and beloved family doctor (good for half-a-sovereign in gold coin to his godson every holiday) and her three spinster daughters: Aunt Nell, the eldest who ran the house, adored my mother and her children (whom she spoilt but in whom she inspired the love of music) and two younger aunts, Mary and Grace (afterthoughts of my grandparents) who frankly found the Lush incursion a noisy intrusion and did not disguise their distaste. Now I don't blame them, for how we fitted into the house was always a mystery.

But the great delight to us, mother and children, was the largish garden with a lawn tennis court on which we all learnt to play both tennis (never on Sundays) and sabbatical croquet. The grown-up ladies played both games, the while holding their long skirts with their left hand. There was also a path round the lawn on which I would ride madly my solid-tyre tricycle, imagining I was a London South Western train, loudly nominating the various objects and corners on the path as the stations between Twickenham and Waterloo. My younger spinster aunts openly doubted my sanity at this very vocal and monotonous progress round and round the garden.

There was also a potting shed which I was allowed to use as a carpenter's shop and where I learnt (self-taught) to make book shelves and string boxes (tongue and groove deal 6" cost ½d a foot) which I sold shamelessly to the family. The transaction was businesslike. I borrowed sixpence off Aunt Mary, bought 10 feet of deal (10d) and 2 dozen screws (2d), fashioned the article and sold it to Aunt Grace for 1/6 (18 pence) and learnt the value and skill of labour.

Let me go back to the house itself, Cross Deep, at the end of King Street, and exactly at the beginning of the Cross Deep Road to Teddington.

There were two front doors - the main door for the family and visitors, the smaller for patients to the surgery, my Uncle Bill's (William Clark) domain, having a two-bedroomed suite built above. The ground floor housed a large dining room, the red walls of which held various sculls won by a non-resident Uncle Frank, a member of the Thames Rowing Club. More exciting, the bookshelves themselves contained bound copies of the Strand magazine containing the original Sherlock Holmes detective stories, Martin Hewitt Investigator and Brigadier Gerard. The morning room with access to the garden lay opposite the dining room and a long passage containing pantries, kitchen, a huge scullery and larder and the "boot-hole".

The first floor contained two drawing rooms which had front windows looking on to King Street and back windows onto the garden - I remember that bats would trespass through those windows on an autumn night. The second floor contained a large bedroom, three single bedrooms and a bathroom having a gas heated geyser. The third floor contained the attics - two bedrooms unheated - for Mrs Taylor the cook, and the maid.

We *did* all fit into that house by night and by day - with much spare space - for the rooms were large.

My worst experience therein was being woken at midnight, on the second floor, by the noise of fierce rattling of a door downstairs - we descend, Mother, Aunt Nell and I, to see from the stairs the dining room door being shaken from within, most violently. Courageously, my intrepid aunt opened the door. An enormous rat from the cellar, imprisoned in the room, sped rapidly to the lower depths! He had gnawed a good inch from the door's bottom edge.

The front 'drawing room fascinated me for on the north and south walls, exactly opposite to each other, hung two large identical mirrors about six feet square; the effect was multiple or endless reflection of any object or individual in the middle of the room, and one had the uneasy feeling of gazing into infinity.

Next door to Cross Deep there was a large orchard where apples and plum trees grew in abundance. Woe betide us if, during the summer, our tennis balls or other articles went adrift among the fruit trees, for Mr Bates was a crusty, mercenary neighbour and the orchard his livelihood. But come the autumn, he always invited us in to pick up the windfalls.

Alas, Cross Deep house, surgery and stables, became a cinema which in turn became defunct but that house and garden gave endless and abiding happiness to the Lush family during the first and second decades of the century.

There were also the stables with Clements the coachman - a character. My uncle the doctor, would do his daily rounds in his trap or (funerals only) his brougham. We were not encouraged to go to the stable yard, chiefly because of Clements' (a drinker and robber) language. Who does not swear or perpetrate eroticisms when grooming a horse?

Then there was my uncle's errand boy. He spent his life in a "boot hole" next to the kitchen, cleaning knives in one of those exciting machines with a handle to turn, and polishing boots and shoes, until summoned from across the garden by a stentorian bellow of "Boy" from my uncle, the doctor (a bellow loudly echoed by my grandmother's cockatoo who stood unshackled on a perch in the garden - except when he flew on to the kitchen roof to be rescued, swearing like a trooper, by Clements, equally blasphemous, or any other man handy, and the exhortations of all the aunts). The boy's main duty was to collect medicines from and take empty bottles to the chemist, Mr Feather, across the road in Twickenham High Street.

Other most important inhabitants of Cross Deep were the dogs - Boscoe the Aberdeen, who growled and bit unashamedly, Jumbo the pug, who wheezed and chased rabbits, both beloved and spoiled by their owner Aunt Nell; the third was Jack, owned and equally spoiled by Aunts "M & G". The dogs caused more noise and more tension in that household of spinster ladies than any human factor. The word "cats" uttered at lunch time (I regret to say, sometimes, quite deliberately by grandchildren) would cause a paroxysm of barking in the dining room, until the brutes could be released to make a wild, screeching and senseless race after the imaginary cat, at the far end of the tennis court.

Twickenham is on the river - in those days the Twickenham-Teddington Reach was really beautiful and we children learnt to scull in our grandmother's 4-oared skiff. My mother was adept with her sculls, taught by her brother, my Uncle Frank, who rowed for the Thames Rowing Club. My brother's early career in the Navy did not prevent our capsizing a skiff in Teddington Lock and a 3-paddled canoe while changing places just above Teddington Weir!

My Uncle Bill once, and once only, took me fishing (floats and worms) on a tributary of the Thames. It was a serious, early- morning outing. We fished all morning and caught nothing - then suddenly my float bobbed under. "Strike, strike you little fool!" cried my cold and frustrated uncle. I did. Tip of rod, line and float and a quite fair sized roach disappeared into the foliage on an inacessible tree - I had struck up instead of diagonally. We rescued the rod; line and hook, float and fish remained a heavenly taunt to us - hanging from the tree. My uncle never took me fishing again - but he did take me in about 1902 to see W G (the great cricketer) Grace batting in a charity match on Twickenham Green.

It was my grandmother's wish, each year, to gather many of her sons and daughters and their children to Cross Deep for a New Year's Eve Party. I don't suppose we were ever more than 20 or 30 people, but after supper the grandchildren were expected to perform either recitations of a poem or the singing of a song or a performance on the piano. In those days it was most unusual for children of our type to be taught solo instruments except, possibly, the violin or 'cello. (In fact, I did learn the side drum, taught by a red-haired orphan from the Shaftesbury Home near Twickenham. He walked to Cross Deep once or twice a week in the holidays, and taught me so well that later I became Drum Sgt Major in my public school OTC Band.)

These concerts and recitations were very grim affairs. We did not much care for our cousins - their parents and ours seemed at variance - but it gave us an opportunity once a year to meet. I think I was the youngest.

One ceremony was always enacted at midnight of New Year's Eve. Electric trams came to Twickenham in 1906 (my mother many years later in Tripoli, Libya, once remarked "Twickenham was a very nice place, until the trams came") and at midnight of each New Year's Eve we children, led by my brother or sister, would run out, stop the first tram coming home from

Hammersmith outside the house, and give the driver a glass of port. No breathalysing in those days!

We were able to extend our wings and "go places" - in the garden, on the river, in London. It was there that I saw my mother happy and relaxed with her mother and sister Nell, much beloved people. It was there that I learnt the joy of doing things - making bookcases, mending broken chairs and bicycles, learning to be resourceful and, to a certain extent, inventive. I built a railway route for my clockwork train by laying wooden rails for quite a distance to a remote part of the garden.

26, Highcroft Terrace, Brighton

Well! All holidays end and the term always began from 26 Highcroft Terrace, Brighton. And so back we went home to work. As we got older we children were allowed to pocket the railway fare (6/8d) and bicycle the 52 miles. Great was the day when I was deemed old enough to accompany my brother and sister. We set off through Teddington and Bushey Park, past Hampton Court, through Esher to Leatherhead where we had "elevenses" at the "wasp-shop"; on through Dorking (no by-passes then) across Holmwood Common, with luncheon sandwiches on the road south of Horsham; on through Henfield and Poynings; then home by Saddlescombe and the Devils Dyke our last climb - a total of 52 miles in 10 hours. There was never much traffic before 1910 and I made my first ride when I was 10 (1906) and was very proud - and only a trifle saddle sore!

My mother was a great promoter of our bicycling, whether for short or long distances. Indeed she could not afford the then luxury of the tram or train even for short distances - most of our friends bicycled. Traffic was not dangerous, in fact my mother used to cite as my brother's only serious accident one in which he was charged and knocked off his bicycle by an infuriated cow on the main road in Sussex.

Mother was also devoted to walking in the country and nothing pleased her more than a walk to the Devil's Dyke and Saddlescombe or Poynings (Sussex) - a good picnic lunch, tea at a farm cottage marked "Teas - 6d" (there were so many in those days) - and home to supper. I blessed her example for many years when my wife and I or I alone walked the Sussex Downs.

CHAPTER 2

School - Holland House and Tonbridge 1905 - 1915

Schools

The holidays over and back to work. Cecil, as already mentioned, went to prep school at Crescent House (Mr Thomas "Tommie") and then to Brighton College Junior School (Mr Belcher - what a name for headmaster!); thence he went to Osborne Royal Naval College and on to Dartmouth. At both places he excelled. He was my hero and almost in loco parentis during his young life in the Royal Navy. Only the foresight, devotion and determination of my mother saved him from death when, as a young snotty, he was landed from HMS Dartmouth in Bantry Bay suffering from serious typhoid fever and sent to the only "hospital", the building attached to the (Irish) workhouse, where on arrival she found that the undertakers had been ordered to arrive next morning.

Christine went to the Brighton and Hove High School where she moved steadily up the school ladder for nine years without missing a single day, except when I gave her mumps. She became Head Girl and as I have recorded gained a Classical cum Musical Scholarship at Girton College Cambridge, whither she went in 1913. She was a fine pianist and only just missed appearing in the Albert Hall as co-finalist in a public competition owing to these mumps. She had a fine incisive brain and was a demon for work. Was she not later founder and Headmistress of the English School in Addis Ababa, Ethiopia?

At the High School in Brighton Chris had made friends with one Marjorie Smithers who had two sisters (and a brother) and a mother who, knowing of our fatherless state, was kind. She suggested that I should join her other two daughters, Barbara and Ursula, and take lessons with them under their most excellent Miss Robson, a first class governess. To this kind gesture my mother gratefully consented, and so at the age of six I accompanied Christine to school, generally walking the 1½ miles (very occasionally by electric tram) and on to The Gables, Furze Hill, Hove where, for two years I learnt all morning from Miss Robson and came home with Chris to lunch. My sister did the journey again in the afternoon. Walking in those days presented no problem to the ordinary child.

This period at The Gables was during the Russo-Japanese war in which Great Britain's sentiment was entirely allied to Japan. Russian policy towards N W India and Afghanistan had alienated British opinion from her and was probably the cause of the Anglo-Japanese Treaty. I can still see the ashen face of Barbara's mother as she interrupted lessons with the news "The Russians have sunk 2 British trawlers in the Baltic Sea!"

Holland House Preparatory School 1905-1910

It was through the redoubtable Miss Robson, no doubt with some vigorous backing from Nellie Smithers, that my mother put herself in touch with W B C Cawood, headmaster of Holland House Preparatory School, Cromwell Road, Hove - a small school of not more than 50 boys, about 12 of them boarders. But it was a good school and the teaching was of the best. Cawood himself was a fine classical scholar and he must have determined that M S Lush was a scholarship boy, for he took me in hand and trained me as such in Greek and Latin from the very beginning. Whether he took me at reduced fees I do not know but, often, if my prep. was difficult he would keep me back (particularly in summer) give me supper and do my prep. with me. I remember to this day what a help and inspiration that was. Holland House was a good mile from home - all downhill there, all uphill going home - so for 4 years I did 4 miles a day and was thankful even when I was allowed to bicycle. Cawood was a man of irascible temper and a howler on the part of a boy would send him to the piano in the classroom where (he knew not a note of music) he would violently churn out dischord after dischord until the irascibility passed. But he could teach Latin and Greek.

His sister, Betty Cawood, was a remarkable character. Tiny, indomitable, she ruled us all, masters included, with a rod of iron, wielded with a hand of great kindness and half a pint of milk daily at 11.00 am. Cawood sent me at the age of 12 in 1909 to sample the scholarship examination for Charterhouse School. Of course I could hardly answer a question except, I believe, the Greek unseen. My success in that paper I attribute to the very hot and strong curry for lunch to which my Aunt Nell treated me, together with a bottle of Stone's Ginger Beer at the Charterhouse Hotel, Clerkenwell. During the next year, however, at the age of 13 I won the Fourth Judd Scholarship at Tonbridge. (The Latin verse paper read "Write ten lines in Latin elegiacs lamenting the death of King Edward VII"; he had died earlier that year.) The night before my journey to Tonbridge to take the scholarship paper there had broken over Sussex and Kent the fiercest and most prolonged thunderstorm I have ever experienced (including countless storms in Africa and elsewhere) - a good omen.

As a preparatory school Holland House was not eminent in games nor I as a boy therein, although I did captain both cricket and football teams. But we held one distinction in cricket, viz. that of being allowed to play on the 2nd XI part of the Sussex County Cricket Club ground and watch all the county matches as members. So I often saw "Ranji" play - Ranjit Singh the famous Indian Cricketer of the early 20th century. I once took my Aunt Nell to watch a county match there. After an hour of dull cricket she awoke from sleep and declared in her stentorian voice, "Well, Maurice, this cricket appears to me to be a game in which 22 idle men saunter through the afternoon doing nothing".

The main enthusiasm of the Cawoods was centred on national service. They enrolled Holland House in the Junior Officers Training Corps, dressed us up in khaki once a week, had us drilled by a Sergeant of the Royal Sussex Regiment and placed us at the disposal of the National Service League, at the head of which was Field Marshal Lord Roberts of Kandahar. The diminutive "Bobs" who had made his name in South Africa and re-established the honour of the British Army by persuading the British government and the troops that they were fighting a force of highly trained guerillas and not a rabble of undisciplined farmers. He saw the military weakness of the nation in the early decades of the century and the incompetence of the army generally and of many military leaders in particular. He strove courageously against the jingoism which erupted during and after the South African war to bring the nation to its senses by advocating the institution of compulsory national service. He formed the National Service League and became its protagonist. But to no avail: we had "won" the war (the "Boer" war); the boys were coming home victorious; Anglo-Egyptian troops under Kitchener had won the battle of Omdurman at the other end of Africa; Gordon had been avenged; we had a new king; the British Navy ruled the waves; the King, Edward VII, and Queen Alexandra put the nation's seal on the Indian Empire; Entente Cordiale survived; the age of graciousness had arrive. Who wanted national service to reduce our glorious army to a force of conscripts? Our treble songs at the NSL rallies, patriotic as they were, proved of no avail. But the movement left its mark on one small boy who later, at the Coronation Review was very lucky and proud to be inspected, as a member of the Tonbridge OTC in Windsor Great Park by both Lord Roberts and Lord Kitchener. But that belongs to the next chapter.

One enormous benefit bestowed upon myself and other boys at Holland House was the realisation that we had good treble voices. The Cawoods, as I have said, were no musicians, but they realised the advantage of music to their boys. The school music-master was no great shakes, but he, with all the help possible from the Headmaster and Bessie, produced *HMS Pinafore* in Hove Town Hall before appreciative audiences, with great success. The orchestra consisted of our music-master at the piano and one violinist! I was billed to play Phoebe to Ludwig Menges playing Ralph. I had a strong and musical treble voice and I thoroughly enjoyed singing - my family had encouraged it and here was my debut in public! Ludwig Menges (afterwards the well-known conductor) sang brilliantly and Betty Cawood had found or made the most fetching wig for me. We had an excellent Buttercup and a splendid boy who sang or croaked Dick Deadeye. It all went very well. Unfortunately, no record remains of the production - there were no cheap instruments or tapes for recording in those days - and the Press comments were lost in the fire which later destroyed the Hove Town Hall in the 1970s.

But to myself that production of Pinafore had a profound effect which brought great and continuing happiness to me for many years. For it made me realise that I could sing and that singing produced pleasure and joy in others and, as I was to find later, great benevolence. It was the music produced by me, both on the piano and (as a boy) from my mouth, indifferent in technique as it was, which moved my contemporaries to acts of kindness and friendship which have brought enormous and sometimes quite unexpected happiness in my life.

My mother was a convinced practising Christian, and took us children to church regularly. She was not outspoken about her faith but she prayed as only those who have suffered can pray, and she taught us quietly to follow her steady example of faith. To her, Holy Communion (Eucharist would have been considered by her to be a very "High" expression) was a very personal relationship between God and the individual. Parish or Family Communion appeared much later in the Anglican Church. The church which I remember best was St Patrick's, Hove - a good 1 1/2 miles from our home, and the vicar of which, Rev Marshal, had a dominant personality, but was a very good pastoral priest. I had a comfortable habit of feeling faint and retiring before the Litany (2nd Sunday in the month) and never shall I forget a Commination Service which my sister and I attended (alone) one Ash Wednesday in 1909 or 1910. "Cursed be he who removeth his neighbour's land mark" intoned the curate. "Laundry mark" whispered Christine *sotto voce*.

The same curate pointed out to us one May evening in 1910 the famous Halley's Comet (I think it may have appeared as the Daylight Comet in the same year). It was a wonderful sight stretching about 15 degrees across the westering sky, vivid, unforgettable. I saw Halley's Comet again in 1985-6 - this time through a telescope at Greenwich Observatory - very dim!

Reverting to faith. My mother implanted into all her children the unshakeable faith which leads one to turn to God and to pray to Him perhaps only in emergencies at first - "Oh God, may it be strawberry jam for tea", "May we win this football match", "May I get a scholarship", "May I get better" - but more regularly and comprehensively "May I understand", "May *she* find happiness", "May *she* recover" - as life goes on; the habit becomes part of daily life, as the life hereafter comes nearer at hand.

A further kindness from the Smithers family must be recorded. For 4 years they invited my sister Chris and me to spend 2 weeks of our school summer holiday with them. For 3 years we visited the Lake District where they had rented a house, and learnt with them to walk up (and down) Helvellyn, Coniston Old Man, Scawfell, the Langdales and many other peaks. Transport in the district was always horse drawn "charabancs", meaning walk up the hills because the load is too heavy for the horses, walk down the other side because the heavy load might over run the horses! There were few cars. We certainly never entered one. Those holidays were very good. How truly has Betjeman said that the joy of the Lake District is that, compared with other countries, everything is on such a small, immaculately miniature, yet perfectly proportioned, scale!

We found ourselves welcome guests in a family who loved the countryside of England, who lived to share that love with their own children Marjorie, Keith (at Winchester), Barbara (my own age) and Ursula; who sensed that the Lush family fortunes could never be extended to cover such a holiday; therefore gave to the Lush children the joy and happiness which their own children could enjoy. We shared everything with them at their parents' expense and to their parents' joy as well as our intense delight. I can still see Ted Smithers, the pater familias, gathering his young family of Smithers and Lushes at the base of Coniston Old Man, encouraging them at half-way (it was cold) and giving us all a wee tot out of his flask at the summit! I can share his anxiety as he shielded us along the Striding Edge of Helvellyn, during an unexpected rise of dangerous wind. I can remember so clearly his and Nelly's excitement as we watched the sheep dog trials on the high fells above Grasmere. What wonderful days were those! Great happiness for Christine and myself made possible by the unselfish love of a family which eventually became closely entwined with ours when Cecil, my brother, fell in love and married Marjorie, the eldest daughter.

But I have jumped a decade ahead of my story.

Tonbridge School 1910-1915

My scholarship at Tonbridge was, of course, a great cause for thankfulness all round. It meant that I could go to Public School! Without a scholarship that would have been financially impossible. I remember, when the news came by telegram to our home, bicycling down to tell the Cawoods at school and suddenly remembering that I had entirely failed to thank the Almighty! Kneeling down on the grubby stone basement entrance to the school boot room I mumbled "Thank you, God!" The offer was followed by a letter from the Headmaster, Charles Lowry, who wrote to my mother offering me a place in his house, School House, whither I duly went. But before that the trousseau for a public school had to be bought and paid for! Hitherto, except for my Eton suit with its bumfreezer jacket which cost 30/- (£1.50) at the Civil Service Stores but which was not acceptable at Tonbridge, I had lived in my brother's or some elder cousin's casts-off - a perfectly natural outfit for a younger son. Here was the appalling list of suits and shirts, of shoes and overcoats and all the rest to be purchased. My mother managed it (I suspect with grand-maternal help); the trunk and playbox were packed and one day in September 1910 my mother and I set off for Tonbridge by train - 2 hours of misery.

Later we sat in the Headmaster's drawing room, both very near to tears, when my mother had her usual stroke of courage and genius. "What" she asked "are those sounds coming across from that building?" "The music master, Mr Stewart" replied Charles Lowry, "is testing new boys' voices for the choir." My mother abruptly left the room with me, took me to the building whence vocal scales could be heard, pushed me inside with a goodbye kiss and went back to Brighton. Stewart tested my voice and enrolled me in the choir and as a piano student, and then I found my own way - one point of happiness made - to my School House study.

That was the beginning of a great tutorial friendship between Hylton Stewart and myself. He taught me to play the piano; he made me sing all the soprano solos for 3 years and recommended me for the school music prize in piano and singing over the same period. He taught me all the music which I know. He was wonderfully patient. He knew that I did not practise the piano suffiently but that this taught me mightily to read music at sight. He knew that my form masters resented time given up from Classics to Music. "Possibly, to some extent, hampered in the Classics by the valuable distraction of his various activities in Music" wrote Vere Hodge, form master of the Lower VI. W M Gordon of the Upper VI was more forceful "Let him beware of music and of the band; he can pipe and drum later in life". Tonbridge had not then reached the standard of musical excellence of which it now rightly boasts, but Hylton Stewart and later his assistant Maurice Besly (very avant garde) not forgetting musical boys like Denis Arundel, laid the foundations of the musical standard which now flourishes there. I am proud to have been associated with them.

I do not think even Hylton Stewart can have known what an immense and kindly benefit he was ensuring for me by encouraging and insisting on my other tutors that I should continue my piano lessons which took place during school hours and involved absence from Virgil and Homer, Tacitus and Herodotus not withstanding. He taught me to play well enough to maintain my just adequate standard, so that I could play the piano (no other instrument) sufficiently well to accompany other singers and soloists of my musical calibre (and some better) and to be able to give a certain amount of pleasure in many different countries all my life, certainly up to the period when the recording of music has reached such a high standard that amateur performances and music in the home is unusual. I record my gratitude to him, to Maurice Besly, to all who sang or listened to my accompaniments and playing and to God for giving me sight and supple fingers until I was very old!

In the meantime, on 15 September 1910 school life began in earnest. But before recounting my scholarly progress, let me tell you about one notable event which took place about a week after my arrival - Novi Singing.

My first days at Tonbridge found me sharing a study, a diminutive room for 2, in the junior end of School House, with Maurice Oxenbould who, my senior by one term, welcomed me most kindly, inducted me to the routine of School House life - fagging, Novi Singing, etc, and found that we were in the same form, Middle V under Laurence (Bobo) Herman. He warned me about Novi Singing, a trial of the stamina of new boys, each one of whom had to sing a song.

I had heard of this ordeal and was prepared, for my redoubtable Aunt Nell had found in the newspaper some political ditty all about current politicians - Balfour, Lloyd George, Churchill, etc - set to the well-known tune of *Clementine*. School House Novi Singing took place one evening 10 days after the commencement of term. Peter Knott, the Head of House, had heard me singing in the choir and insisted on a kind reception. I began with trepidation but when, after the second verse, the audience (Praeposters or Prefects and the whole house) joined in the chorus, I knew that all was well: the house liked it, and I was allowed to continue unmolested. I was "invited" (note the point) to sing again at a "request performance" next evening, earned the nickname of Clementine and heard the tune whistled *passim* in School House for the next 2 or 3 weeks. Performance in public at Hove Town Hall had been good training for this more barbarous ordeal! I wonder whether I was grateful at the time!

The Head of School House chose me as his "fag" - he was Peter Knott, a member of the famous Tonbridge family. He was immensely kind to me and there developed a friendship which, alas, lasted all too brief a time, for he went on with a scholarship to Cambridge two years later. It was completely sexless, (homosexuality was as widespread at Tonbridge as in any school or monosex institution) almost wordless, for Senior boys did not consort or converse with small fry, but it was intense, and to me, very valuable - we both loved music and sang in the choir. We had much in common - though he at the peak, I at the start, of our school careers. It was he who encouraged a very junior and small Maurice Lush to sing solos at School Concerts (eg. Cherry Ripe, etc) and to train and conduct the School House Quartet, which won the coveted prize on two consecutive years, finally to sing *O for the wings of a dove* one heavenly evening in School Chapel evensong.

Let us return to the more serious testing of new scholars. On the first morning of term Maurice Oxenbould took me to the Middle Fifth Classroom which was in fact housed in our Big School for some reason, where I met L H (Bobo) Herman, form master of this preliminary form on the Classical side of the school, and in which we were introduced to the Classics as such - Caesar, Ovid and Xenophon and the rudiments of Roman and Greek history. There I met my fellow Scholars (in those days Scholars wore gowns) and almost at initiation the competition began for removal *quam celerrime* to the Upper V, the second testing ground under G A Floyd known as "Gumph", "a single man with a double chin and a treble voice". Here every year, the form learnt to recite faultlessly a whole book of Virgil's Aeneid: no boy was ever known to score less than 90% when examined by the Headmaster at the end of Summer Term!

As top of the form I managed to move out of Middle V in to this cradle of Latin "Rep", after my first term, having made (according to Bobo Herman) "a promising start"; "his exams good on the whole but not brilliant". This scholastic move also meant promotion from the junior part of the House (a shared study, dormitory, fagging) to a cubicle - a bed sitting "room" (walls only 5 feet high) but blessed privacy in which one could work, if so desirous, at peace. True, for 2 terms I was in a "horse box" with a door but no window: I gained the window at the end of my first year - with a glorious view over the "Head" (School Cricket Ground) and hot water pipes which never failed in winter! School House was part of the main School buildings and enjoyed the very efficient maintenance given to the School by the Skinners Company.

After 2 terms' learning to recite Virgil's Aeneid II (and a good deal more to boot) the Headmaster, Charles Lowry, thought me too young for the Lower VI form. But after 2 days of intense disappointment, the sun shone and I found myself in Lower VI after all and deemed myself on the second set of rungs in the Classical ladder. I stayed in that pleasant form for 2 happy years under H S Vere Hodge's really wonderful teaching of the "youngest boy in his form". "Vera" records: "His work is possibly to some extent hampered by the valuable distraction of his various activities in music" but was grateful for "small services he has rendered to me readily and ungrudgingly" (I had acted as general bottle washer to the form).

Finally in the Michaelmas Term of 1913 I was promoted to the (Classical) Upper VI under W M Gordon, a great Classical teacher, who took me in charge, taught me how to write Greek prose and iambics without recourse to English-Greek Dictionaries and began to train me for the Oxbridge Scholarship. Gordon also taught me (with the rest of the form) English and Greek caligraphy - his own was superb. After one term as my form master he found me "rather superficial" and urged me to exert myself; my Headmaster wrote that I was something of an "amateur" in regard to really solid work at his Classics: "if he put this in first place for a couple of years ...." Later he was more hopeful: "if he can get rid of his inaccuracy".

I loved those 2 years in Upper VI. Gordon instilled in me the love, if not the full appreciation, of Classical literature just as Hylton Stewart was opening my mind (and ears) to the true value of music.

Alas, I fulfilled success in neither - to the extent which both would have hoped - but they gave me enough understanding through Classics and Music to enrich my life, and I have always felt a debt of gratitude to my form masters Bobo Herman, Vera, Gumph and Gordon, and to Hylton Stewart and Besly, not forgetting my House and Headmaster, Charles Lowry.

Charles Lowry never failed to applaud my character and general behaviour, which worried me at times, but, of course, delighted the grown-ups at home. I always thought that school reports should be read to the pupil before despatch!

I did nothing to enhance the position of my House at games and athletics - a most important factor in school life. I was in fact only just of average standard at athletics - gaining my House colours only at Rugby. I remember scoring a try in the vital House Match when School House, who stood at the bottom of the House League, knocked out the Cock House one Autumn Term! I excelled only at fives (Rugby fives, with back wall and a buttress). I could not afford squash (racquets cost money) and failed dismally in my trial for the Colts at cricket (a duck and a dropped catch!). Ten years were to elapse before I could find a game in which I could excel - Polo - the most expensive of all! But I also adopted squash racquets and played that splendid game until, aged 70, my son could give me points - for which, of course, I blamed my arthritis!

I did retain, however, that love of country walking and, in my latter days at school, instituted in lieu of boring runs round the cross country track, a system of walk-runs, with some point of interest half-way. In those days one could walk with impunity on main roads and there were quite a few places of interest. Such exercise was exceedingly good training and in my last year gave me 3rd place in the annual "Cras", the 6-mile cross country race. How wonderful it was to take such walks later when time was of no object and moors and fells took the place of roads - eg. the Sussex Downs, Dartmoor, the mountains of Abyssinia and France.

Lord Roberts and the National Service League had inspired one small boy at Prep School and I joined the Tonbridge contingent of the Public Schools Section of the Officers Training Corps as soon as my age and position in school allowed. Mr Hallam, my Maths master, was Commanding Officer (not a very inspiring teacher) and under his command I was delighted to be included, thanks to the Head of my House, in the selected body of boys chosen to represent Tonbridge at the Coronation Review of King George IV in Windsor Great Park where, before the Sovereign's appearance, we were inspected by the 2 Field Marshals Lord Roberts of Kandahar and Lord Kitchener of Khartoum. I remember our pride and delight in defeating the stamina of the Eton contingent whose line was just in front of Tonbridge. It was a piping hot day! Casualties from fainting Eton 3 Tonbridge 0! I have never forgotten that quite wonderful day in my boyhood military career.

Later I became a lance corporal and joined the Band as a side drummer. Had I not been taught by a small boy from the Shaftesbury Home at Twickenham? Tonbridge OTC Band had a bad and quite undeserved reputation for "sloping off", avoiding the arduous exercises of Field Days and enjoying them as picnics and visits to pubs! "Not so", writes a side drummer, having played and carried his drum across Salisbury Plain!

I was thoroughly and always happy at school. I had plenty of friends, some especial, a kindly staff of 3 Housemasters, under the Headmaster, who never failed to give me a good report (why?). I enjoyed my work in form and my preparation therefore. I had been amazingly lucky in my early days with great if unseen friendship from my Head of House, Peter Knott, downwards. Alas so many of my contemporaries and friends did not survive the War; K H Moore and Jakes Danbery of School House were killed. The boy to whom my music gave enormous if emotional pleasure, Stephen Clark (he gave me my volume of Mendelssohn's *Songs without Words*) died young; many others disappeared in the maelstrom of World War I. One remained - Gordon Perry, a boy of another House, Parkside, whose friendship began in the classroom and remained into the 1970's.

Most of my friends, however, were nearly wholly confined to School House boys and I will give you an instance of their friendship and generosity. It is a story which bears out the continuing kindness I enjoyed throughout my school days. When a boy reached the Upper VI form he was expected to use a full size Latin (Lewis and Short) and Greek (Liddell and Scott) Dictionary or Lexicon. They cost 30/- or 40/- (£1.50 or £2.00) which was a largish sum in those days. I don't know how, but some friends in my House and form knew that this was bound to be a financial strain on my mother. On 2 successive birthdays first a Latin Dictionary and then a Greek Lexicon were presented to me - 2 weeks' pocket money from 15 boys who understood. I have the Latin Dictionary to this day, signed by those wonderful donors, all of whom have preceded me into Elysium!

Skinners Day, before World War 1 was a notable day at school. The Master of the Worshipful Company of Skinners with the Senior Member of the Livery descended upon Tonbridge and lodged at the Rose and Crown Hotel in the centre of the town. At 6.00 am the whole school arose and proceeded, clad in pyjamas or shorts, to the banks of the River Medway and swam naked across its muddy waters. Tonbridge School had no swimming pool in those days and we relied on our local river for rowing and swimmming. Each boy collected a branch of birch wood and leaves, swam back, dressed and marched down the High Street to the Rose and Crown where the Master of the Skinners appeared on the porch of the hotel in pyjamas and addressed the noisy, ill clad throng, all waving their birch branches. Later the whole school, staff, the Skinners Company and many parents attended a special service in Tonbridge Parish Church (Lessons by Headboy, Anthem by Choir, Sermon by Headmaster), the Prize Giving and Speeches in Big School and then the opening of the Cricket Match, School versus Old Tonbridgians. A great day to which my mother usually managed to come and twice heard her son sing the treble solo for the Anthem in church. I gathered 3 good books as prizes (Middle V in my first term and Music for 2 consecutive years), and have read and valued them greatly. I deplore the modern practice of "No prizes". I treasure mine!

At the end of Skinners Day the members of the OTC paraded and marched off with drums beating and bugles blaring, preparatory for entrainment next day to the Public Schools OTC Camp.

It was a great day and I, naturally, especially remember Skinners Day and the ensuing Camp of 1914 when we, with many other schools, found ourselves encamped at Rugby. The Camps were run by the Training Department of the War Office and manned by members of the regular Army: Officers to supervise the administration and training, Other Ranks to run the commissariat, tented camps, etc. On 3 August, after only 4 days of our 1914 Camp, we awoke to find the whole of the regular Army Staff and Camp Administrators had disappeared, called up by Mobilisation Orders to their own Units! Our OTC Officers and we cadets were told to strike camp, entrain for London and disperse. Near chaos threatened but was averted and noon on 4 August 1914 found me, with the Tonbridge contingent steaming into Olympia (Kensington) Station (now the Motor Rail and interchange platform) where we headed for home. I boarded a No 27 Motor Bus for Twickenham. En route we heard much comment such as "My God, they've got some pretty small youngsters in the b___ Army these days!"

And so dawned 4 August 1914.

The outbreak of war made a tremendous difference to my emotions -my outlook - my whole life (nor was I the only victim of change). On 5 August I went to the Twickenham recruiting office of the Queen's (London) Regiment and signed up as a private soldier, sadly to discover the next day, when I went to collect my shilling and my papers that at 17 years of age I was not allowed to join the Army. I spent the rest of the summer holidays in correspondence with my Headmaster, Charles Lowry, and drilling young ladies in Richmond Park - not at all what my military ambitions had dictated! Meanwhile, Charles Lowry, patient and understanding as always, advised me strongly against joining the Army there and then, but encouraged me to take up the Regular Army as a career, change my curriculum at Tonbridge School from Classics to the Army Class and eventually join the Royal Military Academy at Woolwich (The Shop), to which he would "nominate" me (thus avoiding the entry examination) early in 1915, with a view to becoming a Gunner - the Royal Artillery being a Regiment in which I could live on my pay when the war ceased. This must have been bitter advice for Charles Lowry to give, for had he not marked me down for a Classical Scholarship at Oxford? He knew that I had already been offered a Bible Clerkship at All Souls. It was by no means the only bitter disappointment suffered by that fine leader and scholar and it is said that he retired and died heartbroken by the deaths of so many Tonbridge boys and the dashing of so many of his hopes, as a result of World War I. His last Headmaster's report on myself read: "He has the faculty of forgetting himself and devoting himself to a cause - I shall always cherish a faint regret for the University and the career of a schoolmaster: he would have done admirably in this."

My last terms at Tonbridge (Michaelmas 1914 to Easter 1915) were hardly real - I was a School Praeposter and a Colour Sergeant in the OTC. I surrendered Homer for Trigonometry and Cicero for Science. Finally I left after a wonderfully happy school life.

Deus dat incrementum.

Florence Emma Lush, Maurice's mother

Maurice Stanley Lush in 1898 aged two

Maurice as a scholar at Tonbridge School, 1911

Florence and Hubert Lush in Brighton, 1923
'The Proposal'

Capt M.S. Lush, RA with Military Cross and Bar, 1918

Capt M.S. Lush at HQ V Army, Lille, on 'Anzac', 1919

'Mother': a 9.2 inch Howitzer used by 94 Siege Battery

Hubert Stanley Lush, his father,
in the Canadian Infantry, 1917

CHAPTER 3

World War 1: 1915 - 1919

The Shop

In April 1915, dressed in a lounge suit, laden with a suitcase containing, inter alia, a dinner jacket I entered the Royal Military Academy at Woolwich (The Shop) and became, with 400 others, a Gentleman Cadet.

This was a six-month war crash-course as opposed to the normal 2 years. There were no uniforms for "Snookers" (new cadets) at the start but for drill and day work we were soon fitted with the khaki uniforms of Gentleman Cadets. We never, however, acquired the blue "mess kit" but always wore black dinner jackets for evening mess and in the junior or "Snooker" term wore bowler hats on top - the most bizarre turn-out! The drill sergeants for infantry parade (one hour daily at 7.00 am) were picked drill instructors from the Brigade of Guards and every term they turned out 5 companies from RMA Woolwich whose foot drill could match the Brigade of guards. The academic teaching was good, map reading and map-making instructions excellent. We learnt at Woolwich Arsenal how guns were cast. We had no gun drill but we did learn to ride horses. Riding School took place 3 times a week. We all learnt to ride whether we were destined for Horse, Field or Garrison Artillery or Engineers. Riding Troop Corporal Pepper was instructor of our company, No 3, and his language and blasphemy equalled his skill in teaching. Those who could ride, unlearnt what they knew and learnt afresh - the Pepper "seat and hands". Those who couldn't ride learnt the hard way - I fell off 14 times on the first morning. "Mr Lush, sir, you came down here to ride a horse not to kiss the bloody tan!" said the Riding Master. On a later date I fell, broke an arm and was kicked on the head (I have a dent in the skull to this day). Pepper shed his ferocity and blasphemy, drove me to hospital in his own gig and visited me daily until I emerged. But on my next riding lesson he made me take the same jump on the same horse and without stirrups! How I blessed that man later, jumping stone walls in Ethiopia, in the polo finals at Addis Ababa and Khartoum, winning the steeplechase thrice in Addis Ababa and acquiring a handicap of 3 at Khartoum polo!

I fear we Gentleman Cadets were vandals in 1915. One week-end (most of which were "leave-outs") the Duty Officer sounded a fire-alarm for those left in the Shop. An unwarranted intrusion we, who were left, imagined. We turned on a quantity of fire hoses one of which was directed from the roof straight down the chimney of the offending officer's quarters. We all suffered 3 days check parade (double marching - full kit for one hour before ordinary parade at 7.00 am). Captain R H D Love was a very fine officer, a horse gunner who became a General, like a number of the GCs who vandalised his room!

Then in October 1915 came the great day. The best climber of the term ascended the statue of Queen Victoria, armed with a chamber pot which he placed on the Imperial Crown. The staff Sgt Major on duty duly shot it down without defacing the royal head. The Commandant handed first commissions to 250 cadets and G C Lush became 2nd Lieut Lush Royal Garrison Artillery with a stripe and circle round his tunic sleeve.

Entering the Shop as No 249 (a nominated entry, not by examination) I had, by some hard work and luck, passed out of the final examination 3rd. So I had my choice. I chose to be a "bombardier" or officer of the Royal Garrison Artillery, because in that arm of the regiment one could, I had been told, live on one's pay in peace time. I estimated that if I survived the war I had to be in that position - so I chose what turned out to be the most interesting arm of the Regiment, in the war now being waged, for I was later posted to a battery to be equipped with the very latest type of howitzer gun which was mobile, accurate and mechanically very sound; moreover it could kill more of the enemy with a single shell at a longer range than most other pieces of artillery. But that was all to come. I took leave - proudly took salutes from anyone below the rank of officer who cared to salute me - polished my boots and leggings and Sam Browne (and occasional spurs) and enjoyed myself! Those spurs once caught in the lace frill of my hostess's teacloth and pulled the whole cloth - bread and butter, cakes, cream and jam - to the ground. I had to stay to supper and purge my sin by playing the piano! At home I found that my brother was at sea and Christine was at Girton College; my mother proudly enjoyed walking with her officer son.

I was soon posted to a Royal Artillery training depot at Lydd whence on Boxing Day 1915 I proceeded with another Shop subaltern to join 94 Siege Battery RGA, commanding officer Major D A Sandford DSO, stationed at Tynemouth Castle, Newcastle. Sandford had apparently asked for 2 "Shop" or Regular officers to be sent to him from the Lydd depot.

94th Siege Battery RGA, Tynemouth

Sandford had captained 10th Siege Battery in France in 1914-15 and had been awarded the DSO (Distinguished Service Order); he was then sent home to form his own battery, on promotion to Major. 10th Siege Battery had the distinction of being the first battery to be equipped with 9.2" howitzers, each weighing fifteen tons, commonly known as "Mother", the most accurate piece of artillery produced during the First World War. So on Boxing Day 1915 Mike Cassidy and I endured a bleak journey to one of the coldest spots in Northern England - Tynemouth Castle, where we found our Battery Commander Major Sandford. We were his first officers to join the new battery and he seemed delighted to see us. Sandford and I soon established a bond in the person of his younger brother Dick, a naval friend of my brother Cecil's, who had encouraged me to join the RGA "because of his brother Dan" - a bond which was to become even stronger as time went on. The remainder of the officers in that RA Mess appeared to Mike Cassidy and myself to have acquired the age of 70!

Battery Forming and Training: UK

Sandford's first order to his new subalterns was to be on parade at 7.00 am next morning and to take charge of a "scotch-up" exercise. Seeing our blank faces (for we had never heard of such a manoeuvre) he expressed no little surprise for in his day it had been part of the curriculum at the Shop at Woolwich to practise "scotch-up" and we were told to find out all about it from the Battery Sergeant Major in the morning. This we did in perishing dark cold and found that it was the art of lifting and moving heavy weights - eg guns - (often several tons) with no mechanical means other than wooden handspikes, blocks of wood, rollers and ropes. It is an admirable skill and greatly to be commended even in these mechanical days. It seemed Heath Robinson, on first sight, but I have found it extremely scientific and more than useful in many countries in times of peace as well as war. Several other officers joined the embryo battery before the end of the year and young Mike and I enjoyed the feeling of superiority as we initiated them into the secrets of "scotch-up". We did do other drill too.

Early in January 1916 we were brought up to strength by the arrival of the Territorial part of our battery, some 60 men and a couple of officers from the Territorial gunners of Hartlepool, and to Sandford's joy he found that they were mostly Durham coal-miners -expert diggers whose value he had already learnt to appreciate. When the need for dugouts came in France our battery was "underground" before one could believe it - and snugly too. Moreover their courage and endurance were beyond praise.

The Officers' Mess at Tynemouth Castle was not a lively gathering when Mike Cassidy and I joined our Commanding Officer. I never discovered who the old gentlemen were or what they did. I remember on our third night Sandford, hearing that I played the piano, asked the senior officer after dinner, if he would object to a tune on the piano. "I don't mind," wheezed the old (to us) gentleman, "All music is beastly to me." I played Sibelius' Valse Triste! Later when our Battery began to form we livened that Mess not a little.

Among the officers was a distinguished Oxford scholar, Maurice Platnauer. He had been a mathematical scholar at Shrewsbury and a classical scholar at New College. War, the men who had to wage it and the conditions and circumstances of life in a military formation was completely alien and utterly repugnant to his sensitive and meticulous mind. He loathed every moment of his military career but he never faltered from doing his best and trying to help his brother men. It was reported, truly, that he read Virgil's Georgics in the Observation Post. There were of course many like him for whose dedication we have to be grateful. Thank God he survived the war and lived to become Vice-Principal of Brasenose College, Oxford, where he was said to have reformed the College merely by being in it. In contrast to Platnauer, I for the most part, enjoyed the war. I was 15 years his junior.

Maurice Platnauer and Dan Sandford were, for fundamentally different reasons, stars among the members of what was, in fact, a happy officers' mess in "94". Sandford turned out to be a most excellent Commanding Officer, imparting knowledge gained from experience, expecting implicit obedience and loyalty and giving the same to us with great sympathy, and he led a battery which was to distinguish itself in battle. It consisted of a happy and contented lot of officers and men (does happiness exist in war?). But then I was biassed.

As luck would have it, my sister Christine, having left Girton and a teachers' training college at Culham, Oxon., had in 1915 obtained a post as Classics mistress in Newcastle High School. We met at weekends in Newcastle and, as she also knew the younger Dick Sandford, I nervously suggested to my commanding officer that he should join us in a walking expedition on the Roman Wall. He did ..... the consequence was that my sister and Dan became engaged in the spring of 1916, were married at the end of the war, and lived in Ethiopia for 50 years, where, having distinguished himself mightily in World War II he died in 1972.

Reverting, however, to 1916 after visits to Bexhill and Lydd (to observe firing using live shells) 94th Siege Battery at last sailed to France - men and officers in one ship, the guns in another. I had the privilege of moving the guns from Woolwich by road to Avonmouth. They were pulled by Caterpillars and the progress was slow - about 3 mph! It became quite a progress in the Western Counties who turned out a mounted police escort for our procession through the streets of various towns.

France

We arrived in France in time for the preparation of the offensive on 1 July 1916 - the first Battle of the Somme. We came under command of a Heavy Artillery Group of which the Colonel told us what part of the German front we were to cover, to select a battery position and mount our guns. Imagine our excitement. Sandford and the Battery Captain (Bennett) chose a position about 2,000 yards behind the front line. Each gun had an officer in charge with orders to mount the gun - have everything ready for "registration" and ranging shots. Leaving the Captain in charge Sandford took Cassidy and me to choose 2 observation posts from which the German lines and hopefully our future target area could be observed, fire from our battery onto our targets directed (a very complicated business) and, as important, the whole situation on our front watched and reported - whether it had to do with our own battery or not. Mike Cassidy and I had been chosen, in UK, as the Battery's principal forward observation officers and had been trained by Sandford as such. This day in June 1916 was our baptism. Not only had we to find a good observation point from which we could see the maximum of enemy territory but also to build some kind of protection from shell splinters for our tiny crew of six signallers; then we had to supervise the laying of some miles of telephone lines, for a FOO (Forward Observation Officer) without means of communication is useless. In those days the Battery depended for information entirely on telephone wire communication; wireless, as such, did not exist.

The Battle of the Somme 1 July 1916

Dan Sandford took Cassidy, me and our small party of signallers out on our baptism, and the first thing we learnt was that it is no shame to lie flat on the ground when one hears a shell coming. Sandford was always first on the ground. Well, we found 2 likely places for OPs (Observation Posts), one on the right the other on the left of the area - about one mile apart. Mike and I and our signallers could see the whole front necessary. We spent 2 or 3 days preparing our little nests and long before dawn in the night of 30 June Mike and I manned our OPs. We were great friends and deadly rivals! Zero hour approached - dawn on 1 July: the gun crews were ready; Sandford was in his Command Post in the Battery position connected by field telephone to his FOOs in front and the Artillery Group in charge in the rear. The barrage opened. 94's guns fired so fast (2 rounds a minute) for one hour that the barrels of the guns became heated and had to be sponged out with water. The barrage lifted; the time for the infantry assault arrived - no enemy artillery fire yet. Our telephone lines were intact and we reported. Then we heard the crash of shells in no-man's-land between the lines. The smoke lifted. It was very difficult to discover what had happened. There seemed to be no British troops in the German lines, but there were many immobile bodies in no-man's-land. I saw a number of the enemy massing in a trench near a point on which I knew our guns had "registered". I asked by telephone that 1 or 2 guns immediately be "laid" on to that trench and fired. The battery responded - the shells hit the target - the enemy was destroyed. All day until the July night came down, Mike and I reported and reported and asked for our guns to engage various targets. It was clear that the attack on Gommecourt Ridge - our front - had failed. As night fell we were ordered back to the Battery, very excited, very weary. Sandford allowed us to go out next day at dawn and there we saw the unprecedented sight of white flags in no man's land, both sides collecting their dead and wounded. Success had been achieved at other places and the front line moved a fraction; on our front the situation had not changed but the Battery was moved to another position nearer the line. Mike Cassidy and I found other Observation Posts and observed further minor advances until finally it was clear that another "putsch" was imminent; first the Battle of Thiepral, then from a rise called Pozieres Ridge. Again we had our target area laid down; again we found new Observation Posts. My own was so near our front line and the mud was so wet that making a dug out was impossible. In addition some other British Battery had miscalculated their range and kept dropping large shells (8") into our trench - most unpleasant and unsafe. The message sent to the offending Battery was "94 Battery would be grateful if X Siege Battery would confine their attention to shelling German trenches. 94 SB can provide a FOO in the front line to assist them in this task." We survived.

Life in 94 Siege Battery between major battles was never dull. The guns themselves needed continual maintenance: bolts here, springs there; the levelling of the bed of the gun; the intricate business of sighting the gun; immaculate cleanliness and greasing or oiling of all the parts of the mechanism; orderly and invisible storage of shells (they weighed 72 lbs a piece!). Constant gun drill was done to keep everyone of the gunteam (14 in all) on their toes and to ensure that each man knew the job of every other man.

Our Brigade HQ would give us special tasks - destruction by heavy guns would be needed on special targets requested by the infantry division. "Suspect Machine Gun at A4211B7. 94 SB will silence"; "Heavy fire needed on enemy trench running from XY7 to ZAB"; "Church tower at Achiet le Grand suspected as OP. Try to destroy. Not more than 25 rounds to be expended."

Squads of men were organised to visit Medical Officers' HQ. Other squads paraded for kit inspection; dugout inspection and repairs were essential. In periods of long inactivity men were organised to visit the local canteen or the Ordnance HQ for clothes. Officers attended Battery HQ to learn the latest codes and the meteorological information in order to work out the variations to be made at different ranges at different hours of the day.

FOOs were required to study recent map alterations of enemy trenches and fortifications notified by Brigade HQ. SOS (emergency) lines, ranges and orders had to be checked. Orders might arrive by telephone at any moment of night or day. "Fire slow rate, medium rate, rapid rate X rounds for Battery on SOS line (a) at once (b) at 6 pm (c) when ordered during next 2 hours" or

"Stand by to answer SOS call at any time between midnight and dawn."

At night the guns were manned - in quiet times by a skeleton team, with the others at the ready. The guns were always "laid" - ie. prepared to fire on their SOS night lines. In times of emergency a full or half full team would be at the ready. The Battery of course mounted a nightly guard with an officer in command.

Life was never dull in a well run battery and when it was, the Section Officer would arrange section drills, lectures and "new idea" sessions when the men of his section would make suggestions as to gun drill, dugouts or other accommodation and gun techniques.

About once every 6 months the major would lend his limousine car to convey a group of officers to the nearest town where a good dinner and a drink in a *estaminet* could be had. But we were, when in the line, on our toes morning, noon and night.

We batteries with large guns preferred to fire only when other guns were firing in order to avoid being easily spotted by the enemy. But we were often called upon to take on locations of suspected enemy batteries and sometimes had the advantage of observation made by our own aircraft; usually however the FOO on duty would conduct the shoot by field telephone sending back such messages as UN (unobserved) 1 degree R, 2 degrees L, OK.

FOOs were expected to return with full reports of change on the enemy front, such as fortifications, flashes from new sites of enemy batteries or MG (machine gun) posts and movement of men or vehicles. The signals teams of the FOO were never idle - repairing lines to the battery, laying new lines, reconnoitring for new routes, gathering in abandonned telephone lines - and our boys would not hesitate to pinch a whole reel of wire left abandonned, enemy or ally. I remember one glorious find of about 4 or 5 large reels of good telephone wire abandonned by the enemy.

On the Somme and in many other positions in normal country we had no trouble about cover. As I have said our Durham miners had us all underground in no time - and they were good dugouts - deep, roomy, safe and well hidden. At Ypres and on the sea coast we could not take advantage of their skill and, except for one unforgettable day at Nieuport (see below), we never during my service with the Battery suffered exterminating shelling but we were often exposed - or felt so.

On the night of 14/15 September 1916 we finished preparing our Forward Observation Post on top of Pozieres Ridge - it would be quite visible by the Boches. Because of our forward position we were appointed Reconnaisance Officers for the whole Corps to send back valuable information. Why? We had the only telephone line out over those miles of open country and we kept it going. Life without wireless was a difficult business for the conveying of Intelligence, but not impossible if one's signallers carried enough wire and courage!

In the ruins of a village called La Boisele we were quite heavily shelled and had our first fatal casualty - the Sergeant who was leader of my No 2 gun team. Mike Cassidy dug his 2 guns into the side of a road about ½ mile further forward and was not allowed to fire his guns before the coming attack. Our Durham gunners did a magnificent job digging themselves the deepest and safest "dugouts" possible and Mike was comfortable and safe very near to the front line on Pozieres Ridge just ahead - where one of the Australian divisions held the line from which they were to attack. It was always good to know that we had Australians manning the line between us and the enemy - no chance of disturbance in the gunlines with the Australians about. They were magnificent troops and men: I watched them attack a few days later.

I had been told about tanks - very much hush-hush - by our Major who seemed (to his admiring Subalterns) to know everything. They had been shipped and arrived in France enclosed in enormous wooden crates which were clearly labelled "Water Tanks". Hence their name - maintained in spite of military technical nomenclature, for the rest of time. There had been much controversy about their effectiveness and their debut. As a very junior Observation Officer I thought that they, with the Australians, won the battle of the second attack on the Somme that day (15 September); that they engendered a slight hope of turning static, murderous, ineffective trench warfare into mobile warfare; and also that, because we have always bred and produced the finest Cavalry regiments in the world, commanded by men who knew their mounts and knew how to ride over difficult country, the new mechanised cavalry (tanks) and the men who led and drove them enabled us to win the Second World War. (If any reader is interested, let him go to the Imperial War Museum and look at the first tank.)

On the night before the Battle of Pozieres Ridge 15 September figures appeared in the darkness laying broad white tapes right up to the front line. Strange noises as of tractor engines could be heard to our rear. At about 2 am one of my young signallers ran panting into the dugout and slumped down obviously and dangerously frightened out of his life. He had seen the most "bloody awful monster" moving along the lines of those tapes: we tried to pacify the terrified boy (Gunner Edser was only 17) and I went out to meet my first tank. It was 14 September 1916 and they were used, partially successfully on the attack on Pozieres Ridge and Courselette. I always prize the memory of seeing the first tank in action - a fact I remembered when I entered Tripoli with the Armoured Division in 1943. Later the enemy retreated some miles to a prepared position and we had the doubtful satisfaction of being out of range. We FOOs subsequently had great fun operating in wide open spaces with the telephone lines 2 miles long.

At their first appearance we gunners thought that the tanks were partially successful and the cheers of the infantry who greeted their new dancing fortress with enthusiasm showed that they were most welcome aids - until they were hit. They were very vulnerable to artillery fire because of their pace, 3 mph. (I never had the luck to take on a German tank with our 9.2" Hows nor to take a drive in one of our own tanks.)

My co-FOO Mike Cassidy had already left the Battery and was by now flying his own kite. I missed him sorely for our very close friendship was made even more valuable by our keen rivalry. I remember vividly the simultaneous award of our Military Cross. The Brigade Colonel telephoned our officers' mess one evening wanting to speak to Lieuts. Cassidy and Lush. Only one telephone. "Cassidy will then repeat out loud to Lush what I am going to say." "Yes Sir." (Sotto voce from other officers "What on earth have the boys been up to?") Then came the extract from the Army Order that "on the recommendation of the Army Commander, HM the King has awarded the Military Cross to Lieuts D M Cassidy and M S Lush for gallantry in the field during operations on the Somme between 1 July and 1 November 1916." A Gallantry Award in the field was worth 10 of the New Year and Birthday Honours and for 2 young men under 20 it was the day of our lives.

The battle over, we settled down to our first winter on the Somme - memorable to many of us for the intense cold (we had to use explosives to assist in digging dugouts) and at the break-down of the bread ration. Army biscuits for a week caused far more dental casualties than enemy action. Later when the thaw came we fought in front of Cambrai and moved out of the battle area after the German retirement to the Hindenburg Line (a clever move of the enemy which left the Allies the task of building new positions over a long line in the months of winter - hence the near success of the German Offensive of March 1918).

Extract from the London Gazette:

Awarded the MC

2nd Lieut MAURICE STANLEY LUSH, RA. He reconnoitred a newly captured enemy trench obtaining most valuable information. He has previously done fine work. [Gaz Nov 14, 1916]

Battle of Messines June 1917

In the spring of 1917 we moved north to take part in the Battle of Messines (June 1917) and I was able to see some of the work the human moles who burrowed day and night - while the Teuton moles counter-mined against them. There were occasionally some bloody encounters underground. I did not have a fixed OP until the mines had been blown and the battle joined on 17 June 1917 and then I scrambled to the edge of a still smoking crater. The explosions were impressive sights but I think the enemy had removed himself before the attack. I enjoyed the Battle of Messines which is a terrible confession, but the first attacks were successful. It was a bright and sunny day, our OP was not shelled and I was able to move about and gather a good deal of general information. A gunner FOO like myself whose guns were not in constant action, has a splendid opportunity for becoming a fount of information useful to all and sundry and Command Post of 94 SB was well known as a centre of general intelligence. We had good troops in front of us (1st New Zealand Division). I see that "MSL's usual reliable reports kept HQ in touch". Reporting the progress of a battle in those days, even from a smoke filled mine crater was interesting. One of my signallers did some splendid work that day, a young Geordie named Birks and we were able to get him awarded a Belgian decoration. Once before when a French General had visited the Battery to present a French decoration to one of our men (it may have been the Major who received the coveted Legion d'Honneur) his Aide brought a bottle of good red wine to drink. The ADC asked "Could we kindly have it warmed?" *"Mais oui, mon Capitaine."* Our cook, Guy Vickery, said "Right Sir" and popped the bottle uncorked straight into a saucepan of boiling water! When lunch came (Bully Beef or McConachie) the French Aide whispered *"Et le vin de mon General,"* the reply was *"Mais non, mon Capitaine."* Chlorinated water only. These stupid English!

After Messines we went further north to the coast. On our way thither I went with Sandford to visit "Plum" - General Plumer commanding II Army whose HQ was on the well known hill of Cassels. I was duly impressed. Plumer took the name of Messines when created a Viscount. He, like every other British General, has been heavily criticised for incompetence. Scarcely any British military commander of this century - indeed before - has escaped hostile criticism by his own countrymen, politicians, historians, newscasters and others. I suppose they are fair game. It is the General who makes the fewest mistakes who wins the most battles.

It was about this time that Sandford displayed, on behalf of his Battery, a determination and skill which made us all so proud of him (and 94SB). Headquarters needed a heavy howitzer right up quite near the front line to take on a gun or some target which had been harassing the infantry. For reasons of terrain it was impossible to move to the right position except over the most terrible shell-pocked area - the scene of some intensive barrage. All the other heavy howitzers had deemed the move impossible. "We'll do it!" said Sandford (our 9.2" was the heaviest of the lot - all 15 tons of her). Two of our caterpillars were ordered up and for 24 hours we pulled the three pieces of Mother over the most appalling terrain - craters 6' deep almost continuously. We got there: the massive gun was mounted in some hidden dell which had to be done in comparative silence and by night. We lay doggo next day but then took on the offending target - I cannot remember how successfully. The firing of a 9.2" howitzer so near the front line not only made a tremendous noise but caused great consternation among the infantry who expected immediate retaliation. Mercifully it didn't come but we had to make the return journey and thankfully this also was without damage. We earned the thanks of our Corps Commander and the resentment, no doubt, of our fellow doubting batteries.

The strategy on the coast in June 1917 was to have been what we now call a "Combined Operation". A naval force was to land marines and other troops on the enemy coast between Ostend and Nieuport while troops of the XV Corps who occupied positions on both banks of the River Iser, which flows out through Nieuport, were to contain German troops from defending the coast in their rear. Unfortunately the Hun forstalled us - destroyed the bridges over the Iser, attacked and destroyed the British troops on the right bank and gave us all a very nasty day on 10 July 1917. The ultimate British goal must have been Ostend but the strategy may have been a device to pin down German troops and relieve pressure on the Allies further south - Ypres, Paschendale, etc.

The Battle of Nieuport

On that 10 July 1917 east of Nieuport 94 Siege Battery lost our FOO in Nieuport itself, early in the morning. We were heavily shelled all day with many casualties on the gun sites. Dan Sandford was away from the Battery on some conference and, though our Captain who was in command was a splendid officer and as brave as a lion, we sorely missed "the Major". The Hun was obviously prepared for the attack and in addition to annihilating our infantry the Bosches put down a barrage of accurate fire on every battery, including 94 Siege, throughout the day. Every gun was hit and damaged, and as our gun crews bravely stuck to the duties of keeping the guns active, we lost a great number of them killed and wounded. At one time I remember firing my No 2 gun over "open sights" at an enemy aircraft flying very low and obviously "ranging" for the German battery shelling us. We did not see the aircraft hit, but it never returned again. My worst moment of the war occurred that afternoon when a very good gunner of my gun team, badly wounded and burnt, died in my arms begging me to put him out of his pain. Moreover, our ammunition dump - shells and the "charges" of propellant - was set on fire. This was serious for it illuminated the whole area as darkness fell and the danger of an explosion was real and imminent. Luckily RAE Somerville, a splendid officer with some years' experience in the ranks (and a Military Medal) and I found little difficulty in raising a small voluntary fire brigade. Luckily, again, the ammunition was stacked on the edge of a pond and the shells were not fused. So we went round throwing the lyddite cannisters (the "charges") into the pond and extinguishing those flaming shells in which the contents had caught fire. A wet sandbag soon did the trick. It was an exciting 1 1/2 hours for at any moment one of those smoking shells might have exploded or an enemy battery might have opened fire on a night target. I lived to tell you that neither happened but that the language of Gunner Moore might have exploded the lot! I cannot describe the language which poured out of his mouth. He was one of the first volunteers, a good West Hartlepuddlian with a heart of gold but also with a very long crime sheet in the Battery. He was awarded a well deserved Military Medal. I am sure he celebrated it with a hidden store of rum.

Awarded a Bar to the MC
2nd Lieut M.S. Lush RA MC
When a battery ammunition dump and the orchard in which it was placed were set on fire by hostile shelling he called for volunteers and took an active part in the work of extinguishing the fire and removing cartridges, though many were alight, fuses and tubes were exploding, and splinters from burning trees were falling amongst the burning cartridges. [Gaz April 25, 1918; Award, Gaz Jan 18, 1918: MC Gaz Nov 14, 1916]

We had a relatively quiet time for the rest of our stay by the sea and I celebrated my 21st birthday with a champagne dinner at La Panne just down the coast. Sadly, a stray enemy shell wounded our Captain Fred Grant and caused him to lose his leg: the same shell caused my promotion to Captain in his place.

During our stay in the sand dunes there we were honoured by a visitor from the Royal Navy. Lieut Richard Sandford RN, who had 14 days leave from one of our submarines, obtained permission to spend it with his brother in his Battery. Our dugouts on the coast were very shallow, for at about 4 feet of depth one reached sea level. I was showing our naval guest (whom I knew well) to his dugout when an enemy shell arrived and destroyed it completely along with his kit therein! Shouts of laughter when we got back to the mess. "That's how we live, Dick!" cried our Major, his brother. We never had another shell near us for the whole of his visit. Eight months later while we were licking our wounds after the British Retreat of 1918, we heard of HMS Vindictive's raid on Zeebrugge and the blowing up of the mole there by one of our submarines. "I bet that's Dick" said Sandford. It was. His other naval brother, Frank, picked him up from his dinghy in the Channel after the raid. Dick won the VC.

It was about this time that I had my first trip as Artillery Adviser in an aeroplane. There was a very troublesome German Battery which did a good deal of harassing fire and no one could spot its position. It was, we thought, a 6" gun and the plane was to spot it when firing and put all our 4" guns on to it. This meant ability not only to spot but also to check the effect of our gunfire. So I, as the leading FOO of the Battery was sent along. I was absolutely terrified. "Can you use a Lewis gun?" asked the pilot. "N-no" stuttered I. "Then we'll probably be shot down" was his comment. Well, up we went. I soon discovered that fear was overcome by cold and, when I saw the flash of what I thought was the Bosche gun, by professional interest. We could not describe his position by wireless and we soon returned, mercifully, I thought, unscathed and I was able to telephone the map position, as I guessed, to the Battery. The Bosche fired again and we put down about 5,000 lbs of high explosives on or all around him and, let us pretend, he never fired again. This was a "shoot" when the gun teams knew what and where their target was. They could see our aeroplane - "Captain up in aeroplane will soon have the b....s silent" and we all compared notes after the shoot.

After our coast trip the Battery was sent to the "Salient" at Ypres and I went for a temporary break to do Counter-Battery work with the 13th Corps Heavy Artillery Group. I expect I was getting stale, possibly a little white about the gills when under shell-fire, and the move did me good. Besides, it taught me a great deal about what went on behind the lines in the spotting of enemy batteries and the steps taken to silence them by our guns in the lines. I also took a fortnight's leave in England round about Christmas time 1917.

It was during that leave in 1917 that I met my father after 15 years' absence. He had found nothing in Canada before the war which would enable him to maintain a family there, and when war broke out, to his eternal credit, he went to the recruiting office of the Canadian Army, told them that his age was 35 (whereas he was not a day younger than 53) and enlisted in the Canadian Army. After training in Canada - no picnic for a man of his age - they came to UK and were quickly moved to France where he was in action in the Ypres Salient and was, mercifully, slightly gassed; he returned to Blighty in 1917, had a light duty job with his reserve battalion at Seaford. By then the Canadian authorities had discovered his age and determined permanent Blighty duty for H S Lush! He had seen my mother and they were on very good terms, but he was naturally shy of meeting his officer sons. We did meet briefly and affectionately. In 1919/20 he was demobilised and returned home; he joined my mother in Brighton. But as you will read, I had by then gone to Africa and never really met him until 1922 when on leave. I want, however, to place on record my admiration, shared by all of us, at his courage in joining up in a Canadian formation at his age and with his background.

Retreat on V Army Front 21 March 1918

On return from leave I rejoined 94 Siege Battery and found little change except that we were now attached to General Gough HQ direct as Army Troops, and could be ordered about by HQ of the V Army. We all knew during March that the Boche attack was imminent and that this would be launched somewhere in or near our sector. We had no illusions about the bloodiness of the approaching "Putsch". Every man in that Battery was under such perpetual bodily fatigue that mental weariness was forgotten. Of course, only once, on the first day of the battle did personnel of the Battery (except FOOs like myself) see any Germans but we knew they were pretty close and moving fast. Our men were simply admirable - dead tired, grey with fatigue, going the wrong way! But we were much fortified by having a brave and resourceful section of the RASC Commisariat who never failed to bring us food and ammunition at the right spot at the right time, sometimes with a chicken or two snatched from a deserted village. They were very good those RASC attached to 94 SB; I am glad to add that the commander of our ammunition column was awarded the MC towards the end of the war.

We all awaited the German attack. It came at dawn on 21 March 1918, a cold, misty morning. We were in action firing on fixed targets in the mist. Soon after noon, we were ordered to pull out. We were but a few hundred yards from the enemy when the last gun was dismounted and pulled out. All of us went to our Reserve positions but the Germans were too quick for us and we were ordered to the Second Reserve. The next 2 or 3 days were nightmarish. The 9.2" Howitzer was not an easy weapon to manouevre - each piece consisted of a tractor and 3 four-wheeled 5-ton units and normally demanded 3-4 hours to bring into action. The tractors' maximum speed was 3 mph and the French roads were a mass of moving men, animals and vehicles all trying to get away to new positions. But orders did get through; troops were in some kind of order. Sandford having ensured the safe withdrawal of the guns from our First Reserve handed the Battery over to me his 2nd in Command, and stayed behind to give a hand to E Battery Royal Horse Artillery RMA who had sent their horses away, were firing over open sights ie. directly at the enemy troops and were determined literally to obey orders and to fight to the death. They did. Dan Sandford with them - but not to the death. He went from place to place gaining useful information which, somehow, he passed through to higher command and was their most useful and informative officer on those days. (He received a Bar to his DSO for his actions during this period.)

In the meantime, we and all heavy artillery received orders to get back to the River Somme "pronto". We got there, and incredibly, had several guns nearly ready for action when again came the order to retire. This meant turning every gun load in a half-circle; we were spotted and then machine-gunned from the air. Twelve aircraft failed to hit 94 SB! On we went in retreat, reaching our ordered destination by evening 24 March. A gun had been mounted and by 1.00 am we were in action firing on the enemy. But we were soon ordered further westward and given 24 hours to restore ourselves. We collected a seventh gun (9.2" Howitzer) en route, abandonned at a repair depot.

After a good deal of toing and froing we settled in a position behind a ridge - and I got an unexpected treat: our cook gave us a stolen goose for dinner! Our only other loot during the retreat had been an enormous case reported by retreating NAAFI men as chocolate but which turned out to be toothpaste.

This last stand of the V Army at Villers Bretonneux was a tremendous adventure for me. First of all the church tower of the village, which I ardently desired to use, was being unlawfully guarded by a very drunken Australian deserter with a bayonet fixed at the end of his rifle. Somehow we despatched him, and from the top of the tower I watched masses of German troops advancing without a pause, until they reached the top of a rise where they were literally mown down by thousands of rounds from our artillery, who had been waiting for this very advance to happen. The British Army and nation owed a lot to the Royal Regiment of Artillery on 4 April 1918, the day on which we received Marshall Petain's order forbidding any further retreat by any troops. Even 94th Siege Battery managed to fire a few salvos on to the German reinforcements. We also saw "Carey's force", a motley body of cooks, clerks, batmen and drivers collected from V Army HQ under the command of Brig Carey who marched them through our gun positions at midnight on 3/4 April and saved the situation at the edge of the village of Villers Bretonneux. This was my last battle as an FOO of 94 Siege Battery; the carnage inflicted by our Artillery on successive waves of German infantry advancing to their deaths was unforgettable.

The German attack on the ridge failed. It was the coup de grace by the British Artillery who had retired in order and come into action on the right targets at the critical moment - critical for the final victory of the war. I myself as FOO from that church tower at Villers Bretonneux, was lucky enough to observe and report the German defeat, the halt to their advance, the safety of Amiens and the Allied forces and the prevention of further advance by the Germans on 4 April 1918. I record a message sent to me by a runner from my CO:

> Dear Lush
>
> Your messages timed 11.30 and 12 noon read. Just what was wanted.
>
> We may be pulled out but I have asked to be allowed to stay as I think the line ought to hold now.
>
> The line apparently runs practically N & S through P 25 d 9.2 but I understand we have outposts on W edge of Bois de Vaire.
>
> Lovegrove is in - says line OK down S & Boche putting over mustard gas there & so probably won't attack there.
>
> 39 DA tell me they are only drawing out one or two batteries to cover eventual retirement. They say they will keep their Bty up as long as possible.
>
> Yours DAS
>
> 1.40 pm
>
> 4.4.18

Here for 94 Siege Battery ended the great retreat. We were pulled out of the line to reorganise and rest. We were a happy and proud Battery thinking we were the most mobile and efficient heavy Howitzer Battery in the Army! We had suffered fewer changes of personnel than most batteries; we had fought in more set battles; we had a double DSO, 4 MCs (one double), a DCM and several MMs; and at times we must have been unbearable to others. But truth to tell we had an outstanding Battery Commander for 2½ years - Major D A Sandford DSO, Legion of Honour. He was a man of great efficiency himself and therefore expected a high standard in others. His courage was infectious, his discipline stern and his compassion unbounded. He never asked a man to do more than his ability allowed but he expected the best a man could give. He would dress a man down with dignity and blow another sky high for idleness or deceit. He suffered fools gladly, except when they were his superiors, for foolishness in high places was not easy to forgive when it cost gunners' lives. He had a lively sense of humour but never at the expense of others: "Give a man a job to do and let him get on with it"; "Never use sarcasm to a subordinate". 94 Siege Battery was lucky to have him as Commander.

HQ III Corps, Heavy Artillery

And here in May 1918 I left the Battery after 2½ years service. I became Staff Captain Counter Battery at the HQ of III Corps Heavy Artillery. I wore a red band round my cap, red staff badges and thought myself somewhat of a swell! My general was an efficient, kindly soul called Perkins. He had a good and friendly staff including B Ingrams of the Illustrated London News. Julian Lambert, later to become House-Master at Eton, and one Oppe, who became a well-known journalist. I made a close friend of Julian - but our lives went in different directions. I remember one urgent mission which the Brigade Major and I had to undertake either to Army or possibly GHQ. We were driven in a Vauxhall Staff car - wooden wheels - and so urgent was the mission (I cannot remember its nature) that we sucked 2 raw eggs for sustenance - and nothing else!

Two incidents stay in my memory. The Germans were about to spring quite a big raid. The infantry division concerned got wind of the intended raid and asked for urgent artillery help. I obtained consent and ordered an SOS barrage. This meant that every gun in the Corps (about 1,500) fired rapidly on a programmed target for 5 minutes. Having started the racket I felt awful. We had spent one million pounds! We had disturbed the whole Corps and the neighbouring Corps for half the night, to say nothing of the Germans who then thought we were on the raid. But the German raid did not eventuate. We were thanked. "Those bloody cushy gunners made the hell of a noise and of course brought shell fire on us -but no raid, Thank God." Trench warfare was like that. The other incident was a visit to Dieppe with my General - an afternoon on the beach and dinner in a very pleasant hotel.

Then came the British advance when the surge forward became too rapid for Counter Battery work - except over open sights - and soon the pace became too hot for the heavy artillery. But when the end came I was determined to be in the front line and persuaded my general to let me go forward with some other officer.

We reached the village of Enghien in Belgium at 11.00 am on Armistice Day (11 November 1918). Fighting had taken place in the village that morning but now the "sales Boches" had gone and the village was en fete. The *maire* opened his Hotel de Ville and asked us in. There was much jollity and embracing, and we were made citizens of Enghien from that hour (an honour of which I have never taken advantage). It was a scene of joy in a small country village which had escaped much damage but whose men and women had suffered much.

HQ V Army

Then I began to think about the future. It was clear that Staff Captain Counter Battery III Corps was not going to lead me anywhere in time of peace and that to be a subaltern in a heavy artillery battery would be worse. So I pestered my genial general to let someone know that I wanted a working job. He understood and within a fortnight I was posted to HQ of V Army in Lille (commanded by the Australian General Birdwood) as Staff Captain, Demobilisation, under Colonel Holdich RA as my chief. Believe it or not, together we demobilised one million men in the Vth Army! Holdich was a highly efficient staff officer and a splendid chief who delegated - I enjoyed serving under him nearly as much as fighting under Sandford and he wrote to me when he left: "I don't make a practice of writing nice letters to my subordinates but ....."

I had arrived at V Army HQ in Lille to find that the Demobilisation Office consisted of the said Colonel Holdich, some senior warrant officers or staff sergeants to organise the paperwork and an air of expectancy. Everyone else wanted to get quit of the Army and to get home, but most realized that it could not be done tomorrow and in any case a new War Office directive had just arrived to stifle any thinking of that sort. Army Regulations Demobilisation Part I had made its appearance - a fearsome volume. Obviously some civil servants had spent the war years working out these rules and they covered most contingencies. Col. Holdich, greeting me, said "Very glad to see you. Your job will be to administer these Regulations from Army HQ here. I shall go round the various Corps explaining their meaning and watching results." That is exactly what happened: with a splendid sense of decentralisation, Holdich left to me the running of the quite intricate machine from HQ at Lille, while he visited countless units telling them how we did it. Occasionally he would look in and ask questions about the War Office Regulations and give directions. A few more officers joined the staff under me and work went ahead. It was to me a splendid example of good staff work: the Chief went ahead working out principles; the staff did the general work.

I obeyed my Chief's orders and read the Regulations religiously: there was much dealing with priorities and special grounds, compassionate cases and ex-prisoners of war; men with wound stripes, General Officers Commanding (who could proceed to UK by the Cross Channel ferries) and ordinary soldiers who had to pass through concentration camps. I studied paragraphs about Staging Camps, Embarkation Camps and Collecting Units; all these were connected by the French Railways who gave priority, naturally, to the French demobs and shunted every British train into the darkest siding. We found every category of men and women was catered for. We read two thousand paragraphs ..... and para 1,739 read "Regimental Allowances Forage for Horses: Regular Units already receiving this allowance will continue to do so. Regular Units which have ceased to draw this allowance on joining an Expeditionary Force will become eligible for a re-issue on proceeding to a peace station ...." Demobilisation orders missed nothing!

It was very hard work - my first experience (I was 22) of unremitting work which entailed having a ready answer to any question at any time of day or night. I remember the Commander of a Staging Camp ringing me at 3.00 am, and demanding instructions: a train containing 5,000 soldiers "on demob" had been shunted up into a siding by the French authorities alongside a British ration train. The men had raided the wagons of the ration train which inter alia carried large quantities of rum. Two men were already dead, the remainder, without exception, drunk as drunk could be. What was he to do? Why a young staff officer 100 miles away should know better than a seasoned and senior officer on the spot I could not imagine nor enquire. But I suggested a solution and tried to persuade my French colleague to play trains! It worked!

We had our lighter moments. General Birdwood, the Army Commander, lent me his "whaler" (horse for which he drew Forage Allowance) - enormous but very thin - on which to go riding early in the morning. Leslie Henson a well known theatrical star was producing good entertainments at Lille theatre. I had the distinction of demobilising him later as a special Pivotal case (he had a contract at the Winter Garden Theatre, London). There was the occasional concert and I remember lunching, quite by mistake, almost tete a tete with the then Prince of Wales at a public restaurant.

I earned prestige in my Mess by producing a bottle of Jubilee (1897) Port from my grandmother's cellar which my favourite Aunt (Nell) had insisted on sending by Army Post.

Leave was not difficult to obtain (a Staff Captain Demob seemed to have special access) and I got home to one joyous occasion in 1918 to give my sister away in Twickenham Parish Church to Daniel Arthur Sandford, an event which was to have significant influence in my life; not only did I gain 6 nephews and nieces (in good time) but a link was forged with Ethiopia and Africa, the principal link in the chain of my future life. Chris and Dan were to celebrate their Golden Wedding in Ethiopia in 1968 surrounded by most of their 6 children (5 of whom were born in that country) and 23 grandchildren!

I went home in 1919 for a less happy ceremony, the funeral with full Naval Honours, of Lieut R D Sandford VC who, after surviving the Zeebrugge Raid of 23 April 1918, died of influenza in the following summer. It was there that I met the complete family of my brother-in-law Dan - a notable collection. His mother, the widow of the late Archdeacon of Exeter; his sisters: one, Ethel, headmistress of a school in Yorkshire and later in New Zealand, the other, Betty, keeping house for the eldest brother Temple, a housemaster at Marlborough (and a well-known internationl Rugby player); his other brother, Tom, in the Colonial Service (I met him again later in Lusaka, N Rhodesia); John, a Rector in Devon; and Frank, a Commander in the Navy who died tragically in Switzerland; another brother, Ruscombe, had died in Omdurman in 1916 from Blackwater Fever.

The influenza which struck the world in 1919 did not spare the Vth Army. The hospitals and graveyards were full of its victims. It was a quick killer. I remember a young captain on our staff, alive in the office at 9.30 am and dead that afternoon. It was, as I saw it, the aftermath of the physical shortages, the horrors and the mental nightmares suffered by men and women, members of the forces and civilians, during the long and terrible days of World War I.

My own belief is that we emerged from both wars victorious in arms and though we began to recover as a world power after World War I, sufficiently at any rate, to fight another World War after 20 years (often alone) and to save the world from disaster in the 1940s, the immediate effect of the defeats in Europe, of the Dardanelles, of the incredible toll of death and mutilation caused by the Somme and by static warfare, and of the lack of experienced leaders from which Great Britain suffered for almost the duration of the First World War, caused more direct and more fatal disaster among our countrymen than the Second World War, despite its wider scope and effect, in spite of the more terrible impact on the civilian population and despite the more terrifying foretaste of what future warfare might and, God help us, may well become. The influenza of 1919 also left us sorely smitten by death - even more severely than by the hands of our enemies - temporary victims of our own reactions.

But I was not then concerned with such comparisons. Now that the war was over, and happy as I was in my job as a demobiliser, I had to think of my future. Was I to revert as a subaltern officer in a battery of the Royal Garrison Artillery and if not what did the future hold for me? And then in August 1919 in a short letter came the answer.

Sandford (who by now and in future reference in these chapters is to be called Dan) wrote a short note to the effect that Wilfred Thesiger, HBM's Minister at the British Legation at Addis Ababa in Abyssinia was looking for a likely young man to be Secretary to the British Legation whither he was returning. Both he and Dan thought that the Sudan Government would be prepared to take me on in the the Sudan Political Service, if my service in Abyssinia proved satisfactory and I was willing to enter the Sudan Service permanently. Dan had filled this very post in Addis Ababa before the War, after previous political service in the Sudan. He had previously fascinated me with his account of service in both countries. I replied to Dan that I would accept the possibility of a job in Abyssinia without hesitation and seek an interview with the Sudan Government in London immediately. Wildred Thesiger himself wrote to me offering me the job stating that it entailed 3 years service in the Legation at Addis Ababa, where I should "have to help in the chancery work, learn Amharic and generally get to know all I could of the country", and that after 3 years I should pass on to the Sudan Civil Service (he meant Political Service). So wrote Thesiger - so far so good.

Before receiving these letters I had, rather *faute de mieux*, decided to remain in the Army - what other career was open to me? But this offer from Thesiger was too good to be true. All that I had heard from Dan in the past about life in Abyssinia and in the Sudan Service impelled me to accept the offer. Thus I asked for immediate grant of leave from V Army HQ. This last was granted and I was very soon in Wellington House, Buckingham Gate SW, facing General Sir Lee Stack, Sirdar of the Egyptian Army and Governor General of the Sudan, with his Private Secretary Colonel Mervyn Wheatley. Both were charming and the interview was short but positive - "Can you leave for Addis Ababa in a fortnight, Lush?" finally asked the Governor General. "Yes, Sir," Lush replied. "Good! Well, we will take you on probation now, to fill that post and, provided that at the end of your 3 years you and the Sudan Government are happy about your continuing in the Service, we will take you on for permanent service in the Sudan. Colonel Wheatley will arrange the details." Such was my selection for the Sudan Political Service.

One of the clauses of my eventual letter of appointment read that I should be offered permanent service in the Sudan Government on the same terms and just junior to the university candidates chosen in 1919. I did not then realise that the Sudan Political Service ranked second only to the Indian Civil Service and the qualifications were a good honours degree from Oxford or Cambridge, Edinburgh or Trinity, Dublin, and proofs of leadership. I have since sat on a Sudan Selection Board and realised the vigorous tests applied to candidates. Here was I, with no university degree, selected after a recommendation by 2 people and a 3-minute interview with my Governor General.

Colonel Mervyn Wheatley was an expert in arranging details and the result was that I was to go to Abyssinia as a soldier - seconded as a Bimbashi (Major) into the Egyptian Army and accepted as such by the Sudan Government and lent by them to the Foreign Office who paid my passage to Addis Ababa while HBM Minister paid my salary (£432 per annum plus the "run of my teeth") in Addis Ababa. I think I was the only *Bimbashi* in the Egyptian Army who served outside Egypt or the Sudan for 2 years and never wore Egyptian Army uniform! Thesiger never returned to Addis Ababa as Minister, for he was appointed Consul General in New York, and died of a heart attack before he reached his new post. I therefore never met the man whose acceptance of me changed my whole life, but his son, the equally well known Wilfred Thesiger - explorer and writer - was a member of my service and at one time served in my province.

A schoolboy in 1915 and a Probationer in the Sudan Service via HM Diplomatic Service in 1919, 6,000 miles away - fortune had favoured me and my classical education had not been wasted. But at this juncture, clothes were really the problem and luckily Major Hugh Dodds, returning as Charge d'Affaires in Addis Ababa, was in London. I was in Lille - but we corresponded. Luckily for me, he extended my date of arrival in Addis Ababa thereby giving me more time to buy my kit and arrange my affairs.

My mother took the news very well. Thanking God for sparing the lives of her 2 sons during the war she now faced the absence of each child for long, long periods - for was not Dan, now her son-in-law talking of looking for business jobs abroad? I did not know enough about the Sudan Service to know that after the first 3 years I should be home for 3 months in every year. There was, we children knew, a good chance of my father who was about to be demobilised from the Canadian Army, joining the household again, so that my mother would not be entirely alone; we would also be able to add to her small income and Chris, her daughter, was happily married and expecting their first baby. But it was a lonely maternal outlook for my mother. Even then, and especially a year later, we children buoyed her with prophecies of her coming to Abyssinia. Those rash prophecies were fulfilled - but not for many years.

Sudan Political Service

CHAPTER 4

Abyssinia 1919-1922

Preamble

To those who wish to continue reading I most strongly advise a reading of the first four chapters of Wilfred Thesiger's *The Life of My Choice*. Born in Addis Ababa in 1910, the son of the Wilfred Thesiger mentioned in my last chapter who as HBM's Minister in Addis Ababa accepted me as Secretary but never met me owing to his transfer from Abyssinia and death, the writer of this very remarkable autobiography tells the history of events in Abyssinia until 1919 in those early chapters. I commend them to my readers with admiration for a great lover of Abyssinia, her people and especially of her Emperor Haile Sellassie - the Ras Tafari of those early days.

---0---

So here I was, embarked on a civilian career in Africa. My secondment to the Egyptian Army with the rank of *Bimbashi* (Major) assured me the opportunity of return to the British Army in case the Sudan Goverment did not find me satisfactory after 3 years probation, or if I wished to revert to a military career.

No member of my family except Dan knew what it all meant, having occupied virtually the same post before the war. It was all vastly exciting to a young man aged 22 in a world where jobs were becoming increasingly hard to find.

But there was much to do. I was now the baby of the Foreign Office and a charming Mr Sperling had asked me to be ready to sail on 3 September. Major Hugh Dodds who was leaving then to take charge of the Legation (on Thesiger's change of post) sent me an imposing list of saddlery, guns, clothes (including 12 polo sticks and 2 red polo jerseys) and, merciful man, realised that departure on 3 September was really impossible, gave me an extra month's leave with the result that eventually I did not have to sail from Tilbury until 17 October.

This gave me ample time for suit, polo, the purchase of a trousseau for 3 years. Results included a riding suit built by Ross of Exeter, a cerise red polo shirt bought at Turnbull & Asser, a couple of tropical suits built by Plumb & Co, Victoria Street, the "Shop Taylors", and a pair of black polo boots and trees and accoutrements, built in South Molton Street for £10! Staff pay in the Army must have been good for I paid for this trousseau out of my savings and still had enough to pay my annual contribution to the maternal exchequer. Besides my own kit, I had also to take guns and ammunition for the Legation from Holland & Holland, saddles from Whippey and finally 2 confidential bags from the Foreign Office which on arrival at Addis Ababa were found to contain 2 ciphers and some official correspondence, a saddle, a ham and various parcels of goodies. Those, oh Foreign Office, were the days!

A Mr Lidderdale of the Bag Dept at the FO bade me farewell with a Diplomatic Passport (a yard long), the heavy baggage was delivered to Cox and King's shipping Dept in Cockspur Street and on 17 October accompanied by Mother and Aunt Nell, I was locked into a First Class Compartment at Liverpool Street (King's Messenger with Diplomatic Bag) for Tilbury where we boarded SS Devanha, a P & O liner carrying British troops and a Governor of one of the States of India.

Crisis met me at once! Cox and Kings had failed to deliver any of my heavy baggage and the guns, saddles, etc I was carrying for Major Dodds. At once a guardian angel stepped forward. "You are in trouble" he said. "I am Zaphiro, Oriental Secretary of the Brishie (he could never enunciate "British") Legation in Addis Ababa whither I am returning. I do not like the sea. I will return to London with your mother who will please identify your luggage, which I will take personally to Marseilles and rejoin you there in a few days' time." I left Tilbury on that ship on a three-year sojourn in Abyssinia with one suitcase. But Zaphiro was as good as his word and at Marseilles I spottted him on the quay surrounded by all the luggage, and some more which Dodds had lost going across to France in September. Those were the days when one could recover lost luggage from all sorts of places!

So Philip Constantine Zaphiro CMG came into my life as a helper, a friend to whom no trouble was excessive. For 3 years he played an almost daily and important part in my life and I venture to pay my tribute to a very good friend and a fine British official.

We had an uneventful voyage to Aden but to me it was the opening of a new and exciting chapter. At Tonbridge, the Shop and in France, there had been little opportunity to meet young people except one's daily companions. Here on board for 10 days we younger passengers, girls and men, soon formed a coterie which was an entirely new experience for me. I had a pleasant cabin companion named George Jacques, who was on his way to India in search of a job (he soon returned jobless). There were others with whom I maintained a desultory correspondence, but, typical of those days, we used surnames rather than Christian names, and it took a seven page letter from India, for a certain Miss Read to insist that I should call her "Moppet"!

The FO had asked me in London to let them know whether my ship would stop at an Egyptian port long enough for me to pick up a machine gun, which they asked me to take as a present to the Empress of Abyssinia: "although it will weigh a good deal, I don't think you will have much trouble with it as you can put it with your heavy luggage and leave the railway people to handle it". I agreed to pick up the "present". So at Port Said out came a Royal Navy Pinnace to pick me up (great excitement among my friends) and I returned with a large case containing 2 machine guns! My diplomatic immunity waived all customs and military objections in Egypt, Aden, Djibouti and Abyssinia. Sometime later I wrote a confidential memo deploring the French involvement in the arms traffic into Abyssinia!

Arrived at Aden we disembarked and here, of course, Philip Zaphiro was quite invaluable. He spoke every language, knew all the ropes and we were soon ashore expecting to spend the day in a hotel. "Mermaids on view upstairs" was the greeting on the doors! But news had reached officialdom from the FO and I was whisked off to the Residence to deposit my precious Diplomatic bags (saddle, ham, chocolates and all) for security reasons, and was asked to lunch. I was very self-conscious about my tropical clothing. My Shop tailor had made me 2 double breasted jackets of light but creasy material and I felt very awkward (these were the days before shorts and short sleeved shirts). But anyone going to Abyssinia was regarded as an interesting person and I was no exception. I was able to tell the story of Dan Sandford who in 1907, when stationed with his Battery at Aden asked leave personally from the Resident to trek across Abyssinia to the Sudan to meet his brother on the frontier. The Resident (or Governor) of Aden refused permission. "You will only get murdered" he said "and then we shall have a diplomatic incident on our hands." Later Sandford, realising that the Governor was also "Commander-in-Chief", made a second application to the same man, this time in his millitary capacity. "I like to see courage and initiative in members of the Garrison" said the same C-in-C "and willingly give you permission." Sandford made the trip without incident - by mule. He joined a merchant's caravan.

When making my farewell in the Residency, I noticed that the ADC, who had been in military uniform at lunch, was now arrayed like a Turkish sultan - tulip turban, flowing silk robe, boat sandals with an enormous scimitar in his hand. Seeing my surprise he explained that he was "trying on" for a fancy dress party that night! During our wanderings in the volcanic rocks of Aden we came across an Armenian (or was he French?) typing furiously in what appeared to be a cave by the roadside. "Hallo!" exclaimed Zaphiro "fancy seeing you here!" "I don't know if it is worth staying" the typist replied "and working to the bone in this climate - earning nothing!" I met him 24 years later when, having flown solo from Aden to Addis Ababa, in war, he appeared before me and introduced himself as Antonin Besse, who by then had made - and lost - more than one fortune as an entrepreneur based in Aden.

Denys Finch Hatton joined us at the hotel in Aden. He had come from Kenya and was going to Abyssinia as the representative of the Abyssinian Development Syndicate, a British company hoping to open up trade with Egypt. Karen Blixen wrote movingly of him and his death in his Moth aeroplane in Africa in her book *Out of Africa*.

That evening we crosssed in the 200 ton Aden to Djibouti ferry - carrying mainly cockroaches, rolling like a drunken sailor and run by the firm of Cowasjee Dinshaw - I smoked a Burmese cigar with the captain. We sailed into Djibouti harbour by dawn. My diplomatic passport covered all three of us, Zaphiro, Finch Hatton and me, and our pile of luggage, though my machine gun boxes which scarcely disguised their undeclared contents, caused a few French eyebrows to curl. Djibouti was the home of the famous French contrabandist De Montfried, author of *Pearls, Arms and Hashish* and other books on the Red Sea.

The Franco-Ethiopian railway express to Addis Ababa left Djibouti twice a week at 7.30 am. It stopped frequently for water and mechanical repairs, one hour each day for lunch - Greek restaurant at each stop - and 12 hours each night for security reasons: the first night was at Dire Dawa where first class passengers stayed at a delightful Greek hotel; the second night at Hawash where, though the food was edible, the beds were in concrete cells alive with mosquitoes. The train then struggled up to the 8,500 ft altitude of Addis Ababa, hopefully by 4.30 on the third afternoon. One was advised to arrive in riding breeches or jodhpurs for there was quite a long ride before one.

Denys Finch Hatton (the second son of the Earl of Winchelsea) was a delightful person. He stood 6'4" and was quite undaunted by most difficulties, but I must admit that conditions on the first day in the first class carriage of the Chemin de Fer Franco-Ethiopian tried him sorely. The compartment was small (even for a metre gauge railway), the seats were narrow and hard, there was no fan (air conditioning had not then been invented) and the heat in that confined space was almost insufferable. Denys had wisely produced 3 cases of cold beer which he stacked in the toilette at the end of the tiny corridor and at some stopping place we clambered into an empty goods truck on our train, preferring the heat (105°F) and rattle of a large airspace to the baking confinement of a small carriage. At about 10.00 am the bogie wheels of the engine jumped the rails; we stopped. They sent a brave man with a telephone up a telegraph post to report this dire accident, but soon had the wheels in situ again and we reached the haven of Dire Dawa on time. Dire Dawa was (and remains) the HQ of the Franco-Ethiopian Railway. Even in 1919 it had the elements of a French African engineering village and in particular boasted of a small but clean and efficient Greek Hotel with bedrooms, showers and good food, situated in a lovely garden with orange trees and bougainvillea and vines climbing up the house walls. There we ate a good Greek meal with French wine and we slept well.

Next night after a tortuous journey, up to 6,000' and down to 3,000' we stopped by the Hawash River and bridge, ate a railway station supper and slept(?) in the concrete cells with the mosquitoes and were thankful to start the last lap next morning, in which we chugged cheerfully and hopefully up to 6,000' again, past the very obvious but extinct volcano of Sequala and over many miles of red lava, to the river Akaki; approaching the railway station we noticed a shower of luggage, sacks, tins, skins and parcels - descending from the windows of the train on to the ground track whence they were whisked away by expectant crowds. Zaphiro, who of course had been a most interesting interpreter to us all throughout the journey, explained that the Customs boundary ran just beyond the Akaki station and the friends and families of travellers would come out from Addis Ababa to collect the dutiable goods of their kin! Luckily no one threw away my machine guns.

The train rolled merrily along the last 20 miles often to be challenged by Abyssinian youths racing on their ponies - easily out-pacing us! A splendid end to 2½ days' journey when we reached the terminus.

There existed at Addis Ababa quite a good railway station with a platform and facilities but the train seemed to prefer stopping in mid-track outside such conveniences where there was plenty of room for passengers and their luggage and the yelling crowd of their Addis Ababa relations, friends and every *guraghi* porter imaginable to meet. Even so pandemonium ensued.

We were met by Major Arthur Bentinck, Coldstream Guards, badly wounded in the war, from whom I was to take over, plus Majors Darley and Athill, members of the Maji Commission (described later), the *Duffadar* and 4 *Sowars* of the Escort to the Legation (provided for the Minister and his staff by the Indian Army), and a string of ponies, mules and donkeys from the Legation stables. The *Duffadar* took over my diplomatic bags - the 2 Majors supervised custody and transport of my machine guns which were loaded onto mules. Darley and Athill were attaches at the Legation connected with arms traffic and slaving; they were both lately of the Royal Artillery which created an immediate bond, though I saw but little of them. It was a perfect evening and Bentinck was kind (and thoroughly pleased to see his successor in the Chancery, for he did not care for the job at all).

"Would you like a pony, mule or donkey, Lush?" asked Bentinck with a twinkle in his eye. I caught the glint and the summing up and voted for a pony. We had an exciting canter of about 5 miles across the plain of the "Hot Springs" to the British Legation which stands about 300ft above the town on the lower slopes of a scrub covered hill - having a glorious view to the west which I shall never forget. He asked on the way "Do you type, Lush?" and to my negative reply said "What a pity! There are 4 despatches to the FO and 6 tapes of Reuters Telegrams for typing before morning!" For the record, I achieved the job, but the Chancery looked like a paper mill by dawn. I have since typed voluminously through my long life, rapidly but with 4 fingers - it was a terrible omission that I had not taken just a few lessons before leaving home or even on the journey out. A despatch to the FO had to be faultless and my Chief was as particular - but he might have warned me.

Finally we reached the gates of the large and fine estate which enclosed HBM Legation where I met the man who was to be my Chief for just over a year, and a finer instructor I could not have found. Hugh Dodds had served in S Africa and then moved to Somaliland whence he found himself Consul in Harar under Thesiger - his first experience of Abyssinia. When Thesiger took leave in 1919 he left Dodds as Charge d'Affaires in Addis Ababa, an appointment which delighted Ras Tafari, with whom he was very popular - as he was with most people in Addis Ababa.

Dodds introduced me to the other British members of our bachelor mess in the Legation that evening - Cyril Cane the Vice Consul who lived in the small Consulate building in the Legation compound, and Neville Dyce Sharp the Legation doctor who ran a small but very busy Legation dispensary (with 2 beds). They all gave me a warm welcome with a bottle or two of champagne! It was a happy beginning to a wonderful 3 years. My bedroom next to the Chancery was the best in the

Legation and I had, down the passage, my own diminutive bathroom with its wooden bath of lovely red mahogany into which hot water was poured from the adjacent kitchen stove and cold from the stream which ran past the Chancery.

Before turning into bed I bethought me of those 4 despatches and Reuters telegrams, and finished the despatches to "The Most Honourable, the Marquess Curzon of Kedleston, Secretary of State for Foreign Affairs".

Next morning - early - I examined the really lovely buildings where I was to live for 3 years. I do not know who was the architect but he built a beautiful one-storey house. A large entrance hall led to the Durbar Hall which had 2 courtyards with flowers and fountains on each side. On every side of the Durbar Hall were passages and rooms. In the front stood the drawing room, the Minister's study and one bedroom at each end. On one side were 2 bedrooms, on the other the entire Chancery. At the back were a fourth bedroom and the kitchens. There was a large cellar fitted for defence in case of siege and one of the courtyards contained a well. The Vice-Consulate, another one-storey local stone building, was adjacent to the Legation, having the Consular Office, 2 bedrooms and sitting rooms and kitchen. The stables contained stalls for 45 ponies and the quarters for the Indian Escorts, slightly above and up wind. In addition to the dispensary and hospital, good mud buildings, there were 6 or 8 finely built cone roofed Abyssinian *tukls* to house the Oriental secretary and the doctor; these were the original Residential buildings for the Minister and his staff. There were no other buildings in the compound which stretched over 15 acres.

Behind the compound the hill rose steeply and down its slope flowed a stream from a spring which gave abundant water. This was trapped in a small concrete reservoir and supplied the whole of the water resources of the Legation, and the 50 or more souls and the 45 ponies. The overflow watered the extensive garden. One of my duties as estate manager to the Legation included inspection of this water supply. Regretfully one weekly inspection disclosed the body of a dead sheep in the water - a secret shared between myself and the doctor - no casualties!

The garden consisted of a series of terraces - lawn and flower beds. There was a magnificant paddock of some 4 acres in which ponies were allowed to graze when off duty - especially during the rainy season and in which we held our annual gymkhana. For 2 months during the rains that paddock was white with lillies and mushrooms; the latter, freshly picked for breakfast, became almost a drug on the market. I believe that during the troublesome days after the Emperor's departure before the Italian Army in 1935, this paddock was crowded with the tents of British residents in Addis Ababa who had been gathered there for safety (just as they have been subsequently).

In the corner of that paddock, under the trees which encroached into it from the hill above, lie the graves of British citizens. In 1920 two small brothers died, probably of poliomyelitis, sons of Mr & Mrs C F Rey, then Manager of the Abyssinian Corporation, a British firm in its infancy in Abyssinia. Philip Zaphiro - no better resting place for a man who had served the British legation so well - was buried there much later, as were a few others. R I P in the most beautiful setting on British soil.

The climate of Addis Ababa helped the country, carpeted as it is with eroded soil, to produce a profusion of flowers, wild and garden, and the Legation gardens consisted of terrace after terrace of herbacious plants and most colourful flowering creepers. The house was a blaze of colour from bougainvillea and the porch covered with magnificent wisteria. The keen gardener could watch his carnations, sweet peas and lillies grow in profusion and with the speed of cuttings or seeds in a greenhouse in the UK. In 1919 there was but a cluster of eucalyptus trees at the lower slopes of the hill and it was quite normal (though not a daily practice) for one of us to climb the hill before breakfast. In truth, there was so much in the equine world (especially for myself) to supervise in the early morning that pedestrian pleasures were few.

I spent my first 2 days learning from Bentinck my duties as Head (and tail) of Chancery and then the wider aspect of the job from my chief Hugh Dodds, who throughout my service in Addis Ababa taught me many things - not necessarily by word of mouth but by example. Hugh Dodds was no scholar, was self-taught in many things - but he was an excellent teacher especially in matters of Abyssinian life and politics, in equestrianism and in the use of guns and rifles in sport. He was a good shot, a beautiful rider and driver of horses and a devoted friend of Ras Tafari and many leading Abyssinians. He loved his job as Charge d'Affaires in Abyssinia and was far more in touch with the Abyssinians as it seemed to his subordinates than the trained diplomats who took his place. I remember well that he suggested a ride together on my first day - I on his favourite pony Dobbin - and that we took our ponies over some jumps in the paddock and talked horses all afternoon.

A day or two after, Dodds told me that he had decided to put me in charge of the stables and everything equestrian at the Legation. This involved command of the *Duffadar* and 6 *Sowars* of the Central Indian Horse, Sikhs who formed the Escort to the Legation. I had passed my first test with Dodds!

The Escort were a splendid body of men, extremely well disciplined, very smart in their appearance (they all played polo) and ready to accompany any of us into the town, to other diplomatic Legations or into the country. To me they gave excellent and ready advice not only on horsemanship but on the care of horses and of tack. They also looked after our prison cells whither our Consul very occasionally sent malefactors who were British subjects (Somalis etc).

The 45 ponies were in newly built stables (1918) -

brick and stone, beautifully ventilated, water laid on with sick bay, loose boxes and tack rooms - designed by J H Dodds and built by HM Office of Works under his supervision: he was justly proud of them. The ponies were all Abyssinian country bred (about 14 hands high). In August and September of each year it was the custom for pony breeders in the interior to bring in some 20 or 30 animals from which we would select 6-10 and train them for our needs - polo, pulling a four-in-hand or merely hacking (quiet mounts for the women). The Abyssinian country breed is a wonderful pony, absolutely sure of foot in the rockiest or steepest terrain and very amenable to training for polo, jumping or harness. They cost in those days the equivalent of £5 each. The Abyssinian was a born horseman and the Legation had a very good team of 20 grooms under the rule of one Ato Rucka who knew every pony individually. The stables were supervised by the *Duffadar*.

I personally had a great many jobs in HM Legation, the chief of which of course being in the Chancery, but the ponies and the stables were an infinite though equally time consuming source of happiness. How often did I bless Corporal Instructor Pepper at the Shop who had taught me horsey basics - and a great deal more. How I loved those ponies -all 45 of them!

It may well be asked why with such a small staff at HM Legation it was thought necessary to maintain 45 ponies and the buildings and establishment for their existence. The reason was that there was no alternative form of transport other than pedestrian or animal. The use of vehicular transport was impossible because there were no roads. Abyssinia is an exceedingly mountainous country and Addis Ababa was no exception to the national terrain. One road had been started leading north from the city in about 1915. Massive foundations of stone had been laid out but then the work ceased. No person or beast could walk on these stones and the population with their animals used the mud paths on either side of the foundations. In 1919 these stood some 6ft above the tracks which by then had reached rock bottom. In 1919 there were 2 automobiles in Addis Ababa - one had been presented to the Empress Zauditu who could never use it and the other was the property of the (British) Governor of the Bank of Abyssinia and was also unused. The entire population rode or walked. The Ethiopian nobles or gentlefolk rode mules for ordinary purposes. A Ras or leader would own horses which the younger men would ride violently and dangerously and many horses could be seen, most gaily caparisoned, at any festival or funeral. At a chieftain's funeral his bedecked horse would follow directly behind the bier. Most Europeans (*ferenje*) and especially the Legation staff, rode horses, both men and women, and rode to all functions - luncheons, tennis, dinner or a shopping expedition. At the apropriate times a host would feed and water his guests' animals as well as his guests.

There was keen rivalry in equestrian turn out and prowess between the Legations, particularly between the British and Italians, as regards performance at polo or the races. The Legations formed the principal members of the European community - British, French, Italian, Russian (who left in 1919) and German (who arrived in 1922).

The British Legation owned a 4-wheel phaeton which Dodds drove occasionally over certain mud "roads" - the other Legations had no such form of transport and one year we trained 4 ponies to pull the vehicle and drove 4-in-hand to one of the biennial race meetings (this entailed hiring a working party to make some kind of "road" to the race ground) and we drove onto the track, where some 6,000 spectators had arrived, including all the other diplomatic bodies, in a really brilliant cavalcade - the *Duffadar* and 2 *Sowars* of the Indian Escort leading in full *Durbar* dress and with lance pennants flying; then came the 4-in-hand, Dodds driving and myself winding a coach horn from the "tiger's" seat closely followed by 4 more of the Lancers' Escort.

The Jan Hoy Medan, as the racecourse was called, was the only large area of flat ground near the Seven Hills which formed the diplomatic quarter of Addis Ababa. The British, Russian, Italian, German and French Legations had been granted sites on the lower slopes of the enormous horse-shoe of hills which surrounded Addis Ababa. At an equal distance from them all was this area of flat ground. On this wonderful expanse the European community (chiefly Corps Diplomatique) had built a club house with a lawn tennis court, a full sized polo ground and a sizeable racecourse. Incidentally the polo ground was unbordered because any border erected would remain but 24 hours - wood was scarce.

We played polo twice weekly throughout the dry season. Hugh Dodds really took me in hand and taught me to play. He was an excellent teacher and twice ordered me off the field for dangerous riding. But when I later in my life found myself playing in Khartoum where the standard was high, I was rated at 3 handicap. Dodds also taught me how to handle a shotgun (a new experience for me). I never became a good shot except on snipe. As the youngest of the riding coterie I organised the races: no light undertaking. They were very popular and the Empress and Ras Tafari would attend. Also thousands of Abyssinians who, immediately after the steeplechase (the last race) stripped the racecourse of everything - rope, wooden posts, jumps, etc. I managed to win the steeplechase in 3 successive meetings on Dodd's splendid pony Dobbin, and so won the Harrington Cup for the Legation. A charming young attache at the Italian Legation and the *Duffadar* of our own Indian Escort were my chief and very deadly rivals.

Other popular riding pastimes in the dry season were the paper chases. The country around Addis Ababa was lined with boundary walls, some of stone, most of mud. I was generally despatched with a Sowar of the Escort to select a course and on the day to ride as hare. The sight of two *ferenje* (foreign) horsemen littering the country with bits of paper and being pursued by other mounted *ferenje* was a cause of great concern to the local Abyssinian peasants and caused one old man to reach for his gun and fire a shot at the two miscreants with the loot! Farmers' guns were not the only hazard. Hyena holes caused much grief, but also joy, for our doctor, who rode clad in black and white check jodphurs and a shocking pink shirt, found that the bonnie Scottish lassie whose pony had foundered at such a hole needed instant and pressing assistance - she ultimately became his wife.

In the rainy season when hacking was the only equestrian exercise, we put some ponies out to graze, trained our newly acquired mounts in the riding school, and rode many miles in the rain to shoot snipe.

I have written at length about the ponies because apart from work they were to many of us the chief interest in our lives and because riding and polo became part of my life for the next 20 years in the Sudan.

I shall borrow extensively for a description of the town and surroundings of Addis Ababa from a book written in 1922-23 by Charles F Ray who spent 2 short periods in Abyssinia at that time. My own impression is that of one who lived for these years in the Legation quarter well above the town itself and on the south eastern side of the great horseshoe of hills which dominate the town, rising to 12,000ft while the town itself lies between 8,500 and 9,000ft. The altitude, which made the air crisp and champagne-like, bothered some people, especially those of middle age, but temporarily, and it produced an almost perfect climate. Situated 10 degrees north of the Equator the temperature rarely exceeded 80 degrees F or reached freezing point. We always proudly explained that the rainy season started at 2.30 pm on 15 June, with a violent thunderstorm and ended on 15 September, but in reality it consisted of thunderstorms with heavy rain, increasing in number as June turned to July. There were a very few days of unceasing rain. During this period the countryside and the gardens produced their thanksgiving - wild flowers without number - and the Jan Hoy Medan would be white with field lillies and mushrooms. Further afield on the hills surrounding the town the wild flower expert could gather hundreds of specimens from blue delphinia, wild thyme, maidenhair ferns, bird's foot trefoil and yellow rock rose. Then in September the ground would be carpeted with the yellow *maskal* flower, almost the national flower of Abyssinia. The country dried fast but the dry season was refreshed by the "little rains" in February and March. It was a perfect climate, akin to the real summer which, as every Englishman remembers, blessed his country in the days of his boyhood.

In reading about Abyssinia one must always remember that the Emperor Menelik commenced his residence on the edge of a small collection of huts (with probably a market) as late as 1896. He called his new capital Addis Ababa (Amharic for "New Flower") and very nearly deserted it in 1900 because of lack of wood. Sir John Lane Harrington, the British Minister, begged Menelik to remain a few years longer and promised to produce a remedy. He ordered 50,000 seedlings of Eucalyptus tree (blue gum) from S Africa and Australia. These duly arrived and were duly planted in and around Addis Ababa. In 3 years the signs of a miracle were apparent; in 1905 the situation was saved. In 1919 Addis Ababa and the surrounding countryside was well convered with copses and plantations of Eucalyptus and by 1969 there were veritable forests. The Abyssinians used it for all purposes - house and general timber construction, hedging and firewood. In spite of its fast growth it is a noxious tree. The smoke is pungent and full of oil, the grain is crooked and the timber difficult to fashion. But it has proved the salvation of Addis Ababa and many other towns in Abyssinia.

What about the people? At the end of 1919 the Empress Zauditou was on the throne having been chosen in 1916 by the General Council of Chiefs to succeed the deposed Emperor Lij Yasu. Ras Tafari Makonnen (son of Makonnen, Ras of Harar and a cousin of the Empress) had been at the same time designated Crown Prince, and was, in his opinion, plenipotentiary Regent carrying out the full work of government. He was President of the Council of Ministers, Commander-in-Chief of the Army and Chief Justice. He conducted all Foreign Affairs. He was then aged 27. Lij Yasu the deposed ruler was more or less at large. The Empress was 20 years Tafari's senior in age and had little intellect or experience. Ras Tafari had as many enemies as supporters. One chapter in Professor Ulendorf's book *The Autobiography of Haile Selassie I* is headed: "About men who were an obstacle to the work of the Government by coming between Queen Zauditu and myself" (Tafari) ....

The situation of course, especially in Abyssinia where intrigue was the very spice of life, was almost impossible. It is a lasting credit to Tafari that he was able to govern at all. He had no civil service to carry out the ordinary chores of government, and the Ministry of Foreign Affairs, which he conducted, consisted of a couple of rooms filled with packing cases in which papers were bundled or extracted.

The Minister for War, Fitaurari Hapta Giorgis, was the *eminence grise* in palace circles, and we in the Legations never knew whether he was working for or scheming against the Empress or the Regent (Tafari). Outside the capital some of the Rases of the provinces were definitely behind Tafari, notably Ras Kassa who remained a most loyal friend. Ras Hailu was a more doubtful starter and although later he was really responsible for Lij Yasu's surrender, was a man of power and uncertain loyalty.

It must be remembered that in those days the writ of the Empress or Ras Tafari might run through some provinces and not through others. If a traveller or even a diplomat wished to go through Gojjam or any other province he would be wise to obtain the permission of the local Ras as well as that of the Empress.

I have written these observations as I saw them from my inexperienced chair in the Chancery or from conversations with other young men in the other Legations. My chief tutor, apart from Dodds, was of course, Zaphiro, who was a fund of knowledge but extremely temperamental. The British officials in the Bank were generally knowledgable but financially biased in their interest.

We met Ras Tafari privately or unofficially quite often. We liked him for his friendliness and his interest in all that we did. He would come to the Races and to our Gymkhanas at the Legation. He was not often entertained by us (he shunned official entertainment which took up too much of his time) but occasionally a message would arrive from the *ghebbe* (palace) asking Dodds if he would send the cook and some *ferenje* food to the *ghebbe* in the morning; a party of carriers would arrive in the afternoon to collect the piano and the cook and we would all go along in the evening to have dinner with Ras Tafari and his wife Waizara Menen. We were generally able to collect a party of 6 or 8 and rode down to be warmly greeted by Tafari and more shyly by his wife, Menen, who was then, and throughout her life reserved but warmhearted - some would say a little hardhearted when business was to be done!

We came to the conclusion after these parties that Tafari had asked us so as to give Menen experience and practice in Western habits. Nonetheless, we had an excellent meal, detected none of the western food taken by our cook, ate off gold plate and drank champagne, and, before we left the lovely mahogany table, played 5 or 6 excellent rounds of Up Jenkins. In the next room, which was but a round *tukl* with a conical roof, we would sing songs from the Scottish Students Song Book - *Gaudeamus*, *Riding down from Bangor* - a favourite with our host and hostess, and even then I did not realise that it had an American background! Finally we resorted to parlour games and exercises which were always well received.

Ras Tafari liked the English during those early years; for instance, when he went to round up Lij Yasu in 1916 he left Asfau Wassen, his first born, with Wilfred Thesiger and his wife and their small son, Wilfred.

During those early years too, the British Government trusted and tried to help Tafari. "If Tafari goes under there is no one to replace him" went an FO minute in 1920. Dodds was an outspoken supporter of Tafari and the two men liked and understood one another. This relationship was endorsed by the FO: we all took comfort and courage when a telegram from the Most Hon the Marquis Curzon of Kedleston (after being deciphered) read "We approve of your attitude towards Ras Tafari". A CMG for Dodds followed and was even more warmly approved.

We were never sure what was the attitude of our colleagues, the Italians and French. We believed that Count Colli in Rome would have supported Lij Yasu, had he tried to make a come-back. We felt even then that the Italians regretted that the results of the First World War and their joining therein had produced no opportunity for expansion of their own colonial ambitions and the avenging of Adowa. There was an almost audible amount of sabre rattling from the quite charming Italians, Conte Cornegliano and Lieut Camicia - my equestrian rival and a close social friend.

As for M le Ministre de France, Maurice de Coppet (5' tall) and his self confessed anglophile wife Yvette (6' tall), his instructions, we felt sure, were to improve the revenue of the Port of Djibouti and the Compagnie Chemin de Fer Franco-Ethiopien by importing the maximum number of arms through the port and selling them at the highest price to whomever would pay - Tigreans, Danakils, Boranas or Amharas. There exists in some collection of archives at Oxford a memorandum by myself on the Arms Traffic in Abyssinia in 1920. I cannot find the paper nor accurately remember its content, but I think I must have written it after meeting Simon de Montfried, the writer who was *persona non grata* in Abyssinia. He lived on a hill above the sea near Djibouti in a villa where his wife or mistress played Chopin divinely on a grand piano, which was wheeled in the evening haze on to the patio! Maurice de Coppet had two rather attractive daughters Marguerite and Violette and it was the habit of one of our consuls to wear in each lapel, when visiting the French Legation, a small daisy and a violet culled from our garden.

At this point I am conscious of negligence on my part in the years 1919-22, for I should be able to write down all the names of some 20 Abyssinians whom I met in those early days, whose careers I followed afterwards and some of whom I met again as older men in later years. I can give the names of some of the Rases who were neighbours or guests at the Legation - Ras Kassa, Ras Hailu, Ras Getatcho, Ras Imru and Bitwas Hailu Giorgis. I undoubtedly met some of their sons or young followers. After a while I could talk to them in Amharic but situated as I was, hard worked in the Chancery, it was near impossible to meet young Abyssinians either in their homes or at the Legation. I learned Amharic from Ato Tafara Werk, the Ethiopian clerk at the Legation. He became the Emperor's Private Secretary and later Minister of the Pen. I met hundreds of Ethiopians but there was at that time little or no individual social intercourse. The Abyssinian was not a great "mixer" and there are those who said that to the proud Abyssinian mind the *ferenge* was a lesser mortal than such as he, the Abyssinian, to be regarded with some suspicion. My sister, of whom you will hear much more later and who lived in Abyssinia for 50 years until her death in 1974, loved the country, founded the Sandford School through which hundreds of Abyssinians must have passed, and wrote two books on Haile Selassie. She made a vast number of friendships through her devotion to the people, but told me towards the end of her life that, by then, there was one Abyssinian and one only whom she could still regard as a true friend. In the years 1919-22 I was young and totally inexperienced in Africa; very few Abyssinians were educated to speak any European language, and none of my age, and so I spent three years there learning Amharic in order to be able to communicate. I was also learning the politics and the general trend of evolution of the country. But I could never say to the Sudan Government in later years "I will write to (eg) Ato Mangasha, my Abyssinian friend, and find out what he thinks". Of course, as education spread, as outside contacts multiplied, contact between Abyssinians and foreigners increased and when I returned to Ethiopia 20 years later the situation was quite different. (I did not make many friends *then* for obvious reasons, as you will read.)

Here I must for the good name of Abyssinia relate the story of my *syce* (groom) Tasfai, who groomed my ponies in Addis Ababa for three years, watched me grow in equestrian stature and in the art of polo, and wept when I left in 1922. In 1924 this young man left Addis Ababa with three ponies and rode alone the 800 miles to my district in the Sudan, delivered himself literally at my feet and remained as my groom for five years in a foreign country, the Sudan, a Christian amongst Moslems - a friend and adviser and a carer for my ponies such as I never deserved. Thanks be, he returned to a good job with my sister's regime in Ethiopia and died honoured by many of his and my own family.

Legation Staff

So far I have mentioned only casually the others in the Legation for whom I, the youngest and most junior, was to work. First there was Hugh Dodds, the Charge d'Affaires; he had served in the Yeomanry in the South African War and then in Somaliland. Thence, he became Vice Consul and Consul in Harar as early as 1911 when he was present during the massacre of the Moslems. He was moved to Addis Ababa as Consul, and on Thesiger's transfer, became Charge d'Affaires there, a post which the FO allowed him to hold until 1921. There is no doubt that he was an excellent Head of Mission in Abyssinia during those crucial years in the life of Ras Tafari. Lord Lugard wrote of him that he possessed an influence over Tafari, whom he had known from boyhood, to a remarkable degree. He was a very good chief and trusted and helped me in every way while he was in charge. He had enthusiasm and showed it, whether for Ras Tafari or his ponies or his garden or the Abyssinians, which was infectious. He married Lady Annabel O'Neill of whom we on his staff most warmly approved and loved when she stayed with us in the Legation in 1922. They had two sons. The FO, of course, would never admit Hugh Dodds into the Diplomatic Service but he served as Consul in Tripoli, Palermo and Nice - I hope happily. I trusted and admired him and was always grateful to him, my first civil chief, for introducing me into African ways.

He was followed in 1921 by an entirely different person - Claud Russell, ten years his senior, a career diplomat who had a string of posts to his name, and had served as a soldier in Europe in the First World War. He had married a charming Athenian, Iphegeneia, daughter of the British Archivist in Athens. She had a monkey and a Greek cook in tow! The former was a nuisance, the latter a menace. Once, when intoxicated, he began shooting at the Abyssinian staff in the kitchen just before dinner. I served the dinner and locked up the cook who set fire to the prison cell. However I was ordered by my Minister to release the miscreant, return to him his brandy and forget the incident. I obeyed - learning the power of wifely influence!

Claud Russell who was 51 on appointment as Minister, found the altitude a strain. Our Legation doctor, he of the pink shirt and jodhpurs, gave him a "pick-me-up" which produced all the symptoms of strichnine poisoning except the ultimate decease. He was the only man I know to wear a morning coat over riding breeches and boots with a solar topee on top. He retained me because I knew some of the ropes by then and worked hard, but I don't think he liked a Sudan Government *Bimbashi* as Head of his Chancery! He was thrilled, however, by the ceremony of his presentation of Credentials and I give his account thereof. I assisted in full Regimental dress throughout, carrying the Letter of Credence on a black velvet cushion.

Reception of HE Claud Russell, on Presentation of Credentials

"I was waited on, at an early hour by a deputation of *Dejazmatches* whose followers numbering thousands massed in the Legation grounds [ruining the flower beds - MSL]. An Imperial mule was produced for me to ride. I mounted and was followed by the whole Legation staff and escort, and a crowd of some 10,000 accompanied us to the *Ghebbe* (Royal Palace).

"I was received by the Empress Zauditu, sitting cross legged on the steps of the throne round which stood Officers of State in their robes and lion skins. His Majesty King George's letter was carried [by MSL] on a cushion of black velvet, and was handed to the Empress who received it. The Chiefs and their officers were entertained on our return to the Legation. The order and dignity left an impression of picturesque grandeur which, while barbaric, was in no way ludicrous.

"No foreign envoy has been received hitherto with such honour. This is no doubt due to Ras Tafari who wished to emphasise his personal leaning towards England. [A great tribute to Hugh Dodds - MSL]. It remains to be seen how long this desirable frame of mind lasts."

I found life in the Legation under Claud Russell very different from the happy, gay, bachelor days of the Dodds regime, when we worked hard, rode and played hard, and lived a very social life. The Legation was then open house at all times and we had weekend parties and were very much the lively centre of the small British community in Addis Ababa. Claud Russell was a diplomat who, I sensed, did not really care for the job or the country. I retained my room next to the Chancery but I think I had my meals elsewhere.

During his regime an amusing but slightly embarassing visit and shooting trip was made by a well known MP. It all started with a cable from the FO that Mr & Mrs X would arrive at Dire Dawa, stay the night and then go off shooting in the bush. Would Mr Russell and staff and Abyssinians treat them as VIPs and do all we could to facilitate? The Minister delegated Zaphiro and me to meet them at Dire Dawa and we asked the Abyssinians to give them facilities. We went to meet the train and the Abyssinians turned out in force - the local mayor, a police guard (terribly nondescript) and a brass band (terribly unmusical). The train stopped, out stepped the MP impeccable in tusser silk suit and then emerged a very beautiful young woman dressed in a very lovely silk gown. The guard shuffled in their honest attempt to present arms, the band let forth the most cacophonous noise, and Zaphiro and I stood goggle eyed at the vision of beauty on the foot board. Off we walked up the mud road to the hotel, the lovely little Greek hotel covered with vines and which I have already described. Here the MP ordered champagne (sent ahead from Great Britain) and about a dozen of us (the MP and the lady, self and Zaphiro and some six Abyssinians) stood while Mr X made a very good - mercifully short - political speech in good Westminster style to the crowd of Abyssinians, Somalis and Gurahis who sensed high drama but understood of course not one word. The band expired their last blast, the crowd melted, the Abyssinian dignitaries faded away, and Zaphiro and I ate the best dinner the Greek hotelier could produce (Guinea fowl, mutton or goat, and fruit) swilled down with endless champagne. We retailed the local news about Abyssinia to the MP (not that he cared) while gazing calf-like at the apparition of beauty by his side; she was extremely intelligent. Next morning at dawn they were off - mule and camel caravan ready, and we caught the train back.

Back in Addis Ababa at dinner I related the visit to the Minister and wife and also Miss Russell, his middle aged sister, who was staying at the Legation. Having dilated a good deal on the beauty of the MP's companion I remarked ".... but she speaks with a foreign accent". "She certainly does NOT!" said Miss Russell, "She was at school with me." I left the room.

Next day the French Head of the Railway Company telephoned me. "My dear *Bimbashi* Maurice, you have brought me the most lovely English flower that I have ever seen in Abyssinia - but do not believe, *mon brave*, that she is Mrs X! Mon cher Maurice, they have brought with them *quelque chose de fantastique* which I have never seen before: a *double* camp bed! Your famous Harrods provides them, yes?" Alas, I never saw the couple again, for my Minister and his sister were not amused and did not ask them to Addis Ababa! Of course her name became known to us later. I have no doubt that Claud Russell complained privately about the naughty and wanton deception played upon HM Representative by somebody in Whitehall with a sense of humour!

The Legation consisted of two other persons, one of whom, the Vice Consul was C H Cane. He was a good sound official who was not a great horseman and so quite naturally ranked low in the estimation of some of us. He found the Abyssinian Courts and Judicial procedure very difficult and the delays quite intolerable. But, oh juvenile critics that we were, he retired in the 1950s Sir Cyril Cane HBM Consul General, San Fransisco. The other, Neville Dyce Sharp, the Legation doctor, tended to the physical well-being of all of us, British or Indian, and was in great demand by influential Abyssinians as well. He made a study of the tapeworm, lengths of which he had strung round his dispensary. He was an intrepid rider, a dangerous polo player but a most delightful person. His sister Sybil came to stay with him and was for 18 months the only white woman in the Legation. In 1922, I was joined in Chancery by an able and willing assistant named Porter.

Diplomatic Affairs

What was the mission of the British Minister or his Charge d'Affaires in Addis Ababa in the 1920s? What problems really interested the Foreign Office, whose attitude was always to keep a watchful eye on a country but, unless British interests are to be affected, to let sleeping dogs lie?

When I arrived the most serious problem was the future government of the country - would it remain in the reactionary hands of the Empress or would Ras Tafari, Regent and Heir Apparent, succeed in establishing himself, both at the centre and in the provinces, firmly enough to govern the country and to carry out the reforms and measures so dear to his young mind? While Lij Yasu, the deposed Emperor, was at large, it was touch and go. Zauditu's presence would always be a hindrance. Our duty, approved by London, was strongly to support Ras Tafari - which we did, constantly. I suspect that the other two powers were neither so strong nor so unwavering in their support. The results will be seen in a later chapter. Slavery and the supply of arms (by the French) were not forgotten subjects of interest.

The next matter was one which had already been a subject of importance for several years, namely joint control of the waters of the Blue Nile at their source, Lake Tsana, in the north-west of Abyssinia. The irrigation experts in the Anglo-Egyptian Sudan and in Egypt had been pressing for an agreement on this matter for a score of years. At the beginning of the century, Kitchener had authorised Colonel Doughty Wylie, who was acting Charge at Addis Ababa, to "finalise a treaty with Menelik giving Great Britain these powers". (What authority Lord K had, I know not, but the telegram exists.) HMG had established a Consul in NW Abyssinia to prepare the way with the local authorities. Italy and France were oppposed to the scheme. We sent irrigation engineers in the 1920s to survey as much of Lake Tsana as possible. We drew near to partial success then but, with hindsight, it is easy to say that until Ras Tafari became Emperor there was little chance of conclusion. But the words Lake Tsana appeared on my desk and in my despatches in the years 1919-22 more often than any other subject. The great scheme never came to pass and now such control is probably not necessary. But, of course, as a Sudan Probationer I was greatly interested. I may add that I did not manage to see the great lake which still feeds the Sudan (which provides my pension) until I flew there with my wife in 1972! It is still a solely Abyssinian (Ethiopian) lake!

Next on the list of problems which were continually

confronting the Legation was the state of insecurity on the frontiers between Abyssinia and the Sudan (1,300 miles) and Abyssinia and Kenya (about the same). We had British Consuls at Gore Maji and Mega, chiefly for commercial and trading purposes. The Sudan Government had a trading post at Gambeila manned by a British official. A joint Anglo-Ethiopian Commission had just returned from examining a "nasty business" on the frontier near Maji in which lives had been lost. In the Sudan, "Abyssinian" meant "raider" and there was in fact constant trouble. In 1919 I met (on my arrival) the two former British officers of the Maji Commission, Majors Darley and Athill, fine men, who incidentally gave us a great deal of information on slavery, and also Major Brian Hawkins who was appointed HBM Consul for SW Abyssinia to reside in Maji.

Further west on the Kenyan frontier there was perpetual trouble. A water hole called Gaddaduma was frequented by Kenyan tribes who claimed ownership, and by Borana (Abyssinian) cattle owners; in the dry season there were continual bloody fights between them. The Kenyan authorities were outraged, but the Abyssinian local authorities could not care less. Gaddaduma changed hands once or twice each year. When it fell to the Kenyans we walked about the Legation downcast and practically lowered the flag - but somehow the Borana lads won it again. We had a British Consul at Mega who risked his life annually over Gaddaduma and many other problems - he was Arnold Hodson who rightly earned a CMG for his courage. He then left us to become the Governor of the Falkland Islands and later of Sierra Leone and the Gold Coast.

These Consuls were wonderful men who did more for the British name in Abyssinia in those days than any of us in Addis Ababa and kept the peace more assuredly than any police. They used to visit us once a year and great was their rejoicing to be in relative civilization again. Arnold Hodson "played 36 holes of golf" every day on his 30 day trek from Mega to Addis Ababa. He had two caddies aged about ten years each: one carried the clubs and led a goat in milk, the other spotted the ball and milked the goat for the Master every six holes.

In 1922 the establishment of British trade in Abyssinia was one of the tasks which the British Foreign Office were at pains to impress on the British Legation. I don't think that any of us were very expert at this, even then, complicated problem. We knew that the French held and exploited the monopoly of the Franco-Ethiopian Railway, and that their exacting and most immoral customs impositions at the French Port of Djibouti put a virtual embargo on the free and unfettered trade of any importing country, excepting France, into or out of Abyssinia. One example will suffice: Djibouti was a port of transit for Abyssinia, yet a detailed list of the contents of every consignment of goods imported through the port to Abyssinia had to be made in long hand manuscript (typewritten sheets were prohibited) specifying every package and its contents. At Dire Dawa, the Abyssinian Customs insisted on a detailed examination of each package, a procedure which was repeated in Addis Ababa.

Moreover, the Maria Theresa dollar (originally minted in Vienna in 1780 and used for nearly two centuries in the Sudan and Northern Africa as far west as Algiers, all along the East African coast, and in Arabia and Madagascar) was in 1919 the only form of currency generally accepted. Menelik had minted dollars of equal weight and silver value in 1890 but even in 1920 these were acceptable only in the capital - a caravan traveller venturing into the provinces would need Maria Theresa dollars. The weight which had to be carried (every dollar weighed 1 oz) can be imagined. I can see to this day the figure of our major domo riding up to the Legation at the end of each month on pay day followed by a mule laden with bags of coins - wages for the staff. Pay day was fun for we met all the Abyssinian staff of the Legation and heard all sorts of comments. I can remember a British advisor on slavery sitting in his bungalow rather astonished at seeing his first month's pay ($1,000 = 60lbs) lying in a bag on his verandah.

British trade was clearly not in the forefront of either Abyssinian or British Legation ideas in 1919. But then out came the manager of a British firm called the Abyssinian Corporation, a firm formed in London with Lord Lugard on its Board. They sent out a manager, Charles Rey, in 1919 to find trading contacts in Abyssinia and set the machinery of the company in motion. He did not succeed and reported to London the impracticability of so doing. Thereupon in 1920 the Board approached Dan Sandford with, I always imagined, a brief to report on the practicability of trading - if positive to carry on, if negative to wind up and quit. And so in that year I was delighted to welcome my sister with her firstborn child, a daughter Christine, and Dan - whose previous experience in Abyssinia must surely have been invaluable to his company.

Dan and Chris took up residence in the old Russian Legation next door to the British Legation. They brought with them a governess for their baby and a secretary for Dan, who, with his customary vigour, soon tackled the question of the future of the Corporation. Dan travelled widely and had his first experience of living in Abyssinia in an unofficial, commercial capacity. He adapted himself to the change admirably. He persuaded his Board to send Lord Lugard to visit the country. Lugard of African fame (he had been Governor of Nigeria and had written *The Dual Mandate in Africa*, a book which became a Bible to District Commissioners in the Sudan) arrived and was our guest in the Legation. He occupied my room. It was worth it: I had the privilege of meeting and working with a man who had ruled a piece of Africa and found out the proper way to administer it - to change Government into Guardianship and Guardianship into Government by the former-governed. I was too inexperienced to learn much from him then - but I remembered later some of his advice - or did I? I read his book!

Lord Lugard's arrival provoked an event which showed to me, him and all of us the conditions in which he and his Corporation had to work. The Abyssinian

Corporation when C F Rey was in charge had secured from the Abyssinian Government (Ras Tafari) a Concession to search for and exploit oil in the Ogaden territory. They had paid £32,000 for the Concession, a considerable sum of money in those days. While Lugard was staying with us I was visited in the Chancery by a cheerful Armenian, M Boghossian, who said "Capitaine Lush, your Lugard and his company are saying that they have a Concession to exploit oil in the Ogaden. I think it may interest you to see this document." He produced a Concession granted to him, Boghossian, to exploit oil from almost precisely the same area for a much smaller sum. "I am prepared to hand over this Concession to your m'Lord and Sandford for the sum of £32,000!" said smiling Boghossian. In short, Rey had paid to the Government for the oil Concessison which they had already sold to Boghossian. Well! Eyebrows were lifted on the Lugard face, but in the end he and Sandford refused to trade with Boghossian and after some weeks and stormy interviews recovered the cheque for £32,000 paid by Sandford's predecessor to the Ethiopian Government. That ended the life of the Abyssinian Corporation in Addis Ababa and the visit of Lugard (who as I always suspected, came out primarily to look into the question of slavery). Dan wound up the company and then most courageously he and his wife remained on in Abyssinia trying out various lines of business including farming.

All good things come to an end and in August/September 1922 I left Addis Ababa after my first experience of a civilian career. My probation apparently satisfactory, I had been formally accepted by the Sudan Government as a member of the Sudan Political Service with due seniority.

I was sad to leave Addis Ababa where I had made many friends. Hugh Dodds was the man who did most for me. Because of our mutual love of horses, he took great pains to teach me polo and with his discipline I began to respond well. And so, being young and favoured I expect I became conceited: I know that I had that reputation after a year but I hope I reformed. Certainly I made friends, experienced kindness and understanding from men and the few women around of a variety of nationalities. I realised later in my service that it would have been more expedient to have learnt more about Abyssinia and Abyssinians, especially its rulers, but the Chancery, of which I was head and tail until the FO sent out a very willing assistant during my last year, did entail a very great deal of purely office work and I wished to learn Amharic (which I can speak to this day) the hard "book" way instead of by the far more pleasant but less effective route of social contacts. As for travelling, a horse or mule caravan covers but few miles in a day and though I did many weekend safaris on horse and mule (I visited Harar and spent a weekend alongside Ras Tafari's encampment shooting gazelle). I saw but little of the country except from the carriages of the Chemin de Fer Franco-Ethiopien.

I recall little of my journey home in 1922. I travelled by Messagerie Maritime liner from Djibouti and do remember that my first sensation of discomfort, having spent 3 years at an altitude of 9,000 ft, occurred at sea level, when I found my heart pulsating with the vigour necessary to maintain life at the higher altitude.

I found my mother and father had settled down very comfortably, still in her tiny house in Brighton. My father (he was nearly 65) had secured employment with the Pyrene Fire Extinguisher Company and was in fact one of their travellers in Sussex and Surrey. He was very happy in his job for he was never so content as when travelling the country (by train). Occasionally he had work to do in the Isle of Wight which took him across the Solent to his beloved Ryde. Besides, he was home again, earning a little money and helping my mother; the long exile in Canada was over. He never spoke of those years but one could sense his thankfulness. As for his children, we all felt that whatever was the cause of his long absence from our lives, he had redeemed any wrong, any failure, by his magnificent courage in enlisting in the Canadian Army at the age of 53, and enduring until the Armistice.

Julian Humphries, late of Addis Ababa, suddenly appeared with a car and whisked my mother and me off to the Lake District for a fortnight. He was very generous but a complete Philistine and the beauty of the country meant nothing to him; Honister Pass might have been Houndsditch; Windermere and Wolverhampton meant the same. But he was very patient with his more appreciative passengers and my mother enjoyed her first real holiday since her Twickenham home had closed following the death of my grandmother and, later, of my Aunt Nell, during and after the First World War. Chris and Dan were, of course, still in Addis Ababa, their future very uncertain, and Cecil was at sea.

I bought a Douglas motor bicycle for £25 and sought my friends. I found that they were few and far between. I did not realise until then how many of my contemporaries, my school and Shop friends, had died during the War, and the realisation came as a shock. Of course the Empire existed then and many young men like me were serving abroad. Mike Cassidy, my alter ego in the Battery, was one whom I would willingly have discovered, but he was abroad and, in fact, we never met again, though I heard of him and his marriage. His absence was a loss to me, for his gay companionship had meant to me more than can be explained, in the grim moments and days of fear.

Gordon Perry, an old school friend, who had suffered a bad leg wound during the War in which he had served in the Coldstream Guards, was at home in 1922 still attending Roehampton Hospital, and we saw a good deal of each other. In fact we maintained contact throughout his life. He died a bachelor in 1979.

I think I tried to bring some outside interest and even excitement into the lives of my two parents, whose children were either abroad at the time or destined to remain so. My parents at that time never imagined that they would ever see the countries about which we spoke and which my mother did eventually see.

Corporation when C. F. Key was in charge had secured from the Abyssinian Government (Ras Tafari) a Concession to search for and exploit oil in the Ogaden territory. They had paid £32,000 for the Concession, a considerable sum of money in those days. While Lugard was staying with us I was visited in the Chancery by a cheerful Armenian, M. Boghossian, who said "Captain Lush, your Lugard and his company are saying that they have a Concession to exploit oil in the Ogaden. I think it may interest you to see this document." He produced a Concession granted to him, Boghossian, to exploit oil in almost precisely the same area [illegible] form [illegible] similar [illegible] I [illegible] prepared to hand [illegible] this Concession to [illegible] Lord [illegible] Sandford for the sum of £[illegible] [illegible] smiling [illegible]. In short, [illegible] had paid to the Government for [illegible] Concession which they had already sold to Boghossian. What Eyebrows were lifted on the Lugard face, but in the end he and Sandford refused to trade with Boghossian and after some weeks and stormy interviews [illegible] the [illegible] for £32,000 paid by Sandford [illegible] to the Ethiopian Government. That ended the life of the Abyssinian Corporation in Addis Ababa and the visit of Lugard (who as I have [illegible]ested, came out primarily to look into the question of Slavery). One wound up the company, and I am most courageously he and his wife continued on in retirement [illegible] various lines of business including farming.

All good things come to an end and in August/September 1922 I left Addis Ababa and my first experience of a civilian career. My probation apparently satisfactory, I had been formally accepted by the Sudan Government as a member of the Sudan Political Service with due seniority.

I was sad to leave Addis Ababa where I had made many friends. Hugh Dodds was the man who [illegible] most [illegible] because of our mutual love of horses, he took great pains to teach me polo and with his discipline I [illegible] to respond well. And [illegible] being young and favoured I expect I became conceited. I knew that I had that reputation after a year but I hope I reformed. [illegible] many friends, experienced kindness and understanding from men and the few women around of a variety of nationalities. I realised later in my service that it would have been more expedient to have learnt more about Abyssinia and Abyssinians, especially its rulers, but the Chancery, of which I was head and tail until the FO sent out a very willing assistant during my last year, did entail a very great deal of purely office work and I wished to learn Amharic (which I can speak to this day) the hard "book" way instead of by the far more pleasant but less effective route of social contacts. For travelling, a horse or mule caravan covers but few miles in a day and though I did many weekend safaris on horse and mule (I visited Harar and spent a weekend alongside Ras Tafari's encampment shooting gazelle), I saw but little of the country except from the carriages of the Chemin de Fer Franco-Ethiopien.

I recall little of my journey home in 1922. I travelled by Messageries Maritimes liner from Djibouti and remember that my first sensation of discomfort, having spent 4 years at an altitude of 9,000 ft. occurred at sea level when I found my heart pulsating with the vigour necessary to maintain life at the higher altitude.

I found my mother and father had settled down very comfortably, still in her tiny house in Brighton. My father (he was nearly 65) had secured employment with the Pyrene Fire Extinguisher Company and was in fact one of their travellers in Sussex and Surrey. He was very happy in his job for he was never so content as when travelling the country (by train). Occasionally he had work to do in the Isle of Wight which took him across the Solent to [illegible] Ryde. Besides, he was home again, earning a [illegible] money and helping my mother. [illegible] long exile [illegible] was over. He never spoke of those years [illegible] could sense his thankfulness [illegible] for his children [illegible] felt that whatever was the cause of his long absence from our lives, he had redeemed any [illegible] by his magnificent courage in enlisting in the Canadian Army at the age of 59, and enduring until the Armistice.

[illegible] of Addis [illegible] suddenly appeared [illegible] and whisked my mother and me off to the Lake District for a fortnight. He was very generous [illegible] and the beauty of the country meant nothing to him. Honiton [illegible] might have been [illegible], Windermere and Wolverhampton meant the same. But he was very patient with his more appreciative passengers and my mother enjoyed her first real holiday since her Twickenham home had closed following the death of my grandmother and, later, of my Aunt Nell, during and after the First World War. Chris and Dan were, of course, still in Addis Ababa, their future very uncertain, and Cecil was at sea.

I bought a Douglas motor bicycle for £25 and sought my friends. I found that they were few and far between. I did not realise until then how many of my contemporaries, my school and Shop friends, had died during the war, and the realisation came as a shock. Of course the Empire existed then and many young men like me were serving abroad. Mike Cassidy, my alter ego in the Battery, was one whom I would willingly have discovered, but he was abroad and, in fact, we never met again, though I heard of him and his marriage. His absence was a loss to me, for his gay companionship had meant to me more than can be explained, in the grim moments and days of fear.

Gordon Pussy an old school friend, who had suffered a bad leg wound during the War in which he had served in the Coldstream Guards, was at home in 1922 still attending Roehampton Hospital, and we saw a good deal of each other. In fact we maintained contact throughout his life. He died a bachelor in 1979.

I think I tried to bring some outside interest and even excitement into the lives of my two parents, whose children were either abroad at the time or destined to remain so. My parents at that time never imagined that they would ever see the countries about which we spoke, and which my mother did eventually see.

Left:
British Legation, Addis Ababa, staff and Indian escort, January 1921; Arnold Hodson (Consul Mega), C H Porter (Asst Sec), C H Cane (Vice Consul Addis Ababa), MSL (Secretary), J H Dodds (HBM Chargé d'Affaires), P C Zaphiro (Oriental Sec), N A Dyce Sharp (Physician), A D Home (Consul Gondar)

Right:
Presentation of Credentials by H M Minister, 1921
Rear: N A Dyce Sharp, Arnold Hodson, MSL
Middle: A D Home, P C Zaphiro, C H Cane, DGP
Front: Mrs Russell, Claud Russell (Minister), J H Dodds

Below right:
MSL, Dan and Chris Sandford in camp at Monogasha, 1921

Below:
Consulate Building, Addis Ababa

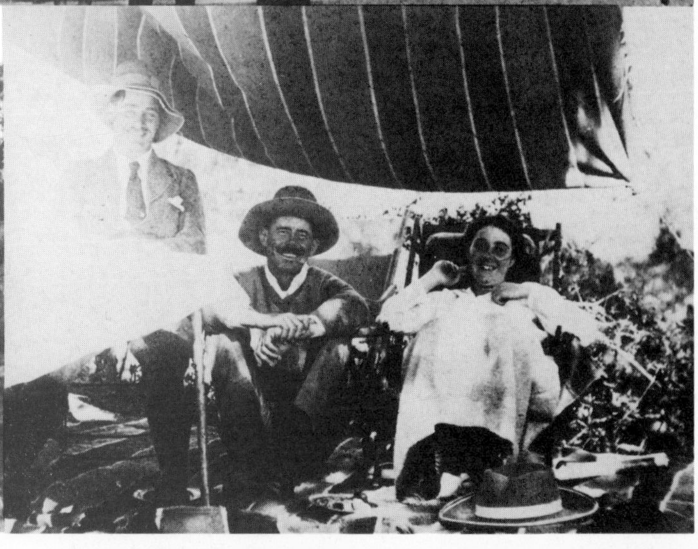

On trek with Philip and Gwen Ingleson, Gedaref District, 1925

Martin Parr, MSL, J Simpson, Rollo Bolton, Dinah Coates; Khartoum, Christmas 1926

MSL on 'Shaheen' with Tasfai, 1926

CHAPTER 5

Khartoum and Gedaref District 1922-26

First Journey up the Nile 1922
Shellal (Aswan) to Wadi Halfa

The two days spent on the Sudan Government Mail steamer (a stern wheeler) as she churned the muddy waters of the Nile between Shellal and Wadi Halfa (the end of the flood was still coming down from the south) would of course have been a proper time to think seriously about the country and service in which I was destined to spend the next 20 years of my life. Naturally I did not. I was far too interested in the completely new surroundings: the interminable sand covered landscape, broken here and there by a riverain village, the extraordinary gyrations of the powerful stern wheeler and her limpet barges, my fellow first class passengers, the chattering third class travellers, Sudanese and Egyptian, who travelled on barges alongside the steamer, surrounded by mounds of personal belongings, the excellent fare provided by the Sudan Railways and Steamers Department (kippers for breakfast) who expected a high standard of behaviour from their passengers (black ties for dinner were not unknown) and finally the dismal intoning of the crewmen who with poles or leads sounded the bends of the river and confirmed the depth to the *rais* or pilot in charge of the craft and knew by instinct the meaning of every eddy or change of colour in the water of the ever varying currents of the vast river; such knowledge was handed down by father to son through generations of these wizards who knew their Nile as the modern bus driver knows the surface of the streets of his route.

Little did I think that I should be making the same journey in eight years time in my Governor General's official steamer as his Private Secretary, with my bride to be, his guest, by my side, and again in 16 years, at the beginning of World War II, as Governor of the Province we were nearing. Here I was steaming up the Nile about to join a *corps d'elite*, the Sudan Political Service, without most of the qualifications which the Selection Board most carefully investigated; no post War year at a University; no sign of a degree; no athletic prowess (one did not get a Blue for polo!); no knowledge of Law or Arabic. My contemporaries had already passed their examinations in these subjects and so fulfilled their probation and had achieved experience in the administration of magistrates' courts conducted in Arabic. How on earth could I ever catch up? But I entertained only a few of these thoughts or fears: I was thrilled (with a smattering of panic) with the first experience of the Sudan.

My first impressions were the immaculate state of efficiency and cleanliness of the steamer, the impeccable manners of the *suffragi* (Sudanese steward) who was the first Sudanese I had ever met, and the friendliness of his British superior, both of whom welcomed me and other passengers on board the steamer at Shellal in Egypt (the southern terminus of the metre gauge railway which ran from Luxor to Aswan, a ghastly 8-12 hour journey). Somehow they knew I was a newly joined official. My fellow passengers included Mr Grabham, the Government Geologist, whom I had met on the boat from Venice; he asked me to stay with him in Khartoum. All of these were interested in Abyssinia and my life there, and made me feel I was amongst friends.

Wadi Halfa

I cannot remember much of our arrival at Wadi Halfa except that it was in complete contrast to our reception at Shellal railway terminal in Egypt. In the Sudan there was order, calm and unobtrusiveness, with a very smart Sergeant Major *(Bash Shawish)* of the Police in charge. One delivered one's baggage to a porter bearing a number - one's ticket to a Sudan Government Railway policeman or clerk and the luggage was automatically taken to the sleeping car allotted to one.

The Sudan Railways ran on metre gauge track - the gauge which Kitchener had adopted in 1899. The passenger coaches were of a width suitable for the wide European gauges - very comfortable, the sleeping cars especially - but clearly they were not appropriate for a narrow gauge chassis at high speed. The trains therefore seldom travelled at more than 25-30 mph. Moreover this speed was suitable to the track itself. The Wadi Halfa - Khartoum express took 36 hours to cover the 581 miles. The first stage of the journey to Abu Hamed (230 miles) was built in 1896-97 by Kitchener's army and runs in a straight line across the desert; the stations are numbered 1 to 10 - but there were no villages at them. Mercifully we covered these miles by night and woke dusty but cool. The rest of the day I had my first glimpses of rural life as we passed villages and towns on the right bank of the Nile; by evening we reached

Atbara, the "Crewe" of the Sudan and Headquarters of the Sudan Government Railways and Steamers; next morning, at dawn, we were in Khartoum Central Station.

In Khartoum I was met by a member of the Personnel Staff of the Civil Secretary's office who normally would have taken care of me on arrival. But Grabham explained that I was his guest and carried me off to his house promising to produce my body later to the Personnel Office. Thereafter my host took charge of me. Grabham was a very efficient Government geologist and specialist in the earth's structure. He was a kind host but he was eccentric: having no apparent leanings towards Christianity his guest rooms were decorated with texts from the Old and New Testaments, which hung untidily on the walls. He was also an ardent photographer and loved to show his slides. "We are having twelve to dinner tonight" he would say "and we'll drink black velvet. Afterwards I shall show my slides." Black velvet (champagne and stout mixed) was an excellent cold drink but a soporific without equal. Dinner, good talk and good drink were the order and then Grabham had his guests in bondage. Comfortably seated on the verandah, our host would begin his favourite hobby. He loved his slides, he knew his geology and his Sudan country and he liked nothing better than to talk about both. He never stopped; a snore or two meant nothing. A veritable plea to get away was met with "But I have six slides about the Miocene period which you *must* see". Grabham was a good friend to a young probationer: he died in his beloved Madeira in his nineties and doubtless some of the heavenly host still watch his pictures of Gebel Marra in Darfur and Lake Tsana in Abyssinia both of which he had visited.

Intelligence Department Khartoum

On the morning of my arrival I made my first contact with the Government in the Sudan. I duly went to the *"Dakhilia"* building of the Civil Secretariat.

Before I enter the august portals of the Sudan Government Offices let me explain very roughly how the Government of the Anglo-Egyptian Condominium was run. Under the Governor General (a British subject, selected by the British Government and appointed by the *Khedive* of Egypt) the principal Departments of the Sudan Government were the Office of the Civil Secretary, responsible for the Administration of the country, the Office of the Legal Secretary, responsible for all aspects of Law and Order including the *Sharia* or Islamic Law Courts under the Sudanese Grand *Qadi*, and the Financial Secretary responsible for all Financial matters. The Heads of most Technical Departments, eg. Medical, Agricultural and Economic had direct access to the Governor General, but as a matter of practice would generally approach him through one of the Secretaries; and in the case of the Irrigation Department it was always after discussion with the Egyptian Irrigation Ministry.

The Head of Personnel in the Civil Secretary's Department was a delightful man by the name of Gibson. He was in fact Assistant Civil Secretary, Personnel (a job I was to handle myself in due course) and he soon put me completely at my ease, showing sympathetic realisation that I was a late arrival among the immediate post-war batches of men who were now established as permanent members of the Political Service, while I, with only my Abyssinian Service to my credit, had much to do to gain permanent and pensionable recognition. The Civil Secretary had posted me to the Intelligence Department based in Khartoum, a job which would, they hoped, give me an opportunity to cram my studies of Law and Arabic into one year. "We are sure that the Director of Intelligence, Mr Willis, will help you in every way to achieve this." To be brief I passed my Law in a year but it took me a second attempt to forget my Amharic and to satisfy the examiners in the stiff Arabic exam. "We are glad to report" these pundits wrote in 1924 "that the persistent candidate Mr Lush has passed the examination."

Charles Armine ("Chunky") Willis, the Director of Intelligence (*Mukhabarat* in Arabic) was 41 when I first met him. He had enjoyed a brilliant career at Eton and Oxford where he was Newcastle Scholar at Magdalen. He was a notable oarsman, won the Ladies Plate when he was 18, gained his Rowing Blue in 1903 and became President the next year. He was one of the early University entrants into the Sudan Political Service in 1905.

After service in four Provinces he started the Intelligence Department in 1914 and became Director in 1919. Intelligence was obviously his "bent" and there is no doubt that after eight years in the Provinces, Chunky was qualified to help form an intelligence service, which had become necessary. Public opinion in the bigger towns (Khartoum, Omdurman, Port Sudan, Wad Medani and Atbara), where politics were beginning to sprout and education was naturally (and rightly) introducing trends of thought which were wider than the tribal background of the rural population, was tending to bear a trace of politics of an Egyptian nature. Some form of collation of public and private opinion - other than personal relation between the governed and the governors or guardians - had to be devised and directed from Khartoum, but in conjunction with the Provincial Administrations; and so the Department of Intelligence was created.

In a country which the *Mahdi* (the Guided One) of Allah and his lieutenants had ruled and despoiled for many generations, and having only been conquered by force of arms, which was ruled by a Condominium in which the active partner was foreign in race and religion, in which the sleeping partner was a Moslem neighbour very much under the supervision of the same foreigners, it was natural that, in the towns at any rate and sometimes in the rural areas, political and religious ideas and even fanaticism should be fostered by men of forethought, of religious, racial and political fervour, or even by malcontents.

In the early days of the Condominium the Army had complete control of the Intelligence Department which was part of the Headquarters Establishment of the Commander-in-Chief *(Sirdar)* of the Egyptian Army in Cairo, who was also Governor General of the Sudan. Reports of, for example, fomenting trouble would come direct to the Chief of Intelligence, and the action, such as further investigation or removal of the trouble maker, would be taken on the orders of Intelligence Staff in Khartoum possibly without previous reference to the Provincial Governor. Stack and Symes, both Directors of Intelligence in those early years, would surely have followed this military practice. But as the government of the very early years became less military and civilian Governors and provincial administrative staff took the place of British and Egyptian military officers, the military methods of Intelligence became outmoded.

In 1922 there was a general feeling in the provinces that the Intelligence Department was infiltrating itself too much into provincial administration. A Governor would believe that his District Commissioners (DCs) ought to know from their ordinary day-to-day contacts what was afoot among the tribes and resent a message sent from the *Mukhabarat* (Intelligence) in Khartoum such as "Agent in X District reports Sheikh Mohd Ahmed in constant contact with Abdulla Omar whose brother is secretary to White Flag League in Assiut Egypt". The Governor would ask his District Commissioner for information but would much prefer that *Mukhabarat* should not be involved in his Province. And yet, in 1922 for instance, extremely serious excesses had been committed in Egypt against British troops and Britons generally. There were Egyptian Army officers on detachment in many provinces of the Sudan, and it was easy for these officers, if they were politically minded and inimical to the Sudan Administration to do a great deal of harm. In fairness to the many Egyptian officers who served in the Sudan, I am happy to record that no extensive damage was effected by them there, but there were definite cases later which added to the demand in 1924 for the expulsion of all Egyptian troops from the Sudan.

I had therefore joined a Department which was generally disliked both by Headquarters in Khartoum and by the provinces on the grounds of interference in provincial affairs. In the course of wide experience in World War II when I was administering civil populations overrun by British forces, I came to learn that decentralisation is the first essential in civilian administration, including intelligence. Military intelligence does not realize this and tends to centralise its activities. The military education and experience of Stack and Symes led them to maintain centralisation. Even Chunky Willis as a civilian Director of Intelligence did not decentralise to the provinces, hence the low status of his Department in the eyes of provincial and central Government.

I was not to know this then. Chunky Willis welcomed me in his office as someone who could remove a load of paper work from his shoulders and leave him free to concentrate on the under cover work which he found was necessary and valuable to the administration - politically - of the Sudan.

My first task was to compile the Sudan Monthly Intelligence Report, culled from Provincial reports, from special reports or private letters from Governors and DCs and from the administrations or British representatives in neighbouring countries. There were, of course, many other menial jobs, one of which was correcting a new cypher volume about to be distributed to all DCs. I liked working under Chunky who left me alone at work and gave good advice about the Sudan. He was a most helpful chief to a newcomer.

I learnt a great deal about the general administration of the provinces but little about the problems with which Chunky had to deal. Although he was a very good teacher he sometimes did not realise how little I knew, except about Abyssinia!

Socially, Clare his most charming wife and he were more than kind: after I had dined once or twice at their very nice house with its small, gay garden, they asked me to occupy one of their spare rooms and to live with them. I suspect that this was after Chunky discovered that I played the piano - he loved to sing Negro Spirituals and Sea Shanties to my accompaniment. This was a kindness which caused me great happiness and which I was never able to repay. Clare Willis was a great-great grandaughter of Lord Holmpatrick. She was a delightful person and gave to me some of the love she should have been able to shower on their only child whose life was a tragedy. Luckily she had many friends and the complete adoration of a young man!

Living in the Willis' house gave me an entree into Khartoum society which was invaluable to me. These were the days of Society with a big S and visiting cards and though my calling list was not so long as when I was posted to Khartoum as DC four years later, it was formidable enough. I had many introductions from Dan Sandford, and Clare was to be the balance, trying to cut my social commitments to a minimum so that I could study Law and Arabic.

She introduced me to worship at Khartoum Cathedral where I joined the choir and later met Bishop Llewellyn Gwynne, whom I had met in France in 1917. He became a lifelong friend and spiritual guide. Never shall I forget finding him at the side of my wife's bed in the Anglo-American Hospital in Cairo 14 years later, praying for grace for Sylvia our newly-born daughter.

Another lifelong friend who was living next door with the Legal Secretary and his wife was John de Courcy Hamilton, who most kindly lent me a pony to ride with him, and afterwards (in 1926) persuaded me to play polo. Our lives came together again in Cairo where I succeeded him as Sudan Agent in 1934. He was the perfect courtier, much beloved of all the ladies in Khartoum - a man whose thoughts and ideas were older than his years and who was immensely popular and sought after by his elders in Khartoum and Cairo. He finally married after his retirement.

The Rev Harper, the new Chaplain to the Cathedral who arrived in 1923, was to the minds of Clare Willis and me bound to be a misfit. His accent! His approach! How wrong we were - "Uncle" Harper, next to Gordon and Bishop Gwynne, was the most potent, the most practical and the most spiritual force the Sudan, during the remaining history of the Condominium, was blessed to experience. I knew him when he arrived new to his charge. I appreciated him even more three years later when I was DC of Khartoum and he one of my spiritual and human aides. (I was one of his co-founders of the Supper Club, Khartoum.) I knew him in later years when I was Director of Personnel, and afterwards as a member of the Palace and Governor General's Staff. Never did Uncle Harper fail us as an international Christian community in a Moslem country. He was the most perfect, yet to himself imperfect, the most patient, yet always impatient to do better, spiritual/human leader that a community such as existed in Khartoum could desire.

Posted as ADC to Gedaref, Kassala Province 1924-26

At last my first, happy appointment in Khartoum came to an end. I was posted in 1924, to be Assistant District Commissioner, Gedaref District, Kassala Province.

This district, in its eastern border, was contiguous with Abyssinia and it was nice to think that my Abyssinian experience and my knowledge of Amharic had been remembered and might be useful. To a limited extent they were, and the Gallabat Sub-District (Metemma to the Abyssinians) became part of my bailiwick. (The Italians captured the town in 1940.)

It was exciting (and a trifle alarming) to know that life as a District Commissioner in the field was beginning and that I was leaving the civilization of Khartoum.

There was much to be done. Equipment for the field, camp furniture including bed, bath, table and chair, *shamadans* (camp candle holders - wind proof) sheets, blankets and the roll in which to carry clothes and linen - all had to be purchased. Luckily the Director of the Stores and Ordinance Department, the great provider for all Sudan officials, knew me because he had been a friend of one of the Sandfords (his wife, too, was a darling and a great friend of Clare Willis) and these splendid ladies willingly saw to it that I lacked nothing. Nor was it very expensive - just within my annual salary of £540. I found the name of the DC of Gedaref, J Guthrie Monteath, and that he had taken early leave. J N Richardson was the Assistant DC and I very soon received from him a warm, welcoming letter. He told me that he would be sending his own riding and baggage camels to the Blue Nile near Wad Medani to bear me and my kit the 150 miles to Gedaref; a Gedaref policeman would meet the train from Khartoum at Wad Medani and take me down to the *meshra* (ford) and my baggage camels would be on the east bank; I had better spend the night by the river and start the journey next day. This was kindness itself and made the journey into the unknown so much more easy in the knowledge that someone, at the other end, cared. I may say he ended his letter "Don't delay in arriving here: Monteath is away and there is a hell of a lot to be done." In the event Richardson sent the district lorry instead of camels, such was the urgency of my arrival. I saved three days on the road and a very sore sit-upon after what would have been my first camel ride. Kind, impetuous Whiskers (for that was his nickname). He was killed ten yards in front of me on the Atbara Bridge in 1940 - but that is another story.

Journey to Gedaref

After crossing the *meshra* near Wad Medani, the capital of Blue Nile Province, I think we spent a night on the road at a resthouse (a mud hut with a roof of millet stalk thatch; water from a well). Eventually we arrived to be met by an enthusiastic Whiskers who was finding life as sole occupant of the *Merkaz* (District Office) of a big district a trifle strenuous, and longed for assistance and company. He himself had joined the Sudan Government in 1919 and spent 3 or 4 years in the Education Department as Tutor in Gordon College. After four years he opted for a probationary period in the Administration Service as an ADC and finally decided to join the Administration. He taught me in a wonderfully kindly way during the year in which we worked together in Gederaf. He was impetuous, with men and beasts and this was often put down to impatience. His ponies were apt to throw up their heads, but he was a most lovable person to whom I owe a great deal. It was a great joy to me to find in later life that he was a senior DC in my Province, where he was, as always, a tremendous support. His tragic death was a great personal grief.

Gedaref

When I arrived in Gedaref there existed only two buildings to house British Political Staff. One was the DC's house, built for a married couple (the Monteaths, who were on leave when I arrived), the other for a single man. This I shared with Whiskers for meals but lodged next door in a circular stone-mud *tukl* with a conical thatched roof, a door on leather hinges and two glass windows which let in the minimum light. I seem to remember a rickety wardrobe slightly devastated by white ants and I had a tea case for my clothes. The floor was loose stone on which mats lay. I bathed in my canvas "trek" bath: the Public Works Department had not caught up with the expansion of Gedaref District Staff.

In 1924 the official buildings in Gedaref consisted of the *Merkaz* buildings plus a reasonably large prison and store, situated at the top of the rise leading out of the one street town; the two residences stood about 500 yards to the west; each had camel and horse stables and apologies for gardens. The school and the dispensary (no hospital) of corrugated iron lay in the vicinity of the *Merkaz*. It was not an inspiring layout for the HQ of a large and important district and was greatly enlarged later when the railway was extended from Kassala.

Eastern Arab Corps (EAC)

The majority of the civilian population of Gedaref lived beyond the town to the east and north and drew their water from a stream which separated the *gebel* (hill) from the town and the *Merkaz*. On the slopes of the *gebel* were the quarters, including the HQ and officers' mess of the Eastern Arab Corps - a unit of the Egyptian Army stationed permanently in Gedaref whose strategic duty it was to protect the eastern border (Abyssinian frontier) of the Sudan. The Corps covered this long frontier with a company at Kassala (120 miles distant), a small detatchment in Gallabat (90 miles to the south-east and right on the frontier) with the remainder in Gedaref under the Officer Commanding, who in 1924 was The Hon Bertram Aloysius Forbes Bey, a very smart, immaculately dressed Colonel: he was brother of the then Master of the Horse to King George V. He was a very good officer commanding a crack unit of the Egyptian Army and was immensely hospitable - even to the young DCs whom he regarded as newly joined Subalterns. I remember my very first day in Gedaref when Whiskers and I were out riding, he showing me the terrain: it was a lovely afternoon, temperature between 80 and 90 degrees and we were in shirt sleeves and jodhpurs. We met the *Bey*. I was introduced. Up went the eye glass. "How de do" said he. "We generally wear jackets when we go riding in the town." He rode on. Whiskers' expletives were unprintable when he was out of earshot and I was a little astonished at even a Bey telling a DC how to dress. But there always, and perhaps naturally, existed that slight feeling of disdain in the minds of the officers of a distinguished military unit of the Egyptian Army - I stress Egyptian, for the young members of the Political Service whose lives were spent among the rather scruffy Sudanese peasants, could never attain the immaculate turnout and discipline of a crack unit of the Army.

In fact I formed a very close friendship with one of the younger officers of the EAC, one *Bimbashi* Gerry Stainer and we sought each other's company whenever possible. Although there were three Political Officers in Gedaref District during the best six months of the year (September-March), two of them were generally out on trek in the very large district and the remaining one enjoyed the company of the officers' mess while Gerry Stainer found the peace of a quiet evening "down the hill" equally refreshing.

Forbes Bey commanded a very fine lot of officers; when we dined in their mess, we all wore black ties, sometimes with, sometimes without, a jacket. There was no heavy drinking and Forbes Bey, with his perpetual sniff, was an excellent host, only to be compared with his Second-in-Command, *Kaimakan* Paddy Walsh, a notable gunner, who was exceptionally kind to me, a younger gunner, both in Gedaref and later at a hunting lodge in Scotland. But that is yet another story.

Rosita Forbes

One evening the EAC mess was entertaining the then well known desert explorer, Rosita Forbes, who with Hassanein Bey (in the household of King Fouad of Egypt) had made a much publicised journey to the Kufra Oasis in Libya. Rosita was in Gedaref desirous of travelling through the north of Kassala Province and through the Beni Amr country (the Fuzzy Wuzzies) in the Red Sea Hills (she later wrote a book *From Red Sea to Blue Nile*). Forbes Bey and his officers had done everything possible to facilitate her journey - put their guest house at her disposal, provided camels, stores and escort for the road. She had been given every facility and shown every kindness. She was herself entertaining and talkative during the evening. As she left the mess room to retire to bed she turned, saying "Good night, Col Forbes, and thank you. I always sleep with a revolver under my pillow." Stunned silence ensued broken only by a short remark dropped by Paddy Walsh.

We played polo in Gedaref, organised by the soldiers, and very good fun it was. One had, among the orthodox rules, to remember an extra rider - "never ride off the Bey"! I once did so - successfully from the point of view of horsemanship but a tragedy in terms of human relationship. I avoided the EAC for a spell - but I knew some years later that I was forgiven when Forbes Bey congratulated me after playing for Khartoum Political team in the finals of the principal polo tournament in Omdurman.

Egyptian Officer Removal 1924

Perhaps my last contact with the Egyptian Army was sad, tricky, humourous and instructive. When Sir Lee Stack, *Sirdar* of the Egyptian Army and Governor General of the Sudan, was murdered by Egyptian political assassins in the streets of Cairo in 1924, the revulsion in the Sudan was widely felt. But except in the towns and in the Egyptian Army units and District HQs the news took several days, sometimes weeks, to permeate. Throughout the Egyptian Army units in the Sudan however the effect was immediate. That same evening, after General Allenby, High Commissioner in Cairo had delivered his ultimatum to the Egyptian Government, an order went to all units of the Egyptian Army in the Sudan that all Egyptian officers were to be removed from their units forthwith and sent to Khartoum, under escort if necessary, thence to be returned to Egypt.

I happened to be in Gallabat, 90 miles east of Gedaref, on the Abyssinian frontier at the time. There was stationed there a small unit of the Egyptian Army under a British Bimbashi and two junior Egyptian officers. The Bimbashi, a charming officer by name of Russell, was ordered to place his brother officers under arrest, if necessary, and send them forthwith under escort to Gedaref: he was also told that I was returning thither and would take care of the party. I received orders a little later in the day to return to Gedaref and bring back the two Egyptian officers to the HQ of the EAC.

Bimbashi Russell was furious. He knew these two Egyptian officers well and would count on their complete loyalty to him and the EAC. He certainly would not put them under arrest and though he agreed that I should escort them back to Gedaref, he begged me not to put them under constraint on the journey, but to treat them as "officers and gentlemen". Bimbashi Russell knew his men. Having met the young officers I was able to agree with his plans and especially after a talk with them themselves.

"*Genabak*" (your honour) they said, "We are sorry to leave our Bimbashi Russell who is a fine officer, but we are delighted at the thought of leaving this dreadful country of exile, the Sudan, and especially the fever-ridden town of Gallabat - beset by scorpions and hyaenas. Now, *el-hamdulillahi* (God be praised) we shall soon be back in Egypt. Have no fear, *Genabak*, we will not try to escape to be the prey for the savage Abyssinians or Sudanese brigands who roam in this area." They were quite genuine and neither I nor my two policemen, who would probably have shot "these sons of Egyptian dogs" at first sign of trouble or a nod from me, had any problem, though we had to spend a night on the road. I handed them over to the Duty Officer of the EAC in Gedaref next day and then with my DC J G Monteath, wondered whether the Egyptian flag would be lowered for good and all (ie Egypt withdraw from the Condominium). It was not - though there were many, including the Acting Governor General, Sir Wasey Sterry (Legal Secretary) in Khartoum and other Britons in Sudan and Egypt who thought that it should be. With hindsight I am sure that HMG made the correct decision. The thought of the Sudan Government administering the country under the aegis of the Colonial Office - which would have been the inevitable result - was not tolerable.

Sudan Defence Force

After the withdrawal of Egyptian troops from the Sudan in 1924, the Sudan Defence Force was established at once under a British Commander-in-Chief who, with all his officers, owed allegiance to the Governor General. I shall write about this gallant force in a later chapter - suffice here to say that I was privileged to be present at the establishment in Gedaref of a unit thereof very soon after the events recorded above.

Administrative Work

Let me now turn to the life and work in Gedaref District as experienced by the recently joined Assistant DC, myself who, with five years seniority to his credit had passed his Legal but not his Arabic examination, who had never tried a case in court nor assessed a *feddan* (acre) of millet nor a herd of cattle or camels and who, indeed, had never ridden a camel. It was a pretty daunting prospect for his DC and to the other ADC Whiskers Richardson who, as I have already described, took me under his wing as soon as I arrived.

Our District Commissioner (J G Monteath)

My DC, Monteath, was not so warm in his welcome - not through lack of courtesy or kindness but because, I think, he was not an embracing man. He was a Scot - not dour but a bit awkward; by no means unintellectual but lacking, as it seemed to me, in the graces. He had ten years service by the time I arrived, seven of which had been spent in Berber Province and Gedaref gave him his first experience of life and administration away from the Nile, with the problems of raingrown crops as opposed to riverain cultivation. He had missed the First World War and spent at least one leave in Alexandria where he learnt to play the whole of Handel's Messiah on the piano from memory! I seldom heard him play any other piece of music though he sometimes asked me to bring such piano music as I had to their house and seemed to enjoy listening to it. He was meticulously careful in court where I sat with him learning to dispense justice. He was almost unbearably slow in movement and decision. He apparently had no idea of time and I remember reporting to him at noon as ordered one day packed and ready to go on trek with him, only to find that he had stripped the engine of the Model T Ford, recently supplied to the District, because he wanted to know the reason for some small inexactitude. He learnt all about the Ford just as he had learnt Handel's Messiah. We delayed our departure by 24 hours. His wife was a Scottish girl whom we regarded as slightly fey. When on trek she refused (a) to motor after dark and (b) to pitch our beds anywhere but on the main road. Camel caravans generally travel by night and are no respecters of beds and camp furniture of government officials!

Going on leave through Egypt

On my first leave from Gedaref I took my Arabic examination in Khartoum en passant and "that persistent candidate Mr Lush" passed (only just, as I suspected). That was a good beginning to a well-earned leave but my DC Monteath had asked me to look after his wife on the way home. The lady and I both were travelling by the same route - down the Nile to Cairo and Port Said thence to Marseilles by ship and home by rail - but "she might find a brother in Paris".

We had a pleasant journey as far as Shellal (Aswan) and my duties towards the lady in my charge were not onerous. In 1925, along the meter gauge railway line from Aswan to Luxor ran a rickety train - no comforts and much dust. There was an apology for a restaurant car at the end of the train. After eight hours travelling a cloud of smoke was wafting down the train: FIRE! - no communication cord, no means of knowing what was happening. In a few minutes all the second and third class passengers were fighting their way to the rear of the train - first class carriages and restaurant car. On puffed the train and it was clear that the engine driver had no idea of the conflagration behind him. We were on a straight stretch of track and our next stop (for water) was, so we gathered from the restaurant *suffragis* (attendants), some ten miles ahead. Two of us got hold of a crowbar and tried to uncouple the last two coaches, to no avail. After about 20 minutes one *suffragi* shouted "A bend in sight" and with great courage managed to climb out on the side of the car waving a table cloth. At the peak of the bend the fireman or driver must have looked back and seen the tablecloth or the fire and its locality - two luggage vans behind the engine. He slowed down but sensibly did not stop until he reached a station two miles ahead where there was water. They soon doused the flames and we all went to inspect the damage: the van was full of luggage but only the roof had suffered. Suddenly I heard a wail behind me "Maurice, that is my cabin trunk in the middle!". It was my DC's wife - in my charge! What could a man do but rescue the trunk, which I did. But at the peak of my success a railwayman poured a last bucket of water on to the roof and most of it fell on me and my tussor silk suit! I travelled with a suitcase and had few clothes. We passed Luxor, Cairo and reached the ship before I could change.

All went well on the ship as we steamed on one of those never-to-be-forgotten trips along the Mediterranean - and I managed to shepherd my charge and her abominable trunk on to the train at Marseilles. At the Gare de Lyons in Paris the lady descended from the sleeping car still wearing the very wide and rather dirty solar topee which she wore in Gedaref. (In 1925 the discipline of clothing was more rigorous, even in Paris, and I believe that even I myself was wearing a Homburg.) We took a taxi to the address where I had been asked to hand over my charge to her brother. The concierge of the block of apartments was full of concern: "But Monsieur is out of town - he left for the country yesterday; he gave no date of return." I translated with a sinking heart; my lady had no French and I could only hope that her travellers' cheques would get her home to Scotland. At that moment providence opened the door of the neighbouring apartment and a buxom lady said how glad she would be to entertain the English lady (whom I think she mistook for a nun - that helmet) and there I left them - the buxom lady might have been the madame of a *maison de plaisir* for all I cared. I ran - reached the Gare de Lyons and Dover!

(Many years later I had an amusing finale to another trip home looking after another Sudan wife - a very beautiful woman. We missed a connection in Paris and had some difficulty in securing cabins on the Dieppe-Newhaven night boat. In fact we could secure only a double cabin which my companion allowed me to share with her. On arrival at Newhaven my wife met me on the quay (by car) and we escorted Mrs X to her railway carriage, where she secured the last seat. As the whistle blew I said "Goodbye Mrs X - a good journey". She replied "Considering we shared a cabin last night, you might at least call me by my Christian name". Tableaux in carriage and on platform!)

And yet my DC and his wife were kindly folk and tolerant of a young untrained recruit as the Assistant *mufettish (Commissioner)*. But we were glad, Whiskers and I, when they handed over the District to a spendid couple in Philip and Gwen Ingleson - very different people: full of charm and youthful elegance, but quite ready to teach ADCs their jobs and the secrets of good administration. They soon had the administration of Gedaref District on a longer rein and relations with the Army became more relaxed.

Work among the Shukria

Let me now consider the people whom it was my job to administer.

I was lucky enough to start my field career among the Shukria tribe - people who to my untried experience were wholly pleasant, friendly and law abiding with a standard of good manners unparalleled even in the Sudan. The various members of the Abu Sin family taught me more good manners and gave me more sound advice (even in court) than any one I had met in the Sudan.

The Shukria in the 18th century were a great power in the land exercising authority and being held in great respect in the territory east of the Nile - the Burana, the Gezira and the Atbara regions: tribute is said to have reached them even from Meroe on the Nile. But they showed no inclination to join the Mahdi and so lost authority. In the famine of 1889 they were largely decimated but recovered under the "Turkia" (a common name for the initial Military Government established in 1899-1900) who gave them much and widespread authority.

They were good farmers who grew their millet and their sesame oil both for home consumption and also for market produce and were good practical herdsmen of camels and cattle. My first job soon after arrival was to go round part of the District and assess the crop - chiefly millet. Under the paternal and direct form of government in 1924, the assessment of the crops and the counting of the camels was one of the direct duties of the DC and his staff. I had been briefed in the field by Whiskers Richardson before I set out riding my own white *abeid* (riding) camel, with three *hamla* (baggage) camels behind me and a couple of policemen, also camel mounted. We sent the *hamla* on a couple of hours ahead and joined them at a place called Shasheina where at sunset we found the resthouse ready for me - my table and chairs put out and dinner on the boil. A local sheikh was present (there were few villages or crops around Shasheina) and I had a leisurely bath, dinner (clean shirt and black tie) and afterwards retired to rest, ready for the dawn start next morning for Doka, an important centre. Arriving there at noon I was able to talk to sheikhs and arrange a programme for the next day's crop assessment. About sunset a sheikh from a neighbouring village turned up. A woman had been in labour for 48 hours. Could I help? I went into the *tukl* where the woman was groaning in travail. In those days at 28 I had no experience of child delivery! I ordered all the 30 women in the *tukl* to leave; I sent for a basin of clean hot water and asked for the local midwife. (What the hell was the Arabic for midwife?) I urged her to massage the expectant mother's front with hot water and to clean her altogether. (What was the Arabic for a lady's privates?) I then returned to Doka. At 10 pm a panting camel rider appeared with the news (so I understood) that the baby had been born and that both mother and child were well!

Next day when I returned from assessing the crops a very old man was brought to me. "Many years ago " he said "we had a case just like Fatima's - and a *mufettish Inglize* just like you came along. He arranged the birth of a good child, just like you: and that year we called all the male children by his name - SANDIFORD." Later that year I checked with Dan Sandford and learnt that the story was true. But there were no children by the name of LUSH in Doka in 1924-25!

Ushur

The assessment of crops, a preliminary to the payment of *ushur* or tithe, and the counting of cattle directly by the DC or his senior Sudanese or Egyptian officials (*mamurs*), were all part of the direct administration of the Sudan which had been established, of necessity, when the Condominium Government began the administration of a country decimated by 11 years of the Khalifa's rule. (The population, it was estimated, fell by six million people during those terrible years of Dervish rule.) The Sudanese sheikhs and *nazirs* in 1899 were in utter disarray and had little competence, however willing, to enter into proper administration of their tribes. It took a generation of patient but direct rule, of education to win and make possible the introduction of "indirect" rule, of guardianship rather than governorship; to introduce, in short, the tenets of Lugard's "Dual Mandate" (already in 1925 a Bible at Province HQ if not in the field) which spelt out "indirect rule".

In any case here was I in Doka about to set out on an assessment of *ushur* - the tithe. I had told the *omda* (sheikh), after consultation and discussion, that we would visit a large area of the plain about three miles to the east. We left an hour after sunrise and after a hearty breakfast - I had a long day before me and carried some corned beef and a few dates. On arrival at a fairly large area of crop (millet which stands 6-8 feet high) the inhabitants of all the surrounding crop had already assembled. "*Wallahi*" (By God)" I had been told "It's been a bad year - short rains - strong winds and the birds - they have eaten every head of millet on the land." These were natural and annual declarations of disaster which were belied by the sight of very good crops, large high heads at regular height with no empty patches.

"Here" I said "we will assess five acres." "Wallahi" the crowd murmured "the *mufettish* is assessing the best crop in this area. Mohd Ahmed was lucky with a freak shower which watered his crop - and he had no birds. As for ours, the millet is black." (All this because I was to use this acreage as sample for others.) Then started the assessment. Of course I was accompanied by a dozen sheikhs and farmers who knew to the nearest tenth of an *ardeb* what the crop would produce. I had with me the *Omda* of a neighbouring locality and it would be interesting to see whether Shukria loyalty would overcome possible neighbouring enmity. We finished our first area and did others in the same area and yet others in different localities. The sun came to meridian and we stopped for an hour or so to do a *shishna* (trial) which entails marking out precisely a small area, say 100 x 2 yards, cutting the maize therein, winnowing it and then weighing the grain. All sorts of hanky panky was practiced, generally quite openly and every one was full of fun, trying to hoodwink the young *mufettish*. It was a good *shishna* and gave a bigger yield than even I had imagined. On we went to other areas until the sun told us to go back to camp at Doka. This went on perhpas for five days - long, long days when one felt that really this assessment ought not to be one of the duties of a British Administrator. It is true that one lived with the *nas* (people) and got to know them personally and their way of life, but one was a tax gatherer with police in attendance and, truth to tell, one was too weary in the evening to do oneself or the *hakouma* (government) justice. Of course there was always a large number of people who wanted to see me - to complain, to ask for help, to pay respects even and glean news. They were all so nice, so courteous - even the loudest complainer.

A camel was the only animal on which to ride when assessing crops: he was slow, seldom stumbled, never fell and one had the complete birds eye view of the maize above the crop. He would munch the heads contentedly during our progress but sometimes he would seize a head and fail to bite it off! Would he drop the dainty morsel? Never! He would cling to that head with this teeth, his body still moving forwards until his muzzle would be behind my left leg and I had a complete void in front. For performing this infuriating act of posterior mastication I once hit my own camel so hard on the side of his long neck that I must have unsettled a muscle or nerve. The result was that when we emerged from the maize his neck instead of protruding straight in front of him, had a distinct kink in that long line of vertebrae. There were a good many clucks and side glances from the Shukria villagers who are good camel owners themselves. Thanks be to God, the camel recovered

Assessing the herd tax was a more rapid, less wearing process. One would give notice of the check in an area of herds of cattle or camels who were to be concentrated at a certain water hole. One would go thither oneself but always having sent a small posse of mounted police to reconnoitre in the vicinity - another water hole, a clump of trees or a dried out wadi where, invariably, the remainder of the cattle or camels (all identifiable by local marks) could be found. This was really a splendid game of hide and seek which everyone, including the culprits, always enjoyed - they confessed to their attempted deceit quite guilelessly.

A source of comparative wealth to some tribes in Gedaref District was gum Arabic which in those days formed a valuable export for the Sudan which at one time supplied seven-eighths of the world's demand. The gum was tapped from a species of the acacia tree which had become diseased and when tapped exuded this extremely glutinous resin. There was an art in tapping in such a way that the maximum could be collected without killing the tree. But the acacia forests also were the home of the wild bees and honey was a precious liquid which supplanted the expensive sugar. The *suqs* or markets of Gedaref, Mefaza, Doka, etc. were full of honey pots - most of them with dead bees floating in the liquid. Now to obtain the honey the bees had to be driven away - what better than by fire? So the honey seekers fired the honey trees and of course never extinguished the fire which then attacked and devasted acres of gum forests. It was typical of the Sudanese of those days and one of the inevitable results of direct rule that noone would dream of organising a village to contain or extinguish the forest fire until some Government official - a policeman, a *mamur*, or the *mufettish* himself - came on the scene to organise the affair. On my third evening in Gedaref I saw Whiskers Richardson galloping *ventre a terre* on his pony in the direction of smoke on the horizon. I soon caught the same fervour to persuade the peasants to do something to save their own wealth - for gum Arabic fetched a good price in the market.

Our journeys and sojourns in the villages outside Gedaref were not always on tax assessment forays or forest fire affrays. I myself, the reported *Habash* (Abyssinian) expert, had been allotted Gallabat Sub-district as my special child.

The 90 miles between Gedaref and Gallabat - or to give it the Abyssinian name, Metemma - meant a three-day journey by camel or a day and a half by car on mud roads. There was a good deal of animal traffic on the road and the journey was never without incident. The stop-over villages of Shasheina, Doka and Sarraf Said always had interesting cases or matters for discussion. The last day took one through thick scrub where guinea fowl abounded and once my policeman hissed "Lion! Lion!" I never saw any beast and I am pretty sure it was a hyena.

My worst journey was on camel just before the rains - 4 extra *hamla* or baggage camels were carrying the poles and rig for the scaffold on which I duly supervised the hanging of a murderer (whom I had sentenced to death a month before). I think I can count that as one of the worst journeys on my life.

Another bad journey was a year later when I had to entertain in Gallabat (1) My Provincial Governor (2) the Financial Secretary of the Sudan Government, Huddleston - a very big man with a most hearty appetite and (3) the Director of Agriculture - a malleable, charming Scotsman. I travelled with my Governor "Pull-through" Browne, so called because of his thin and tall stature, and his quite charming wife, Brownie. We were travelling by car. At Doka, the first stop, the resthouse had been transfigured to accommodate the *Mudir* (Governor) and his Lady. A half hour after arriving the Governor's wife interrupted our conversation with the dire report that her nightie had not been repacked in Gedaref where they had spent the night. "That's all right, m'dear" said the Governor "I will lend you one of my shirts." (I would willingly have laid my pyjamas on her bed for she was a sweet person.) "No need to send the car back 50 miles." Half an hour later the cook appeared before the Governor and me to say "By God, Satan has overtaken me - I have left behind the cold ham!" "God be praised!" exclaimed the Governor "There is still time to send the car back and retrieve the ham from Gedaref. Go at once and if there is room bring the lady's night attire." Alas, I, not she, wore my pyjamas - and that ham kept us happy and fed for three days! That particular trip nearly ended in disaster. I had taken sufficient food to feed six people in my very small, blue-walled, entirely unfurnished house on the Abyssinian border. I had an excellent cook; the Governor had his - and the ham! The big man from Khartoum arrived. We had chops for lunch - wherein the EAC Bimbashi Russell nobly supported me. Huddleston ate two large chops and asked for more - we were all messing together. We discussed the main issue - rain-grown cotton and irrigated cultivation in Gedaref and Gallabat Districts. After lunch Browne, my Governor, took me aside. "Lush" he said "I cannot bear to sit out another meal with Huddleston - he revolts me. Please arrange for us to feed apart." Crisis! But we managed it. Governor and wife had early supper of cold ham and went to bed, while Huddleston and the irrigation man ate more chops with Bimbashi Russell.

The railway never came to Gallabat: it was, *ab initio*, an area completely unfit for irrigation, but that meeting of top people was the beginning of the Kassala-Gedaref-Medani Railway and the Rahad-Dinder Irrigation Scheme of many years later.

Well to the east of Gedaref ran the head waters of the River Atbara which rises in Abyssinia. The people on that river were different from the camel owning Shukria. Samuel Baker and his lady knew them in 1861: they were less settled, rougher, mountain river folk. It was a great treat to go thither on trek to try to help them in their more difficult problems of cultivation - lots of rain but poor soil.

I once went there and met a black mamba en route at which my camel shied, and nearly had me off! I met for the first time dog-faced baboons who threw stones at me for fishing at their watering place. My bull terrier was badly wounded by a small crocodile whom I had hooked on a big fish hook. We thought the crocodile was dead but when pulled ashore he became very much alive and made for me. My bull terrier raced from the bank and went tooth-and-nail for the croc - turning him into shallow water where I shot him dead. Bully, the terrier, was lacerated across the back (luckily not on the stomach) and fortunately I had the strongest detergent, picric acid, which I poured into his wound. He suffered valiantly and lay on my knees on a palliasse for the rest of my journey. At every village where we rested for an hour or for the night, a bowl of milk and a small *angareeb* or bed had been supplied for the dog who saved the life of the mufettish. My bull terrier recovered completely though his coat was yellow for a year. He had saved, probably, my life - or at least, my legs!

Mefaza was also in our district and I remember visiting that rather poor and dull village (now part of the Rahad-Dinder Dam Project) and riding back to Gedaref 64 miles in 24 hours on my splendid *abeid* camel because news had come by telegraph, that my young ADC Kit Haselden, was a very sick man. The episode of his *kala azar* (Dumdum fever) is described below.

It was the policy of Robin Bailey, my first Governor in Kassala Province and his successor, and indeed, of every DC in the districts, that time spent in the field among the *nas* was time well spent - worth many times driving a pen at your District HQ, in the magistrates court, among the files, or drilling police and confabbing with the merchants and townspeople. I think Gedaref District maintained a healthy record of life among the people. Moreover as an enthusiastic young man I learnt greatly about their normal life. It may have been because Whiskers Richardson was an educationalist by career but their lack of education impressed me as vividly as it did him. In 1925 the spread of education was going ahead steadily and widely but it was confined to the towns.

I would not like to give the impression that one learnt nothing at one's District HQ. The hearing of cases as a magistrate was an education in itself. We sometimes tried cases, especially civil suits over land, cattle and camels in the villages, under the traditional tree, and it would seem quite natural to the magistrate (myself or another) when a witness had made some declaration of issue to the case, to require him to proceed to the nearest holy man's tomb, lay his hands thereon, repeat his oath to tell the truth and repeat the declaration or denial. I have known witnesses flinch from the ordeal. There was a legend that in Gedaref itself a witness had repeated his assertion, his hands laid on a very holy man's tomb (a *feki*) and had dropped dead. Judgement for the other suitor!

It was during one of these civil suits, lengthy and boring (I think a land case), that a leading Shukria sheikh took me aside and said "Your Honour, please take my advice and never give a judgement in a land case or any civil case. Neither party expects judgement or a decision - in fact there probably is no final word in this case. If you bring it to a decision the parties in this case will have nothing to do for the rest of their lives. Make a *sulh* - a compromise: then later one party will break the *sulh* and they can happily begin all over again."

He was quite right and I never again gave a final judgement in a land case, or in suits concerning legacies. (A date tree could quite legally be bequeathed or become the property of 327 persons.) Debts of camels and cattle or money had to be settled but only if after much argument, the parties could not come to a *sulh*.

It must be remembered that lawyers or advocates did not exist then in the Sudan. There were no trained Sudanese lawyers (in fact I am uncertain whether the law school had been instituted) and foreign lawyers or Sudanese with foreign law diplomas were not allowed in any but the High Court, and there only in special cases.

Work in the Merkaz

One could not, of course, be on trek for ever and a return to Gedaref had to be made to let others go out among the *nas* and to do one's stint of office and court work. One generally wrote a short report on one's trek and some reports might go to Kassala Province HQ and thence to Khartoum. At Province HQ there might be technical inspectors - agriculture, veterinary, irrigation - and they were grateful for reports on matters in their particular field. In line with Government policy, we generally kept writing to a minimum and tried to push everything into the monthly report, the compiling of which was the job of the junior ADC. A famous Governor General once wrote on the wall of a DC's office "Often the best work which a DC does, is that which he leaves undone."

The Merkaz at Gedaref

Besides the DC and two ADCs, the District HQ comprised the following: Chief Clerk, Treasurer, Chief Accountant, Sanitary Inspector; other Clerks, Translators for written work, and 120 Sudanese Policemen.

The Mamur, an Egyptian, was in full charge of the Sudanese and other native staff. Although several Egyptian Mamurs were evacuated with the Egyptian officers in 1924 there had grown up in the Sudan a class of Egyptian civil officials of great integrity and loyalty. It was on these Egyptian Mamurs that the first DCs and Governors depended as far back as 1900 and in few cases was their faith misplaced. They must go down in history as junior but important civil servants who helped build the Sudan. As education progressed Sudanese entered the administration and were appointed Sub-Mamurs and subsequently, of course, became Mamurs, and in a few cases Sub-Inspectors.

The Mamur was responsible for the conduct of the police. Except in the large towns, there were no police officers: in fact I cannot remember a police officer in Kassala Province HQ and the policemen in the district were rather jealously regarded as the children of the DC, disciplined by the Mamur. We had a force of about 120 Sudanese police in Gedaref: some were mounted and were sent on patrol to look after security on the roads and larger villages: the foot police were used chiefly in Gedaref and Gallabat to keep order in the market and town. They were recruited from the Shukria tribe and were a splendid body of men maintaining a high standard of discipline. In a District HQ which contained a large number of troops (such as the EAC) there was always the danger of trouble between the soldiery and the civilians (and therefore the police) - eg. in the brothel quarter. But I cannot remember, during my three years, that any serious incident of this nature took place.

The Mamur and his assistants were responsible for the proper administration of the *suq* or market. Gedaref had a big *suq* which on market day would be filled with produce, maize, millet, *simsim* (sesame oil) and of course gum Arabic - to say nothing of herbs and spices, rases of sugar and semi sacks of salt. Indeed Gedaref *suq* is, as is every *suq*, a wonderful sight typical of the produce of the country and the people who live therein.

Cleanliness of the town was, of course, one of the easy ways for a Mamur or Sub-Mamur to acquire merit and indeed it was a very necessary duty to insist on the merchants maintaining orderliness. It gave proof of relations, good or bad, between merchants and Mamur when the time of assessment of business profits tax came along: immediately after the payment of the crop and herd tax. This appraisal of the merchants' wealth was then an example of direct administration. The DC with a board generally composed of the head merchant (probably an Armenian), a Sudanese merchant, the sheikh of the *suq*, the Mamur and a Sub-Mamur would convene primarily to discuss trade and business in general. The DC would then inspect a statement of profit and loss submitted by each merchant. It was very necessary to assess this tax as accurately as possible. There was a natural feeling among the rural peasants that they were *muzloom* (oppressed) on all sides: the government ground them to dust with heavy taxation on crops and animals while the merchants completed the punishment by paying ridiculously low prices. This complaint was generally well-founded in cases of preemption - forward buying was very general especially when times were hard: the peasant devoured the grain which he should have retained for seed and from that moment was bled to death by the more intelligent and opportunistic *khawaga* (merchant) whose livelihood depended on making money out of ignorant peasants. That after all is common practice - but in those early days it appeared a practice which should and could be stopped. We younger *mufettishin* would be wracked by the tale of woe poured out by some cultivator from the countryside, send for the merchant and try (unsucessfully) to effect an immediate repayment. "But Your Honour, I have broken no law!" the *khawaga* would declare - and indeed he had not and neither Whiskers nor I could force him to pay. The older DC would send the peasant away telling him not to be such a fool next year, and would remember to warn the sheikh of his village against the merchant - and to soak the offender well and truly when his tax assessment came under scrutiny.

In the office section of the merkaz the *bashkatib* (chief clerk) was responsible for the whole gamut though the *serraf* (cash clerk) was independantly responsible for the Treasury was concerned. There was often conflict between the two, both of whom had responsible jobs. The *muhasib* (accountant) not only kept the day-to-day accounts but had to advise his DC on the state of revenue and expenditure compared with his budget. This was part, of course, of the Provincial budget, approved by the Central Government and by which every District was expected to abide very closely. With a Central Government budget balancing at a minimal level, the reins were kept tight.

There was the *mutergim* (translator), who saw to it that all Arabic letters and petitions were submitted to the DC with a summary of contents, if not a full translation. Outside every *merkaz* there were generally several petition-writers, who, for a fee would write down on an official petition paper (available for 1 piastre) the gist of anyone's complaint. One always tried to see a petitioner: after all he had paid his entrance fee and some of them undoubtedly had a case, while at least they had the satisfaction of telling their friends on return to their village and reporting that the *mufettish* had listened to their complaint. In some cases, dare I say in most cases, the complaint was of no consequence, without foundation and sometimes malicious. It gave us the rulers, the notion that by hearing petitioners we were flying the flag of patience and tolerance. In fact, of course, though the justice we administered was clear and certainly uncorrupt, I am sure that we had a lot to learn about patience and tolerance from the elder statesmen among the Arabs. I regret to say that I always, as a *mufettish*, arranged for petitioners to be heard at the end of a morning's work and many seekers after justice or sympathy were apt to receive short shrift if their complaints were deemed empty or malicious talk.

There was generally a mass of correspondence and many matters needed answers - questions from the Governor's office on budget and finances; matters of high policy (indirect administration was greatly under discussion and the means to bring it to effect must come from the Districts). There was correspondence on agriculture, roads and transport, veterinary matters and the condition of herds, education (very much up Whiskers Richardson's street), Abyssinia and the state of the border, the police and the army. It was amazing what a pile of files could be amassed on one's desk - especially if the other two *mufettishin* happened (as they should) to be on trek, or on leave.

The provision of annual leave for expatriates in the Sudan Service was of infinite value and probably ensured sanity and good health in the Service - but it meant that for six months in the year a Province or District was running with only 60% of it's establishment.

Magisterial Work

I now come to an important and, to myself, a very interesting part of a DC's work, namely his position as a magistrate administering justice.

It has been said that the Sudanese understood fully two things about the British in their country - their complete impartiality in the administration of justice and their abstinence from corruption. I believe that to be true.

Ignorance of language, of the finer points of religion (Islam) may have led to errors but can never have swayed the impartiality of judgements. I became extremely interested in my magisterial work and felt that I learnt a great deal about the Sudanese from the figures I met in the court - and I enjoyed dispensing justice.

The Sudan Penal Code was based on the Indian Code - with necessary alterations - and, by and large, was simple to administer. No lawyers or advocates existed in the Sudan nor were they permitted in any court except the High Court in special complicated cases. "Prisoners' friends" were definitely excluded and so the magistrate found himself counsel for the both prosecution and the defence - trying to extract from the witnesses the truth and often (by what he thought was clever cross examination) obtaining such a welter of conflicting evidence that prosecution and defence evidence was apparently quite false! Case adjourned for midday: a game of polo, a quiet hour alone on the case in the evening. By next morning all seemed clear. I was not, I am sure, the only magistrate in the Sudan courts to whom beads of perspiration on a witness' brow, nay his whole face and neck, were clear evidence of his veracity or falsehood. I have seen witnesses led out shouting that their evidence was true - and who later, when questioned, laughingly admitted that their story was slightly *shuya* (incorrect). I found many men (and women) who found it difficult to accept that an eye for an eye and a tooth for a tooth, so acceptable to them in the theory of Islam, was not acceptable under the Sudan Penal Code.

After a year as a third class magistrate I became a first class magistrate with powers up to the death sentence. In homicide cases one sat always with two assessors, Sudanese sheikhs, who advised one throughout the case and particularly as to the sentence. They, naturally, tended towards clemency and in these cases I hope that we always took complete consideration of their views. I remember one terrible case in Gallabat where I had to swear in the local Abyssinian *shoum* (chief) as an assessor. It was a very clear case of brutal homicide and the Abyssinian chief was most outspoken in his verdict. In purely Sudanese cases one felt always that one was protected.

The Sudanese or other assessors were not magistrates (although as time went on Sudanese were appointed magistrates), but their duty was to advise the magistrate (the DC) on the evidence, the guilt or innocence of the accused and the sentence. I found such assessors most valuable on the validity of the evidence, valuable as to the guilt or otherwise but not so good on the sentence. This was only natural. They were assessing the punishment which a village or higher form of Sudanese assembly would impose: I was administering the Sudan Penal Code which was and had to be the yardstick of penalties and the printed word supporting law and order. Here was one of the problems facing the introduction of indirect rule.

The setting of a court case in Gedaref in those days was very different from the dignity of a magistrates court in the UK or even the larger towns of the Sudan. There was one largish office for the DCs and ADCs. The DC's portion was raised about 12 inches - the ADCs occupied the "ground floor". Quite often Whiskers or I would be engaged in the noisy process of hearing a case in one half of the office while, simultaneously, the unfortunate Monteath with the *Serraf* (Treasurer) or *Muhasib* (Accountant) was trying to unravel some intricate problem in the Treasury or budget. When a serious case was tried the magistrate generally tried to arrange for silence to be maintained but the braying of a donkey immediately outside one's window might still occur as a cataclysmic disturbance.

The Shukria and the other tribes round Gedaref were a law-abiding lot and the calendar of criminal cases was not a long one. Of course a great deal of petty crime, theft and wife-beating was settled out-of-court in the villages. But the sheikhs of the village had a duty to report a serious crime and produce the accused before their court. Police patrols brought some miscreants along and it was always essential that they should be charged within as short a time as possible. When carrying out the weekly inspection of the prison one was prone to find some unfortunate person sent or brought in from a village, and having lingered two or three days forgotten by all, was likely to do so for another week. The prison incidentally was just a long stone building with a concrete floor kept spotlessly clean in which all prisoners convicted or on remand were kept, each having a straw mat and a blanket or two and a bowl for water and food. Prisoners were adequately fed. A prisoner under sentence of death was kept in solitary confinement as was any recalcitrant prisoner. Death sentences were carried out by hanging: a macabre business fulfilled (in the corner of the Merkaz building) with great dignity by the senior police sergeant. An ADC was present with a doctor, the Mamur and the sheikh of the victim's village. The public were kept away - in fact, except in Gallabat, I never experienced much public interest. During and after a murder trial one was always (at any rate, in my experience) at pains to ensure that the accused had every help, every chance. In fact, the death sentence was rarely imposed. The magistrate was required by law to send a written transcript of the whole case, with his reasons for conviction and sentence in writing through the Governor of his Province (or the province judge) to the Chief Justice in Khartoum who could quash the conviction or reduce the sentence. If the sentence of death were upheld the Governor General could exercise his prerogative of mercy. In my experience in the Sudan I know that the death penalty was necessary in cases of culpable homicide amounting to murder. I have both convicted accused and acquitted them. Between sentence and execution I knew that the exercise of mercy was always present in the minds of those who judged. The end was always in an atmosphere of dignity.

Visitors

We were always entertaining visitors in Gedaref. During my three years there we had our annual visitation from our Governor, "Pull-through" Browne whom I have already mentioned, and others from Khartoum. The Brownes left the Sudan soon after, on retirement. He was a silent man and made little impression on me as my Governor. He was followed by Robin Bailey - a complete contrast; ten years younger, a man of action (I remember that he was chief fireman at a blaze which badly damaged a shop in Gedaref during his first visit) but nevertheless a thinker who was an ardent supporter of indirect rule without delay. I learnt to know him later in my life in the Sudan and was always glad of the breath of fresh air which he brought - sometimes it was almost a hurricane.

A Governor's visit was always a serious matter. Problems which had become old chestnuts needed solutions; new questions arose, prompted from above or by the DC. The Governor had to be careful not to appear to administer the district; the DC must let it be seen that he was the Governor's trusted deputy; the Governor must see as many of the locals as was possible and be allowed to show the *nas* that he too was trying to help the Sudanese rebuild their country.

By no means annual but periodic was a flying visit from the Governor General. In those days the vast majority of the people regarded the *Hakim el am* as the ultimate authority; there was no question of his representing the King of England or Egypt. His authority was ultimate - and so it was. It was imperative therefore that the *Hakim* should be seen to rule and that he should visit as many of the population as he could. The Sudanese loved a party and they were always ready to join a gathering, line along the road or gallop in front of the *Hakim's* procession, thereby smothering the unfortunate followers in clouds of dust. The roads were mended and lined with white stones, the market was cleaned, buildings were whitewashed and flags and bunting appeared in the town. (The main street in Gedaref was, in my day, only just passable for the Rolls Royce.) The *suq* was thronged, especially if the GG came on Saturday and banners or arches of Welcome and Goodbye were erected at the boundaries of the town. Nor was the Army forgotten - a parade for the Sirdar on the polo ground and lunch at the EAC mess.

We were visited by Sir Lee Stack in 1924 - his last visit to a Province before his assassination in Cairo a month or two later.

In reaction, there was felt and shown deep resentment and dismay among the people of Gedaref District and members of the EAC. This was echoed in every province of the Northern Sudan and many devoted messages of condolence were brought personally by Nazirs, Omdas and Sheikhs. The Hakim el Am may have been remote who ruled from Khartoum - but had he not been with them all last month and presented a Robe of Honour to one of the Nazirs?

Among ordinary folk whom we were always glad to see were (British) Inspectors of Agriculture, Veterinary Officers, Irrigation Officials (with an eye to the long future), sometimes even Auditors who would pretend to spring on us without warning. When two or three people live alone visitors are always welcome and we *mufettishin* who "lived among our people" and their crops and cattle and thought we knew a great deal more than the technical experts, really learnt a great deal of sensible practical disciplines in their various fields.

I myself had three notable visits which gave me immense joy and lasting pleasure.

I was in the office one late morning when the policeman on duty came in, saluted and said "*Wallahi* (By God), there is a *Habash* (Abyssinian) outside who demands to see you and won't say for what reason!" I remonstrated but finally said warily "Oh show him in." The policeman grinned, opened the door and there was a rush of something I had experienced before - the scent of Abyssinia and horses. In a flash my feet were clasped and my ankles embraced and then disengaging myself from this tornado I recognised Tasfai - my beloved syce (and mentor) from Addis Ababa leading two ponies to give to me and begging once more to enter my service. "Come and see the ponies" he said "they are weary like me but they are yours!"

The Merkaz staff and the police and general crowd outside then saw the strange sight of the mufettish with tears rolling down his laughing cheeks, being led by a pretty scruffy looking *Habash* or Abyssinian towards two equally scruffy looking ponies, one grey, one chestnut. It really was a wonderful meeting and another example of the personal loyalty of which we found an example later in life in our personal servant, which was new to me and so utterly unexpected. We found a friendly policeman, half Abyssinian, to look after Tasfai and the ponies and he gradually took the place of my existing groom and took over two Sudan countrybred ponies as well. I extracted from him the story of his determination and his journey. Dan and Chris Sandford of course financed him and got his permit. He joined the mule caravan of a merchant friend of Dan's and had an uneventful journey except that one of the ponies (for he had set out with three) died en route. "Is there polo here?" he asked and was delighted to hear "Yes!" In a year or two he had the great joy of grooming and preparing one of the ponies to carry me in the final of the big polo tournament in Omdurman, for he stayed with me loyally when I moved from Gedaref and only left my service to return to Abyssinia when I gave up keeping ponies. He fraternised wonderfully with his Moslem fellow *syces* and was a great favourite, especially in Khartoum, when we went there. In Khartoum he fell completely in love with the statue of Lord Kitchener (pronounced by him and the Arabs too as "Kisschener") the first Governor General, mounted on "the biggest, most wonderful horse" he had ever seen. Whenever he was away from his ponies he could be found lying on his back almost under the statue gazing at the monstrous charger. I don't think that I ever appreciated Tasfai sufficiently - he became very much part of my life, for

I became very horsey and a polo enthusiast in Khartoum. I saw him many times after he returned to Abyssinia for he became head boy on Dan Sandford's farm outside Addis Ababa which we used to visit many years after - there he died, much respected and beloved. But I always believe that he remembered that meeting at Gedaref as one of the moments of his life, as indeed it was of mine!

Soon after Tasfai's arrival, I received a visit from a total stranger who also later became a devoted and much admired friend.

The policeman on duty walked into my office and presented me with a visiting card - a really genuine visiting card. In Khartoum as I knew, visiting cards were de rigeur but hardly so in the rural districts of Kassala Province. The inscription on the card was also unusual. It read:

PRINCE ALBERT HAMILTON
COLPORTEUR
British and Foreign Bible Society

"He came on a wheel (bicycle)" said the policeman. "What colour?" I asked. "Black as that book" was the reply. "Show him in" I said. I could not think what a colporteur could be - nor had I met, at that time, the BFBS of which I became a Vice President!

In walked an ebony black man. He was extremely good looking and dressed in black travelling clothes which were dusty but not travel stained. Here indeed was a great character though I did not recognise that at the start of our meeting. "Where have you come from?" "I have bicycled from Wad Medani" said the Prince. Gedaref is 148 miles from Wad Medani along a mud road which was manoeverable by a very strong motor car or lorry - not exactly a bicycle track. We discussed his bicycle trip (the first in history along that road). I was beginning to like him - as I used to bicycle as a boy, I somehow became in sympathy with him.

What was the object of his journey? I asked. I did not confess that I knew not the meaning of colporteur. "I am a British subject" came the astonishing reply, "I am carrying 50 Bibles in the basket of my bicycle and I have come to ask whether I may sell or distribute them in the market or town of Gedaref." I told him at once that the proselytising of Christianity among the Moslems of the Northern Sudan was forbidden but that I could not stop him selling his Bibles. He thanked me courteously and took his leave. When he finally left Gedaref a few days later he most courteously called again, thanked me and told me that he had sold all his Bibles (mostly to Christian, Greek and Armenian merchants in the town) and was off to Kassala whither he had been offered a ride in a lorry.

Would that I had invited him to lunch or tried to know him better even in my office, for I missed the early friendship of a very fine, gifted and spiritual man. I had another opportunity 15 years later when we were both in Addis Ababa together, but I was then a Brass Hat and he a lowly representative of the Bible Society and our paths did not cross. The next time on which I met him was in our house in Sussex in the sixties, when on a visit to England to mark his retirement from the BFBS, of which I was then a Committee Chairman, he came to stay.

When he left for Kassala I had not the courage to ask him his origins. But I can explain it now. His parents, devout Christians, were citizens of British Guiana and proud to be British, had a deep regard for the memory of the good Prince Albert, beloved husband of their Queen and Empress. So, Prince Albert was born in Georgetown, British Guiana (now Guyana). He fought in the First World War, based in Palestine, and then was employed by the British and Foreign Bible Society for whom he did sterling work in the Sudan, ubiquitously, and in Ethiopia for over 30 years. He was responsible for a Bible House in Khartoum (30 years after his visit to Gedaref) and the Emperor Haile Selassie, as a reward for work in Ethiopia during the Italian War, granted him land in Asmara (Eritrea) on which to retire and end a wonderful life devoted to Christianity. I was grateful to have him as our guest at our home in Sussex after my initial inhospitality to him in Gedaref!

Colonel and Mrs D A Sandford

Almost the last visitors I received in Gedaref were Chris and Dan Sandford who after a journey of some eight weeks on horseback from Addis Ababa crossed the frontier at Gallabat and came on to Gedaref, by motor transport which I had sent for them. Dan had arranged this journey in an attempt to open up a more regular and orderly trade of hides and skins in which, after the dissolution of the Abyssinian Corporation, he had tried to start business as a private trader, but he was finding it hard going. It was notable that in the year 1926 a Briton and his wife could ride 800 miles through the wildness of Abyssinia unscathed - in fact in complete peace.

Indeed had it not been for his brilliant handling as counsel for the defence of a well-known and very rich firm of Indian merchants before the Abyssinian High Court, Dan would have been in very low water. In the event he won his case and the Indian firm was bountiful in their gratitude, paying not only Dan's substantial fee but also my sister's return journey to England. For the rest of the Sandfords' lives in Addis Ababa they showed gratitude and gave help. Dan sold his legal practice for a substantial sum to another Briton, a barrister, who found it profitable for some years.

Chris and I went home to England together and Dan rode back to Addis Ababa. It was good to have had them both in Gedaref. Dan had been there before, as a locum tenens in about 1910. He was to visit Gallabat again after another 14 years - in time of war - entering an Ethiopia occupied by the enemy, the leader of a small body of British soldiers to rouse the tribes and finally take the exiled Emperor along the route he was now riding alone.

Leave in UK 1926

I cannot now remember much of the journey my sister and I made to the UK. On arrival at Wad Medani whence she and I planned to take the night train to Khartoum, we found that a large party of the Sudan Defence Force had commandeered the sleepers and their first class carriages and it was too late in the night to turn anyone out of bed. So I persuaded the station master to open an empty cotton truck and in it we rigged our camp beds and passed a very comfortable if noisy night.

When I reported to the Assistant Civil Secretary later that morning I was received with asperity:

"I understand, Lush, that you spent last night alone in a cotton truck with a lady! Well, that is not the usual practice of members of the Political Service, and I must ask you not to repeat the performance!"

I do not know to this day whether Martin Parr who became and remained one of my best friends really knew the identity of the lady. At any rate I told him that he would meet her at dinner that evening.

General Strike in the UK

On arrival in Brighton I found my brother, whom I so seldom saw, staying with my parents. But we were all faced with the threat of the General Strike and indeed Cecil had been recalled to his ship in Plymouth - but not before he had made a most wonderful apparatus with an enormous gramophone horn. This was a wireless. "Turn this screw and rotate that disc" he explained "and it will work!" And it did. My parents listened to the first News Bulletins ever broadcast, every day of the strike, which began on 6 May.

I myself went off to the old Town Hall in Brighton, signed on as a "Special" (Constable) and joined the Mounted Police. We groomed our horses and rode in the Brighton streets for a couple of days. Police chargers at 16 hands on hard roads were a rather alarming change from 14 hand ponies on mud or turf! But the Brightonians were peaceful: they didn't want trouble at the beginning of the summer. The police were keeping a low profile and we were asked to bring our cars and help in ordinary police duties. I ferried in my car the Police Inspector delivering summonses, warrants, etc. Only on the penultimate day were we summoned urgently to the Brighton Tram depot - whither we went, 50 police in eight cars, lights blazing, horns hooting, at 40 mph. But there was no trouble and we all went home. There was however, bitterness in many places - there were a good many motor buses in London carrying the slogan "Dear Mother, I have no pane." But the change from strike to peace was well-handled.

HMS Royal Oak

At this time Cecil was serving as Lt Commander and navigator on the battleship HMS Royal Oak. He was in the good books of his CO, Captain Fortune, who was well known in the Royal Navy. Cecil wrote suggesting that if I cared to make a trip in Royal Oak he had the Captain's permission to invite me: he as Navigator had two cabins; we could share his officers quarters cabin for ordinary purposes and he would sleep in the Navigator's cabin on the Bridge - where he would inevitably be for a great deal of the time, as Royal Oak was to sail on 29 May for Cromarty. Would I sail in her? I accepted willingly and had the best ten days of my life so far. The Captain sent me a message of welcome and the wardroom received me warmly into their company. I joined at Plymouth and it seemed to me that a conference of officers present in the wardroom decided which course we should follow to get to Cromarty in ten days - west or east. The distances were equal. We were still on economy expenditure of fuel. We went westward. We sailed at dawn - Cecil steering the great ship out as if she were a lugger. Every morning the officer of the watch assigned me to the care of some luckless technical head - Engineer Commander, Torpedoes, Gunnery, Flags, Wireless etc, and I was examined as to their skill in teaching a landsman every day at lunch or dinner.

I learnt a fair amount, albeit that naval skill and language is rooted in itself.

Evenings in the wardroom were wonderful; we were at sea and very little gin flowed. One evening I dined with the "Snotties" and Sub-Lieutenants and loved it. The Snotties still slept in hammocks. On the Saturday afternoon the Commander signalled STOP to the engine room and the whole ship's company jumped into the sea off the Western Hebrides.

We went north and passed through the Pentland Firth. Cecil had asked me to join him on the Bridge: at about midnight he said to me "There is a 12 knot tide running against us - we, economically, are forbidden to steam at more than 12 knots: we are therefore without movement, forward or astern." When we reached Cromarty we joined forces with other RN ships and engaged in gunnery practice. At one time I was more or less dared to ascend to the Spotting Top, to what looked like a large crows nest - hundreds of feet, or so it seemed, above the water when the ship was amidships but almost on the water when she rolled to port or starboard. Of course a ship of the size and bulk of Royal Oak did not roll much, but to a terrified landsman she certainly did not lie still in the northern seas. Of course, the guns were so controlled that they fired only when plumb level. I spent some part of the practice in one of the 16" gun turrets and fired one of the guns. Cecil, by putting a degree too much turn to starboard, and I, by firing the big gun fractionally too late, managed to demolish the whole of the wardroom glass which (I claimed) ought to have been stowed away! That day of tense action, of real naval discipline, was a climax to a most wonderful experience of the post-war Royal Navy at sea. I have never forgotten it.

In the evening, my last, Cecil and I were bidden to dinner with Captain Fortune. We found quite a party

had been invited - principally the officers who had been my tutors during the week. The Captain knew that I was a gunner and teasingly had me involved in some gunnery problem about which I knew nothing. It was all great fun and at the end of dinner a half-carafe of port wine was placed on the right of each guest and he was expected to finish that carafe and retire in good order at the end of the evening.
We all managed both, but bacon and eggs on a very *mouvemente* harbour tug which took me into port at dawn looked slippery in the extreme.

My next dinner on one of HM ships was in Diego Suarez Harbour, Madagascar in 1942, two days before she was torpedoed. Royal Oak had a stormy history and a sad end. She was one of the ships in which mutinies occurred in 1931 over cuts in pay (Captain Fortune and Cecil had long before left her) and she was sunk by a German submarine in Scapa Flow at the beginning of World War II.

Gedaref, Sudan in July 1926

The Sudan in July is a hot country but Gedaref, to which I returned after my strike-ridden and naval leave, enjoyed the edge of the monsoon rains which watered Abyssinia and broke in June or July, so we were spared the dusty heat of Khartoum and the Nile Valley. I returned prepared to enjoy life: for with the DC's absence on leave I would be in charge. Moreover I should not be single handed for E C (Kit) Haselden, a Probationer, was posted to us and would not be taking leave during his first year. I should, therefore, have help in the work and companionship in the house.

Haselden was a very able probationer and a charming person, but he developed a recurrent, undulating fever which we all thought was malaria or sandfly fever until he found that quinine had no effect. He would go for a week in perfect health and then suddenly go down with a high temperature. We had no British doctor in the place; we depended on the Eastern Arab Corps for their Medical Officer, Bimbashi Cantlie, who was on leave. One day, when I was on trek in Mefaza, I received word that Haselden was very sick, so as already recounted, I rode back to Gedaref quickly and consulted the Syrian assistant doctor who said, in a very serious manner:

> "I think that Mr Haselden is suffering from *kala azar*. He displays all the symptoms. It is very serious and he should go to Khartoum, for the only way to be sure is to make a liver puncture and I would not do it myself here."

He convinced me and I sent a telegram to Khartoum reporting the suspected *kala azar* which I must have worded badly for I received a blistering reply ordering me to send Haselden in and adding that the Medical Authorities in Khartoum would decide what treatment to prescribe without any advice from the District Commissioner! To my great relief Haselden recovered. I had read that if *kala azar* was not detected and treated early, fatal results could ensue.

Years later I suspected similar symptoms in a nephew by marriage, Leslie Casbon, who arrived home from Ethiopia with similar symptoms - with great humility I had my fears conveyed to the staff of the Hospital for Tropical Diseases in London: they began treatment just in time.

Leprosarium Gedaref

Mention of Bimbashi Cantlie in the last paragraph prompts me to write of medical work in the District. The EAC were very good in providing regular medical service. They had a full medical unit headed by Neil Cantlie, and two or more Egyptian or Syrian medical officers for no Sudanese had yet been fully trained. The Kitchener Medical School in Khartoum was not yet built. The EAC boasted a good hospital and could also put one in the field. The civilian District had a more primitive hospital - a red corrugated iron building with about ten beds, a simple operating table, a pharmacy and out-patient department. One of the Army doctors attended on alternate days and was always on call. Cantlie was exceedingly good at servicing the civilian side of his duties: he and I became great friends and he taught me a great deal about medicine and surgery. He would always call me down to the hospital for a postmortem, especially if crime were suspected.

Our great combined effort was to reconstitute the small but terrible leper colony outside Gedaref where the lepers lay and literally rotted to death. They were fed and some were physically able to cook for the whole colony; otherwise they did nothing. There were 20-30 of them cast out from their villages.

Cantlie and I altered all this. We chose a village site near by with a well, good soil and good drainage. We had new huts built (prison labour) and Cantlie had a dispensary constructed. We gave them cultivating tools. We visited them weekly to begin with and Cantlie injected all but those in the last throws of the disease with a solution - chaulmoogra oil - which, while it could cure only those at the outset of the disease, did, at any rate, alleviate pain and delay the onset of loss of toes and fingers and, later, limbs.

I persuaded Sudanese officials and notables to visit these unfortunate folk and bring them food and comfort instead of sending such things by unwilling servants. The results were almost instantaneous among the lepers. They became living creatures instead of outcasts and began to sow their maize and simsim and milk their goats.

Cantlie and I were proud of our Leprosarium. His cooperation, indeed his initiative therein, was typical of his concern for the civil population of Gedaref. In later years he became Director General of the British Army Medical Services, Lieutenant General Sir Neil Cantlie KCB, KBE.

Last days in Gedaref

My DC Phil Ingleson had returned from leave with news

that I was on the transfer list - he did not know whither.

I was sorry. I was still learning a great deal in my first administrative post and how really attractive the *nas* could be and were. I had had good experience; of administering the really attractive Sudanese people, for it was a good trekking district; of judicial work; of the intricacies of the finance and accounting. I had begun to know and like the merchants, some Sudanese but mostly Levantines. I had been absorbed in my scruffy little Sub-District of Gallabat with its Abyssinian connection. I had learnt to ride a camel and how to fall off - and that it is safer to fall off a camel than a donkey. I had learnt not to resist an army of marching ants whose queen insists on swarming in your bathroom. I had shot and killed a cheetah but missed hundreds of duck and sandgrouse; in short, I had been thoroughly happy.

Then later came the blow. I was to return to the the capital - not into some department but as District Commissioner Khartoum! My spirits dropped. I had always heard that DC Khartoum was a job to be avoided - and I must say that my friends did nothing to change my opinion. The present holder of the job was known as *Abu Ishrin* - Father of Twenty (strokes of the whip or cane). I was not a little anxious. I knew my Arabic was not good. Was that the reason for the transfer to a town? Was I to be condemned to service in towns for the rest of my career, etc, etc? I need not have worried!

So - soon after Christmas I sold my camels, said farewell to my much loved district, despatched Tasfai with my two ponies down the road with a couple of policemen (a friendly DC in Wad Medani had them entrained for me) and took myself on the same route by car and train to Khartoum.

CHAPTER 6

Khartoum 1927-30

Khartoum Province 1927

The structure of the administration in Khartoum Province differed somewhat from other provinces. There were three Districts - Khartoum with a population then of 30,000 - 40,000, Omdurman the biggest town in the Sudan having a mainly Sudanese population of 150,000 or more with two DCs and Khartoum North across the Blue Nile with a population of well under 10,000.

Each district or town had one or two DCs under the Provincial Governor who also had on his British staff a Police Magistrate (a Political Service man), a Commandant of Police and a Superintendant of the Central Prison. Whereas in other provinces the districts lay often hundreds of miles from Province Headquarters, in Khartoum Province a mile or two at most separated them, although Omdurman and Khartoum North lay the other sides of the rivers. The population of the three districts varied not only in race but in occupation and education. Khartoum North District was a mostly rural district but boasted the Sudan Steamers Department dockyard and the Central Prison. The Kfouri Dairy, an ever expanding herd of cattle and consequent industry, was situated there.

Omdurman District's population was principally Sudanese, a large number of whom were Government and other officials; the remainder were merchants some of whom were very important. There was also a large military contingent in Omdurman whose soldiers (1924 excepting) were well disciplined and orderly but woe betide anyone who thwarted their women folk! I knew of one DC Omdurman who had to ride *ventre a terre* in full retreat from an infuriated mob of ladies, the women folk of the Engineer Troops, whose illicit brewing of *araq* he had unwisely stopped on some military festival.

Khartoum District proper had a motley population. The Governor General and his Lady headed the list of some 1,500 - 2,000 British residents who were divided into three blocks: Senior Officials, Commerce and Industry, and Junior Officials. There must have been a similar number of Levantine merchants and professional persons - white-collared gentry and the backbone of the commercial community of the city. The remaining 25,000 were a motley of Sudanese, representing many tribes but without tribal cohesion, a few Government and commercial clerks who could afford the high rents in Khartoum. Most of the *effendia* or white-collar Sudanese preferred to live in Omdurman and commute to their offices by steamer or, after 1927, by train. There was in those days of low wages a large number of Sudanese cooks, servants *(suffragis)*, watchmen *(ghaffirs)*, gardeners, cleaners and regularly employed municipal workers. There was little community spirit except among the British Senior Officials who had their club (the Sudan Club) which was exclusively senior and British, and the Junior British Officials who had their own club, the Khartoum Club. Senior men did not go to the Khartoum Club and junior wives did not drink coffee or lemon in the houses of the seniors. This class distinction occurred only visibly among the British and in those days it was considered to be and was quite natural. Perhaps it was not so exclusive to the British for I do not suppose the Grand Qadi or the Mufti or the few leading Sudanese who had houses in Khartoum but lived in their mud brick houses in Omdurman came very closely together with their more mundane, less holy brothers. It must, I repeat, be remembered that the date was 1927.

Throughout my service, particularly in Khartoum, I considered that the Governor Khartoum was never given his rightful position in the hierarchy of the capital. He could accept the presence of the Governor General, but he was regarded as of little importance by Members of Council (of which he should have been a member), by Heads of many Departments and to a lesser degree, by the Army; the Sudan Defence Force Headquarters were in the city. Truth is that he should have been styled Commissioner Khartoum but I, for one, could never inspire anyone, Civil Secretary or Governor General, to take very much interest in the matter.

I have not mentioned that there was stationed in Khartoum (and had been since the Condominium) a battalion of British infantry. As DC Khartoum I never had to remember, from the security point of view, their presence and it speaks well of the British Army between the Wars that they were an ever present but never a visible force of security. I must add that they had attached to them one section of Artillery: their armament was one 4.5" Howitzer.

How was DC Khartoum to do his duty with this polyglot, class divided (and yet so kindly), population in Khartoum? Before I discuss that I must write a word or two about Pat Munro, Governor of Khartoum, because he put me on the right track.

Pat Munro entered the Service in 1907 - 20 years before I reached Khartoum. He had before that, and throughout his service in the Sudan, the reputation of having been Captain of Oxford University and Scotland Rugby teams. He was, in the Sudan (I don't suppose he played elsewhere), a first class polo player and I fell for him, as did many others, at our first meeting. He greeted me with "Glad to have you; a difficult, very difficult job ahead of you; you will accomplish it. Don't get involved in Sudanese politics or the political movements of the *effendia*. Neither get involved with the Holy Men - call on them, as you should, but any further dealings with them are my pigeon. Run the District as you would any of the districts, for the good of the people in it especially the Sudanese, but not forgetting all the others. The others, not the Sudanese, will be the first and the most evocative to insist on your help. Good luck - come to me for anything you want. (I did!) D'you play polo?"

I cannot remember "taking over" Khartoum from my predecessor. I do remember that every morning for a week I rode round the succession of Union Jacks which bounded the city of Khartoum. I took one of the Sudanese Sub-Mamurs with me and I began to know the intricate pattern of streets and quarters to which Kitchener had condemned the unfortunate inhabitants of the town. Once a month we had a right royal town ride when the Police Officer and the Mamurs and various local sheikhs joined in. The Governor should have been at our head but I could never persuade him to lead us! It really was rather a showing of the flag and belonged to a bygone generation - but the merchants seemed to enjoy the procession. A succeeding Governor instituted a monthly gubernatorial ride.

In the office there was a rare medley of problems all of which, seemed to me, should have been solved by someone else - the place was full of technicians: there was a Police Department and a Police Magistrate, to say nothing of a Superintendant of Gardens and a Game Warden. I soon found (I had been warned) that the DC's office was thought to be a veritable domestic servants' agency. One would be asked by Mrs X to find her a "really good cook" or by Mohammed Ahmed to warn Mrs Y that if she hit him again he would bring a case against her. I was soon able to rid myself of that nuisance by establishing away from my office a real domestic agency which charged a fee.

I think in some respects I was a bad *mufettish* of Khartoum. I should have lived far more among the dwellers in the town - I should have sipped coffee on the pavements with the merchants in the evening and attended the Boy Scouts' (*Bya Skeet* in Arabic) rallies. I did not do so; I fell for the social pleasures; I closed my office at 2 pm and - to my Governor's great delight - joined the Polo Club. I was soon playing in the Khartoum Province team, with a handicap of 3 and we reached the final of the big tournament but did not win. Pat Munro captained our team which contained Peter Clarke, a charming Political Service man who was then in the Finance Department, Dinah Coates, a contemporary of mine, and myself. Peter Clarke did me the infinite kindness of lending me his very fast (though hard to handle) grey pony for the final match, as my Abyssinian 14 handers were a shade too slow when pitted against Sudan country breds - some 15 hands.

Polo was played in Omdurman on a half gravel, half sand ground. It was extremely fast and we played without boards. A fall meant abrasions on the skin and gravel rash. But the polo was of a high calibre - most of the players were military SDF officers and we encouraged Sudanese officers to join in. The loyalty of the women folk was amazing. We left Khartoum by the Governor General's steamer at 2.30 pm (by his kind permission), often changing clothes on board, rode up to the ground, began playing at 4 pm and caught the special polo steamer back with tea and drinks on board just before sunset. The colouring of the setting sun and, once a month, of the rising full moon - both reflected in the waters of the Blue Nile - were stupendous. I am sure a number of romances of that period began on the decks of that steamer. When the Nile Bridge was opened the romance of steaming to and from Omdurman receded: the ponies had to clip-clop over the hard road surface and the players went by car. We arrived more quickly but I doubt if any romance started in a Ford Model T driving along the unmetalled dusty roads of Omdurman.

On the opening of the White Nile Bridge, the Sudan Light and Power Company and the Governor decided that this should be a real occasion. Lady Maffey, (wife of the Governor General) was asked to drive the first tram. His Excellency, Members of the Governor General's Council and the leading Sudanese were asked to be the passengers and Khartoum District and the Company arranged quite a party. Lady Maffey kindly came in the morning to learn how to drive a tram (not everybody's forte) and we all assembled. After tea and speeches, the HE's party with Members of the Council and the eminents entered the tram - Lady Maffey on the footplate. For some reason all the passengers were standing up - maybe the tightness of levee dress trousers prohibited a sitting position, maybe the band was playing the National Anthem. The sign to proceed was made. Our lovely (she really was) lady driver started the electric motor perfectly and then pushed in the clutch handle, or whatever a 1927 tram had, and the vehicle shot forward like a Derby winner leaving the starting box. Her eminent husband by her side was flung back but remained erect; she clung to the handle as it surged ahead; every passenger in the tram - tall or low, fat or thin - fell backwards just like a pack of cards; the crowd roared their merriment and approval. Lady Maffey kept her head! She did not stop but she remembered the rest of that morning's lesson and quickly brought the tram to a steady pace. She never looked back, I am told, and at the entrance to Omdurman, brought the vehicle to a regulation speed and finally to immobility. I cannot remember who drove on the return journey - I suspect HE.

That bridge was and is an enormous boon to all and sundry. Khartoum market was filled with produce next morning and every morning in record time; government and other junior officials could bicycle from Omdurman to work. Omdurman and Khartoum were more closely linked. DC Omdurman felt a little dismayed; hitherto he had been very much king of his castle, remote, away from the distractions of Khartoum with its western jargon and ideas. If the Governor wanted to see him it had taken at least an hour for either to visit the other by river. Now, with a land-live telephone, the DC could be summoned in ten minutes. *"Abu-Shoke"* (Father of Thorns) or DC Bramble, to give him his proper name, didn't much like that bridge. I may say that the security plan for the defences of Khartoum in the event of civil commotion needed a deal of rethinking as a result of this economic link.

I have twice mentioned social distractions of Khartoum and of course life there was gay. From the Palace (the Governor General's Residence) downwards, hospitality was abundant but seldom lavish. The longevity of many retired officials and others from the Sudan has been ascribed to the fact that spirits were practically never (in those days) drunk before sunset, and that wine would not keep and was seldom drunk at all.

But cocktail parties there were - and up to the 1930's in the winter one wore long dresses, dinner jackets and boiled shirts for dinner. At the Palace official dinner parties, of course, it was white ties and gloves for the ladies. When the ladies had gone home (by April) shirts became soft and jackets were not worn. Palace staff (military) wore their full mess kit while the Private Secretary wore dark blue tails. It was their duty after dinner to make up to His or Her Excellency, breaking into conversations quite ruthlessly. Every female or male guest had a very strictly limited conversation time of not more than four minutes (more or less according to the size of the party and also to the look on the host or hostess' face).

Most married senior officials lived in well built houses (not always bungalows) with a garden and more often that not a grass tennis court or two. There were electric fans in most living rooms - everyone slept on the roof and there was no need for mosquito nets. Dawn in Khartoum, daily, was much like the medieval idea of the last trump and the resultant resurrection - the white population arose in their nighties and descended to the verandah for tea. Thereafter it was a busy day. I think that most offices in Khartoum in the late 20s were busy: we were still building. There had recently been appointed a vigorous, imaginative Governor General who with long experience of India came entirely wedded to native administration but after his first impact with the Sudan had faith in the integrity of the British administration.

Women folk of this heart of government in Khartoum were, in my opinion, no less responsibly minded, no less devoted to the country and to the menfolk's life and work therein than the men. I saw these women - living in comparative luxury but in a difficult climate, separated for nearly six months of the year from their menfolk - and had them very much in mind when dealing with Personnel affairs in Central Government. I became quite certain that the carefully selected political and technical officers of the Sudan Service had the good fortune (or perspicacity) to choose wives who could and did very quickly, very fundamentally realise that the interests of the Sudan and the Sudanese came first, not only in her man's but in her own estimation and that their lives were dedicated to the country in which they were serving.

These were my thoughts very much in embryo, as DC Khartoum. Experience later - and again much later after a long retirement, seeing them at meetings of pensioners - convinced me of the rightness of my, perhaps, youthful views.

But let us return to Khartoum.

I found allotted to me a bachelor suite in a group of dwellings known as Peabody's Buildings - also as the Yellow Peril. There were 12 apartments - bedroom, sitting room, bathroom with a large verandah, one electric fan, no kitchen or refrigerator. Next door, a few steps away, was the Sudan Club - that comfortable, cool building with a good restaurant, wide verandahs and a shady garden, with many tennis courts. (No bathing pool then, as exists now.) I was able to hire stables nearby and accommodation for Tasfai - who had miraculously arrived with the horses, and had already made his acquaintance with "Lord Kitchener".

I took my meals in the Sudan Club and soon found myself sitting, at any rate at breakfast, with Martin Parr, Dinah Coates, a Junior DC in Finance, and a fellow gunner C E Fouracres who was an Assistant Private Secretary in the Palace. Dinah Coates contracted diabetes but returned to Kassala Province for a couple of years after he left Khartoum. But district life was too much for a diabetic and he died in Khartoum in 1929. It was said at the time that he refused to be invalided home. He was a most lovable person and a fine polo player.

Ted Fouracres was an Assistant Private Secretary to Sir G Archer at the Palace at the time. We all supported him in his attempts to join the Political Service but he did not succeed. He served the Sudan in a number of posts - Intelligence, the Governor General's staff - and finally became a fixture, and a very valuable fixture in the Sudan Agency in Cairo.

Martin Parr as Head of Personnel under the Civil Secretary, MacMichael, was the character of the table: a bachelor, who had lost one eye in the war, a professed despiser of women and horses, an ardent and cynical Wykehamist, a strong and outspoken Christian who could beat any of us at squash racquets or tennis.

The Club was a pleasant place - always frequented by a small number of permanent Khartoum residents like ourselves and a much larger number of transient soldiers and civilians. When the Honorary Secretary, a very bright character named Brock Bridgemen, went on leave, I took his place and enjoyed the experience. On the tennis courts (grass) a very high standard of tennis was played - Martin Parr with his one eye often appeared in the finals of the Club tournament. There were ladies' nights with the SDF Band and dancing on the verandahs.

But Club life allows one little privacy and I was always glad, especially in the hot weather, to accept an invitation to share a private house with some married man whose wife had sought early leave. The dog days of summer when work was doubled required the peace and comfort of private life in a cool private house.

My name went down to posterity by personally supervising the attachment of brass or iron number plates to the door of every house and business place in Khartoum. That was the kind of menial work to which one was reduced at times, in those days, as DC Khartoum. Very direct administration! I must admit it was a most popular though exhausting innovation.

The summer in Khartoum was particularly oppressive for there was little open space. The young forests around the perimeter were only then being planted and irrigated and 1927 happened to be an extremely bad year for *haboobs*, the dust storms which were always compared with the darkness of a London pea-soup fog, accompanied by a 40-60 mph scorching hot wind and sometimes by rain turned to mud. *Haboobs* in Khartoum had a habit of making their first approach from the east and then returning several hours later from the west. The heat and dust were unspeakable during and after such visitations. In those days there was no swimming pool anywhere in Khartoum.

The hospitality of the British residents in the cool season was wonderful and a bachelor had little time to himself in the evening or even by day, with tennis parties vieing with polo in the afternoon. I made a host of friends, some renewed from my previous sojourn, some new. The parents of members of the "fishing fleet" threw their nets but I was definitely a non-starter with the young ladies. Life was too busy and I was, financially, not much of a catch. Besides I loved their kind, sensible, hard-working mothers so much more!

I did help to found a club - for all kinds and conditions of people, Senior, Junior, British, Sudanese and other nationalities - for which Rev B J Harper had the inspiration and I arranged literally the sausage and mash. We met on Sunday evenings at the back of the Clergy House. It began during my first tour of service in Khartoum but we put it firmly on its feet in 1927. We had unexpectedly large attendances for Uncle Harper never failed to lure to the platform the interesting men resident in Khartoum and was especially good at trapping the unwary enterprising traveller. The Supper Club brought together all kinds of people in Khartoum. It reached its peak during the war, lapsed for a year or two afterwards but was revived in 1948 and continued, I believe, long after.

On the whole, as I have said already, I assessed myself poorly as DC Khartoum and maybe others thought so too. But to my great surprise my Governor told me one day at the end of the year that the Civil Secretary desired to see me. Weak at the knees I was ushered by Martin Parr into MacMichael's office. I did not know MacMichael personally though I am sure I had dined and played tennis at his house. He wasted no time. "Lush, you have served a year in the job as DC Khartoum and Munro tells me that you have done that job very well" (MSL's knees braced themselves) "Now I want you to come into my office and run Political Service Personnel instead of Martin Parr. He will make all the arrangements for a quick transfer. I hope you will like the job!" I uttered thanks and went to Martin Parr's office astounded for it was a quite unexpected promotion to a Grade II post. Other factors were clarified by Parr: he was going to the Palace as Private Secretary to the Governor General and MacMick wanted me to replace him.

The exchange was effected quickly. I cannot think to whom I handed over - the luckless man - but I do remember two days with Martin Parr in which he initiated me into the Jug and Bottle Department -which was his name for the job I was taking over.

Assistant Civil Secretary (Personnel) 1928-29

There followed for me two years of service under a man - Harold MacMichael -whom I feared at first, admired immensely, and was very proud eventually to know as friend. It was good to serve as Assistant Civil Secretary to a man who was completely devoted to the people of the Sudan, about whom he knew more than most. He was determined that the administration of Arab North and Nilotic South should achieve the best results possible for the Sudanese; devoted to the Political Service and determined that each member thereof should give of his best, and be in the best post possible to achieve that. MacMichael was a man who devolved work on to his juniors, expecting them to think and act for him. He was meticulously careful in composition of letters and it took a year before I learnt his style well enough to submit a draft letter which was not returned with correction in blue pencil. He taught me (and many others) more about staff work than I could have imagined. He abhorred slip-shod or unprepared work, be it spoken or written. He could see the real nub of a problem generally before one had stumbled through an explanation. He could be sardonic about people, often almost cruel but never to their faces. He insisted on seeing every member of the Political Service, young and old, who travelled through Khartoum (generally during the leave season) and there were very few who did not emerge from his office feeling inspired.

The Civil Secretary's Office in 1927 consisted of MacMichael himself, the Great White Chief we called him, J D Craig or "Sarah" Craig as his Deputy was always known (who acted for the CS during his absence on leave and who had been Governor of Kordofan; he was brought into the Civil Secretary's Office, I believe, to strengthen the policy of Indirect Rule), his Assistant on the Administrative side, R K Winter, an old hand but very wise and being gentle and artistic rather the antithesis of MacMick, and the Assistant Personnel (myself) with two Deputies in the persons of G R F Bredin, a future Governor and later Bursar of Pembroke College, Oxford, and A R C (Rollo) Bolton.

But there were other and most valuable members of the Civil Secretary's Office without whom we could not have functioned. They were the almost permanent "junior" officials who knew the files and the routine. Battalion Sergeant Major B C Shea DCM was in charge of the Personnel files which included the personal file of every member of the Political Service. A more efficient, more loyal and silent officer than he, one could not imagine. He knew the history of every current and some past members of the Political Service. He never uttered a word about any personal file unless asked by the Assistant Civil Secretary Personnel - and to him only would he speak. I relied on him immensely, every day that I occupied that chair.

The job was to administer, that is minister to, the Provincial Administration and the Political Servants therein throughout the Sudan. There were 200 of them with 8 or 9 Governors accustomed to wielding wide authority who sometimes thought little of "Khartoum's policy in sending Tom, Dick or Harry" to their Province and "must absolutely insist that X be allowed to continue in the Province for at least another two years because he and he alone could handle a tribal or administrative situation." Governors, of course, had liberty to move DCs about within their Provinces but the Civil Secretary through his Jug and Bottle Department must be the authority for entrances or exits.

Of course changes had to be made, DCs removed from and injected into Provinces. Casualties occurred every year - retirements, deaths, sickness (medical advice would sometimes insist on a constant malarial subject being moved into a non-malarial Province).

The Sudan at that time had two types of DC: (a) University candidates chosen by the Selection Board in London for regular service or (b) Army Officers, generally seconded or retired in their late 20's or 30's, chosen under contract for service in the Southern Sudan. No contract DC could become a Governor - probably few of them aspired to that exalted position.

We always tried to have our changes for the year settled (on paper) early in the year and during January I would submit to my Civil Secretary that, for example 4 Governors would retire this year; that I presumed 3 Deputy Governors and one other would take their places (1 Deputy Governor obviously unsuitable and would have to remain Deputy); I proposed the name of the fourth. For appointment of the new Governors, I prepared a memorandum for submission to the Governor General. The four changes and other casualties probably meant some 30 changes in provincial establishments. The game of keeping the provinces fully and happily manned involved a pretty good paper knowledge (confidential reports, letters, etc.) of every member of the Service, and one tried to ensure a personal interview with as many as possible, as each one passed through Khartoum.

The problems of course raised by the men as they came to the fountain head were multiple and various. They could talk to me in confidence, in a way which sometimes would have been difficult with their Provincial Governor: "Could I be posted to some province away from the river? I am tired to death of irrigation, pumps, *sagias* (water wheels) and *shadoofs* (water raisers)." "Any chance of a tour among the Arabs in the west or in Kassala?" "I have been in Port Sudan for 5 years and have eaten my meals out of a table drawer in the dust of Tokar!" "For God's sake let me see a bit of the Nile!" or from a Governor "Young X is quite hopeless with the *nas* and I can't keep him as a bottle washer in my office for ever. Can't you post him to some office job in Khartoum?" Sometimes from a Governor on a different note - "The bumph (paper) which pours out of these palaces in Khartoum would run the railways and steamers: can't you get MacMick to put his foot down on this evil production?" "Can you stop the Posts and Telegraphs asking for a return of telegrams received mutilated?" As a fact the outpouring of paper in those days was not excessive - but G Schuster, our Financial Secretary, was trying to place the Sudan on a sound financial basis and really did need information.

There was the DC from a southern district who, greatly daring, brought a party of Dinkas to see Omdurman and was much incensed at being asked to have his friends cover their nakedness on the river steamer when it steamed into Moslem Arab country 300-400 miles south of Khartoum. Khartoum to those southern contract DCs - the Bog Barons, some of the bravest and finest administrators in Africa - was anathema and many of them were anxious to spend the minimum of time in that "sink of indulgence". Even a very civilised western Governor when transferred to the Civil Secretary's Office wrote "This place is the nearest approach to hell that one can imagine: a mixture of heat, noise, boiled shirts and very many people. I have a drinks party tonight, then dinner. It is now (4 pm) 113 F; it may drop to 94 F by dinner time."

The request which I remember best came in all seriousness from a fine contract DC in the south who asked whether I could persuade his Governor to give him leave next year so that he could be in the UK on 1 July 1929. I promised help and then asked why. "Well my family and I all belong to the British Israelites Society and we believe that a tidal wave at Weymouth on July 1 will signal the end of the world!" He got his leave the next year but I had him examined medically and told his Governor confidentially on his return.

Then there was marriage. In MacMichael's words "Marriage is frowned upon until at least four years have been served." I would go further and suggest that a minimum age of 30 was the test. The stipulation was well known and a few good men left the Service because they were not prepared to wait. Others fought the restriction. One or two arrived back from leave married with wife in tow. The bachelor Jug and Bottle Department had to deal with these young lovers and their beautiful wives.

It was very hard work; MacMichael was a hard task master. The lights used to burn late in the CS office throughout the year. But how worthwhile it was working for a man who directed, with a very special standard of efficiency in his mind, with a mouth which uttered crisp harsh words, sometimes, but which were never totally undeserved; a man with a heart of gold ready to help anyone who served the Sudan.

He was very loyal to his subordinates. I remember that he had a confidential clerk who would type and keep his private and very personal correspondence immaculately - as well as produce, also immaculately, his official papers. (Typing long or even pithy memoranda in a shade temperature of 110 F, with no cooling system in the room except a fan which blew all the papers about, was no parlour game.) He was an excellent clerk and he kept his mouth shut. But off duty he drank and no woman was safe from his advances. One day he had obviously attacked the bottle vigorously and been as vigorously attacked by one or more outraged husbands. He had a black eye and a split lip. The Superintendant B S M Shea gave him one horrified look and sent him home: I agreed and we replaced him with my best clerk. "Where is B_____?" asked MacMick. I explained and said that I had not been able to allow this dreadful sodden looking fellow to sit on the threshold of my Civil Secretary's door. "I don't care if he has raped all the women in the junior club and been beaten up by all their husbands! So long as he can do the work required of him, he will remain my clerk! Send for him please!" Of course he got his way.

One made contact, of course, with all the Heads of Departments in Khartoum for all of them were involved in work in the Provinces and many, if not all, provincial DCs carried out Departmental policies in their districts, eg. Agriculture, Education, Irrigation, Veterinary work. It was as well to discuss provincial appointments with them and by so doing one learnt about the technical problems in all parts of the country. Some DCs were excellent with cattle or camels and not so good with crops; some had green fingers and couldn't tell the difference between a *hamla* or a riding camel. I made a point of discussing appointments with Departmental Heads which they all appreciated. Again one had to be careful not to send to a garrisoned place - eg. Gedaref - someone who could not appreciate the SDF point of view. In both my provincial posts I had been in close touch with the soldiers and now, in Personnel, there were appointments which concerned them greatly.

There were certain characters in Khartoum who on no account were to be allowed to penetrate to the Great White Chief - MacMichael. He could not abide X, Y or Z and it was up to me as Personnel to keep them out. He had no Personal Assistant (except the confidential clerk) and I have wasted many half hours talking down aspiring callers. (I learnt, from MacMichael, always to have a Personal Assistant in later life.)

The social round in Khartoum was pretty terrific but we in the Civil Secretary's Office were generally excused cocktail parties. For a year my addiction to polo kept me off the tennis courts but work made the long afternoon at polo impossible during my second year so I sold two ponies and kept only my blue roan Rataplan - Tasfai went back to Abyssinia. I turned to lawn tennis again.

It was at tea in Mrs MacMichael's garden after tennis, at which her two small daughters were making themselves pleasant, that in one of the silences that does sometimes occur, Nesta their mother, who had been deep in serious conversation with her neighbour, suddenly declared in a voice which broke through the silence "Well, I don't know who is the father of my two!" In the ensuing "let's try to cover up the gaff" conversation which greeted this statement MacMick was heard to say "Having failed in my conjugal duties I will see what I can do in the office" and left abruptly. Nesta was quite unabashed; her Harold was prone to sudden exits - and continued "One was born brown, the other black; I had their tails docked very early."

Nesta was a splendid person - the ideal wife for our Great White Chief whom she adored. We on his staff were often her guests and always at her service. One day she confided to me that "I'm going to get rid of that dreadful sports jacket of Harold's in the clothes sale at the Cathedral Bazaar." (This was an annual affair which, well organised by a committee of stalwart wives, brought in large sums for church expenses.) Now we on the staff knew this coat which was green with age and full of decay, but much beloved by the GWC and worn only, of course, in winter. We conspired but said nothing. At the opening hour of the Bazaar three of us approached the clothing stall. One engaged Nesta (who was running the stall) in conversation while the other two bought the coat from some hapless girl helping Nesta, and disappeared. That evening a delegation of his staff waited on the GWC bearing a document basket on which the jacket was neatly arranged - with the £1 ticket still attached. "What's all this?" And then he smiled - "I'm most grateful!" He wore the jacket home in triumph. "Beasts!" said Nesta when we next met.

It was about this time that Araminta MacMichael aged 6 proposed marriage to me.

During my service in the Personnel Department I moved out of the Yellow Peril and shared house with Marcy Huish, a gunner serving in the SDF as *Kaimakam* (Colonel) whose wife had gone on leave in March. It was very pleasant to live in a private house, with a garden, to meet his friends and be able to invite one's own friends.

Every year Bishop Llewellyn Gwynne organised a children's party. Huish and I and others became involved by building a pirate ship in the garden, manning it as pirates who would then be attacked by the children, some armed with truncheons of newspaper. The attack commenced and was prosecuted with great vigour - we pirates gradually suffered defeat and lay groaning on the deck of the very fine ship: we were then belaboured with the paper truncheons. Suddenly I heard a warning shout "Look out Maurice! Serious!" I did look up to find a small boy of eight advancing on me only two feet away, with a large knife, the blade shimmering, ready to plunge it into me!

In November of 1928 12 probationers of the Political Service arrived and became my wards until we could post them to their Districts. We did all we could to make their arrival easy: they were shown round Khartoum, wined and dined, and the Governor General invited them to dinner at the Palace. I was to shepherd them there; rendezvous was the Sudan Club for drinks; all were present on the club verandah in dinner jackets and patent leather shoes. I suggested an advance to the waiting vehicle at the gate, but omitted to say "Keep to the path!" All 12 of them with one accord walked the shortest route to the gate across a lawn which had been irrigated that evening and therefore was 2" deep in soft mud. It was rather a terrible moment for them and me. Luckily the club servants came forward en masse and not much mud eventually stained the Palace marble passages.

Of that group of young probationers 8 became Governors or attained Governor's rank, 3 died in the Sudan and one was invalided from the Service. He - as you will see - had a most profound influence on my life.

During my leave in 1929 I became Secretary of the Sudan Political Service Selection Board in London. To my shame I cannot remember the names of all the members but I know that MacMichael was Chairman and also present were Huddleston, our Financial Secretary, and the Legal Secretary.

It was an interesting exercise. We interviewed some 30 young men. The original 200 initial applications had been reduced by two Governors on prior visits to Oxford and Cambridge and other universities. We saw them one by one, I having interspersed their curricula vitae and academic or other distinctions. I remember so well one young man who was, after all, hoping to serve in a country of Blacks ruled by Blues. He was asked to tell us of his favourite recreation. "Bridge" he said. "Post him to the Legal Department" said MacMick. (The Legal Secretary was well-known as a Bridge player.)

It was hard to tell very nice young men that we could not have them - but a joy to inform others of their selection. One young man on being told of his acceptance buried his head in his hands on the table.

During the two years in which I served MacMichael I learnt more about the Political Service than I could have learnt in any other way. I met every type. Some of the older Governors about to retire were not quite certain about the trend of devolution to the Sudanese native administration which, still in its early days, was very definitely the policy laid down; "Never mind them" MacMichael would tell us, " They are on the way out, having fought their good fight. Get hold of the younger Deputy Governors and the DCs like X and Y and instil the policy into them!" Of the younger, more progressive Governors, many liked to rehearse their views on me before seeing the GWC. All the DCs with one accord, rightly, off-loaded their views on personnel and their own personal problems on to me and Rollo Bolton my deputy. I soon established a waiting room with a telephone which became quite a club where members of the same batch of probationers who had been posted to different and mutually far distant stations met again.

I was privileged to claim close contact if not friendship with MacMick. The subject which I prepared for him - Personnel - was of a very personal, intimate nature touching the lives of men whose principal aim was or should have been to help the Sudanese and better their lives. Having little experience himself of the Southern Sudan and he was all for delegating as much as possible to the Bog Barons - the contract DCs - for whom he had the greatest respect. I was always terrified when he agreed to see one of them in his office (Romilly or Wyld or Alban or Stubbs) for he became so absorbed in their stories - which could have come from Rider Haggard - that even he lost sense of time. They were, of course, the salt of the earth and were truly fathers of their people with whom they identified themselves far more than was possible for the *mufettish* among the Arab northerners. There is still being administered a trust fund bequeathed by one of them to a section of a Dinka tribe who were his adopted children.

Away from the office I found myself appointed as official Starter for the Khartoum Racing Club. The method was primitive. The Starter, mounted and carrying a large white flag, would line up the ponies and jockeys behind a white line. 50 yards down the course stood the Starter's Assistant, a Sudanese with a large red flag. At the drop of the Starter's white flag the race was started; if the white flag remained lowered the red flag was lowered at once and the race proceeded; if the white flag went up again, the red flag remained up and a false start was signified. On my very first race two of the British riders came through at a gallop and I raised my white flag at once - a false start. No one took any notice however, until I cantered down the course and called them all back. I hated that honorary job but I did enjoy displaying my very good looking blue roan Rataplan to the racing crowd. He was the best looking horse at the meeting!

It was a hot summer and I was about to get away. I had missed my leave in 1928 (the Sandford finances had taken a tumble and needed replenishment). So I was due for 4 months in 1929.

Throughout these two years in my Personnel Department I had kept in touch with Martin Parr, my predecessor now Private Secretary to the Governor General, and perhaps because of this I had met Sir John Maffey at tennis and lunch or perhaps dinner at the Palace. I had also helped the Palace staff at one or two Palace parties and had also seen a number of HE's short pithy minutes and some memoranda. I had formed the impression of him which was one of great admiration - enhanced by stories which Martin Parr told me.

But it was a complete surprise when MacMichael told me one day that Martin Parr was leaving the Palace and that HE wanted me, if I were willing, to succeed him as Private Secretary. When, after consideration due to my respect for and enjoyment of work with MacMick, I accepted, he was glad. An amenable Private Secretary who understood secretariat ways was an important link with the Palace.

I had of course a personal interview with Sir John

Maffey and it was arranged that I should join him as PS after our respective leaves that autumn. He generously extended an invitation to me to stay with them in Scotland.

This was indeed a wonderful period of anticipation and I spent the rest of my days in the Jug and Bottle with my head very much in the air. I handed over the Department to my Deputy and gladly joined the train to Port Sudan, there to join a Bibby Line ship destined for Marseilles, whence by train to Paris, spending a night in the Gare du Nord Hotel, to cross the Channel just 10 days after leaving Khartoum! A very restful start to 90 days leave in Britain. I think that the joy with which I hailed the first sight of the shores and countryside of England explains to a certain extent my dismay in later life at the millions of Britons who seek their holidays abroad.

Shortly before my departure, one of the probationer ADCs whom I had mothered on arrival in the winter was taken ill in Darfur. He had suffered terribly bad luck in having been licked by the puppy of a rabid dog and had been compelled to make the long journey from his province to Khartoum to undergo the painful and tedious anti-rabies injections (the serum needed refrigerated storage and this did not exist in Darfur). During his anti-rabies treatment the doctors in Khartoum found his general condition very low and strongly recommended that he should not return to Darfur. He came under my official care and I had him transferred to Khartoum Province (North) where DC Springfield could look after him. But he did not improve and was given sick leave to the UK there to undergo a further examination by a Medical Board. In Khartoum he stayed in the house of G R F Bredin who was not in the CS Office and with whom I was sharing a house for the summer. His name was Alan Hill.

I found he was booked on the same Bibby liner as myself sailing from Port Sudan. I found Alan a charming young man and bitterly disappointed at his breakdown in health. We became friends. We arrived in London together on 10 July: he went to his home in Queens Gate Terrace, I to my parents in our old small house 24 Highcroft Terrace, Brighton. I found that my brother Cecil had arranged for them to move to a nicer small house in Hove and the move was imminent.

On Leave: Summer 1929

Residence for nearly 30 years, even in a tiny house like my mother's, entailed momentous decisions when a move has to be made. I was glad to be at hand to help two aging parents - both over 70. I was able to put in a good week with them before commuting daily to London, to begin learning my new job as PS from Martin Parr at the Sudan Government London Office in Wellington House, Buckingham Gate.

On 18 July 1929 Alan Hill's mother and sister picked me up in a car from the steps of Wellington House. That meeting changed the course of two lives.

We drove to Harrow School where 5 years previously Alan Hill had been Head of School (he replaced suddenly a Head Boy expelled for illicit attendance at London night clubs in term-time). I spent an enchanted afternoon with his mother and sister and we talked and talked.

A few days later I dined at 30 Queens Gate Terrace with the Hill family. I met Alan's father, Charles Alexander Hill who was Chairman and Managing Director of British Drug Houses, and one of Alan's elder brothers, Mervyn. They were all very grateful to me for kindness shown to Alan in the Sudan. I accepted their very flattering invitation to spend a week with them at Sidmouth where they had rented a furnished house on the sea. I expect I unwisely played their lovely Bluthner piano not knowing that Beno Moseiwitch used to practice on it. It was a warm night and the music could be heard all the way down Queens Gate Terrace. I knew I was with friends.

Two days later Alan's sister drove to Sidmouth and there on 31 July celebrated her 21st birthday with all her family and friends. I was not there.

Early in August I drove from Brighton to Sidmouth. I had bought (on hire purchase) a Morris Cowley saloon with wooden wheels. It took 10 hours to complete the journey.

I found myself in a whirl of gaiety in a house-party of which most members were a good deal younger than I, and, judging by their motor cars, not quite so poor! But they were all quite marvellous to me. We rode horses and played tennis; we bathed and drove or were driven madly in sports cars and others (not my Morris Cowley); we danced; they forgave my evening pumps, my demon handled tennis raquet, my bowler hat and umbrella when I had to go to London for a day. My hostess, Ruth Hill treated me as an elder; my host, Charles Hill, who came for the weekend only, was sorry I didn't play bridge. (He was Chairman of the Portland Club.) We walked up Peak Hill and when the sun shone we bathed and then basked in it. After a little I got their names - Elizabeth Lindsell, Herbert Ferdinando, Jimmy Ridell, Olive Seon, Owen Howell and wife, the Sleman girls, Mervyn and Kitty his wife: we were quite a party. On about my fifth day Alan's sister did insist that as we had known each other for at least 10 days I should call her Diana. We were standing under a merillo cherry tree. That evening we went to a house called Sidholme close by, which had been rented for the summer by very old friends of the Hills - Mrs Dora Carson Roberts and her brother Bertie Davidson. The house had a most lovely hall which they had converted into a music room, for Dora was a great patronne of music and staying with them was Puishnoff, the celebrated pianist. He played to us for several hours and life for two of us began, sitting on the stairs of that house Sidholme, listening to Puishnoff. He played mostly Chopin - beautifully, robustly - "If I hit the piano as hard as Puishnoff does" said my host "I would break the note - he doesn't!" He was supreme.

I stayed a fortnight - a lovely fortnight; I was surrounded by kindness and happiness!

I returned to Brighton to be present at my parents'

move and to organise my mother's journey to Abyssinia - she was to go as far as Port Said in my company. I also had to prepare clothes and equipment to join my future chief whose guest I was to be at their Scottish shooting lodge early in September. I moved my parents from 24 Highcroft Terrace, Brighton to 39 Wilbury Crescent, Hove. I bought a pair of good walking shoes, but I did not stay long in Sussex.

A telegram was read to me over the Post Office telephone asking me to go to Sidmouth - it ended "Wallahi" (By God). The girl read it as if it rhymed with wallaby.

I had thought and prayed hard during my five days in Brighton. I remember as if it were yesterday, walking down Convent Hill, Hove - between my parents' old and new houses - praying that "THIS" might not be a passing friendship but "LIFE".

I drove to Sidmouth in seven hours. I found to my delight that Diana had won the women's handicap lawn tennis tournament which she had shrunk from entering. This seemed to be a good omen.

We danced at some hotel. It was Saturday night. Richard Hill, Alan's eldest brother, and Tuppy Headlam, a master at Eton, had arrived for the weekend. We were a full house at Seaview.

At the end of the garden of the house was a tower which consisted of a sunbathing platform on top, a junk room with a sofa and much rubbish inside and a long staircase down to the sea. Whenever the sun shone and we were at home we ran there to sunbathe - not often that summer - but we seldom went inside. It was, and still is, called "The Kell".

After supper that Sunday evening 25 August Diana Ruth Hill and I went out to The Kell - on a not so fine evening. There on the musty sofa we plighted our troth - but I would not have it binding on DRH until next morning when during a 7 am walk up Peak Hill I told my beloved of all the worst circumstances and conditions which life in the Sudan could produce. I spared her nothing. At the top of the hill both breathless with walking, talking and hunger, Diana kissed me, accepted the lot and we walked home to breakfast. Minnie, the housekeeper-cook, had already broken the news "Miss Diana must be in love Madam, she's just gone up that hill before breakfast!"

I hoped I was not slow in asking my host, Charles Hill's permission to marry his daughter. I postponed it however until a late hour in the morning when I begged leave, etc.; told him of my present position and hopes - and ultimately "in 1946, Sir, a pension of £1,000 per annum."

Of course both my parents-in-law-to-be were splendid - and I hope their innermost thoughts did not dismay them either then or later; their love and generosity in thought and in substance was very real, very welcome and very much appreciated.

I left next day to acquaint my parents with the news - for part of the way I had Tuppy Headlam as my passenger. Tuppy, a famous master at Eton, great friend of the Hill family and admirer of R H Hill, Diana's eldest brother, cricketer and real tennis champion, spoke to me most kindly and very seriously about my engagement to Diana. "Maurice" he said "I think that I should warn you quite seriously now you are about to become a member of the Hill family that they will have your appendix out of you without compunction, without delay! Diana has lost hers; Kitty, Mervyn's wife, was the next early victim. They have appendicectomy on the brain. I beg of you be careful. Thank God you are leaving the country soon!" (I still have my appendix safely inside me!) Diana and Alan went to London and Diana and I spent the weekend in Hove, apparently visiting the zoo with Marjorie Lush, my brother's wife and her family en route. I see an entry in a diary 31 August - "Glorious day on the Downs after choosing an engagement ring" (in Brighton).

We decided not to publish our engagement until later in view of my appointment as PS to the Governor General and his known antipathy to married Private Secretaries. We both thought that in fairness to him, publication should be postponed until he had decided what to do with an engaged PS.

HE was helpful in the extreme: still extending his invitation to me to stay with them in Scotland - and even there blessed the engagement, of which he approved an announcement in October, after our arrival in Khartoum.

I was not at my best at Ben Kilbrek where I joined the Maffey family and Joe Ross, the ADC, early in August. Diana with Alan motored me up to Edinburgh with a night at Shrewsbury en route. Larig was the nearest railway station - 7 hours from Edinburgh. Ben Kilbrek lies in the heart of the Sutherland country and the hunting lodge was in quite beautiful scenery. I found Sir John and Lady Maffey happily installed with their four children Penelope 18, Alan 15, Simon 10, Diana 4. Penelope and Simon I had known slightly in Khartoum (it was in fact Simon from whom the knife was taken on the pirate ship in Khartoum). Paddy Walsh who was second in command of the EAC in Gedaref was a fellow guest.

They were without exception wonderfully kind to a fish-out-of-water and a love-sick one at that. I had shot at duck and snipe in Ethiopia and the Sudan but never had I joined a highly organised grouse shoot with dogs and beaters - all experts! I wrote to Diana that "one cannot shoot grouse in flannel trousers!" I had never pulled a fish out of a loch (Alan patiently taught me one wet afternoon), I had never stalked a 16 pointer stag (Paddy Walsh took me on that day and fired the fatal shot) and believe it or not, young reader, I had never been in love or anywhere near that state in the 33 years of my life! They were all overwhelmingly kind and even Lady Maffey forgave me when I asked if I could go for a walk without having to come back with a trophy. "No you cannot Maurice" she said "What state do you think my larder would be in if everyone just went for walks!" - but then relented.

In another letter I wrote about resolving my hero worship of Maffey to a more natural understanding and of losing the apprehension in the presence of their

Excellencies which was felt in Khartoum. We also made plans for the future. HE was attending the Coronation of the Ethiopian Emperor Haile Selassie, in September at Addis Ababa. Although I knew Ethiopia HE saw no reason for a Private Secretary on that journey: he would take two ADCs. The proper place for the PS was with the Acting Governor General MacMichael, and I should join him in London next week. This was proper but disappointing.

The night before I left Kilbrek the Maffeys gave a ghillies dance at which I find from letters that I was horrified to see so many young Scotsmen in the trouser and not the kilt. My last letter from Kilbrek written about midnight reads:

> ".... Just now on arrival in my bedroom here I found the most entrancing figure lying on my bed - to wit my pillow dressed in Penelope's dress with a most beautiful face painted on top of it (I won't tell you painted on what!) and a bundle of skeins of wool to represent hair - ragged again!"

I left Kilbrek happy (but with how much should one tip the head ghillie, the footman, the cook? I think they had a staff box) with the knowledge that the Maffeys had accepted me into the family and found me clean about the house.

Diana and Alan met me in Edinburgh - we drove to Armathwaite south of Carlisle and spent two nights with their uncle Norman Fletcher and Aunt Jess. Nancy their eldest child was there - a little older than Diana. Norman was Ruth Hill's eldest brother and head of the family. He owned a coal mine, Ladyshore, in Lancashire and was a JP and a prominent figure in the north country. The Fletchers lived in a lovely house called Edenbrows, in the heart of East Cumberland on the River Eden. Although our engagement had not been announced it was common family knowledge and our host and hostess kindly arranged a small dinner party on our second evening. In the middle of the dinner I noticed Diana's eyes streaming and I realised that she was suffering from a bout of hay fever: no hay about in September but she was also allergic to cats. Boldly I asked my hostess whether the cat could be removed from the dining room. "Cat!" exclaimed Aunt Jess "We haven't a cat in the house!" But the butler was a kindly soul: very quietly he forced out a large grey stray who was hiding under the sideboard.

We three left in the Chrysler next morning - the drive was known as the first jet-propelled motor drive in the UK - a brace of very high grouse in our boot, a gift from Nancy Fletcher who left Cumberland by train two hours later and was in London well ahead of us.

For a month then I settled down to work with MacMichael at Wellington House - sometimes I commuted from Hove to Victoria (7/6d 3rd Class return, breakfast on Pullman Car 2/6d extra), other nights I spent at 30 Queens Gate Terrace, crowding into 3 weeks the joys of an engagement which was to last 9 months. There was a lot to do in Wellington House and the Foreign Office who delighted in the presence of Sudan Officials below the rank of Governor General but senior enough to tell Under Secretaries what was going on in the Sudan. The less they had to do about it the better for them (and for the Sudan) constitutionally and in fact relations between the Governor General and Residency in Cairo were soon to be on my plate.

At my home I was preparing my mother for the journey to Ethiopia where she was to stay with my sister and Dan Sandford. We were to sail from Marseilles together as far as Port Said and my mother alone from then on to Djibouti.

Diana came to meet my family and Cecil, my brother, approved mightily. Diana became accustomed to a way of life which she had not met before. I, too, had much to learn in a family where with a long family background on both sides, the old school ties, games and Society were important. The Wykehamist tradition was very strong with C A Hill and Richard who had played cricket for Middlesex; thus the house was often full of well-known county cricketers; he had also won the Silver Racquet at Real Tennis. Charles Hill, my father-in-law-to-be, was the acknowledged English expert at bridge. Diana herself had won the Bronze Medal of her year at the Royal Academy of Dramatic Art. I, who had no family background whatever, injected into the family the very slightly "older generation" atmosphere of someone who had actually fought in the First World War and had spent the last ten years in Africa. The fact that my father-in-law-to-be was the very active director of the British Drug Houses, who were first in the world to produce insulin in commercial form and quantites, and whose initials "BDH" was well known in the dispensaries, even in the Sudan, was to me of more importance than the fact that he was going to the USA to help them formulate the new laws of Contract Bridge or that Nigel Haig Captain of Middlesex was coming to dinner.

My meeting with Aunt Marie (Soeter, nee Hill) was not propitious. She was precious or had become precious after her marriage to a rich Dutchman with rubber in Java, Uncle Henri Soeter. Aunt Marie came to call at 30 Queens Gate Terrace after lunch. At 2 pm precisely there was a cloudburst and the River Thames flooded London: the basements of most London houses were flooded within an hour. The basement of 30 QGT contained the kitchen, the larder and the coal store. Minnie the cook and pillar of the household was in despair. Diana and I donned bathing trunks and baled out that kitchen - I don't quite know how. Aunt Marie's voice was heard above the gurgling black water crying out - "I must go, I must go, but I must meet Maurice!" I was led up the basement stair, half naked, wet and black, to be greeted, I must admit, effusively but at a distance, by this very well dressed and quite charming relation who was most kind to us both during the next year. Aunt Marie died 16 years later in the Hotel Negresso in Nice.

Diana and I went to see and hear Noel Coward's *Bitter Sweet*, the haunting refrains of which have lived with us for over half a century. *I'll see you again* has kept us alive though tearful for a hundred partings or more. We saw *Journeys End* and laughed with the Cooptimists.

Diana had decided that after my departure she would do a further course at RADA until she should go skiing at Christmas.

A typical Hill-Lush affair happened the day before I left. I parked my car illegally outside the Grosvenor Hotel where my mother was staying. We emerged to find a police officer, notebook in hand. Diana's mother, Ruth, rushed at him and flinging her arms round his shoulders whispered loudly and brokenly "They just got engaged and he's leaving her to go to Africa tomorrow! Please let them off." The constable shrugged her off. "Your address, Sir," he said. "From tomorrow" I replied "The Palace, Khartoum." "Where's that?" he asked. "The Anglo-Egyptian Sudan" said I. "You don't say so" says he shutting his notebook: "Well, don't do this sort of thing down there" and walked away.

My mother and I had booked on a Messagerie Maritime Boat to sail from Marseilles on 19 October. She was in her 70th year and a journey to Abyssinia as it was widely known then was regarded as quite an adventure for any one, let alone at that age. Little did her gloomy friends and relations know that my mother would be making the journey by air between Ethiopia and North Africa again -a quarter of a century later!

We left by the well known 11.21 train from Victoria, just made our connection in Paris and duly embarked on Athos II in Marseilles. This was the usual quick route to the Sudan.

We had a good voyage though my mother spoke no French. On arrival at Port Said I sadly handed my mother to the care of the ship's officers and some friendly passengers (American, for very few of the French travellers spoke English) and left her to continue the journey alone to Djibouti where she arrived in good order a few days later to be met by my sister Christine. Together they continued on up to Addis Ababa to the home of the Sandford family.

Private Secretary to the Governor General (Sir John Maffey) 1929-30

My initiation to my new job was interesting and I shall describe it and the personalities involved. I was to meet my Governor General on his arrival in Alexandria.

In early 1930 I went from Khartoum to the Sudan Agent in Cairo, one R E More who had joined the Sudan Political Service in 1902; after service in the Provinces and in Khartoum, which he governed, he was 11 years in Cairo as Sudan Agent. I had met him in 1922. I formed a high opinion of his knowledge of Egyptian affairs, not shared by everyone. He and his wife were always more than kind to me, especially when, after his retirement, I myself went to Cairo as Sudan Agent in 1935.

More had, in his office (Sudan Agency) in Maidan Tewfik in central Cairo, a box of papers for me and HE. I dined at More's house to meet the MacMichaels, Russell Pasha (Head of Egyptian Cairo Police), and Shoucair Pasha (a Lebanese of great distinction) who was Financial Adviser to the Sudan Government in Cairo. He was a charming man of great repute in the early days of the Sudan, his daughter Celeste marrying in 1937 Frank Roberts, then PS to Sir Miles Lampson, High Commissioner in Cairo, and eventually becoming British Ambassador in Germany and USSR (Sir Miles and I were combined bestmen at the wedding.)

More and I went to Alexandria where the then High Commissioner, Sir Percy Loraine, was spending the final week of his summer residence. My Governor General arrived by ship and was met by a host of Egyptian officials and a large number of police since the Governor General of the Sudan required a heavy guard and armed escort. His car, headed by motor cycle outriders, was driven at top speed along the wrong side of the dual carriageway - a hair raising experience. Leaving Joe Ross, the ADC to bring the luggage, the party was thus conveyed to the summer Residence.

High Commissioner was the title given to the representative of the British Government in 1921 after Egypt had been granted independence under a King and Parliament; however, four points had been reserved viz. Communications, Defence and Foreign Interests, Minorities and the Sudan, which were to be settled by Treaty. An Egyptian delegation led by Nahas Pasha had been in UK all summer to negotiate such a Treaty. It was they who had suggested the return of the Egyptian troops peremptorily banished from the Sudan after the assassination in Cairo of the Governor General Sir Lee Stack in 1924. Sir John Maffey, anxious to help HMG in the Treaty negotiations, had suggested that "in certain circumstances and under definite conditions" the presence of a battalion of Egyptian infantry might be acceptable to the Sudan. The news reached the House of Commons where a Parliamentary question was raised. In the departmental reply, the Foreign Office omitted to include the conditional quality of the GG's statement, which thereby laid him open to strong criticism at home and abroad. We of the Sudan in Alexandria, knowing that official conversation between the two Excellencies was apt to be difficult (Loraine's predecessor Lord Lloyd had been a frequent critic and mentor on Sudan afairs) feared the worst. But Sir Percy Loraine, whom my HE invited to visit the Sudan for Christmas, agreed to postpone raising the subject of Egyptian troops until he could meet him and his Council on Sudan soil.

All then was peaceful between their Excellencies. We in the lower echelons of the Chancery were busy enough arranging dates and doings for our visit. The Cairo Chancery in the '20s was very "Foreign Office" and tended to regard those from Khartoum as if still arrayed in shorts and open necked shirts. Mercifully, this feeling of superiority gradually disappeared and in later days (the mid '30s) I was glad to help fashion a change in outlook; by the time of the signing of the Treaty (not till 1936) all was as it should be.

I cannot say I found Loraine an easy host at luncheon, although noone could have been more vivacious than our hostess. But it took me well into the cheese course before I, who was seated next to him, luckily mentioned that I was the starter at the Khartoum Races after which conversation never lagged with the man who later had the distinction, as Ambassador in Istanbul, of being able to talk the Turkish PM under the table before dawn!

Next day Ross the ADC took HE to pay his respects on King Fuad and I took him to call on the Prime Minister (suave and polite but with little knowledge of the Sudan). We Sudanese then proceeded by train to Cairo, called at the Sudan Agency on R E More and Samuel Bey Atiyeh who knew more about the Sudanese, the Egyptians and the Middle East than any of us. We had tea at the Gezirah Sporting Club and then caught the evening Mail, extended by a private coach for HE and staff, for Luxor and Aswan (Shellal). HE was somewhat mystified and not too pleased from dawn onwards at the reception parties at Egyptian stations of *sheikhs* and *omdas* to greet the *Hakim al Am al Sudan*.

We reached Shellal at last to find HE's steamer, spotless after a refit, with peace and order and lots of room on board, all ready to sail just after noon. We found MacMichael, the Civil Secretary, on board and I felt that my job had really begun. We all shook the dust of Egypt from our feet, thanked heaven that the fleeting visit had passed well and would soon be in the good order of our own country where HE's word held sway.

This reminded me to look out extracts from the four London Times of March and April 1900 carrying articles by Our Own Correspondent in Omdurman on "British Rule in the Sudan 1900". These articles describe the position and powers of the Governor General in highly disparaging terms: "Never in her history and in no part of her dominions has England ever set up a more thorough-going despot than the Governor General of the Sudan". May I, who served under Sir John Maffey throughout his service, and in particular as his PS, testify that I never knew him to abuse those powers. He was most careful to respect the considerable authority vested in him. But he did draw the line at married Private Secretaries!

This personal problem raised its head next morning when HE asked MacMichael to tell me that, contrary to the impression given to me in Scotland, HE now felt that I could not continue as his PS after I was married; that he would like to have me for a year if I was prepared to stay for that short period, but that on no account was I to postpone my marriage. I gave the problem much though, wrote my reasons out in a long letter to Diana and went off to HE to tell him I would stay the year as his PS. I had a charming chat with HE himself which cleared the air and the subject was not raised again. HE most certainly proved to Diana and me within a few months that his decision was based on principle rather than on personalities. I never regretted the decision for a moment and I spent a supremely happy year as his PS.

I finished my letter to DRL that evening as follows: ".... This trip up the Nile is really very wonderful. The River's width is nearly a mile wide throughout its length here - narrowing down only at certain points. On each side are low sandy hills coming to within about ¼ or ½ mile of the water. In the day time these hills are yellow and glaring in the sun; at dawn and in the evening they take on the most wonderful colouring. At sunset they go from every shade - from red to purple to blue to grey and finally black, while behind them stretches the most wonderful golden, then purple then blue grey sky. Close to the waters' edges is one continuous line of green cultivation - just a narrow belt stretching right down to the river, with maize, beans, lucerne and at the back the inevitable palm and acacia trees. There are many villages with houses made of mud, all square, some white-washed if the owner is rich. The water is a muddy brown and one's bath water just the same. This boat is most comfortable and we have had two wonderful days, with every comfort and all of us enjoying a very jolly family party. I think we must try to do this next year: it is such a wonderful introduction to the country ...."

During my first month in the Palace I was anxious lest my ability and knowledge should fall short of standard (my predecessor Martin Parr was a very able man) and cause HE to regret his decision to take me for the year. I tried to direct all my thoughts and energies into making the Governor General's position vis a vis his people and the Sudan Government a relationship which was free from misapprehension due to ignorance of facts, opinions or feelings. The PS had to know what was going on behind the scenes: what were the fundamental reasons for popular movements and Governmental proposals. In this I had the powerful help of a host of friends - for I found that many people appreciated a change from the very proper and logical relationship of my predecessor to the perhaps more flexible attitude of the not so clever PS en poste. I repeat that my friends from MacMichael downwards gave me every help a PS could want. Moreover I was well known in Khartoum from my previous three years' presence there (had I not as DC numbered every house in Khartoum?) although there were now certain activities from which, as PS, I had to retire.

The first people to tackle in Khartoum were members of the Governor General's Council - the Civil Secretary (MacMichael), the Legal Secretary (Bell), the Financial Secretary (Huddleston), the Kaid or C-in-C of the SDF and the Director of Economic Affairs (Hewins).

One soon knew what Members of Council or Heads of Departments could talk straight and intelligibly to HE. Others had to be helped by careful and tactful preparation. HE, for instance, hated Finance and so disliked the presentation of financial problems by the Financial Secretary. I remember a minute which read:

"I cannot understand this flabby argument submitted by the FS. Kindly ask him to resubmit."

The FS and I together submitted a cast iron document! HE's relations with MacMichael were ideal. They both had incisive minds and HE understood Mac-

Michael's devotion to the Sudanese - which he shared.

Of the rest of his Council, Maffey found his first Legal Secretary slow to appreciate the wider inference of some of the political problems facing the Council, especially at this time, and he preferred Humphrey Bell who succeeded in 1930. He was more reticent perhaps but sounder in judgement. A minute of 1932:

"The LS is as uncommunicative on paper as he is by word of mouth."

The Kaid, the Commander in Chief of the SDF, HE tolerated (he was not attracted by soldiery) though he found him ponderous.

Council meetings were apt to be dominated by Maffey and MacMichael but HE was more than generous in insisting that the views of each member should be heard - and recorded. On the whole I found that he listened to his Councillors' advice and that Council meetings were useful to all concerned. Among my duties were to ensure that HE was approachable and to differentiate between the man who would do well at a proper interview or whom HE could dispose of as a guest at lunch and a talk afterwards.

Naturally there was any amount of work to be done during the first month of HE's arrival in the country and HE insisted on becoming fully "in the picture" of every aspect of life - political and administrative, climatic and irrigational (how flowed the Niles), cattle and camels, and lastly but by no means least how fared the people: the everlasting and perhaps insoluble problem of the South - the enigma of Islam and Christianity, the Arab and the Animist, with the Ethiopian beginning to twinkle over the border. MacMichael managed to bring into Khartoum the Governors of all eight Provinces (distances were immense in the days when air travel was in its infancy) and HE had each Governor as his personal guest at the Palace.

One Governor brought to lunch his newly wed, second wife who was of South American birth: as it happened a portrait of General Gordon (a head and shoulders painted by Collier) had just been returned to the Palace after cleaning. We discussed it during the meal - perhaps too exhaustively: as the *helu* (sweet) arrived, the newly wed wife turned to HE and asked "And who, Sir John, was Gordon?" Without a flicker HE replied "Oh he was a famous man who planted many roses in the garden below - after lunch I will tell you all about him." For one hour and a half an overworked ADC entertained a perspiring Governor while his wife learned "from that most beautiful man", as she described him, about one "whose labour was not in vain!" Luncheon parties were generally light hearted affairs from the staff point of view - but not so, of course, on the part of many young and shy guests. But we tried to reduce the apprehension so many people felt on entering the marble front hall of the Palace and ascending the spiral staircase. That was one of the main duties of the Staff - the breaking of barriers!

There were of course many guests from other countries. I remember one hot day, having ushered four guests into HE's presence, each of whom bore the title and name of Prince or Princess Lichtenstein, asking the fifth for his name: "Prince (would you believe it?) L...."

HE was enthusiastic about daily exercise - riding in the morning and lawn tennis in the afternoon. Of course he preferred men's fours and the best players in Khartoum were on frequent call. He never resented defeat at their hands and I as his partner learnt some good tennis. HE likewise never despised the poor player. Indeed he was always merciful to the "not so bright".

Dinner parties were generally designed for two or more bridge fours. HE was a good player; his PS a very poor performer. "Lush, whatever other fault you commit here NEVER please lead the Queen of Hearts" is a warning written deep on my heart.

Official dinner parties were a different entertainment altogether - they were confined to the cool winter months and were, under the Maffey regime, really vice-regal affairs - but with a great deal of friendship pervading the ceremony. Boiled shirts, stiff collars, white waistcoats, decorations and for the staff blue tailcoats with brass buttons. I have known myself dash up to my bedroom during the evening where a clean stiff collar would be awaiting me! I have also had to extract from a lady's handbag a silver ashtray (she was a visitor to the Sudan!)

In December the High Commissioner in Egypt and staff together with Lady Loraine and friend and Lady's maid descended upon us for Christmas. Sir Percy Loraine arrived by air (quite a novel method of travel in 1929).

During Loraine's visit, the question of the acceptance of Egyptian troops in the Sudan was discussed in Council and HE had to persuade the members that, from the Imperial point of view, the conditional acceptance of one battalion was politically wise and could do little harm - it would be stationed in Wadi Halfa. Neither Excellency had an easy task but in the end Council accepted their views. We shall see in a later chapter how HMG reacted. This was my first experience of Council meetings.

During this week we staged for our guests a garden party, two official dinner parties of 40 guests, a quiet Christmas Dinner and on Boxing Day a ball for 360 guests. Descriptions of these are to be found in letters written to Diana at the time. I must say we entertained the High Commissioner royally. In spite of official differences of opinion and outlook (Administrator versus Diplomat) the two Excellencies got on well together and we younger men liked Lady Loraine considerably.

Finally the High Commissioner's stay in Khartoum came to an end and we drove him and his not inconsiderable party to join a steamer which was to take him up the Nile for a glimpse of the cotton country in the Gezira and the edge of the Sudd where dwell the Nilotic tribes of the Sudan. They all flew north at the end of this river tour and we saw them no more.

HE and I took time off and went by train and steamer to Berber Province immediately north of Khartoum. We went to Shendi, the HQ of the Sudan Horse, the cavalry of the SDF, where we found the soldiers not at all up to standard; thence we slipped across the river and camped en plein air on the battlefield of Abu Klea having ridden across the plain of Metemma. These were two engagements which had been fought by the unsuccessful Gordon relief column in 1884, our troops wearing the red tunics of those days.

A little later we also set out on a very happy, almost private tour through the two northern Provinces, Dongola and Wadi Halfa. A night in the train took us to a place near the Governor's HQ which bears the ancient and delightful name of Merowe (I knew a DC who lived there and named his daughter Merowe). Then we steamed in the Governor's steamer or rode ponies in a leisurely manner for two or three days, visitng the Jaalin and Dongola people who cultivate the riverain land, irrigating it with thousands of *saqias* (water wheels). It was good country; crops of wheat and barley and date palms covering the land.

On our return, I learned from the Residency in Cairo that the Governor General was expected to go down to Cairo at the beginning of March 1930 to put the finishing touches to a joint Residency-Khartoum despatch to the FO concerning the Anglo-Egyptian Treaty as it bore on the Sudan. Plans for the journey were made accordingly for HE, his staff and Lady Maffey.

Diana and I had corresponded frequently and fully since I left England and I shudder to think of the number of grey sheets of writing paper marked "Palace Khartoum" which arrived at 30 Queens Gate Terrace during the months of our engagement. They are preserved and have been read. I had every reason, as I saw it, to write at length and in detail so that Diana should have no doubt as to the kind of country and variety of people, white and native, to whom she was about to dedicate her life, so different from her past experience.

Diana had gone back to RADA when I left and been immersed in finals, in which she was awarded a "Highly Commended" for her performance. She joined her companion in arms at RADA, Barbara Beauchamp, to stay with her mother, Helen Beauchamp, who owned a chalet in Chateau d'Oex where the skiing was excellent - and at which Diana was outstanding. She found that abroad as well as at home she had to submit to a spate of information on the Sudan.

But it had not all been plain sailing for Diana. As soon as she heard (in Switzerland) that the Palace Khartoum party, including myself, was to be in Cairo again in March 1930 she bethought herself of a possible meeting with me there. She wrote to me and I, envisaging a brief few days in Cairo, thought the journey worth planning. And plan she did. She moved south to stay with her rich Aunt Marie and Uncle Henri Soeters in Nice. She discovered details of all ships from Nice calling at Port Said and found a liner due to arrive on a suitable date.

She found plenty of opposition. Tante Marie thought she was throwing herself at her fiancee; Uncle Henri remarked that if she was likely to remain married to this man Lush in the Sudan for 50 years, why could she not wait till after the wedding? Her father cabled to the effect that the trip seemed inadvisable - a cable which one regrets to report was discarded in tatters down the WC. Then came a stroke of luck: friends of the Soeters were leaving for Java in March and offered to chaperone Diana as far as Port Said on the very liner she had picked. Thus, knowing she was acceptable in Egypt and having the means of access, with admiring disapproval from her Aunt Marie and resignation from her Dutch uncle, she accepted the chaperonage, booked her passage and cabled me and her family.

In Cairo, the talks at the Residency proceeded but with MacMichael present, I had little part in the discussions or drafting of the despatch. But I was present in attendance on HE at an official dinner given for him by the Wafd with Nahas Pasha at the end of the table. In accordance with Security Orders, we the members of the Staff were all armed with revolvers (borrowed from British soldiers). A large Smith & Wesson is not easy to conceal in evening dress; I remember that mine fell out of my trouser pocket during the meal - retrieved without much alarm.

Mercifully the talks came to an end; HE saw Lady Maffey off to England and announced his intention of spending four days alone at Mena House, the then country hotel close to the Pyramids. I was free to go to Port Said and meet Diana's ship.

On 11 March 1930 in Port Said, I met a very self-possessed and exuberant Diana off the good ship Athos. We travelled physically by train but in spirit in mid-air to Cairo and went straight to the house of good friends, Rev and Mrs Colquhoun who had agreed delightedly to house Diana and lend us their car.

I will draw a veil over those few days in Cairo. We did buy summer frocks in Sicurels (then the Marks and Spencer of Cairo) and on the third day we did ask ourselves to tea with HE at Mena House Hotel. At tea, HE found that Norman Fletcher, Diana's uncle with whom we had stayed in the summer, had been "a very good friend" at Rugby in the '90s.

I thought I knew Sir John pretty well by then but I was astounded when he said to Diana "Well, if you are going to marry this young man, you had better see, first of all, the country to which he is taking you. So will you accompany us on our journey to Khartoum? Joe" as he turned to Ross the ADC, "will you please arrange for Miss Hill to come with us?" Tableau.

We spent the next morning buying more frocks at Sicurels, and left by the Wagon-lit from Cairo that evening en route for Luxor (dawn arrival) and Aswan by evening.

There we embarked on HE's stern wheeler, and made that wonderful journey up the Nile. We had two days and nights with a following wind. We made an excursion stop at Korosko, an evening visit to the Abu Simbel temple (then at water level) and reached Wadi Halfa on the morning of the third day. There we were met by Jackson, the Provincial Governor, who took HE and me round the town where they were putting finishing touches to the new and successful hotel. Diana was kindly welcomed by the DC's wife and in the evening we left in the GG's Sudan Rail saloon; Diana occupied the ADC's compartment. Next morning Diana saw the Nile again on the banks of which we were to spend so much of our lives in the Sudan. The Omda of Abu Hamed greeted us at his station where we stretched our legs before the warm, not too hot, journey along the bank of the river to Atbara, passing through after dark so as to avoid the need for official greetings. Early next morning we reached Khartoum by which time, despite Diana's presence, I had managed to deal with three black boxes of correspondence and reports sent to me from Khartoum. Diana was ensconced in the guest-room of the Palace overlooking the Nile with a view of Tutti Island and North Khartoum across the span of water. HE had been wonderful to us throughout the journey, not sparing me from work but with a regard for Diana which was unforgettable.

It was the same with all my friends in Khartoum. Mary Humphry called shyly at the Palace and took charge of Diana; the MacMichaels had us to dinner our first evening; the Sarsfield Halls (he Governor of Khartoum) on the second. As Nesta MacMichael (a close and wise friend) said "We all want to meet the notable young lady who makes her first entry into the Sudan as the GG's guest". We managed to include Diana in an official dinner party at which HE spared her the ordeal of the two minutes tete a tete after dinner.

True to herself, Diana threw herself into this whirlwind of hospitality and sightseeing with an infectious *joie de vivre*. She even invaded the holy ground of the Palace tennis courts (showing who had won Joe Ross' heart as well as HE's) and acquitted herself well; by special request to my Chief, she did not play bridge.

The reader can imagine the wonderful happiness that HE's invitation and kindness produced in both of us; I only hope that I repaid the debt which I owed John Maffey for the gift of his personal blessing. Diana herself was brilliant on her entry to the Sudan Service and society; her courage and determination in reaching Port Said, her acceptance of the invitation to Khartoum after her quite natural mention of "Uncle Norman" and her conduct on that halcyon journey. I observed and learnt a lot during those few days about balance of behaviour - Diana trying to convey her young appreciation of her host's generosity, HE trying to tell her that he approved mightily of her presence and future. This first cupful of loving kindness was the foundation of our happy service in the Sudan.

Abortive Anglo-Egyptian Treaty

When considering the negotiations for a settlement of Anglo-Egyptian relations by Treaty one has to go back to the report of the Milner Commission of 1922 and the special declaration on the subject of the Sudan made by that Commission.

Referring to the past the Commission wrote:

"The Arabs of the Sudan speak dialects of the same language as the peoples of Egypt and are united with them by the bond of religion. But the Sudan has never been subdued by the Egyptians or in any sense amalgamated with Egypt. The Egyptian conquest of the Sudan in the last century was especially disastrous to both countries and ended in the complete overthrow of the Egyptian authority by the Mahdist regime.

Since the conquest of the Sudan by British and Egyptian troops under British leadership the government of the Sudan, which under the convention of 1899 (The Condominium) takes the form of an Anglo-Egyptian protectorate has been virtually in British hands. The Governor General although appointed by the *Khedive* is nominated by the British Government and Governors of all the Provinces are British ...."

The Report went on to stress the success of the administration in its first 20 years of life and to declare that the present form of government should continue:

"…. always bearing in mind the policy of gradual increase of native administration, the government of the Sudan should continue without alteration in structure …."

Egypt's undoubted rightful claim to proper division of waters of the Nile was safeguarded by the Nile Waters Convention. The presence of large forces of the Egyptian Army was acknowledged (pre-1924), as was the presence of junior Egyptian officials:

"…. officials of local origin are still outnumbered by those introduced from Egypt with whom service in the Sudan is by no means popopular …."

and it was hoped Egyptians would gradually be replaced by Sudanese. It was strongly recommended that the then combination of the Governor General with the post of Commander-in-Chief of the Egyptian Army would be abolished.

After the publication of the Milner Report, the Wafdist or nationalistic party in Egypt who maintained that the Sudan was an integral part of Egypt, did their utmost to make impossible the negotiations for the implementation of the Milner recommendations. HMG therefore took dual action. They deported Zaghlul, the leader of the Wafdists and his lieutenants to the Seychelles and then made a unilateral declaration of the end of the Protectorate over Egypt and the institution of Egypt as an independent state. But in an accompanying declaration they affirmed that four matters were absolutely reserved in the discretion of HMG - communications within the British Empire, the defence of Egypt, security of foreigners in Egypt and the Sudan, and fourthly, the future of the Sudan could not be discussed except in negotiations agreed upon by Britain.

The Nationalists in Egypt however did not diminsh their attempts to create political pressure concerning the Sudan. There was great agitation when the first King of Egypt was enthroned to call him King of Egypt and the

Sudan.

In the Sudan itself during 1922 and 1923 grave disturbances arose, in each case initiated by Egyptian officers or officials. A political organisation called the White Flag League was formed at the instigation of Egyptians. At Atbara the Headquarters of the Sudan Government Railways, the Egyptian Railway battalion mutinied but were quickly overpowered by British and Sudanese troops and packed off to Egypt; there was trouble in Malakal, the then Headquarters of the Egyptian Irrigation department and there were two mutinies among the troops in the Khartoum area, all subdued with but few casualties and all traced to Egyptian initiative. HMG in 1923 had issued a declaration of intention to support the Sudan Government in its determination to uphold law and order in the Sudan and denouncing the intrusion of Egyptian agitation.

Then came the assassination in Cairo in November 1924 of the Governor General of the Sudan, Sir Lee Stack - a crime which caused horror and anger among the Sudanese and resulted in the removal of every Egyptian officer and official from the Sudan.

Since then, although the Egyptian flag of The Condominium still flew, Egyptian agitation had disintegrated. The disorder which had been confined to the towns and headquarters of Egyptian units disappeared. But the troubles of 1922-23 and the murder of their Governor General lay not forgotten by those responsible for the government of the Sudan.

Incidentally, as a result of the withdrawal of the Egyptian Army from the Sudan (thereby reducing Egyptian expenditure in that country) and of the formation of the Sudan Defence Force, (the cost of which would be born by the Sudan government), it was arranged that the Egyptian Government should in future pay a fixed annual subvention of £E750,000 to the Sudan, one of Egypt's obligations under the Condominium.

"…. Periodic attempts by the British Government to settle by Treaty the issues left outstanding after the declaration of February 1920 were the dominant feature of the political situation in Egypt from 1924 onwards, but these as such had no direct effect on the Sudan and excited little interest except in official circles …."

There were, the Report adds, departmental agreements on matters of Irrigation which were to the benefit of both Egypt and the Sudan.

Let it be noted that HMG "declined to agree" in 1926 to the formation of a Wafdist Egyptian Government under Zaghlul and insisted on a coalition with Egyptian Liberals and when that Government proposed an increase in the Egyptian Army, HMG sent warships to Alexandria to endorse its disapproval - and the Egyptian Government resigned.

Sarwat Pasha, the next Prime Minister, visited London in 1927 and personally arrived at a basis for agreement on a Treaty - but he faced the grave difficulty of persuading the Wafdist, Anglophobe party in the Egyptian Government to accept the agreed terms. They were very near to terms accepted by Zaghlul in 1920 - but with him died any hope of those particular terms being accepted.

In all these discussions between the two governments the stumbling block to possible agreement - ie. the question of the Sudan - was omitted.

However, Sarwat was able to extract the Wafd leader, Nahas Pasha's agreement to return to London and try again. He did so - concessions were made on both Egyptian and British sides and near extraneous agreement reached on the Nile Waters question. Sarwat returned to Cairo to be told by the Wafd that he had overstepped his mandate and that they could not accept the draft proposals. Again it should be noted that the Sudan question was not included in the draft.

Sarwat, of course, resigned and Nahas became Prime Minister of a coalition which, however, insisted on introducing legislation which in the opinion of HMG would have endangered the security of foreigners in Egypt. Only the arrival of five warships in Alexandria induced Nahas to withdraw such legislation.

At the end of 1928 King Fuad prorogued parliament and dissolved it in the mandate of 1929. Mohammed Mahmud Pasha was left as Prime Minister and virtual dictator but still having to remember that the Wafd under Nahas was still the dominant political party.

In London a Labour Government had come into power with Ramsay Macdonald as Prime Minister and Arthur Henderson as Secretary of State for Foreign Affairs. There is no doubt that they were anxious for political reasons to establish a Treaty with Egypt and that the Foreign Office were equally willing to eradicate a seemingly insoluble problem from their files. Moreover the retention of British troops in the Middle East or at any rate in Egypt might become unnecessary. With hindsight one is thankful that the moment for the removal of British troops from Egypt was delayed for many years.

Mohammed Mahmud who had come to London to discuss the admission of Egypt to the League of Nations, suddenly found himself dealing with politicians who would be quite ready to discuss a Treaty. There is little doubt that the Foreign Office took the lead about the Treaty and Mohammed Mahmud promptly produced, as it were from his pocket, Egyptian draft proposals. Conversations proceeded on these lines and a draft Treaty was drawn up.

From the point of view of the Sudan the clause affecting Sudan (No. 13) was neutral and acceptable - we knew it almost by heart before the end of the year:

"(13) While reserving liberty to conclude new Conventions in future modifying the Conventions of 1899, the High Contracting Parties agree that the status of the Sudan shall be that resulting from the said Conventions. Accordingly the Governor General shall continue to exercise on the joint behalf of the High Contracting Parties the powers conferred on him by the said Conventions."

The draft Treaty agreed upon by Mohammed Mahmud and the British Foreign Office was considered by the Ministerial Committee and the British Cabinet - with certain modifications. (I quote from H A MacMichael's book.) Of these the most important referred to the return of Egyptian troops to the Sudan. (Let it be said here that no Egyptian soldier personally wished to see the unfriendly, hot, humid, malaria-infested country of the Sudan, ever again.)

My Governor General when in London that summer of 1929 had been called in by the Foreign Secretary and sounded on this very vital question. He knew that from the point of view of his Council (representing British Officials in the Sudan) we hoped never to see Egyptian troops in the Sudan again - they were anathema. There is no doubt that he expressed that sentiment, that firm hope, to the Foreign Office and the Cabinet committee. At the same time he had to think as a subject of HMG - that is Imperially (his own words). He - and I have no doubt that he consulted MacMichael - came to the conclusion that a battalion of Egyptian troops stationed at Wadi Halfa - and no further south - could do no harm to the Sudan. HE decided to take the responsibility of agreeing "in certain circumstances and under definite conditions" to the return of one battalion of Egyptian troops to the Sudan concurrently with the withdrawal of British troops from Egypt. He decided to consult and persuade his Council on return to Khartoum.

As mentioned earlier, the phrase with which he conditioned agreement was overlooked. As often happened even in those days, the news was leaked and the next he heard of his private conversation with the FO was a statement in Parliament giving effect to his agreement! All this happened before I joined the Palace Staff and I learnt of it only when I met Martin Parr in Alexandria where HE and the High Commissioner discussed the whole matter.

The concurrence of the Governor General to the return of an Egyptian unit to the Sudan was not included in the Sudan clause but was embodied in a letter from HMG to Mahmud Pasha and specifically related the return of one battalion of Egyptian troops to the withdrawal of British troops from Egypt.

When Mahmud returned to Egypt he had to face the general election which he had promised. The Wafd said nothing about the draft which Mahmud had brought from London until they were swept into power with a thumping majority in January 1930. In the meantime, HE had summoned Council and, taking advantage of a visit to Khartoum of Sir Percy Loraine, the High Commissioner in Cairo, explained to them the reasons for his (the Governor General's) acquiescence in London in the summer, to the return of an Egyptian battalion to Sudan - and to Council he stipulated not further than Wadi Halfa.

After his appointment as Prime Minister, Nahas spoke cordially of the Egyptian Treaty negotiations and obtained a mandate to go to London with three of his Ministers with full powers to negotiate a final draft of the Treaty. Thus, in March 1930 the Labour government sat down to negotiate with the Wafdist Government of Egypt. We all realised from the beginning how anxious HMG was to conclude this Treaty with Egypt - it would be a feather in their cap politically at home and internationally. As MacMichael writes in his book, "the omens seemed good". The Governor General made it plain where his government stood on the draft Sudan clause (13) of Mahmud's negotiations plus the letter concerning the Egyptian battalion. When we visited Cairo in March HE made this perfectly plain to the High Commission in Cairo who left us in no doubt that Nahas' terms would be far more difficult to accept. I think HE and MacMichael felt satisfied that at any rate the Residency had been fully briefed on the Sudan question.

It soon became quite clear that the Wafdist draft was very different from that of Mahmud. Telegrams began to flow thick and fast. They were of course all in cipher: many were prefaced with the ominous group "to be deciphered by the Private Secretary only". Such telegrams were gleefully brought to me by my cipher officer.

Fourteen plenary meetings with the British Government took place between 31 March and 17 April, with the High Commissioner for Egypt and the Sudan, Sir Percy Loraine, in attendance. The basis for discussion was the Mahmud-Henderson draft of the previous year. Every conceivable point was thrashed out, every avenue of possible agreement was explored. The purely Egyptian issues, and even that of the defence of the canal zone, were eventually disposed of, but the Sudan problem proved insoluble. To put the matter in a nutshell, the Egyptians claimed in effect that the words, in draft Clause 13 "The status of the Sudan shall be that resulting from the said Conventions" (viz. the Condominium Agreement of 1899) must be interpreted to mean "the status of the Sudan shall be that which in our view should have resulted from the Agreements of 1899" ie. they implied Egyptian sovereignty over the Sudan and a share in its administration. The British contention was that the words meant that the status of the Sudan would continue to be that which had, in fact, resulted from the Agreements of 1899 in accordance with their original intention, ie. that they implied the maintenance of the existing position. England claimed no sovereignty - neither must Egypt. The sovereign rights of both had been merged into a Condominium. Other points, particularly the right claimed by Egypt of unrestricted immigration for her nationals into the Sudan, presented difficulties and caused delays, but these could probably have been settled sooner or later. On the main question, sovereignty and the political status of the Sudan, a complete deadlock was reached and on 8 May the negotiations terminated.

The two telegrams which were the prelude to the breakdown of negotiations are printed below. The telegram from the Foreign Office (direct to Khartoum) arrived at about 11.00pm on 7 May. I woke HE soon after midnight (it was a very hot night) and suggested a

Council meeting for 2.30am that morning. Having received sleepy concurrence I roused the Palace Staff to prepare sandwiches and coffee and set off to warn the members of Council themselves. Having persuaded astonished watchmen to let me pass I ascended to the roof of each house and woke eight weary men. On a hot night they had probably just dropped off to sleep. Attendance was complete at 2.30 and while they munched their sandwiches and drank their coffee HE explained the matter of sovereignty and administration and it was, I think, MacMichael who summed up the Wafd policy more or less as he wrote in his book:

"…. It was certain that there was nothing that the Wafd (or any other party in Egypt) wanted less than to have their claim to sovereignty over the Sudan conceded with the corollary of having to accept responsibility for its control …."

There was discussion, for HE left Council in no doubt that rejection of the clause as contained in the telegram would lead to the breakdown of negotiations.

To EGYPT

Cypher Telegram to Sir John Maffey (Khartoum)
Foreign Office 7 May 1930 2.30pm

IMMEDIATE

On resumption of negotiations after Egyptian delegation had consulted their colleagues in Cairo they began by putting forward entirely unacceptable proposals regarding the Sudan. This was made clear to them and eventually they have come down to the proposal that the Sudan clause should read:

"While reserving liberty to conclude new Conventions in future modifying the Conventions of 1899 and settling the Sudan question, the High Contracting Parties agree that without prejudice to Egypt's rights and material interests the status of the Sudan shall be that resulting from the said Conventions. The Governor General shall as one of the consequences of the 1899 Conventions continue to exercise on the joint behalf of the High Contracting Parties the powers conferred upon him by the said Conventions."

The Cabinet are meeting tomorrow morning at 10.30 and I am most anxious to be able to lay your views and those of your Council before them.

Repeated to Cairo No 158.

A reply to the telegram was drafted and agreed.

Telegram Governor General (Khartoum)
To Foreign Office No 1
Repeated to Cairo No 83
8 May 1930

IMMEDIATE

We would earnestly ask His Majesty's Government to consider whether the course now proposed is not a historical and moral "non sequitur" which cannot be reconciled with the ultimate interests of this country and the definite trend of His Majesty's Government's policy in the past. While anxious, if it were possible, to introduce a solution of most difficult position that has arisen, we for our part feel that it is our duty in the permanent interests of this country to maintain the position stated in our second telegram unnumbered of May 7 and restated with succinctness and force by Mr Hoare in his telegram No 217.

The conclusion of a Treaty leaving open to immediate discussion the participation of Egypt in the administration of the Sudan would immediately give rise to grave unsettlement and ultimately undermine the fabric. Now that the object of Egypt in respect of the Sudan has been so clearly disclosed, viz. a share in the administration …."

I had asked our GPO to clear the lines as far as possible and it reached London in time for a Foreign Office minute to begin:

"In view of Sir John Maffey's telegram we have no alternative …."

Negotiations were broken off that morning. It was curious that though the Foreign Office notified the breakdown to Cairo they failed to inform the author of the coup de grace, to whom they had appealed directly.

It was a silent day in the Palace and when I took Reuters telegrams (no kind reply from the Secretary of State!) to HE, he made no comment.

I shall refer to another Anglo-Egyptian Treaty in another chapter.

1930

HE and I flew to Erkowit to get ready for discussions in Cairo and London. I also had the Herculean task of preparing the Annual Report for the Sudan in 1929.

Lake Tsana and its possible advantage to the Sudan reared its watery head (the problem had lived with me 10 years before). The Abyssinian Government, in the person of Ras Taffari, suddenly took the unilateral (and perfectly proper) step of calling in an American engineering firm to construct any works necessary to conserve the water and sell it to Egypt and the Sudan. The project came to nothing but was important while the notion lived.

The price of cotton on which the success of the Gezira scheme and other smaller cotton based schemes depended slumped. The whole future of this relatively important scheme fell into doubt. How could we finance the deficit? Heavy rains - welcome over the grain growing part of the Sudan (99%) had caused havoc to the cotton crop (representing 70% of the country's revenue).

Lastly and to add a calamity to what was clearly the start of a bad period economically as well as politically, a new type of locust made its appearance - a locust whose breeding powers were (if possible) greater than the desert locust and able also to lay its eggs in harder soil, thereby enlarging its area of attack. These and many other matters needed quick decisions and a note of sympathy to those provinces badly affected.

Finally we left for the north - spent a week in Cairo and were in London by 10 June, just 16 days before our wedding. HE gave me leave of absence as his PS from the date of our arrival in Great Britain.

MSL and DRH Wedding

Diana had, of course, kept me in touch with plans for our wedding and I knew that so long as I appeared suitably clad all would be well. Many of the preparations which the bridegroom should have planned and achieved had been wonderfully accomplished without him.

We were married at Holy Trinity, Brompton at 3pm on 26 June 1930 by Rev Harold Kittermaster who had been Alan Hill's housemaster at Harrow.

My best man was Martin Parr. A host of friends of bride and groom had bothered to support us both including Sir John and Lady Maffey and their lovely daughter and most members of the Sudan Council!

After the marriage service we all (210 of us) walked across the Brompton Road to the Rembrandt Hotel where my parents-in-law had kindly arranged a heart-warming reception. No couple could have enjoyed a happier start to almost 60 years of married life! At the appointed hour Diana and I retired and donned our going away attire, drove round to Queens Gate Terrace where we changed into "dog robber" clothes and departed in our Morris Cowley en route for Dunster in Cornwall for our one week's honeymoon.

Martin Parr was not to take over from me as PS (again) until the Governor General went to Ethiopia in October for the Coronation of the Emperor. But Martin stood in for me for 10 days and then had to attend Bisley so I was able to support Eton v Harrow at Lords with my wife. Best frocks for girls and morning coats for men in 1930!

And so ended four years of Service in Khartoum - one in the Province and three on the staff. I enjoyed every year. In two I served under remarkable chiefs. As DC Khartoum I learnt the satisfaction and the joy of getting on with my fellow men; I did not learn much about administration. Under MacMichael, a hard taskmaster, I learnt to work in an orderly manner - MacMick could extract more work out of his staff and rub more awkward knobs off his subordinates than any man I knew; but he did not fail to let his gratitude be shown and known. Maffey, I frankly hero worshipped from the start and it was one of the greatest privileges and joys of my career to have served a man of such wisdom, strength of character, sympathy and understanding. He did much for DRH and me at a time in our lives when we needed advice.

HE went off to Abyssinia in September 1930 and DRL and I went to the Army and Navy Stores in Victoria Street where at the export counter a little gnome of a man knew without reference exactly what we needed in the way of provisions from flour to strawberries in brandy ("one bottle Madam for your Christmas") to take with us to el Dueim, White Nile Province. "Take *coloured* towels, Madam, the water tends to be rather discoloured."

Diana R Hill, on engagement to MSL, 1929

MSL on engagement in Sidmouth, 1929

Their wedding on 26 June 1930

Ruth and Charles Hill, at the wedding

Left and right:
MSL and DRL riding, El Dueim, White Nile Province, 1930

Right:
The Governor General, Sir John Maffey, with MSL (Private Secretary) and other staff, Khartoum, 1929

Left:
King's Day, at the Palace, Khartoum, 1930

CHAPTER 7

WHITE NILE and UPPER NILE PROVINCES 1930-34

Deputy Governor, White Nile Province, el Dueim: 1930-32

In October, we embarked at Marseilles on a City Line ship and happened to be the only honeymoon couple among the several scores of Sudan officials sailing in her. We survived and were soon in Khartoum buying furniture and there embarked on the Province steamer which Guy Pawson, the Governor of White Nile Province, had sent down to bring his District Commissioner to el Dueim. The old title was Deputy Governor and although "those bureaucrats in Khartoum" (for that is what we provincials now called my erstwhile fellows) had changed the title, in Arabic the name was *Naib el Mudir* or Deputy Governor.

In fact, for a newly married couple, there could not have been a more pleasant assignment than Deputy Governor, White Nile Province, deputy to Guy Pawson and Helen his wife. Not only was he a first class Governor but Helen was the kindest, most amazing person who laid herself out to help the wives of DCs and other staff - and, as we thought, rather especially Diana.

White Nile Province was the smallest province in the Sudan; in fact in later years it became a sub-province of Blue Nile Province on the other side of the river. The land area was 16,000 square miles but it boasted a population of nearly half a million people - more than Kassala, my first Province. One noticed at once that the towns and villages were larger and the people were more clustered together. The vicinity of Khartoum and Wad Medani affected the northern half of the province. Kosti in the south was the gateway across the Nile, especially for the thousands of pilgrims who annually crossed on their long, long pilgrimage from West and Central Africa to Mecca and Medina and their return the next year. The report of 1930 states that 17,000 westerners from Nigeria, French Equatorial Africa and the Western Provinces of the Sudan passed through the quarantine at Kosti, many of them seeking work to enable then to reach home.

Kosti was a growing trade centre where we had a DC (first M F A Keen and then Geoffrey Hancock) with an ADC at Tendelti. Native Administration was in an advanced stage by 1931, many degrees further than I had known it in Kassala Province. I cannot do better than include extracts from the Annual Report for 1931:

"…. During 1930 great strides were made in Native Administration and in freeing it as far as possible from bureaucratic control. The sub-districts of Gateina, Tendelti and Gebelein were withdrawn, the heads of the two Native Administrations were given definite financial responsibility and they assessed and collected their own taxes. 1931 has been a year of consolidating these advances. The most important step has been the giving to the two *nazirs* budgets of their own on the expenditure side. Each *nazir* now pays his own *omdas, sheikhs*, scribes, retainers and other members of his administration; he manages and pays for his roads and fire-lines and he administers his minor local services, such as repairs to temporary buildings, feeding and working of short-term prisoners and clothing of minor retainers. It is hoped that next year it will be possible to go further and give each *nazir* his own complete budget with a definite percentage of revenue to be credited to his administration.

"On the judicial and administrative sides also there has been steady progress. In each of the two Districts there is a main *nazir's* court and this court is divided into a number of local panels presided over by Vice-Presidents who are generally relations of the *nazir*. Under the panel courts are the *omdas*, with small punitive powers to deal with minor offences. Thus, there is a complete chain of judicial machinery starting with the *omda's* court and ending with the main court presided over by the *nazir*. Similarly, on the administrative side, the *nazir* has his executive agents, who generally coincide with the Vice-Presidents of the panel courts. Under them again are the *omdas*. In both Native Administrations the underlying principle is a confederation of tribes united either by consanguinity or by historical associations.

"Public security was satisfactory, although both the Hassania and Baggara are prone to crimes of violence generally connected with drink or women. During the year eighteen such crimes occurred and of these thirteen resulted in death. The Native Administrations have effectually dealt with local thieves, but the semi-professional criminals who operate from province to province present greater difficulties. These, no doubt, will be overcome when the local administrations begin to co-operate and co-ordinate with each other to a greater degree than they do at present ...."

This advance was due in great part to the patient and sympathetic efforts made by Guy Pawson. His Deputy, myself, had much to learn.

Education too was well advanced and the Sudanese themselves had organised and were financing girls' schools in two centres. Forestry was a new industry in White Nile and large areas were being taken over for tree planting by the Agricultural Department. There existed a "pump scheme" at el Dueim managed by the Agricultural Department who rented the land to the former owners from whom they had purchased it. Cotton was grown as well as other crops, notably *berseem*, clover, for our ponies.

Then there was Aba Island, the home and large estate of Sayed Sir Abder Rahman el Mahdi KBE CVO (the posthumous son of the Mahdi of Allah) who had risen from obscurity to become a religious and political leader in 1926, a position which was a factor in the departure of one Governor General, and from which he was gradually reduced to the status of a country gentleman with a government subsidy on Aba Island.

Here he controlled a powerful pumping scheme, grew cotton, employed practically unpaid labour in the form of hundreds of pilgrims from the west to whom the *baraka* or blessing earned by serving the son of the Mahdi was supposed to be worth the gift of their labour. This form of unpaid labour (some called it slavery) was a practice which Governor White Nile Province had especial instructions to detect and forbid. Thus a general surveillance of the practice and finances of Aba Island was one of the Governor's political duties. Guy Pawson and I would visit the island, often taking our wives, and we both well remember breakfasts there at which both porridge and turkey were on the menu and had to be devoured. Sayed Abder Rahman el Mahdi was politeness personified but I found it hard to like his ingratiating ways.

After four years in the busy, crowded, tense atmosphere of Khartoum it was a wonderful change to live in rural surroundings with the duty of tackling rural problems - the daily lives of men and women, their food and water, their crops and subsistence, far, far away from international or national crises.

The British community in el Dueim was not large. John Humphry was DC Northern District. He and his wife Mary were old and beloved friends from Khartoum. He suffered from hay-fever and matutinal sneezes from the roof of his house were the reveille for his neighbours.

We had a pleasant and moderately commodious house on the river's edge shaded by trees and having a good garden: it was here that we both learnt from Helen Pawson the rudiments of Sudan gardening. I must admit, however, that never before or after have I dug up roses in May, preserving them in a shady store to prevent the summer heat from burning the roots. We had no refrigerator and our drinks and butter were maintained in a *zeir*, an enormous porous amphora filled with water which lowered the temperature by evaporation.

There were mud lawn tennis courts, a small swimming pool and a polo ground about 2 miles away. It was hard to find surface in those parts which was not composed of the black cotton soil which became glutinous mud in the rainy season and developed enormous and ubiquitous cracks throughout the rest of the year. The ground was in fact adjacent to the so called aerodrome and I remember the chaos caused by the unannounced landing of an aircraft during a chukkah of polo. It was probably Maori Coningham who stayed with us in Dueim and was, I think, on the staff of the Air Wing stationed in Khartoum. He was a well known figure ten years later in the British VIII Army.

Living on the banks of the Nile - as indeed we did for the rest of our service in the Sudan - was an ever-changing experience. Not only did we see the usual fishing and sailing traffic, the government and irrigation steamers and the very occasional crocodile (one of them even had the effrontery to lay 99 eggs in the governor's sailing boat) but, before the building of the Gebel Aulia Dam, we experienced annually the extraordinary sight and movement of the White Nile flowing backwards. Most years, the Blue Nile came down in spate and with great force some weeks before the White Nile's waters were swollen by rains in the south. The White Nile was at its lowest level on arrival at Khartoum, where it met the Blue Nile; the latter flood, due to earlier rains in Ethiopia and anxious to get away from its comparatively high enclosing banks, found an easy overflow up the White Nile - still sluggish and at its lowest ebb. Thus in our years, 1931 and 1932, we had the unusual vision of the White Nile flowing in a southerly direction past el Dueim. The irrigation experts blandly called it "ponding of the White Nile" - it sometimes seemed to us landsmen that the earth might be rotating the wrong way!

The Gebel Aulia Dam, approved by the Nile Projects Commission (an Egyptian body) in 1920/21 was now about to be built under Egyptian direction. Its purpose was to store and regulate flood water for Egypt. Although the building of the dam would provide labour for the inhabitants of White Nile Province, the resultant storage would inundate land for long periods, much longer than the annual Nile flood. Compensation would be forthcoming but the compensation payable to the Sudanese who would or might suffer from the effect of the Dam all had to be evaluated -an obvious task for the Deputy Governor and I was put in charge of this wearisome job. I estimated these figures but whether they were ever used I know not.

We found a British community in el Dueim in 1930 of some 12 souls, six on the political side, six on the technical side. The tradition of the place was that all of us should meet, by rota, at someone's house, each day (except Sunday) for tea (after games), then bridge and drinks and home to dinner. This appalling daily round was accepted by both Governors in my day and therefore by ourselves. The bridge was generally bad and one player always became aggressive after 7.30 pm. If one belonged to a drawn out rubber, dinner could be postponed for one hour; there was little home life in the evening. However, such was the chosen life in el Dueim and we accepted it.

The Pawsons were posted to the Upper Nile Province next door and they were succeeded by a Governor who was their very antithesis, officially and socially. John Reid spoke Arabic fluently, not only classical Arabic but the colloquial idiom which differs from tribe to tribe and which seemed to require many words to tell a short story. He knew the difference between the Ahamda and Baggara dialects; he would talk for hours on end with the Sudanese. He disliked anything that resembled pomp and circumstance, and would really have preferred to govern the province from a tent visiting the various parts of it on camel back. He was less tolerant of white officials and had little use for the bureaucrats of Khartoum. That distaste was part of the mantle of his previous post as DC Omdurman.

I never knew what the Sudanese thought of him. My belief is that they liked their Governor not only to be able to talk to them and understand them but also to display some of the outward forms of authority. Except for a fluency in both languages one missed that display. He was an excellent speaker, but the Arabs were wary of him: was he not, they asked, a little too like one of them?

I believe that no-one I knew as Governor could converse in Arabic better than John Reid, but that never have I served under a more exasperating man. He was unpredictable and completely intolerant, almost intolerable - especially at bridge after 7.00 pm. Mercifully we were transferred to Upper Nile Province in 1932.

White Nile, being a small province, we were proud in 1931 to write that most places in the area were accessible by motor car - which is not to say that there was a network of roads. Moreover, the black cotton soil with its gaping fissures when dry, was unmotorable when wet and created havoc among our lorries and cars. Nor were the inner tubes of the '20s and '30s fashioned to tolerate 110°F for six months of the year.

One could however drive by car (Model T Ford) to the northern limit of the province and also to Kosti, our southern district, spend the day in discussion and be home by nightfall. At any rate, cars and lorries had replaced the camel for DCs' transport. Diana and I used our ponies daily for exercise and I found a pony very useful for local inspections. We played polo when we could find 8 horsemen in the station. DRL and I trekked 100 miles or so to the south of the province where we entrained our ponies and went to el Obeid, the HQ of Kordofa Province, for a polo tournament. That was a great day for Diana - her first glimpse of living among the Sudanese away from the river. Then at el Dueim we had the *felucca* or sailing boat - useful as a ferry to the other bank of the Nile which was almost one mile away, but often used for fishing. The most pleasant form of transport was the province steamer. SS Tamai was a sternwheeler built at the end of the nineteenth century, one of the smaller, sturdy type used on the northern stretches of the Nile. She had three or four good cabins and plenty of saloon accommodation. By steaming north to Gateina one could reach Khartoum in 12 hours and Kosti to the south was a night's steaming - a very delightful way of visiting the province for one could sleep the night en route. The trip took much longer when the Nile came down in flood.

Reverting to pony trekking, I remember a memorable visit which Diana and I paid to the *ferik* or nomad encampment of Sheikh Mekki, *Nazir* in 1932. This was a repetition of a visit I had paid with the DC (Hancock) the previous summer. After our polo tournament in el Obeid we detrained, ponies and all, at Tendelti. Thence we rode about 20 miles in the afternoon and evening light. The Nazir met us and we chatted. After dinner 2 beds with mattresses were produced and a vast brass bound chest was carried along, out of which the Sheikh produced 2 pairs of silken white sheets so, for the first and last time, we slept between silken sheets under the stars. It was a great experience too, next morning, when, I having discreetly disappeared, Sheikh Mekki brought his wife (or wives) to visit Diana.

Coming back at noon we both rocked with laughter to watch a hen standing in front of and under the open mouth of a cow who was quietly dribbling out of her open mouth. The saliva was the only fluid for miles and the hen was well watered.

During the summer months of 1931, after Diana had left as normal for England, she and I corresponded almost daily and it is interesting to note how the standard of my letters diminished as the weeks went on and the weather deteriorated. Looking back I do believe that it was remarkable that any work was done or any movement or visiting achieved in the heat, the sandstorms and the rain during those months. Our small community continued to meet each evening. I accompanied songs at my piano once or twice, a bathe in the swimming pool every morning and evening and I see that I read *The Universe Around Us* and *Undertones of War* by Bertram Thomas.

Diana and I spent the start of our first leave together, in 1931, in Northern Italy. Diana met me in Milan where, on arrival at about 10 pm, I was astounded and delighted to see her young and beautiful figure in full evening dress standing on a trolley where a kindly porter had placed her against the arrival of the train. We walked up Monte Rosa and stayed a few days on Lago Maggiore before crossing over by train to Lenno on Lake Como. At the Albergo St Georgio there was a musical box in which in addition to the brass cylinder a figure played a violin. On the other side of the lake we espied the Villa Lucertola. Thence she and I went to stay at Chateau d'Oex in Switzerland with Helen Beauchamp.

On our next leave in 1932, which we took "early", ie. in March, we decided to accept warm invitations to go to Ethiopia and spend the full three months with the

Sandfords in Mulu, some 40 miles north of Addis Ababa, which Dan had just taken on lease from the Empress Waizera Mennen. This was a happy return for me and another experience for Diana who took it all in her stride and enjoyed every moment of those months. We took a P & O from Port Sudan for Aden, found an immediate connection in the Cowasjee Dinshaw ferry from Aden to Djibouti and there had to wait for two days before the Addis Ababa express pulled out for the two and a half day journey to Addis Ababa.

Hotel de Louvere in Aden was much the same as in 1922 and it must have been on this occasion that we found in our bedrooms, among the various "Avis" about keys and meals, etc, the following, printed in red:

"Messieurs et Mesdames les voyageurs sont priés .... de ne pas se promener dans les couloirs nus."

We passed a night at Dire Dawa, charming as ever with memories for me of the MP and his lady, and found the same mosquitoes at Hawash and a foul Abyssinian customs man who turned Diana's case inside out. At last the run down to Addis Ababa we were met by Dan and Chris and those of their children who could ride; then up the road to their new house. It was a wonderfully happy gathering and Chris and Dan and such of their children who were articulate gave a great welcome to Diana - who never turned a hair at finding this part of Africa and the way of life even more wild and woolly than that of the Sudan. We stayed a week or so in Addis Ababa, paid homage to the Emperor and were given a real welcome at the British Legation, my old home. There we found Sir Sidney Barton well installed as Minister - with his wife and two daughters Esme and Marion (who was about to marry a young Italian officer). They kindly had us to meals and gave us the run of the garden and grounds where we met many of the staff of my apprenticeship there. I was especially glad to see Ato Rutta, the then head syce who was led to me blind and very old but very loyal, who remembered the names of all my ponies as well as those of Dodds. A very moving meeting - I cannot remember whether we met my beloved Tasfai in the Legation or whether he had already joined Dan Sandford's household or farm staff. One of the greatest joys was to be able to share the memories of those three happy years with Diana.

We met in Addis Ababa, apart from many others, the Padre, the Rev Austen Matthew, who, having come out to Ethiopia to study the Ethiopic Coptic language, was also Padre of the British and Anglican and many other communities in Addis Ababa. He was a good friend of the Sandfords - devoted to my sister Chris and to Dan of whom he was a friendly critic. When the farm at Mulu was established, Austen Matthew would *walk* out there on Saturday, all 40 miles at 9,000' of altitude, give them Holy Communion on Sunday and walk back home later that day. In the difficult years to come he was to show himself the bravest of the brave, a staunch friend of the Ethiopians and a great defender of the faith.

After the week of gay life of Addis Ababa - which had not altered much socially - we all prepared to ride out to Mulu. Let it be stressed that there were still few roads in Ethiopia outside the capital and that in the country one rode everywhere.

The short rains had already started and the going was good: the country was turning green and we had but 40 miles to go - and then the heavens opened and the streams came down in spate, especially one which earned the name of Wanty River. This river we crossed with difficulty - I seem to remember a rickety bridge for humans, the last span a fallen tree, and a real swim for the ponies and mules carrying our saddles. The ponies shook themselves on the bank and were saddled by very wet syces.

Having arrived, Mulu Farm (at 9,000 ft.) came into action and we became thoroughly happy residents; Diana and I were given the task of building stables for 24 ponies, and if ever the reader has had the task of fashioning Eucalyptus trees - cross grained, twisted, unamenable to *adze* or saw - he will know what that meant. The building was finally erected and was still standing at our last visit in 1972, 40 years after completion. Diana and I, with the Sandford family (youngest then four years old) went down the steep descent to the Mugger River where the Sandfords grew coffee. We stayed there for a night, seeing the coffee plantations and also, at 5,500', birds and vegetation which does not exist at higher altitudes. We saw many, many Colobus monkeys leaping, running, vaulting from tree to tree in the forest, their bright eyes and white tails flying in the suffused sunshine.

We spent nearly two months at Mulu, refreshed and exhilarated by the climate of the country, with its long periods of wonderful sunshine and enlivened by sudden but short and sharp intervals of cloud and storm, with the thermometer never above 75° and no lower than 50° at night. There was a green, glorious landscape, with high hills and deep chasms; two waterfalls in half spate with 800' drops both within riding distance of the farm; good wholesome fresh food; any amount of physical labour on that stable interspersed with family picnics attended by several children. In 36 years' time we were to repeat that visit to Chris and Dan, with these same children, on their golden wedding in 1968 could toast a quiverful of 23 grandchildren, 17 of them in Ethiopia at the time.

Our leave was running to a close and we returned to Addis Ababa - and sadly bade farewell to family and friends as we climbed into the Franco-Ethiopian 1st Class coach for Djibouti.

(Who would have guessed that in nine years I should return as a soldier and as Chief Political Officer take, with the Commander of the British Division, the surrender of Addis Ababa from the Italians, finding a city modernised with roads, electric light and modern buildings, full of defeated Italian soldiers?)

At Djibouti we uneasily boarded the ferry to Aden. We slept throughout a storm in beds lashed to the main mast, temperature 100°F at midnight, all the ship's crockery broken. We just caught a Norwegian timber ship bound for Port Sudan, crewed by golden haired Norviks. The captain gave us a "British breakfast" in the Red Sea in July - a menu of eggs and toast, enormous chops, potato and veg followed "because you are British" by a good plate of porridge!

No wonder Diana threw a blackout in his cabin as we went to bid the Captain farewell and that I was extremely ill en route in the train from Port Sudan to Atbara where indeed two doctors and an ambulance were awaiting me with a view to immediate operation! Thanks to Diana, a sponge and half a bottle of champagne produced by the ever-ready Sudan Government Railway buffet staff, I had quite recovered by Atbara, thanked them profusely and apologetically and we went on to Khartoum, then to el Dueim to relieve an anxious Governor straining for leave.

Diana had courageously agreed to return to el Dueim prematurely, for the rainy, humid and hot season had not ended. She suffered no harm and indeed the climate of the rains, though hot and sticky, did not produce a great heat. We had three months before the north wind began to blow so we were in good training for the damp sticky climate of Upper Nile Province, to which we were transferred at the end of the year, 1932.

On Reid's return in November, Diana went to Khartoum for a medical check in view of the fact that she was expecting our first child!

As a fact we were quite happy in those months of 1932 in el Dueim but I was glad to leave my Governor who had little use for an all rounder ie. one who had wider interests, looking beyond the confines of White Nile Province - for he regarded that kind of outlook beyond his ken. I felt that I had failed him but that I had not done badly for the DCs and the staff of the Province.

Deputy Governor, Upper Nile Province 1932-34

While Diana was in Khartoum I moved south and she joined me in Malakal, some miles up river from el Dueim. I went in SS Tamai to rejoin Guy Pawson, Governor of Upper Nile Province in the Southern Sudan. Diana, I may say, arrived a month later in a magnificent Egyptian Irrigation steamer, the guest of the Head of Egyptian Irrigation.

So I arrived alone - and there was no lack of warmth in my welcome. I was woken in the early hours by a cacophony of noise coming from the other bank of the river. "The Shilluk tribe have risen and are advancing" was my first thought. My second reasoning came to the conclusion that the noise was caused by some millions of frogs in a predawn chorus. It was indeed a nightly performance.

I, knowing nothing of the Southern Question, had made up my mind to take all the other administrative work off my Governor and let him tackle the question of the policy of Southern Sudan. I had known many "Bog Barons" (the contract DCs) and knew their skill and their wish to be left alone and undisturbed in their districts.

North of Malakal I knew I had sufficient experience to guide DCs in self administration of the tribes - but they were so adept themselves in their lead towards this that advice was almost unnecessary; however, when they did ask for advice, they received it.

Here I was in the Southern Sudan for the first time with four months to learn the job before I became acting Governor of the Province while Pawson went on leave.

The south was quite different from the north, in practically every way. The northern Sudanese are of Arab stock, generally pale of skin and Muslim by religion. The Sudanese in the south were black of skin, Nilotics by race, having no religion and wearing no clothes. Arabs of the north had owned slaves, and had acquiesced in, if not practised, slave hunting and trading. The most common word of human abuse is "you slave". The southerners had been their prey - hunted, traded and owned as slaves.

The proselytising of Christianity was, under the Kitchener Charter of the Condominium, forbidden in the north. It was permitted, in fact commended, in the south. Whereas in the north the spread of education was in Government hands and represented one of the main principles of Government policy, in the south the task of spreading education was left principally to the missionaries, with support from the Government. The missionaries were taking up their responsibilities in this respect - especially in the towns and larger tribal centres.

In the north, Government policy - eg. on Native Administration - emanated from the Governor and it was expected that DCs would apply it, with local variations, to the circumstances of their tribes and districts. In the south, certainly as we tried to administer Upper Nile Province, the DCs would explain the varying administrative problems of their tribes and we at Province Headquarters would attempt to help them solve these, along the lines of Government policy.

It was in fact, far more difficult to generalise in the south than in the north. In Upper Nile Province several Nilotic peoples were represented and the problems of the Shilluk, the Nuer and Dinka (all speaking different languages - not dialects) were far more varied, indeed different in principle from those of the essentially similar Arab tribes in the north.

My Governor, Guy Pawson, was wise enough to realise that his DCs - some on contract, some permanent members of the Political Service - knew far more about the Shilluk, the Nuer, the Anuak and the Dinka than we at Headquarters, however much we travelled, could ever hope to learn. We DCs in the northern, Arab Sudan were prone to boast of our understanding of the people of our districts. I, for one, believe that the men who administered the southern tribes of Nilotics knew their people better, more intimately.

Pawson's policy was to hold a large province conference once a year at Christmas when communications were at their best - plenty of water in the Nile and roads becoming passable. Every DC came in and, with the Governor in the chair, we had a good ten days of conference when everyone was encouraged and expected to speak his mind. I assumed the job of recorder and by much night work saw that today's talks were summarised in writing for tomorrow. We conferred all morning - took exercise every afternoon and were convivial most evenings, though many of these were devoted to personal discussion between DC and Governor or neighbour.

Luckily for me we arrived for the 1932 Christmas conference and I learnt much. Those DCs in the south were very much the fathers of their people, living courageous but amazingly happy lives in sometimes appalling conditions.

Upper Nile was a huge province, with 700 miles of the White Nile flowing through the centre which, in flood time, became one gigantic marsh called *sudd*. To the east were the mountains of Ethiopia which drained an immense amount of water into the Nile Valley. Throughout the province, the hot and humid climate produced mosquitoes and malaria was rife. We all lived and slept in "meat safes" and bread would go mouldy overnight.

The Nile created the climatic conditions while the state of the river itself reflected the result of the rains which fell between March and October in the Upper Nile Province. The river was also fed in Sudan and Kenya and Uganda Colonies further south, and particularly in the mountains of Ethiopia.

Nearly three-quarters of a million people lived in this area - and by and large were amenable to the loose rein, as one liked to call it, of the British Administration (one should correctly have called it the Condominium Administration but the tribesmen, and to an extent the administrators themselves, were unaware of the Condominium).

In the north was the large, historically well known tribe of the Shilluk, whose leader the *Ret* was elected for life when his predecessor died or became incompetent. They were an attractive though unpredictable people who through their connections with their northern Arab neighbours had adopted some of the agricultural habits of the north - eg. rain grown cultivation of cotton. I remember seriously discussing with a DC the introduction of some form of game like hockey as an antidote to the throwing of spears, their usual Saturday afternoon form of inter-tribal athleticism.

In the centre, and particularly the east, were the Eastern Nuer, cattle-owning folk who followed their local leaders and were less accustomed or even ready for any form of agriculture except the cereals which their sparse land would produce. Evans Pritchard, the well-known anthropologist, was living among them during my service in the province and though wonderfully interesting, was generally thinking and talking some way above my comprehension. The Eastern Nuer were often at odds with the Anuak who came from the western boundaries of Ethiopia and were therefore well armed.

A few instances will illustrate the volatile nature of the southern tribes, and the very great different strains imposed on public security by their temperament.

The Anuak tribe living in the north east of the province were divided. Some lived in Ethiopia and were unadministered but the main part lived in the Sudan. In 1931 the Abyssinian Anuak made a fierce raid on the Sudan part of the tribe, killed many and took away many hundreds of cattle and some 40 women and children. We demanded instant action by the Ethiopian authorities which of course was not forthcoming. Khartoum cabled Addis Ababa and, to give the Emperor his due, a commission was set up under which a high ranking Ethiopian met Governor Upper Nile Province and a plan for retribution was agreed. A Syrian adventurer named Majid Aboud was appointed Ethiopian commander and given troops and police with which, after some delay and not until our DC had come to his support with mounted police, a couple of RAF aeroplanes and the Sudan part of the tribe, he punished the offending Anuak, recovered the stolen women and cattle and generally extended dire retribution.

At some other time a portion of the Shilluk tribe who inhabited the northern part of the province, dismayed by crop failure and general shortage, blamed, very naturally, the *ret*. A section of the tribe in fact was about to attack the *ret* and his supporters and serious trouble was only averted by the prompt action of the ADC who arrested the ring leader and kept the peace. Shortage of food was always a possibility in many areas and famine relief stocks, including grain, seed and food, were kept ready for distribution.

A critical situation arose among the Dinka at Bor in April 1933, with fears of an attack on the Government. Here are two extracts from my annual report to the Governor:

> "Aeroplanes, followed by 25 police sent in lorries from Juba, put an end to the danger. A further 30 police came next day by lorries from Malakal, while a company of the Equatorial Battalion Sudan Defence Force arrived from Torit the same evening. The sudden arrival of these Government forces greatly impressed the Dinka, who, accustomed to seeing only the DC with a handful of police, had begun to forget that Government had other resources at its command. The trouble arose through a witch-doctor, Kuca, whose son had been condemned to death by a Government court for killing another Dinka. Kuca threatened to withhold rain for five years unless the tribesmen rescued his son from the government. A head chief, Deng Cuol, supported Kuca in his subversive propaganda, while pretending to assist the Government. The Equatorial Company, under the command of Captain Leslie, accompanied by the DC, subsequently marched through the district, and the persons responsible for the trouble were punished and Deng Cuol was dismissed. His dismissal proved popular with the tribe as there was no doubt that he had been abusing his position. Fortunately in spite of Kuca's threats, both rains and crops have been exceptionally good this year in Bor District. The presence in Bor of certain chiefs of the Aliab Dinka

tribe - which was responsible for the killing of Majors Stigand and White in December 1919 -put suspicion upon them, but subsequent investigation have proved this suspicion to be false."

Lastly comes the story of the road workers and the lion:

"Public security during the year was exceptionally good, but the time is yet distant when primitive and warlike tribes, such as the Shilluk, Nuer and Dinka will give up fighting among themselves. Satisfactory features, however, of these inter-section fights are:

(a) That the participants are now almost always brought to justice and the cases settled according to tribal law and custom;

(b) That the desire is growing up among the chiefs to ask for imprisonment or even for the death penalty in cases where a feud is reopened after proper settlement or where some unfair advantage has been taken by the guilty party.

"An incident that occurred early in the year shows how uncivilised, primitive and incalculable the Nuer still are. An Englishman in charge of the road grading party in the Zeraf Island was asked to shoot a lion that had been killing the village cattle. The lion was chased out of the long grass, but, owing to the number of excited tribesmen, it was impossible to shoot and the lion mauled one of the Nuer. The Nuer considered the grading party to blame for this, and surrounded them in a threatening manner, refusing to allow them to continue work; the party was forced to retreat until the prompt arrival of the DC restored peace and enabled the work to continue."

Roads were in constant need of upkeep and therefore expenditure. It is hard to recommend outlay of money and labour on a road which will carry light lorry traffic regularly for only four months in the year, uncertainly during two further months and negatively for six months. But we and the DCs reckoned it was worth while and they were built. Diana and I motored from Malakal to Bor on a mud road in 1934 with success and stayed in Bor over a weekend. We were fearfully hopeful as we approached Bor of running across the then famous heard of elephants for the road was much disturbed by their droppings.

My chief memory of Bor is a splendid Sunday service of Anglican Matins conducted by the then, locally famous, Archdeacon Archibald. We said or chanted Morning Prayer; we sang hymns out of Ancient and Modern translated into Bor Dinka, in which language the lessons were read; we all prayed, I feel sure, to God and were part of communal worship (most of it through Dinka minds), and of that congregation of 200, Diana and I and the Archdeacon were the only human beings who wore any clothes at all. It would have seemed to us quite unnatural and certainly unhygienic if the Dinka had worn clothes.

The men, women and children among whom we were worshipping were themselves perfect physical specimens of the human race, beautifully formed, male and female, without outward adornment. Nudists in Europe would clothe themselves with double blankets rather than stand comparison with these splendid figures. Diana and I despised the Roman Catholic missionaries who would "clothe the people and suppress nudity". They impressed us not necessarily as the ideal of Christian Africans, but as completely natural people who were, like ourselves, seeking for Truth and finding it in Christ - a straight-forward faith, a perhaps rather wonderful discovery that they could believe in the God whose message and faith had been brought to them by the white men - some of them the rulers.

Diana and I did little or no "trekking" outside Malakal during my first year of service there. This was understandable for Guy Pawson, the Governor, had been more in Headquarters than out during his first year of service in Upper Nile Province, and was therefore anxious to journey around the province himself. A Deputy Governor's lot was generally to man headquarters during the winter months and fit in his movements abroad during the Governor's absence. Moreover, Upper Nile Province was no easy province to cover in short visits. Except in the Shilluk area, since permanent roads did not exist, visiting was achieved mostly on the province steamer SS Nasser, a slightly larger version of our White Nile craft SS Tamai. Moreover, Diana arrived in Malakal pregnant, and brave as she was to come to a malarial climate bearing her first child, she decided to take quite early leave and I followed her in March 1933. (Our son Julian was born in London on 20 June 1933.)

Diana was voluntarily accompanied on the journey home by Aileen, wife of Hasler Skeet who had been a contemporary entrant to the Sudan and was serving in Kordofan at the time. He became Deputy Governor and later Governor of Equatoria Province during World War II. This act of kindness by Aileen for Diana started the closest, life-long friendship between the two families - as you will read. Aileen became Sylvia's godmother and, following Hasler's retirement to West Tytherly in Hampshire, he and she acted *in loco parentis* to the three children while at school in the 1950s.

We came to know Malakal well. One must own that the capital of the great province of the Upper Nile was not much to look at from the air, river or land, for the terrain was as flat as your hand. The town was small, the Sudanese quarter was clean (we had a DC Malakal Market Town) but ineffably dull and the only two bright areas were the Government residential area (for the Governor and British staff) and the residences of the British and Egyptian staff of the Egyptian Irrigation Service whose quarters were far superior in every way to those of the Sudan Government officials. The Egyptian Service had larger houses, electric power, fans and refrigerators, superior fittings; squash courts, tennis courts and everything Egyptian money could afford and which the Sudan taxpayer could not.

But our houses were not too bad. It is true that the Governor's house had no glass windows but only iron shutters which plunged the house into Stygian darkness and hellish heat, but I own that his Deputy had glass windows and mosquito proofed verandah. We had a *punkah* erected in our verandah and enjoyed a puff of moving air at the low time of the day soon after sunset.

We all competed in cultivation of gardens; here in the damp air of the south the canna lilly thrives and our own garden had three terraces full of these lovely flowers. The coral creeper grew well on our walls and we planted pawpaws in profusion behind the house - but forgot that they are sex-distinct plants and we had the bad luck to have the male trees only. We had our ponies and kept two cows which gave an average of two pints a day. However we owned a separator and Diana made pots of butter! The Governor's garden was notable for an avenue of mahogany trees and Diana and I planted quite a lengthy avenue in front of our house.

Humans were not the only lovers of gardens - one had to be very wary of snakes, large and small. Several cobras were killed in our compound and a very colourful flower called gerbera was much favoured by a small and extremely poisonous snake called a crite - small enough to coil itself round a door handle. I once, to my dismay, spotted one coiled round our doctor's leg - and only with difficulty encouraged it to climb elsewhere. I also shot a crocodile, a 14' beast who had the temerity to be making for our canna lilly bed.

We played tennis - of quite a high order - on mud courts which deteriorated considerably in the rains - and squash in the Egyptian Irrigation court in which many very damp games were played. We even played polo which entailed crossing the half-mile of river.

One incident comes back to my mind. We had in Malakal a DC, James M, who was a very good mimic. It was during the DCs' conference in 1933. Late one evening during a party at the Governor's house a bugle call suddenly rang out; the lights went out, and after a pause shone again. Then into the room strode Adolf Hitler - the Fuhrer. It was the precise image, the dead spit as one might say of that evil man - the black boots, riding breeches, black shirt, features, eyes, moustache and the smarmy hair. It was a complete tour de force.

I was busy with our province cypher book next day and we continued our DCs' conference as usual. Two days later I noticed that James M (for one of his duties as DC Headquarters was to decipher any incoming telegrams) had left the meeting with a telegram in his hand. An hour later he returned, rather white, and handed me the decipher of the telegram. It read:

"To Governor UNP from Civil Secretary Khartoum.

Following received from High Commissioner Cairo, urgent, reads: German Ambassador has just called on me to complain about an incident which he stated took place at an official party in the Southern Sudan, at which the figure of the Fuhrer was held up to ridicule and contempt. He asked that an immediate official enquiry be held by the Sudan Government and demanded that an apology be sent and those responsible punished.

"I assured the Ambassador that his fears must be groundless but that I would make enquiries. Should be glad of any information which will give the lie to this report and confirm my assurance to the Ambassador. Glad if you would send any information on this curious story."

We finally put James M's mind at rest - and he had his revenge on the next 1st April.

Our communications with Khartoum and the outer world were confined to the telegraph line (wireless was not yet in practical use) and the steamers of the Sudan Steamers and Railways Department which ran a fortnightly service from Khartoum to Juba in Equatorial Province to the south. Mail from London took 21 days with the result that, for instance, the London Times would arrive in bundles of 14, just three weeks out of date. The Times, let me tell you, then ran to 26 pages (Mondays included), weighed just under half a pound and cost twopence. I forget the postage but we considered it a necessity. Diana, anxious for English news, opened the last number first: I, pretending to be more methodical, began at the beginning.

The arrival of the mail steamer and the departure of the northward bound vessel to carry our letters home, were times of great emotional importance in our lives. The despatch once every 14 days of letters home should have made one orderly writing one letter every day. The arrival of all a fortnight's news (and that nearly a month old) in one glorious bundle, dispelled, of course, any hope of order. But woe betide the host who planned a dinner party the day before or after the steamer, to or from Khartoum. So often friends would be on board the vessels and we always wanted to see and entertain them - but many a wistful eye would be turned to the unopened sack of mail!

All this was in the process of change, for Imperial Airways were opening their Cape to Cairo, or, more correctly, their London to Cape route, and Malakal was an essential staging point in the trip, amongst others in north and central Africa as far south as Durban. One must congratulate Imperial Airways for their initiative in establishing this route, the prototype of many international air routes throughout the world. They had the courage to overcome the practical difficulties of flying from temperate to tropical equatorial zones, and had the foresight to make all the necessary arrangements for flying staff, their machines and the flying public, of whom I was very much one. [Shell was a leader on positioning fuel supplies and a refuelling service at all the staging points - AJML]

In Khartoum, in White Nile and Upper Nile, we were grateful to the Royal Air Force for the help which they sometimes gave us, most readily, in flying from A to B regardless of the official demarche. There was always a job to do - Air Force and civil - and we generally managed with a wink and a nod to assimilate the two purposes of the flight. To the RAF, and to the pilots who flew us, we owe much gratitude. I know the RAF authorities were more than ready to help. The wing commanders at Khartoum (eg. Sholto Douglas, Maori

Coningham) were not blind to the difficulties in the administration of the Sudan, and as early as 1930-33 their assistance and readiness to help greatly strengthened the administration of the south. I should add, however, I was generally terrified at take-off on these flights, but I used the good services of the RAF nevertheless.

Our most interesting trek, however, took place in November 1934 when Diana and I, as Deputy. made the annual Governor's visit to Gambeila. We left the voyage until late in the year when the rains in Ethiopia were over (in September) but before the water coming down from the Ethiopian Highlands in the Baro and Sobat Rivers had diminished. We set sail from Malakal on the province steamer SS Kerreri bound for Gambeila Trading Post 340 miles east of Malakal and some 80 miles within Ethiopian Territory.

Gambeila had been leased as a trading post to the Sudan Government (under the aegis of the British Government) by Treaty between Great Britain and the Emperor Menelek in the early years of the 20th century and the Sudan Government had maintained an official in that remote place for many years. Gambeila was the centre of the coffee growing areas in NW Ethiopia and there was, in good years, a large export trade. The only roads leading out of Gambeila went in an easterly direction, none in the direction of the Sudan. The Baro River from Ethiopia joins the Pibor River from southern Sudan, to become the Sobat River, which itself joins the White Nile; all are navigable for smaller Nile steamer traffic during and for some time after the rains. The rivers are meanderers with continuous twists and turns. Steaming upstream is a steady slog and the *rais* or helmsman on the bridge of the steamer had two assistants to help him at the wheel. We did not travel much by night. We left Malakal in the afternoon and progress was slow even on the Nile which was still running strongly, brown with flood water and islands of *sudd* which hit our little steamer with a bang. After 25 miles we altered course and entered the narrow, more rapid and muddy (with no *sudd*) waters of the Sobat still pouring its silt down from the highlands of Ethiopia. Progress became slower but next morning we reached Abwong, the home and headquarters of the DC of the Lak Nuer tribe. I inspected his mule-mounted police while Diana tidied the garden: not far from Malakal but what a place to inhabit! The DC, Captain Alban, was a splendid contract DC - very outspoken but his heart was really in his job and with his people. Incidentally we saw very few of the tribesmen on the trip - they were all well away from the malarial swamps formed by the river, grazing their cattle on the lush pastures of the hills to the east. We chugged on, steaming all out against a 5 knot stream and seemingly making little progress. Small boys running on the bank could outstrip us. There were crocodiles sunning themselves on the banks and muddy spits - jaws wide open. Whenever we emerged from some tortuous manoeuvre into the straight we would sight our escort - a largish flock of some 30-40 pelicans, swimming in a most dignified and unhurried pace ahead of the steamer. Gradually we steamed nearer and nearer to the birds, until when only 100' separated steamer us, up they would fly nonchalantly to settle in the water at the "regulation" distance of about one-quarter of a mile ahead. This would be repeated on every straight reach, hour after hour - a most impressive sight. When we came to a bad bend, the pelicans would take to the air, fly over the obstacle, and be found waiting for us as we rounded the corner. I don't know where they went at night - but they were *en poste* next morning.

We next came to Nasser, for long the site of a splendid American Mission Station which we visited, taking tea with these wonderful Christians and learning of their way of life. We visited the Mission and their school on our return journey. Nasser was also Headquarters of DC Eastern Nuer who was away on leave.

At Nasser we came to the confluence of the Sobat coming from the east and the Pibor River coming from the west. We steamed up the Pibor to Akobo - Headquarters of the DC looking after Anuak Beir. We spent the evening and night there talking to the DC, who had a great deal to tell me about the Anuak.

Next morning we went on upstream to join the Baro River and reached Gambeila. Here we were met by the DC Jack Maurice and his staff. It was quite ridiculous and yet rather dignified and very British to steam up this narrow muddy river to the remote enclave outside the small town in western and almost unknown Abyssinia, and there to find the Union Jack and the green Egyptian flags flying, with Jack Maurice the DC dressed in his No 1 uniform, with his staff (three clerks) and half a dozen Sudan Police and to hear the Royal Salute for the Acting Governor sounded by the police bugler, in answer to which the *rais* of our ship lowered and then raised his two flags! I hoped the Ethiopian townsfolk would be impressed.

Jack Maurice (JK) was a great character. He was 50 years of age when we saw him at Gambeila and had already been there 15 years. He loved the job, in that lonely, God-forsaken place, working among the Abyssinians of pretty low mentality and few words. He knew a great deal about the frontier, was a very good shot, and insisted, in that fly-ridden country, in keeping two strapping ponies who lived in mosquito-proofed stalls and were injected personally by JK every day of their lives. He stood 6'2" and though he suffered from fever - who wouldn't at Gambeila? - he was otherwise a very fit man. He ran a good establishment and one of his show pieces was his gramophone (no wireless in those days) and his 200 records. He kept a small native boy (either Anuak or Abyssinian), who somehow knew every single record by its look. If JK's guests or he requested, say, the Merry Widow, Bitter Sweet or Chopin's Marche Funebre, JK would ask for Gay Woman, Vinegar Sweet or Dead Man, without delay the record would be found. JK was a very good host. He and we had a great deal to discuss about Abyssinia and also about the customs dues imposed by the Abyssinians at Gambeila. He was in touch sporadically with the DCs at Nasser and Akobo and with Malakal and the outer world in the short wet season when steamers like ours could navigate the rivers and when trade was at its height. But in the nine months of dry weather his nearest British contact by land was the British Consul at Gore. The Consul was, of course, responsible to the British Minister in Addis Ababa but I believe that later, when the Italians occupied Ethiopia, some such contact was maintained. Had I known what was to occur in 1935-36 and where I should be in 1941 I would have spent another day or two consulting JK Maurice!

Diana rode his ponies and she was able to visit the grave of General Gatacre, a connection by marriage with her relatives the Pembers: the General died probably from sickness when game hunting. He was the inventor of the Gatacre Gun, forerunner of the machine gun. Old specimens of this gun used to reside in the hall of the Palace in Khartoum.

The return journey on SS Kerreri was faster than our approach. The *rais* always had control of his steamer, for engines were maintained at half-steam. The rivers were running at about 5 knots and in rough places, where the meandering of the river necessitated great navigational skill, the *rais* allowed the bow of the steamer to hit the projecting headland - BUMP; the current then forced the stern downstream and we took those parts of the river in a series of circular movements. At one moment the steamer hit a headland in such a way that a crocodile fell headlong on to the lower deck. The Nilotic foreman stoking the furnace in the bowels of the steamer suddenly espied a crocodile on the gunwale above him, gave one strangled cry and spent the next two hours gibbering on the bridge - far away from water and land of crocodiles. The croc, equally alarmed, scrambled off before I could get my rifle!

This girating method of procession was not without discomfort but mercifully we tied up at night; and so we arrived - corkscrewed, battered but unscathed - at Malakal. The return resembled Alice's return from Wonderland.

In spite of rapid movements and air currents on the way home, humidity throughout those nine days had been approximately 100%. Our two loaves of bread became mildewed 36 hours after leaving Malakal. There was, of course, no refrigerator on a 1933 province steamer. We had fresh milk from our own cow until Nasser but then the poor beast died. We had a taste of what a DC at Abwong, Nasser and Akobo endured. We then returned to the cocktails and relative highlife of Malakal.

The Duke and Duchess of Gloucester stayed with the Governor. He "borrowed" my trousers for keeps and hated Helen Pawson's starched napkins. The Governor of Nigeria (Bourdillon) plus Lady B. stayed the night. The Secretary of State for Air with an escort of nine aeroplanes stayed the night (no hotel in Malakal). Intrepid private air travellers thought Malakal was Kosti (some 300 miles north). An Under Secretary of State for Air ditched in the Nile and spent two nights up a tree with a girlfriend (embarrassment and rescue). We had our year-end conference and our Christmas parties and all the festivities. And so one year passed into another (1933-34).

During these months, on two occasions, during two years, Diana had left her first born baby, Julian, in England - in good care but not in her arms - so that she could be present at my side, at my job and as my support. Throughout those two periods of utter separation of mother from firstborn son, she maintained what she conceived to be her duty to her husband and *their* job - courageously and uncomplainingly - and carried out her loving duties amazingly well. Her sense of duty, which was shared by many other wives in the Sudan, made the men's lives so well worth living, so wonderfully shared. I believe that this self-sacrifice by so many wives in the Sudan was a tremendous factor in the success, if there were one, of our Service.

Malakal

I have mentioned some of our many visitors in Malakal, but there was one especially delightful guest who stayed while Diana was away. Who she was and what doing I have no memory. On her southern journey she played our piano - well; she passed through Malakal again a fortnight later, sat down and played two of Schubert's Moments Musicales, again well. She swore to me that she had not seen a piano since leaving, but had studied the pieces with such effect that she could sit down and play them without the music. I thought, then, that she was a prodigy but have learnt since that I ought to have been able to do the same myself. That little piano which we had brought down from el Dueim suffered terribly from the hot damp climate - but gave the greatest pleasure.

Reading Diana's diaries of life at Malakal - "dinner parties, drinks parties, tennis, squash and polo" - one feels quite ashamed at our gay existence at Headquarters while the stalwart DCs lived their lonely, hot and often damp lives, often punctuated with fever, at places like Reuk, Kodok, Abwong, Akobo and Gambeila. But there was little object in avoiding what comfort we could find - and in those days there were few enough aids to comfort as are known now.

We lost our beloved Helen and Guy Pawson late in 1933 when they left on final retirement after 23 years' service in the Sudan Political Service. One of the initiators of Native Administration among the Sudanese, he spent his last two years gently instilling this policy into the minds of the southern DCs and the Nilotic chiefs. DRL and I had the luck to serve under Helen and Guy for three years and we found them to be, both of them, the finest couple and the best teachers of those whom we met in the provinces.

There had been notable changes at the top - in 1933

Sir John Maffey resigned as Governor General on his appointment as Permanent Under Secretary of State for the Colonies. He was on leave when his new appointment was announced but came back to Khartoum in November 1934 to take leave of the country he had ruled so wisely for seven vital years. He had established with solid foundations the principles and practice of Native Administration during the years of political instability in Egypt, the effects of which the Sudan could not escape. He established the Sudan's position viz a viz both Condominium partners with precision and firmness. The Sudanese and the British soon recognized the value of his long experience as an administrator in India and took him warmly to their hearts. Some 20,000 people attended his farewell in Omdurman and heard his message of farewell.

Sir Harold MacMichael, Civil Secretary, left the Sudan soon after Maffey, on his appointment as Governor of Tanganyika Colony. Many people, British and Sudanese, had hoped that he would succeed Sir John Maffey as Governor General, but since the Milner Report [recommending the split between military and civil roles] the British Government had chosen as (civil) Governor General a man from some other service. Harold MacMichael had entered the Political Service as one of the earliest University candidates in 1905. He served three of the northern provinces until 1915 when he became Political Officer to the Dafur Expeditionary Forces which secured the capture of Al Dinar and the inclusion of Dafur Province within the administration of the Sudan. He won the DSO for his services in this minor war. He was devoted heart and soul to the Arabs of the Sudan. He worked for them, wrote a remarkably penetrating and detailed work on the Arab tribes and their genealogies which is a classic in Sudan Arab history, and also wrote a shorter work on the Sudan itself and its administration up to 1935. He was attached to the Foreign Office for the First World War Peace Conference and returned to the Civil Secretary's Office for the next 14 years, becoming Civil Secretary and Head of Administration for seven years. He was a great leader and worked closely with Maffey as Civil Secretary throughout Maffey's Governor Generalship. His detractors would tell you that he disliked and suppressed the intelligentsia, and that never having served in the south he did not understand the very vital southern question. It was fortunate indeed that he and Maffey saw eye to eye, for the Governor General was compelled, from the date of his appointment, to concentrate his skill and wisdom on the economic problems leaving with full confidence MacMichael to tackle the administration of the country. Incidentally the KCMG with which MacMick was honoured, after much pressure on the Foreign Office, was the first knighthood conferred on a Sudan official since the Condominium. The Foreign Office was seldom generous, even if they recognised their foundling infant of the Condominium.

And so I personally lost two friends and leaders whom I served with admiration and devotion and from whom I learnt to work with loyalty not only to a principle but to a person, with devotion not only to a cause but to a man, because he was the leader of that cause. They taught me that loyalty was worth several hours of sleep each night! Let me not dismiss those two great men without telling of their wives who were mirrors of themselves and in differing ways succeeded in accomplishing personal solutions, even triumphs, which their menfolk could not have done. Among those of my particular generation the names of Dorothy Maffey and Nesta MacMichael would bring an aura of happiness and help to many who needed both.

Sir Stewart Symes followed Maffey - an old Sudan hand, formerly in Intelligence, but coming now directly from the Colonial Service, from Tanganyika Colony.

MacMichael was succeeded by Angus Gillan who became a great Civil Secretary - and after retirement a great ambassador of the British Council. He lived, healthy in mind and body until he was 95. It was he, as Civil Secretary, who wrote to me in November 1934:

Civil Secretary's Office

10 November 1934
Dear Lush
I am glad to be able to tell you that, subject to any unforeseen happening, His Excellency proposes to appoint you Sudan Agent in Cairo in the near future ....

Please accept my heartfelt congratulations. I have every confidence that you will fill the post admirably.

I think you will probably have to go to Cairo in January, but I shall let you know as soon as possible.

Kindest regards to your wife. I hope she will like the prospect of Cairo.
J A GILLAN

I remember very vividly the actual receipt of this letter - for some reason it was delivered to me in the Public Works Store at Malakal where I was inspecting a large length of mahogany which was lying in the seasoning shed, awaiting fashioning into a desk for us at the end of the year. I managed to gather enough breath to ask Salmon, our most excellent Public Works Inspector, kindly to arrange a rapid construction of the desk, then rushed home to share this astounding message of happiness to DRL. The final words of Gillan's letter must have made him and the stenographer smile. Oh joy! Oh rapture unforeseen! It meant that we could have Julian to live with us. No more of those almost unbearable partings from her child for Diana.

I had never envisaged the Sudan Agency in Cairo which was a job unlike any other. Just as Great Britain was represented in Egypt by a High Commissioner and not by an Ambassador during the British Protectorate, so the Sudan was represented by an Agent and not a Minister or Consul in both capitals of the Condominium. It was true that it was another appointment to Civilization for myself but if my abilities were assessed as more fitted to such work - tant mieux; if it meant that my chances of becoming a Governor of a province were reduced - tant pis. There were two very happy people in Malakal on that day.

We prepared for the trek north; we sent urgently to our families in the UK for warmer clothes. I cannot remember how or when they appeared in Cairo, but they did.

Dinka at Kongor, 1932-34

A *haboob* approaching the Palace, Khartoum, August 1932

A steamer on the White Nile

R J Johnston and MSL, Kongor, 1932-34

Shilluk, 1933

Left:
Shilluk dancing, 1932-34

Below:
Dinka women, Bahr el Ghazal Province, 1932-34

Above:
Shilluk with shields, 1932-34

Right:
'Upper Nile Delegation to Disarmament Conference'
Caption to Christmas card, 1933

CHAPTER 8

CAIRO 1935-38
Sudan Agent

We left Malakal in January 1935 and stayed two weeks or more in Khartoum with Margaret and Angus Gillan - they were more than kind to us. I was briefed by Gillan and Sir Stewart Symes, the new Governor General, and made it my business to find out what was expected of the Sudan Agent in Cairo, not only by HE (with whom I was to have direct personal contact) and the Civil Secretary, but by the many Departments of Government, several of whom had strong links with the Egyptian Government. I also paid a visit to Blue Nile Province to become better acquainted with the cotton industry, and the Gezira Cotton Scheme in particular. Diana and I knew (through polo contacts) a good many of the splendid body of men and women in the Sudan Plantations Syndicate who made that scheme such a success. Thank goodness that in 1935 the price of cotton was beginning to rise again.

My special briefing of course came from HE and Gillan. HE knew Egypt (he had been on Wingate's staff when Sir Reginald was High Commissioner). I cannot remember that I was given any specific instructions in Khartoum except that the Civil Secretary required the Sudan Agent to conduct himself on a low key - as a Deputy Governor - and the Governor General warned me that on no account should I become mixed up with Egyptian politics; I was only too happy to steer quite clear of them - I found them sordid and greatly disliked the *Wafd* who had done much to harm the Sudan.

We reached Cairo in February 1935. John Hamilton, from whom I took over, was my best advisor. I found him absorbed in Egyptian security problems and Egyptian politics. He advised me firstly, to make my number with and secure the friendship and advice of the staff of the British Residency, from the High Commissioner downwards, especially the Oriental Secretary and the member of Chancery who dealt with Sudan Affairs, Henry Hopkinson, later Lord Colyton; and secondly, to secure the confidences of the Senior British officials in the Egyptian Government Service. Hamilton himself did a great deal in the way of introductions and himself accompanied me to the Chancery at the Residency and to the office of the Senior Anglo-Egyptian officials. R E More, John Hamilton's predecessor-but-one, had built for himself a position which was out of proportion to the requirements of the Sudan Government (as I knew full well in 1930), and John Hamilton had done his best to bring the office onto the right lines. The title "Agent" was well-known in Egyptian and British circles. Lord Cromer was British Agent in Cairo for years; the title was changed to High Commissioner only after the establishment of a British Protectorate in Egypt. (In fact the Canadian and Australian Dominions maintain Agents-General in London to this day.)

The role of Sudan Agent was described by MacMichael in his book *The Anglo-Egyptian Sudan*:

> "…. He (Wingate) retained a strong Intelligence Department as a kind of Bureau of Native Affairs and Foreign Office combined. Until the Great War its Headquarters were nominally in Cairo and the Sudan Agent there was also Director of Intelligence, performing the double duty of acting as Liaison Officer with the British Agent (Cromer and his successors) and supplying information to Khartoum about affairs in Egypt …."

Indeed there lived in Cairo in 1935 a certain Colonel Roger Carmichael Robert Owen who, seconded in 1903 from the Egyptian Army to the Sudan Government, served in Suakin and Khartoum and became Director of the Intelligence Department, Egyptian War Office and Sudan Agent 1905-08. In 1935 he was a daily frequenter of the Gezira Sporting Club, where he kept a particular eye on the flower gardens. He generally wore a kilt and was quite charming. He was succeeded as Sudan Agent and Director of Intelligence by Lee Stack (later Governor General). R E More was the first civilian from the Sudan to become Sudan Agent (in 1920) after he had served as Governor Khartoum. He remained Agent until 1930 to be succeeded for a year or two by Charles Ryder who had served in the Sudan in Land Settlement in the early days (1905-07) and thereafter in British Military Intelligence and Egyptian Public Security. He remained in Cairo in Egyptian Government employment after handing over to John Hamilton who came down from Kordofan in 1931 and became Sudan Agent in 1933. He too went over on Secondment to the Egyptian Government (Public Security) when I replaced him. He had been a great friend when I arrived in Khartoum in 1922 and he renewed that friendship with great hospitality to Diana and me on our advent in Cairo in February 1935, and throughout our service in Egypt.

I therefore found no less than four previous Sudan Agents resident in Cairo on my arrival! Let me say in warm gratitude that not one of them proffered advice unless I especially sought their counsel, and they were all of them scrupulously careful to avoid even the remotest intervention or unsolicited help. Their kindness and that of many others, British and Egyptian, helped to make our four years in Cairo one of the happiest and most fulfilling periods of our Sudan Service.

The doyen of the British Officials in the service of the Egyptian Government was Frank Watson, Advisor to the Ministry of Finance who, as such, was concerned with the annual payment of £750,000 to the Sudan Government. The British Advisers formed a remarkable body of men, absolutely loyal to the Egyptians and yet able and ready to advise Britons with equal sincerity. They all took a great and fatherly interest in the Sudan and were of course very ready to help the Sudan Agent in every way. In fact I personally had more to do with them over Egyptian Sudan Affairs than with the Egyptian officials or Ministers themselves. Indeed I cannot remember ever going to an Egyptian Head of Department for information or advice, and I doubt whether I could have said which Ministry took care of Sudan Affairs. In London one would have gone to the Foreign Office, but though I knew one of the Ministers for Foreign Affairs, Watif Boutros (a Copt and a most helpful friend and adviser) one did not approach his Ministry on Sudan subjects. To tell the truth the Sudan (with the exception of the Irrigation Department) was a political pawn, and no Egyptian official really wished to take administrative action in a country about which he knew little, except that the Sudan frontier was 1,000 miles from Cairo, that to be sent there was to be exiled and probably to die of malaria or exile itself. Egyptian sovereignty over the Sudan was a great cry for the Wafdist politicians, but not so great for Egyptians when they were posted there.

I did rightly sign my name in the King's Book at Abdin Palace, and when my Governor General was given an audience by King Fuad he took me with him. On such occasions visitors had been supposed by Egyptian loyalty to wear the *tarboosh* or fez on our heads: I regret to say that this custom was disregarded in my time.

With the other partner of the Condominium, the British Residency (after August 1936 the British Embassy), my duty was obviously to keep in very close touch; for though the High Commissioner did not give instructions to my Governor General, he was the Foreign Office link with the Sudan Government and it was the Sudan Agent's duty to ensure that the Residency, from the High Commissioner downwards, was kept in full knowledge of circumstances and conditions "up the Nile" together with the intentions and actions of the Sudan Government and their conclusions and results. I had a weekly personal meeting with the High Commissioner, Sir Miles Lampson, who had arrived from China only a month before ourselves, and was anxious to be properly informed about the Sudan and very ready to listen. He was always well briefed by his staff who pointed out to me also the matters on which they thought their High Commissioner should be generally informed. These weekly interviews were a matter of great pleasure to me and, I hope, of interest to him. I remember one of his observations to me, after we had discussed some problems and the Sudan Government's approach there: "You know Lush, you administrators always hope to be able to see and know your fences before you jump them. We diplomats just hope we catch a glimpse of them *as* we jump them." He was meticulously careful in his relations with my Governor General (and incidentally, myself, whom he always treated as he would the head of a foreign diplomatic mission) and he showed no sign of the exercise of authority in the Sudan which had so spoilt relations between Loraine and Lloyd vis a vis Maffey. I only wish he had visited the Sudan while I was in the Agency - but that is another story. Both he and his Lady were quite charming to both of us.

The staff at the Residency were equally helpful and anxious to learn about the Sudan and I was a frequent visitor to the Chancery and the Oriental Secretariat under Smart and Grafftey Smith, who knew more about Egypt than the Egyptians themselves. Arthur Yencken, a member of the Australian Diplomatic Corps, was Head of Chancery, and the man who managed the Sudan dossier was Henry Hopkinson, who was the most typical member of the Foreign Office, but utterly charming. I had the freedom of the Sudan files in the Chancery.

With "Smartie", the Oriental Secretary, I shared that Egyptian picture, because, in the Sudan Agency, as one of my staff, sat Samuel Bey Atiyeh, a man who had lived in Cairo since boyhood and knew as much about Egyptian social and political society as anyone. We gave him our confidence and complete trust: he gave the same. I had the good fortune, through him, to be one of the best informed Britons in Cairo; I had not the background - on the official side - but Samuel Bey could tell me the ins and outs of Egyptian developments which were invaluable to the Oriental Secretary and the Chancery. Samuel Bey served long and courageously the Sudan and British Governments for many years. But he fell suspect to Nasser's regime in 1956, was arrested and died in prison. I should like to pay tribute to a fearless man of great intelligence and high integrity who served his country with unflinching courage and loyalty for many years.

My other great pillar in the Agency was DC Shea who in 1927 had been my right-hand-man in the Civil Secretary's Office in Khartoum. He had willingly gone to Cairo and his wife and he were thoroughly happy. He took care of all my immigration and passport anxieties - and he did it so well that I was almost unaware of the existence of the Visa Section. He did more than anyone to ease the passage through Cairo of Sudan officials and their wives, often unaccompanied.

He could not, however, curb the desperate need for economy on the part of the daughter of my Governor General. This beautiful young lady was travelling to the UK through Cairo, unaccompanied. It was my natural and official duty to ensure her safe passage. She spent three hectic days and nights in Cairo and finally left that city by train for Port Said. She was seen off from Cairo station by most of the *jeunesse dorée* of the Kasr el Nil Barracks (Coldstream Guards) and arrived at Port Said to join a P & O Liner for Marseilles. She was booked first class as befitted the daughter of a Governor General. No-one knew that she had exchanged in Cairo, her first class ticket for a tourist class ticket - and cash. On arrival at Port Said she went on board the liner to her cabin. Minutes later appeared at the top of the gangway the Governor of Port Said, the Chief of Police, the British Consul, all with large and expensive bouquets of flowers. The donors hoped and expected to present the flowers in the almost Royal Suite. Instead they were conducted through corridor after corridor, down at first wooden and then later metal staircases, to deck D/E and to a 6-berth economy cabin 610D where, in the absence of the maiden (drinking cocktails in the first class bar) they, perspiring and greatly fatigued, deposited their flowers. I managed to gather the maiden to the gangway to give thanks - but sad, sweaty and footsore four Egyptian officials trudged home and wrote an official complaint to the Sudan Agent!

Incidentally I had many interesting trips through the Suez Canal when I went to meet my Governor General or some Sudan official of interest steaming north, dine with him, talk Sudan and local "shop" and leave the ship at Port Said 12 hours later.

Part of the job was, as I saw it, to keep in touch in so far as possible so that, although one lived in Cairo, one was still part of the Sudan. For that reason, during the leave season every Sudan official (together with wives and babies) going on leave through Cairo (rather than Port Sudan) was met, even at 7 a.m., at Cairo station (after a very tiring 24 hours from Shellal) and given comfort and probably breakfast before continuing his or her journey north to Alexandria or Port Said. Tuesdays and Fridays during the months of March to August were busy mornings for Shea, Diana and myself. Thus we collected much personal news from the Sudan and were able to send our friends on their journey refreshed. The same routine took place on their return. Thus we were very much Sudan Consul to all travellers to and from the Sudan.

On the other hand, the Sudan Agent was generally invited to Khartoum once a year (in the winter) to stay as a guest at the Governor General's Palace (generally coinciding with the Palace Ball) and again to touch with reality in the Departments. We went twice and thoroughly enjoyed "going home" again.

So far as the Sudanese themselves were concerned we did not, in 1935-38 come across many either resident in Cairo, though there was a Sudanese Club, nor passing through. There were students both resident and transient, and any Sudanese merchants passing through might pay a courtesy visit or come for advice. The politically attuned Sudanese I passed on to Samuel Bey Atiyeh.

After my first few months in Cairo, I concluded that what was expected of the Sudan Agent was, first to give information and advice about every aspect of the Sudan, to the High Commissioner (who was entirely new to Africa) and the Chancery at the Residency. All of them appeared eager, I found, to be informed, if not advised. Secondly my duty lay to the Egyptian Government which did not seem so eager to know - with the exception of their British officials.

Thirdly, I was expected to keep the Governor General and Government in Khartoum fully posted on the situation in Egypt - political, economic and military and the reactions of the Residency (and therefore possibly the Foreign Office) to the situation in Egypt, the Sudan and their neighbours.

Fourthly, I was really the Sudan Consul on Egypt for Sudanese and British officials and for all those visiting and travelling in or through the Sudan; not forgetting officials of my Government passing through Egypt.

Fifthly, (determining to follow my predecessor's example) to enhance the name of the Sudan and its peoples in the eyes of the Egyptians, the British and the large international community of which Egypt was composed.

I knew that I should have the full support of Diana, especially in this last resolve. When Angus Gillan had told me in 1934 that I was to go to Cairo he had finished his letter "I hope your wife will like the prospect". The qualities of wives counted for much in the Sudan, and I knew then that Diana's qualities had played no little part in my selection for Cairo. How grateful I was, for how wonderfully she supported me. She was beautiful, vigorous and active, and amazingly unselfish to all and sundry. Our lives entailed a great deal of entertaining and social activity and Diana's charm and magic, together with her powers of organisation and her wisdom ensured that our lives in Cairo were devoted to these four aims. We were very happy and of course extremely lucky to be in Egypt at such a time.

Surely at no other time had the British presence been so eminently represented. A new British High Commissioner whose avowed and obvious policy was to make and retain peace between Great Britain and Egypt quickly attracted the admiration and even co-operation of the Egyptians - politicians and public alike. Lampson was a fine man - he could laugh and make others laugh with him. He was very approachable to all and was determined to make a success of his job. The *Pashas* loved his obvious popularity in high places - in England and abroad. He was even admired by the *Wafdist* politicians who liked his frankness. He had married a young and charming wife and the Residency hummed with social life of a high social order - Viceroys, Dukes, etc. The Grenadier Guards were in the Kasr el Nil Barracks (despite the bugs) and the Cavalry Brigade and the Royal Horse Artillery were in Abbassia.

Friendship was in the air (it wasn't always the same on the ground when trams were upturned and British police officers' skulls cracked - but the *Wafdist* crowds were the exception). On the surface, relations were good and Lampson was determined to keep them so.

Diana and I, despite financial difficulties, decided that

the Sudan would benefit if we jumped into the "swimming pool" of Cairo with the top swimmers. Thus we enjoyed every moment of our three years. We had a happy family life, we lived beyond our income, but survived thanks to the National Bank (under the British Governorship of Sir Frederick Rowlett, and Management of Reginald Adams), and to my life insurance company who financed us, not forgetting wonderful help from Diana's father.

It is true that the storm was gathering in Europe - a fact which made it more imperative to have peace further east. Coming from the Sudan it was not only natural, but indeed right and proper, that I should retain a Sudano-centric outlook. As such I found friendship towards my country, official and unofficial, and I looked forward to three years of peace in the two countries of Egypt and Sudan and their neighbours. By the end of the year 1935 we all had to look very much over our shoulders as the first lightning struck Abyssinia.

Social life in Cairo

From the very beginning our social life in Cairo broke upon us with great force and gaiety. Diana and I of course paid our duty calls: the Residency, on British diplomats, on Senior Anglo-Egyptian officials and their wives and on other notables.

We had decided of course, that after our leave we would bring our son Julian to Cairo. We had also determined to enlarge our family and before Diana went home in May 1935 we knew this would occur in December. So we had to look for a sizeable flat with plenty of room for entertaining. In the meantime in our early days in Cairo we partook at home of scarcely a single meal, such was the friendship we found.

By March 1935 we had found a very adequate flat in New Grotto House, a newly built block near a public garden (The Grotto) in Zamalak, Gezira within walking distance of the Gezira Sporting Club, which we knew would be the recreational centre of our family's life - tennis, squash, polo, golf, a bathing pool and excellent facilities for children and their nannies. The ex-Sudan Agent, Colonel Owen, voluntarily tended the garden and a Sudan Defence Force retired officer later became secretary there. It had a long waiting list for membership but luckily a Sudan Agent was elected automatically. The Club had extensive acres - a gift in perpetuity from a *khedive* of the past - sufficient for it to contain a racecourse, two polo grounds, a nine-hole golf course, eighteen very good sand clay tennis courts (no grass as in Khartoum!), ten squash courts (which produced at least two international champions), a swimming pool, a very good restaurant and indoor facilities for bridge and billiards. In those days a cricket team (Mr Molyneux's) visited the Club annually for a weeks' cricket season.

I have described the Gezira Club before the flat for it really took priority in our lives.

Reverting to our home, for which the monthly rent was £18, we could boast of a relatively spacious hall, two reception rooms (the dining room would seat ten with difficulty) and the drawing room managed to accommodate a grand piano. We had five bedrooms and two bathrooms and, best of all, the flat faced two directions so that a courant d'air was the rule rather than the exception. We had brought a certain amount of furniture from the Sudan and were able to fill the gaps with Heliopolis (the furniture centre) cheap necessities. By the time Diana left in May 1935 we had accommodation, at any rate, for our small family, present and expected. The reader can imagine her second re-union with Julian whom she had not seen for eight months. We were quite determined to make our first family home a very happy place in spite of the amount of official entertainment which we knew lay before us. We succeeded.

I followed to England in August and found a very happy Diana staying at Glenfarne, my brother Cecil's house in Lindfield, Sussex. He was then at the Admiralty and he and Marjorie had very kindly lent us their ex Nanny (Pearson) and given a home to Julian and her, but were now willing to release Nanny to accompany us to Egypt in October. This time we should all be together and Diana would no longer suffer that traumatic experience of leaving her son - twice in two years - in the hands, very loving but not maternal, of someone else. I am sure it was done by other mothers in the Sudan and that our Imperial mothers suffered even more - they failed to see their young for years - yet the trauma was no light experience.

On our return to Cairo we had another happy addition to our family party: Diana's mother Ruth Hill was with us and during her six month visit on this trip and during the subsequent year added greatly to our happiness and that of our friends, and I dare to say, of herself. Her health improved enormously, and she too was happy in Cairo. She made a host of friends and her paintings have made beautiful the walls of our homes in the Sudan, Pakistan, Libya and finally Sussex and London - happy and perfect memorials of a very lovely person.

I associate the years we spent as a family in New Grotto House, as a period of great happiness. We were exceedingly busy on the official side. Diana, as well as being a mother of two, was a hard-working and associate wife of the Sudan Agent. It was she who charmed Prince Mohammed Ali, who dined us at the Mohammed Ali Club; it was she who persuaded Jacqueline Lampson to relax chez nous when the High Commissioner worked all evening; it was she who at the last moment when I could not, arranged for members of the Chancery to meet Sudan DCs and their wives as the latter passed through Cairo. To Diana the work of the Sudan Agency had top priority - as indeed "the job" has always had all through our lives.

Of course I am writing of the days when domestic service was available, and I am not blind to the fact that the lives which we led in the 1930s were entirely different in many respect from modern experience, especially in Egypt today.

We had two excellent, most sure, most responsible Sudanese servants. I have no hesitation in using the word "servants" because they gave service of the highest personal standard. Abder Rahman Suleiman our butler and house servant was first engaged by us before we went to Upper Nile Province, where he proved to be a servant of the highest quality in the insalubrious parts of his own country. He came from a most respected family in Omdurman where he owned house property and was most anxious to purchase agricultural land. He had a family (both of his sons became well educated and later found good employment, one in the Ottoman Bank and one in Sudan Airways). I remember his dignity and sagacity in calming a fellow *suffragi*, the Governor's butler in Malakal whom the cook had bewitched. Abder Rahman not only restored the twitching victim to sanity but asked me to accompany him in a rowing boat on to the Nile at midnight where we sank the cook's box of magic! We could not, however, save the Governor's cow who died that night, her intestines perforated by a bodkin which all and sundry knew had been mixed in the animal's fodder by the said wizard cook - who was put on the next mail boat to Khartoum!

Abder Rahman was even more anxious about the welfare of his master and mistress in the savage and dangerous city of Cairo (whose citizens he scorned) than in the swamps of Malakal. He scarcely ever left the precincts of New Grotto House and he tried to ensure that nothing was missing from our home lives which would bring maximum comfort and efficiency and dignity to the Sudan Agent and his wife who were, to him at any rate, the senior officials in Cairo. He adored the children, and I have known him sleep all night in the passage outside Julian's room when the little boy was out of sorts and the parents were short of sleep as the family grew to four. He had a cure for every ill: eg. to swallow whole the yolk and white of a raw egg (no easy feat to achieve) would cure tonsillitis. He shook his head sadly with disapproval if ever I had occasion to spank Julian for some misdemeanour. There were many of his like among the British families in the Sudan - but we thought that there was none like him, and he really came into his own in my next appointment when we took our little family to the Sudan.

Mohammed Dhahab, our admirable cook, was of the same build and displayed the same loyalty. He catered and cooked well and patiently helped Diana in the appalling feat of prescribing meals, ordering and procuring food. He never let us down and like all Sudanese cooks could always rise to an occasion and overcome a crisis. One evening we had a small dinner party and while waiting for the meat course after the soup we heard an ominous fall and crash of four dishes between kitchen and dining room. Abder Rahman the butler came in and filled our glasses and after the shortest possible pause re-entered with slices of a joint of beef and the usual vegetables. Diana, who had expected chicken in sauce Hollandaise was astonished but of course made no comment. We heard afterwards that immediately after the accident in which the chicken and sauce had been strewn over the floor, Mohammed the cook had run up the outside spiral staircase to the flat above where a dinner party was also in progress, and arranged with our neighbours' cook the immediate swap of their joint of beef (all ready but not quite yet needed) which he sent in to us and then deftly restored the chicken from the floor, adorned it with some more sauce and took it upstairs. Slight surprise on our neighbours' part but nothing said until we all - cooks and all - had a good laugh the next morning.

There was great camaraderie among the Sudanese staff in that large block of flats and our own couple were regarded as the doyens of that good company. How very lucky we were to have such good staff - indeed, to have any servants at all: fifty years later the scale of wages has made such a luxury impossible.

Christmastide of 1935, therefore, was a very happy time for us. Sylvia, our daughter, had made a fairly rapid and easy arrival on the evening of 7 December. She was born in the Anglo-American Hospital situated just outside the Gezira Club. As Diana and I walked into the hospital (we had suddenly abandoned a visit to a rugby match) we saw Dr Pochin, gowned and masked, as we thought, awaiting us. Not at all - "There's been a riot and a senior British Police officer has had his skull cracked. You go along to Sister Maclean who will look after you." And in fact Fiona Maclean delivered the baby deftly at 7 minutes to 7pm that evening. I was chairman of the Hospital Committee and knew that mother and child were in good hands. But we were all overwhelmed when, the very next morning, the Egyptian gardener from the Residency somehow insinuated his charming but grubby person into the nursery for the newly born with four pots and four very long streamers of rambler roses in full bloom. The pots he put at each foot of the cot, the streamers he deftly wound round the bars. The nursery staff were horrified. "I" said the grubby gardener "have been sent by Her Excellency the Lady of the Residency (the English Palace) to arrange these roses. She will shortly come to visit my handiwork. Kindly allow me to carry out Her Excellency's wishes." It was all rather like a fairy tale, and it all came true. Jacqueline Lampson, arrived soon after. Fiona Maclean, after a feat of nursing in which she accompanied a patient disabled by polio and pregnant, from Cairo to the USA and there assisted in a successful delivery, came to the Sudan where five years later she nursed me from near death back to life. She later married one of our greatest friends and I proposed the bride's health at her daughter's wedding. So wonderfully do lives become intertwined.

Diana returned to New Grotto House before Christmas and we entered 1936 a happy family of six - Ruth finding life very good with the warmth of Egypt, two grandchildren and making many friends. Nanny was very adaptable and soon found that the dirt and dust and the flies and creepy insects were not so terrible (she had experience of Malta) and she too discovered other nannies who were kind to her.

Diana and I had made a host of friends but the international sky had become overcast: I was to become involved, for the High Commissioner and the Chancery asked me to keep them fully informed of the effects on the Sudan of Mussolini's threat to Abyssinia and, knowing that I had served in Addis Ababa, to be ready to tell them as much as I could of events taking place in that country.

Abyssinia: Italian aggression

5 December 1934 marked the first obvious and ominous step by Signor Mussolini in his determination to acquire an empire overseas by force of arms - a policy which he sought to legitimise by declaring that he was doing in the 20th century what the British and French had achieved in the 19th and the Dutch, Spaniards and Portuguese in the centuries preceding them.

The Italian Duce's attack on, military defeat and ultimate occupation of Ethiopia was an international crime. The inability of the League of Nations to prevent the perpetration of this crime was really strengthened by the refusal of first France and then Great Britain to bring their forces - ie. their fleets - into action. The combined fleets of France and Great Britain could have bottled up the entire Italian fleet in harbour and prevented any troop movement to Port Said and through the Suez Canal. In spite of bold words by the then Foreign Secretary of Great Britain to the League of Nations in August 1935 - words which gave great joy to us all in Cairo - by September France and the then British Foreign Secretary had initialled a disgraceful surrender to the Italians which made one's blood run cold - and spelt "finis" to the Emperor of Abyssinia. Instead of a task force there were to be "sanctions", a new form of economic preventative which meant nothing to a nation intent on conquest by war.

For Britons in Cairo, and I was in very close touch with the Chancery in those days, 1935 was a year of great anxiety and no little dismay. Here was the British Mediterranean fleet assembled in the Levant - many ships based on Egyptian ports - and yet Italian transport after transport laden with soldiers, blackshirts (the Fascist elites) and their vehicles sailed through Port Said unmolested, to reinforce an Italian Army in Eritrea which had but one declared purpose - to exterminate the Ethiopian Army and occupy Ethiopia. HMG and the League of Nations talked of sanctions, but while they may have caused discomfort to Italians at home they did not deter one soldier from travelling to Ethiopia.

Why was this allowed to continue? The answer is FEAR. Fear of Germany, and immediate German support of Italy in any military action causing a war, for which neither France nor Great Britain was ready. Moreover there was in the minds of the Foreign Office a contempt for Ethiopia and even for the Emperor, a contempt shared by Churchill himself, who had described Abyssinia as "a wild land of tyranny, slavery and tribal war" and "a country full of armed men who love fighting against each other". I have seen Foreign Office comments on the country written in the 1930s far more scathing, and I remembered in the 1930s and experienced in the 1940s, the views held by the permanent staff of the FO that the Ethiopians were held of little account by Whitehall.

But what was I as an official of the Condominium doing in my indulgence of these purely English thoughts?

The Sudan Government, whose servant I was, while deploring the outrage being committed by a European country on an African state, had really little sympathy for the Ethiopian regime whom they regarded as quite incapable (even if willing) to prevent their border tribesmen raiding and pillaging the border contiguous tribes of the Sudan. The border tribesmen too must have welcomed the idea of a *Hakouma* (Government) who would prevent the raiding of their women and cattle. Perhaps! The educated and certainly the politically minded Sudanese must have seen in Italy yet another European state with power to rule a large portion of Africa.

I am not sure that I kept all these reactions in my mind - I should have. I watched, powerless, the rape of a country in which I had spent my first three happy years in Africa. The fact is that we Britons thought very fully, and sometimes despairingly about our native country's position, but we were in duty bound to think of the countries in which we lived and served - and life became complicated if one interspersed British national ideals with British and Sudanese policy in the Middle East. But it was galling during those 18 months to know of and actually to see Italian ships steaming south through the Canal, packed with Fascist armed forces, and to know that they were to be launched against virtually unarmed Ethiopians. As I have already noted, I made it my duty (and pleasure) to motor to Suez and spend the dinner hour with such people as my Governor General, Sir Stewart Symes, and the Civil Secretary or others going north on leave - but during those hours in the Canal I passed (and pointed out) not a few Italian transports bound south.

I remember so well the mental agony of David Kelly, Counsellor or even then Minister in Cairo, when we learnt that not even oil sanctions were to be imposed on Italy.

The aggressive activities of Italy on a neighbouring African state and the strained relations between Italy and Great Britain had a marked effect on Egyptian politicians and leaders. If Abyssinia were overwhelmed and annexed, they argued, might not Egypt, a far richer prize, be the next to be attacked? If war broke out between Italy and Great Britain, Egypt, willy nilly, would become a battlefield. Surely it was time to put Anglo-Egyptian relations on a far firmer and better basis, so that the Egyptians might have some independent voice in their future.

Anglo-Egyptian Treaty

Toynbee, in the *Survey of International Affairs*, 1936 (p 670), described the position admirably:

"…. In the first place Egypt's sympathies were engaged on behalf of a fellow African country. In the second place decisions were required of her in face of war between two of her neighbours. In the third place she found herself at closer quarters with the belligerants than any of the other countries not actually involved in the struggle. In the fourth place her dangers and difficulties were vastly increased by the consequences of her anomalous relation with Great Britain ...."

Later he explains the fact that Egyptian territory, waters and ports were all at the disposal of the British commanders - a fact most satisfactory to the British but equally disconcerting to the Egyptians who might ponder well on the fact that Great Britain was mobilising her armed forces in a much more civilised African country which she had been holding without any legal title for more than half a century. Whatever passed through or remained in the minds of Egyptians and Britons they both came to the conclusion that the time had now come - in fact was urgently presenting itself - to regularise the Anglo-Egyptian position. Sir Miles Lampson was an eminent promoter of such a settlement and after a turgid political year in 1935 the Wafd and the other parties realised that some kind of a national if not a united front was essential.

I cannot remember whether I reported such changes or even was aware of them, but I did know that the members of the Sudan Government, that is the top layer, who suffered both personally and politically the tragedies (Egyptian made) of 1924 had gone, that 11-12 years had passed since our Governor General's assassination, and that we all realized that the Sudanese themselves were 12 years older (though still very young) in education, in administration and in experience. My Governor General was not such a sound administrator as his predecessor, the new Civil Secretary was less concerned with the wrongs perpetrated by Egyptian politicians and intelligentsia on Sudanese effendis than MacMichael, and they were more ready to accede to the more liberal approach of the High Commissioners. Sir Miles Lampson found the British Military Commanders, curiously enough, more flexible once they had to face a real, as opposed to an ephemeral, objective, and 1936 opened in Cairo with a real will on all sides to find a solution - in fact an Anglo-Egyptian Treaty. Political parties in Cairo seemed to sense the urgency and although pronouncements by the Foreign Secretary at functions in London aroused crises, the treaty parties seemed to get on well and the Military were near to acceptance. I remember that Noel Coward was in Cairo, a guest of the High Commissioner, and he seemed to add soothing oil to troubled waters (by his very presence) and then we came, as a finale to Clause 13 - the Sudan. My instructions were that the 1930 Clause was sufficient and needed no change. The Egyptians could not take this. Impasse arrived. I think it was I who suggested that my Governor General, Sir Stewart Symes, then on leave in London, should be asked to join the negotiating parties. He arrived "straight from the Cafe de Paris", as he described his summons, and briefed by the High Commissioner and myself, he agreed to meet the Egyptian Delegation en masse and talk to them about the Sudan.

We went to the Zaparan Palace in Alexandria on the morning of 29 July 1936. "I have never felt so nervous in my life" declared Sir Stewart as we approached the Palace. However as we entered there were some 20 or 30 delegates or Egyptian Ministers. I had primed my Governor General as to names and luckily he had known some of them as junior officials in the Sudan 20 years previously. These few he at once addressed in Arabic using their former Sudanese titles and caught himself up saying "Your pardon, Your Excellency!" This raised a laugh and soon Egyptians were laughing at Egyptians; and then Sir Stewart changed into English and told his audience very succinctly what he and his Council and the British-cum-Sudanese Administration had tried to achieve in the Sudan and the steps they were taking; the actual work - administrative, technical, education and medical - to achieve their ends. He told the Ministers very frankly that he did not think that Egyptians would be able, in that climate and among those people, to achieve those ends. Some of his audience, he reminded them, had been administrative officials in the Sudan and they could remember the very special qualities needed. He doubted, for instance, whether any Egyptian administrative official would want to go into the Southern Sudan or whether he would be acceptable there.

So far as immigration of Egyptians into the Sudan was concerned the Governor General asked the Minister for the Interior whether, if to allow unlimited immigration into Egypt, he too would not insist on the safe-guarding clause.

His whole address was a masterpiece of good, truthful sense spoken with the maximum of tact. He carried his audience with him - or let us say, that his audience could not but agree with him.

The Egyptian Delegation applauded him and, through Nahas Pasha, thanked him. I was very proud of my chief and as I recorded his words in the Residency afterwards I could not but wonder whether Sir John Maffey would have used the same approach or, if he had, whether he would have moved the Egyptians in 1930. I came to the conclusion that 1930 was too soon after 1924 (the murder of Sir Lee Stack) for the first to be possible and that the Wafd were too inexperienced then to be moved by sensible arguments.

We had a wonderful day and evening on that 29 July, for having recorded my Governor General's tour de force at the Residency, I accompanied him to an audience with King Fuad, had a long talk with Hassanein Bey, the King's Chamberlain, already a good friend of mine, and finally, with Diana went out with him to an immense banquet which Nahas Pasha gave that evening on barges moored in Alexandria Harbour. Already the news had got round that the Treaty negotiations were on the right road for Nahas had roused the crowds in Alexandria, and for the first time, possibly in history, the High Commissioner and the Governor General were cheered and clapped on their way down to the docks. It was an almost eerie experience. The dinner was a sit down affair on very mobile barges and the belly-dancing afterwards was of a standard well below the navel - which one did not associate with the supra-umbilical affairs usually put on for dignitaries. However it was all great fun and Sir Stewart Symes returned to London chuckling, next day, to continue his leave.

The Egyptians accepted the Sudan Clause as presented to them by the English Delegation and the whole Treaty was initialled in Cairo and later signed in London on 26 August 1936. I can testify now (as I wrote to the acting Governor General in Khartoum, Sir Humphrey Bell, at the time) that without Sir Stewart's lively and liberal intervention in Alexandria the Treaty would probably have foundered, as it had in 1930, on the Sudan Clause.

He was present at a Cabinet meeting in London later when HMG approved the Treaty and I hope he was suitably thanked. It is curious that neither in the *Killearn Memories* (the edited diaries of Sir Miles Lampson) nor in Professor Toynbee's chapter on the 1936 Treaty in the *Survey of International Affairs* (1936), is any mention made of the decisive part which the Governor General played in that drama of negotiations. Sir Stewart's own version of the matter stresses the fact. It reads:

> ".... For the first time the Governor General appointed by the King of Egypt on the recommendation of the British Government was given the opportunity verbally to explain to leading Egyptians the results of British stewardship in the Sudan ...."

And so for the second time in the history of the Anglo-Egyptian negotiations the Governor General of the Sudan had been instrumental, at the last moment, in deciding the contents or at any rate the character of the Sudan Clause; his advice had been accepted and in both 1930 and 1936 had sealed the fate of the Treaty.

Fall of Abyssinia to Italians

For the Sudan Agency the Treaty had occupied a great deal of time and thought - and correspondence - during 1936 but we had not forgotten the far more serious, internationally speaking, crisis developing in Abyssinia. The Italians invaded the country in October 1935, entered Addis Ababa on 5 May 1936 and formally annexed the country the next day. The Emperor left by British cruiser from Djibouti after making appeals both to the League of Nations and to the British Government for help. The rape of the country made an impression on Egypt and certainly had its effect on the Treaty negotiations described above. In the Sudan, the Sudanese may have felt a tremor of anxiety at the presence of a European power on their 1,200 mile border but had sufficient confidence in the *Hakouma* (Government) to deal with another white nation. The said Sudan Government almost immediately sent its Commander-in-Chief (the *Kaid*) back to London for immediate consultation on Imperial (and Sudan) defence, while the Governors and DCs of border provinces felt sightly reassured that at any rate the raids and incursions by the *Habash* Abyssinians into Sudan Territory could not be worse and might even become less frequent, less bloody and more subject to resultant agreement and compensation. Let it be said that there was little sympathy for the local *Habash* who had not been very good neighbours.

I, of course, and Diana who had visited the Sandfords in Addis Ababa and Mulu in 1932, had a great personal anxiety. Dan Sandford had entered the Emperor's service in 1933/34 and had accepted in one of those years the post of Adviser to the Ethiopian Governor of Maji in South-West Abyssinia. The post had been created by the Emperor as an assurance to the Anti-Slavery Department of the League of Nations that everything was being done to abolish slavery in SW Abyssinia - and in the country as a whole.

Dan showed great courage in accepting the post at his age in a remote and most insalubrious part of Ethiopia, and in a provincial administration which was incompetent and corrupt. The Central Government in Addis Ababa completely failed to send either the Ethiopian Governor or Dan Sandford any funds or material or assistance. There was a British Agent, Whalley, (also a watch-dog against slavery) at Maji, but he and Dan did not see eye to eye - officially neither man would be prepared to acknowledge the other's point of view, ie. the British official view by Dan, nor the Abyssinian very untidy administration on the part of Whalley. However both had the good sense in the circumstances, fraught with danger, local and international, and almost complete lack of information from British or Abyssinian sources, to get together in the evening and have a drink. The local danger was very real. The Abyssinian tribes and their local *rases* were at enmity - which meant bloody affrays - and had no confidence in or respect for the Abyssinian Governor. Dan made one successful tour and managed to secure a temporary truce, but in conditions of appalling uncertainty from foreign invasion and the complete lack of information or money; it could not last. The absence of news from Addis Ababa and elsewhere made life a complete nightmare and even when rumours came of a debacle - the Emperor's flight into exile - it was difficult to piece together the scraps of uncoordinated news. Imagine Dan Sandford in a very wild corner of Abyssinia, striving desperately to weld together antagonistic tribes and to shake an incompetent and frightened Abyssinian Governor into some kind of action. Then, unexpectedly, they received or gathered the news that Addis Ababa had fallen - that the Emperor had left the country. In Sandford's courageous mind there lay the hope that Maji was a long way from the capital and that resistance might be - would be - exerted south of the capital. He at first thought it was his duty to remain en poste at Maji but wiser counsels prevailed and he decided to get to some British or Sudan territory to find out truthful news. Having learnt, in Lokingtaing the reality of the fall of Addis Ababa on 5 May 1936 and the departure of the Emperor, Sandford had the courage to return to Maji - in order to encourage the Governor, of whom he had a high regard before he left, again to give service to the Emperor his master in what he conceived to be a possible last ditch attempt to maintain some form of Ethiopian government in Western Abyssinia.

In the meantime Chris, his wife and my sister, had sailed from London before the fall of Addis Ababa in a most brave attempt to join her husband and help him serve the Emperor. Before she reached Port Said the capital had fallen to the Italians and it was clear to me that her journey further would be but a forlorn hope. I therefore met her on the ship before it docked and was able to persuade her, not without difficulty, to disembark and join us in Cairo until we had news of Dan. I brought a very sad person home to Cairo that evening - she had been thwarted in her purpose, had no news of Dan and was desperately worried.

I had, some weeks' previously, organised the despatch of a few cables to the Governor of Mongolla or Equatoria Province in the Sudan which we hoped would ensure that if Dan again entered British or Sudan territory every effort should be made to prevent his returning to Maji. He did not appear again until the end of June and came straight to Cairo convinced that Abyssinian resistance could still be organised in Western and South-Western Abyssinia, and that he, given authority and funds by the Emperor, could organise an Abyssinian Government based on Gore in the west (quite near Gambeila). It is curious, for I do not think that Dan knew that the idea of setting up a provincial Abyssinian Government based on Gore had already been mooted by the Emperor just before he left Addis; it was coupled with a desperate plea for help, warmly supported by Sir Sydney Barton, the Minister in Addis Ababa, whose last telegrams from his Legation in April 1936 read as some of the saddest which I have ever read in Foreign Office prints. He recommended:

"…. the minimum steps to be taken to save something of the honour of the League of Nations and of England …."

Immediately on arrival in Cairo, against my advice, Dan prosecuted this idea with the Residency, in Palestine where there was a sizeable number of Abyssinian refugees, and finally in London which he and Chris reached at the end of July 1936. He discounted the views of the two British Consuls at Gore and Maji, which, of course, antagonised the Foreign Office. Moreover the permanent official whom he met there was a man who disliked the Abyssinians intensely, and Dan received short shrift from the Foreign Secretary. Nor of course, could the Emperor act against the advice of his host government - in any case, he had no money.

We all felt deeply for Chris and Dan. They had lost their livelihood, their home and all their possessions. The looting of houses and property in Addis Ababa and the outskirts had been very bad. They had five children; they had no home; they had jobs in neither Abyssinia nor in England - and precious little money.

The following extract from a letter shows some of the complete loss in Abyssinia which faced the Sandfords, written by Chris to Diana and me, dated November 1934, showing progress on their farm at Mulu:

"…. Jam is the latest venture - strawberry and blackberry - with orange marmalade, quince and guava jelly, chutney, tomato sauce, all on sale in the new depot in Addis Ababa. I can recommend our chutney made of papaya ….

"We're very busy on the farm - reaping, threshing, grass cutting and hay making; laying in new nurseries of fruit trees and putting out a bed of 1,000 rose cuttings to send to HM the Emperor in two years' time when the new palace will be completed and the gardens need laying out …."

But they had great faith and great courage. My sister returned to her professional career of teaching and Dan was the original organiser of the Appeal Fund to build Guildford Cathedral.

Within four years Dan Sandford had re-entered Ethiopia to raise the tribes against the Italians and within five years he was riding into Addis Ababa with the Emperor whom, as a Brigadier in the British Army, he still served; they found me waiting to receive them in the city! Within ten years my sister was Principal of the English School which at the time of her death in 1975 numbered 800 boys and girls - but of that we shall tell hereafter.

Leave

Our four periods of leave from Cairo had differed. In 1935 Diana had gone to England in May to be followed by myself in July. Diana's mother lived then in a very lovely flat in 219 Knightsbridge - opposite the Old Barracks. Diana went also to my parents in Hove and on my return in July we spent two great months between London and Hove. Ruth had happily decided to come out to Cairo with us and we all travelled in the good P & O ship Strathnaven in October 1935, with not long to wait for Sylvia's birth in December.

In 1936 Ruth went back to England in May and we decided that, in view of Treaty negotiations, we might experiment with leave to Cyprus, instead of the UK. Diana and the children and Nanny went there in August and had a splendid month under canvas in a very well run tented camp near to the summit of Mt Olympus. Here I joined them in September and we continued a very happy two weeks in the camp, during which it is recorded that I achieved some mighty walks - 30-40 miles. My figure made them imperative but I enjoyed every step. We then, the last inhabitants of the camp at the end of the season, moved down to the Berengaria Hotel in Prodromos at a lower altitude, with real rooms and a landlord who went "for the shoot hunt" and left us to order lunch and run the bar! We motored north to the coast and walked 24 miles to Kykkou Monastery, thereby ruining Diana's toes for life. Finally we had to quit this "do as you please" hotel, motor to Limasol and so home to Cairo. I see that Diana won a Ladies'

Singles Championship at the Gezira Club. One notices also that we lunch and dine at the Embassy not the Residency. I think we found life, therefore, more relaxed: it is easier to represent than to be in charge! Social life grew to daily proportions in 1937 and life was really full. I thought "good for the Sudan representation". We were often at the Embassy for we were friends with the Ambassador, Sir David and Lady Kelly. We went one evening to hear Richard Tauber (a great Austrian tenor) sing in the drawing room.

Diana's father, Charles Hill, "CAH", came to stay in January 1937 and we really gave him a rousing fortnight. I notice in the diary entries recording a visit to the Pyramids, the Fayoum, cocktails at Irish Guards, the American Embassy, a tour of the Agricultural Museum by the sub-Director, a ball at the Embassy (bed at 5.00 am), a motor tour to Suez and Ismailia, and a cocktail party given by CAH at the Continental. We loved having him because he enjoyed himself so much.

Life in Cairo after the signing of the Anglo-Egyptian Treaty seemed to be more intense both officially and unofficially than before. The conquest of Abyssinia by the Italians, of course, added to international anxiety and in 1935-36 the spectre of Mussolini played a more haunting part in the world around Sudan and Egypt than that of Hitler, for Egypt, being North Africa, was less aware and less disturbed by Germany than the powers in Europe. The Mediterranean to them seemed an effective barrier to Nazi threats - in 1937. But the British Embassy had never been so busy.

As far as the Sudan was concerned the 1,200 miles of Eastern frontier was our first concern. The then Governor General wrote "whatever might be the ultimate outcome it was clear to us in the Sudan from 1936 onwards that we must set our local military establishment in order". Sir Stewart had told the Egyptians in his 1936 Treaty talk that Sudan Military chiefs were already discussing future plans with the British Commanders in the Middle East assembled at the War Office.

The family went on leave in May and I followed in July 1937, meeting Diana and brother Alan in Paris where, with Noel and Betty Moreton, we had a day at the Paris Exposition, a most exhausting but enjoyable experience.

We spent most of August and September 1937 in my brother's house in Roborough near Plymouth which Cecil had temporarily vacated on his appointment as King's Harbourmaster in Plymouth - a not very arduous but pleasant job which entailed living in the harbour at KHM's house. On that leave Nanny Pearson retired from our service and we had the great good fortune to discover Pamela Crowther Smith, who joined us in Plymouth on 3 September 1937: we knew at once, children and adults, that someone rather special joined our family on that day - and we were abundantly correct. Pam was one of three daughters of Vivien Crowther Smith who was Comptroller to the Corporation of the City of London. They lived in Hampstead Norris, Berkshire - where our little family was to enjoy many happy holidays - thanks to Pam's parents.

So began in 1937 one of the happiest friendships the Lush family has ever known. Pam came out to Cairo with us in 1937 and to the Sudan in 1938. On the outbreak of war in 1939 when I left the Sudan Pam most loyally stayed with Diana in England, to be with her during and after the birth of our third child, Meriel, and through a time of intense anxiety in 1940. Pam later joined the WRNS and served until 1946 when she joined us again, this time as my Personal Assistant in the Allied Commission in Rome - again she joined our family which she left on the happiest of occasions, for she was married from our villa in Rome to a young diplomat, and, after a brilliant career in the Diplomatic Service, they became Sir Roderick and Lady Sarell. Philip, their first born, became my godson.

Christmas 1937 came and went - was it to be our last peaceful festival? In fact for us, it was not, although it was our last Christmas in Cairo, for at about Christmastide 1937 I received a letter from the Civil Secretary (Angus Gillan) saying that the Governor General had decided to appoint me as Governor Northern Province to succeed Donald Purves in 1938. There was also an invitation to attend the Governor's Conference in Khartoum in February 1938 and a suggestion that I might like to accompany Donald Purves from Khartoum to el Damer, capital of the Northern Province, and have a look at my new job with my predecessor.

This was a wonderful Christmas present - a Governorship was the goal for which we in the Sudan Political Service all aimed, and the Northern Province was no small territory to govern - covering nearly 1,000 miles of the Nile riverain territory from the Shibka (the first cataract) just north of Khartoum to Wadi Halfa and the Egyptian boundary.

The year 1938 therefore brought to our little family mixed feelings - the professional satisfaction and joy of "getting a Province" and the sadness of having to leave Cairo which was such a happy family home - indeed our first - and a home where Diana's mother had twice been able to join us. Nevertheless it was good to think of a second family home in Damer, and a period of country life in the Sudan.

I had already seen the highlights of the province when I accompanied Sir John Maffey on one of his winter tours of the then three provinces of Berber, Dongola and Wadi Halfa, now amalgamated, and Diana and I had spent a day or two in Damer and Wadi Halfa under the hospitality of Donald and Mabel Purves on our return from our annual visit to Khartoum in 1937. We knew therefore, that our next few years would be spent among a quiet, law-abiding riverain population and that the water in the Nile was to be our very life blood - and the main topic of conversation. I also knew that the same Nile passed through some lovely scenery of which I had taken numerous photographs on those tours and that some river scenes and villages had appeared to me rather beautiful. Moreover the climate during half the year was temperate (and even cold) and the province boasted of one of the bigger towns in the Sudan, Atbara, Headquarters of the Sudan Government Railways and Steamers where shops of reasonable size existed with such things as furniture and household goods. For Diana and me to go on a personally conducted tour of the province with the retiring Governor and his wife, was a positive stroke of luck (and a very real holiday). So we accepted the invitation with alacrity.

As before, when making quite a long absence in the Sudan we had no qualms in leaving the two children in the capable hands of Pam who, by now, had many friends in Cairo. We took Ruth with us as far as Wadi Halfa where she spent ten happy days or so in the particularly pleasant hotel on the Nile there - and accomplished some beautiful paintings. We had as our official proteges as far as Khartoum, Sir David Kelly, the Ambassador in Cairo, who was a delightful and very helpful colleague (as concerned as anyone over the Italian invasion of Abyssinia) and Marie Noel, his beautiful, lively and intelligent Belgian wife. We took advantage of a conducted tour of the Aswan Dam and locks, provided for David Kelly by the Egyptian Government, before joining the Sudan Government steamer at Shellal. We also had great fun on our journey to Wadi Halfa and had then the free run of the Governor General's railway saloon which had been sent to Wadi Halfa to meet the Kellys. We handed them over to the Palace staff at Khartoum and, though we were staying at the same place, saw little more of them. I believe they moved south very quickly.

A visit to Khartoum for any "outlier" always involved discussions with many Departments and individuals. The Director of Finance was anxious about the annual payment by the Egyptian Government of their £E7,500,000 laid down in 1924. The Sudan Agent was responsible for persuading the Ministry in Cairo to make punctual payment of this important provision to the Sudan Budget. Various Departments were interested in the political situation in Egypt, and the Italian aggression was of particular concern to the *Kaid* of the Sudan Defence Force. Socially there were many old friends to see - the first of whom had to be Sayed Abder Rahman el Mahdi on whom I paid a most friendly duty call (I next saw him in Geneva ten years later).

The climax of a busy social week was the Palace Ball which was a great occasion and tremendous fun - the world of Khartoum and his wife were there. There was a tradition in the Palace (at any rate under the Maffey regime) that no woman should remain partnerless for any dance at this function, and the palace staff saw to it that the tradition was maintained.

Almost the next day we left Khartoum on 11 February 1938 with Donald and Mabel Purves in the Governor's saloon attached to the mail train for Shendi, the southernmost district of Northern Province. Here Donald Purves began his farewell tour of the province which he had governed for three years; he was due for retirement from the Service.

We reached Damer (our future home) next morning. Here the Purves held a levee and we met a good many of the Sudan Railways officials and the sheikhs and notables who had come in for the ceremony. Emley, the then General Manager came to dinner and we visited Atbara, his headquarters, next day. He was an efficient and pleasant man and I wish he had not retired that year. We spent a day with the Railways and then took rail again for Karima, opposite Merowe at the head of the Dongola Reach of the Nile, the last 400 miles in Sudan territory. Merowe, like its name, is a charming place full of gardens and date groves and I remember we had a fire in the grate of the DC, Titherington's house. Our next stop was at Dongola where Fred Keen, the DC had organised an Agricultural Show. I have always found Dongola people charming and they certainly gave the Purves an enthusiastic farewell. Across the river on the east bank we took to the road again, and finally crossed the Batn el Haggar (the Belly of Stones) well known in the days of the 1899 (Kitchener) expedition. We broke a spring and mended it with the starting handle and finally reached our haven, the Wadi Halfa hotel, for dinner and the night. After a day or two in this delightful frontier town, Diana and I headed for Cairo and home after a most exhilarating introduction to Northern Province which gave us great hopes of a happy sojourn in the northern Sudan. We were not to know the international and personal traumas which were to make that happiness all too short.

We arrived back in Cairo to find all well at home, and then settled down to our last three months there. In spite of mounting international anxieties they were months of intense social activity in Egypt. The King had just married his first Queen, Zulfiah; Diana went to a presentation party; we all went to a Royal Soiree - 1,500 guests at Abdin Palace; there were "white tie" parties for David Kelly who was leaving; we met the Athlones at the Embassy; we had David Barran, a junior manager in Shell, to dinner; Jack Gibson, and the names of Generals Godion, Austen and Weir appear in our dinner lists. Cairo was gay and we began to give our farewell parties. In the middle of it all Diana found time to visit St Catherine's Monastery in Sinai and Petra and thoroughly enjoy a desert journey on camelback.

Our climax came at the end of April when the Ambassador gave us a farewell luncheon at the Embassy and almost next day we attended the Consecration of All Saints Cathedral by Archbishop William Temple of Canterbury on 28 April 1938.

Thanks to Bishop Gwynne and the Archdeacon Frank Johnston we had been able to play a great part in the final stages of the furnishing of that well-known building and had delayed our leave departure from Cairo to attend the Consecration.

It was a perfect day. All Cairo was in that lovely building; the Archbishop was led to the throne. Bishop Gwynne knocking at the door of the building, begging entrance to his second Cathedral, knocked too strongly and broke his crook. His Chaplain, Rev David Hoare, accompanying the Reverend Bishop, held it together both by manual dexterity and by the prayers or rather instructions of the Rt Reverend Bishop who interpolated the Lord's Prayer, which it was his office to recite proceeding up the nave of the building with such sotto voce commands as "Our Father which art in Heaven, Keep it straight David; Hallowed be Thy Name, Hold it firm, my boy; Thy will be done on earth, It's wobbling, ..." etc, etc.

The Archbishop moved to the pulpit and spoke but the architects, with all their skill and care for beauty, had forgotten the acoustics so few of us heard his sermon; many of us met him later.

The Cathedral caught the eye and pen of the journalists. The New Cathedral, the Anglican Cathedral and the English Cathedral were three of the most common descriptive epithets used for that lovely building. We who worshipped therein immediately after its building and dedication came to love the sanctity of our new church. Little did we know what an inspiration the Cathedral and the worship therein would be to the many thousands of men and women who in five years' time were to worship there before going westwards - sometimes to fight and be beaten back, sometimes to fight to the death and, ultimately under Alexander and Montgomery, to fight to victory and to succeed in repelling, defeating and in the end annihilating those forces, enemies of the British Empire, whose object it was to conquer Egypt and the Suez Canal and whose end was written in the surrender and debacle at Bizerta.

The stained glass window was designed by Carl Edwards and erected at the east end. It was unveiled on 3 March 1951 by Field Marshall Viscount Montgomery, consecrated by Bishop Llewellyn Gwynne in the presence of the representative of the King of Egypt, the British Ambassador, Sir Ralph Stevenson and an immense congregation. The dedication of this beautiful window reads:

"In memory of the men of the Eighth Army who fell in the fighting in Egypt, Libya, Tunisia and Italy."

I have included this episode out of its time because the window put the finishing touch to the lovely building which was All Saints Cathedral for just over 40 years and now is no more. In its short life one can be certain that the Cathedral poured out the fullness of the glory of God, not only to the normal congregation which worshipped there, but especially to the servicemen of the Armies who, serving in a foreign land a long way from home, found comfort, solace and inspiration in their greatest hour of need.

On 15 May 1938 the Lush family with Ruth Hill and Pam left Cairo for the last time. It was a Sunday and Diana, Ruth and I went to Morning Service at the New Cathedral, as we called it, before joining the train for Port Said and embarkation on the Japanese liner Harune Maru of the Nippon Yuxon Kaisha Line, bound for Tilbury. The air was already thick with ugly international rumours and I remember cabling Cecil in Plymouth for advice as to whether the Japanese were dependable. We experienced very good weather and had a splendid time on board this very fine and well run ship - on her, judging by the snapshots, the children were thoroughly spoilt!

Steaming along the blue Mediterranean, a piece of water which we knew pretty well by now, we thought with great joy of the very happy time which we had enjoyed in Cairo - high social life, yes, but very interesting. We had been able to rub off our "up-country" shyness (if we had any) and our decision to swim with the other fish in the pool had been successful.

We had experienced three years of family life when Diana could be with her children and separations from myself had been short. She had the joy and companionship of her mother - a blessing to both of us and we had enjoyed the visit too of her father. We had, as it were, enfolded Pamela Crowther-Smith into our family. We had experienced the presence of a British High Commissioner in Cairo who was determined to bring Anglo-Egyptian relations out of the slough of suspicion and enmity in to the smoother stream of mutual respect and confidence. I had seen, once more, my Governor General put the finishing touches to the Sudan Clause which made the Treaty possible. We had watched the rape of Abyssinia by Italy and had watched our own Government desert Abyssinia in its hour of need and jettison the honour of our country in order to aid France in her vain efforts to appease Italy and Germany. Living as we had been at the southern end of that most evil Axis we had the opportunity of realising how inexorable was the next step. We scented blood in the air. We feared the worst on our voyage home in 1938 and all the letters which passed between Diana and me when we were apart during the next two years show how the fear of war was ever present.

Leave in UK 1938

Our leave in 1938 was really centred on Hampstead Norris (now called Norreys) where two splendid ladies - the Misses Scrivener - rented apartments with food and lodging; and from our diaries of that time, they apparently had unlimited accommodation not only for our small family, but also for most of our relatives who seem to have camped in that hospitable house immediately opposite the home of Pamela Crowther Smith. Of course it was she who had organised this and not only was it perfect for us and our children, all of whom had the run of the Crowther Smith garden and tennis court, but it was home for Pam.

I left this happy family in August to return, this time to the Sudan, to take up my new job as Governor Northern Province and allow my Deputy to go on leave. The Purves had already left on retirement. Diana and I wondered with no little anxiety whether they would be able to return, for war seemed so very imminent by that summer. I left England with the threat of occupation in Czechoslovakia imminent. The Czechs had mobilised, and England under Chamberlain and France under Deladier were dithering in their declared policies of what to do.

Crocodile, Upper Nile Province, 1934

MSL and DRL with 'Bully', the bull terrier who saved MSL from a crocodile, Malakal, 1934

Governor's car, Northern Province, 1938

Above:
MSL as Governor,
Northern Province, 1938

Left:
Shaikh Zubair with DRL and others,
January 1939

Shaikh Zubair, Omda Abdullahi, Freddie Keen, MSL; January 1939

MSL, J and S with Dalmatian

DRL and children, Governor's House, Damer, December 1938

Above:
MSL, Pam and children, Damer, December 1938

Right:
MSL at home, Damer

CHAPTER 9

NORTHERN PROVINCE 1938-40
Provincial Governor

Governor, Northern Province

I arrived in Wadi Halfa sometime in August 1938. I had deprecated any civic welcome usual for a new Governor. Summertime with a number of officials on leave and with the maximum temperature at 110° was no season for parties, but I was received by a Guard of Honour and the DCs. I cannot remember whether Geoffrey Titherington or Rex Harrison met me; they were both friends, the former a contract official who had served principally in the south, a man of intense loyalty to any institution or person whom he had served. He retired soon after and I met him next in Port Elizabeth, South Africa, where Winifred, his wife, had gone ahead of him. She was a niece of Arthur Bryant, that most eminent historical writer. Rex Harrison was then a young ADC with immense energy and a lively sense of humour. It was, I know, a tonic to meet either of them at my initial take-over. The Sudan Railways had kindly sent down the Governor's Railway Saloon, a roomy, comfortable, easy to clean home on wheels, built to carry two - ie. a sizeable office or sitting-cum-dining room, two sleeping berths, a bath and a kitchen with servants' quarters. In the saloon I found my two staunch servants, Abder Rahman and Mohammed Dhahab; all this made one feel at home and we were able to give my small party of welcome a drink and off we went with the mail train through the miles of completely empty desert (stations 1-10) which was the threshold of my province. We reached Abu Hamed, on the Nile, by dawn and I was up and able to greet a few dignitaries who had turned out to greet me; similarly at Berber the Head of Native Administration had brought coffee on to the platform. At Atbara, the railway town on the junction of the River Atbara with the Nile, and also a major railway junction, Bill Crawford my Deputy Governor came over and joined me, introducing a few Sudanese notables on the platform, before we travelled the last few miles over the Atbara Bridge to el Damer, the small town on the banks of the Nile which had been the headquarters of Berber Province and became the Headquarters of the Northern Province in 1937 when it swallowed the three small provinces of Berber, Dongola and Wadi Halfa. It was an insignificant place with scarcely a shop or store, but my predecessor and Crawford had managed to convert the whole of the *Mudiria* (Governorate) area into a very pleasant compound consisting of about seven houses grouped fairly closely together with gardens, orchards and vegetables. We had four grass tennis courts which, of course, gave us only two to play on at any time. But Northern Province HQ did not form a large colony and the nature of provincial work led to almost constant visits up and down those 1,000 miles of river throughout the working year.

Crawford left a day or two after my arrival - indeed I had advised him to get away speedily before the international situation closed the ordinary means of travel. International politics, of course, left the population of this rural province untouched. The Nile was rising steadily when I arrived and reached its peak at Atbara early in September recording flood above normal. So my feet were "wet" as far as the river was concerned; on the other hand the southern district of Shendi (the only district in the Province affected by rain) suffered from poor rains. I see no mention of locusts in 1938 - they were to trouble us in 1939.

I spent the first two months - and what hot months they were - trying to find out what conditions existed in the Province, what were the people's problems and how we could help them. I had paid three visits to the area but never before as the *Mudir*.

Luckily communications were good - and half my British staff were on leave. I paid my first visit to Shendi District in the south - not 200 miles from Khartoum; a thriving town and Headquarters of the Sudan Horse. The DC, Whiskers Richardson, my tutor of Gedaref days, was on leave and so was the OC of Cavalry; but I met the young ADC Lumsden who seemed to be in good shape and gave me ample evidence of a local Native Authority in full swing - still a bit shy of taking responsibility.

It was on a later visit to Shendi in 1939 when we crossed the Nile with quite a posse of Sudanese leaders and police to cope with a vast swarm of hopping locusts reported on the west bank of the river. The swarm had just developed and covered a front of some three miles and, say, half a mile in depth. They came from the uncultivated lands and were advancing relentlessly towards the bank of young cultivated *dura* just showing near the river. Sacks of poisoned bran previously stored in villages in the area were now hastily laden into lorries or loaded on camels and their contents strewn on the ground in a line before the advancing enemy. It was successful for the most part but the "enemy" penetrated a gap of about half a mile and thence pursued their way relentlessly, devouring any crop or green thing in their path until they reached the Nile. The river was flowing in moderate flood but this did not stop the advance for as some insects drowned others hopped on their backs and some - one's romantic imagination says many - reached the other side. In any case the town and environs of Shendi had by now been invaded by a flying swarm of locusts (hoppers who had developed wings) and there was much consternation in that town; it was even said that a small baby had been devoured by the pest (its swaddling clothes certainly formed a meal!). My other experience of locusts in this province was seeing a Sudan Railways mail train stranded by a swarm which was three miles in breadth, the crushed bodies rendering the track unusable owing to the slippery condition of the rails. The train lost three hours while the locusts made their way. I may add that an expert on locusts has told me that hoppers swim - so maybe it was a feat of aquatics by these brutes which I saw.

The remainder of the Province relied on the Nile for its livelihood. As the river rose, reaching its peak, as we have seen, in September, the lands which lay by the banks were covered by the natural flood and the farmer, knowing in his uncanny way when the peak had arrived, would sow his crop - maize, wheat (our winters were cool enough for wheat), sesame, chickpeas - on the flood lands. Basin irrigation was used on a wide scale. There were numerous depressions or basins especially on the western bank into which flood water was guided by carefully planned canals. Kerma Basin extended over 50,000 acres and another large one near Shendi contained 5,500 acres, whence a good crop of cotton could be harvested. The date crop was valuable, especially in Dongola - famous for producing the best dates in the country and at about the time of my arrival a brochure on date cultivation had just been issued by the Agricultural Department and, mirabile dictu, had been accepted with "great interest" by the Dongolawi farmers and others whose ancestors had been growing dates for centuries.

When the river dropped, water had to be raised by mechanical means, in low Nile as much as 30-40'. The Persian water wheel *(Saqia)* and the *Shaduf* (for shallow lifts) were the apparatus of antiquity - the former worked by camel, ox or ass; the latter by man. The 4" petrol pump, or in large schemes 6-9", were now in increasing use (100 4" pumps were raising the water in 1938) and were popular. The larger pumps were used for areas under Government control and irrigated sizeable areas used as experimental or educational farms. The Agricultural Inspectors did excellent work in teaching and encouraging not only the farmers, but also the Local Authorities, to improve the farming of traditional crops and fruits and in the introduction of new cultivation - citrus and other orchards. There existed several co-operative schemes managed by Local Sudanese Authorities. Agricultural shows were popular in the big centres of the Province such as Shendi, Berber, Merowe, Dongola and Wadi Halfa. The stock may not have had much fat, nor the sheep or goats much wool.

Cotton was grown not only in the south by a Sudanese Co-operative Society, but on some 5,500 acres on the west bank of the Nile opposite Damer, under the auspices of the Sudan Plantations Syndicate (who ran the Gezira Scheme on the Blue Nile).

Such was the agricultural picture of the Province and the Sudanese therein were becoming fine agriculturalists as I was soon to learn when I did a quick visit to the northern reach of the Nile from Abu Hamed through Merowe and Dongola. When I set out on this journey by train and steamer, at the beginning of September 1938, such was the international situation (Hitler's threat to overrun Czechoslovakia) that I had left instructions in Damer to recall me by telegram if things became worse, and sure enough I received a warning in September advising my instant return to HQ. My saloon and special engine were sent for me and for some reason I travelled the last 60 miles by motor railway trolley, to find "Peace with honour" proclaimed at Munich - panic over.

Diana - in England with passages to Port Sudan for herself and the family in the autumn - was, in the meantime, becoming frantic at the ups and downs of the menace of war. "Munich" solved her doubts and she arrived in Damer in October with the two children and Pam and I remember riding out to meet them at the first station outside Atbara. I had added a day nursery and a third bathroom to the Governor's house and here, in mid October we set up our second home - and our last for four years. The winter of 1938-39 was a very cheerful season in Damer. Bill Crawford had his wife and family living next door; we had an excellent and most loyal staff, and Damer was, we hoped, a very happy community. We ourselves found the house, the garden and especially the life, entirely to our liking. I had no compunction in my visits to districts in taking the whole family so long as we were self-contained and caused no bother or confusion to anyone, Sudanese or British. Our railway saloon and the province steamers made excellent bases and entertainment or accommodating visitors was one of the joys of any DC and especially any wife. So my family saw nearly as much of the Province as I during the winter and spring of 1938 and 1939. We took our horses and donkey (ridden by Julian) and the donkey cart (Sylvia's transport) when we could, and at home in el Damer our *syce* Abdalla made gallant and successful efforts to teach Julian to ride. Christmas was of course very special. We had children's parties in Damer (the bachelors and childless married couples so often organised the most successful) and at Atbara the large staff of the Railways organised Christmas parties on a really big scale. In Atbara too, lived our Province doctor, Leigh Henderson and his wife Diana. The big Atbara Hospital of which he was Director catered for all Sudanese and British in the Province. To that hospital also came Fiona Maclean, the auburn-haired Sister who had brought Sylvia into the world. We had advised and helped her to join the Sudan Medical Service and she soon moved to Khartoum.

All was going well in the Province. Native Administration which had found its feet firmly and perhaps earlier than elsewhere was thriving like a growing young man; the Local Authorities were laying their hands successfully on much that went on in the land eg. law and order (perhaps not very strong yet in urban areas); agriculture (eg Cooperative Societies, basin irrigation, pumping schemes). As Governor I realised that the power in the land was now far more in the hands of the Sudanese leaders; that my DCs were more guardians and guides than governors; that the people themselves were beginning to understand that they could talk and discuss matters judicial, agricultural, educational or even domestic more easily - and with better results - with their Sheikh, Omda or even Nazir, than with the uniformed DC. It was a great eye-opener to me to see the marked progress that had been made among these northerners in the last ten years. I was enthusiastic to give the Sudanese leaders all the encouragement possible.

There were interests in Northern Province other than those which brought money. In the 1938 Annual Report I wrote:

> "…. The steady exodus of men in search of casual or permanent work in Egypt or in other parts of the Sudan continued. This is no new problem but it creates a permanent shortage of labour in agricultural enterprises. On the other hand the amount of cash sent to their families by these emigrants is considerable …."

The other import was that of tourism; as far back as those days I was able to report that tourist traffic through Wadi Halfa had increased and that great satisfaction was shown at the decision to keep open the Nile Hotel at that attractive place throughout the year. Moreover 1,049 aircraft landed at Wadi Halfa Airport which was reconstructed for the purpose.

Education was well advanced in the Province. There was a general and insistent demand for more education, more schools both primary and secondary (as we call them now). I see that, in 1938, Parents' Day was "adopted in all schools and proved to be most popular". At Atbara the demand for vacancies in the boys' elementary schools exceeded the supply five-fold.

We had an excellent and most progressive British Educational Officer who was tireless in his (successful) efforts to increase and improve education in this very fertile area.

As a matter of financial or fiscal interest it is proper perhaps to record that in 1938 the direct taxation - date tax, land tax and animal tax - of the half-million people in the Province amounted to £88,000 and was collected efficiently and without difficulty by the Local Authorities.

River Nile

To give a picture of the Nile as it flowed through the Northern Province, I cannot do better than extract a few passages from a book written in 1936 by an eminent biographer, Emil Ludwig, who wrote in the preface of his book *The Nile* (George Allen & Unwin Ltd London 1936):

> "…. Only once have I beheld in a river the image of man and his fate. Here (at Shendi) the Nile enters the desert which it only quits in Cairo. 200 miles below Khartoum, at the most easterly point in its whole course, it receives its last tributary, the Atbara, which rises in the same volcanoes of Abyssinia from which the Blue Nile flows. The Atbara, called by the Arabs the Black River, is the last tributary of the Nile …. from now onward it is alone to the end with its ancient waters." (p264)
>
> "In the thundering desert sunshine, the water wheel wails its melody along the Nile valley - the old gnarled water wheel groaning and creaking turns the fringe of the desert into emerald green land." (p265)
>
> "This is the ancient magic wheel by means of which men on the Nile Valley replaced rain. Here the sweetest dates of the whole Nile Valley ripen in a peculiar way. There are too few male palms; in spring therefore the boys clamber up the male trees, pluck twigs with flowers, and with them fertilize the female trees. The dates of Allah grow with their feet in water and their heads in fire …." (p282)

In latitude 20°, 250 miles below Khartoum the rock is so far master of the river that the basalt forces the Nile - the only time in its entire course - to turn round and run a few hundred miles to the south; then it turns as abruptly to the north and pursues its northern course again.

This is very much the cataract region which is not navigable except in short stretches - eg. the 100 miles between Merowe and Dongola - and is, as Ludwig points out, the reason why the Nile has not become one of the great waterways of Africa like other rivers in the continent, eg. the Congo and the Niger.

Water passing over the cataracts creates a deafening noise to newcomers; the Romans gave this as the reason for the lack of inhabitants, but of course it has in history known pagan, Christian and lastly Moslem populations for millennia. The present inhabitants have certainly overcome the noise for they can hear messages shouted to them across the river, even across the cataracts themselves.

The fifth cataract is above Abu Hamed when the river turns west and south; the fourth at the southern extremity of the bend turns it north again; the third below Dongola is the noisiest; the second, just above Wadi Halfa, was the frontier of Egypt in ancient days and marked the resumption of the steady navigable flow of the Nile. It and the first have now disappeared under the waters of the Nasser Lake formed by the raising of the Aswan Dam in 1956-58.

It is interesting to note that in the time of Amerophis III, 1,000 BC, the Nile in low flood ran 25' higher than in 1936 AD, i.e. 25' of erosion in 3,000 years.

Family

The family went to England in early May 1939 and I was to follow in July. Diana by now knew that a third baby was expected in November and my letters home during those summer months of 1939 were filled with anxiety owing to the ever-increasing international crisis. My Deputy Governor was on leave; I was writing a document called *The Northern Province in Time of War* and the chances of my getting home at times seemed minimal. It also happened to be a very hot summer in which *haboobs* were all too common.

A visit to Khartoum when I stayed in my beloved Palace as a guest of the Governor General, somewhat restored sanity. I met there the new *Kaid* - the Commander-in-Chief of the Sudan Defence Force - General William Platt, whom I greatly liked. Luckily I think he reacted in the same way, for he was to be a strong factor in my life. I also met and liked immensely our new Bishop elect, Bishop Gelsthorpe.

I was thoroughly heartened by news from home that Ruth my mother-in-law and Diana between them had signed a lease for Westlands in Ewhurst, Surrey - a charming, small house in the property next to my sister and Dan's house. Here at any rate, come what may, was a suitable birthplace for the new baby and a home for the family in time of war. I was worried about the coming babe, for Diana had not enjoyed an easy time even after her third month of pregnancy; moreover, the summer of 1939 was a particularly bad summer for hay fever and so Diana transferred to London for a spell.

But notwithstanding the critical international situation I did get home on leave, flying, for the first time, by Imperial Airways. Travelling very comfortably in a flying boat we took off from Alexandria early and reached Marseilles that evening; here the flying boat stopped for the night so I took the Paris express train and flew thence by light aircraft to Croydon, beating my flying boat by several hours.

Then started a leave of relief and happiness to be with the family again and in an established home; a time too of growing anxiety and turmoil of emotions; it was clear early in August that nothing could deter Hitler - that British hopes (Chamberlain's "Peace with honour") of 1938 had been born from vain hope rather that good judgement and that war was inevitable. In August Dan Sandford was recalled to the Army and sailed for Egypt at 48 hours' notice, thus preparing for his magnificent work in Abyssinia in the years to come. At the same time I wrote to Gillan recommending that all Sudan officials be sent back to duty while it was possible and on 31 August my summons came (as to all Sudan officials on leave) to report to Glasgow on 1 September with a view to immediate return.

And so on 31 August 1939 I said goodbye to Diana and my family - and the babe to come - from the guard's van at Reading West Station. I was not to see them again until June 1943, an absence of nearly four years.

Outbreak of World War II

Throughout those years that family which I left behind, led by Diana and her mother, and including my own mother and sister next door, sustained each other (and myself by letter) with the courage and faithfulness which was common to all British families at home, but no less supreme. They suffered, with others, fear of death or injury and saw tragedy around them; they suffered from bodily hunger and mental anguish; they waited in vain and in tears for news which was delayed, sometimes inevitably, sometimes avoidably - but they never faltered. At home the children were well tended, well fed and well educated. The adults suffered first and always; self was obliterated.

The first weeks of World War II for myself and others of the Sudan Service, comprising about one half of the total strength of that Service, are described in my note of October 1939 "on convoy". We sailed in the Montcalm - a comfortable Canadian Pacific liner equipped for sailing in the Arctic waters, not the Mediterranean. Of the 400 of us from the Sudan - in fact we made up the bulk of the passengers - at least half had been torn away from wives and families and were about to face long absences; as I wrote, homesickness and anxiety shared with 399 other men became less acute.

The outstanding personality on board was Bishop Llewellyn Gwynne who had the love and sympathy to appreciate the personal turmoil affecting our minds and thoughts and had the experience to find a remedy for our troubled minds - prayer. He led a daily meeting every morning at which with a few prayers, a psalm and a lesson he calmed us and made us men. I mentioned him in almost every daily letter to Diana and seldom can a body of troubled men have been made more stable, more sympathetic to each other by the personality of one man. We were a great party and we withstood the rigours of that voyage (every porthole shut fast with outside temperatures of 80° in the Mediterranean and no fresh water for baths) for three sweltering weeks. In times of stress good friendships are made and I certainly came to know others in the Service far better and with a deeper feeling of sympathy on that voyage than I could have otherwise.

They took us to Port Said while the Sudan Agent with a special train was sent to Alexandria - but somehow we reached Shellal where the Sudan Railways had assembled four river steamers with every cabin allotted. And so the Sudan Government was brought up to strength a month after declaration of war.

Certainly my first concern when I returned to Northern Province was to make various assessments of people, Sudanese and British. The Sudanese were splendid. Crawford, my Deputy, spoke highly of them and was much moved by their immediate and overwhelming expressions of loyalty to the *Hakouma Inglese* on the outbreak of war. The Levantines -

merchants and clerical staff alike - had assumed the same role. The British staff were those most hard hit and Bill told me that he himself was getting a little frayed (his wife had spent the hot summer with him and gone home on the outbreak of war). But problem No 1 was the suburban minded town of Atbara with a large British population, wives of railway engineers, mechanics, etc, led by a General Manager who was not of a high calibre and had recently suffered family loss. Into this town the military had transferred a battalion of British troops (Atbara was the railhead nearest to the Sudan-Abyssinian frontier). I described the white population there as jittery and suburban and set about to put it right by trying to abolish its remoteness (in spirit) from the Province and absorbing its people into Provincial rather than railway affairs - no easy job but achieved later by the appointment of James Macphail, an old friend from Malakal days, as District Commissioner.

At home near Damer we at last enjoyed electric light (although shut down at 10 pm even for the Governor) and I made it my business to invite Atbarians over to tennis and golf.

I had also to watch my British staff. My Deputy had already confessed that a month's grass widowerhood had rendered him short tempered and crotchety. A holiday in my favourite town of Wadi Halfa brought him back no better. A senior DC from the south suddenly appeared in my house to stay - unannounced. We were very old friends and with his wife in England pregnant, he couldn't bear to be alone. I thought it right to establish a regular system of writing to my DC's wives in England - not very often, but at sufficiently short intervals for them to realise that there were others about who cared for them.

For myself I had some months of imminent fatherhood, which affects the husband as much as the wife and on 11 November came the glad news of the birth of (I thought) Helen; but she became called Meriel! It was the happiest news and buoyed me up tremendously! Diana had been particularly clever about the birth which she had at home and produced a fine baby in the minimum number of hours without her own mother, who was in the house, knowing that anything was going on! I wrote "Helen" above because for weeks - 11 November to Christmas - no decision had been taken about her name, and I hoped she would be so named. Other names were bandied by air mail and telegram for two months but Meriel was produced (by Diana) as a very late starter - on the eve of her Christening. Of course I fell for the name immediately and so she was thus named in Ewhurst Church. I read her horoscope (Scorpio) as

"a person of extreme activity, who takes life at a gallop, and eagerly gathers the golden harvest which fate so often puts in her path; but being open handed and kind hearted gives away to the less fortunate almost as much as she garners for herself; who goes through life smiling; who is ambitious; who dreams of glory and often attains it. So give her blue and violet ribbons for her christening and plant pansies in her flower bed."

My letters were also much concerned with our possible reunion. The ban on wives joining their husbands in the Sudan was still enforced but there was little doubt that it would be lifted (it was lifted by Christmas 1940). But basing my argument on a feeling of certainty that the war must soon erupt into action I was compelled to advise Diana not to think of joining me in the early future. Whatever happened in the UK I felt that Westlands was the best place for our three children. Little did I know then of the traumas and tragedies which 1940 was to bring, not only to the world, but also to our family; far less did I foresee that 1940 would be my last year of Service in the Sudan. Diana did agree, though the decision tore our hearts badly!

Our first Christmas of the war in Northern Province was, for me, as happy as family disruption would allow. First of all, I had to comfort my (younger) DCs; secondly the Governor General, Sir Stewart Symes, had accepted a suggestion made earlier that he and his party might spend a week of holiday in my province, living on a steamer in the most delightful scenery, among really pleasant and forthcoming Sudanese (whom I should expect him to meet) and enjoying the best climate the Sudan could give him in winter. The visit I knew would involve a good deal of organisation on the part of the Steamers and Railways Department, two of my DCs (who were most anxious to be his hosts) and our Province Police and Local Authorities. But it would be an honour (as well as a pleasure) to the Province to have HE on holiday among us and I knew that everyone, from the second fireman on the steamer upwards, would enjoy the experience. HE paid us the compliment of accepting the invitation and brought in addition to his staff (Arthur Hankin, Private Secretary and Mark Leather, Comptroller) the Legal Secretary John Gorman (a stranger to me) and his wife Serena who was easy to look upon and who made herself friendly and one of the party. Throughout the visit and also at the end we all, HE included, vociferously voted the party a great success. The Governor General arrived by train at Damer where the Legal Secretary did his stuff with our Province Judge Maxwell Harrison a most charming person. HE went on to Atbara to talk with the General Manager of the Railways, Lee Spalding. I joined them and we looked at the military forces in Atbara (this all very official) and then we rolled on north by train in three saloon cars - HE's, the Legal Secretary's and the Governor's. HE had been very good with the large British community in Atbara and had charmed his hostesses at the Club. We climbed on to that train weary men - I wrote to Diana:

"It was a very good day." I see I had a comforting hot bath and "slipped into the Doctor's Hospital Car for dinner".

We reached Karima, where the Nile turns north again and embarked on our first steamer - and the holiday tour began. I wrote to Diana:

"…. The river was looking lovely. A cheerful evening, and now I have left them to play poker. Dr Ali Bedri and his wife were at Merowe and were quite charming. He told us all how his father had been one of the military leaders under both the Mahdi and Khalifa and etc. In Sheikh Zubeir's house there was a most beautifully run tea party. Everything was well and very happily done …."

I described (truthfully) our picnic spot for Christmas lunch as follows:

"…. We all went off to Kerma Basin. We found a pool called *Birket el Maluk* (The Pool of the Kings), with perfectly lush grass growing round a young crop of hay; greensward by the lake; the *sunt* trees heavy with yellow blossom and the ground underneath carpeted with yellow; lots of duck in the lake for HE and staff; a strong north wind - perfect temperature and no *nimittee* (small flies). Could you have had better conditions? HE loved it. "In half a moment I am going to roll in this grass!" he said …."

That almost royal Christmas trip was greatly appreciated and was of enormous benefit to all of us in the Province who had the fun of organising it, for it took our minds off our own homesickness for Christmas at home.

It was at this time that I heard from my brother Cecil, of the death of our father (Hubert Lush). He had been for months in constant and severe pain and death must have come as a merciful release for him. In a letter to Diana I quoted the passage from the book of Wisdom:

"…. 'The souls of the righteous are in the hands of God and there can no torment reach them'. I feel that so deeply true that I could not but feel …." (near Merowe 29 December 1939).

The year 1940 opened with the continuation of the phoney war in Europe (and for all that, in the rest of the world). Before Christmas the Sudan Government had lifted the ban on entry of wives into the Sudan but it remained so far as children were concerned. Our position was clear. Diana and the children should remain at home. The Governor General however at Christmas time had told me that leave for certain Sudan officials would be opened if the situation remained static and he told me that he wanted me to take leave. I recount later the two valiant attempts I made in April and again in May 1940.

The birth of Meriel and the very successful Christmas party in the Dongola Reach had done much to mitigate the beastliness of war and the separation caused by it. As 1940 dawned I see from my first letter home that I had no little difficulty in getting Diana's letter of 1 January 1940:

"…. I had to go to the Post Office and then the Railway Station (at Damer) whence the train was just moving out. However we soon stopped that, pulled out the mail bag, opened it, and extracted the letters addressed to Northern Province (a duty which should have been carried out by the Postmaster). There was a good deal of restrained comment on the part of the Railway staff but the "goods train and the el Obeid train were only held up for 10 minutes *and* I got your letter!"

My first letter describing the above train robbery and subsequent hectic days in Khartoum ends:

"…. It's all right about leave *if* the war allows; so don't count too much."

My next told of the purchase of a Dalmatian pup:

"I'm going to have my baby too!"

I spent the second week of the year in Khartoum travelling by night - achieving as usual a great deal by discussion and personal explanation which saved a packet of paper, making my number with the Governor General (dinner at the Palace) and seeing a host of old friends. I wrote in good spirits and after a couple of days went down to Shendi where I wanted to see for myself some of the problems of riverain agriculture. I boarded the district rivercraft with sails and auxiliary engine and had two excellent days visiting not a few villages where "I spoke chiefly about the war as the conflict between those who had no faith in God and those who did". I also learnt a great deal about riverain crops and their cultivation. The *gyassa* or sailing boat was comfortable with day and night cabins and hot water for a hip bath. I talked all day long to the *nas* but always insisted (as I did through all my Service) on privacy in the evening until dawn. I had my ponies with me which gave me exercise (some of it in the dark). I wrote in good spirits to Diana twice a week - incoming mails from UK were very regular and fast. I reported faithfully my problems:

"…. This morning my *syce* Abdalla went sick and one pony was lame …. The *Omda's* horse bolted and he was heavily thrown on his head …. The *gyassa* suddenly proceeding broadside on and finally crashed, stern first, into the bank - the auxiliary engine would function only "full speed astern" and we broke our rudder. We rigged a jury rudder actuated by ropes …. We had to walk the last three miles into Wad Hamed as the *Omda's* horse collapsed under me. On arrival at Wad Hamed the villages didn't know whether to welcome me or speed me on - for the oldest inhabitant had just died. However I had a pleasant morning at Wad Hamed and had just started the return journey by river when blowed if I didn't go down with fever! I went to bed with everything on top of me and a very warm whisky and lemon inside me. In spite of all the mishaps I have enjoyed this trip enormously …."

Well I had to pay the price and had my first bout of malign tertiary malaria for two years. I recovered but found later that my quinine course had side effects:

"…. I am not at all depressed but rather short of temper!"

In the meantime my house was seldom without guests and when I was in hospital, I was told they enjoyed themselves immensely!

At this time Dan Sandford was in the Sudan making contact with the SDF and the Intelligence. His object was (under instructions from HQ Middle East in Cairo) to sound out the Sudan Authorities on organising a return of the Emperor Haile Selassie through the Sudan to Ethiopia, in the event of hostilities breaking out between Italy and the UK. He was finding the going very sticky and HE particularly averse to any such international entanglement on the part of the Sudan. Dan went on to Kenya to discover the thinking there about Abyssinia and her exiled Emperor.

Writing cheerfully from Wadi Halfa on 1 February - I had gone there on Sudan-Egyptian Irrigation affairs and provincial matters - I report myself as fit and well and cheerful, having met many good friends and new acquaintances. I also report two of my province wives ill with diphtheria in Atbara; they do not appear again in my letters and I know they survived.

I record a very good annual report from Whiskers Richardson of Shendi which he begins by saying that:

Shendi District won the prize for decrepitude: it had the oldest DC, the oldest *Mamur* (Sudanese Executive Official), the oldest doctor, the oldest inhabitant (140 years) and the oldest Abyssinian concubine who won the prize for concubinage for over 50 years".

Apparently I received The Times of 17 January by surface mail on 2 February, and this after 4½ months of war! This fact shows how remote the idea of hostilities was and explains how plans for leave in the coming spring became credible.

I wrote of my unhappiness at having to tell a probationer ADC that I couldn't recommend him for confirmation and of my intention to chloroform my Dalmatian puppy who was stone deaf.

I repeat my conviction in the next letter that:

"…. we shall win this war and that the world will be a happier place with people like Hitler removed therefrom …. my trouble is that I am doing nothing to help win this war …. we cannot discount the Italians as potential enemies - and that being the case I reiterate my conviction that England is the best place for Diana and the children …. in the meantime one must continue to try to inspire one's DCs and to trust and hope that we may be together in April. But don't hope too much on that score!" (February 1940)

Soon after I wrote:

"…. Come what may we have had some glorious times and naturally, our years in Cairo when we were all together were the best!"

Visit of Egyptian Prime Minister

I went to Khartoum as ex-Sudan Agent, and advised HE and Douglas Newbold for about two hours on the programme most likely to please the Egyptian Prime Minister and several of his Ministers who had accepted the Governor General's invitation to visit the Anglo-Egyptian Sudan. This was in fact made to Nahas Pasha and his Wafdist Government at the time of the Treaty denouement in 1936, and only taken up by Ali Maher four years later.

It was the first visit of an Egyptian Prime Minister to the Sudan during the 40 years of the Condominium and the initiative came from Cairo. I never knew what was the reason, advertised or otherwise, for the visit and I never really learnt of the results. But it was for the two countries an historic visit.

As usual no date or plan, however firmly accepted, was regarded as firm and the Egyptian party, as always, were adept at last minute alterations. I quote from my letter to Diana of 20 February 1940:

"…. I arrived at Damer by train (in my saloon) from Shendi at 9 am to find the PM and party were unexpectedly landing in Atbara instead of flying to Khartoum as arranged. So I jumped into uniform and off Bill (my deputy governor) and I drove to Atbara. I called in on Lee Spalding, the General Manager of the Sudan Government Railways and asked him to accompany me in the party of welcome. He absolutely refused. I gave him HE's message: that had no effect. I asked him to meet the PM at my house at lunch next week: he refused. So I have written him off as any help in that way! Well the Egyptian machines began to land and I had a talk with two old friends of Cairo days. Then landed the big Misr Airways machine and out stepped Ali Maher (the PM), Abdel Kawi (the Minister for Works) and Suleiman Harb Pasha (the Minister for War). All were very amiable and greeted me as an old friend. I think they rather liked seeing a face which they knew. I introduced them all to Bill Crawford (rather intolerant of it all), to Macphail, the *Mamur* and the *Omda*, and off we drove to the Club where they sat and had drinks and were extremely pleasant. I wondered what Ali Maher thought of driving in my car with both British and Egyptian flags flying - and hoped he noticed them! By noon they were gone.

"I wonder what the PM has up his sleeve. He obviously can't go back from the Sudan to Egypt without saying he has got something out of us!"

The whole party returned in a weeks' time and spent the day in Atbara and Damer. This is how I described the visit to Diana on 4 March 1940:

"…. Well, our visitors have all gone and I hope by now have left the Province and the Sudan. The show on Wednesday was not too bad. They all changed their minds about five times as to how they would come to Atbara and when, but finally arrived at 9.45

am by plane. Lee Spalding and I were there to meet them with a Guard of Honour by Harry's police. An introduction by the General and then by me, and then off we went to the technical workshops. They were interested for half an hour and asked intelligent questions. Ali Maher and Abdel Kawi went round as the Minister for War had gone off with the General Manager to see Colin Fosdich do some exercise. But then the PM wilted - made straight for the EXIT and left the Railways almost an hour before time! I then took him to the Coptic School when the perfectly [blank] headmaster worked up the otherwise decent and well-behaved boys into a frenzy of mass hysteria. Through sheer yelling he got the boys yelling too and finally pandemonium broke loose. The boys mobbed the PM, yelling, and with the sweat running down his face I finally took him away - again early. Even the Egyptian Press said "This is awful!". Then we went to pay the grand visit to the Egyptian Club. We arrived there to find it locked and barred! However we finally got them to open it (the President had run all the way from the school with the keys) and drinks were handed round. The Coptic boys had by then streamed into the Club and were likely to be a confounded nuisance so I got Harry Dibbes going. Somebody made a speech and Abdel Kawi replied (the Mother Nile and the sister countries). The PM then left suddenly (we were by now a good hour before time) and we went to the Sudanese Club where we found the President and 10 members only. More coffee and speeches and then we went to Damer. I had sent a message across but of course Bela of the ferry was on the wrong side. However I turned to the PM who was by then pretty tired and told him that officialdom was finished and that he was now coming to my country house out of Atbara (he still thinks my HQ is in Atbara). I may say that on arrival he had said "Please don't ask my staff to lunch but ask the newspaper men"; so instead of *beys* and soldiers we had the most awful collection of thugs and stiffs including the camera man who ran about on his hunkers taking marvellous pictures of the PM arriving here and leaving there. He took about 200 feet of the General's backside because the latter was leaning over the table on the verandah explaining military strategy to the Minister for War. The General hates being photographed and this monkey cinema man would crawl around suddenly popping up and pressing the button. The next instant the General would shoot round the table and present a full backside to the camera. However we shall probably see it on the film with the apostrophe misplaced - ie the Generals' behind. Abder Rahman had got the house looking wonderful. Lunch was laid before I came down from the roof at 6 am and the rooms were full of flowers. I had Ali Maher led to the bathroom and WC where he remained for fully 25 minutes. Luckily we had lots of time. John Rowley did the perfect aide de camp with Maxwell Harrison, James Macphail, Daoud Khalife (new Sub-Inspector), and May of the Essex and William disappointed at not getting money out of them. As the PM left my house he handed me three cheques - two for £100 (for the two clubs) and one for £50 (for the poor). He has been doing this all round the country and it really is rather foul. The result is that the Damer Club and the Atbara Kadi and this and that institution all tried to meet him in the hopes of extracting a bit of *baksheesh* from him. And in fact that's all the Sudanese really thought of the show."

I described a flower show in Atbara at which the prize presented by Mrs Diana Lush went to the Horams, the Secretary of the Flower Show and his wife. They were the most lovely flowers and beautifully arranged in a large round low basket.

I was finding the grand piano the greatest companion and comfort and had found a good woman singer in Atbara who would come over of an evening and give enormous pleasure to me and many friends. She sang good music, sang well and enjoyed singing. I too tried to practise and keep my fingers and my reading in good fettle. The tuning of the piano was not easy but I generally tuned it quite well.

I wrote in March 1940 tentatively and later strongly advocating trying to buy Westlands, our home in Ewhurst. Price then about £2,500 - I intended to pursue this matter if I managed to get leave.

The Shendi Agricultural Show organised by DC Whiskers Richardson, the Agricultural Officer Bill Ross, with Bill Crawford very much in the offing, went very well. We invited a large and distinguished company from Khartoum, eg. the Civil Secretary, the Assistant Financial Secretary, Bill Davies, the Director of Agriculture and a number of others.

"…. Altogether there are two saloons and nine service cars in Shendi station …. I have remained myself in this noisy station so that my Khartoum guests cannot say that I am more comfortable than they …."

I was very anxious to give Douglas Newbold the Civil Secretary a good holiday. We rode to the ploughing site:

"…. a mile of land with at least 120 pairs of bulls ploughing. I was glad we rode for it added to the rural feeling of the scene. Then at 9 am we all adjourned to two tables and chairs set out quite near the ploughing. The tables were groaning under the plates of *sinkert* (camel's hump), tongues, beer, marmalade, butter and coffee. I must say it all went with a swing and everyone much enjoyed themselves. Beer at 9 am is a good way to start the day and Douglas Newbold said he felt completely squiffy when we rode off to the Sudan Horse Sports. After that we did the round of the booths - a miniature bank; miniature house; broadcasting by the Post Office. Then we went down to the cotton auction market. By

1.30 pm I had a very tired Civil Secretary on my hands! ... Now it is time to take them out again and see the ploughing and meet some more chaps ... We were soundly beaten at polo: 10-6."

The Show was a tremendous success and we won the second polo match. The party dispersed and I wrote two days later:

".... sitting in the *gyassa*, preparatory to sailing or rather riding the odd 100 miles back north to Damer".

In fact I rode at least half of those 100 miles on the most lovely pure Arab pony, lent me by the Sudan Horse. I told Diana that the prestige of the Governor was enhanced a hundred-fold as I ambled or cantered sedately, on this lovely golden chestnut pony into this village and that. It was the perfect trip - one's home on the water, one's transport a true Arab pony.

I end my letter envisaging a journey to Merowe en route to Wadi Halfa - and home - but always without much confidence.

Writing of our garden in Damer (in mid-March):

".... The garden is looking rather lovely: the south bed is a mass of colour, petunias for the most part but some lovely patches of blue larkspur, salvia and clarkia - and four or five quite big masses of plumbago. The poinsettias are still in flower and also the single hibiscus. The bed on top of the terrace is not so thick but quite a splash of colour. Here we have marigolds and small sunflowers and cosmeas among the reds and purples of the petunias. Oh! How I wish you could see it all!"

At the end of March I gave dates to Diana indicating leaving Damer on 14 April. But I was still very doubtful of getting away - although Khartoum people told me I would. But on 10 April - four days before I hoped to go - I wrote:

".... The testing time has come - as you say in your letter - the war seems to have started in earnest, and I know you will have courage if I cannot get away with ....

On 13 April - my suitcase packed - a wire came from Khartoum indicating leave for Governors and senior staff postponed indefinitely. I had been warned by a friendly telephone call the news was not unexpected. Our friends locally and elsewhere were most sympathetic. I wrote to Diana on 21 April:

".... so long as we can win this war and put a stop to this disruption of our life which you and I and countless thousands and millions of people are now suffering, then our own disappointment and sufferings will seem as petty things compared with the issues at stake ...."

I asked her to try to explain to Julian the meaning of the word "duty":

"It's a hackneyed word but it helps tremendously if one can get it engrained into one's make-up".

I little knew what fear and anxiety she would soon have to suffer.

I finally managed to meet Dan Sandford in Khartoum in early May and had long talks with him about possibilities if the Italians declared war against us. I found him full of optimism and quite selfless. I wrote to Diana:

".... Dan makes me feel very selfish when I think of him uncomplainingly carrying on, financially much harder hit, older than I by 10 years and after a hard and disappointing life. But he has the confidence of his superior now (in Cairo) and has won the difficult battle of winning them over to his ideas. He has not won over people in Khartoum, particularly HE ...."

Writing on 12 May after the German invasion of the Low Countries:

".... I, a non-fighter in this war, still have the utmost confidence in the AEF and the French. We certainly have the superiority of air personnel, I am sure of that. Of course, unnaturally, I long to be back with 94 Siege Battery .... here we prepare."

The DC at Wadi Halfa was a bit surprised when no fewer than one dozen Italian Military Aircraft landed at Wadi Halfa in a *haboob*!

I end my letter of 8 May:

".... WC will make a grand PM and we shall win the war, I hope, under his leadership .... the battle has been joined but perhaps because I am out here, but also because I have the greatest admiration for our own and also the French armies, I have no doubt as to the result."

Then, for some inexorable reason the authorities in Khartoum lowered the embargo on leave for "key" men who had not had leave "if they could fly home". I myself did not think there was the barest chance of our achieving any flight to Europe but, as I wrote to Diana, I felt it right in fairness to her and to my Deputy (who would also take leave when I returned) to have a try; and so I started by train and steamer - only to be caught at Aswan by a telegram recalling me to the Sudan at once. However the steamer timings gave me three days so I decided to go on to Cairo and there at last met Dan, very smart "full Colonel at GHQ" and with him the Sudan Agent, at 7.30 am. I breakfasted at the Gezira Club and met a host of friends including my Governor General's daughter "being photographed by a young Guards Officer", and of course visited the Sudan Agency "where it was lovely to see again Miss Coy!" We had a splendid luncheon party for 12 - all old friends - watched cricket - visited my bank - attended Evensong in the Cathedral and had tea with Frank Johnston the Archdeacon and his family, catching the 7.30 pm sleeper train from Cairo to Shellal. I found my best man Martin Parr on the train - a tremendous boost to my morale. I reckoned that I had used well the eleven-hour visit to Cairo!

I confessed this latest escapade on the northward bound steamer in a letter to Diana. She of course understood and took the disappointment with great courage which infected me too. She kept me fully and bravely au fait with all the family news and some news of friends. She has always been a wonderful writer of letters and one of the tragedies of her and our lives was the destruction many years later, without her knowledge, of all the letters written to her mother and to others during our later life.

The next time I attempted to go on leave I was successful - but I had to wait over three years before I finally achieved it in 1943 - and Meriel, my youngest child, whom I had never seen, was 3½ years of age.

I found my province staff wonderfully sympathetic on my return but it was clear that the strain of the uncertainty regarding Italy's position was having even more effect on people's nerves than the news of calamities we were suffering in Europe.

Bill, my deputy, and his wife went off to Shendi - she was worried about her children whom she had left in the UK, when she joined Bill. I found my Chief of Police in Atbara, very near to a breakdown; James Macphail the DC of Atbara told me he felt "disembodied". My immediate job therefore was to take firm hold of the morale of my staff and through them of the Province. There were the loners whom, because we were in touch through good railway connections, it was easy to call in to HQ or visit regularly and often. The Sudanese in the districts were generally, if not unaffected, certainly unmoved - as yet. Then there was the sizeable town of Atbara with a heterogeneous population of 20,000, practically all railway employees or their families: a couple of hundred British, the same number of Levantines and the remainder Egyptian and Sudanese mechanics. The population of Atbara was still jittery and there was lack of good leadership. It was clearly my job to help my staff to overcome that weak spot in the Province morale. I wrote later that I thought of asking HE to come down and talk to the Atbarians himself.

"…. I wish you could be wafted out here to show the female Club members of Atbara what the women of England feel!"

I had asked for James Macphail to be sent to the Province to do this - and right well he justified my request - but he needed handling. I think it was he who said that some of my younger DCs were terrified of me!

I was writing at the end of May with a high heart ready to face a long separation which I knew to be inevitable, confessing that I had sagged in courage after my first failure to get home - much emboldened by personal news of Diana from friends who had seen her.

My Deputy's wife, Marjorie Crawford, flew home to look after her children and now he was added to the list of anxious spouses.

My letters show how deeply I was moved at the fall to the Germans of the French town of Amiens, around the debris of which we had fought in the first World War. I was not so distressed at the fall of Paris which, of course, became inevitable and

"once more one's thoughts are tumultuous …. once more one thinks of what happiness means …."

I write of us all as very busy. I remember asking my staff in Damer to my house as soon as the Italian news came in. There was nothing much to say but we all knew that our Sudanese were completely loyal to a man. As Stewart Symes wrote in his book *Tour of Duty*, their attitude was:

"…. We are all in this war whatever happens: it is our war as well as yours."

I had a grand Province and a wonderful small band of DCs to run it. I wrote:

"…. I won't have despondent talk; our friend GM was fined the other day by my Province Judge for passing on depressing talk."

By July 1940 surface mails were probably all going round the Cape and there seems to have been a hiatus in our correspondence. In a letter of 5 July I write at length about Diana and the family moving from Surrey. There was the possibility of going to Julian Humphreys in USA but I dismissed them all and advised her to stay put:

"…. Whatever may befall you, you will be among your own people - the best place - I do not intend anything to happen to me!"

I explained how terrible it was not to be able to look more than a day ahead into the future:

"…. I cannot think that the world has ever seen such amazing and quick change scenes in the whole of its history as we have seen in the last two months. To think that we should be solemnly and deliberately sinking French ships. Every single prophecy and sense of value has crashed in 60 days and we have lived to see what must be one of the finest military achievements in history. I still think that we are going to see Germany undergo, through lack of sea power, a military defeat …."

Atbara Bridge

Then on 23 July 1940 Diana in Ewhurst received the form of telegram which, in time of war, every wife and mother dreads - the telegram which begins "Deeply regret to inform you …."

The sender was Douglas Newbold, Civil Secretary in Khartoum, a close friend and it read as follows:

"Deeply regret to inform you Maurice was severely injured at Atbara yesterday evening by railway engine and sustained ruptured bladder and broken pelvis. Dr Mayne operated this morning. Maurice stood operation well and result hopeful though not definitely out of danger for next 48 hours. Have courage. Douglas Newbold."

Bill Crawford and Dr Leigh Henderson's wife Diana both wired hopefully next day from Atbara, as did Newbold every day until he was able to telegraph "Out of danger" on 28 July, the day after I had sent a telegram "sitting up and taking notice" on 27 July.

The accident took place on a moonless night at about 10.30 pm on the Atbara railway bridge. When the River Atbara was in flood the ferry did not function at night and it was an established custom for officials to cross from north to south and vice versa by the railway bridge, walking along the footplate between the railway lines. There were safety hatches on each side of the line into which a pedestrian could step if he saw or heard a train approaching. We always enquired from the watchman at the entrance to the bridge and received the all clear as regards any rail traffic.

Bill Crawford, Deputy Governor, Whiskers Richardson, DC Shendi who was staying at my house, and Maxwell Harrison, my Province Judge, and I had all spent the evening in Atbara and arranged to meet at the bridge entrance to return to Damer. Bill was the first to start and I the last, with my policeman behind me. We all clambered on to the footplate; one of us had a torch; Bill Crawford was far ahead of us by the time I had started. I remember no more until I recovered consciousness lying in Atbara Hospital three hours later, and found the Atbara doctor, Louis Brown, standing over me, Diana Henderson at my side and Bill Crawford on a chair, looking grey and haggard. Instinctively I asked - "Were Maxwell and Whiskers killed?" They all nodded. A light engine travelling at 20 mph had come from Atbara, to our rear, and had picked four of us neatly off the line with its "cow catcher", viz. my policeman, myself, Whiskers and Maxwell. The two latter and the policeman had been thrown clear of the bridge structure into the flowing river 80' below; they died instantly. My body had been caught by the superstructure of the bridge. Bill Crawford was far enough ahead of the engine to hear the noise of its approach and stepped into one of the shelters - and safety. The engine was driven on to Damer station, the driver quite oblivious of the carnage he had caused. Bill walked back, horrified to receive no response to his shouts. Mercifully he espied my body on the side of the bridge, prevented me slipping riverwards and somehow carried me to the bridge entrance, thence by ambulance to hospital where I was found to be alive but obviously badly battered and bleeding internally. Louis Brown was no surgeon and having briefly questioned me, before I again slipped into oblivion, he telephoned Khartoum (this at 1 am) and by dawn the senior surgeon, Dr Mayne, was on his way to Atbara by RAF aircraft to save my life. I was by then in the operating theatre. He diagnosed a ruptured bladder, proved his opinion correct when he opened me up, stitched up the wound, satisfied himself that I had suffered no further major internal injuries nor serious fractures of bones other than my damaged pelvis (I was by now blue from head to foot as a result of bruising), gave orders to pump saline into me as often as possible (I came to and heard that order) and flew back to Khartoum. He had decided to allow the ruptured bladder to heal entirely before tackling the various orthopaedic problems which my rather battered body presented. How wonderfully right and foreseeing he was. He reported to Douglas Newbold on return to Khartoum that I had a 50:50 chance of recovering from my ruptured bladder and the side issues of peritonitis etc. But he was too modest. Within 48 hours I had in my hand a telegram from Diana "Holding you fast in undying love". That gave me the courage to make the supreme effort; the matron and two British nurses in Atbara Hospital never failed me; Bill Crawford with his brusque emotion told me to "buck up" and Di Henderson never left either the side of Leigh her husband, very sick with sandfly fever, or myself with curious tubes dangling from my body, until five days later when Douglas Newbold could telegraph Diana that I was out of danger. Dr Mayne had flown to Atbara again, bless him, pronounced himself very satisfied with my internal organs - but should I ever walk again? My pelvis was not fractured but split and though they made a few "posture" suggestions for me while I was in Atbara, Mayne told me that he would not tackle the orthopaedic side of the case until I had been moved to Khartoum, where he had the necessary X-ray apparatus and would have me under his eye every day. Luckily I could not see my bruising which was total - head to toe - but it was one of the show pieces of Atbara Hospital. I was to remain in Atbara for a fortnight before transfer to Khartoum.

During that fortnight I had time to accommodate my mental reactions to the shock of losing, by tragic and terrible deaths, two of my best friends in the Province.

Whiskers Richardson I had known practically all my Service. He had inaugurated me into a *mufettish's* life in Gedaref and I had been immensely grateful to him then. He should have returned to Education wherein his metier lay, but his choice was to remain in the administration, and when I overtook him on the ladder and came to Northern Province as his Governor he gave me all the loyalty and help I could have wished for. He was about to retire and enter the Church; his wife Betty was about to present him with his third child; his death was a terrible tragedy to his family - a tragedy which I felt sure he would try to minimise by prayer and guidance when he died. He was a man of God - irascible but loving, and loved; and I with others, Sudanese and British, cherish his memory.

Maxwell Harrison I did not know so well but I admired him as a man and as a Province Judge. He was quiet, absolutely frank and honest in his opinions, and I often felt that he was more troubled by the untidiness and injustice of the world than most of us; he had courage and great loyalty and his loss to the Province would be incalculable. He had no children and his wife, Phyllis, suffered from ill health which separation had not improved. Maxwell's integrity was always a shining light in the dark days of the War.

Their bodies were found on the river bank and they

were buried in Atbara Cemetery. A Memorial Service to them both was held in Khartoum Cathedral on 24 July 1940.

Letter from MSL to DRL:

Atbara
29 July 1940

"…. I am alive as by a miracle and I say it with all humility and thankfulness. I wish I could say the same of Maxwell and Whiskers. Of all the people in the world whom I would have wanted to be kept, it was those two. But they were both killed instantaneously, and Bill C and I saved. Bill C is quite unhurt.

"We had been to the flicks in Atbara. The river was down and it meant returning over the footplate and so motoring home. Whiskers was staying with me; Maxwell had just come back from Shendi and Bill was under the weather. So we picked up Di Henderson in Atbara (by Jove she has been splendid since) and went to a flick. Dropped Di at home and started back over the bridge. Bill No 1, then MABH, then Whiskers, then I and lastly a policeman. I asked the *ghaffir* (watchman) if there were any trains and was told "No". We cannot have gone more than 50 or 60 yards when a *single* engine must have silently entered the bridge and it just picked us off one by one, except Bill who had the longest time to hear and realise its approach. It threw the policeman over the edge; it got me on the right head, elbow and boco and flung me on to a strong cross girder which I hit with some force and was apparently just conscious enough to cling to while pouring blood, but not myself, onto the ground 40' below. It picked up Whiskers and, I think, broke his skull before throwing him into the river, and Maxwell also though only breaking his arm. JNR died instantly and Maxwell of shock due to a dicky heart, *before* hitting the river. Bill leapt to a shelter and then came back and picked up my bits. The engine went on, unconscious of the tragedy, to Damer.

"They got me along here, half conscious by then, and in some pain in front. Leigh Henderson was ill and Brown wisely telephoned to Khartoum for Mayne who came by plane at dawn with Miss Hills Young. They thought I had all sorts of injuries - I was a bit vomity all night. However Mayne diagnosed, rightly, only a split pelvis and the usual accompanying ruptured bladder. He had me open and played about for 1½ hours inside and sewed me up very nicely. I was back and eating lunch quite fairly comfily. The pelvis is split in the middle and it's more a split than a crack; the bladder is going on well too. My marvellous escape was to avoid rupturing the urethra which is quite sound and my parts which although a bit swollen and discoloured are in good order! The whole of my right side is just black and blue and I have two stitches on my head and one on my right elbow. *But* I got over the shock very quickly and 48 hours after the op. I was shaved and happy and comfortable. I have *never* suffered much pain and very little discomfort, though catheters are nasty things and my bladder still drains through a tube coming out of my navel, and trickles when I don't mean it to!

"Di Henderson has saved my nerves and morale. She was here as soon as daylight would let her and just knelt and held my hand and comforted me, and said "Just hold on and think hard of your Diana". She has been the same ever since - giving me her vitality and preventing me from worrying. She is a great giver and a tireless one. Please thank her for her letter.

"Today, the 8th day, I was X-rayed and had 13 stitches removed from my navel; I am eating and reading and sleeping well. I *am* weak. Lost a lot of blood and I am going very slow. I have got to lie supine for 4 or 5 weeks on a/c pelvis. Everyone has been marvellously kind and I am overwhelmed with my safety and their kindness …."

I end another letter from Atbara:

"…. I have been spared and it gives me tremendous hope and faith that a good deal more is required of me here and that we shall meet again soon."

I remained in Atbara for two weeks. From the surgical point of view Mayne required a complete healing of the perforated bladder and this occurred. From the mental standpoint he (no doubt advised by Leigh Henderson, my GP as it were, and his wife Diana) deemed it wiser for me to absorb the shock of the tragedy in my own surroundings with my own people and I would have added especially Di Henderson. Two quite wonderful remedies were sent to help and comfort me, and defeat the demons of horror at the terrible destruction of my friends, the sudden bereavement of their wives and families, the self pity at my own battered state and the anxiety caused to my own family. One remedy was of course the telegram of five words from Diana "Holding you fast in undying love"; and the other was Di Henderson's hand which was in reality holding my own in loving sympathy when I recovered consciousness in that night, which I found again on my return from the operating theatre and which was there whenever she could be spared from a sick husband and her children. "Don't worry" Di in Atbara telegraphed to Diana in Surrey "I am holding him". "Don't worry" she would say to me, "Just think of your own Diana." The nursing was excellent and my guardian (she had after all the authority of my doctor's wife) kept visitors, who were many and wonderfully kind, Sudanese, Levantine and British, to a minimum of time. When Mayne returned he found a patient far more near to restoration than he had hoped. He gave me another week in Atbara, to strengthen my innards, to give my shocked nerves further time to settle and have me ready to face the relatively more painful and more difficult orthopaedic treatment which lay ahead of me. I myself could see the good sense of this. I was not idle - supine on my bed I hired a young stenographer and polished off 72 letters of thanks and several messages to Egyptian and Sudanese newspapers. The Press in both countries had been wonderfully sympathetic and kind, especially to the widows of Maxwell and Whiskers. The Egyptian Gazettes had a daily bulletin of my health until I was out of danger. The kindness from all and sundry was a tremendous help to the morale of someone who had been literally hit for six.

I went to Khartoum on 6 August on the Hospital Train. The driver was warned "No jolts" and the result was an arrival of one hour late in Khartoum - normal passengers furious! I was met by my surgeon Mayne and my golden-red-haired Fiona who in 1935 had delivered Sylvia in Cairo and had come to the Sudan at our instigation. Now began the serious business of orthopaedics, viz. how to close the gap in the pelvis joint. Mayne confessed that he had never seen a case like mine and asked for my constant help. He received it! After multiple and intensive X-rays they started me off in the tightest maternity belt Fiona could manipulate; they then put me in a plaster of Paris from navel to below the knee for four weeks - lying for ten days on my back, then another ten on my right side, then on my left etc. I made up my mind to endure anything. I could always read and write and I slept reasonably well - even whilst going through this strange time. Then they allowed me to sit up. After six and a half weeks I wrote to Diana:

"I started this business supine; I became lateral; today I am vertical!"

On that day two months after being struck down I was walking again - stiffly but straightly and with no limp. Dr Mayne told me that he wanted me walking without crutches and to continue walking to within the limits of tiredness and of course any pain. The rest was really up to me. I wrote:

> ".... I cannot tell you how wonderfully, truly, utterly thankful I am. The whole shock, no, that is the wrong word - the whole meaning of the accident and my recovery; the shock and anxiety caused to you; the wonderful way I have felt, physically, the strength of your thoughts; the kindness of friends here and everywhere, all came over me yesterday with a rush. I felt overwhelmed and not a little humbled. One cannot go through an experience like this without realising - well - just the love of God ...."

It is meet at this stage to bear witness to the immense kindness, understanding and sympathy of my many and dearly devoted friends in Khartoum and elsewhere. Their devotion perhaps not so much as to one personally but to a man who had suffered mentally and physically and whom they wished to help. Most of them now need no earthly help but I owed to so many during those two hot months a debt of gratitude which I never repaid and can now only record in loving gratitude. It was said in the Sudan that my speedy recovery was an example of mind over matter. I believed it to have been a shining example of God's love and of man's love towards a man in trouble.

I suppose my most exalted visitor was an old friend whom I had never expected to see in such circumstances, namely the Emperor (in exile) Haile Selassie who was one of the first to see me. He also saw through a window Richard Dimbleby who had been struck down with German measles. Dan Sandford had just penetrated into Abyssinia to prepare for a further endeavour to raise the central Abyssinian tribes against the Italians and prepare a way for the Emperor's return.

My Governor General and General William Platt were frequent visitors; also Douglas Newbold who was handling the administration of the Sudan with a Political Service "dwindling into nothing before his eyes". Major "Pongo" Barker brought an almost daily bulletin from the zoo (he was Game Warden) to cheer me. There were literally countless others who never failed to bring their sympathy, news and good stories, often sacrificing part of their precious leisure hours in the evening.

As for their wives - I shall never forget the love and understanding shown by so many women, young and not so young, who made it a duty - a pleasant duty I hope - to come and tell me all the stories and all the scandal of Khartoum and elsewhere. When I overcame the first hazards of hospital life I asked permission to spend an hour on a wheeled stretcher (known as the drunkard's trolley) under a golden mohur or some other shady tree in the garden. Noon day temperature was about 100°F but it was cooler earlier. Fiona, my darling sister-in-charge (of me) would say to enquiring visitors "Mr Lush is under the golden mohur tree with his usual bevy of lovelies."

One day, soon after I arrived, Rev "Uncle" Harper and a fellow chaplain arrived to give me Communion in my private ward. The news immediately became current in and beyond the hospital that I was on the point of death! I stifled the rumour by asking them to come every week - and so Tuesday morning was church morning for my ward. It was lovely later to visit the Cathedral actually on foot.

The matron Miss Butcher, a kindly soul, was overworked but never too busy to pay her daily visit. But my guardian angel and daily joy was Sister MacLean - Fiona to me - who ruled me with a rod of iron. I was terrified of her with a very deep love and respect. She knew if I had altered from this position to that (wrong) position - "Just for a tiny second, Sister!"; she knew if I had read too late on her nights off duty. But when a horde of marching ants swarmed out of my bedside table and went straight into my plaster of Paris she was nearly defeated - nearly but not quite! She seized a flitgun full of anti mosquito liquid and pumped and pumped down the crevasses of my poor body. She herself shaking with laughter! The corpses of the ants were found when they cut off the plaster a week or two later!

My most tragic visitor was Sir Stewart Symes who came to say "Goodbye" after he had been instructed, almost peremptorily by the Foreign Office, to terminate his appointment and hand over his job to General

Huddleston who was to succeed him. I never knew the reason for that decision. I liked him greatly and always admired his handling of the Egyptian Cabinet when he addressed them in 1936 and saved the Anglo-Egyptian Treaty. I knew that he was, in the first year of the War, averse to military plans which might unnecessarily involve the Sudanese in a war "which was not theirs" and he found plans to re-establish Haile Selassie from the Sudan border (mooted even before Italy declared war on Britain) distasteful - Dan Sandford was very wroth with that attitude. I think his metier was more in the international field than in administration. But he was good with his staff and I was sorry to see him go as it were, so unceremoniously.

Douglas Newbold was always full of interest, a tonic to an invalid, and very naughty in discussing provincial problems with me instead of with my Acting Governor, and, I know, used to make me an excuse to quit his office to try out some of his ideas of administration on this or that, on an old invalid dog! It was a great honour - and very amusing and interesting.

I felt much the same with General William Platt who now told me plainly that he wanted me to take charge of the administrative-cum-political affairs when his forces entered Abyssinia, and that he was personally very anxious that I should be fit to do so in the near or not quite so near future. He had, since Mussolini had entered the war, changed his opinion about Dan Sandford, whom he had dismissed on first meeting in 1939 as a "dreamer" and he sounded me out about him and his "schemes in Abyssinia". Dan had been quite secretive to me when we met in Cairo and elsewhere, and he never made it his business to come to visit me or let me know what was in his mind as to the Middle East. Of course he could not - for I was a senior civilian in a Condominium Government to whom British military secrets could not be passed! However I was able to convince Platt of Dan's integrity, of his complete knowledge of the Abyssinian situation and his confidence in his Emperor (now in Khartoum) - a confidence which was mutual.

These visits by General Platt started, I hope, a friendship which was not scarred by later differences in military rank and established in me a loyalty to a not-so-easy commander when I became his subordinate. I was always "Maurice of the Sudan" to him.

Khartoum Hospital lay adjacent to the railway station and so we were in the target area for any Italian air raids on the station. We had three while I was in hospital. I was bundled onto the "drunk's trolley", taken to ground level in the lift, and wheeled into a sandbagged enclosure in the yard. Here, one evening, I sat throughout a raid, with Di Henderson holding one hand and Fiona the other. Unfortunately the raid, unsuccessful, was of short duration!

Slowly, slowly, as it seemed, but how wisely determined by Mayne and the medical staff, I was allowed to arise from my supine state - first to sit up, then to dangle my legs from the bed, then, Praise be to Allah! to walk a step. It all took weeks, but strength returned quickly. Fiona massaged and pummelled me; I ran a temperature - pure excitement and thought all was lost; I returned to normal and was quite amazed at the speed with which normality returned. There was an exciting future at stake.

Khartoum Hospital; 13 September 1940

I can dangle my legs from the bed!
The thought of it goes to my head.
To hell with the bedpans
Tamergis and headmans
I shall WALK to the closet instead!

Away with my aches and my pain
I shall soon be out walking again!
It was not an ice-creamer
Who cracked up my femur
But a highly respectable train!

Murderous! (DL)

General Platt would "pop in" and wag his head in disapproval at excessive speed and nod his head as I obviously gained normality. I was given a pool car to take me hither and thither; I went to see all the girl friends who had visited me so kindly; I looked in at an office or two; I returned thanks to God in Khartoum Cathedral. Then came the real tussle. All the pundits from Governor General through the doctors and the personnel staff encouraged me to take leave in Kenya (six months was suggested). I had a small battle with all the authorities about my existence on emergence from hospital. The official (medical and some administrative) view was that a complete change was essential and that I should go to Kenya or some other African colony for 3-6 months. I, who knew my capacity for rehabilitation and my present fitness, was convinced that a short rehabilitation in the surroundings which I knew and loved, ie. my home in Damer, would be the better if not the best convalescence. Leigh and Di Henderson mercifully aided my plea to this end by agreeing to move en famille to Damer to look after me.

Newbold, my immediate chief, was convinced. It took a little time and a good motherly talk by Di Henderson to Mayne and the other medical high-ups, to convince them.

In the end I was discharged from Khartoum Hospital and permitted to go to Damer on convalescent leave on 2 October - just over two months after the Atbara Bridge tragedy.

I found a wonderful reception party at Damer when I arrived by train. The Hendersons in full possession of my house with Bill Crawford and a new young DC. I went home to peace, to memories of home, to my piano and to the love and ministrations of the Hendersons. Our servants were in terrific form and we had a wonderful return - the ghosts of Whiskers and Maxwell *were* there - but we tried and succeeded in thinking of happiness.

In such luxury in my home, but supervised by my doctor and his Di, I lived for a month, gaining physical strength, moral courage, and a deep thankfulness before taking up the reins of office again.

I found Damer far more peaceful than Khartoum where during my first week of release from hospital I exhausted myself by calling on all my friends, to thank them for their kindness.

Walking was my principal form of exercise, apart from the physio-therapeutic exercises prescribed by the medicos in Khartoum. But I found that acting as a ball boy at tennis was an excellent form of voluntary unexpected exercise - and the presence of the *mudir* attempting to do their job simply delighted the ball boys who longed to see His Excellency get the clip on the ear which the Deputy Governor generally gave them. I was lent a very sure-footed mare and by the end of October I was riding. I was able to practice hydro-therapy in the baths at Atbara and by 20 October, three months after the knockout, I was at work again in the office and living my normal life. I had the complete agreement of Mayne and the Civil Secretary, Douglas Newbold, and I quote:

"…. General Platt took me furtively into a corner in Khartoum and told me that there were STRONG (code word for Abyssinia) reasons why I should get fit and strong soon …."

A later visit to Khartoum confirmed all that we, Dan and I and other cronies of Abyssinia, had hoped for - the Italians were to be driven out of Ethiopia. Sir Stewart had also warned me of this and of my future service with STRONG.

In November I was on trek between Shendi and Damer - in fact I sailed down that reach with a DC (Keen) and my ponies aboard the sailing boat. I weathered a visit from General Hubert Huddleston, the new Governor General, whom I liked (I knew him of old) but found almost dumb! I wrote to Diana:

"…. He won't speak - he never utters a word; one has to get people to speak to him. He fell asleep in public on three occasions and I had to go back to Metemma to say to the people all the things which HE *should* have said …. this tomb-like business is carrying the strong silent man a bit too far …."

My hours as usual were always full and our cook Mohammed Dhahab swore, laughingly, that it was like a hotel.

"…. The boys have been splendid. Abder Rahman won't let me wear my new socks and has hidden some of my best shirts …."

By October 1940 mails between UK and the Sudan were becoming very patchy, but letters did get through though I suspect some were lost. I find mine full of praise for Diana's great courage at the time of my accident; of my concern for her to take some kind of holiday (she had 14 days in Wales in the first three years of war); of praise and thankfulness for the indomitable courage of the people of England (she among them); of my thankfulness that she did not leave Ewhurst to join me even after my accident. I console over measles in January 1942 and take to heart the warnings Diana sent me about "overdoing it!" I tell of a new pony, Ewhurst, with myself about "to take a toss" but remaining up. Another attack of malaria bothered me but was soon forgotten.

At the end of the year, writing when on a visit to Merowe, I say:

"…. To me 1940 has brought a realisation of what pain and helplessness mean, which I shall never forget, and an appreciation of being saved from death by what was a miracle. That I hope, I shall never forget. It has brought to me the realisation of what human loving kindness from friends and even acquaintances can do - I hope I shall never forget that, nor the friends who gave it to me …."

I had spent the inside of a week in Khartoum before Christmas that year:

"…. forgetting the Province and looking at a few maps and files, listening to other people and generally finding out what STRONG is all about. For when I am called I had better know something about it."

Christmas came and went - I wrote home that I had wept in Atbara church at the old familiar Christmas hymns. I was at last beginning to feel happier about Atbara and the difficulties among the various divisions of the British, Levantine, Sudanese and now a strong element of military. I did another tour in the northern part of my Province and found my beloved Wadi Halfa "packed with people", many of them military. I took the Sunday Evening Service in their little church and preached my first ever (but not my last) sermon, and I came back to Damer most grateful that I had such a loyal and steady British staff - DCs, agriculturalists, doctors, customs men and railwaymen and such a splendid half-million Sudanese.

The New Year came and January must have been a busy month of which I have no record. But on 4 February 1941 a telegram reached Diana in Ewhurst which read:

"Leaving Province joining army rank Brigadier for Strong Administration staying Hester where hope see Dan soon hope measles better much love Maurice Lush."

The story of the STRONG administration will be told elsewhere. On that day there ended quite abruptly my Service in the Sudan Political Service - over 20 marvellous years in a Service which received me "on tic", retained me in spite of Service out of the Sudan, taught me the elements of administration, promoted me to serve personally first of all the men and women throughout the Service and then the finest Governor General in the history of the Condominium; which sent me to represent them, again outside the Sudan, and finally gave me the honour of Governorship - 20 wonderful, happy years - happy because of the people we tried to serve and the Service to which we belonged.

Letter to The Times Saturday 20 November 1982

"Shendi Sophistication" from Mr Maurice Lush

Sir,

In his article "Isolated in the Sudan" printed in the overseas section of your issue of 13 November, your reporter describes Shendi, where the PLO camp is situated, as a primitive village in the Sudan.

Forty years ago Shendi was the Headquarters of the largest district of the Northern Province of the Condominium Sudan. There was a number of good brick buildings, some offices, some shops, some residences. The Headquarters of the Sudan Horse (Sudan Defence Force Cavalry) were there. There was a thriving market and the Sudan Railways maintained a busy goods and passenger station.

Writing to my wife in March 1940 of the Shendi Agricultural Show (attended by a number of British and Sudanese guests from Khartoum) I remarked on the number of saloon railway carriages (for the "high-ups"), service cars and rail-buffet cars "now parked on the lines in Shendi station".

I described the ploughing match in which 120 pairs of bulls took part; the judging of some hundreds of cattle, etc. I tell of the booths erected by the Shendi schools, by the Khartoum banks, by the Post Office, etc. (the last gave a display of broadcasting, a novelty in the Sudan). There was a booth erected by ICI. In fact it was a veritable Southern Counties Show in miniature!

All this did not take place in a "primitive village", even 40 years ago!

Perhaps your reporter approached the PLO camp direct by that dreadful road instead of through the town of Shendi?

Yours faithfully
MAURICE LUSH
The Athenaeum
Pall Mall SW1
15 November, 1982

I served for a further 20 years in the British Army, in the United Nations, in industry and thereafter in many voluntary organisations; never did I find the fulfilment nor the happiness which the Sudanese and the Sudan Political Service gave to me.

I hope that I was able to give a little in return.

The Home Front

Throughout the 18 months since the outbreak of the War, how had matters fared with the person I loved most in the world - my wife - and my family, my mother and sister, my mother-in-law? How had they faced the stresses and strains, the fears and hopes, the nearly darkest news, during those first 18 months of War?

Needless to say - but with thanks to God and to them - they met the break in family life, the absence of husband and father, the problems spiritual, physical and mental, the family loneliness, difficulties of finance and food, family education and discipline, in an atmosphere, at any rate at the outset of the War, with magnificent fortitude and success which they succeeded in passing on to the absent father of the family in letters and messages of happiness which meant everything to someone who felt powerless to do more than write, advise and pray.

There was for both Diana and myself one consolation - we now both had our separate problems to handle - and to handle alone - she our home and family; I my job. Diana had experience of this when alone on annual leaves. Although mails were regular and prompt at first and we sustained each other with advice, during that first year and a half the individual decisions on our family problems were made and rightly made by Diana. I can think of no false step in the progress of our home or family.

Here I must repeat a former assertion which is to render a paeon of thanks to the foresight of Diana's mother in acquiring for us the tenancy of Westlands which was the Lush family home in Ewhurst from 1939 to 1944. And, with one rather terrible and unhappy blot, was the ideal home for Diana's mother and our family. The house was just large enough for a new baby and a growing family, the garden was spacious and lovely; it was within easy reach of London by road and rail so that visitors were always plentiful and welcome. The property abutted onto the house and garden owned (through my brother's foresight) by my mother and sister. Westlands and Brookside constituted a formidable territory of the very old (my mother), the old (Diana's mother), parental age (my sister and Diana), their seven (and an eighth to come) children and one very sweet and very formidable adjunct to their families, Pam Crowther Smith, who loyally stayed with our little family for the first 18 months of the War to be with them at Meriel's birth and infancy.

The Westlands-Brookside households - about half a mile apart across fields - were complementary to each other, though my sister at Brookside had a slightly different, older and more severe outlook on life. She knew that her husband Dan, had volunteered (at an age of well over 50) to enter Ethiopia while the country was still under the rule of the Italians in order to prepare the way for the return of the Emperor. She could share that news with noone. Their financial future was by no means secure, her children were approaching the age when expensive education had to be considered, and they were six in number. She was however a good planner - and a qualified teacher herself - and soon the elder Lush children were sharing some lessons with the Sandford youngest. Diana wrote:

".... Julian does his numbers with me, his reading with Granny, writing, history and nature also at Brookside, and Pam teaches him the piano .... I do hope that Granny lives long - she is the link that binds our households together."

Moreover there came to stay and finally to live with

my sister at Brookside a formidable lady, Miss Katherine Stephenson, commonly known as KT who had been a teacher of girls and women all her life, culminating in the post of Principal of a Teachers' Training College with Chris my sister as one of her pupils. Her devotion to my sister was strong and unbreakable, and she became one of the Sandford family in England and then later in Ethiopia, for better, for poorer, in sickness and in health, till death took her. She was a wonderful rather terrifying lady.

So the first foundations of the children's education were established, and this responsibility lay on Diana's shoulders for three and a half years - the choosing of nursery schools, the dancing classes and finally Preparatory School for Julian - indeed it was she alone who put him down for Winchester at a very early age - and saw to it that he became the third member of her family to become a Wykehamist.

Westlands had a modest but lovely garden containing most joys to delight children - a swing, a pond (very muddy), horses in the next field - and an ever-enlarging vegetable area. There lived in the bungalow attached to the house a married couple, Watts, of whom the wife was supposed to cook and help in the house (but whose varying tempers made life a hell to Diana and the family), while her henpecked husband did help somewhat in the garden.

Diana's mother Ruth - the tenant of Westlands - was, of course, the saviour of the personal and housing situation - but her health became a great anxiety to Diana and to her brothers Richard, Mervyn and Alan. Richard enlisted in the Royal Navy soon after the outbreak of war. To his eternal credit, he had to endure for some time the rigours of an able seaman's life, which, compared to his life of county and club cricket combined with real tennis (though both exhausting pastimes at which he managed to excel), was an extreme contrast; he gained his commission to the RNVR, which indeed he deserved. Covered by the veneer of his apparently easy going and ineffectual life of athletics, bridge (from which he earned a moderate income) and "bar propping" there was an inherent courage in Richard which carried him to commissioned rank and the tough life on a frigate in the Atlantic; it taught him to endure much pain with great courage at the end of his short life.

Mervyn and Alan were both busy about the business of British Drug Houses in war time, amidst the unspeakable dangers and horrors of ARP work in London during the whole of the blitz of 1940 and 1941. Yet they, especially Alan, found time and petrol to come to the country to be with their mother and sister, and give them company with mental and physical help and comfort in adversity.

Diana's letters were to me a pattern of what letters from home should be: stressing the beauty of the country and the happiness of the family; describing the difficulties of wartime conditions (the winter of 1939-40 was rigorous in the extreme); the restrictions, the shortcomings, the anxiety and indeed sometimes the fear:

> ".... I expect we shall be the next on Hitler's list for invasion ...."

Yet they always brought the troublesome facts and anxieties, the dangers and discomforts to a happy conclusion.

The initial desolation of separation was enlightened by accounts of the children's happiness and fun; the boredom of the last months of pregnancy, coupled with the uncertainty of the "phoney war", were alleviated by the business not only of the ordinary nursery life of the elder children but by the extra discomfort and toil necessitated by war precautions.

Westlands and the beloved inhabitants thereof lived a hard self disciplined life which cannot have been ideal for a mother whose mind and body should have been chiefly concerned with the coming infant; there were constant last straws:

> ".... if only Mrs W would behave normally, I could be happy and settled ...."

but Diana's letters without exception were written with one intent - to send peace and comfort with a real story of family life to a lonely husband who felt, as he must feel, that he should be at home to help in the zone of war.

When other wives were allowed to join their men in the Sudan, Diana was quite firm in her certainty that her duty was to stay with the family and her sick mother:

> ".... Would that I might come out even for 48 hours to talk ...."

However I was thankful that she agreed with me on this vital problem. Of course there were moments and periods when we both longed to be at the other end - I had malaria twice and Ruth was ill.

And so after nearly 22 years in the Sudan Political Service, I was seconded to the British Military Administration of Occupied Enemy Territories and became a soldier once more.

Service in a *"service d'elites"* perhaps spoils one for the hurly-burly of the army or the United Nations; but in neither service during the next 10 years did I find that freedom of thought and action without the interference from superior echelons or individuals as I had in the Sudan. The bureaucracy of the War Office, Foreign Office and whatever power guided the UN agencies was very hard to bear, and often quite maddening to one who was accustomed to:

> ".... control by one man occupying a position which gave him the most autocratic power in the British Empire." (The Times March 1900.)

I write this in retrospect because in the army I served under chiefs of worldwide reputation who had no regard for rank - Wavell, Cunningham and Platt; Sturgess of the Marines; Alexander, Montgomery, Leese and Robertson.

MSL and DRL, Sylvia, Julian and Pam Crowther Smith, 1938

MSL and Julian in the garden of Westlands, Ewhurst, 1939

Meriel; Daily Mail, 25 May 1942: 'This little girl has never seen her father'

Diana with her three children, May 1942

WESTLANDS, EWHURST

MSL, Ruth Hill, Christine and Eleanor Sandford, Meriel, Julian and Sylvia during MSL's first leave, July 1943

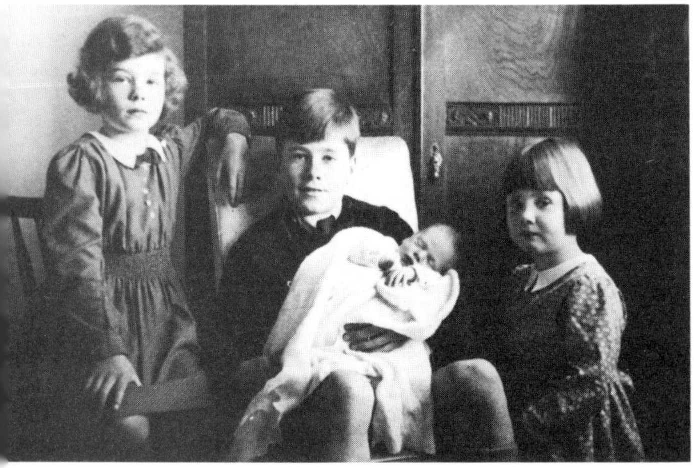

Sylvia, Julian with Nicola and Meriel, June 1944

Family group with Hills: Peter, Mervyn, Julian, Kitty, Charles Hill, Sylvia, Alan and DRL with Meriel; September 1940

A family gathering in April 1945: Cecil Lush, Audrey, Judith with Meriel, Julian, MSL, Granny Lush, Christine, Marjorie Lush, Sylvia with Eleanor

World War II - Military Administration

CHAPTER 10

ETHIOPIA 1941-42
Chief Political Officer, Occupied Enemy Territories Administration

The Ethiopian Campaign 1941-42

For those who are sufficiently interested and kind to read on, the following chapters on Ethiopia 1940-42 embrace my first experiences as a reinstated soldier in World War II. I have thought it kinder to give the chapter a preface, as one would a play - Place, Time and Dramatis Personae.

Place

The area was the Horn of Africa, then comprising the new Italian East Africa and Italian Somaliland - formerly and for the purpose of this narrative known as Eritrea Ethiopia, British and Italian Somaliland, with the ports of Leila, Berbera, Mogadishu and Kismayu, and additionally French Somaliland with the port of Djibouti. The neighbouring countries which provided bases for the British Forces concerned, were the Anglo-Egyptian Sudan and Kenya Colony; the Belgian Congo produced a small force which entered Ethiopia by Gambeila.

The whole campaign in the north and in the south, culminating with the final engagement in Ethiopia in 1941-42 can be read in the excellent precis: *The Abyssinian Campaigns* 1940-43 and in pages 1-10 of *British Military Administration in Africa 1941-47* by Lord Rennell of Rodd, KBE CB (HM Stationery Office 1948).

Time

The period of time was from June 1940, when France our ally had just surrendered and Italy had joined the Germans and when Great Britain found herself alone, desperately short of military equipment and aircraft, enduring the Battle of Britain and the imminent threat of invasion, pressed by our enemies on several fronts and especially in the Middle East, until February 1942, when, with the knowledge that we could win victories in battle, we still fought alone.

Dramatis personae

I shall give the dramatis personae characters from the chessboard in accordance with their importance in the military game which was to be played: mark well the word "military" for we were playing the game of war and not politics.

The King on the board was General Wavell, the Commander-in-Chief of the British Forces in the Middle East whose aim and duty were the defeat of the enemy; his two **Knights** were Generals Cunningham and Platt, who fought battles under his direction; his **Bishop** was General Mitchell who unwound the political knots which were bound to occur.

There were three **Pawns**: Dan Sandford (DAS) who planned a small part of the military scheme and took a courageous personal part in it; the exiled Emperor Haile Selassie who, though a military Pawn, thought he was a King; and M S Lush, whose principal duty was to maintain peace in the country from which the enemy had been driven. If the restoration of the Pawn Emperor to his throne would help to achieve such peace, then it would be wise to fulfil such a restoration; to me, British military interests were paramount.

The King on the chessboard was General Sir Archibald Wavell, a "student of war, gifted in high degree with the imaginative daring which is the hallmark of a great commander" (London Times 27/2/41); he had gained a victory in a campaign of outstanding brilliance in Cyrenaica, only to see his victory turned to defeat at the end of that year with the arrival of the German Forces in Libya under Rommel. Wavell was the inspiration and the driving force behind the Ethiopian Campaigns from the Sudan (Platt) and from Kenya (Cunningham).

Wavell endeared himself to me on 26 January 1941 at our first meeting in Khartoum when he promoted me from Captain RA to Brigadier. I shall describe the scene in a page or two. I was indeed lucky to serve under Wavell. He left his command at the end of 1941, and finally became Viceroy of India. Incidentally, he produced *Other Men's Flowers*.

The Knights - Lieutenant General William Platt was Commander British Forces in the Sudan; had been *Kaid* or Commander-in-Chief of the Sudan Defence Force since 1939; and I had known and liked him when I was Governor of Northern Province. His job was to attack the Italian Forces in the northern sector, striking from the Sudan, then to turn south, occupying Gojjam and eventually Addis Ababa. I was appointed, at his request, his Deputy Chief Political Officer and was happy to think of serving under him. In fact his advance, though successful, was held up, and I entered Addis Ababa as DCPO to the other Knight, Lieutenant General Alan Cunningham, General Officer Commanding Troops in East Africa. Cunningham arrived in Nairobi in November 1940 to take command of a composite force of East, West and South African troops who were to oust the Italians from their outposts in Kenya Colony, advance through Italian and British Somaliland, proceed north to meet Platt's forces in Addis Ababa. Such was the plan. His forces attacked the Somaliland border on 24 January 1941. By 6 April they had covered 2,000 miles, taken 22,000 prisoners, routed the Italians all the way and entered Addis Ababa. I flew south from Khartoum and became General Cunningham's DCPO in March. I thoroughly enjoyed service under Cunningham who gave me his full confidence even during the tricky times of the Emperor's return to his capital. He was every inch a soldier.

The Bishop, whom I will insert between the three Generals and the Pawns, was Sir Philip Mitchell, lately Governor of Kenya Colony and very much imbued with the ideals and practice of a colonial officer who had spent most of his service in Africa. He had been given the rank of General and created Wavell's Chief Political Officer for Africa - which comprised Cyrenaica (then under British Administration, alas temporary), all the Somalilands and Eritrea, and finally Ethiopia, the future and indeed the administration of which demanded all his skill and diplomacy. It was quite a new experience for him to deal with an independent African leader at one end, and the Foreign Office at the other. Mitchell was thus my superior; not only did he and I find complete agreement on policy, not without argument, but he finally found goodwill in the Foreign Office, though never with Dan Sandford (for whom however, he procured a CBE).

The three **Pawns** come next in order of appearance in the military scene. Dan Sandford was first. Oh! how I envied him in 1939! The movements and actions, the intentions and reactions, of Dan and I were so interlinked, at some times so mutually at variance and at others completely united, both having one object - the success of our own country in the prosecution of the war - that I have written at some length about his work in the early days of the war.

Dan was warned for active military service in the Middle East as early as August 1939. He was in Cairo by September attached to Intelligence Middle East Force, Cairo, where he found himself definitely in charge of the section dealing with Ethiopia, then part of the Italian East African Empire.

I had, as related, rejoined the Northern Province in October 1939, and for a year was entirely absorbed in Sudan civil duties. Dan could not share with me, a civil official of the Condominium, any military secrets whatever. In fact, during that year we met but little; I however, knew Dan's general intentions in case of war with Italy - revolt in Ethiopia to assist operations of British forces and the return of the Emperor to his throne.

While Italy remained neutral the British Government's policy was one of her appeasement: the British fleet showed a low profile in the Mediterranean; Mackereth, the British Consul General in Addis Ababa, was directed to make no attempt to communicate with Abyssinian elements hostile to Italy; the Italians were permitted, openly, to increase their air fleet in Ethiopia; priority was given to Italian ships in the Suez Canal; a general policy of appeasement to the Italians was adopted until 10 June 1940.

I remember myself, how a whole squadron of Italian military aircraft landed in Wadi Halfa in my Province, spent a day or two there, reconnoitred the surrounding country and flew away - all with our permission, in March 1940. The Intelligence Department in Khartoum were compelled to remain inactive; the Sudan had more information than other countries, eg. Egypt and Kenya, but all were coloured by friendly relations with the Italians. Dan formed the impression of views held in high places in the Sudan that it was doubtful if, on Italy declaring war, it would be morally justifiable to involve the Sudanese in a war between European powers. I too had heard this mooted by a senior executive in Khartoum and this view was undoubtedly thought to be in line with

British appeasement policy.

Before Italy came into the war, the plan of 101 Mission (a mission led by Sandford, and designed to enter Ethiopia and raise the revolt among the tribes) had been definitely decided upon and British and Ethiopian personnel had been selected. Dan wrote later: "I knew that active support to the Ethiopian rising would be the first and main action taken by us on the outbreak of war, and that I was cast for the role of Head of the Mission to go to Ethiopia."

Dan found the Governor General (Symes) and General Platt sceptical of the wisdom of backing the Emperor. "We had to break this down" he wrote; and he did.

In 1939 and 1940 Dan had made extensive tours of inspection to Nairobi and East Africa, the Somalilands, Djibouti (with General Wavell) and, of course, the Sudan.

Now we come to **Pawn Number 2**, the Emperor Haile Selassie, "the Pawn who thought he was a King".

It is necessary to go back in time to February and May 1936 when the Emperor, in desperate need, asked HMG's Minister in Addis Ababa whether the British Government would consider establishing under the League of Nations, a Protectorate or Mandate of Abyssinia. The request was made twice and twice refused by the Foreign Office in London. The British Minister's eloquent pleas that "the honour of his own country", Great Britain, and of the League should be vindicated by some further token of financial or material aid was likewise refused - a natural policy on the part of HMG but a refusal of help in the eyes of the defeated Emperor.

The Emperor soon after his arrival in the UK in 1936 had visited Geneva and delivered a speech to the Assembly of the League of Nations there with great dignity; but in spite of cogent arguments and demands for justice, the Assembly ignored him and in that very year of 1936, lifted sanctions against Italy - Great Britain and France were among the nations who supported the motion - and thenceforth the position of Abyssinia deteriorated sadly in international circles and annexation by Italy was affirmed. In 1936 the status of the exiled Emperor was very low in the eyes of the Foreign Office who still believed their consuls' stories of disaffection among the Galla and treated Dan as a disappointed exile spreading inaccurate information; indeed most people in England and other countries, came to regard the Italian conquest as permanent, the Emperor as one more exiled sovereign in our country.

Dan however, had always and especially during 1939 and 1940, envisaged the return of the Emperor to his own country as one of the essentials to the military success of the patriot plans. He knew the opinion of the Foreign Office and to his eternal credit he succeeded in over-riding that opinion. At some time - probably in June 1940 - a message from Wavell to the War Office definitely demanded the presence of the Emperor in Khartoum, ready to enter Abyssinia at the earliest possibility or when recommended by 101 Mission. This was a demand on tactical grounds from a C-in-C to Chiefs of Staff who would have found it hard to disregard - and so the Foreign Office were forced to agree - much against their own views. That is why Haile Selassie left London unbriefed.

The Foreign Office really disagreed with the return of the Emperor and, therefore, would not or did not, cooperate by properly briefing the returning "little man". This was a grave error of judgement which caused countless difficulties. They more or less washed their hands of him.

Wavell and his staff, with one exception, regarded the presence of the Emperor from a purely military point of view, viz. the undoubted impact on the patriots which could be made by Haile Selassie, their former commander, leading the Abyssinian forces to victory. Nevertheless, no-one, with the memory of 1936 not greatly dimmed, could have failed to realise that here was the case of an exiled ruler hoping to return home - to rule! But the soldiers had a war to win; such realisation was the job of the Foreign Office.

Of course return to his throne must have been in the hopeful mind of Haile Selassie when he was told by the Foreign Office that he would be flown out to the Sudan. George Steer tells a delightful story of the departure of the Emperor and his son, with three staff, from the Great Western Hotel, and the influence of Sir Sydney Barton, the former Minister in Addis Ababa, Thompson of the Foreign Office and himself in persuading the Foreign Office to allow Haile Selassie to join his "troops" in the Sudan. There is no doubt that the military chiefs had their say and that the Chiefs of Staff persuaded or overruled the Foreign Office, for the latter, six months later, were still averse to the Emperor entering his own country from the Sudan.

In fact Haile Selassie left the UK with the unwilling agreement of the Foreign Office who was his official host in London. He had a short interview with the Under Secretary of State for Foreign Affairs, R A Butler, the Permanent Head of the Department in the Foreign Office, who in 1936 had written most disparaging remarks about Abyssinia minuted "If we are going to send the Emperor out, we had better do it at once", and on 24 June 1940 the Emperor, accompanied by his second son Makonnen, two secretaries and George Steer, left Southampton in a Sunderland Flying Boat and arrived at Alexandria the next evening. They were met by Colonel Clayton of Middle East Intelligence (Dan's colleague at GHQ) and Chapman Andrews of the British Embassy Staff whom the Foreign Office had attached to the Emperor. There was *no* official recognition by the British Embassy and indeed Lampson the Ambassador had protested strongly at Haile Selassie's arrival "which will cause trouble here". The Egyptian Government was equally noticeable by their absence; the party were pushed on with great haste to the Sudan where the Governor General, equally strong in his disapproval at being made the unwilling host of this Emperor without a throne - indeed without a country - kept the party in the hotel at Wadi Halfa for a week. I, as Governor of the Province, knew he was there, but for obvious reasons of secrecy, refrained from visiting him. Dan arrived in Khartoum, full of enthusiasm and, according to Steer, "slapped his files down on the table and began to speak". Dan explained the strengths of the patriot movement in Gojjam. He talked of the 101 Mission about to enter Abyssinia - five officers with six radio sets, who hoped to contact the two (quarrelling) chiefs of Gojjam; arms and ammunition were being collected and a force of some 2,000 Sudanese troops was being formed to guard munition supply routes; some 20,000 rifles might be available and Dan hoped to have 3,000 rifles for an Imperial Bodyguard in Gojjam. There was no artillery; there were no aircraft detailed for the mission. In fact, at that time, the Italians had vast numerical superiority in numbers - and so he went on.

The Emperor, we are told, was "deeply distressed" at the paucity of arms and men earmarked for his use. "In England, I was promised full air support." He declared "It would have been better had I never left England." Steer relates that Dan was not in the least perturbed by this outburst.

The British Government, personified by the FO, had no policy for the future of this exiled Emperor, who, in the minds of many in the Abyssinian Department, was a "doubtful starter" in the Abyssinian stakes. Wavell and Dan, the soldiers, knew exactly what his role was. Later Winston Churchill himself was surprised to hear of the hesitation of the Foreign Secretary in approving of his crossing from the Sudan into Abyssinia in January, and it was he, Churchill, who "rather liked the idea of his crossing into his own native land". Churchill saw the military reason therefor - and as often, had the genius to understand the political advantage.

But at this moment, in Wadi Halfa, at the end of June 1940, less than a month since the Italians in Abyssinia had become our enemies, Haile Selassie must have begun to ponder on one or two facts. Why had there been no consultation with him before he left England? Why had his request for an Anglo-Ethiopian Treaty and the provision of British advisers been refused before he started? Why no reception in Cairo or the Sudan, as the Emperor returning to his throne? Why was he left incommunicado on entry into the Sudan, rather than be welcomed to the Governor General's Palace as the ruler of a neighbouring state?

The answers, which he could not possibly understand, were that Great Britain was at that moment fighting alone for her very existence - and for the existence of free people. In Ethiopia, thousands of miles away from the hub of war, there was a chance that the presence of the Emperor in his own country, would help the military success of British Forces - no less, no more. Haile Selassie was, therefore, brought nearer to that scene of possible hostilities. The decision to fly him to the Sudan was a military one, and nothing but, just as Orde Wingate's transfer to that theatre of war a few months later was a military decision. The future government and the political future of Abyssinia itself, had nothing whatsoever to do with this military decision. Haile Selassie, was a pawn, not a king, in the military chessboard. Locally in Khartoum, where he was practically incommunicado except to Abyssinians and a few officials who were wondrously good to him, he remained a pawn; but across the frontier among the *Habash*, the word spread like wildfire that *Janhoi*, the Emperor was about, spreading alarm among the Italians (for his presence surely presaged invasion from the Sudan?) and excitement with some degree of cohesion among the patriot Abyssinians. They saw that *Janhoi* was clearly the friend of the Sudani whom the Abyssinian rebels respected and feared and the Inglese who had aircraft. He was a rallying point which brought many doubters from *Rases* downwards to fight the "dogs and donkeys" of Italians.

Here we will leave Haile Selassie, still in Khartoum, for a spell, the focus for many Abyssinians who came to revere him in Khartoum (and possibly get a rifle and some cartridges). The task for his entertainment fell on Jose Penney, the Director of Intelligence, whose able and foreseeing mind kept the "little man in the Pink Palace" happy; George Steer who in a more personal way could amplify Penney's intentions, and Chapman Andrews, who probably never really understood how political problems must give way to military exigencies in time of war. If only they had brought me in! And so we come to the **Third Pawn** - myself.

Appointment as DCPO Ethiopia 15.1.41

I was summoned from Damer to Khartoum in mid-January 1941 to report to the Civil Secretary, Douglas Newbold, who told me that I had been chosen to lead the British Military Administration in Abyssinia, as our troops occupied the country, and that Kennedy Cooke, Governor of Kassala, had been chosen to do the same in Eritrea. We should receive our Commissions and orders at a meeting at the Palace the next day. Douglas was so nice: "I am devastated", he said, "at losing more political staff, but I am proud to be able to give two of our best Governors to the Army!"

It was clear that the battle in Ethiopia was about to be joined; that the goal was the defeat and eviction of the Italians from Ethiopia; that the first stages of creating revolt against the Italians by the tribes of Gojjam was succeeding (thanks to Dan); that the Emperor was already within his own country. I, myself was to play a part in this battle.

Off we went to the Palace and there we found our Governor General Huddleston, who introduced us to the Commander-in-Chief, General Wavell, the Secretary of State, Anthony Eden and General Dill, Chief of Staff. General Platt, of course was there, and Major General Sir Philip Mitchell, who had been appointed Chief Political Officer himself only a day or two before.

Invasion of Ethiopia : The Plan

The meeting had been discussing the plan of campaign in Ethiopia where the offensive was to take the form of a pincer-like attack on the Italian Forces throughout the territories. Platt would invade Abyssinia and Eritrea from the north and from the Sudan - the 4th Indian Division had been brought from Libya and Egypt to form the main force of this attack and assist the Sudan Defence Force and other troops. Platt was expected to enter Eritrea and then hook south to overcome the Italians in Central Abyssinia, and with the help of the Abyssinian patriots in Gojjam led by the Emperor, Sandford and Wingate, to march across the Blue Nile (Abbai) and capture Addis Ababa.

At the same time General Cunningham with southern, eastern and western African troops was to oust the Italians from their outposts in Kenya Colony, advance on Mogadishu through Italian Somaliland and drive the Italians from British Somaliland; advance north through Jig Jigga and Harar and meet Platt's forces in Addis Ababa.

We were also told at the meeting in Khartoum, that Mitchell, just appointed Chief Political Officer for the Administration of Occupied Enemy Territories, would delegate his powers to Deputy Chief Political Officers for the administration of Italian Somaliland, British Somaliland (rather a special case), Eritrea and Abyssinia. All personnel of the administration would have military rank and act under the military orders of either General Cunningham or Platt, through (for administrative purposes) the Chief Political Officer, General Mitchell. Our meeting at the Palace was the final item of a long and vital planning day for Wavell who came up to Khartoum to approve Platt's plans in the north (and we are told, instil some "pep" into that already peppery little man).

Turning to political matters, the first local administration would clearly be that of Eritrea, and Wavell himself appointed Kennedy Cooke to that assignment. As regards Abyssinia, he of course knew Dan Sandford, and admired greatly what he had planned and achieved. Turning to me he said: "Very glad to have you Lush. You know your sister is the king pin in this little outfit." For a C-in-C who was responsible for a vital battle then being fought in Libya, to remember details of this kind was typical of Wavell and it certainly touched my heart. He then turned and asked my rank as an officer in the Reserve. "Captain, Sir" I replied. "Well, I suppose you ought to be a Brigadier. You are a Brigadier!" And so, once more, I became an officer in the British Army and life became military again (and highly diplomatic and political to boot). I must record that "Huddle", by now my ex-Governor General, was fast asleep at this juncture in the meeting; it is also for the record that in Khartoum that evening Wavell had been told that a large part of his forces in Libya were to be diverted to Greece. It was good to have such personal contact with Eden and Wavell - the latter, now my Commander-in-Chief, who came to visit me later in Addis Ababa.

Of course the question of the Emperor's position was the first problem to discuss with Mitchell, my immediate chief and with others. Wavell had been adamant on the institution of British military administration and my first duty was to warn Mitchell that this decision would cause grave difficulty with the Emperor. It was decided that I should take an early opportunity in discussing the whole question with the Emperor, Sandford and Chapman Andrews.

So there we were, at the beginning of January 1941. Platt's attack from the north had as its objectives first Asmara and its port Massawa on the Red Sea, then turn south, driving the Italians into the guns of Cunningham's forces moving up from the south. DCPO Eritrea, Kennedy Cooke, would remain in Eritrea with Asmara and the active port of Massawa to keep him busy. This, in due course, he did most successfully. DCPO Abyssinia, myself would accompany Platt's force when they hooked south and advanced on Addis Ababa. Platt's zero hour was on 15 January, a week after our meeting, and my appointment was dated 15 January. General Cunningham in Nairobi, after several attacks on forts on or near the Kenya frontier, began his offensive against the Italian position from Juba, and the subsequent invasion of Italian and the then British Somaliland occurred on or about the same date in mid-January. But he had over 1,725 miles to cover through defended territory before reaching Addis Ababa which was not, at that time, his goal.

So DCPO Abyssinia and his staff, based on Khartoum, planned for the advance to Addis Ababa from the north. Luckily, a skeleton staff was already in Khartoum, headed by Travers Blackley of the Sudan Political Service, who was to be my No 2 or Secretary to the Administration. He worked wonders, planned wisely, managed to find and secure the men we wanted both for provincial and technical administration (mostly from the Sudan). I left recruitment and such to him. This gave me time to think out and discuss the political problem with those who knew Ethiopia and had seen the Emperor in Khartoum. I often wondered why I was not recruited earlier, to enable me to discuss and plan with the "little man" when he was in Khartoum. Would it have made any difference?.

I took a few days to return to Damer, hand over my Province to Bill Crawford, pack my belongings, store our furniture and finally dispose of myself, my property and my papers as Governor of Northern Province and, though I did not know it then, as a Civil Servant. It was very sad to pack up our family house which had so many memories of Diana and the children. But there was little time for sentiment, and hardly time to write to Diana telling her what was happening. I did write fully in January, a letter which one of Eden's staff agreed to take home. It arrived on Diana's desk in April!

Extract from letter to DRL from Damer 16.1.41:
"…. I was winding up the office, saying 'Goodbye' to the chaps, making speeches to clubs and ARP in Atbara"
Extract from a letter to DRL from Khartoum on 9.2.41:
"…. We are starting OETA (Occupied Enemy

Territory Administration) from O. I have got Travers Blackley, a tower of strength; and a young ADC called Laurie. I have a very good Indian Army Officer called MacLean .... I have Helen Foley as my secretary while I am in Khartoum. We may of course move at any moment. KC (Kennedy Cooke) has already gone with Duncan Cummings. I hope that Dan (DAS) may get in next week .... I am sure you would have agreed with me about leaving the NP and accepting this job. This is a duty which I could not turn down; it may lead to greater things; it may be a temporary job, but I feel it is my duty to make Abyssinia a better and happier country. It will be grand to work with Dan again, and with a mission about which he feels even more strongly than I do. No "Apostles" in the order, that is we must try to lay on sound administration before thinking of sentimental "returns to the fold" - and that is where I can help. Because, although I am desperately sorry for the "strong" man (ie. the Emperor) I do see the amazing difficulties before us. *And he may not come into the picture as soon as he would like.*"

Another extract from a letter dated 15.2.41:
".... The General (Platt) asked for me, and I could not refuse, even though it meant chucking our house in Damer, and security there for you. But it was my duty and also, I feel a call towards it. And, being a careerist, or so my friends call me, it may mean a lot, with employment after 50; there are more reputations lost than made in Ethiopia, but - well I am not going to start diffidently; and never have I been faced with such a job."

To re-trace my movements in time, I must record a memorable visit which I paid to General Alan Cunningham (and his staff) in Nairobi, Kenya, at the beginning of February 1941. Here, things were clearly about to move. I was very glad when the General, whom I liked immensely, asked me to stay and after dinner we discussed the possible problem of the Emperor's presence and desire to rule. Here, as with General Platt, I took a strong line as Chief Political Officer Abyssinia on the inevitable necessity of the restoration of the Emperor to his throne, and the difficult effects that would have on our attempts to administer Ethiopia. The General, as always, was frank and sharp to the point: "I don't care a damn, Lush, about your b....y Emperor; he can ascend his throne or go and boil himself; the territory occupied by my troops will be under my military administration, and you, Maurice Lush, will be the man to carry out my orders." Such were the very definite opinions of the other. My next move was, clearly, to find out the Emperor's intentions.

At last Dan returned to Khartoum from his 101 Mission far inside Ethiopia, a very disconsolate man because, under orders from on high (one suspects Winston Churchill), General Wavell had sent Erskine Wingate to take over from him the military side of the 101 Mission and the military operations which that Mission had made possible. Dan was to become principal military and political adviser to the Emperor, with Chapman Andrews (CA) as his assistant. It had all been done in a curious impersonal manner, without sufficient, if any, regard to the most courageous and highly successful work of 101 Mission, achieved entirely due to Dan's initiative, intelligence and great courage. However, Dan's new appointment was a very good choice for everyone concerned. As such Dan's views and my own often clashed, but never did our personal mutual respect fail.

I discussed the whole issue with Dan in Khartoum, received a grave warning from him of "rocks ahead" and so went to see the Emperor. We left Khartoum in a captured Italian Caproni aircraft (filled with petrol and ammunition) and flew to the airstrip at Belaya, 150 miles inside Abyssinia. The flight was alarming but uneventful; the landing on the hastily prepared strip was hazardous, bumpy and bruising. The aircraft was immediately surrounded by "revolting" Abyssinian patriots (all loyal to their Emperor) who then cleared a way for Dan to conduct me on mule, some miles into the vastness of Mt Belaya, as far as the hide-out of the Emperor.

The following extract from a letter dated 21.2.41 to Diana, describes the scenery, written from Belaya, Ethiopia (enemy territory) some 150 miles from the Sudan frontier. We were about to discuss the future of Ethiopia, a country not yet in British hands, with the erstwhile ruler of that country, not yet on his throne:

".... One step forward for OETA. I am sitting in a towel by the side of the most lovely rippling stream, having flown out with Dan yesterday to hold "strong" discussions. It is a lovely place miles from anywhere, the tops of which look so near but are, as I am told, 5 hours away. I am entering the diplomatic stage of my job (which grows bigger every moment) and have had two long and I suppose pretty important discussions. Dan has been present, of course, and CA to take notes. It hasn't been easy to get across this dual control business, but I hope, with patience, to carry it off and get back in a day or two, also by air. My staff is gradually filling up and our plans are becoming more and more crystallised, and we are ready to leap forward at a moment's notice.

"I can't tell you what fun it is and how I am looking forward to the immense difficulties ahead - difficulties which will not be made easier by the "strong" presence. Dan and I see absolutely eye to eye over this and the only snags are my restricted terms of elasticity and "strong" amour propre and considerations for the future. In the meantime, between discussions and "strong" tea-parties I sit on a rock by the running water and think of you. It is good to be in real country again and to think that we may all enjoy it as time goes on. I hope very much that Dan doesn't feel that he ought to have my job - he certainly will work with me whatever he feels, but we shall both have many difficult corners to get round, and honestly I don't believe that any other two people could navigate them without foundering. (There is the most lovely kingfisher, red and green and gold, sitting on a branch just by me and the noise of the water is filling me with good health!).

"Dan returned from Cairo [to Khartoum] on Saturday last (about 15th February) and we had three busy days with him before setting off. We treat Skeeto's (Hasler Skeet) place just like a hotel and the evening before we left my room looked like the cloakroom of a railway station, with all the gear strewn about. I travelled very light and am sleeping on the ground (no bed!) but find it most comfortable; certainly not less so than in a plaster of Paris. Blackley came in on Sunday and Lizzie Laidlaw. They are getting down to their particular jobs of work and I shall have a lot to do on the paper side when I get back. Dan is in his tent, dictating letters and Donald Knott, his erstwhile Staff Captain is working in another hut. The "strong" position is down stream; all I long for is a couple of days to climb the hills .... Must go now and bathe."

I returned to Khartoum and reported to General Platt on my failure to move the Emperor's insistence on "L'Ethiopie c'est moi". Platt, busy with his own war in the north, packed me off to see Wavell in Cairo who was similarly intransigent and told me to make the best of it on the spot. Mitchell, with more understanding of the impossible situation in which I should find myself, agreed, and so I perhaps foolishly accepted the well nigh impossible situation of administering parts of Ethiopia in the name of the British Commander, without the goodwill of the man who insisted on wielding his authority, which that same British Commander had enabled him to exercise, by British military skill and force of arms. The Ethiop is difficult enough to administer (by anything like modern means) in ordinary circumstances, as the Emperor was to find himself, but when the white face of the interloper is added to the difficulty, only trouble could be expected and we in the British Military Administration received rebuffs and refusals almost daily - without, thanks to the stamina and loyal understanding of my team, any grave crisis. I quote from a letter to Diana written at the time:

24.2.41

".... Well, I'm a long way from where I began this letter and am now in the air making for our home '35-38 (Cairo). I had such a jolly three days with Dan and though discussions brought out the immense difficulties ahead, I came away feeling that we were all friends and all out for one objective.

".... Got into Khartoum for tea .... found Travers Blackley had been doing great things .... I just worked on at my particular headache which is the matter of form between my show and "strong"; you can imagine what they are like; but do tell Chris that I am full of sympathy and not hide-bound or rigid. Yesterday I had a long talk to the *Kaid* (Platt) who was most awfully helpful and said "Off you go to Cairo and do what you can" .... I am simply delighted that they have made Dan a Brigadier. Don't tell Chris, but I did it - at least I wrote to the *Kaid* .... the *Kaid's* wire to the C-in-C got there just before Dan, and the C-in-C promoted him on the spot! I was glad and every one was tremendously pleased. He is a very well known and much admired figure, is Dan, and fully he deserves it. He has not had a bed to sleep on nor any European food to eat for months.

(Continued from Cairo:)

".... I think we have found a formula (with the C-in-C in Cairo) which will give us a modus operandi with "strong" .... Had Francis Rodd to dinner, Financial Adviser to PM; seems a first rate fellow .... Saw HE (Lampson) and had a long talk."

10.3.41

".... I am off tomorrow to see Dan and "strong" again."

We were at a good altitude (6,000ft) and the climate was very good compared even with the "cold weather" in Khartoum.

My job was to bring the Emperor round to the C-in-C's way of thinking. Dan and I, with Chapman Andrew, discussed how to overcome the insuperable problem of British Military rule of Ethiopia (or those parts of Ethiopia conquered and occupied by British Military forces) with government by the Emperor as ruler of his country. After a meal, we were received by the "little man"; he was charming, asked after my health since my train accident; we talked about the old days when I had stayed in his camp in the mountains (Wochecho) near Addis Ababa twenty years before. He was truly and outspokenly grateful for Dan's exploits in 101 Mission. But when we embarked on the subject of how Ethiopia was to be administered, he had but one answer: "By me, the Emperor; the ruler of the country." We talked. I submitted all the compromise possible - Proclamations to be issued by the Emperor only; Platt's and Cunningham's orders to take the form of local orders only. I met a complete negative answer. After a subsequent, no more successful interview next day, I told the "little man" that whatever my orders were from my Generals - Wavell (whom I would consult in Cairo), Platt and Cunningham commanding the British troops who would drive the Italians from his country - that whatever orders I received, I would earnestly try to assist him in the return to his country. I added that I hoped that any troubles from dual administration would be small and that I would do my best to overcome them. He was not obviously impressed.

I flew to Khartoum the next day. In Khartoum I handed to General Platt a memorandum of reconciliation, proposing a form of administration which I believed would work and would have the goodwill of the Emperor. In particular I strongly recommended that the issue of Proclamations should be a matter for the Emperor only, and that the C-in-C should be content with Public Notices - which would have the same force in law. Platt endorsed my memorandum which I took to

Cairo next day by air.

In Cairo my CPO, Philip Mitchell, and I had a long discussion and conference with Wavell's staff, and finally with the C-in-C himself, finishing with a cable to London which indicated that the C-in-C required military administration in occupied territories. And that was that! I was expected (with great sympathy from Wavell and Mitchell) to do what I could. On 3 March I flew again in my Italian Caproni to a landing ground near Burye (a good deal further east than Belaya), met the Emperor, gave him Wavell's message and assured a stony faced little man of my personal help in carrying out my orders; Dan and I had a look at Dongola, where we were bombed, and I flew home - slightly alarmed at spotting another Italian Caproni in the air - but he sheered off and we reached home.

These two air sallies, 150 miles and 300 miles inside enemy territory in captured Italian aircraft which flew slowly but surely, laden with petrol and ammunition for the patriots, would have been a wracking experience had it not been for the faultless courage of the RAF pilots who had entered into the spirit of 101 Mission - an operation planned with the knowledge of the tremendous obstacles presented by the landscape, with faith in the spirit of the Abyssinians whose loyalty to their Emperor was undoubted, certain that the Emperor at the head of thousands of patriots would return to his throne supported by the population of Ethiopia.

It was quite an experience to land this far inside enemy territory - even though Sudanese and patriot forces were in complete control. We felt perfectly safe on land knowing that the Italian forces feared us more that we feared them, though this thrust was but a spearhead into hostile territory. The flight back to Sudan territory exposed one, as it seemed, to dangers in a stratum where the odds were not so balanced in our favour; one was wrong; the Italians, at that time, did not dare to expose themselves to their British-Sudanese enemy, even by air - and we returned to Roseires and Khartoum unmolested. In a way one felt that one had earned ones spurs!

British Military Administration in Africa (Rennell) page 64; paragraph 2;

> "After his visit to Cairo, Brigadier Lush returned to Ethiopia to meet the Emperor at Burye, and communicate to him the C-in-C's detailed and preliminary decisions taken in Cairo on 24 February .... after some modification had been made a modus vivendi was worked out with the Emperor at Burye."

Let me say here that the Emperor never intended any "modus vivendi" to work!

DCPO under General Cunningham

On March 4, we had the great news of General Cunningham's advance from Mogadishu and during that week, I packed a small suitcase with a change of underclothes, and took advantage of BGS (Brigadier General Staff) from Cairo, by the name of Whitely flying south to see "how things were in Nairobi". We landed at Kampala in Uganda, motored to Nairobi (a terrible road then) and found that the bird had flown! My BGS raised a small aircraft and in we bundled en route for Jig Jigga, the northern town of British Somaliland. Cunningham had made a tremendous leap forward through British Somaliland from Mogadishu which was captured with stores and personnel and 400,000 gallons of petrol! It's a long way from Nairobi to Jig Jigga (in a 1941 small aircraft) and the sun was setting as we approached. "For God's sake, Sir, can you spot two landing bulbs'?" said the pilot "before dark otherwise we are lost." We did and landed at dusk. It was a hair-raising end to a momentous flight.

In Jig Jigga I slept and shaved "rough", but at 10 am next morning arrived at General Cunningham's HQ and reported as his DCPO Abyssinia. He was in tremendous form, gave me a great welcome, and when Brigadier Whitely, my air companion had left to go and have a "look see" with the forward troops, he threw all his political problems at me. Brigadier Seapham, the DCPO Somaliland had, rightly accompanied Cunningham to Jig Jigga, and was very anxious to remain with the HQ until we reached Addis Ababa - equally was he sorry to see me! However, I insisted on taking over there and then, for Cunningham's troops were well on their way to Harar, the second most important town in Abyssinia, the good administration of which was essential to the good name of my General's (and my own) administration.

Harar

Harar was my first administrative and political problem: the second largest town in Abyssinia, the native country of the Emperor's father, Ras Makonnen, centre of a Province having a large Moslem population (Harar town itself was divided into two parts, half Moslem, half Christian); it had in truth belonged to Egypt until late 19th Century, a focus of attention and encouragement, well favoured towards the Moslems by the Italian Government. It was a ticklish proposition for British Administration to handle as a first endeavour, with no political staff whatever, except myself.

However, on that point of staff, Brigadier Seapham was more than generous. He whistled up several officers, destined to administer Italian Somaliland, led by Lt Colonel Dallas, a magnificent character (notable for his gait, for he had but one leg) and several others, and between them they had a dual administration (Ethiopian and Italian) running in no time. Alas, the administration of Harar on this satisfactory basis was not to continue for many weeks, as will be seen in later pages.

I quote from my own DCPO's report to OETA for Feb-Sept 1941: paragraph v:

> **HARAR:** Lt Col Dallas began his administrative work in Ethiopia as Political Officer in Harar Province immediately after British occupation of that place. He instituted Italian Committees and ran a dual administration, that is to say Ethiopian in the walled

native city, and Anglo-Italian in the European commune. After his transfer to Addis Ababa and prior to the arrival of Prince Makonnen, Duke of Harar, whom His Majesty appointed Governor of the Province, his successor substituted Ethiopian for Italian administration and police throughout Harar and Dire Dawa. Lt Col Feasey arrived with Prince Makonnen and took over the duties of Senior Political Officer.

Harar had sent the white flag of the surrender of the city and although there had been heavy artillery fire immediately before the capitulation, our East African troops and after them the South African gunners entered Harar without a shot being fired. The official account reads:

"Here again was encountered the remarkable friendliness of the native population. The European inhabitants were segregated from the native quarter and it was comparatively simple to start the dual administration of the native and Italian quarters which, under my orders, Dallas established speedily and with excellent results. Here he used the existing forces of administration and police, at first leaving it to his successors, for as will be seen I was compelled to take him with me to the capital."

I do not remember details of our occupation of Harar, in fact I do not think that I passed a night there. General Cunningham did not move his HQ to the town, leaving his Divisional Commander, Major General Charles Wetherall in charge, with the Nigerian Brigade under Brigadier Smallwood. General Wetherall's troops had captured Harar on the evening of 25 March and the South African Brigade took over the next advance. I quote the official account of the military operations from *The Abyssinian Campaigns*, (HMSO 1942) p98:

"It is 35 miles from Harar to Dire Dawa. One crosses at first the well-watered, high plateau, where there are many native villages, but the last 15 miles contains some of the craziest scenery in this part of Africa. Here the motor road pours, as it were, between twin peaks over the edge of the 7,000' tableland and plunges down a 10-mile, 4,000' cascade to where Dire Dawa, hot and mosquito-ridden, stands at the foot of the hills on the Addis Ababa - Djibouti Railway. It is a perfect road for demolition, and the South Africans found that the Italian engineers had made the most of it. They had blown up several bridges at points on the plateau itself, and further on they had blasted the mountainside creating chaos and dizzy drops at five of the steepest places. One of the craters caused by these demolitions was 70 yards long and together they formed such a serious obstacle that it was originally believed it would take eight days to fill them. However, the 1st South African and the 54th East African Field Companies and the Nigerian Regiment, which was moved up to assist them, attacked the task with such vigour that, working day and night, they had cleared the road in only 36 hours.

"It is remarkable that the Italians used these demolitions merely as a means of gaining time. They made little effort to defend them except in the case of the first, where two companies of machine-gunners, consisting mostly of officers of the regular army type, whose original units had disintegrated, put up a really gallant resistance from nearby peaks and held up the advance until nightfall. But this was a delaying action rather than a rally, and two companies of the 1st Transvaal Scottish, who set off on foot before the road was open, entered Dire Dawa unopposed on 29 March."

There had been a devastating attack on Dire Dawa airfield previous to the unopposed occupation of the town which was more of a European railway colony and had little place in the Ethiopian centres of authority. The population was extremely bomb-shocked, but its surrender was important, for immediately General Cunningham was able to whistle up from Italian Somaliland his railway engineers and mechanical units, already occupied in railway reorganisation there; for with the fall of Berbera, lines of communication, even without the Djibouti - Dire Dawa stretch of railway, could be considerably shortened. With my previous knowledge, albeit that of a layman, of the Franco-Ethiopian line I was able to help from the vital communication point of view. I also managed somehow to arrange a pattern of (Italian) administration in the very European town.

The little town, where the Abyssinian brass band had entertained the rather typical but slightly haughty MP and his lady friend, was terribly changed. A long conspicuous hotel had been built and I was nostalgic for the orange blossom and bougainvillaeas of the little Greek albergo where Diana and I had slept on our railway journey to Addis Ababa in 1932, now gone. But we, the British, were there again.

It was tremendous to foresee an *Anglo*-Ethiopian Railway! I quietly left Harar in the good hands of Dallas and remained thereafter for a week based at Army HQ. For not only were problems of geography and topography prominent on my reference board, but the surrender of Addis Ababa, 300 miles away, was not only very much in the air but the GOC and the military commanders wanted to know what were my intentions therein.

Towards Addis Ababa

The official report states that I arrived at General Cunningham's HQ only just in time to make arrangements for the taking over of Addis Ababa, and that is what we tried to do.

The Italians had let it be known that Addis Ababa would be an "open city" that is to say, British troops when they reached the outskirts would enter the city unopposed; of course had the advance from the south not swept forward with such rapidity, I should have had my skeleton staff by my side, and we should have been armed with plans and photographs of the city, political and technical offices would be available and we would have known where to go. As it was, there was only Lush and one Political Officer borrowed from Italian Somaliland Administration. There was also one important personal factor - General Cunningham and his staff consulted me on all political matters, appeared to trust me, and took me unto themselves.

We were all agreed that the protection of the white population was serious and of the highest priority and the avoidance of incidents of paramount importance. We arranged for segregation of the Italian population under Indian armed guard and British protection. I myself vouched for the good behaviour of the Ethiopians. Plans for contact were finalised.

We asked for permission to drop leaflets by air on to Addis Ababa, signed "Wavell". The terms of surrender presented by General Cunningham were handed to an Italian officer, who arrived by Italian aircraft at Mieso on 3 April. The officer was extremely courteous and arrived bearing a case of wine which General Cunningham refused. He returned next day with the Italian reply.

The Army Commander, Alan Cunningham, was a tower of strength to his DCPO whom he sent forward with the Divisional Commander, General Wetherall, to make all the administration plans.

Throughout the last days of March and the first days of April 1941 I worked out in detail with General Weatherall the way in which I would like security and the plans of the campaign for the investment of Addis Ababa, containing 12,000 armed troops and 150,000 Ethiopians. I am not sure that I had any accurate idea of these numbers in my planning discussions with General Wetherall who elected, very wisely, to select one Brigade only of troops to occupy the straggling town.

We had a map, not a very good one, of the city. I recommended allowing the Italian troops to remain in situ when our troops entered and invested the quarters of the town delineated for them. I arranged for a company of South African police to take over the existing Italian *Carabinieri* and to use them in the divisions of the city agreed upon. I took the responsibility of disarming these Carabinieri at my discretion during the initial stages.

I cannot describe the air of confident, hopeful excitement which filled our hearts and minds during those few days before the fall of Addis Ababa. Italian morale had broken. Demolition of bridges and roads were now their only means of opposition and even these they failed to defend or make more difficult the overcoming of the destruction which they caused.

The abandonment of that great defensive obstacle the Awash Gorge was typical. The Italians had intended to hold it as a last obstacle to save the capture of the capital; both road and railway bridges were destroyed. But the King's African Rifles crossed by a ford slightly higher upstream and charged the Italians defending. The Italians replied with inaccurate field fire or fled; the road bridge was in action again at sunset that day. I cannot remember accurately but I think I drove over that evening. I looked at the railway station; the "hotel" with its almost cell-like rooms where I had often passed the night, had gone!

Entry into Addis Ababa

At last the day came, the day I had hoped and worked for since January - the British entry into Addis Ababa, 6 April 1941. British patrols had reached the capital on the evening of 5 April and indeed white flagged Italian officers had come out on that evening, entreating us to enter the town. For the Italians, from top to bottom, were terrified that, left without the protection of British soldiers, their civilian population of 50,000 men, women and children would be exterminated by the Ethiopians if left to their mercy, in spite of 12,000 armed Italian soldiers and police which they were allowed to retain for their protection.

However, General Cunningham decided to occupy Addis Ababa on 6 April and on that morning General Wetherall and I (bearing flags) with his Divisional Staff and Brigade Commanders and I think one or two armoured cars, were met some miles out of the town by a representative of the Military Governor and the Head of Police, who were to conduct us to the Italian HQ in the Duke of Aosta's Palace for the formal act of surrender.

Before we started, the Chief of Police confided to me that, knowing that traffic regulations in Great Britain differed from Italian rules, he had, for some days, been instructing his police and traffic officers to drive on the left - a courteous gesture, one of many other such examples.

It took a good half hour before we reached the town of Addis Ababa itself, and found the streets lined with Italian and native troops, large crowds of Ethiopians, all of whom gave us the Fascist salute, many Ethiopian women, a few quietly ululating, a largish number of the non-Italian population including women, Armenians, Lebanese, Greek and even a few Italian civilians. Italian officers and officials peered down at us from inside the buildings.

A vanguard of press representatives had preceded us in a few miscellaneous vehicles, but the thousands on the streets could not really believe that our score or less of cars and vehicles represented the might of the British Empire, arrived in triumph to take the surrender of the capital of Ethiopia. No tanks? No guns? No bands? They did not understand the British way of conduct. To the Italians (and the Ethiopians) the seat of the mighty Italian East African Empire had fallen - an epoch-making event. To the British, this was no political conquest with the object of changing the history of the Horn of Africa; to us, the advance and occupation was all part of a military undertaking which had as its object the destruction or capture of the large Italian Army in the Horn of Africa - an Army which was a menace to the British intention of destroying her enemies and winning the war; the political effects of this day's surrender meant nothing to Generals Cunningham and Wavell who left Addis Ababa as soon as the troops had established security in the town, taken the surrender of the 12,000 Italian troops within and many more from the forts outside; they left with their Brigades to destroy the remnant of the Italian forces in the north.

On we went that morning; I had the General's procession deflected so that we could pass the Emperor's Palace which I pointed out to General Wetherall as the scene of the second flag raising ceremony. But let me quote a paragraph on the ceremony from *The Abyssinian Campaign* p105:

"Inside the gates of the Duke of Aosta's palace all was ready for the ceremony. In front and a little to one side of the massive, rather heavy building of grey stone, with the sculptured eagle, stood a Fascist Guard of Honour, while on the central steps General Mambrini, the Military Governor of the capital, dressed in all the greens and yellows and buttons of Italian senior officers, awaited the arrival of the British. The ceremony was short and extremely to the point. A squad of Italian police, riding motor bicycles and dressed in shiny black, swept up the drive. Behind them, in cars, came Major General Wetherall, Divisional Commander, Brigadier Pienaar, Commander of the 1st South African Brigade, which had forced the Juba line and captured Diredawa, and Brigadier Fowkes, Commander of the 22nd East African Brigade, which had captured Afmadu, Brava and Merka, and later led the advance from the Awash. They had their staffs with them, but no troops. The only show of force was one armoured car, which flew a Union Jack home-made by a daughter of Kenya's Attorney-General, Mr Walter Harragin. This car parked itself under a convenient tree a short distance from the palace, and seemed to eye the ceremony with an attitude of apologetic benevolence. The British officers were greeted by the Italian representatives, received the salute from the Fascist Guard of Honour, and went immediately into the palace in order to complete the necessary arrangements.

The only touch of pageantry concerned the flags. In the centre of the lawn before the palace stood a 40-foot pole, from which the Italian flag had been hauled down a trifle prematurely. General Weatherall ordered that it should be re-flown and saluted with full honours. After that the Union Jack was raised in its place and greeted with Fascist salutes from the Italian officers and the Italian Guard of Honour. That was the end of one of the most businesslike ceremonies on record."

The "necessary arrangements" mentioned in these paragraphs consisted of a repetition of the terms of surrender agreed upon on 4 April in the field, and General Wetherall's introduction of myself to the assembled Italian counsellors. Among the latter I noticed, and exchanged bows and smiles with Commendatore Piacentini who had been Italian Minister in Addis Ababa in 1921, and had distinguished himself only by seducing and marrying the very attractive wife of the amicable French Doctor Germaine. He, however, did not last long and was sent down to Nairobi as a prisoner of war.

A very appetizing luncheon had been prepared, and was served to us in the hall of the Palace, which we demolished heartily. The Italian host prisoners excused themselves. It was a typical Italian gesture we had every right to accept.

Immediately afterwards, I was in touch with the hungry Italians, and chose from them the men I wanted to consult. I also managed to get hold of the leading Ethiopian - be he pro-Italian or not, I knew that I could extract news from him.

Two facts of temperament astonished us all during that memorable 24 hours; firstly, the courtesy and good manners of the Italians - soldiers and civilians in defeat; the day's programme of surrender had gone without a hitch or a sour face; the behaviour of the leading Italians had been impeccable and although we knew then, and discovered later definitely, that dirty games were afoot, nothing was done, so far as I could see, to stop the wheels of their administration from functioning smoothly. Secondly, as soldiers, those units well away from Addis Ababa who had not surrendered continued the battle, and our forces continuing northwards found effective opposition in places.

Immediately after the hoisting of the Union Jack and the surrender of the Italians and their city by General Mambrini, the Italian military Governor, I took General Wetherall and his Brigadier to the Emperor's Palace, or little *Ghebbi* where we had a ceremonial hoisting of the Ethiopian flag amidst scenes of great rejoicing. General Wetherall made a short speech which I tried to translate and the General was mobbed by the delighted population which ululated in the queer Ethiopian way: they wrung his hands and kissed his feet. I was able then to tell the Ethiopians that I had seen their Emperor at Burye last month and that he was ready to join them in Addis Ababa soon.

The capture of Addis Ababa thus took an entirely practical form. The troops of the occupying army went straight to their appointed places, guided by Italian officers and police; the Ethiopians welcomed their deliverers (with the Fascist salute!) and were on the streets in crowds. The non-Italian fraternities - Greeks, Armenians and Lebanese - were there too, some throwing flowers; the Italian civilians appeared at windows, always apprehensive and especially of the fact that so many of the victorious troops were African.

After the ceremonies my first duty was to learn the new (to me) Addis Ababa, and this I did with enormous personal and nostalgic interest; at the same time I managed to visit the locations of the British Army units garrisoning the town and the locations of the Italian Army units who had remained behind as a protection against the possible Ethiopian attacks, being allowed to maintain their arms.

It was a really wonderful day and the scene was quite

extraordinary during that sunny, almost peaceful afternoon: the 150,000 Ethiopians and the many thousands or so of mixed races - Levantine, Indian, African - all wonderfully but peacefully happy. The Italian civilians, guarded by Italian troops, were numbed and fearful. Some of them must have heard stories of, or even seen the results of the shooting, rioting, looting and killing which broke out in Addis Ababa when the Emperor departed, defeated in 1936. It certainly passed through my mind. But we need not have been anxious: a happy Ethiopian is controllable. The British entry into the surrendered city had been typically British: no sign of triumph over a beaten enemy, no gesture of aggression or superiority. The quiet, unassuming behaviour from the General, who took the surrender, to the private soldiers of the Nigerian and East African Brigade, who went quietly to their appointed area, all created an atmosphere of quiet dignity and peacefulness on the part of victor and vanquished alike:

> "The atmosphere in Addis Ababa during the first 48 hours" writes the official chronicler, "seemed curiously unreal. Here were British, Italians and Abyssinians all living together in the same city, yet everything was peaceful and no-one was cutting anyone else's throat."

The fact was that the surrender had been peacefully made and peacefully accepted. Everyone, including the Ethiopians seemed determined to continue that atmosphere of peace. And to me, the maintenance of that peace was a primary duty.

I visited as many parts of the Ethiopian quarter (which were segregated from the Italians) as I could, and met as many leading Ethiopians and Levantines (ie. merchants and shopkeepers) as I could. I left the Italian civilian population, guarded by the armed Italian soldiers, to the watchful eye of our own troops who were at their appointed stations. The Ethiopians were still policed by the Italian-appointed Ethiopian police - armed. I spoke to many Ethiopians and was able to talk to some of their leaders. I told them that their Emperor was at Debra Marcos, ready to come in when the Italians had gone. So far, so good - but I learnt a disturbing piece of news: that there were in the city some thousands of Blackshirt Polizia, in and around the city, all armed - the Italians regarded them as soldiers.

I told General Wetherall that he would have a quiet night (which he did) and then went off with Dallas to disarm those Blackshirts - the only people who might have proved me wrong.

Either then, or possibly before our entry, I had, on a brain wave, suggested that one Colonel Hayton - Deputy Provost Martial of the South African Brigade - with his company of South African Police, should take over the entire policing of the city, using the Italian Chief of Police and his men until such time as we could raise an Ethiopian police force in the city. Colonel Hayton was magnificent: his South African Company was the backbone of the initial Police Force of Addis Ababa. Their very presence and really wonderful relations with Ethiopians and Italians assured the security of the city.

Dallas and I spent most of the first night disarming the Blackshirts in various police stations on the outskirts of the town, reassuring ourselves of security and finally found two beds, baths and breakfast at dawn, in the old Italian Consulate way outside town.

It had been an anxious dramatic night, dealing with men in a defeated force - once the most blustering, cruel part of the force - who were fearful, approaching panic. I was glad to know that these had been rounded up next morning as prisoners of war, and joined by another Blackshirt force of 1,000 men, undeclared, but discovered on the race course - an isolated case of not Italian but Fascist duplicity.

The next day, 7 April, I set up my HQ in the old Italian office of the Palace - begged, borrowed or stole some clerical staff from Divisional Headquarters, sent Dallas and a charming young man named Guy Shipp (from Aden) who had joined us in the previous day as my Chief of Staff, to make contact with men of note, while I tried to lure leaders among the Ethiopians, Levantines and others to visit me and help me in making a plan for the administration of Addis Ababa and the parts of Ethiopia which we had already occupied and would hope to cover in the near future. I was at pains to eliminate irate Italians from my visitors though I welcomed the Italian commercial or industrial groups. I made it abundantly clear that as soon as the military situation permitted - and this included the removal of all armed Italians from Addis Ababa - we hoped to bring the Emperor himself to his capital.

I heard from General Wetherall that day that Rommel had begun his operations in Libya.

I gathered an immense amount of information from my many visitors in that first week; my two stalwarts, Dallas and Shipp, learnt as much on the matter of local day to day administration. We combined it all at meal times; where we had those meals, or indeed where we lived for the first ten days in Addis Ababa, I cannot remember with certainty. I think I found a cubbyhole next to my office. And there I made my personal HQ. For, although I visited the city (and sometimes the environs) once a day and reported and probably had a meal with my Divisional Commander every day, I found that my small office on the ground floor of the Palace, approachable to all, had become a great centre of civil information.

Let me now turn to a quandary in which the DCPO found himself. During the first week the Roman Catholic Bishop, the representative of the Vatican in Italian East Africa, called on me with no little ceremony. He committed to the care of Great Britain the earthly lives of his flock; he was assured of their safety so long as they obeyed the regulations of the British Military Administration.

Having learnt the art of protocol (in Cairo) I repaid the visit at no long interval. He lived on Entotto Hill, a mile out of the city. I entered his sacred house; I found a British Lieutenant and several British NCOs. The Holy Father - I don't think he was a Cardinal - the

Monsignor, was in a state of agitation. "A bit of bother here, Sir," said the Lieutenant, who was from Intelligence, "found a packet of rifles in the chest in the hall and a transmitting wireless set in this auto outside." It all seemed true enough. "Could the Holy Father give an explanation?" I asked the Monsignor, explaining that I had come to return his call. "The wireless set transmitted only to the Vatican" he explained; the arms he had forgotten.

It was with difficulty that I prevented the officer, perfectly correctly, from removing the Bishop to a POW camp forthwith. He was a sensible young man and had the wisdom to accept advice from me. We shipped the Monsignor away, quam celerrime, with the next batch of high ranking POWs, en route (by road) to Nairobi.

A few years later I told this story to HH Pope Pius XII who already knew it from the miscreant Monsignor and had posted him to Northern Italy.

Incidentally throughout my service in Military Administration in the theatre of war I found that the Intelligence Corps were not really in touch with OETA whom, I know, they distrusted. Civilians were interrogated and removed from the theatre without reference to me or my officers and information was seldom exchanged.

On about 10 April a notable visitor arrived in his own aircraft, which he had piloted from Aden, braving the French (Djibouti) and British air defence. I had last seen him in Aden in 1919 typing his own correspondence in a small office in the Crater. He was Antonin Besse, and he came to place his oil distribution facilities at British disposal in Ethiopia and to ask for "most favoured nation" treatment for the Shell company, whose agent he was.

A curious visitor was Gaston Palewski, who arrived from nowhere with no credentials. He was of course, General de Gaulle's confidant and had undoubtedly been sent to spy out the land of Ethiopia. He was friendly and sympathetic, but would not stay to lunch saying he wished to examine the state of the French Legation in Addis Ababa; whence he came and whither he went I never discovered.

The Emperor's man Dejaz Makonnen came too - by air from Debra Marcos; also Dan. They of course, with others, had the same question. "When will the Emperor come into Addis Ababa?" To which I and my staff gave one stock reply: "When the military situation permits."

My CPO, Philip Mitchell, arrived and of course our Finance expert, Francis Rennell, anxious about currency. This was indeed a difficult matter, for we intended to replace the Italian paper currency with the old Maria Theresa dollar which we had arranged to be especially minted in Bombay.

Then on 16 April, eleven days after the surrender of Addis Ababa, there arrived a transport aircraft from Khartoum carrying my OETA team, led by Travers Blackley. Their late arrival on the scene should not be laid at their feet; the eyes of Khartoum were fixed on General Platt's exploits - indeed his hard struggle - in the north. Keren had not fallen until the last days of March and Asmara on 1 April. Massawa, vital port for the allies, fell only after we had entered Addis Ababa. No wonder the carrying of Political Officers to Addis Ababa took a low priority.

Nevertheless they came: Travers Blackley my most valiant second in command; Frank Stafford from Nigeria who managed the Finance of Ethiopia; Laidlaw, who began forming an Ethiopian Corps of Police almost before he left the aircraft; Derek Lomax, my Magistrate and Justice who had taught Maxwell, my Legal Adviser in the Sudan; fairly aged but nice. There were also Corfield, Elliot Smith, Laurie, de Bunsen all from the Sudan, and destined to go out to Ethiopian Provinces; Jack Maurice for Gambeila and Dick Whalley for the south west. For a month or more, they had been studying their jobs on paper - there were no precedents - and never have I seen a team tackle the unknown in practice with better heart or more satisfactory results; never were a dozen men more warmly welcomed.

The unpublished history of the campaign by one Colonel Barton records that the arrival of the OETA team was much appreciated by the military. My team just had time to get their teeth into their jobs before the Emperor entered his capital on 5 May.

Telling Diana about my staff later in a letter I wrote:

> ".... I, at last, have a staff which is out to assist me and indeed prevent work reaching me."

Again:

> ".... The most intimate of my staff is my young Personal Assistant John Lawrence, who is destined for the Uganda Civil Service and has been a gunner for 18 months."

He, like the rest of them, served me magnificently. With the arrival of this really splendid team I was able to turn my thoughts and actions to a more personal matter. Where should we live?

With the help of the Provost Martial and his men I took charge of the keys of His Brittanic Majesty's Legation and Consulate, with the many extra buildings in the Legation area and compound which I had known so intimately and maintained 20 years before. Normally the residence and buildings would be sacrosanct until a member of HM Diplomatic or Consular Service arrived; but in the circumstances then prevailing it seemed ridiculous that this fine estate should not play its part in the military salvation of Ethiopia and give comfort and amenity to part of the military forces - and what better part than either the General Officer Commanding or his Political Officer? In these terms, I put the case to General Cunningham and my chief, Mitchell, and they to the Foreign Office. I did not wait for an answer - I occupied every building using the Legation as my own Residence and Mess. We had twenty officers housed in the estate and when, bless her heart, Lady Sydney Farrar, the Queen FANY in Nairobi, sent me 10 clerical FANYs from her force I put them in the cluster of *tukls* or Ethiopian round buildings in the centre of the compound (all had H & C and all furnished) where their safety was assured.

Residence in my old home of 1919-22 with its lovely garden and glorious view made all the difference to my physical and mental condition during the 12 months ahead, which formed, I know, the most difficult period I have ever experienced.

The purple bougainvillaea which I had planted against the front wall of the Legation House in 1922 was doing nicely and the "Mrs Butt" bougainvillaea which I planted in 1942 on the other side of the front porch had kept it good company when I last visited the Embassy in 1974. My wire fence erected on the perimeter of the land (which was British) in 1921 had stood the test of time for the same half century.

Practically all the old Ethiopian staff of the Legation suddenly appeared, ready to work as before, and we were soon busy preparing the houses for residence.

Here let me say that the Italian authorities respecting international protocol had maintained the buildings in very good state of preservation. The interiors were quite intact. I managed to borrow an officer of the Royal Engineers who, with some very expert and hard working Italian POWs, not only repaired any damage but installed two new bathrooms and a hot water system to replace the wooden baths and the carrying of pails and kettles of hot water which the Ministry of Works and members of the Diplomatic Corps and their families had tolerated for 40 years! The Foreign Office to whom I sent a nominal bill of £100, and the Office of Works neither acknowledged the value of the work, paid the bill or sent me word of thanks! We tackled the garden and the trees, the water supply and the roads, also with free but enthusiastic Italian POW labour.

So we were, rightly, established in residence and in an environment worthy of the British representative which General Cunningham and we, his deputies, were. The Legation and its capacious grounds were "open house" to all members of OETA and all visitors of whatever nationality, military or otherwise. Our guests included General Wavell our C-in-C; Generals Cunningham and Mitchell were frequent resident visitors; we seldom sat down to lunch without guests at our table. Of course, the Emperor and his chiefs and officers were honoured guests.

With others dealing with the administration of Addis Ababa, it behoved me to concentrate on the return to his capital of the Emperor. Pressure to bring him back at an early date was intense - from London, from my CPO Mitchell, from the representatives of the press who had somehow appeared in Addis Ababa, and of course, from the Emperor's HQ, vociferated by Dan, quite calmly, and by Wingate, loudly and without thought; by British officers who were bored at inactivity at Debra Marcos and wanted to "get shot of this little man and get on with the war". I had no pressure from the Ethiopians in Addis Ababa or elsewhere. To all pressure bearers I replied "When the military situation permits".

I took the line that so long as there were armed Italians in Addis Ababa and until the Ethiopian Police Force of the city was on its feet I could not advise the Emperor to risk his life at the hands of a patriot Italian or a dissident Ethiopian. This was a matter which depended on one's judgement and my judgement turned out to be correct. General Cunningham now left the ultimate decision to me. I also remembered that 5 May was the anniversary of the Italian entry into Addis Ababa. This would be good press news and I suggested that day. My General was convinced and all went well.

Before describing the Emperor's return to his capital let us turn for a page to the military situation. I quote largely from the official history of the campaign. On the day before Addis Ababa surrendered, the British Forces in Cyrenaca were in precipitate retreat before Rommel. After the loss of Addis Ababa it is very probable that the remaining Italians in Abyssinia would have preferred to surrender than to fight but due to the news from the Western Desert they received instructions from Rome to continue resistance for as long as they could, in order to delay the move of the much needed British Forces from East Africa to Egypt. The Italians chose Amba Alagi, a veritable Monte Cassino 10,000ft high, and here were concentrated remnants of the Italian Army from Asmara in the north and from Addis Ababa itself with the Duce d'Aosta - a total of some 5,000 troops. But the Italians had retired to other places along the roads which radiate from Addis Ababa: to Nekempti, to Jimma in the west and to the Lakes in the far south west. After bringing in the fearful Italians from the parts around Addis Ababa (there was a veritable cordon of them all begging to be saved from the Ethiopian patriots) General Cunningham sent out his troops - the main force towards Dessi and Amba Alagi, the others in the other directions. I was now able to send out Political Officers with these forces and very useful they proved to be.

The disarming of the Italian troops and their concentration as POWs and subsequent despatch to Kenya were military operations very efficiently performed. Their feeding alone was not without problems.

My slight relaxation of mind was evident at this stage in an exchange of correspondence with GHQ Nairobi, POW Department:

GHQ to DCPO (MSL): "On arrival in Nairobi POW General Frusci's suitcase was found to contain a revolver. Please enquire and report."

No reply from DCPO to GHQ Nairobi.

GHQ to DCPO: three "reminders" to above telegram. "My .... Report required urgently."

DCPO to GHQ: "Pull trigger; report will follow."

In the meantime OETA was not idle. I sent a letter to Dan Sandford at Debra Marcos, with a Report to tell the Emperor what OETA had accomplished in April 1941, the first month following occupation of his capital by British forces under General Weatherall. It was a lengthy document and I suggested that the Emperor might like to listen to a recitation of it. I don't know whether he listened or not; I do know that when I flew to visit him a few days before his entry he never mentioned it.

There follows a resume of this Report, with my own comments added to it. It included:

- *The local military situation* and steps taken to organize defence of the city, entrusting the manning of forts to Ethiopian patriots and holding British troops ready to be sent out in any direction to deal with threatened attack. Dejazmatch Makonnen, as HM the Emperor's representative, worked in close cooperation with the Military Commander, Brig Smallwood, regarding defence. He was invaluable to the Military as well as to me. Incidentally, the Military Commander played no part in the administration of the city.

- *The Administration*; the takeover from the Italians and the explanation to Ethiopian leaders that the British "had come to re-establish the independence of Ethiopia and to assist HM the Emperor to return to his capital and re-establish his government". We found both Ethiopians and Italians only too willing to assist in the day to day work of administration; but the Ethiopians had no training or experience and the Italian officials did not know much about the Ethiopian ways - in the past five years fascism had ruled the country centrally.

- *The Police* force organization following the disarming of the Italian Police, regular and irregular, the Garde Civile, and Blackshirt battalions (found on the race track), who were all heavily armed and equipped. I was amazed at the speed with which Colonel Hayton organised the existing police - gradually weeding out Italian officers and the rapidity with which Colonel Laidlaw had his Ethiopian recruits drilling and then most efficiently policing the town - and here comes the amazing truth - *unarmed*. It is a fact that we managed to achieve, at any rate on the surface, total disarmament among police and civilians. What happened later when unemployed "patriots" seeped in to the capital I cannot say; I expect the Emperor smiled when he heard of our optimism.

- *Segregation of Italians*; segregation and a curfew were measures to which the Italians agreed readily at first. Their fear of reprisals during the first week must have been very real.

- *Evacuation of Italian civilians*: this became one of the most difficult problems which arose. I was involved not only in the general principle (wherein the Emperor behaved with extraordinary and impersonal lack of sympathy) but also through the suffering, quite inescapable, which the long journey from Addis Ababa to Berbera involved; this was unavoidable.

- *Remaining Italians*: The numbers permitted to remain in Ethiopia became a matter of frequent and sometimes unintelligible changes of decision on the part of the Ethiopians.

- *Finance*: Frank Stafford was a tower of strength to me and to the whole administration during my tenure. After a distinguished career he returned to Eritrea in 1951 and was Financial Adviser to the Ethiopian Government from 1953-1960. I was most fortunate to have him by my side in 1941-42.

The reinstatement of the MT dollar was popular but its actual introduction was delayed owing to the sinking by enemy action of a ship carrying a quantity of the coin.

For the rest and for the institution of any financial or fiscal order, the absence of educated, let alone trained, Ethiopians complicated our outlook.

- *Food and other supplies*: Luckily the Italian organisation for the supply of food for Europeans existed. It remained for our OETA officers to organise transport and distribution; the Italians cooperated with goodwill.

We found that the Italians had, by and large, left the feeding of the Ethiopians to the Ethiopians themselves and we gladly saw to it that the normal Ethiopian way resumed. It was interesting to note the rapidity with which the people renewed their customary mode of marketing as soon as they were free. Very soon the long slow lines of animals - donkeys, mules, horses - came back on the roads to the utter detriment of order amidst military traffic; but whereas the Italian conquerors had driven these motley, undisciplined caravans off the roads and onto bypaths (their proper place), the British were far more tolerant though equally exasperated. There was much patience and good humour shown by South African, Nigerian, East African and even English military drivers whose road discipline was obliterated by these Ethiopians heavily laden, bringing their food and firewood from their villages into the capital. So gradually the accustomed ways of animal transport of food and the vast Ethiopian market in the capital returned. Mighty glad were we to see the sign of plenty, or at any rate, sufficiency in that market.

- *News broadcasting*: I had asked for George Steer to be released from Khartoum (Intelligence) to come as my Press Propaganda Officer. He was the husband of Esme Barton the daughter of HBM's Minister in Addis Ababa from 1932-36, and George was a godson of the Emperor, accompanying him on his flight to Khartoum from London. He later published a book called *Sealed and Delivered* which tells the story of the Emperor's return. I much admired his attitude to OETA, the British Policy in Ethiopia, and to his Godfather. He most sadly died in South Africa.

- *Prisons*: I myself had feared trouble in the prisons and visited the main jail within 24 hours of our entry into the city. My fears were well founded and I discovered signs of bloodshed. I had the Italian warders and prison Governors arrested. They were subsequently tried under some of the first British-Ethiopian courts which we set up by mid-April. In the meantime I had the jails emptied of all political and petty crime prisoners but left further clemency to the compassion of the Emperor whenever he should arrive.

- *Medical*: The British Army medical chiefs were splendid. Accustomed at home to equal medical treatment for every race, they applied this principle to Britons and Africans alike. The Italians had discriminated: good and well equipped hospitals for the Europeans; mediocre and bad facilities for the Ethiopians. We were not able to do much in the first month but later managed to devote one hospital to the care of Ethiopians - for the first time in five years.

It was all tremendous fun. Here was an administrative, racial mess, created by the fascist idea of colonisation in Africa, being converted into the nucleus of an Ethiopian administration. In that first month, we in OETA tried valorously to blot out the vile poison of fascism and give to the Ethiopians the taste of what Britons thought was a decent life for them. We only had a month, but we made the most of it and the paper which I sent to the Emperor (and which received neither thanks nor acknowledgment) was a deliberate attempt to show him that with a handful of experienced administrators, much could be and was done. But, of course, it employed methods to which the Emperor had no access and would not have employed had he that access.

I have quoted from this paper on our administration in Addis Ababa not only for historical reasons but because it gives a pattern of what every DCPO or head of a British Military Administration had in mind when preparing a plan and taking over an occupied territory in war.

At the end of April I paid a visit to His Majesty at Debra Markos some days before his entry to tidy up details and explain where my GOC, General Cunningham, would welcome him to the capital of his country which the enemy had surrendered to British Forces. I also needed information from Dan and others on the number of patriots who, fully armed, would accompany or precede their *Janhoi* (Emperor), possibly remaining to the detriment of security in the city. I failed to receive any definite information. How could they guess?

The Emperor's entry into Addis Ababa

My General had determined to send General Wetherall and an escort to meet the Emperor at the top of Entotto Hill, the summit of the ring of hills 9,000-10,000ft high which surround Addis Ababa, and over which the Emperor's route from Debra Markos passed.

Once more, with the arrival of the Emperor and his patriot army, General Cunningham quite naturally and rightly was concerned at the behaviour of some thousands of fully armed "wild and woolly" fighting Ethiopians, many of whom might be regular *shiftas* - he and others (every Italian!) were nervous as to what excess might be perpetrated when such patriots were "let loose" (my General's words) in Addis Ababa. "I am anxious, Maurice" he said "and I want you to limit the numbers of patriots in the procession accompanying the Emperor to 2,000 men."

I submitted to that command, knowing that I had no power on earth, save a fully armed Brigade of the General's troops, to prevent a much greater number from entering the city. I told my General (who I am sure didn't believe me) that the number of the patriots would be limited to 2,000 - and I assured him that no trouble would be caused by them. Luckily General Alan Cunningham and I knew each other by then.

Luckily I had met Ras Ababa Aregai. He had but recently come into town and to see me; whether he had been to Debra Marcos to visit the Emperor I am not sure, but his history was as follows: son of one of Menelik's generals, Emperor Haile Selassie had appointed him to be the Chief of Police - a position which he held until 1935. During the Italian occupation he never submitted to the enemy but lived a life of resistance and was the leader of the patriots in Shoa Province; his title of Ras was conferred on him by his own people during the Italian regime. I am sure the Emperor confirmed it later for he was made Governor of Addis Ababa - a very popular appointment.

I consulted Ras Ababa Aregai before 3 May as to the numbers of the patriots to be allowed into the city on that day - and whether indeed we could refuse them entry. "*Gid yellum*" he replied in Amharic "No matter; I Ababa Aregai will control the patriots and I can assure you that there will be no *chic a chac* (trouble)". I was perfectly happy with that assurance and did my best to comfort the General. There was in fact, not one single incident, and the 7,000 or more patriots who entered the city went out the same evening to carouse in their camps outside. General Cunningham in his official dispatch (*LG 10.7.41*, para 82)was good enough to give me a mention in that respect:

> ".... From the moment my troops entered Addis Ababa I was being pressed continually by the Emperor to permit his return to the capital at once. This I was most anxious to accomplish at the earliest possible moment, both to hasten the structure of an Ethiopian state which might eventually stand on its own legs and to get the fullest use out of the patriot movement in conjunction with my forces which were still engaged with the enemy, thus compensating to a small degree for the loss of troops and equipment sent up to the Middle East.
>
> "It was however, quite impossible to allow the Emperor back until I had settled the various internal security questions in Addis Ababa and disarmed the Italians. I had some difficulty with the Emperor on this question and he appeared distrustful of our future intentions towards him. I was, however, in a position to let him in on 5 May on which day he ceremoniously entered the city on the anniversary of the entry of the Italians exactly five years before. In view of the complete disarming of the city there were no major incidents. Considerable credit was due to Brigadier M S Lush MC, the DCPO who was in charge of the civil administration, for this happy result."

The great day 5 May 1941 dawned. I had discussed and defined General Cunningham's reception of the Emperor in Addis Ababa and I determined to remain in the city where my staff and especially the police had their specific duties. The crowds began to assemble bright and early - a quiet, joyful lot, every one dressed in clean linen, many women and young girls; Italians were not to be seen, all having been very willingly confined to their quarters. Our OETA police were splendid and I was very proud at what they had accomplished. At about 9.00 am I was suddenly besieged by a whole posse of press reporters, photographers and the like, bemoaning the complete lack of transport for them and their utter despair. With a brainwave I dispelled their wails - I summoned the lately Ethiopianised fire brigade of Addis Ababa with several brand new motor fire engines and escapes which had but recently arrived. Off went the press and the capital was defenceless against the ravages of fire for several hours.

My greatest delight on that day - shared by many - was to see the patriots from Shoa Province (Ras Ababa Aregai's men) march early into the town led by the Ras's young son, a boy of 12, dressed in fine clothes on which were fastened two bandoliers of ammunition, his belt bedecked with a large pistol, he himself carrying a very modern rifle (probably loaded and at full cock), riding a gaily caparisoned white pony. He was a fine boy and he looked as proud as well he might be, as the son of his gallant father. He stole the limelight that morning!

Extract from *Sealed and Delivered* by G L Steer

"Towards midday the Emperor arrived at the summit of Entotto, where he prayed in the church of St Mary, from whose other side he could see for the first time Addis Ababa floating in the billows of eucalyptus far below, like a mirage that might be stolen away.

"The procession formed among the rocks. Ahead a South African motor-cyclist; next, my loudspeaker van flying the Ethiopian flag; six South African motor cyclists abreast; three South African armoured cars; two red Italian fire-engines carrying a scramble of the press; Wingate, close shaven, carrying a long leather whip on a white horse; the 2nd Ethiopian Battalion under their flag; a cloud of Ethiopian mounted police on white horses carrying carbines round a car containing the Emperor and Major General Wetherall, commanding the Addis Ababa Division; cars with the Princes, the Rases, the *itchegi* Dan, Andrew, Lorenzo; the Sudan Frontier Battalion in clean turbans and grins, with a rich green flag of silk sporting their badge, a golden lion; lorries of Ethiopian exiles; some more armoured cars.

"We moved slowly down the steep incline and through the crowded streets of Addis Ababa, through many thousands of waving flags and stooping bodies. Lij Yelma, at my side, called into the microphone: "Today, five years ago, the Italians entered into our city to murder and pillage; today, five years after, our King returns with the aid of a just God and of the English!" Looking through the sides of the van one could see the expression of the crowd as we descended through the skirting forest. The shock of the first news; the recognition; the faces wrinkling up in a mixture of sorrow and memory; and of release from sorrow; tears starting suddenly from faces of old people; wrinkled women raising their arms in ecstasy to the sky; lines of men and women going flat on the ground and kissing it; dignified judges of the Quarters, at one moment lifting high their inscribed silk standards and flowers, then bowing low till their foreheads touched the earth; before the centre of the town was reached and the streets were clogged, flocks of people running alongside the Emperor's car shouting proverbs and throwing flowers; old faces in the crowd that one had not expected to see again. Addis Ababa means the New Flower and as the car entered the town somebody shouted "The New Flower has flowered again!"

"The ranks were serried, the individuals were lost in the mass, the expressions grew more uniform, there was no room for bowing, the women only cried out like a swarm of bees on the wing, the men gave the short triple clap. At the gates of Menelik's old palace an artist encouraged by the propaganda section had set up a most horrible representation of the Ethiopian Lion disembowelling the Roman Wolf; and beyond, waited Lieutenant-General Sir Alan Cunningham, GOC East African Force, and a Guard of Honour of the King's African Rifles and a battery of captured guns whose Italian ammunition was to be touched off twenty-one times as the Emperor mounted the rostrum to speak, and everybody fell as flat as in the book of Daniel!

"The morning wore on - more and more patriots moved in. Not a shot was fired - even into the air - even on this day of days. Was it the result of Italian discipline instilled during the last five years which prohibited the carrying of arms by Ethiopians? Was it the undoubted presence of British troops and armoured vehicles dotted unobtrusively at random points? Or was it Ras Ababa Aregai?

"On reflection, exemplary behaviour of the 7,000 patriots fully armed made the Imperial procession a most brilliant, happy occasion; their behaviour was due neither to past discipline of the Italians, nor to the Emperor's words or influence, nor to the presence of British troops who had been their allies in real battle, but to the influence of one of themselves, who had never left them, who had endured the five years of enemy rule as an exile it is true, but an exile in his own country, always actively exploiting the conqueror and helping brave Ethiopians like himself - I refer of course, to Ras Ababa Aregai. He kept the peace that day and led the patriots out of the town at nightfall. No wonder the Emperor agreed to appoint him Governor of Addis Ababa.

"The Emperor's speech was moving - 'Thanks be to God; gratitude to my brave patriots; gratitude to our allies - We should thereafter fasten our friendship for ever in an indissoluble bond .... our allies are our friends and our own blood. Take them to your hearts.'"

For the fighting troops of the British Army and their leaders, the Emperor had nothing but real gratitude and praise - and those sentiments lasted throughout his long life. The British political approach to his country in the past gave him little for which to be thankful or confident. The administration now imposed, as he saw it, on his country, imbued him with no sense of gratitude but, per contra, resentment and suspicion. Proper relations he felt could only be restored when all forms and signs of inequality between the two countries had been removed, at any rate in so far as the right to govern was concerned. The fact that the military forces of Great Britain had to administer as they went along because they were in the act of conquering the common enemy made no impression on him.

But we all went to bed on 5 May thankful that the day had gone well, that the Emperor was now in his capital and that the patriots appeared to have returned to their camp fires outside Addis Ababa. We, in OETA, had experienced a wonderful month or few weeks really achieving our initial purposes, in administrative peace, but with the knowledge that we should not work really independently in the future; that is to say, we should always be in the shadow of Imperial criticism, and sometimes opposition; that we, for the most part, realised that fact, was probably our salvation.

Administration after Emperor's return

It was May, the Emperor was on his throne; my staff, both in Addis Ababa, and in the Provinces were in situ if not in officio. I paid almost daily calls on the Emperor and established, through Dan, that I had the right of almost instant access. I then left "the little man" to settle down at home and - with an eye on the coming rainy season - went out on trek to see my political officers, leaving Travers Blackley to hold the fort in my absence.

I had travelled but little in Abyssinia in 1919-22; this had been a pity but unavoidable; transport on four legs curtails distance covered. Now I found Italian constructed roads, built for motor transport and I determined to go out to my political officers who had the most difficult task of us all.

Before describing my travels, let me quote from letters. 23 May 1941; MSL to DRL:

"…. We moved in to the Legation after 3 weeks here (AA). It is *so* nice. We have a mess of 6 in the top house, and of 8 in the bottom house. I have commandeered a Bechstein piano and found some old music. But I never get time to play. The garden is a delight and I am cutting trees to clear the view. We are very happy here; the weather is wet but lovely - fires every evening. Strawberries from Mulu are a delight and I wax fat!"

1 June 1941; MSL to DRL:

"…. We are getting the tennis court ready and filling the stables …. it is grand being among good solid English furniture. All the "old boys" (servants) have come back, and the place is going very much like old times. My old servant is now head *sebagnia* (watchman), and Tasfai (my old *syce*) comes in from Mulu still with strawberries and cream and butter. I sent some strawberries by air to Aden the other day to an Admiral and an Air Marshall: they were delighted."

What a letter to write to one's wife in war-wracked Britain, suffering nightly bombing at home and reeling from defeats in Greece and Crete and the grave losses sustained by the Royal Navy in the Mediterranean.

I waited in Addis Ababa long enough to give the Emperor on 18 May 1941 the good news of the fall of Ambo Alegai, where the forces of Generals Platt and Cunningham (the Indian Brigade, the Sudanese Brigade and the South African with the East and West African Brigades) met and forced the Duke of Aosta, Governor of Italian East Africa and the Commander of the Italian forces, to surrender and enabled the Indian and South African Brigades to leave for Egypt and the desert battle area.

Just before I left to visit the Provinces in early May, the Emperor, without notification to me or even to Dan, appointed seven Ministers of State - a gesture which, made in consultation, could have been one of confidence towards the British Administration; we could have helped at once in giving them staff and offices. As it was, the announcement appeared quite contrary to our policy of informing the Emperor of all our senior appointments and introducing the officers concerned. Gradually, however, the British Administration were able to use these Ministers, some of whom were most helpful.

I motored to Dessie in the middle of the month through the famous Mussolini Pass, on that masterpiece of Italian road engineering, which links Asmara with Addis Ababa. I found Riches there as Political Officer (he later rose high in the Diplomatic Service); the problems were legion and typical of those which beset most of my Political Officers. His duty was to keep the peace in that area so that British troops could come and go through the important road junction on the route from Addis Ababa to Asmara and also to Gondar which was still in Italian hands. There existed the inevitable dissension between the neighbouring chiefs. Food in the country did not seem plentiful, but the rains would produce a good crop and there was no sign of famine. Loot from Italian stores was no doubt hidden away throughout the area. I had to warn him that the Emperor's officials, if and when they came, would have different ideas from Riches' and mine but that so long as order was maintained he must try to give way to the Ethiopian ideas; this would mean that an Ethiopian way of life would find its way into the area, probably at variance with some of the tidy administration plans which Riches had set in motion (and which the local Ethiopians warmly appreciated).

Dessie itself was a pleasant place. MSL to DRL 1.6.41:

"…. We went over the Mussolini Pass (from the

summit of which one has views on to the country 6,000ft below) and through the road tunnel (attempts by the Italians to destroy it had failed), and had a lovely 10 hours' drive through beautiful country .... Dessie is quite lovely. A Swiss chalet town (dirty in the market!) in the midst of most lovely country - green valleys (it was May, after the "little" refreshing rains), trees, water; a good deal more beautiful and more European in scenery than the country around Addis Ababa."

On another occasion, I visited my brother DCPO Eritrea, Kennedy Cooke, and flew to Asmara in a Wellesley 3-seater fighter sent to Addis Ababa for me by General Platt's Air Commodore:

".... I have flown a tremendous amount - Harar, Dessie and the other day I flew to Asmara and stayed with Sir William Platt KCB. We hurtled through the air and over this appalling canyon-like country at 200 mph doing the trip from here in 3 hours. I was frozen it was so cold and we went so fast that I could not look over the edge! .... Never before or since have I felt so cold or so completely terrified in flight. The Wellesleys were fast fighters and with the exception of a face visor, the three occupants who sat in separate seats one behind the other, had no cover whatsoever. The Simien Mountains of Ethiopia rise to 14,000ft and are snow clad. Cold and fear at a height of some 16,000ft produced in me, a landsman, a sense of panic and despair, physical as well as mental and I landed, a chattering and very damp, exhausted Brigadier. I had every sympathy with the Sergeant RAF who on a similar flight took leave of his senses and jumped overboard! Luckily he was well equipped with a parachute which he knew how to manipulate; mercifully the air currents were calm, and providentially he landed in one of the green welcoming valleys 15,000ft below and fell among an equally frightened bunch of Tigrean peasants, who thoroughly humbled (it takes a lot to humble a Tigrean) by their heavenly visitor, succoured him reverently and took him over the mountains to the nearest *ferenji* (foreigner) who happened to be one of my officers who had him sent back by the slower, surer route by land. The story is told that the pilot of the Wellesley, on arrival at Asmara, when informed of the empty seat behind him remarked 'That explains the sudden lurch upwards which my aircraft gave, going over Simien - I thought it was an air current.'"

I enjoyed my 36 hours in Asmara (and Massawa) and General Platt was a very kind host. My fellow DCPO's job was quite different in style from mine - no less difficult and full of problems, but no Emperor, or Italians who have to be evacuated.

Asmara was also very different from Addis Ababa. The place was, of course, full of Italians and a great many of them were employed in the administration - in fact, as in Addis Ababa, Italians were the key men in many of the technical departments (food, transport, power, etc.) and of course, in the port of Massawa. How Kennedy Cooke (the DCPO) was ever to succeed in training Ethiopians for much of this work was, I said to myself, his problem, just as much as we had to train Ethiopians in Addis Ababa. Writing to Diana I likened Asmara to Alexandria in the '30s, though on a smaller scale: ".... It has a good hotel and a good cinema - in which we saw *The Scarlet Pimpernel* in Italian."

In the meantime in June 1941 my Chief Political Officer, Mitchell had flown to London where, after discussions with the FO, produced a draft Convention - the result of his visits to Addis Ababa and "a great deal of vague and rather unsatisfactory talk with the Emperor" which produced six points as representations of what he wanted. These included the appointment of advisers for his minsters - Political, Judicial and Financial - and a general administrative arrangement. In his report to the War Office written in London, Mitchell reported the Emperor's position from a practical point of view, very well:

"We the British have stopped withholding recognition of him as Emperor by restoring him to his palace by force .... On the other hand he is far from being safely on the throne and has no money, no disciplined force and no means of establishing an administration."

So far so good; but Mitchell did proceed to lay down as one of the conditions which HMG should secure from Haile Selassie an agreement to abide, in all important matters touching the government and in the administration thereof, by the advice tendered by HMG and their deputies. This would have been splendid but we really all knew that, however greatly the Emperor had desired a protectorate in 1936, he would not accept such a situation now. The word "protectorate" had been noised abroad in Addis Ababa among representatives of the press and sundry other bodies and associations. One editor dubbed the CPO and me as Cromerites. Mitchell, who as a colonial governor had at first rather enjoyed the thought of protection of Ethiopia, dropped the notion; and Sandford, when he visited London on leave, persuaded the War Office not to countenance such a policy. Mitchell and I were very close in our considerations during those months of July, August and September 1941, and many were the consultations and deliberations concluded during after-breakfast horse exercise which Mitchell loved. (In a letter to DRL I had told her of the establishment of my personal stable with four ponies, good Abyssinian stock, just as I would have wanted, and named as usual after our abode in England, viz. Westlands, Ewhurst, Guildford, Surrey.)

The plan in *our* minds (and that of General Cunningham) was that Mitchell should be High Commissioner for all East African occupied territories (Italian Somaliland, Eritrea and Ethiopia), based on Nairobi and that I should be British Agent in Ethiopia transmitting, through British advisers to the Emperor, the suggestions of policy and administration emanating from HMG. In fact, rather a Cromerion style of cooperation! The Agent (MSL) would remain a soldier until a Treaty had been signed, probably post bellum. With good will on both sides it would have worked and the British staff employed would not have been excessive. From my own point of view it appeared most attractive - a job I could manage in a most lovely country; the whole family could join me and so far as anyone foretell, a three-year appointment. But it was not to be. I think it was by October 1941 that we had indications that HMG did not really desire such a commitment; that the Emperor certainly was against any such advisory official over him; and definitely did not want General Cunningham's political officers to remain any longer than necessary in Ethiopia.

As regards British policy in the negotiations, one must realise (and naturally this was not apparent to us in Africa at that time) that Winston Churchill, as PM, had envisaged in 1940 a period, after the intended defeat of the Italians and their clearance from Ethiopia, when it "could then be allowed to sink back into its former mire" once the Emperor was back on his throne; his (Churchill's) emotional picture of an Emperor re-instated caused him to declare "give the little man what he wants". Not so easy for the administration on the spot!

Lyttleton had been appointed Minister of State in Cairo, and Mitchell was summoned by him and told to draft a less proprietary Agreement giving the Emperor "more freedom of action" and, I think, the supplanting of the DCPO and other OETA personnel by ordinary diplomatic staff. We therefore all turned our minds to the preparations and execution of an Agreement between HMG and the Emperor giving him what he wanted. The preparation of the Agreement took some months and it was not until January 1942 that we staged a suitable ceremony with pomp and circumstance, sealing wax and seals.

In the autumn of 1941 we began to reduce the activities of OETA to a minimum. We removed our HQ from Addis Ababa to Dire Dawa; my Political Officers in the provinces resigned en bloc. It was they who, in trying to carry out the provincial policy of OETA, had found instant and continued collaboration from the local chiefs (British Administrative policies and procedures were generally popular among the ordinary peasants and townsfolk of Africa) until the "dead hand of the Emperor's governor and officials arrived, when trouble and *chic a chac* at once ensued". The last sentence is a quotation from reports of practically every British provincial officer. Under the Agreement we handed over the peasant population of Ethiopia to the *gabar* system which continued for the remaining 30 years of the Emperor's reign. Haile Selassie was a man of vision who ruled his country with wisdom and achieved much progressive success throughout his reign; education, medical progress and social reforms ranked high in the benefits he bestowed on many subjects in his country. But though he achieved the extinction of many wrongs in the feudal system he failed, really, to ameliorate the lot of the ordinary peasant who ploughed and who still ploughs his land and milks his cattle, because he, the Emperor, did not possess nor succeed in training an administrative class of devoted men and women to whom the betterment of the lot of Tasfai or Zallake peasants was first priority.

The men who represented OETA had as their first priority the keeping of the peace for the sake of British troops in their areas; their second aim - eschewing imperial or feudal personalities and views - was to raise the standard of living of the peasants of Ethiopia. The lack of experienced men at the Emperor's command and his own suspicion and his subordinates' of the country (Britain) who had driven out the common enemy prevented the success of the British officers' aims.

It was only after signature that the Emperor told Mitchell that he did not want any of General Cunningham's Political Officers to remain in Ethiopia. He accused them of rudeness! This complaint fell in with the FO's design (backed by Sandford and Chapman Andrews) to send out a British diplomat as before, to represent HMG.

Marjorie Perham, that eminent historian and writer, was surely wrong in declaring that British officials had undoubtedly failed the inhabitants of the provinces; we had merely found stumbling blocks in the men sent to the provinces by the Emperor. My sister Chris Sandford suffered from the same delusion.

During the latter part of the year 1941 and while all these machinations were going on in London, I was often in Nairobi where I had the great joy of receiving "fastmail" - ie. 10 days from UK to Nairobi - from Diana. She knew what was going on both from Mitchell (who had been in London) and Dan. I think Diana realised more than I, that hopes of future employment in Ethiopia were nil.

MSL to DRL 16.10.41; Nairobi:

> ".... I have spent 3 hectic days here in Nairobi, talking and writing, getting PEM fully briefed. He has been absolutely grand .... whatever they want me to do for the War, I will do .... I don't think I should worry about what DAS told you .... Individual lives have got to go by the board until we get these Huns defeated, and I would love to feel that I had done something even more active to defeat them than the administration of 9 million Habash and 40,000 Italians for 9 months."

At some time during that autumn of 1941 the Empress, Waizera Mannen, with her daughter Tshai and a younger son, arrived in Addis Ababa by air. For some reason the Emperor did not meet them at the aerodrome, and it was left to me to do so. I had known her before in 1922 and I was pleased to receive a smile from her and her most charming and efficient daughter who, professionally trained and properly graduated as a nurse at Great Ormond Street Hospital where she had worked as a most popular member of the staff, at once threw herself into the medical side of the administration and worked most helpfully and loyally with the really first class service, chiefly confined to Addis Ababa, which the British medical officers had so successfully instituted. We were thankful that the Emperor realised that in this field, at any rate, he had no right or reason to interfere.

Naturally I had a sense of failure - failure to carry out an impossible task; the only ways to avoid that failure would have been to refuse to attempt the task after I had first met the Emperor. That would have been cowardice in the eyes of my Commander-in-Chief and myself.

Neither the Emperor nor Dan Sandford, with all his courage and knowledge of the country, nor Philip Mitchell nor I, really fully realised that the five years of Italian occupation - however brutal in so many ways - had advanced the thinking of the Ethiopians in the country, if only from material benefits such as roads and transport, to a stage of evolution which had to be admitted and recognized by the rulers of the country.

After the Agreement, the Emperor ruled well and bestowed great benefits on his country, and his many admirers thanked God that he had rid himself of yet another alien race who would feign have helped him do better.

The drafting of the Agreement took two months and many comings and goings between Palace and British Legation before the final drafts were accepted.

Signing of the Agreement

On 31 January 1942 we signed the Agreement in the Emperor's *Ghebbi*. It was an impressive ceremony - the Emperor and Sir Philip Mitchell taking the principal parts with General Cunningham alongside, and other Ethiopian and British notables dotted about. My OETA staff were present, candles and sealing wax were not forgotten and at last the Emperor had obtained what he desired - freedom to run his country as he wished with financial, judicial and military advice provided by HMG.

That evening we staged a reception at the British Legation, the birthplace of the Agreement, to which the Emperor and his staff came. He was polite - and no more - and we were relieved when he departed. He never offered Mitchell or me or our staff any hospitality in return. We were in his opinion General Cunningham's officers who had been "rude" to him.

It might be noted here that hospitality was freely exchanged in the Provinces between the national Chiefs and my officers, but never between the latter and the Emperor's appointees.

Under the Agreement, OETA was to be contained in certain "referred areas" where the interests of British troops were paramount. One of them was Dire Dawa, HQ of the Franco-Ethiopian Railway and I had persuaded General Platt to appoint Travers Blackley to be my successor as Head of OETA. Platt had recently taken over as C-in-C East Africa Command from Cunningham and had warned me to be ready for another job. He demurred at Blackley's appointment: "The chap's always dropping asleep in the evening - I'll talk to him after dinner." That evening I ordered my PA, Douglas Grant, and another to keep Travers away from the General and we kept him talking all through dinner, after which, I led them to my study, sat them down beside the fire, and Travers fell fast asleep! However, he got the job.

Platt was soon told that HMG's representative Mr R Howe, would arrive on a certain date, and that Chapman Andrews would be on his staff. This was arranged, and Mr Howe duly arrived. I lunched with him a few days later, in the Legation, which was, of course, now a diplomatic building. I handed him a few of our files which I thought he should have - including my full report. Mr Howe never asked a single question about the country, the situation or the Emperor. After lunch I went to the drawing room to take my leave of Mrs Howe. Chapman Andrews and I found a written notice on the door "Not at Home". That was the last and only contact I had with either of them.

I took my farewell of the Emperor telling him how sorry I was that he had found it impossible to work with an administration set up by Generals Wavell, Platt and Cunningham; an administration which had done its utmost to prepare the country and especially Addis Ababa, for his arrival; which had as he very well knew done a great deal for the welfare of his country and which had been wholly necessary for the well-being of the British troops who had driven the Italians from Ethiopia. I received a polite message of farewell, not a word of thanks nor an expression of good wishes.

My adieu to Ato Taffara who had interpreted every interview between me and the Emperor was warmer. Forgotten were any memories of 1919-22: I often thought that Taffara was not my friend in those days.

By this time, many of my Political Officers in the Provinces had gone or were about to go - few wished to continue service under the aegis of an Emperor who didn't want them. Most of us wanted to devote our lives and services to defeating the real common enemy. I had said goodbye to my beloved Legation house and garden and to my ponies - one of whom, Wilbury, I gave to Mitchell in whose stable he died some five years later.

To the Emperor I personally was persona non grata for 30 years and the doors of the Ethiopian Embassy in London were closed to me so far as hospitality was concerned. I could never imagine or find out any single insult that singled me out for such treatment. I was not included in the party of British officers invited to Addis Ababa 25 years later for a week's free festivities to celebrate the anniversary of the "little man's" return to his throne in 1941. I was however, the only officer concerned in that return who wrote to The Times telling the world of the Emperor's munificence; I was able to make an after-dinner speech at the Anglo-Ethiopian Society's Dinner about the Emperor and his work for Ethiopia and Africa. He had just negotiated a peace between the warring Arabs and the rebellious Nilotics of the Sudan.

I was very disappointed at the time, for my first war effort outside the Sudan had ended in failure, and my dreams shared with Diana of a three-year job in a lovely house in a lovely country, with our whole family with us, had been shattered.

Extract from a letter written by Colonel Travers

Blackley to DRL; Addis Ababa 20 November 1941:

"…. where I am administratively and professionally interested in this Ethiopian experiment, Maurice has a far deeper personal and, I think, almost religious belief in our mission, and although he is bearing this disappointment in a way which is an example to anybody similarly placed, he is feeling it very deeply …. If we were to start the same show over again, I should recommend the same policy which we have followed to date. Nothing that can happen in the future …. can mar the recollection of the past seven months. They have been the most interesting experience of my life, and in working with Maurice, I have found a friendship and an inspiration which comes but rarely in a lifetime.

Travers"

Of course, with hindsight, both Diana and I were delighted that such a dead-end job did not eventuate. For the FO would not have raised a finger for one who did not belong in their service, and I should have missed the next three appointments which really brought me into the War - in two theatres which were important under Commanders who were world famous and in one theatre where Diana and the children were at last able to join me on the job.

When I undertook the job of DCPO Ethiopia and was promoted to Brigadier by General Wavell I accepted the honour as a task towards winning the war against Great Britain's and her allies' enemies and as such carried out to the best of my power and skill the task set before me by my Commander-in-Chief. The restoration of the Emperor Haile Selassie was incidental, not fundamental, to that task which locally in Ethiopia was the peaceful imposition of rule in that country and the evacuation from it as quickly as possible of British troops which were needed to defeat the Germans and Italian troops, first in the Western Desert and thereafter elsewhere. Thanks be we achieved this task on time; additionally, thanks to British policy during and after the occupation of Ethiopia by British troops, we were able to ensure the installation of Haile Selassie as Emperor of Ethiopia for a further spell of years. This took place in accordance with the policy of HMG and with Britain's willing help - political, administrative and financial. It was not the task of the British Military Adminstration established under OETA and myself as DCPO.

Dan and my sister Chris Sandford were together again at last in 1942 after an epic journey of risk and excitement by Chris, accompanied by K T Stephenson and two children, Philippa and Stephen, of a sea passage from Liverpool to Cape Town, thence by railroad to Lusaka, Northern Rhodesia where Tom Sandford, Dan's elder brother was Colonial Secretary; he somehow transported them to Nairobi where in spite of every barrier raised by government, the military and banks (lack of money), they bought a car, and arrived triumphant with a military convoy to meet Dan a day or two outside Addis Ababa.

They lived in Addis Ababa where Dan was advising the Ministry of the Interior and then the Municipality. Chris wrote another book on Haile Selassie and Ethiopia and founded the English School, later known as the Sandford School and ruled by her daughter Eleanor and son-in-law Leslie Casbon with 700 pupils; it became well known, not only in Ethiopia, but also in UK (Wycombe Abbey educated many of the girls from the Sandford School).

They established Mulu Farm where they both subsequently lived, cultivating acres of strawberries and later on, cattle, a highly successful agricultural project, some 40 miles north of Addis Ababa, on land rented from the Empress - a focus for hundreds of Ethiopian and foreign visitors (including Louis Mountbatten and Donald Coggan) who journeyed there first of all by horse, then by car to see the GOM of Ethiopia. They loved the country and the people.

Chris had no use at all for OETA of 1941-42 nor the exploits therein of "my younger brother", but Mulu was still a lovely place to visit and she maintained her skill as a pianist until she died there.

As for that younger brother, he reported to General Platt on arrival in Nairobi; found him alone with Mitchell and was told the top secret news that the British were to attack Madagascar next month and that MSL was to be DCPO.

Where was Madagascar?

ETHIOPIA

Dan Sandford with MSL and a patriot leader, Ethiopia, 1941

MSL with Ras Ababa Aregai and others, Addis Ababa, 1941

Emperor Haile Selassie signing the Anglo-Ethiopian Agreement on 2 February 1942, together with Major General Sir Philip Mitchell and MSL

TRIPOLI 1943

Left:
Surrender of Tripoli 23 January 1943: MSL with General Montgomery saluting Italian Governor, Alberto do Pirajno

Right:
MSL as Chief Civil Affairs Officer, Day of Deliverance, Jewish Quarter, Tripoli, April 1943

Left and right above: MSL with leaders of local community, Tripoli, 1943

CHAPTER 11

MADAGASCAR April 1942 - October 1942
Chief Political Officer / Military Administrator, British Military Administration

The whole concept of occupying Madagascar, in order to deny the harbour of Diego Suarez and airfields in the rest of the island to the Japanese, took form in March 1942 after the Prime Minister had been told on more than one occasion that South Africa (not necessarily Smuts) was interested in Madagascar. There was talk of allowing de Gaulle to send a small Free French force but on 8 March, Churchill had told the Admiralty that:

> "the Free French are 'out' of the Madagascar business, and should be kept out. But all the more is it necessary to establish ourselves there".

Later the PM told Ismay on 30.3.42

> "It is of the greatest importance that de Gaulle's people should be misled about Ironclad. Once they know, the secret will be out."

Smuts was now fully au fait and in accord with the assault. De Gaulle was not told of the intended expedition, and the whole question of inclusion of the Free French presented a conundrum at the very beginning of the assault - as will be read later.

General Platt, with Philip Mitchell and I, went to Platt's office in Nairobi where the General told me that HMG had decided, in order to forestall similar action by the Japanese, to seize the port of Diego Suarez in Madagascar, if necessary by force of arms, and that Mitchell, called upon to produce a Chief Political Officer, had chosen me. I was to join the invading forces, then on the high seas at Durban, very soon. "You are, of course, to keep this absolutely top secret, Maurice, but we have told you in order that you can find out something about Madagascar. The invasion is being mounted direct from London, and will be under the orders of Chiefs of Staff, not myself (Platt): no one on my staff has an inkling of the operation, so you must not consult any of them - not even my Intelligence boys!"

Of course, I was honoured and delighted; but where was Madagascar? Who lived there and why? And how in a fortnight was I to find out? I asked for one favour - or even necessity. "Two brains are better than one, and four eyes quicker than two; I have a first class and very intelligent Personal Assistant whom I trust implicitly (Douglas Grant: Philip Mitchell knew him); I shall take him with me but I must tell him now and use him as my guide to Madagascar." Agreed.

What fun! What a splendid opportunity after the disappointment of Ethiopia. Here we were - off again and this time to a Combined Ops affair.

I told General Platt and Philip Mitchell that I should let it be known that I was soon off to Syria (where there was every chance of British intervention becoming necessary) and asked them to substantiate the supposition. I then went off to find my young colleague in deception, Douglas Grant, who had just arrived from Ethiopia where he had been my (very good) PA for 6 months or so. We changed into mufti and spent a week in Nairobi Public Library and the libraries of various clubs in Nairobi soaking ourselves in any information we could scrape out on the subject of Madagascar.

I am afraid that Douglas Grant and I learnt little about the Grande Ile de Madagascar, except that it was a very large island, 1,000 miles in length (about the size of Italy from the River Po southwards); had been described, but not seen, by Marco Polo from Arab travellers' accounts; had been discovered by Vasco de Gama who mistook his first sight of land there for Mogadishu on the Horn of Africa; that Diego Suarez was a magnificent harbour and that Tamatave and Majunga were the island's secondary ports; Antananarivo (Tananarive) was the capital, near the centre of the island. We learned of its indigenous population (Malagaches from Malaysia) and the French occupation of 1888, of their exports of graphite but nothing of great interest to invaders! Later in these pages I will try to give my impression of our sojourn there and of another visit which I paid to the island 20 years later - and I would give advice here that the National Geographic Journal of October 1967 (Vol 132; No 4) has an excellent, beautifully illustrated account of this curious island.

Finally, off we flew (with our not very full knowledge of our final destination) to Durban where some kind staff officer of the Imperial Movement Control, had booked us a very sumptuous suite of rooms in the big hotel on the quayside. In Durban we were to join Major General

R Sturgess, Royal Marines, Commander of the landforce operation "Ironclad", which was the code name of the operation.

The convoy carrying the troops with their landing craft, tanks, guns and vehicles had arrived from the UK where training had taken place near Loch Fyne in Scotland. The expedition consisted of two brigades of infantry and many supporting troops and aircraft. At the last moment an offer of a bomber and reconnaissance squadron of the South African Forces was gladly accepted - at a late assembly date at Durban.

The port itself - a busy place at any time - seemed to be humming with soldiers; two brigades of men who had to be fighting fit in a weeks' time, had just landed after a wartime convoy journey from UK and as the despatch put it "all units engaged in daily route marches to harden and get them fit after their voyage out".

Sitting down to dinner on our first evening in the hotel in Durban I heard the familiar high pitched voice of the wife of one of my late District Commissioners in the Sudan, Winifred Titherington, famed for her *"mauvais mots"*. "Hallo Maurice" she exclaimed "You must be going to Madagascar!"

I introduced myself next day to Major General "Bob" Sturgess, the Land Force Commander; he was charming, had no idea what a Chief Political Officer did, but "For God's sake, take that white band off your cap and dress like a proper staff officer with red tabs," he said "if you are on *my* staff!" I was only too glad to comply and sent my PA to have the necessary changes done - and my CBE ribbon sewn on! Bob Sturgess was very welcoming. He invited me to join his "A" Mess and also his brigade "talk" immediately after sailing.

I took the opportunity in Durban of calling on General Salisbury Jones, the Head of the British Military Mission in South Africa. He was most interesting - and interested; he gave me an insight into the wonderful assistance being given by the Union of South Africa to the Allied war effort - and the influence in imperial, but not necessarily South African affairs, of General Smuts. I was to meet him later.

My passage to Madagascar with my PA Douglas Grant, was booked on SS Winchester Castle - a magnificent Union Castle liner which was to carry some thousands of men and vehicles. In Durban she was HQ ship and I attended two demonstrations in which the operation was fully explained with the aid of models for the benefit of Commanding Officers, Ships Masters and Naval Liaison Officers concerned, with military and South African liaison personnel present.

The naval despatch reads:

"Special security measures were taken which included the sailing and routing of all ships for Madagascar .... by the ordinary procedures. The real orders were issued quite separately and only opened after proceeding to sea."

There were two convoys to carry and protect this expedition of some 10,000 men - Y, the slow convoy which left Durban two days earlier than Z in which was the Winchester Castle. It was in fact a very pleasant few days at sea from 28 April until 4 May when by the mysteries only known to the navigators, some 70 craft met together in one ordained area on the high seas at the appointed hour.

Leading the armada was HMS Ramillies, a fine newish battle cruiser which flew the flag of Admiral Syfret commanding the armada. Admiral Syfret was, I believe, of British South African parentage - a good leader and a likeable person. General Bob Sturgess had joined his Admiral in HMS Ramillies, and the HQ of the assaulting or landing troops was transferred to a small vessel, HMS Keren.

None of us could understand how this considerable convoy had been allowed to assemble so near to its objective without being detected from the air.

After our meeting at the rendezvous, which I suppose must have been about sunset, ships proceeded to their prearranged stations. A study of the naval despatch now is most interesting and brings back moving moments of that night when I stood by the side of Captain Sebastian Newdigate, Master of the Winchester Castle, as he steered his 20,000 ton liner through the minefields and gradually reached her appointed station. "Brigadier," Newdigate said to me, as we proceeded to the anchorage "I don't know what my owners would say if they knew what I was doing!"

At 0154 Winchester Castle anchored silently (earning great commendation for so doing) in her prearranged position off Diego Suarez Bay (in the extreme north of the Island) and landing craft took commandos and other troops ashore at Red Beach in Courrier Bay.

It had been one of the most interesting and, I suppose, hazardous journeys of my life - on the bridge of a large liner, moving through a partially cleared minefield to disembark troops on an enemy shore. At first light I had to leave the Winchester Castle, which was returning to a safer berth, to visit the Senior Naval Officer (Landing) on HMS Keren. We disembarked like gentlemen from our Winchester Castle, were rowed to Keren close by and there, dangling apparently 80' from the deck, was a steel rope ladder up which visitors were invited to climb; and climbing with a full pack and a tin helmet up the side of a merchant corvetted warship is no early-morning exercise fun for elderly Brigadiers! Having done so, to be piped on board by the duty watch, was adding insult to injury. I had paid the call because Diana's family knew the ship's captain, Captain Burgess Watson (Bongo for short), and I must say I deplored the friendship half way up! However, he was an amusing person and an eminent Naval Officer in his day, having landed all his troops without casualties, and we "swapped lies". I believe he did disembark me in some more gentlemanly manner than my arrival. On shore was a jeep about to go to Brigade HQ near the battle - my destination too; so in we jumped. "Oh Sir! Sir!" came a voice "Please may I cadge a lift?" It belonged to a journalist. I agreed on condition that his paper told my wife of my presence on the island. He promised and was as good as his word. In fact, some days later Diana was called upon by a posse of Daily Mail men plus cameras, and a very good photograph of young Meriel appeared with the caption "This little girl has never seen her Daddy". Alas how true it was!

We were driven along the deserted track to Brigade HQ whence Grant and I walked up to the front lines - and a proper line it was, almost a trench. The men had been held up on top of a ridge. This was Brigadier Frankie Festing's Brigade and things weren't going well. Douglas Grant and I had to leave to go up to the forward positions and he and I managed to apply first aid to an infantry lad who had been hit by a sniper's bullet in the backside: pints of blood but no real damage. He rather enjoyed being bound up by a wandering Brigadier.

I stayed with Brigadier Festing's HQ that night in some kind of civilian shack by the roadside. I remember that there was an enormous bed and seven of us managed to doss down thereon and get some sleep. Things had not gone well on Day 1.

Day 2: Next morning the French had moved up artillery; so had we. The enemy opened fire on the forward positions before our guns were in action and I regret to say that both the Royal Artillery and the forward infantry beat a hasty retreat under their first baptism of fire. It seems quite absurd and not to be believed, but Frankie Festing and I both went up to try to rally the infantry, and found ourselves quite alone in front! The shelling was quite spasmodic but the troops preferred to be behind the brow of the hill rather than in front. Festing and I came back also, and found Bob Sturgess, the General, sitting under a tree; I sat down next to him and he asked "Lush, do all British soldiers these days retire when shelled?" To which I replied, "Well General, it's only breakfast time now; you'll find them back by lunchtime." It made him laugh and he remembered the retort for a long time - but it was true. The men had a brew-up out of a shell fire and advanced again at noon.

A few minutes after I had spoken to General Sturgess, there was a sharp CRACK in front and a thud as a sniper's bullet entered the trunk of the tree under which we were sitting - just between our ears! Honour forbade me to move, and the volleys fired into the blue by the General's escort must have hit or frightened the sniper. We had Senegalese troops opposite to us and they were good fighters.

That evening a body of Royal Marines cleverly landed from a small corvette commanded by a young RNVR officer and took the enemy by surprise in his rear; four of our tanks came up and although they suffered 75% disablement, the fourth went on. More artillery had by now arrived and the General ordered a night attack on land and asked for a naval bombardment of the dockyard of Antsirane, the town which was under attack by land. The General's despatch goes on:

"Brigadier Festing now pushed forward 29 Independent Brigade and the remaining tanks right through to the main town, Antsirane, with little or no opposition, and reached the main harbour; he then continued to mop up the town with little or no resistance. He entered the Residency at 0100 hours and, assisted by Brigadier Lush CPO, at once commenced to take over the town."

Day 3; 0100: I had actually entered Antsirane independently of Brigadier Festing and in the harbour walked into a building which was clearly some kind of headquarters. Imagine my feelings, not to say embarrassment, when a good looking young French Naval Officer jumped to his feet, whipped out his sword (from somewhere) and, handing it to me hilt first, exclaimed "I surrender to you - I am your prisoner." I returned the sword with a first class Royal Military Academy salute, and said "I accept and return your sword, with honour." (All this at 1.00 am in French!) "Now tell me who you are, and come with me to the Brigade Commander - I am the Chief Political Officer and shall want your help." He turned out to be Capitaine de Vaisseau de Maertens, Naval Officer in Charge, Madagascar, and we went to the Residency of Antsirane, up the hill, where Brigadier Festing had taken the surrender of Colonel Claerebout, French Officer Commanding the Defences and was with other officials of the port. I segregated those who had to do with the administration of the town and region, and established, quite easily, friendly relations. While Festing and others of his staff were arranging ceasefires and cover for the troops, I began, at about dawn, to establish local civil security and maintenance of law and order as our first requirements, and met the Chief of Police and the Administrator Maire for that purpose, having assured myself that they would play the game. I suggested a brief rally and rest (I was given a room with a sofa and washing material in the Residency which was unharmed) and fixed a civil meeting for 0800 that morning. En passant I accepted an invitation from Capitaine de Maertens to lunch at a nearby estaminet later in the day!

Douglas Grant and I slept - somehow he had collected some of our gear and I had a shave and general "clean up". He was splendid in arranging the 0800 meeting at which I explained that the Admiral Commanding would stipulate the terms of surrender to the naval and military leaders and that I would ask them to help me and my administrative officers maintain law and order in the feeding and the welfare of the population, and in the return to normality of business. I could assure them that, as administrators of the occupying force, we would try to accommodate military and civilian needs and that I would do my best to alleviate suffering caused by the Allied Blockade (which had been going on for two years).

During that night, HMS Illustrious, an aircraft carrier, reported that her aircraft had sunk a French submarine (Le Heros; her survivors were rescued) and HMS Indomitable was attacked by another submarine while about to enter Diego Suarez Bay the next day. Her "screen" vessel destroyed the submarine.

My civil administration meeting went well and the will to help expressed last night was repeated and again appeared to be in good faith. I believe that there had been one or two dissenters among the local administration but nothing to worry about.

In the meantime, General Sturgess, in addition to the occupation of the harbour of Diego Suarez and town of Antsirane, had to make sure of the capitulation of the forts on Oranjia Peninsula, which commanded the entrance to the harbour, and asked the Admiral for support with some well aimed shells from the guns on Ramillies, Hermione and another ship, at 0950. However, the time was postponed because *pour-parlers* were going on at Oranjia, not once but twice, and in his despatch, Admiral Syfret wrote:

> "I was tired of the delays which were keeping the fleet steaming up and down in dangerous waters .... three ships commenced bombardment of the Peninsula to encourage the enemy to surrender .... It was obviously successful."

"Cease fire" was ordered ten minutes later on news of surrender.

This last bombardment began during the end of my meeting with the French at the Residency, and I had just given a strong affirmative to a query which "supposed that all hostilities had now ceased?" Was my face red!

Naturally, I spent a busy day discussing problems and especially urgent needs with the French officials. I also made a thorough inspection of the town and harbour, requisitioned a good car, discussed the situation with Festing and at midday lunched with my captive, Capitaine de Maertens. He was charming; properly, we both avoided military subjects, except for him to tell me that he would not have fought against us at Diego Suarez had not his own ship of the French Navy been sunk under him by British Naval Forces in Oranjia in 1940, after France's collapse and his refusal to steam the French Fleet into British waters before surrender. De Maertens told me a great deal about the absence of Free French feeling: "de Gaulle has not yet had much influence in the French Colonies overseas; witness Syria and Dakar." He asked me to arrange for him to join the French Forces in Europe. This I did and, alas, lost sight of him; but I did hear that he had joined some part of the de Gaullist Navy.

At 1730 hours on that day, the waters having been swept, Ramillies, Hermione, Lightning and Paladin, all Royal Navy ships, proceeded into Diego Suarez Bay, putting "finis" to the military side of operation Ironclad - or so we thought at the time.

Day 4: This was a day of military disposition - defence of the Bay (which was a vast area with a very small entrance), positioning of troops, occupation of the aerodrome by the squadron of the East African Air Force, and the choice and establishment of the General's "A" Mess in a former French Mess on an eminence overlooking Diego Suarez Bay. It was a very comfortable building and had the most lovely view of the Bay with the whole fleet, especially HMS Ramillies who lay just opposite our window.

It was a very busy day for me, but heaven compared with my first day in Addis Ababa. Douglas Grant with some French colleague found a small but pleasant house for us both wherein also I opened the CPO's office, and that soon became a centre of business and information.

Day 5: The Admiral received the French military leaders on Ramillies and then held a conference in the Residency which the French and British commanders and I attended and at which the "Conditions" regarding the French Forces in Diego Suarez were discussed, accepted and signed. Commander Thorold on the Admiral's staff and I, with one of the French officers to help, had finalised the document prepared in London for final signature. It was 1100 and as we finalised our assurances and French acceptances, HMS Birmingham loosed her last salvo on Fort Caimans: "Perfide Albion" muttered the oldest French officer!

On the same day we tackled two of our main problems which lay ahead at a British conference on Ramillies chaired by Admiral Syfret.

First, should we immediately continue operations by occupation of Majunga and Tamatave? We could do so either with existing British brigades (whose presence in India was urgently required) or later with the help of South African Brigade promised by Smuts and East African Brigade from Mombasa. We decided in Ramillies to continue at once.

I remember that I slept through most of this technically military conference. Suddenly I received a resounding blow on my back delivered by Thorold sitting next to me and woke in time to hear the Admiral asking the CPO (myself) for his views. "Majunga" hissed Thorold. "MAJUNGA!" I almost shouted - and Majunga was approved as our next task - and that soon.

Second, the participation of the Free French was an extremely serious complication. My secret orders opened on Winchester Castle stated quite definitely that Free French participation in administration would not be employed. This was in accordance with original thinking in London. In announcing the occupation on 7/8 May, however, the BBC communique quoting the Prime Minister stated the Free French participation in administration *would* be used. This was confirmed on 13 May by GOC; it had been decided for overriding political considerations to issue a communique stating that the Free French would be associated with the administration of Madagascar. I advised Sturgess and Syfret that my view (confirmed by reports in Diego Suarez) was that such an association would alienate the bulk of the French population, provoking civilian unrest which the military would have to control. Syfret added that in view of the above, he would require more troops in any extension of our occupation. The Chiefs of Staff bluntly told Syfret "to get on with the job". For other reasons, however, the furtherance of our occupation was postponed in spite of Smuts' strong recommendation that we should continue with it at once; a recommendation most wrongly ignored by Chiefs of Staff.

Now Eden, the Foreign Secretary, or shall I say the Foreign Office, was in favour of using the Free French. De Gaulle and the Free French who had been most outrageous in their behaviour in the Middle East were now, apparently, behaving better, and Churchill cabled Syfret that he was being pushed into indicating association of the Free French and therefore to seek a modus vivendi. This was completely understandable but surely the Chief of Staff or the FO could also have cabled Syfret explaining this change of policy? That is how we at the northern tip of Madagascar were viewed!

It is right to record here that the Foreign Office always expected as a matter of policy that no approach or response to a foreign power, government or representative be made except by a member of the Foreign Service under instructions from the FO, or, exceptionally, independently. Their argument was that, in the end, the Prime Minister (or the public) would lay the reponsibility at the door of the Foreign Secretary for any dealing with a foreign government. The FO as a department cordially disliked the word "political" in the title of CPO and DCPO, and did their best to supplant him by a Foreign Service Officer with direct access to the FO. In peacetime this policy was surely correct but not in war, especially under a Prime Minister such as Churchill.

On Friday 27 May an unidentified aircraft flew three circuits round Diego Suarez Bay and then disappeared eastwards. It was not challenged. The RAF thought it was a South African machine; the Navy dubbed it RAF and the South Africans put it down as Naval. At next morning's conference the lack of identification was confirmed and alarm procedure followed; all ships, including Ramillies, raised steam and cruised round the harbour while it was properly swept for submarines and mines. At 1900 they returned to moorings; we landsmen thought that Ramillies had returned to her original anchorage. At sunset, that same day of 28 May, there was a series of explosions under water; a tanker sank immediately and Ramillies, not suddenly, but quite slowly listed several degrees to port. She had obviously been torpedoed. We soldiers in our Mess on land, saw the whole episode from the shore. Ramillies was clearly damaged (she had two torpedo hits below water level). Luckily the damage was not fatal and she limped back to Durban under her own steam but was out of action for six months.

Next morning, the wreck of a two-man submarine was found on the rocks at the entrance of the harbour. I was also informed that two suspicious figures had been seen by Malagaches - Madagascar natives - walking in a NW direction across the Anoritabe Peninsular, north of the Bay. I passed the news to the military and a platoon of troops was sent to reconnoitre. They caught up with the two men, obviously Japanese, who, when they were overtaken and surrounded, stood back to back and opened fire on the troops. They were both killed. On the bodies were found aerial sketches of the harbour and Bay showing, inter alia, the exact position of Ramillies. Diego Suarez was an expensive foray for the Royal Navy.

We - which really meant I, as the political adviser - were in deep trouble over a response which we made to Monsieur Annet, the Governor General of Madagascar in Tananarive. It happened this way and indicated the coming and going which went on between the British and the French on the island.

There arrived in Diego Suarez a few weeks after the occupation, a Mr Barnett, Manager of the Standard Vacuum Oil Company in Tananarive; he gave me and others every confidence that he was trustworthy. He told the General and me that he had been sent by the Governor General Annet to find a "basis for agreement with the British whereby French sovereignty could be safeguarded and consequent neutrality would save further bloodshed". We were impressed by Mr Barnett and he seemed to have the blessing of the United States. I drafted an aide memoire which Sturgess approved and we sent it back to Monsieur Annet the Governor General.

The FO had, even before this demarche, decided that, the fighting having ceased, a Foreign Service man with direct access to them was right for the Madagascar situation, and they cabled to say that Lawrence Grafftey Smith had been selected to relieve me and that I, MSL, was to go to Cairo where "I was required to replace John Hamilton". I discovered when in Cairo the following year that this story was a complete myth!

When the cable reporting our response to Annet was received in London, Eden deplored such an approach and was strongly supported by Smuts in Pretoria. The FO added:

"…. particularly as *our* political representative had not arrived".

Smuts was most upset also at any approach being made to Annet and made clear his distrust of Sturgess' political and, indeed, military wisdom.

The Prime Minister Churchill, however, while approving replacing Lush by Grafftey Smith, strongly vindicated the approach to Annet as being part of direct instructions to Syfret to seek a modus vivendi:

> "I wish you to know that Sturgess in sending an aide memoire, was acting in accord with my instructions to Syfret to seek a modus vivendi."

He cabled Smuts in the same manner:

> "This is not 'appeasement'"

General Platt likewise was utterly loyal in his very strong support of me as his Chief Political Officer. He considered that the conduct of negotiations and the administration of the area must come under my, and Platt's, control:

> "I have no objection to Grafftey Smith coming out to serve under Lush, my political and administrative officer, as his diplomatic adviser."

He added in a separate cable:

"I propose to take Lush with me, Sturgess and Festing, to confer with Smuts in Pretoria on future plans."

London resisted General Platt's defence of me, but in the end agreed to a compromise which seemed utterly wasteful and nonsensical to us, that Grafftey Smith and I should divide the responsibilities, he doing political and propaganda work, I continuing as CPO to run the administrative side. Luckily Grafftey Smith, whom I knew and liked well enough, accepted the division with good grace, though this stupid departmental row, stemming from the *idée fixe* of the FO, caused trouble and distress to two individuals and waste of good brain power. Lawrence Grafftey Smith has written several clever pages about it all in his book *Hands to Play* (Routledge and Keegan Paul 1975), though his attack on General Platt is unworthy of an amusing book which gives an excellent account of Madagascar's history, people and countryside where he, poor mortal, spent two years as British Consul General.

In the book Grafftey Smith records:

"I was always treated with great kindness and consideration by General Sturgess and all officers in Diego Suarez, enjoying in that military world where I was the only civilian, the same amused and general tolerance as a regimental goat."

He was. I remember on about his second evening in the Mess, he came out with some classical expression for an ordinary occurrence, to be greeted with a withering demand from one senior officer not to introduce these Foreign Office translations of English into a soldiers' mess. Nor shall I forget almost his first evening when I was showing him his quarters; he and I were discussing matters of moment when I suddenly was aware that he had disappeared! He had indeed fallen into an anti-aircraft slit trench in the garden - I always feared that he suspected a trap.

His same book, incidentally, contains a most excellent account of the emergence of Pakistan into Dominion status. I met him there again in 1947 where he had just been appointed Deputy High Commissioner.

Let us return to Diego Suarez where we sat for five months. A CPO is always busy and in accordance with the policy of making the inhabitants under British rule more affluent and comfortable than in the rest of the blockaded island, I set off to Durban to buy, literally, a shipload of necessities for, chiefly, the French and Creoles but also the Malagaches. I had noticed, for instance, that clothing was in noticeably short supply and many people wore raffia suits; more than one officer had his medal ribbon colours sewn into his tunic in different colours of raffia - a locally grown grass product.

In Durban I found Messrs Mitchell Cotts - well known throughout the south and east of Africa - only too ready to help with expert advice and foods and I came back feeling like a fairy godmother.

I could never understand why Grafftey Smith, who took over the supply side in Tananarive, did not follow my example and order provisions from South Africa, instead of suffering interminable delays by ordering from London - 6,000 miles away!

By this time a few most welcome staff were arriving, kindly provided by Political HQ in Nairobi, who also assisted in our currency affairs. Incidentally, the Banque de France in Tananarive kindly supplied a large quantity of low currency (1, 5 and 10 Fcs) in exchange for the equivalent in high currency notes which were useless in the economy.

There was always a flow of correspondence between the British and French administrations located respectively in Diego Suarez and Tananarive, which somehow penetrated through police and military barriers set up by the French about 100 miles south of Diego Suarez. There was no regular overland route by road or rail between Diego Suarez and the south but determined travellers could get through.

Our other correspondence with Tananarive, indeed with the Governor General himself, concerned a British "agent", one Lieutenant Simpson Jones who had been captured, stark naked, on Reunion Island where he had foundered his craft while on espionage duty. He had been condemned to death as a spy and I or Grafftey Smith had sent successive telegrams demanding, if not his release, then certainly a reprieve - this was granted by Annet. The young lieutenant turned up later as you will read.

General Platt, the GOC in East Africa, took over from the Chiefs of Staff the Madagascar operations and all of us in the administration - including the bicephalous establishment of Grafftey Smith and me. Platt was ordered to consult Smuts in Pretoria regarding the future operations on the island. He took General Sturgess and me. We were invited to stay at Liberty House, the Residence of the Prime Minister, and were well entertained by General Smuts himself.

Platt guided the conversations primarily to the attempts Sturgess and I had made to find a modus vivendi with Annet at Tananarive; we hoped we had satisfied the Field Marshall and then passed on to the operations needed to secure the rest of the country. Eventually Smuts agreed on a joint assault by 29 Infantry Brigade and 22 East African Brigade, if negotiations were unsuccessful. These negotiations included attempts by us at Diego Suarez to reach a settlement with Tananarive, which were gradually proving abortive, and by London to reach an agreement with the Free French to take over or take part in the administration of Madagascar. Both approaches were doomed to fail.

On our last day at Liberty House (22 June) I met Smuts coming down the stairs to breakfast, a telegram in his hand, his face as white as a sheet. He said nothing but later told me that he had just received news of the surrender of Tobruk to Rommel's forces with the capture of the remnants of the South African Division defending the port. This was a most bitter calamity for Smuts and the Union of South Africa, whose people were by no means whole hearted in supporting this "British war".

Smuts asked me to go with him to his study afterwards. "I want to draft a telegram to Churchill. I am no good at English and I want your help." We drafted the telegram as he wished (of course he knew English very well, but he needed support). The telegram for Churchill began:

> "Just heard of the fall of Tobruk. This is no time for recriminations. We must render secure what we still have. If you decide not to go on from Majunga to Tananarive, I offer the South African Brigade now at Diego Suarez for the Middle East. The Division which we have lost will be replaced within six months.
>
> Smuts"

I felt absolutely miserable as I bade farewell to that great man who was far more an imperial statesman than Prime Minister of South Africa - and who found the former role easier to carry out than the latter.

The Smuts conference was followed by a staff conference at which I developed a cracking rigor due to malaria which was as quick to go as it was severe. We had a hazardous flight back to Diego Suarez; the pilot, new to the terrain and sea, missed his cue and rather than risk another miss hit went back to the Comoros Islands and landed by flare lights. I was glad, for being a plane load of Generals, the RAF looked after us well, and I persuaded the party to stay next morning on land so that we could see some of the spice producing gardens for which the islands are famous.

We spent two months longer in Diego Suarez. Amongst the Political Officers Nairobi had by now provided me was an old friend from Cairo, Geoffrey Parker, whom I had known well on the staff of the newspaper Egyptian Gazette. Luckily, he and Grafftey Smith got on well together and indeed shared a house and mess with young Grant and another.

But it was an unhappy situation and I personally was most unhappy at the time - for I guessed rightly that personal feelings of rancour on somebody's part, probably in the FO, had brought it all about. It also made my future again very uncertain and my letters home mirrored this: only the loyalty of Platt and my work kept me sane!

We had much to do administratively in preparation for the attack on Mujunga and Tamatare and the possibility of administering Tananarive. More Political Officers arrived. A further attempt through Red Cross officials was made by Tananarive to secure a *modus vivendi* for the whole island.

During the first week in September 1942, then, I embarked on yet another convoy; this time starting from Diego Suarez - destination Majunga. This was the start of operation "Stream Line Jane" (General Sturgess' code names for the occupation of Majunga port on the west coast of Madagascar, Tamatave the main port on the east and Jane the capital, Tananarive.)

I had been delegated to accompany the landing force which occupied Majunga and thence continue with Brigadier Dimoline commanding an East African Brigade on the road to Tananarive. We landed at night just before dawn. British troops all went to their allotted places and there was no resistance. I and my officers routed out the French administrative authorities whom I found willing to cooperate. I heard that there was a Bishop in the hotel who was disgruntled at the inconvenience - so I went to soothe him. I then reported to General Platt and Francis Rennell who was by now CPO instead of Mitchell (assigned as High Commissioner to Fiji). All the top brass had come on this venture which was to end in Tananarive.

I then went off in a very pleasant Colonial Body Ford (allotted to me) with Douglas Grant to join Brigadier Dimoline who proposed to fight his way to Tananarive. This advance took the troops 10 days. I found the French officials en route very helpful and ready to repair the appalling and wanton damage which the French troops had done to their country, destroying a 12 million franc bridge - but not so badly that we could not cross - cutting down lovely avenues of trees and blowing up culverts. None of this really impeded our advance but put back the economic life of the colony by some years.

> Extract from a letter from MSL to DRL 17.9.42:
> "…. Yesterday I went up on a fantastic mission helping a French District Commissioner telephone to his Government or even Governor General begging them to stop this "imbecile" war. He took a Malagache postmaster with us who was compelled to climb every telegraph pole until he could find the line "through" to Tananarive some 200 kilometres distant. The French DC and I followed: we advanced beyond our front line who were at that moment dislodging some French (Moroccan) troops from high ground. No man's land was paradise to our French man when he fina'ly "got through". I heard him speak with an official who purported to be in the Secretariat Generale at Tananarive. My friend then emitted a torrent of desperate requests demanding, pleading that Tananarive should end this "imbecile" war. The postmaster on top of the telegraph pole was by now sitting target for the enemy snipers at some 800' - we were only 16' less, also sitting targets. However the plea to Tananarive failed and we retired behind our lines, my Frenchman disconsolate. I asked him to recommend the brave postmaster for a Croix de Guerre after hostilities."

On 23 September we occupied Tananarive. We had been told, Brigadier Dimoline and I, that the capital was an open city. We formed a small convoy and arrived at the city at 2.00 pm. We were met by officers in spotless uniforms who greeted us at the entrance politely but with a request that we should make our entry the next day and in any case "Please do not send your troops to the north of the city as our (French) troops are evacuating the place southwards, by that route." "To hell with that!" said my gallant Brigadier, "We are coming in right now!" and he at once sent armoured cars to the north to intercept any troops.

On we went to be greeted by really friendly crowds of cheering French and Malagache men and women, some with flowers, all with smiles. As we drove through the suburbs, a French car came hurtling down and tried to join the procession. I got very angry and tried to stop it. At this moment, out popped a young man, obviously an Englishman, dressed immaculately, even if it looked a trifle home made, in the uniform of Lieutenant RNVR. "Lieutenant Simpson Jones at your service, Sir. I served with your brother [Cecil], Sir, in Devonport. Thank you for saving my life. I am now liaison ADC to the French Secretary General to help him assist you, Sir." Here was the British agent captured in Reunion and condemned to death, but reprieved and imprisoned in an oubliette, which he was wont, by bribery, to quit and call on young damsels in the city. He indeed persuaded some of them to build the uniform he was wearing.

During our first evening in Tananarive I asked my worthy PA whether he would be good enough to summon a midwife to my room the next morning. With all his skill and intelligence, I am not sure that Douglas Grant knew the French for a midwife and, even if he did, how could he procure one within 12 hours? However, he did rustle up the chief "sage-femme" in Tananarive, and next morning she arrived all smiles, knowing exactly the reason for her summons, and bearing the necessary equipment. Curiously enough, the other Brigadier, Dimoline, had made a similar request.

The reason for the presence of these obstetric ladies was simple enough - we two officers, like every other man who had marched through the sandy river beds en route from Majunga to the capital, were suffering intense discomfort, if not pain and agony, in our toes, owing to the presence between the nail and the flesh of one or more eggs laid by the female sand flea, named "chigger". These minute but ever-procreative insects abound in the sandy river banks or beds of the many streams which we, gallant troops, had crossed in our ten days' walk from Majunga. The mother would find the human foot an ideal habitat for burrowing, and the human toe nail perfect protection for the eggs; ovipositing took place and the mother would then die under one's toenail, forming a really delightful sac of poison which only the "sage-femmes" of Tananarive could remove painlessly and effectively.

I had been given a pleasant suite in the big hotel near the main square and here I bathed and changed and then met the principal officials of the city. The Secretary General left behind by his Governor General, who had quitted Tananarive with his "army" for the south, having refused the terms of surrender offered by Grafftey Smith and Rennell in Majunga, refused to lead the Government; it was therefore very necessary to find a personality respected by the French and Malagache who we could appoint as figurehead of the French community.

I discussed the possibility of finding some such person with various Frenchmen, with the American Consul General on whom I called, and with several British businessmen, eg. Mr Barnett, who had remained in Madagascar throughout the war: I imagine they may have been impeded from leaving by the Vichy French. General opinion pointed to Monsieur Reallon, an ex-Governor General of Madagascar, who had retired, married a most charming Malagache wife and lived in Tananarive. I was guided to his house. The first things which thrust themselves upon me in the Reallon salon (a large room) were two life sized portraits of King Edward VII and Queen Alexandra of Great Britain. Clearly they had once hung on the walls of the British Official Residence in Madagascar. It was a shock to find them in this particular house! I saw Reallon, explained my mission and said that if he were willing to cooperate I would take him to my General next day. General Platt and Francis Rennell were bound to follow us to the capital rapidly and I handed over that problem to them while I tackled the administration of the country. This was not difficult, *en principe*, but we had to find ways and means, food and necessities and I waited for the very considerable staff to arrive in order that they could find out what were the real necessities: more than those, I was not prepared to give.

General Platt and Francis Rennell came along in a day or two with Grafftey Smith. We were a very heavy-weight team compared to what I had been accustomed to.

Grafftey Smith handled the Free French problem and as we had warned London and him, found that the Free French element were of very low calibre. I thankfully left that matter to him. Our paths did not overlap unduly; when Rennell went (he was inclined to make heavy weather over ordinary problems) leaving General Smallwood the chief authority as Chief Military Administrator and a Chief Staff Political Officer, all seemed tidy in the bicephalous administration caused by Grafftey Smith's infusion. I made it my business to go out and about in the districts.

The British press were remarkably good about both assaults in Madagascar. The reporter to whom I gave a lift from the beaches in Courier Bay was as good as his word and spelt out the story mentioning that I was the Political Officer. Press comment on the reasons for the occupation of the Grande Ile was well founded and good, and their reports on contacts between ourselves in Diego Suarez and Annet were accurate. But naturally Madagascar was reported in a low key, ie. the inside pages. English people generally, like their soldiers on the spot, thoroughly disliked taking up arms against a spineless colony of our ex-ally. And the ordinary people were spineless. The officials were the dregs of the French Civil Service and the surrender of their homeland, perhaps unwittingly but really because they were low grade French subjects, made them easy prey to the excuses broadcast by the Petainists. I myself found one person only who expressed any shame for his country, and Monsieur Reallon, having decided to retire into the Malagache community, had taken on the mantle of his wife's people and now thought little of his homeland. It was depressing living and working among such people and I longed sometimes to learn more about the leading Malagasy or Malagache citizens. Twenty years later as you will read, I found a much closer rapport with them and found them delightful.

General Platt was very good to me and while he was on the island I went to Tamatare by rail with him and also to various other places. The rail journey from Tananarive to Tamatare took about ten hours. The line was single track in almost, it seemed, everlasting loops and curves through the forest between Tananarive and the sea shore at Brickaville. The curves on the line appeared too sharp ever to be manoeuvred and one's heart was in one's mouth at practically every other bend. We were sitting in the small forward car immediately behind the driver who - motorists as we all were - appalled us by never apparently attempting to guide the train by steering wheel or arm. Of course he didn't need to - the wheel flanges on the rails kept us on course. But it was uncanny. The forest through which we passed looked primeval enough - I should have hated to wander more than ten yards from the railway line. At intervals of 30-50 kilometres there were clearings where small railway enclaves had been built. The line was scarcely ever straight and in one stretch spiralled downwards and then across itself in some indescribable loop. We felt fairly groggy until we hit the sea at Brickaville, and ran north some 30 miles along the coast to Tamatare. Here we found a good harbour and a seaside town. I had a Political Officer here and one or two technical experts and here I met Robert Adeane, Controller of Transport, our great railway expert who was part of the political branch, and achieved great things for Madagascar on the railway system.

Here I came across the new Madagascar fuel for motor vehicles - a mixture of rum and petrol. Cars had been running well on this mixture for two years, no doubt intoxicating the driver and passengers, noisy but moderately efficient. I also saw the effect of rum on a most hardened black East African private soldier who after knocking back a hefty draft of it fell flat on his face and was unconscious for half an hour!

Extract from letter MSL Tananarive, 28 September 1942 to DRL:

"…. We had a really good trek by road. It took ten days and we had lots of luck, a tremendous amount of hard work and a little fighting. The country was very lovely in fact, rather like the foothills of the Ethiopian Plateau, but was entirely ruined by devastating grass fires which were both embarrassing and dangerous. I spent quite a lot of time saving Brigade HQ from destruction by fire. My job other than that was, of course, to settle down the administration as we went along. This I found really quite easy in all cases except one. The local French District Commissioner or Chef de District as they call it, always had a set piece about *l'honneur* and loyalty. Having got that off his chest he got back to work and was generally correct and helpful. Some, of course, welcomed me with open arms. All wept a little over a whisky in the evening. I am going to ask the Administration here to write a small essay on *l'honneur*. I simply don't know what it means.

"Well, we came to the last day when, after a hectic night of filling in holes, building broken bridges and pulling down barricades, we reached Kilo 15. Here the local DC met us and said the military Commander would meet us at Kilo 11 and the Mayor of Jane at Kilo 9. So off drove the Brigade Commander and self. First of all the road blocks were still up and being pulled down by the usual prisoners (the French civil administration depends on prison labour just as we did), then we found no Military Commander but instead the Mayor or DC of Jane who said that we could come right away into the city but would we mind not going to the north of the road because the French troops were still retreating there! Then the Mayor went on to say that all arrangements had been made to receive and billet us, but would we mind waiting till tomorrow as they weren't quite ready! An explosion from the Brigade Commander and we formed a procession of two armoured cars, French Mayor, Brigade Commander, MSL, Staff and our leading troops. And so we drove into the second capital I have occupied. Only, whereas Addis Ababa showed few signs of welcome even from the Habash, Tananarive gave us an enthusiastic welcome; French and Malagache alike cheered and clapped and flowers were thrown.

"Since then I have been cabinet-making and got an administration working yesterday. We are continuing the French Administration as it stands, making few personnel changes at the top. I am in charge of it as liaison, controller and guide. Francis Rennell came here yesterday just after I had finished cabinet-making and will stay here, I hope, a few weeks to deal with the rather abstruse financial and economic affairs. Grafftey is dealing with trade and propaganda.

"Tananarive is a most attractive town. It is built on the faces of a very high hill and the Queen's Palace stands out on the very top. The flowers and fruit are lovely and the climate very like Addis Ababa. There are a good many British people in the place and yesterday I called on the Carters, the American Consul and his wife. There is an Anglican Cathedral with a (Missionary) Bishop and Archdeacon. All rather bats!"

Extract from letter 8 October 1942 MSL to DRL:

"…. Well, we had an amusing if semi-tragic end to our march up here. It took us ten days of hard work and hard living, though the HQ I was with (Brigadier Dimoline) lived well and I kept them a good deal in meat and eggs. But the imbecile destruction of bridges and roads (one bridge which cost 12 million francs less than 10 years ago) has been heart breaking. Imbecile, because in their own words which I culled from one of their Orders of the Day, the French had no hope of achieving even a modicum of successful defence and the destruction has merely damaged the well-being and interests of the colony and the unfortunate Malagache natives who live therein. The roads were blocked with trees and tank blocks, the bridges were destroyed and holes blown in embankments - but it didn't stop us for more than a day or two and the troops soon pulled them down. I went along fixing up administration as one progressed, getting the French DCs and Police Inspectors to realise that their job was to keep law and order going and that we were ready to help them do so. Most were cooperative and willing; all were only too pleased that the war had passed them over; most again were ready to help as long as their "honour" could be preserved (nobody quite knows what this honour means). It was, of course, quite fantastic to see the people who a week before had been busily blocking roads and demolishing bridges, now removing the blocks and repairing the bridges. The unfortunate Malagache, which is the generic term for the inhabitants of this unhappy island, look on with amazement at the extraordinary behaviour of the white races. The Malagache are a pleasant but ineffective race. They are lazy but not lazier than any African; they are timid and most unwarlike and most of the Malagasy troops have deserted before us. The others have fought moderately well. I think one could get to like them quite a lot and certainly the way they rushed forward as soon as we occupied a village and prepared to undo what the French had made them do was most satisfactory.

"In Tananarive there followed visits from the Head of Government who was correct, but hated it and us, and ended by becoming emotional; the head soldier who had turned his coat from being very anti-British to the other way of thinking. The next two days I spent cabinet-making and didn't get much sleep - interviews with people who knew what was what and who was who and more interviews with possible candidates for the chief posts. As a matter of fact we have made very few changes except at the Head of the Government. The Governor General has departed with his troops and is on the run, so we have made the Civil Secretary or Secretaire General the Head of Government. Then we had to intern a few undesirables; meet Heads of Departments, some of whom were very cordial, some not. Then we had a meeting of the Conseil d'Administration and finally in five days the show was running again, the courts functioning, the banks open, the Government officers at work and all was going well. I expect there are a good many working against us but on the whole the show is functioning with good cooperation. It is interesting to study French Administration at work and to compare it with our own in the Sudan. They have a vast number of French officials and *no* tribal leaders. They had a system of Native Administration but the Gouverneurs Indigenes are chosen from intelligent young men of the educated class who go through an administrative school and who are then appointed as Gouverneurs Indigenes, rather like our Mamurs and Sub Mamurs. Some are really very good as executive officers but they are as French in their ways and their thoughts as the French themselves, and there is, so far as I can see at present, no real native or Malagache structure - it is all French.

"There is a very extensive and influential missionary organisation here - largely Protestant with a number of Anglicans. We found a British Bishop at Majunga who has now come to Tananarive, an Archdeacon here and a large English Cathedral. Then the London Missionary Society is much to the fore with a very pleasant Secretary - they will do us a lot of good and will help, I hope, a great deal, in impressing on the Malagache that we have come here not to take over the country but to let the French carry on. It's no easy thing to make the Malagache understand that! There are a number of British commercial people all of whom hope we are going to run the show and clean up the graft and gestapo methods of the recent regime. The last we shall do but I doubt if we can make the leopard change its spots - and I have come to the conclusion that *all* Continental officials make their living by corruption. The American Consul General and his wife are very pleasant and forthcoming and most sensible. They have open house and one meets all and sundry there. Many of the French are very sociable too and though I haven't been yet to many of their homes (deliberately); I shall have to begin being sociable now.

"At the moment I live in the best hotel where I have a sitting room, a bedroom and a lovely bathroom and am comfortable enough, though hotel life with a number of British officers is inclined to pall, and I am on the look-out for a house to share with Grant and my Legal Adviser Major Bellis, lately Mayor of Southport.

"My present appointment and title is Military Administrator, Madagascar, but the whole organisation here is very temporary and none of us knows from moment to moment what the future will be. I shall probably be here at any rate until the end of the year and thereafter it depends on what happens and what our policy here is to be. I did ask yesterday whether I could not be given a spot of home leave - but I am wanted here for the time being and we must be patient. Francis Rennell is going home next week (with a letter for you I hope) and I shall discuss with him plans for (a) my going home (b) you coming out to E Africa. So much depends on what happens. But I am determined that we must get together this next year somehow. I feel you have had so many family decisions to make and that I have failed you so utterly - and I do want a rest. I am terribly *well* in fact and the climate here is lovely - too cold if anything; how lucky I am to have had nearly two years in the temperate climates of Ethiopia and Madagascar. My only recent bother has been chiggers, little fleas that burrow into the feet and especially under the toenails where they lay their eggs and die. I have removed 25 from my two feet and, though it's an easy extraction one's feet look like a grid iron. I got them one night which I spent without shoes or stockings, getting the troops across a ford - but they are endemic here. Malaria is very common too in spite of the height of Tananarive. Seeing that it is surrounded by rice fields which look very like the cultivation in the Nile Delta underwater, one cannot be surprised at mosquitoes. Since my attack in Pretoria I have been free of it.

"Tananarive is a most attractive place perched on several hills. The houses are of red brick and red tiles and are built apparently on the precipitous sides of the hills, and the light and shade effects are marvellous. There are many lovely flowers - lilies, carnations, roses, larkspur, etc., and the jacarandas are just coming out. There are many hibiscus shrubs and a lovely bush which is called "Yesterday, Today and Tomorrow" because the flowers which smell just like jasmine are first white, (a lovely sight), and then turn purple and then into leaves. They are a beautiful sight. People don't go in for large or very lovely gardens but have beds of cut flowers - and the Malagache grow numbers for sale.

"The other day I went by railway down to Tamatave on the east coast. It is Madagascar's commercial port. It was a most lovely journey down, very winding (tortuous), a most beautiful valley with running streams, thick green forest and waterfalls. The railway is a fine effort and twists and turns like a corkscrew.

"To return to Tamatave. It's a jolly seaside place - warm and balmy. It rains a lot there and the grass seems perennially green. We went to the Botanical Gardens and saw vanilla plants and hundreds of trees and palms and had a really grand afternoon. On return from there I went south to Antsirabe which is the Harrogate of Madagascar and has the most enormous hotel where we had the most gargantuan lunch. I shall do a good deal of travelling I expect; I have Political Officers in most places and have to go out to see them. Rather like running a biggish province in the Sudan! I, at least, have a good station wagon or Colonial Body Car.

".... One afternoon there walked or rather ran into my office in Tananarive, a distraught French official. He turned out to be the Resident Administrator of Tamatave, the harbour on the north east coast. Without any preamble he almost shouted at me "I demand my instant arrest!" and that was all I could extract from him during the next half hour. I examined him this way and that way; had he pocketed the cash and been found out? "No!" Had he assaulted anyone? "No!" Reference to others disclosed that while he persuaded his wife to remain within the comfort of Tananarive he had been running a second matrimonial establishment with a Malagache lady in Tamatave; the wife had found out! We sent man and wife to Durban for repatriation!

"A small town on the coast, name forgotten, and on the railway, demanded a tricolour surrender - ie. a ceremonial surrender with honour. So I sent by rail a platoon of West African infantry and a young Political Officer with orders to arrange the ceremony at the railway station. All went well; our troops arrived; the French Guard of Honour was there; mutual salutes; the young Political Officer began a short speech and as he spoke the words: ".... and we have come in peace and with peace in our ...." a bullet was fired! At that moment an African askari (private soldier) playing about with his rifle, managed to press the trigger. Luckily the bullet went vertically upwards injuring no-one, but it passed directly through the glass roof, parts of which crashed to the ground. Red-faced Political Officer paused in his speech and then had the sense to carry on. Honour was satisfied; but, "Why do these *peaceful* Anglais come down and break up our railway station?"

Then came my release. A telegram from Political Headquarters Nairobi summoning me thither for the onward journey to Cairo for a posting as DCPO North Africa - in fact Tripolitania; they did not say so because the battle had not yet begun but British Military Adminstration was in training (in Cairo) for work in those parts and I was to head it.

It was as if an angel had arrived with a white cloth to wipe away the miseries which the Foreign Office (and I detected the evil genius therein) had poured upon me, unsuccessfully thanks to the loyalty of my Generals in Nairobi, but not without spoiling the freedom and happiness of life. Moreover the fact that we were fighting and imposing an administration on Frenchmen who should have been our allies but had lost their souls, repelled me. The words which North Africa spelt for me was war against our real enemies, work which could help terminate the war, freedom from intolerant Emperors and jealous Foreign Offices - and I quitted Madagascar with a light heart and a sense that I was about to tackle a straight-forward job. I had suffered a bad dream.

So far as Madagascar was concerned French troops capitulated in the extreme south of the island on 5 November having prolonged hostilities since 5 May for exactly six months - which gave them all increased pensions - a deliberate plot! Annet was sent as POW to South Africa and later handed over to the Free French who tried and imprisoned him.

General LeGentilhomme arrived in Madagascar on 7 January 1943, and formed a Free French administration. He was met at Tamatave by General Platt. Grafftey Smith remained as British Consul General. General Platt remained GOC East African Forces.

CHAPTER 12

TRIPOLITANIA November 1942 - October 1943
Chief Civil Affairs Officer, British Military Administration

Cairo November 1942

I heard that Montgomery was in Cairo and asked the Chief of Staff at GHQ (Macready) to take me to meet him: "Too busy!" says Macready. So I went to the Embassy, where I was known, and met Montgomery there, just to salute and click heels. He was suspicious but polite (he had not chosen me and he suspected all but "the chosen").

Somehow, on Christmas Day, I had a cracking bout of malaria in the apartment in *Kasr el Nil* street which I had rented, bed and breakfast, for a week, but I recovered. I then, at last, put my finances in order (I was now in another theatre of war and my paymaster was in Jerusalem) and found my old friend Reginald Adams, Manager of the National Bank, ready to ensure a monthly sufficiency going home to DRL "come what may". I missed hearing my children speak over the BBC wireless: "Daddy I have read your letters; I have seen your photographs; I would like to meet you!" (MHL aged 3¼.)

I met many old friends in Cairo, but, as I wrote to Diana, the city was full of ghosts - and my thoughts were with my own people in camp in Maadi - I cannot think why I was not with them!

To come back to my new administration, I must have arrived in Cairo towards the end of November 1942 and there found that a great deal had been achieved to form the skeleton of the British Military Administration in Tripolitania. A Colonel Sillery had been placed in charge and he and other stalwarts had organised a team which, thanks to Headquarters Political, was growing daily. By the end of November we had moved out as a unit to a better camp at Maadi, a suburb of Cairo, which was then blessed with some open space. Here we began intensive training, including lectures on administration, the country of Tripolitania, administration in a captured territory, Arabic lessons and, as I have noted, early morning PT. We soon formed six provincial groups to cover the six areas in Tripolitania and had the manpower to find Political Officers, and especially Agricultural Officers, for each group. I was insistent on the necessity for a strong agricultural group for I foresaw that our principle problem would be FOOD.

Our Director of Agriculture was a Major R L Robb from South Africa and well did he serve the administration, the Arabs, the Berbers, the Jews and the Italians in his fine and farsighted agricultural policy in Tripolitania.

The camp was a happy organisation and we were well served with capable transport officers who obtained at any rate some of the transport which we required; we were a proper military organisation.

Meeting with General Montgomery on Tripolitania Frontier

Our Legal Adviser was a Colonel Dawson, also a South African, and his time was filled with the drafting of the various Proclamations which I took to General Montgomery on 15 December, the day after he crossed Cyrenaica's frontier with Tripolitania. Montgomery, as was his custom, had set up his tactical Headquarters miles ahead of his Army Headquarters, and was actually at the border town of Agedabia some 100 miles south of Benghazi. Here I bearded him one evening, having flown from Cairo. I asked for a short interview in order to obtain his signature on the Proclamations. I was ushered into "the presence" in one of his caravans - now in the Imperial War Museum; I begged to congratulate him on entering yet another territory in North Africa and asked him to sign several Proclamations. "I sign originals only" said Montgomery, "No copies!" I told him that I had arranged for a few of my Political Officers to enter Tripolitania at the right moment, in case they could be of any use to the fighting forces. "Well, you can't stay here" was the seemingly unwelcome remark made by the General, and I took my instant leave.

It was the only uncouth word he ever spoke to me, for after our entry into Tripoli we became the best of friends and he was very good to me and my administration. I even had a mention in his Memoirs - to say nothing of his despatches.

British Military Administration: First Moves

I had already arranged for the doughty Peter Acland and a few others to enter Tripolitania immediately after occupation, and the team followed him in early January 1943. I myself flew back to Cairo to make final arrangements. It was so completely novel to me to have under my command an organisation which could be fitted into the occupied territory as circumstances permitted. Gone were the days of my entry into Ethiopia singlehanded or into Madagascar with only my Personal Assistant. One was able to look ahead and plan and know that one had a team, and a good one, ready for action and with the transport to move. It made a wonderful difference to efficiency and peace of mind!

My letters to Diana from Cairo at the beginning of January were thoroughly happy pages - mails were reaching each other in weeks instead of months. I was very optimistic: Tripoli (though we never mentioned the name) was a good deal nearer to the UK than Madagascar or Ethiopia, and clearly I foresaw a smoother passage with the VIII Army:

> "All my black days and memories of last year have faded and we will make a good show of this .... We are in the thick of the struggle here .... I was delighted to see so many friends from the Sudan, and to see old faces from Ethiopia .... I have a grand team and great confidence in them! .... So many of the Ethiopian team have joined - and many more applied to come - that it warmed the heart and made me realise that 1941 was not a year entirely wasted ...."

By mid January 1943 Montgomery's forward HQ had advanced along the shores of the Bay of Sirte as far as Buerat. Somehow, my very spacious Colonial Body Ford and my bedding, food, etc., was driven to near Buerat by 15 January where I joined Peter Acland. We were able to attend a meeting of officers and men representing the units in the two columns, at which Montgomery, in his own words:

> ".... took special steps to work up the enthusiasm of the troops before the battle and to impress upon them the need for firm determination that the attack would not stop until Tripoli was won."

I was very glad to be present at this meeting of about two or three hundred men of all ranks, sitting in the sand quite close to the sea near Buerat. Montgomery spoke well, frankly and fearlessly, and with clarity and without hesitation; his style was quite simple - without arrogance or superiority, but as one would have expected from a British General of whatever generation or century, leading his troops into battle. I was most impressed; far more impressed than by a lecture given in Tripoli some six weeks later to a posse of generals, admirals and air marshals from many theatres of war (including UK) when he, very lucidly, told his audience (all of general's rank except myself) how he won the battle of North Africa from el Alamein to Tunis.

When I saw Montgomery in Agedabia, on the frontier of Tripolitania, on 1 December, he was planning his forward advance. Administrative problems (the maintenance of his army with its long line of communications and the vital necessity of establishing forward aerodromes) weighed heavily on his thoughts. He determined that the next battle must and would involve a drive straight through from Buerat to Tripoli 200 miles away. He had to have the possession of that port to maintain his army once they advanced into Tripolitania. He also had to consider the possibility of Rommel attacking the VIII Army once its lines of communication became too long. Benghazi, the most eastern port in his hands, although importing more than 3,000 tons a day by early January 1943, was far too distant to support the VIII Army, once they had begun to advance west of Agedabia. Moreover, a gale which raged from 4-6 January destroyed many installations in that port and reduced the intake to 1,000 tons per diem.

He resolved, therefore, to attack Rommel from his position, Buerat, on 15 January and to push straight forward for the assault on Tripoli. The city and port had to be captured within 10 days of the start of the operation. He made his strategic and tactical battle plans accordingly. There were two axes: the main thrust was to be along the coastal road Buerat - Misurata - Homs - Tripoli, a direct thrust to be made by 51st Division with Montgomery himself in command from his tactical HQ; the other axis would be commanded by General Oliver Leese, Commander of the XXX Corps with 7 Armoured Division and the New Zealand Division. This force would strike inland to outflank the enemy and converge on Tripoli via Tarhuna from the south.

I detailed Travers Blackley, whom I was delighted to welcome into my show, to accompany Montgomery and the 51st Division on their coastal thrust, while I took Peter Acland with me and was given a warm invitation to join Oliver Leese's Headquarters of XXX Corps. I made the decision to accompany the inland force because I knew that we should be fighting over and passing through areas of colonisation by Italians, and from my administrative-political view, I thought that I could learn more from the reaction and plight of these folk than from the coast dwellers. I also wanted to see the country.

Delay was Montgomery's worry. Unless we could capture Tripoli port by the end of January he could not maintain his division on that long line of communication. The betting on the winners was not on the race between Montgomery and Rommel, but between Montgomery on the coast and Leese on the left flank.

I join VIII Army in battle

We set off among the troops of XXX Corps, with guns, tanks, armoured cars and lorries for the infantry to join their Headquarters that evening - it must have been 1 January.

Then came one of life's unforgettable episodes. I was at the wheel driving along a desert road, which moments before had been crowded with tanks, guns and other vehicles. It was now deserted, fore and aft. "Why have all the others left the track?" asked I, the recruit to the VIII Army and desert driving. Small voice of our driver from the back of the vehicle "I expect it's the MINES, Sir!" And, of course, it was. I had missed the warning at a turning and was driving merrily through a minefield. I stopped. We discussed and considered the wisest route. To turn round meant driving off the road and DEATH. To back a mile would probably inadvertently take one off the road. My decision was to drive on in prayer. There was a sign some 50 yards ahead which meant, probably, the beginning and the end of the minefield. We reached safety a shaken but thankful party; I handed over the wheel to the driver who said he knew the desert and they all forgave me!

We found General Oliver Leese, XXX Corps Commander, and his forward HQ in the thick of battle - but received a warm welcome. It was either then or in some later action that I was with General John Harding when a shell splinter wounded him in the arm putting him out of action for some months. We were able to be useful with the Arab and Italian population; of the latter we found on one occasion a number of men, women and children in one of the Italian colonial centres. All were desperately frightened. A German detachment had just left them taking all their grain and food and they were in the centre of a battlefield; we were able to pacify them, restore some sense of confidence towards the British, appoint leaders and promise peaceful occupation. It wasn't easy.

MSL to DRL 18.1.43

"…. Found the (Corps) HQ and the most charming GOC (Oliver Leese) just in time for bacon and tea; immediately after we set off (a night attack) and it reminded me exactly of the naval convoy approaching Madagascar; everyone keeps station and away we went across country which was very like the White Nile Province (without the Nile). Very few of my indigenous parishioners were about - they have mostly disappeared with their flocks from the warring Europeans. They are unattractive, white skinned Arabs rather like the Fellahin of Egypt - and they cannot believe it when you speak Arabic …. it is an amazing experience watching this part of the campaign from close up; and my word, it is efficient! It's all on such a grand scale after the smaller campaigns of Ethiopia and Madagascar!"

Indeed, we were in the midst of the tank and infantry advance to capture the Tarhuna Ridge, south of Tripoli.

MSL to DRL 16.1.43

"…. We have had a busy 6 days and my job really began yesterday when I found 4,000 odd Italian colonists in their farms on the edge of the battle and had to start administering them and the Arabs all around."

The enemy continued to fall back but as Montgomery writes:

"…. on both flanks we lost contact owing to difficulties of the 'going' and, on the coastal road, cleverly placed demolitions."

The going on our flank was devilish - there was one very tricky pass, mined of course, with demolitions and we slowed down. That evening came an imperial rocket from the Army Commander on the coast, ordering us to put in a night attack and press home our success with urgency. We took the large market centre, Tarhuna, on 20 January and there I found myself at once laying down the law with a vengeance. As the Germans withdrew, the Arabs had looted every sack of stored grain, and there was nothing for general distribution among Arabs or Italians. I summoned the Arab leaders - the *Kadi* and some local *sheikhs*. To their great surprise I scourged them with my best Sudani Arabic. This particular form of Arabic is well understood in Libya and the Libyans were so astounded at hearing their mother tongue flowing from an *Inglese* officer that they listened and obeyed! 80% of the grain was restored by sunset and the *Kadi* and his brethren were allowed their sunset prayers. The little Italian mayor of the place was astounded and must have forgiven me, if ever he discovered, for having used his bath which was filled with wonderful cold water - intended for drinking!

General Oliver Leese had, by this time, found that Political Officers were useful as well as being good companions, and we had tense but most interesting days in his company for we had found that Corps Commanders could be very human persons. The rivalry between his XXX Corps and the coastal advance under Montgomery was intense! Finally we pitched XXX Corps HQ Mess in an Italian Public Works clearing by the side of the main road, some 30 miles out of Tripoli on the evening of 22 January 1943. Immense columns of smoke were emanating from oil stocks in or near the harbour. Our armoured cars had entered the city; the coast force was still 10 miles out. Oliver Leese invited me to accompany him into the city next morning.

I must record that the Public Works clearing where we had all dined, slept and breakfasted blew up at noon on that very day, the work of a delayed action mine!

We started after breakfast on 23 January. General Oliver in his khaki "plus four" trousers (which looked very suitable on that tall, handsome officer) was driven in his white Scout car which he used when camouflage was unnecessary (it was packed full of cigarettes for the troops past whom we drove) along the main road crossing the plain south of Tripoli. We passed hundreds of vehicles - armoured cars, lorries, anti-tank guns - and to every party of men, Oliver tossed a packet of cigarettes from his inexhaustible supply.

Surrender of Tripoli

MSL to DRL 27.1.43

"…. Well, here we are and my entry into the third capital I have helped to occupy was really a thrill.

We stood by all night - sleeping, but ready, while fires and volumes of smoke rose from the city 30 miles away. At 8.00 am after breakfast the General and I climbed into his open car (in which he always stands) and so we drove in the cold of the morning, down a lane of transport of all sorts and conditions; then past a few Italians in the outskirts into the city itself. A brief halt at the gate and then we went round the city itself and saw what it was like ...."

At some point or other we must have met the Army Commander, Montgomery, who had entered from the east along the Corniche, and he ordered a rendezvous of the Italian Government and officials so that he could take a formal surrender. The Governor, Mayor and Provincial Governor were extracted from their offices (by me) and brought before General Montgomery at the Porto Benito, the north gate of the city, where they formally submitted to the Army Commander. I use the word "extracted", for it is true that the officials remained in their offices until they were ordered to leave the building and accompany me and a British Captain interpreter to the Porto Benito. The Italian Governor, Alberto Denti di Pirajno, who was a qualified doctor with experience in Italian East Africa and had been sent out to act as the last Governor of Tripoli, wrote a book called *A Cure for Serpents*. Describing the summoning of himself and his colleagues from the Government Offices, he mentions the British Captain interpreter who had once been British Vice Consul and with him "an irate and self-important Brigadier-General who shouted orders and curses, both in Arabic and English, at sentries, motor cyclists and passers by" (natural exaggeration of the vanquished!)

In fact, we brought the three men up to the Army Commander where he stood near to the gate with a motley escort of trucks containing military police - otherwise there was little ceremony. I produced the three officials and introduced them.

General Montgomery (I quote the Italian di Pirajno) "spoke in an abrupt nasal voice, emphasising his short sharp sentences, warned the population to refrain from provoking disturbances, imposed a curfew, etc., etc.. If they carried out instructions, he said, the Italians had nothing to fear."

The General then turned to me and said "Lush, keep your eye on that chap on the right, (the Governor) he is obviously a bastard." He then handed over the city and its population - indeed the country - to me.

Blackley, Acland and I then went back to the Government Office and talked to the three officials whom we found quite useless and, therefore, confined them to their houses. By contrast, there were subordinates who were very ready to serve and assist and those we used, of course, mostly in the technical services.

And so I took over my third surrendered capital, and I estimated then that it was the tidiest and most satisfactory occupation so far. Above all, the fall of Tripoli was a signal date in the gradual elimination of Axis forces in Africa and their ultimate defeat. Secondly, the victory had been won by fine strategy and the exploits of a great army. I was proud, and so were my team, to be called upon to assist that army by maintaining security on their lines of communication and helping to make a full use of the country's resources.

We three early birds (Blackley, Acland and I) had a good look at the city, conferred with as many responsible Italians as we could find (very few) and settled down to discover the realities of the food situation. Mercifully, quite a number of my officers reached Tripoli next day and we soon had a skeleton staff splendidly at work - and knowing where to look and what to do. To me, with memories of Addis Ababa and Diego Suarez it was almost a miracle.

Food Situation - The Haversack Order

I was surprised to see so many (principally Jewish and Italian) food shops and restaurants open and it was clear, firstly, that some people had food to spare and were prepared to sell it for good money, and secondly, that the troops of the VIII Army would soon eat the town out of food - for after four months slogging over the desert on battle rations, a taste of macaroni with a glass of red wine was just heaven! The food consumed in the first 48 hours did not amount to a very great volume but obviously Tripoli could not stand this very natural depredation and, though I knew the measure would be unpopular, I went straight to Montgomery and told him of the state of affairs and within half an hour he issued the "Haversack" order to all troops. It was a most unpopular move and many were the criticisms levelled at me, but it had to be done. The nub of it was:

> "It is therefore, my (Army Commander) order that no member of the British Forces in Tripolitania whether officer or other rank, shall have any food, breakfast, lunch, dinner or supper - at hotels or restaurants in Tripoli. Officers and other ranks when visiting Tripoli must take their rations with them."

I, on my part, had made it an offence to provide food to British troops, except tea and buns!

I knew within 48 hours that I had the Army Commander behind me and that gave me great confidence in the work ahead.

Our two first and very serious problems were food and labour to help reconstitute the harbour. In my first monthly report I wrote:

> "Food is short and will remain short until the harvest is on the markets .... There are 600,000 mouths to feed and there is practically nothing to put in them .... I expect no imports for at least two months - I reduced the food ration in Tripoli City to 50 grammes a day .... to give the population their due there was very little squealing; no Arab will starve, so long as there are good crops coming up."

I went on hopefully (writing in April)

"…. the harvest will of course, make things easier but the exercise of control over the crops and distribution will produce difficult problems."

It was with this in view that I had enlisted a large number of Agricultural Officers who, under Major Robb, were able to give tremendous help to Civil Affairs Officers of the Provinces in this difficult task when the harvest was due. Tripolitania owed a great debt to this team of South African agriculturalists under Robb, especially in the early months of occupation.

The Harbour

The restoration of the harbour was, of course, the toughest job facing the naval and military forces remaining in Tripoli. I quote Gerald Norman of The Times, who wrote:

"The lighthouse, which stood 200' high, is now nothing but a heap of rubble on the promenade. Two key wharves have been blown up. The Spanish Mole, battered by the RAF, has been demolished to water level and the breakwater is breached. Two battleships have been sunk in the harbour mouth."

But trust the Royal Navy; they, foreseeing the state of the port and its inviability from the sea, had managed to transport by road from Benghazi or some other port not less than 1,000 miles away, two motor craft of some size which they launched on 24 January from the shore side in Tripoli Harbour and were thus able to inspect the port from their own element and to transport crews and inspectors from point to point in it.

Here I can do no better than to include part of the despatch to The London Times by Gerald Norman, then special correspondent for that newspaper, dated 26 January 1943. He had come "up" with the VIII Army with whom he was popular and I, finding him sympathetic and interested in civil administration, arranged for him to be well advised; he wrote an article on Military Government for which I was grateful, as indeed I was to the press in general and the BBC who continued to take an interest in our affairs - possibly with an eye to the political future of Libya and the Italians, a problem which was not to be solved for nine years.

"Almost as soon as the VIII Army entered Tripolitania, a British Military Government was set up to administer the territory until such time as decisions are taken at the end of the war regarding the future of the Italian Empire. Profiting both from experience gained in Eritrea, Italian Somaliland and Madagascar, as well as in the previous occupation of Cyrenaica and by the certainty which our leaders felt of capturing Tripolitania, more than 80 officers of the Occupied Enemy Territory Administration had been already trained and accompanied Brigadier M S Lush, Deputy Chief Political Officer, into Tripoli.

"Indeed, Brigadier Lush, who will administer the province under the orders of the Army Commander, was at General Montgomery's side when he received the formal surrender of the town from the Italian officials. There has been a splendid opportunity for careful and thoughtful planning of the territory and of the future administration and the change over has taken place without a hitch.

"Officers of the Administration have been trained in the geography and history of Tripolitania, its system of government, its agricultural and mineral resources and in all other relevant matters.

"The basic note of the administration will be to carry on the civil life of the country in so far as it does not clash with military exigencies. Towards the estimated 40,000 Italians remaining of the pre-war population of about 90,000, the British Administration will adopt a firm and just attitude.

"Lists of 'war crimes' such as sabotage and destruction of communications have been posted up, and offences will be tried by British Military Courts. There are also military guards on all public utilities, etc., in various centres.

"Fascist leaders and prominent members of the Fascist Party will be interned. Fascist clubs, cultural centres and similar institutions will be closed. The teaching of Fascist ideas and political economy or subjects with a Fascist bias will be forbidden. The display of Fascist emblems and flags is banned as well as the wearing of Fascist uniforms. Fascist funds in the banks will be permanently frozen, and in private hands they will be taken into safe custody. Otherwise life will be allowed to go on much as in normal times."

The reader will note the absence of any reference to the indigenous population, the Berbers, the Jews and the Arabs, and I have thought it worthwhile to include a note on these, not unimportant, elements of our population. They arrived in Tripolitania in the following order of time - Berbers, Jews, Arabs and I have included notes on the Arabs together with the Berbers with whom they have coalesced and outnumbered.

The Berbers are generally considered to be the oldest inhabitants, probably an invading tribe from Central Europe or the Caucasus who entered via Spain. They are to this day pale of countenance with an occasional pair of blue eyes; their women especially were noted for their beauty; they never, however, coalesced and scattered but they remained and became a prey to subsequent invaders - the Phoenicians from the Levant, better known as the Carthaginians; the Romans who defeated them, and with their enforced labour, built the magnificent cities of Leptis Magna and Sabratha and established extensive cultivation; the Vandals who threw out the Romans and were in turn re-conquered by them under the Byzantine Emperors who set about restoring the ruined cities and some of the ravaged cultivation of Leptis Magna. The Berbers were still a danger to the Byzantines, but both succumbed to what proved to be the most potent of all influences on the population of the country, viz the invasion of AD 643 by Moslem Arabs under Omar bin Ali, followed by a second and larger incursion in the 11th Century of the Beni Hilal from the east which was a veritable human flood, thought to amount to nearly one million souls. Men, women and children poured in and devastated the country, destroying in Tripolitania every sign of Roman cultivation. The desert claimed its natural suzerainty and advanced inexorably, reducing cultivatable land to a few oases. Tripoli became a population centre for several centuries and although the Sultan of Constantinople turned the country into a Turkish vassalate and tolerated the rule of a semi-independent dynasty - the Karamanli Dynasty - from 1711-1835, the Sublime Porte only asserted her rule at the latter date, from which time the people suffered much persecution until the 20th century. Then in 1911, Italy, anxious to establish some authority in the southern Mediterranean, oblivious of the indigenous population, declared war on Turkey, defeated her with difficulty, and established a not too stable regime in Tripolitania and Cyrenaica; after experiencing much difficulty from the Arab-Berber inhabitants, it limited its occupation to two posts. The indigenous population was too strong for them. However, in 1921, the Fascist regime under Mussolini recovered the colony and by 1928, after some savage onslaughts on the indigenous inhabitants, began the demographic colonisation scheme which settled Italian peasants on the land, to the exclusion of the Arabs.

Indeed, under the Fascist regime, which ended in 1943, the indigenous Arabs and Berbers took decidedly second place. They were excluded from the best agricultural areas, now allotted to the Italian "colonial" farmers, educational facilities were practically nil and medical assistance was poor. Very few Italians spoke Arabic and administration of the tribes was effected by a system of Italian speaking native liaison officers called *mudirs* (governors) who often did not reside in the areas administered.

In 1943, the loose administration of these half million Arabs (including Berbers) on a care and maintenance basis but with the primary object of ensuring that the basis ensured peace and quiet, without danger or embarrassment to British Military personnel, institutions or plans, involved a good deal of forethought and much hard work on the part of my Political Officers in the provinces. I found the attitudes of the Arabs was one of "wait and see". They had hoped for more food and were disappointed in that, but they began to recognise that the new governors took a more friendly view of them than their predecessors.

The Jews were second only to the Berbers in their date of arrival in Tripolitania. The first immigrants probably accompanied the Phoenician merchants who later, as Carthaginians, ruled Tripoli. The Jews were the clerks and accountants of the traders. A second incursion took place in the 4th century BC, and their numbers were greatly increased after the fall of Jerusalem in the 1st century AD. I had little doubt that many had also come after the diaspora from Spain.

The Jews had endured, and probably profited from, the numerous vicissitudes of Tripolitania, and especially Tripoli city itself, where most of them lived, and had doubtless become the financiers and bankers of the city and territory. The Italians oppressed them without definite persecution, especially since 1940. The Jews, however, evacuated from Benghazi in 1942 and confined in a camp near Gharian in Tripolitania, were in a terrible state of hunger and neglect which defied description: luckily it was not too late to save them.

As Gerald Norman wrote to The Times, "the 20,000 (no less) Jews in Tripoli welcomed the VIII Army as an army of deliverance" and I shall describe in due course the scenes of spontaneous welcome with which I and my staff were greeted at their feast at the end of April 1943. Administratively they were a slight nuisance owing to internal squabbles, and the Rabbinical courts lagged behind the others for this reason. I had no idea before entry into Tripoli that their numbers were so large and I found it hard to believe that so large a population could exist so well housed, so well 'turned-out', so self-confident.

Lastly the Italians. As I have already described, after their defeat of the Turks in 1911, the Italians experienced great difficulty in occupying any territory in Tripolitania, except two towns, Tripoli and Homs. In 1921, however, Count Giuseppi Volpi, a man of vigour, was appointed as Governor and was allowed to replace the policy of 'scuttle' by one of slow recovery, and by 1925 he had established Italian rule in the west and as far south as Gebel Nef. By 1928 modern weapons, aircraft etc., had made possible the extension of power to the east and in the Fezzan - not without some brutal massacres against the Arabs. Count Volpi was a noted Governor and his name was well known among the Arabs even in 1943. (I eventually in July 1943 took over his house in Tripoli.) It was under Count Volpi's rule that the agricultural development of the country was set in motion. It began well. Italian agriculturalists and farmers were imported, provided with land and encouraged and helped to establish their own farms in the best parts of the country. Cereals, olives, figs and citrus crops were planted and flourished. These were the farms which we found in good condition in 1943 and which formed the only really successful Italian agricultural effort in the country. They were owned and maintained by experienced farming families. The 'demographic' agricultural colonisation which followed and which aimed at settling 100,000 impoverished and unemployed Italians outside their mother country was disastrous. The principle of the scheme was admirable - free land, free well stocked houses, etc., but the immigrants were deplorable and had no idea of farming. The initial ideals of the scheme could not be fulfilled - splendid water pumps will never produce water from non-existant wells; machinery requires spare parts ab initio; even primary farming requires some elementary training. The immigrants were dependant for the most part on assistance from the State. They were third class citizens.

The attribute 'third class' could be applied to most of the Italians who remained in Tripolitania; the cream of the colonists and officials, if it ever existed, had obviously left before the surrender in January 1943. The remaining fascist officials were gradually removed as POWs and, with a few exceptions, we found the remainder poor representatives of their country.

Administration

So far as justice was concerned, race made very little difference. Lionel Dawson, my legal luminary, and a very efficient and charming officer to boot, "saw to it that substantial justice was given in every direction, with the shortest delay possible". British Military Courts set up without delay did extremely well. Italian Courts of Assize and Appeal functioned almost at once. The *Sharia* (Arab Moslem Courts) functioned and only the Rabbinical Courts lagged behind, due to an internal petty squabble.

I was extremely lucky to have, as my Principle Medical Officer, Colonel Beamish, a fountain of energy and good sense. He arrived in the van of the VIII Army very soon after myself. He had been working in Cyrenaica studying the medical administration in that territory and was quick to arrive in Tripoli to take over the Italian Medical Service in toto, with 73 Italian Medical Officers en poste. The latter's standard of hygiene may not at first have been as high as that of their British counterparts but they gave us a very good service. Colonel Beamish found a bad outbreak of typhus among Jews expelled from Cyrenaica by the Italians and lodged in the camp at Gharian in the hills, and there were sporadic outbreaks elsewhere. But I knew that health among Arabs, Jews and Italians, to say nothing of ourselves, was in excellent hands. I never worried about health problems.

We even boasted of a hygiene officer - a British Captain - and his first and vitally important duty was to clean up the "filth and destruction" into which the city of Tripoli had fallen - a state typical of a beaten army and administration. We soon had it restored to a state fit for the many members of the VIII Army who passed through, going westward at first and then returning to refit and prepare for battle overseas after the final victory in Tunisia.

Colonel Stewart, my redoubtable Controller of Finance, concerned himself with a careful financial reorganisation of the Italian Financial Departments under British control. He closed all Italian banks, arranged for Barclays Bank to open without delay and organised the circulation of BMA currency.

The local criticisms of our Adminstration (especially in the minds of some pundits in the fighting forces) were lack of control of prices and the scarcity of labour urgently needed eg. in the harbour. I had refused to take the obvious line (according to critics) of issuing a Proclamation controlling prices - proclamations are useless unless they can be enforced.

"The very small police force in Tripoli" I quote "have better things to do than enforce the terms of a Proclamation controlling prices when there do not exist any fresh stocks on the market to be sold at the reduced prices."

Lack of food and low wages reduced the voluntary supply of labour; we increased it by including a loaf of bread partly in lieu of wages.

Looking to the future, Major Robb, our eminent Director of Agriculture, with his dozen or more Agricultural Officers, tackled all their important tasks with most heartening vigour. They made plans not only for the coming 1943 harvest but for the 1943-44 crops which they hoped to increase by 100%. Luckily they were able to occupy the Italian Government Agricultural Farm at Sidi Mesri near Tripoli and to keep the most valuable acres free from "becoming a billeting area for troops". Given good rains I had no concern about the crops - some grain and citrus on small holdings under irrigation on the acres near the coast and on large amounts of acreage inland. Luckily the VIII Army had wet feet and rain in plenty assured us of good crops.

The 6,000 privately owned Italian farms (olives and grain) were already prosperous and gave us no worry, provided we could supply fuel for pumps and water for the inhabitants.

Robb's difficulty was to repopulate the 30,000 Italians on the colonisation schemes to the south, many of whom had been evacuated by the fighting; he also introduced some 3,000 Italian refugee colonists from Cyrenaica. All these colonisation schemes depended on imported fuel to raise the water and there were no spare parts for broken pumps. Nevertheless he promised me 10,000 tons of grain therefrom in 1943 and kept his promise. The bread ration in Tripoli increased form 50 grammes in January to 180 grammes in May.

But before the merry month of May, and in North Africa May 1943 saw the total surrender of the German Army in Tunisia, many things happened to lighten our lives in Tripolitania. We were deadly serious over our jobs and feeding 3/4 million people on insufficient food makes life serious; but most of us managed to keep light hearted.

For myself I was delighted to serve men like Montgomery and Leese and they showed confidence in me and my staff. I myself could not have been served better, especially in those early days when initiative was essential and lack of 'nous' unpardonable.

From the outset of our occupation of Tripoli, the VIII Army and especially their Commander and Headquarters stayed out of the city. Thus wrote Montgomery:

> "I saw certain dangers in the proximity of my army to a large city .... I installed my Headquarters in the fields some 4 miles outside the city."

And every fighting commander and his troops did likewise. As a matter of fact, Montgomery's Camp Commandant pitched his tents, huts and the famous caravan in a *wadi* or dry water course which, I was warned by the local Arabs, would certainly come down in a spate in the event of rain. I passed the warning on to "Tac HQ": they decided to stay. The rain came; the *wadi* behaved as a *wadi* should; one soldier was drowned and the Camp Commandant lost his job.

I had the privilege of dining at Tac HQ one evening at Montgomery's invitation, when he was there. It was also a privilege to have that entree extended to the other members of the Mess at the invitation of his staff when Montgomery was not there. I was vastly impressed at meeting those comparatively young men - from de Guingand (Chief of Staff) downwards - who were Montgomery's closest advisers. They had a timbre about them which made me realise that the Commander VIII Army knew how to pick men. It was as a result of these contacts that I became CBP or Chief Bath Provider for the Army Commander.

Our first villa in Tripoli had several bathrooms, one of which was constructed of a black, very shiny marble-like substance - one saw oneself mirrored on all sides in this remarkable and sizeable room. I must have described this master lavabo to my hosts at Tac HQ, failing perhaps, to mention that the only drawback was the absence of hot water, for the General's ADC appeared next day and said that the Army Commander would much appreciate a good hot bath in this black and shining paradise and would be at the villa at 10.30 am on Tuesday. I detailed my Camp Commandant, a man of imagination and initiative to provide hot water in plenty, and I can still see the 6 primus stoves lined along the passage corridor of the villa, each with a gerry-can aloft preparing for the General's ablution. On the first Tuesday, there was a near fiasco because the water was cut off from our section of the city in the early hours and it required almost a Proclamation to secure a mobile water cart to be sent to my home. Montgomery arrived, friendly, but a little "Army Commanderish", as if he didn't quite know the attitude to adopt when about to be conducted at 1030 hours by his Chief Civil Affairs Officer, to a hot bath. He refused coffee while waiting for the bath to be filled; his ADC produced sponge bag and towel; he entered (the menial Italian house staff male and female trying to catch a glimpse, even while he was fully dressed!); but once there, it was clear that the General was delighted, and became a boy, childishly thrilled at the multiple mirrorscope effect - to say nothing of the hot water! He emerged after nearly 3/4 hour wearing his uniform and his generalship. But he was charming about it all and repeated the thrill twice before he left for Tunisia. I am not sure that we did not restore the tap water by then. The press later reported:

> "Lush was valuable to Monty because he had commandeered the only reliable plumbing system in Tripoli and there was a ceremony at his Mess known as 'Bathing the Army Commander'."

I liked Montgomery. I never wrote or thought of him as "Monty". I admired immensely his generalship in the desert, a generalship which evaluated the adminstration of supply as highly as the tactical movements of fighting troops; who put on a 'proper act' towards his seniors and his troops before battle; who could be remote to his seniors (C-in-C Army, Navy and RAF, Chiefs of Staff in London, etc.) and to his staff but never to the private soldier; who understood that the impact on a civilian population of a victorious army coming on the heels of a defeated army presented a problem not to be ignored; who was indeed a very human person who liked his hot bath!

The reader may remember his words "You can't stay here!" which greeted my presentation to Montgomery of the Tripolitanian Proclamations at Agedabia. When in March the VIII Army crossed the frontier into Tunisia I received a telegram from Montgomery which read:

> "Hand over Tripolitania to a suitable officer and re-join the VIII Army in order to organise civil administration in Tunisia."

This was indeed a compliment not to be rebuffed - although compliance was not possible. I telegraphed back:

> "Much appreciate your telegram but my appointment here is territorial and stems from GHQ Middle East; submit that French Administration functionaries will insist on governing Tunisia."

To this I received an urgent telegram:

> "Please do not disobey my orders."

So up to the front I went and reported firstly to General Oliver Leese in order to obtain his advice. He advised that I make contact with Montgomery, explain to his staff, try to rally up some French Officials, stay two or three days with him, Leese, and see what happened. This I did. Having reported to Montgomery, he was charming and allowed me into his caravan while reports of a battle were coming in. I don't think it can have been more than a 'serious contact' on the Tripolitanian-Tunisian frontier - but it gave me an inkling of the news which came through to the Army Commander and the use he made of it. I was astounded at his intimate knowledge of the extensive terrain over which his troops were fighting.

I managed to make contact with a couple of French District Officers whom I directed to Army Headquarters and slipped away home. It was nice to be wanted by Montgomery.

Visit of Winston Churchill

But before this a splendid act was staged in Tripoli before VIII Army moved westward in strength. In February 1943 I was informed officially (but oh! so hush-hush!) that Winston Churchill would be visiting Tripoli on 3 February. Internal Security was up to me - Army Intelligence wished to impose a curfew on all Italians who were to remain unseen behind closed doors. I resisted this and won my point. Let Intelligence take military precautions, but my police such as they were, and essentially my Sudanese Battalion, would ensure absence of trouble. As for locking the Italians up, I assured Oliver Leese that they would be waving from their houses and shouting a welcome to the great man.

The plan was for Montgomery and Oliver Leese to meet Winston Churchill at the airport and the PM to inspect VIII Army, meet the officers, then lunch al fresco with Leese and Montgomery in the open country beyond Tripoli. I was asked to lunch.

Churchill's reception by VIII Army was thuswise. The *Lunguomare* or Corniche above the inner or south side of the harbour runs for about a mile in a gentle slope down to the Romulus and Remus statue which marks the shore or pedestrian entrance to the harbour, close by which stands a double archway (one arch above the other) at the eastern entrance to the old Turkish castle or castello. At this point the largest square of Tripoli is laid out.

Along the mile of the *Lunguomare* was paraded a long line of the infantry of 51st Lowland Division - and, I think, some New Zealanders. They were in an irregular single line; every man had somehow found a No 1 uniform or washed and *ironed* his shorts or battledress trousers, and they looked, some 2,500 of them, as if they had marched out of their Scottish barracks; in fact they had walked and fought over 2,000 miles of desert in rough wintry weather. At the very end of the Corniche, standing in the upper arch, high above the ground, stood one single Jock, his rifle at the slope.

In the main square of the city into which the *Lunguomare* led was assembled a mass of armour - every conceivable tank, self-propelled anti-tank gun and their famous crews - together with the New Zealand Division under General Greyberg. At the south end of the square was a platform on which stood the generals and the senior staff officers.

The Prime Minister's progress, slowly driven past the cheering ranks of the Highland Division waving their caps and cheering lustily, was suddenly hushed as the Highland soldier 40' from the ground on that old Turkish arch proudly presented arms. John Patton (Montgomery's ADC who was driving the car) stopped and the PM with tears streaming down his cheeks, acknowledged the salute; it seemed to most of us and I am sure the great man himself, that the salute came from those who were not on parade - many thousands buried in the desert or lying in hospital. On that sunlit harbour of Tripoli - the capture of which had been "the aim of all British offensives" and had now been achieved - amid the enthusiasm of Churchill's presence and the VIII Army's victories, I knew - perhaps we all knew - that the 'present arms' by that Jock was a salute not only to the Prime Minister, but to absent friends. If Churchill's face was wet with tears, so were our own who followed him.

Then we turned into the main square - an imposing square at any time - now filled with the mechanical might of the VIII Army. Then the brave men who not only drove and fought that armour with such elan, such disregard of death, but maintained it and serviced it night and day, gave Churchill a welcome which must have moved the stones of the old city of Tripoli lying next door. He came out onto the platform and shook us all by the hand - even the *Kadi* of Tripoli was included.

The troops in the square marched past him. Either then or later he spoke to both officers and men:

> "Ever since your victory at Alamein, you have nightly pitched your moving tents a day's march nearer home. In days to come, when people ask you what you did in the Second World War, it will be enough to say: 'I marched with the Eighth Army'."

The chosen few among us then followed the PM and the Army Commander along the southern road for about six miles. Sure enough, Italian householders along the way came running to their gates shouting "Viva Churchill!" Then in a patch of desert (now green with recent rains), Oliver Leese had laid out an al fresco lunch for about 20 officers. The area was heavily screened by anti-aircraft guns and I believe there were a dozen aircraft on the alert to ward off attack from the air. What a prize it would have been for the enemy! But we were left in peace and in the sunshine.

Lunch over, talks began and I was called over to meet the PM and with Alexander, Montgomery, Alan Brooke and Leese, to tell him what the civilian population contained and how we administered them; he knew I had been in Ethiopia, listened well, asked very good and pertinent questions and I being the last to join the party, we broke up.

That evening we met again on a Royal Navy ship which had somehow penetrated the blocked harbour and I met, really for the first time out of office, my C-in-C, Alexander.

Official photographers were in their element and many were the snapshots taken, but few I think, reached the press until a year or two later; all are now in the Imperial War Museum.

I felt rather sad at dinner that night to think that not all my staff had had the opportunity of talking to Churchill. I am sure that I was the first man on earth to tell him what a Civil Affairs Officer did; but as will be read later, it was not wasted on him.

Military and civil affairs

One evening, just about the time of this ministerial visit, I was told that a French Officer was looking for me, and there outside my office I found General Leclerc, the French Commander of that remarkable force which had started from Lake Chad and with incredible valour had rounded up Italian troops in the southern districts of the *Fezzan* (Tripolitania), and advanced as far as Homs, one of the northern towns of the desert district. This was an astonishing feat of desert fighting and we had no objection to the French effecting French Administration over the far distant and sparsely populated oases of the *Fezzan* - an arrangement which I made with the French General and Montgomery's Headquarters; the General approved and then drafted Leclerc's forces into the VIII Army where they provided good assistance and fought well in Tunisia.

Soon after the Prime Minister's visit Tripoli Port

began to look like a harbour again. Some of the wrecks had been removed or blown up, the entrance was made clear of sunken ships (how I never quite knew) and by the end of February the port was working well and we were discharging up to 3,500 tons a day on the quayside. Montgomery writes:

"My administrative worries were over and I could bring 10 Corps forward to Tripoli from the Benghazi area."

The fighting troops of XXX Corps moved on to be replaced by I Corps who, up to that time, had been used as Carter Paterson conveyors of supplies from Benghazi to the forward echelons. I lost the company of Oliver Leese whose Corps was to be in the van of the Tunisian battles.

I missed Oliver Leese. He had been a most splendid supporter and adviser and he, like Montgomery, understood the problems of the impact of thousands of troops - battle troops - on a civilian population, especially when a proportion of that population were ex-enemy but still resident on the lands of the indigenous nationals. Oliver enjoyed coming to our Mess though I cannot remember bathing him!

So much for the military side of affairs. In the meantime, civil affairs administration had progressed well and my Chief Secretary, Miller, had the administration well in hand; and in his capable hands I left the details. I was installed in a vast office, generally known as "No 10" in the government building and was very well served by my most excellent PA, Douglas Grant, who had wheedled his way to Tripoli from Madagascar, bringing in my luggage from Nairobi - no small feat for a junior officer - and I was delighted to have him. He and others had found us a villa, The Villa Volpi, once occupied by the Italian Governor, and suitable for "A" Mess which gave Douglas and me private office accommodation as well as good bedrooms. We were without electric light or water for some time but our capable Director of Public Works, Colonel Slingsby, was a member of the Mess and no doubt priority was well arranged. Douglas secured a grand piano (very properly through the custodian of enemy property) and we had a lot of music of an evening. A press report had it:

"When the bombs from raiding German aircraft were being showered on Tripoli harbour, Maurice Lush who had his Mess within the target area would sit at a requisitioned piano and play Mozart!!"

My HQ Mess was open to all 'visiting firemen' to Tripoli and was much sought after by itinerant Generals, Admirals and Air Marshals, who preferred a B & B in comfort to a draughty night in a tent , hut or caravan in the scrub.

We seem to have employed a goodly staff of Italians, cooks, cleaners, etc. and I wrote to Diana that during the first week I had cleaning women in my study marooned all night by the curfew. But we were moderately comfortable and thanks to the efforts of others, well fed.

As an example of our guests let me quote from a letter written to DRL in May:

"…. (General) Howe has been staying here during the last month, to say nothing of Lady Spears (wife of Sir Ronald Spears), the Turkish Ambassador to Egypt, Sir Ronald Storrs and Bishop Gelsthorpe (of the Sudan)."

Then on 3 June 1943:

"…. We now have to the house practically every nationality. We had a Chinese delegation to lunch the other day - such charming people - and last night a minister of the Greek Government and Archbishop Spellman of USA (once 'tipped' as the next Pope). I remember the said Archbishop getting me up at dawn one morning in order to celebrate Mass with the Italian Bishop - only to find the latter still asleep in his house."

One notable guest was Fiona Maclean - my nursing angel in Khartoum in 1940 - who came from the Sudan on 'working leave' and did much good with Colonel Beamish in our main hospital and elsewhere. It was so very good to see her.

My guest, General Howe, was my chief in Cairo; he had succeeded Philip Mitchell and Francis Rennell as Chief Political Officer. The visit was a great success and he wrote foreseeing further promotion for me. But in my letter of 21 March 1943, I wrote to DRL:

"…. It is grand to have had the privilege of being Montgomery's political adviser and of being in close touch with him (he also bathed in my house and we talked much) …. I may have missed promotion by coming here, but I would not have missed it for the world. It is the best job I have held or done so far, and I have such a grand team."

It may be interesting here to record extracts from a letter I wrote in March 1943 to Douglas Newbold, Civil Secretary in Khartoum, giving him my first impressions of things achieved and problems in the future. They reflect my thinking in the early stages of administering Tripolitania - and I do not think I realised then, as I do now, what a very small area of the country our administration covered!

MSL, Tripoli to Douglas Newbold, Khartoum 9.3.43:

"…. I was lucky enough to have two months in Cairo getting together a team for the administration of this country. We went into camp at Maadi and spent the time recruiting and training with Arabic and Italian lessons and lectures on all the aspects of administration. I have been very lucky in my staff and we were a really cohesive body before we ever entered the country, instead of coming in bits and pieces.

"From the Sudan I have been fortunate enough to have Travers Blackley, Peter Acland, Richard Cambridge, Henshaw and last, but not least, Bill Shaw, who has just joined me as adviser on Arab

Affairs. In addition to these there have been allotted to me two Battalions of the Sudan Defence Force for gendarmerie purposes with a call on a third. They had their first crack at the Germans near Misurata when entering this country and, although taken by surprise in the middle of the night, killed nine Germans at the cost of six of their men. They are terribly proud of themselves and they certainly have reason to be. As Gendarmerie they have done extraordinarily well and get on with the local Arabs and Italians and are really very happy. I have got them settled all over the country in small bodies helping the Political Officers on police work in general, while my Commissioner of Police recruits a real Tripolitanian Arab Police Force. It has been nice seeing the friendly faces of the SDF in every single district. They are really happy and they are getting news from the Sudan; this year it is news of good rains and a high river.

"I had the good fortune to come up with General Leese Commander of XXX Corps, and Peter Acland and I entered Tripoli with him. It was an amazingly interesting experience and although it was my third capital the thrill of entering an occupied town never decreases.

"As we came up we had left Political Officers and other technical experts at the various Province and District Headquarters and we soon got the full staff into Tripoli and west of it and I suppose within a fortnight we were working as a going concern. I have divided the country up into six small provinces with a staff of about 36 Political Officers and 150 officers in all.

"We found about 50,000 Italians of which 18,000 are in Tripoli City and the remainder on either the big colonisation schemes which spread all along the coast or on private farms chiefly around Tripoli itself. There are 22,000 Jews, mostly African Jews, who date back I suppose to the times of Titus. They present a considerable problem and naturally expect the full effect of liberation to come into force at once. The Italians did not treat them badly but there were local restrictions and we found 2,500 Benghazi Jews cooped up in a concentration camp, the conditions of which baffle description. The 600,000 Arabs are mostly sedentary agriculturalists or nomads, with the exception of about 100,000 dispossessed from their land by the Italians who are wage earners in the towns along the coast.

"The Arabs on the whole are watchfully friendly. The questions as to the political future of the country naturally arise and here we cannot say that the Italians will never come back. Duncan Cumming is lucky in this way in Cyrenaica. The Italians are numb and I think pretty disillusioned. There are very few signs of ardent Fascism and portraits of the King and Queen are far more numerous than those of Mussolini. The food situation is deplorable. The Italians have rendered the country unable to support itself by importing thousands of Italians, dispossessing more thousands of Arabs from their land and raising the standard of living from the rest of them without increasing production.

"Food supplies from Italy have failed to arrive and the price of wheat on the black market is £100 a ton with sugar and tea at similarly fantastic prices. Previous to our occupation they had distributed what little stocks they had to their friends among the Italians and the Arabs managed to pillage a great deal of the rest. Military operations naturally made it incumbent on me not to ask for transport of food in the initial stages. And so I was faced with a very hungry population and practically nothing to feed them with. However, we put them on to a ration of 50 grammes per head per diem in Tripoli and warned everybody to tighten their belts and I would not let anybody scream for food to be imported. Luckily however, we have a bumper crop coming up after three years of drought and I managed to get a promise of 1,000 tons by sea before the end of this month. We may just tide over without any real starvation. But it is an anxiety and I shall be glad when the crop is on the market.

"The Arabs in the towns are naturally disappointing. They seem rather a degenerate, uninteresting lot, but when you get out into the villages and especially where there is a mixture of Berber stock they are much more like the Arabs we are used to dealing with in the Sudan. The Arabic is much more like Sudani Arabic than any I have come across outside that country.

"It has been interesting to study the Italian colonisation schemes, demographic as they are called. There are seven or eight of them here with a number of private farms and I suppose the total Italian agricultural population is round about 30,000 to 40,000. The whole plan is beautifully carried out in its inception. Houses were built, land was ploughed, olive trees were planted and then the colonists came. But they have been a burden on the rates ever since for they cannot produce sufficient food to be self-supporting and even now, some 10 years in some cases after their inception, it is going to cost us at least £50,000 a year to keep them going.

"The administrative problem consists of keeping the balance between Italians and Arabs. We are maintaining not the central government which was a very 3rd XI affair, but the Provincial Administrators. We are using them in an informatory and not executive capacity and I am trying to bring the Arab leaders on to the same level. The Italian system was to maintain a body of intermediaries between the *sheikhs* and the administrators. They were Arabs and were called *mudirs* but they were seldom domiciled in the same area as they worked and were very much *"Kelab el Hakouma" [Government curs]*. The *Kadis* are the same here of course as practically everywhere but all seem to come from one family. Of course one would love to develop the whole system on a different basis and really bring the Arabs into the picture but, on a care and maintenance basis such as we are working, that would be impolite and unfair to everybody. God knows what is going to happen to this country after the war but we simply cannot afford at the moment to make any promises or to give any assurances which will upset such equilibrium as exists."

I am sure that Douglas Newbold replied but I have not preserved the letter.

Before I wrote my first monthly report to my HQ in Cairo in April I had given myself the enormous pleasure of a visit to every Provincial Headquarters in my endeavour to help my senior Political Officers with such experience as I had. My first visit was to the Western Province having its HQ at Zuara. A railhead with its western boundary forming the frontier with Tunisia, this area had naturally become the main LOC of the VIII Army and I had sent Peter Acland thither - experienced as he was in their ways; he did well - cleared the Arabs from the frontier (the Italians had already for the most part gone) and those Italian officials who had stayed did well. "Contraband has long been the most lucrative business of Zuara (the frontier town) and the shortage of food and possible differences of fixed prices will prove an irresistible temptation to the Arabs."

On the coast at Zanzur was the HQ of the tunny fishing, normally one of the only industries in the country. The Royal Navy however, had removed all the fishing boats (I have no doubt for Tripoli harbour) but we hoped for their return by May 1943.

The famous Roman city of Sabratha with the remarkable mosaics had not suffered but was not on my visiting list yet.

The province immediately east of Tripoli was known as the Eastern Province with its HQ at Homs, a small market town with a harbour for fishing boats. Homs is also close to the famous Roman city of Leptis Magna with its really wonderful theatre, forum, basilica and bathing establishment. In the theatre later I was thrilled to hear a most excellent concert organised by ENSA for British troops; a truly moving performance in perfect surroundings. The Province also contained the *Cussabat*, probably the largest Arab market in the territory. Colonel Wisdom also had the responsibility for two Italian "demographic" colonisation schemes in the Tarhuna area. He had found grave insecurity about, due largely to the incompetence of the Italian police, but soon rectified by the Sudan Defence Force. I liked Colonel Wisdom, a competent administrator, quiet but determined and never unduly fussed. I noted that the area was rich in cultivation with large areas of Arab grain and irrigated crops as well as the Italian Scheme.

Further east lay Misurata, HQ of Eastern Province which contained two Italian Colonisation Schemes and then stretched through Sirte and Beni Awlid to the Cyrenaican border. The Political Officer at Sirte had been in residence since the early days of January, compelled to live in a tent because the town itself was completely out of bounds owing to mines. Except at Cassino, in 1944, I have never seen a whole town so completely mined. Colonel Schofield - a very steady PO - foresaw tribal problems later among the Arabs in the east.

In the centre of the area, I found at Gharian, Travers Blackley my erstwhile deputy in Ethiopia, who had voluntarily joined my administration as a Provincial Officer after a gruelling time in the reserved areas of Ethiopia. It was delightful to have him with us - an enormous compliment - and his brief stay in Tripolitania was a prelude to his brilliant success as a lecturer to Military Government Officers of the USA Army in training at Charlottesville University. In the meantime I knew I had an expert studying the Arab and Berber problems in the Gebel Nefusa area as far as Nalut and Mizda, from the administrative and anthropological point of view, the most interesting job in the territory. It was good to see him again after what he had done for me in Ethiopia. I cannot remember going to Hoa, in or on the edge of the Fezzan, where Colonel Richard Cambridge was in close liaison with General Leclerc's men who were administering the people of the Fezzan - there was an arbitrary and by no means rigid boundary.

[MSL's report of this tour of the provinces, in *Monthly Report* dated 26 April 1943, is held amongst his papers in the Imperial War Museum's Archives.]

My impressions of the native population, Arab and Berber, were related in my letter to Douglas Newbold, quoted above.

I reported in May that "the Italians have shown signs of an early return to normality". They were all, I reckoned, Fascists, but no outward ostentation of that cult was permitted - nor made evident. The enormous Fascist placards or signs "Mussolini" etc. were removed, forcibly if necessary; the Fascist blackshirt police had been interned ab initio; we found little evidence of ardent Fascism among the remaining population. Pictures of the Italian King and Queen of Italy were more common than those of Fascist rulers but I gave warning in my early report "while Rommel and the German and Italian forces remain in North Africa there is still hope in the minds of many Italians."

I myself found it very hard to become interested in any Italians or in their problems, and indeed fraternisation was forbidden. I repaid the Bishop's courtesy call on me; I attended the Cathedral services once or twice and used the Roman Catholic church's educational system throughout the town and rural Italian population. The Roman Catholic hierarchy was not particularly helpful to the British Administration in the towns or in the countryside and I told His Holiness the Pope, Pius XII, in private audience in 1944, that his Bishop in Tripoli bore the nickname among the British of "the old fox". "An excellent description!" laughingly replied the Holy Father.

I wrote in April 1943: "The Jews in Tripoli are very African. They probably date back to the Jews expelled by Titus." They had probably not been badly treated by the Italians - no worse at any rate than by the Turks - and I reckoned that they were among the oldest inhabitants in Tripoli, certainly having arrived before the Arabs.

The Jews in Tripoli however, had managed to live in amity with the Arabs; at least they did so in 1943 and indeed the first public welcome given to the British Administration was in the form of a play performed in Arabic by a combined cast of Arabs and Jews in our honour, recounting very faithfully, according to the Old Testament, the story of Joseph and his brethren, the sons of Jacob. The performance began at 11 am; the acting was good; the speech very audible in colloquial Arabic, and every verse of the Bible was portrayed. I had been warned to take sandwiches for which I was devoutly thankful at 1.30 pm; at 3.30 pm the silver chalice had just been found in Benjamin's sack and I had perforce, to leave to conduct the business of the administration. We were all most impressed with the standard of presentation of the play and the complete rapport between the players. It was for many of the audience a memorable experience to listen to that well known Bible story produced by men whose faiths were not Christian yet to whom the story was just as traditional as to their Christian audience. It made one ponder - if one had the time.

But on 27 April 1943, the Jews of Tripoli manifested their joy and gratitude at deliverance from their enemies and their bondage, for though they did not suffer persecution at the hands of the Italians and Germans they suffered an inferior status. Yet not so inferior as the Arabs and Berbers! The occasion of the Jewish rejoicing was the last day of the Feast of *Pesach*. Major Rabinowitch, the Senior Jewish Chaplain with the VIII Army, had, during the *Seder* celebrations, as he wrote in the Jewish Chronicle (London) on 14 May 1943, arranged a well attended feast for some 250 Jewish soldiers in the VIII Army for which he had bought 850 litres of wine, 1,500 eggs and 500 kilos of vegetables (that did not give the impression of a starving nation!) The banquet was followed by a parade service next day and other private entertainments.

But the last day of the feast was the traditional climax of *Pesach* and took the form of a kind of Jewish St Valentine's Day when bridegrooms chose their brides. The Jewish community invited me to perpetuate the custom whereby the Governor of the city visited them and I must say they turned out in force and with a really wonderful display of gratitude and rejoicing. The Jewish soldiery mounted a guard of honour; the leaders of both factions escorted me on foot through the streets of the old city which was festooned and decorated with flowers and banners. Men put on their best suits (a morning coat and stock was to be seen). Girls - and the Jewish girl is a beautiful creature - ran before, on each side of and behind me and my staff, pumping scent through flit guns all aimed at me; a right and left on both eyes left me helpless just before we entered the synagogue. As I and my party entered the sacred building, the white clad choir of young ladies clapped loudly and long and sang a very good imitation of "God Save the King" at the same time. The newspaper report continues:

"The Brigadier, accompanied by his party and an escort of Palestinian officers, went through the streets. They pelted the Brigadier with flowers, sprinkled him with perfume, shrieked 'Viva l'Inghilterra! Viva L'Ottero Armata!' till they were hoarse and he very damp with perfume. The women gave their famous ululation of joy called the *Zgharit* .... In the synagogue we held a short service .... a blind old Rabbi of about 80 with a long white beard solemnly blessed the Brigadier, placing his hands on his head and said 'Yerorach'cha'. The Brigadier electrified us all by answering in Hebrew!"

We afterwards repaired through "a layer of flowers about a foot thick" to the Maccabi Club where there were speeches and songs and so we departed to "God Save the King". "It was a fitting end to the Festival of Deliverance" wrote the Jewish Chronicle. I was impressed by the spontaneity of the demonstrations and my staff made rude comparisons of the aroma of scent on my person when I reached my office!

The Arabs gave a more restrained and unisexed demonstration some weeks later at Cussabat, the big Arab market some miles away. This took the form of a parade of horses and camels; some speeches on both sides and I think it was on this occasion that possibly the *Kadi*, or some other notable, presented me with a black robe of honour (jellaba), generously decorated with gold braid and a long tassle, which was clearly destined by the Italian authorities for some Arab notable, but which I accepted with pleasure and keep as a momento until this day. I could not help comparing the spirit behind the gift and a very charming message sent to me by General le Gentilhomme when he took over Madagascar from the British, with my relegation to the list of personae non gratae presented to me by the Emperor of Ethiopia.

In May 1943 I lost Douglas Grant, my young indefatigable PA; he had served as such for over 12 months and was anxious to put his hand to more practical work in administration. He had served me with great loyalty and given me his best in three countries and I hope that he, now Sheriff of Ayr, has as happy memories of those 15 months as I who owed him a great debt of gratitude.

Luckily for me, I was able to appoint as his successor, an officer who maintained the standard of personal service in a different way but with complete success. A personal job of this sort is not easy and demands a great deal of self sacrifice, but when fulfilled selflessly and successfully it creates an atmosphere of mutual understanding in the whole circle of people involved. Prior to a difficult interview, a good PA can often prepare both parties before they meet or may deem it wiser to do nothing. At a social or semi official gathering a conscientious PA has quite a responsibility in 'getting the party going' and saving his chief from the boredom of a 'sticky' guest or guests.

Ian Carr came to me as a Captain after fine military

service in Crete where his battalion was left to delay and harass the German invaders, knowing that they could not be withdrawn or rescued and that their superiors would expect a temporary resistance followed by surrender. Not so, for Ian Carr and some of his men. They fought and then slipped away from the aerodrome which they had been defending, into the bush among the high Cretan mountains. They lived for four months 'enjoying the hospitality' of friendly Cretans and hunted by Germans, until they made contact with naval units off the coast and were rescued by one of HM submarines, the Torbay. After that experience he deserved a peaceful billet; at first he was dogged by illness and accident but by the late summer, after he had enjoyed home leave, he showed his true mettle and made our lives at the Villa Volpi as happy and peaceful as could be. He paid me the great compliment of following me to my next job across the water. In Tripoli he was excellent in dealing with some of the sometimes odd and quite frequent visitors whom it was our lot (and joy) to entertain. I have mentioned many and Ian was as good at persuading a Corps Commander to sing after dinner as he was at extracting sensitive information from a Turkish diplomat. Here is how he pumped the wily Turk. This is Ian Carr's story:

June 1943

"Among the interesting persons who stayed with the Chief Civil Administrator Tripolitania, in the summer and autumn of 1943, one particular individual remains in my memory. He was Captain Orbay, a senior officer in the Turkish Navy and at that time representing his country (Turkey) as Ambassador at the Court of St James.

"On his way home to London after consultations with his Government he had arranged through the Foreign Office in London to spend a weekend in Tripoli and it befell the CCAO to entertain him adequately.

"We were somewhat mystified before his arrival as to the reason for him wishing to spend two whole days in this comparatively unexciting town of Tripoli, when the lights and attractions of Cairo lay just six hours flying time away.

"However, the reason at once became clear (on the drive from Castel Benito aerodrome). We were informed that he had been born, educated and, later, a cadet in the Military Academy in Tripoli when the country was still part of the Ottoman Empire.

"Arising out of such an unexpected background, this totally charming man wished to visit all the places, buildings and other spots of childhood and adolescent memories.

"I recollect that our hearts sank slightly. Another full weekend of entertaining but with still all the day to day work awaiting attention when our guest had finally retired to bed.

"Nevertheless, Saturday went off well. He was allowed everywhere (Turkey was still neutral); he saw just about everything he had hoped for; and in some cases met old people who recollected him too. He was no different from any of us resurrecting the past. I lost count of the number of times he said "Ah, now I remember" and off he would go on yet another story of those by-gone days. Sufficient to say the weekend passed and Monday morning arrived. It fell to my lot to accompany him back to his aeroplane (to make sure he got safely on board).

"As we drove out to Castel Benito, I could not resist asking a question which in 1943 was foremost in the minds of many governments.

"Excuse me, Sir" I said, looking him straight in the face, "But will Turkey come into the war?"

He smiled, paused and then said "We are a country which receives some of our arms from Germany, some from France, Czechoslovakia, so ...." and he stopped.

We drove on in silence, but I had my answer. And so it was - his country remained neutral till hostilities ceased."

During my travels round the provinces I could not fail to come across the cave dwellers or troglodytes in their subterranean villages on the comparatively high ground near Gharian, but south of the Nefusa Gebel. In describing them I shall quote from Casserly's *Tripolitania* written before, but published after our occupation of 1943. After describing the plentiful cultivation in the district he reveals that:

"the stranger is struck by the curious fact that no villages or even stray huts are visible. From the road one could see grass covered mounds of earth covered with grass or scrub. If he continued the visitor would find a cluster of square pits, 40' square and 40' deep. May I disclose that there was little or no warning nor obstacle before one came to the edge of the pit? These are the work of the cave dwellers of Gharian. The soil is a kind of sandstone - easy to dig and to fashion. During construction ropes are used for access and for the removal of earth. When the pit has been finished stables are excavated for the animals (goats and donkeys) and then more regular and larger rooms are excavated for humans possibly at a higher altitude; these rooms are well wrought, roomy and having windows on to the pit, and considering their depth, a moderate amount of light. *After* completion of pit and accommodation therein, a sloping tunnel is excavated with a moderate slope and large enough for humans and animals to use. At the top and bottom of this sloping tunnel are built strong doors and sometimes off the passage are built living rooms so that accommodation is available at different heights. The main living quarters, nevertheless, are at the bottom. What better form of accommodation for man and beast in a country prone to lawlessness are these pit habitations? They are warm in winter and cool all the hot summer and impregnable to enemies."

I used my official standing to visit one (the dwellings were not very 'open to visitors') and found them comfortable, spotlessly clean in the rooms outside and amazingly fresh smelling; attempts had been made to collect the animal dung in the centre of the pit (for burning) and one marvelled at the apparent ventilation which existed. Thus have these people lived for centuries and no-one has ever really to my knowledge discovered the origin of this novel and sensible form of existence. I should not care to be an inhabitant during a long period of rain; but such climatic risks do not exist. Rain does come - even snow - but not for long periods.

I was told in 1943 that these pits were first excavated by Jews - but they are most certainly now inhabited by Arab and Berber people. Other members of the staff were either not interested enough or had no time to explore the origins of these cave dwellers and I was indeed disappointed not to find any reference to them in Professor (then Squadron Leader) Max Mallowan's book which contains a chapter on his experience in Military Administration in 1943. They were, however, still in existence in 1953 when Diana and I visited them and Anthony Thwaite in *The Deserts of Hesperides* (Secker and Warburg, London 1969) writes:

"The open-courtyard homes centering in a well with rooms running off it is typical of Libya. This is the plan followed at Gharian, the only difference being that these 'houses' are 40 to 50 feet deep in the ground, cut out of rock and earth. Most of them are wired for electricity and there are plans for piping water to them."

Again there is no mention of their historical origin. Reference can also be made to The National Geographic magazine September 1911 and August 1925.

I, therefore, shall make my assertion based on what I was told by Arabs and Jews in 1943, that these cave dwellings were first excavated by Jews of the Spanish Diaspora (XI Century) - a settlement which raises an historical and archaeological problem!

I have mentioned Max Mallowan and I would like to record here what a pleasure it was to have on my staff even then a distinguished archaeologist whom we 'happened' to post, on his arrival, to the Province which contained Sabratha, an

"…. ancient Phoenician foundation, overlooking the sea, rich in Roman ruins, temples, baths, house and endowed with a superb theatre …. some guardian angel must have directed me to this heavenly spot where in the cool of the evening I perused the memorial inscriptions or visited the little museum with its beautiful peacock mosaic and browsed in the library, well stocked with the classics and books on history and archaeology." (Mallowan's *Memoirs*, Collins 1977).

It is nice to have been styled a guardian angel by the late Sir Max Mallowan! His second posting was to Homs, the most remote oasis in our territory. Homs itself was riddled with mines but Leptis Magna was nearby.

Diana and I came to know him and his distinguished and famous wife, Agatha Christie, when they stayed with us during our second incarnation in Tripoli and afterwards invited us to their lovely home, Greenway. To visit Leptis Magna with Max was a memorable event - only to be compared with the sight of Greenway magnolias for which it and the Mallowans were so famous.

Visit of King George V1

"Headquarters and some of the divisions of the VIII Army moved back to the Tripoli area as soon as their task in Tunisia was completed and, before starting on the next enterprise, were honoured by a visit from His Majesty the King - a fitting climax to our campaigning in Africa." (*El Alamein to the River Sangro*; Montgomery; Hutchinson).

I missed King George's visit for reasons of utter happiness to me - but before I went, Montgomery gave a lecture to a collection of 'brass hats' the like of which I certainly had never seen before. Alexander was there - many Generals from I Army in Tunisia and also from Cairo (I well remember Godwin Austen) and I think two from Chiefs of Staff from London. The subject was El Alamein to Tunisia: how the VIII Army achieved it. The lecturer began as usual "No coughing, please, while I am speaking. There will be an interval." The lecture was superb and the audience went away knowing how it was done and how the VIII Army would do it elsewhere.

My PA, Ian Carr, organised the hall and meeting and wrote his account of King George's visit *Red Tabs and Red Faces*; Tripolitania 1943:

"During the latter part of that summer whilst the Governor of the Province was on a short leave in England, a visit was paid to North Africa by His Majesty King George VI.

"The main purpose of this exercise was to present to the people of Malta the George Cross Medal and a beautifully fashioned sword inlaid with precious stones. All of this was to be an expression of profound admiration by the British Government and the citizens of that island to their opposite friends on what was after all, a much smaller but equivalent piece of territory.

"However I digress.

"His Majesty arrived in Algiers where the programme, lasting three or four days of visiting a number of units in I Army had been laid on. The King dutifully carried out these inspections but unfortunately on the last day contracted 'gippy tummy' and anyone who has ever experienced this short lived but thoroughly unpleasant illness would be the first to sympathise with the Monarch's state of health and indeed feelings, when on the fifth day he arrived in Tripoli. Here he was to carry out a series of much shortened inspections of VIII Army personnel.

"From Tripoli Harbour he was to embark on the cruiser Aurora and proceed thence to Malta heavily escorted by destroyers and aircraft.

"None of the foregoing might seem of the slightest importance but for a small incident which took place just as the King was about to board the Admiral's barge at the slipway.

"At that time I was combining the duties of PA, ADC and Private Secretary to the Governor of Tripolitania and all of it involved attempting the smooth running of his busy life; and as he worked quite frequently 20 out of the 24 hours of each day, much careful forward planning and anticipation of his demands were necessary.

"Clearly the effects of the 'gippy tummy' still held the Monarch's stomach in thrall. He alighted with reluctance from General Montgomery's Humber Staff Car and proceeded slowly towards the sailors holding the barge ready for him to step on board. Then suddenly he realised that he had not got his brief case with him - a vital perquisite in which lay the pills to ease the aching pains. He turned peremptorily to the first senior officer behind him - General "Jumbo" Wilson Commanding Middle East Land Forces from Cairo and demanded his precious case. Not unnaturally General "Jumbo" had not got it, so without further ado he turned to the officer behind, General Sir Alan Brooke Chief of the Imperial Staff. Confusion and embarrassment reigned. I watched the scene with full enjoyment. Makes a change I thought. Someone else in the hot seat.

"General Brooke turned to the Army Commander, General Montgomery. He hadn't got the briefcase either. There were only two more people left now: the Corps Commander General Horrocks and the driver of the Humber car. Once the latter realised what all the fuss was about he smartly produced the missing piece of luggage which was then handed forward from officer to officer until once more restored to safety in the King's grip.

"At that point His Majesty stepped carefully aboard, moved slowly away from the quay side and four clearly relieved top brass commanders returned to their staff cars and were driven away."

Leave - June-July 1943

And then I went on leave! After four years I saw Diana again; I met Meriel aged 3½ for the first time in our lives; saw my mother and Ruth (Diana's mother) and lived in paradise for five weeks. I flew via Marrakesh where, oh horror! I was delayed for 24 hours; I visited the famous *suk* (closed to the public because of smallpox). The aircraft following us next day was shot down in the Bay of Biscay; we were diverted by fog to Prestwick, Scotland. But the blessed sight of Diana at Euston was the start of five weeks of utter happiness and thankfulness for all that she had done to bring our little family so far - so wonderfully far. My first meeting with Meriel was exactly as I had hoped. She was sitting or standing by the little gate that led to our front door and Sylvia let her have first welcome to the stranger father. That welcome was one which I have never forgotten - shyness and confidence and love - all instilled into her by Diana and strengthened by Sylvia, who, bless her, was happy to renew actual love and by showing it made Meriel know that "she had felt the right thing". Complete happiness reigned!

Next day to save petrol, I decided to bicycle to Liphook (24 miles) to see Julian, who quite rightly, had not been moved from school. I was very fit but the muscles used in walking, riding and swimming are not those used in bicycling. I arrived at Highfield School in time for a very good welcome from Julian (in the swimming baths), lunch with him and the Headmaster Canon Mills, an afternoon with Julian and then the long push home. MSL not so mobile the next day - but it was worth it! My mother, then aged 82, was in great fettle in Brookside which she was keeping warm for my sister Chris, who had just joined Dan Sandford in Ethiopia and did not return for some years.

I was summoned to London first by the BBC to give a nationwide broadcast on Tripolitania which began "I was mowing my lawn today and cutting the daisies ....". The broadcast had a long life and was repeated many times!

Immediately after the broadcast I was asked to stay for "messages". Sure enough there were several who had recognised my voice and it was very good to hear old friends who had. One voice, however, said "I am Mrs Biggs and my son is in your administration. Would you ask him if he could send a line to his mother just to say all is well?". I promised to do so and on return fulfilled my promise in an avuncular and commanding officer style. Ewart Biggs was a very fine young officer and administrator who afterwards joined the Foreign Service. I met him again in 1952 when he was Political Officer in service at Doha, capital of the state of Qatar in the Persian Gulf and he died in 1976 as British Ambassador to Eire, foully murdered by the IRA outside his Residence in Dublin.

The HQ of Civil Affairs in the War Office greeted me uncomfortably, as well they might, knowing that I had been asked for by Eisenhower to head AMGOT (Allied Military Government of Occupied Territories) into Sicily and Italy and that they had sent Francis Rennell instead; of that anon. I found no sign of interest in past endeavour and was merely told that if the Portuguese proved difficult about our occupation for strategic purposes (air) of the Azores, I might be sent to administer those islands. In fact Frank Roberts of the FO and an old friend went there. I must say that I found my London Headquarters most uninspiring: I found in Colet Court, Hammersmith, a group of officers training for Military Government in Italy, Austria and Germany and the Far East; I did not stay! I had better thing to do on five weeks' leave, after four years absence, than to discuss my future with bureaucrats who did not care.

The passing of 40 years has by no means dimmed the ecstasy of those five weeks, nor the realisation, which then was made clear to me, of the courage and selflessness which womenfolk of our home at Westlands had shown and were still determined to show on behalf of our small family, in order to protect them, as far as was possible, from the evils, the dangers and deficiencies and even the discomforts of war. That they had suffered was very apparent - that they were prepared to endure more was as apparent. Shortage of food, of comforts, of any luxury and of petrol were 'inconveniences' which Diana, Ruth and my own mother, were prepared cheerfully - with thousands of others - to tolerate for the sake of the children and for the sake of ourselves overseas. I realised that their deepest anxieties were caused by lack of news, for uncertainty and doubt generate fear and despair. I knew that the military postal service was, generally speaking, as good as circumstances would allow, and I determined then and there that I must never allow myself to be responsible for that particular deficiency in their lives. Diana, besides our three children, had the anxiety of her mother's frail health and my own mother's ever increasing age. Ruth, my mother-in-law, did not survive the war and I was to see her no more after my return to Africa at the end of July. My own mother lived for a further score of years.

But the end of the happiest five weeks had to come and I flew south from Lineham to Gibraltar in an Anson aircraft one night at the end of July.

Extract from letter MSL to DRL 25.7.43:

"…. We emplaned at 1 am nicely clothed in airdress and Mae Wests (inflatable lifebelts) …. I had a mattress. On taking the run for his take-off, the pilot jammed on all his brakes saying he could not see a yard ahead. However, off we went and I fell asleep and literally never woke until the General (one of the two other passengers in this small aircraft) pointed out the Rock. I telephoned brother Cecil (Commanding HM Dockyard Gibraltar) and we had a bath and breakfast together and talked until 11 am when I had to leave."

We reached Algiers at 3 pm where I was delighted to find General Jock Whitely with whom I had flown from Khartoum to Nairobi and Jig Jigga in January 1942. I dined with Roger Makins in the Minister of State's (Harold Macmillan) house and learned a great deal about North Africa and Sicily (invasion had taken place on 10 July).

Back in Tripoli

It took me 10 hours to fly from Algiers to Tripoli next day - we stopped at every airfield en route - to a warm welcome with cool drinks at the Villa Volpi, and so to begin again. I managed several quick tours of the territory and found all moderately well. I visited General Brian Robertson who had been the Senior Military Commander in Tripoli with VIII Army, and was in Tunisia preparing for Sicily. We had our usual stream of visitors at the Villa Volpi which *was* an attractive place. General Sir Sergeson Brooke, Head of British Red Cross, Barrington Ward, Ronald Storrs, General and Lady Huddleston, the Governor General of the Sudan were all welcome guests and many others. We, being the more permanent residents, were naturally a more interesting group of hosts than the ever-changing transient fighting men.

One day, a very smart, suntanned (as I thought) officer was ushered into my office by Ian Carr who had a smirk on his face which I knew spelt something unusual. The officer handed me a personal letter from General Alexander which read:

"Dear Lush,

The bearer of this note, Major Ali Khan, has been stationed in Cairo for some months and has succeeded in painting even this city pink. I have ordered him to be transferred to your administration and I would strongly recommend that you post him forthwith to the outpost of your domain furthest from civilisation!

Yours, Alexander"

Luckily I had one or two "ends of the world" stations on the edge of the Fezzan and Major Prince Ali Khan - for the offender was no other - was despatched (after dining with me that evening when he delighted us all) to Nalut and Ghadames - to the ultimate Thule - where, as an Arab speaking Moslem Civil Affairs Officer, he was a great success and a most efficient administrator. Wait, however, one moment! A month after his arrival at his station, I had occasion to visit on business the French Administration of Tunisia, at the sea coast resort of Gabes. The little place was beginning to return to normal vitality after the battles of the Mareth line and thereafter and at least one hotel was open wherein my staff and I were booked. On going up the stairs to my room a handsome, clearly British, officer brushed past me, obviously in a hurry to leave. I had recognised him however, and I stopped him. "Major Ali Khan, what duty has brought you from Nalut in Tripolitania to Gabes at least 400 miles away in Tunisia?" "Sir" he replied "Stationed as I was on or near the border of Tunisia I thought it was my duty to visit that country and get to know the inhabitants." Well, I warned him that if he did not return to Nalut by sunset next day he would be court martialled. I heard a jeep remove itself from the hotel during dinner. Act II of this episode will be presented in my chapter on Pakistan, 1958.

In my journey to Tunisia I drove on from Gabes to stay in Tunis with the Monypennys (he was the Consul General) old friends of Cairo times. I met there Roger Makins who was on the staff of the Minister of State and between us we kept the Monypenny establishment awake most of the night with cypher telegrams. We also managed to see a little of Tunis:

"an enormous town and absolutely packed with people of every nationality …. It is dirty and hot and utterly French. The French have the ability to make their towns, wherever they may be, French in every way. Every little village in Tunisia has a Cafe de la Paix and a Rue Thiers."

I returned to a busy Tripoli - MSL to DRL 12.10.43:

"…. What a week I have had! Jewish New Year's Day on Thursday, Synagogue and teaparty; musical evening at our Villa on Friday - an English professor at the piano played very well; 30 people in our music room; Beiram (Moslem feast) party on Saturday - 200 guests in our courtyard - Italian food contractor turned up late! Sudan Defence Force band did wonders. High Mass at the Italian Cathedral on Sunday when I made my first official appearance - they all thought I was Badoglio (Italian Prime Minister) and I was thanked in the Bishop's sermon for coming; lovely music and most impressive service; lunch with *Mufti* (Moslem Religious Leader) where the second course of eight was 14 chickens for 14 people! Afterwards Arab horse show with speeches by Arabs and self; and then last night a dance in our Villa for 40 couples (Hospital Nurses), a very nice party with very good guests."

Thoughts on the future

My interview in London and the general trend of the war had caused me to think seriously beyond Tripolitania and to my future. With an early retiring age from the Sudan I was due to go on to a pension of £1,000 per annum in 1947 and, as in the First World War, I had to be a wage earner with a second career when the war ended. My eyes were turned therefore to jobs which possibly had a future. But these were secondary thoughts. I was longing to go to Military Government in Italy. I guessed that I had been asked for by Eisenhower and that London had seen fit to send instead Francis Rennell my senior, in spite of his lack of field experience in Military Government. I also heard that Military Government in Sicily had left much to be desired. The question had been asked "Why not send us men with experience in this business?" They required administrators, not just 'sensible people'. A good many people failed to recognise that administration is a profession which is learnt after hard experience and that the rudiments of administration are much the same wherever they are applied - be it in Africa or Europe.

It is obvious from my letters to Diana that I was unsettled again; chafing at the bad repute of the Allied Military Government in Sicily which I might have commanded (with greater success) and anxious about the long distant future.

[Here MSL had intended to quote from his letter to Douglas Newbold of 3.10.43: this letter is now held amongst MSL's Papers in the Imperial War Museum's Archives.]

I had by now no friends in high military places in Cairo - my HQ - except one, General Ronnie Scobie. We had known each other in the Sudan and now he was Chief of the General Staff in Cairo and was good enough to keep his ears open on my behalf. I had opened my heart to him on one or two occasions. Ronnie knew of my anxieties and throughout the autumn of 1943 he advised me that in the end all would be well for me. So I turned away from future dreams - good and bad - and addressed myself to the job in hand which was quite enough to keep me happy and busy. I was, after all, very lucky - with a good independent 'show' to run; I had an excellent and, I hoped, contented staff and had enjoyed five weeks of wonderful leave. To tell the truth I expect the kindness of many people and especially the London press had gone to my head and I wanted to go off and win the war elsewhere!

Travers Blackley returned from the USA where he had earned many laurels instructing in military administration and I was able to send my No 2, Miller, to replace him there and put Travers in his old position as my second-in-command. He was indeed able to support me through the only difficult period of personal animosity which I had experienced - that with the new Civil Affairs Chief in Cairo. The War Office had appointed a very odd card to take charge of the Civil Affairs Office there. He came from India where he had been in the ICS and was an

"old bachelor with very preconceived ideas …. Is out to debunk us and cut us down; he doesn't understand the difficulties of initial administration. He is quite determined not to move any of us."

The last sentence written to Diana in September was very distressing. I had been hearing from many people what a mess Francis Rennell was making of AMGOT in Sicily and Blackley had heard Rennell himself say that he was "all in" and his show was in a terrible mess. My new Chief returned to Cairo after a week's visit to Tripolitania and was particularly silent and uncommunicative. He had damned himself utterly in my eyes by saying that he thought John Maffey was a failure in the Indian Political Service and that the Sudan Political Service was over-staffed.

Then early in November I had a cryptic telegram from Francis Rennell in Italy which read: "When do you arrive?"

After a bout of telephoning and telegraphing to Cairo it transpired that 18 days previously they had asked if I could be spared for Italy, and they had acquiesced (not a word to me!) and now I had been appointed Chief Civil Affairs Officer, Italy, in my present rank. It was typical of the bachelor sexagenarian from India that I should not have been informed!

MSL to DRL:

"It is *rather* exciting and my fourth adventure; it will be good to be with the forefront again and not back material …. the next good news is that Travers Blackley is to succeed me in Tripoli - I *am* glad!"

There followed some more busy days handing over, saying goodbye to the governed and my fellow governors and, as I thought, to Africa for ever. I left

Tripoli by air on 13 November 1943 after 12 months in charge of a splendid and, I hoped, happy team of men who had supported me wonderfully and as I knew would find service under Travers Blackley less of a strain. The Arabs, Italians and Jews had all given me a warm farewell and I discovered that among my flock had been a group of Indians whom I had never really met. Indeed in retrospect, I realised that I had never come very close personally with any of the population - but that was deliberate as regards the Italians and inevitable with the Arabs and Berbers who lived away from the capital. The Jews had given me the warmest welcome and were vociferous in their farewell.

Governing Tripolitania had been the smoothest and easiest of my three administrations so far, and I left, after a wonderful farewell party at the Villa Volpi, for a very different kind of experience.

Proudly I quote Travers Blackley's airgram to Diana on the day of my departure, 14.11.43:

"I wish you could have been here last night when BMA gathered in force to give Maurice a send-off. These parties are normally rather sticky and involve a good deal of brain-searching for the right thing to say. Last night was quite different: it was spontaneous. Each member of this administration is tied by feelings of personal loyalty to Maurice. The party let him see it. It would have made you feel very proud - we hate him going but know that he is wanted on the other side. For me it is delightful to see his very real happiness at me being selected to succeed him. We've had a great war together and I like to think we've done our bit on the home front too! The country needs more Lushes and Blackleys!"

The last sentence refers to increase in both our families; Diana was expecting our fourth child.

Travers Blackley administered Tripolitania wisely and successfully through many vicissitudes and uncertainties from November 1943 until December 1951 when, after finding itself the helpless pawn on the international chessboard it was, by the vote of one single country, granted independence on 25 December 1951. Soon after, I again found myself landing at Castel Benito Airport - but in a very different capacity.

TRIPOLITANIA
February 1943

Above:
Prime Minister Winston Churchill with MSL, General Montgomery and others

Right:
MSL with Winston Churchill

Below:
Winston Churchill reviewing VIII Army troops in Tripoli

Brigadier MS Lush, Chief of Staff, Allied Commission, Italy 1945

Rear Admiral Ellery Stone, Chief Commissioner, presenting US Legion of Merit to MSL, December 1945

ITALY

Harold Macmillan, Acting President (UK), Allied Commission, 1945

Prince and Princess Doria Pamphili, with daughter Orietta, he posing in disguise with limp

CHAPTER 13

ITALY 1943-1946

Chief Civil Affairs Officer, Allied Military Government — Nov 43 - Jan 44

Executive Commissioner, Allied Control Commission — Jan 44 - Sep 44

Chief of Staff & Vice President, Allied Commission — Oct 44 - Oct 46

1943	
10 July	Sicily invaded by Allied armies
25 July	Mussolini dismissed by the King and made captive
17 August	Sicily conquered
3 September	Allies land in Italy
8 September	Italy surrenders; armistice; King and Badoglio flee to Brindisi
9 September	Allies land Salerno
27 September	Capture of Foggia by Allies
1 October	Allies capture Naples
1 December	Allies on Garigliano-Sangro Winter Line
8 December	MSL takes over AMG & Army Group as CCAO (Bari)

I arrived in Bari, the large port on the south east coast of Italy on 26 November 1943, three days after my 47th birthday, to take over command of Allied Military Government (AMG) Italy from Major General Francis Rennell as Chief Civil Affairs Officer Italy, on the staff of General Alexander, Commander-in-Chief Allied Forces in Italy, then known as XV Army Group. It was almost a year since I flew to Cairo for the Tripolitania exercises. On the way to Bari the pilot had very graciously circled round Pantellaria, the island occupied by the Allies just before the invasion of Sicily.

I found Francis Rennell at the airport. He seemed pleased to see me; he was obviously not happy, not himself, and told me that he was longing to get away from it all. His Mess, a mile or two outside Bari, was a gloomy house once used as a home for therapeutic patients. I had sent Ian Carr, my PA, "in advance" of me by sea with all my luggage; he had not arrived by 3 December when I enquired of him in Naples. I found the weather wintry and terribly cold.

I tried to explain to Diana that the job in Italy which had put *finis* on any hope of Christmas leave, was a "must".

Thus began my first job in Europe since World War I; it was to last for three, onerous, stimulating if personally disappointing, years during which I worked with British and Americans and met an amazing number of men of many other nationalities - Royals, soldiers and politicians; I suffered in absentia two grievous personal tragedies at home, and ended with Diana and the children *en famille*, with me in Rome.

I had no experience of Italy except as a visitor, although I had of course, governed in two occupied Italian colonies, and had seen the Italians in defeat in Ethiopia and Tripolitania. I did not speak Italian and, to my shame, never found time even in Italy to learn the language.

I was about to take charge of an Allied administration and had taken no part in the early days of training and preparation therein. There had been heavy criticism of AMG during the initial stages and my predecessor had not been offered a leading part in the new organisation when under urgent consideration for the future administration of Italy.

Francis Rennell told me of his grave misgivings at the outset of his handing over. To DRL I wrote on 3.12.43:

"I have been taking over this untidy show. The whole lay out is desperately untidy and nobody knows what is going to happen next."

Rennell told me that I might find my own post disappearing soon.

But General Alexander who had been my Commander-in-Chief when I was in Tripolitania gave me a warm welcome which at once inspired confidence and determination, both of which were greatly strengthened by General Eisenhower exclaiming: "Are you Lush? Why, we wanted you from the beginning! Right glad to have you now!"

Thus began the only conversation I ever had with Ike.

But his greeting and Alexander's welcome were my shield in those difficult early days.

So, when Francis Rennell after a most unsatisfactory handover which told me very little, did at last depart, I was able to write to DRL on 8.12.43:

> "Hope to take over completely from FR today and really run this show. I want it badly! It *is* fun and I am beginning to see daylight .... There is so much to be done which FR has left undone and which I know I can tidy up."

Francis Rennell retired to banking life in the UK and I pulled myself together knowing that I had "one hell of a job" in front of me. Luckily I had found several first rate officers on my Headquarters Staff who, I hoped, would come forward with help and advice, once they had confidence in me. My hope was amply fulfilled and I was and still am most grateful to men like Thorne, Grafftey Smith and other stalwarts who had helped me in those early days in Bari and Naples.

At the same time, Ian Carr, my admirable PA, and our batman arrived; he gave one quick look at the headquarters Mess and within 48 hours:

MSL to DRL at Christmas time

> "Ian has revolutionised this house and now we have a home with a sitting room and a fire and good food well cooked; all is very comfortable - except that I have a WC next door to my bedroom which works all night at 10 minute intervals - some pneumatic principle! The horrors of war!"

At any rate our home life was in good hands and this was much appreciated by my Headquarters Staff.

On the military front, the Allies had achieved their first strategic objective on the mainland of Italy - the capture of the Port of Naples (October) and the airfields of Foggia, whence they could bomb southern Germany. Although the invasion of Sicily had led to the downfall of Mussolini and the subsequent Armistice between the King with his Prime Minister Badoglio and the Allies, the Germans had forestalled an Allied airborne descent on Rome and had all but beaten back the landing at Salerno in September. German decisiveness had prevented the expected Allied occupation of Rome by Christmas 1943.

Alexander writes (page 17 *Memoirs*):

> "I had to report (early October) to General Eisenhower (C-in-C SACMED) that the Germans had decided not to withdraw but 'to stay in Rome and defend it to the utmost of their power'. I warned that further progress would be slow and that direct assaults on the enemy's positions in the mountains .... must be costly."

The German decision to stand and to fight the Allied armies throughout the length of Italy was, in many people's minds, including that of Churchill, a strategic blunder, for it played into the hands of the Allies who, through the Combined Chiefs of Staff (CCS), had directed Alexander to "carry out such operations (in Italy) as would be best calculated to contain the maximum number of German divisions in Italy." These were known as the "stated ends" and I shall use that phrase in this connection as we go through Italy.

Alexander continues, writing about that autumn of 1943:

> "Here was the true moment of birth of the Italian campaigns. I and my commanders were determined to have Rome - but Rome was not the end of the story. This side of Rome, and beyond it, the Allied armies were to be faced with a seemingly unending succession of difficulties of terrain .... they were to experience a savage versatility of climate without any parallel in north east Europe."

Nigel Nicholson writes:

> "In the early winter months of 1943-1944, V (US) and VIII (British) Armies were fighting almost separate campaigns from river to river divided by the central mountain mass of the Abruzzi, slowed down by mud mountains, supply difficulties and stiffening German resistance until at great cost and diminishing elation, they reached the line of the rivers Sangro on the east and the Garigliano on the west, some 40 miles north of Naples."

Our AMG Forward and most important units were looking after civil affairs in those areas. Although attempts were made to break the winter stalemate, the Allied advance had to await the spring and Rome remained in German hands until June 1944.

With regard to the administration of Civil Affairs, the Armistice of September 1943 altered the plans of the Allied Forces HQ in Algiers, who had formed Allied Military Government of Occupied Territories (AMGOT) and the Allied Control Commission (ACC) on paper in anticipation of an occupied enemy territory. I am not, even now, and certainly was not then, in a position to comment on their thoughts or planning because, extraordinary as it may seem, they neither consulted nor advised my predecessor Francis Rennell of what was in their minds when they began to formulate new ideas emanating from the Armistice when he was Chief Civil Affairs Officer, and certainly made no contact with myself, a mere Brigadier, his successor!

According to Harris (*Allied Administration of Italy 1943-1945*), from whom I shall quote extensively in the following pages:

> ".... the functions of the Control Commission were .... to enforce and execute the instrument of surrender and secondly to ensure that the conduct of the Italian Government conformed to an Allied base of operations. The implications of co-belligerency seem to have been ignored as was the experience of officers on Rennell's AMG Headquarters. Francis Rennell was offered Head of the Economic Section which he refused. It was anticipated that General Mason-MacFarlane who had been Head of the Armistice Commission appointed in September 1943, would

eventually be appointed Chief Commissioner of the Allied Control Commission; but as the Head of the Commission had to be of the same nationality as the Supreme Commander (Eisenhower) the post of Deputy President was invented and given to an American General Joyce whom Harold Macmillan in *Blast of War* described as "elderly, well mannered .... he did not appear to have any particular qualifications or any great disqualifications for the task."

I found him quite spineless, but he did not bother us for long.

In the meantime, there existed Allied Military Government (AMG) under myself, the new Chief Civil Affairs Officer (CCAO) at Bari, with authority over all occupied Italy except the four southern provinces in the "heel" of Italy handed over to Badoglio and called "King's Italy".

It had taken the Headquarters Allied Forces at Algiers three months to evolve the most enormous (1,500 Allied officers) and amorphous mass of untrained men of the Allied Control Commission with literally no real plan of operation or distribution of work for them to do. I had found their "leader" (Joyce) and their Headquarters in Bari doing absolutely nothing. Quite clearly this could not be allowed to continue; Rennell had taken umbrage some weeks before and taken no further part in planning of the future of the ACC.

After Rennell's departure, therefore, I visited General Joyce, titular head of the Commission, in an attempt to discover for what portion of Italy it was responsible; neither he nor his staff knew, and I therefore told them that, failing any orders to the contrary, I regarded myself as Chief Civil Affairs Officer responsible for the lot, excluding King's Italy! I repeated this to their political advisers, Harold Caccia and Chuck Spofford (USA) whom I found ensconced in a bathroom in a Bari hotel which was Headquarters ACC, Harold on a bidet, the other on a bath stool using the bath as a table. They were most welcoming and agreed with my decision. I also had Alexander's tacit approval. After research I now find that I was wrong, for in some extraordinary way Rear AMG formations, including Sicily under the personal command of the Deputy Chief Civil Affairs Officer, were supposed to report to Allied Forces Headquarters in Algiers. This never took place during my regime!

Before recounting further action, let me now mention some of the top personalities whom I met in those early months of my new career in December 1943:

General "Ike" Eisenhower
Supreme Allied Commander Mediterranean (SACMED). He commanded all theatres of war in the Mediterranean: Egypt, Greece, Dodecanese, Balkans, Italy, North Africa and the South of France. He left in January 1944 to take command of "Overlord" - the famous Channel invasion.

General "Jumbo" Wilson
Came from Egypt to succeed Eisenhower as SACMED.

General Alexander
Commander XV Army Group but later became SACMED and Field Marshall. Moved from Bari to Caserta. Ideal Commander-in-Chief.

Lt General John Harding
Chief of Staff to Alexander. Saw him but little; had known him in Libya.

Major General Brian Robertson
Q man (Quartermaster) to Alexander; very efficient; very good to AMG and MSL; neighbour in Naples.

General Montgomery
General Officer Commanding (GOC) VIII Army.

Major General Leese
Succeeded Montgomery as GOC VIII Army, when I renewed my friendship of Libya.

General Mark Clark
GOC V Army (USA); saw but little; not impressed.

Harold Macmillan
British Minister of State; became Acting President of ACC; a valuable and kind adviser and friend.

Lt General Sir Noel Mason-MacFarlane
Head of Military Mission for Armistice, First Chief Commander, ACC.

"Bob" Murphy
US counter-part of Macmillan and very good; saw but little of him.

Roger Makins
On Macmillan's staff; not often in Italy.

Harold Caccia
British and US political advisers.

Sam Reber
on original ACC (General Joyce) staff.

General Kenyon Joyce
First Acting President of ACC in Bari; handed over to General Mason-MacFarlane on latter's return in January 1944.

"Chuck" Spofford
AFHQ representative on Civil Affairs and for some time political adviser to ACC; most helpful.

In the foregoing list I have not mentioned the Italian King (Victor Emmanuel III) nor his Prime Minister, Marshal Badoglio. I visited them in Brindisi soon after my arrival and found them in the portion of Italy known as "King's Italy" which had been set aside from the very beginning (ie. after the Armistice and the Royal flight from Rome to Brindisi) as completely Italian territory. These comprised the four southern provinces of Apulia Region viz Bari, Brindisi, Taranto and Lecce. Over these four provinces Allied writ never ran and Italian government was supreme (with Allied Liaison Officers in residence therein) particularly, of course, in the ports of Brindisi and Taranto - a state of affairs which the Allies hoped would gradually come to pass in large parts of Italy. I never went to Taranto during my total service in Italy.

It was now mid-December and my first duty was to visit as much of occupied Italy as I could while military activity was quiescent. We knew that General Alexander would not suffer a long spell of inertia.

When planning my preliminary visits to areas of administrative importance I omitted "King's Italy" and in fact decided that Naples and my Spearhead Military Governors (AMG's) clearly took priority. Naples came first because here was a city of over two million people, the port through which came the bulk of the Army's supplies in which disorder might easily affect the outcome of military action not so many miles to the north. The place, never a haven of peace or good order, had been heavily bombed by the Allies and cruelly devastated by the Germans before evacuation; this had led to acute food and water shortages and an outbreak of typhus. Bad planning at the HQ of the embryo Allied Control Commission (Joyce) and at SACMED (Supreme Command) HQ in Algiers and Washington had left the food supply far below Rennell's earlier demands and on my arrival in the port I found that Brian Robertson had formed a committee to coordinate food supply and distribution; the US Army engineers had effected urgent repairs to aqueducts and reinstated a fraction of the water supply and a Rockefeller team under General Swan had the typhus epidemic in hand. General Swan was a typical Texan sharpshooter and boasted that he had spat into a hundred rivers or more over the world in his war against typhus - only he used a function which was not expectoration! I was reminded of him in later life by a Texan troubleshooter who was on hand to subdue fires at oil drilling sites - but Swan certainly earned his pay and bombast in Naples and we were grateful to him.

Brigadier General Hume, Chief of V Army (USA) Spearhead AMG, had done a fine job in the first days of Allied occupation of Naples (October) and on his departure northwards, I transferred the administration of that post to the Senior Civil Affairs Officer (SCAO) of Region III AMG who seemed to me to have all the courage and foresight necessary in a desperate situation. Nevertheless, Naples was also a political trouble spot of infinite importance and I decided there and then to call forward Colonel Poletti from his post in Sicily to take charge of this very grave emergency. Charlie Poletti was, like many of my US officers, an American Italian and Lieutenant Governor of New York State. Writing about him in *Blast of War*, Harold Macmillan describes his effect as Governor in Sicily:

"He was in his element and seemed to be loving it. The Sicilians seemed to love him too. I think they felt rather proud that one of their own kin should have made good in America and now be sent to hand out good things with a kind word and a joke for everyone."

Colonel Poletti had a sterner task to tackle in Naples - but he did not shrink from it and showed his powers of courageous patience and determination, his understanding of the Allied and the Neapolitan and Italian problems - human, military, administrative and political - above all human. In continuing the initial work done by Hume, he transformed Naples from a disaster area, first to an administrative headache and, by June 1944, to a difficult but manageable problem.

The reader will hear of Charlie Poletti again for he was one of the kingpins of my team and appreciated, I hope, the confidence which we all placed in him as warmly as we valued his wisdom and power of compassionate administration.

My visit to Naples warned me of the tremendous problems which faced all of us in Italy and the necessity of very careful selection of staff; good selection meant having a knowledge of the men concerned and their capacity. I could only acquire that by visiting as many administrations as was possible. That I determined to do after Christmas 1943.

In Bari, earlier in December, we had been reminded that war was not so far away when on 12 December there was a sharp and, one had to admit, a fairly successful enemy air raid on the port. Badoglio, the Italian Prime Minister, who was nearby wrote an account of it in his book:

"As there had not been any other attacks in Bari the fear of raids had practically disappeared and so had air precautions. There were about 30 ships in port some loaded with ammunition, others with petrol and nearly all were tied up alongside each other .... some bombs hit the town but the chief attack, however, was on the harbour where additional damage was done by an ammunition ship blowing up and by the fires in the tankers. In all, 24 ships were sunk!"

I think he exaggerated but it *was* a bad raid. I happened to be standing at the front door of our Mess watching the aircraft in the sky; the house was about half a mile from the harbour. The blast of the ammunition ship's destruction blew me 15 yards right through the house; a rather battered Brigadier went to bed that night! Next day General Joyce won no laurels by issuing an order to all ACC personnel in Bari to evacuate their billets in the town, seek new residence in a village 40 miles away and commute daily therefrom!

In Bari I began to know my staff and by Christmas time 1943, I was able to get to know some of our other ranks - clerical staff, storemen and motor transport drivers. We were able to arrange the traditional Christmas football match and festivities for them on 25 December, thanks to the excellent services of one

Captain Scully who looked after the mens' and the officers' personal interests. Here in my Christmas letter home:

MSL to DRL 25.12.43

"…. I have had a hectic week but today took a complete day off. Church at 7 am; football match (officers v other ranks) at 9.15; an hour's work, talking; round the mens' Christmas dinner at noon, speeches and singing; this afternoon, listening to the King's Speech broadcast (George VI) and an hour's walk with my Chief of Staff Col Thorne whom you met in Cyprus (1936) …. It's fun working with Americans - but tricky!"

After the football match in which I played "back" for the officers, one of my American staff was heard to say "Well - I have heard a lot about the British Army and 'sakes, I admire them, but I never thought I would live to see at football a British Brigadier put on his butt by his batman!"

By the end of the month I was finding my feet:

MSL to DRL 28.12.43:

"Things go well but there are many snags ahead. I cannot get my people (nice at last to write "my people") to be *administrative* and not *political*."

That indeed was a perpetual problem which I encountered throughout my service in Italy - so many people jeopardised their success at administration by playing politics. A few played other games but that is a different story.

After Christmas 1943 I gave orders for AMG HQ to move to Naples. Having appointed Colonel Poletti as Senior Civil Affairs Officer of Region III AMG which included Naples, I imposed my own HQ onto his parish, for Naples was big enough to hold us all - and I knew that no HQ would hold down the irrepressible Col Poletti!

Soon after, I went north to visit the Spearhead Units of AMG attached to VIII Army (British: General Montgomery). In this campaign just as the Army had artillery and engineer units to fire the shells and construct necessary engineering projects with their Commanders on the Army Commander's Staff, so there existed a force of Allied Military Government units whose job was to deal with the civil population and their civil affairs in the areas occupied by the Army; such units were under the command of the Senior Civil Affairs Officer (SCAO) who was on GOC's Staff and directed operations in the name of his Commander throughout the army area. These AMG units were expected to control and maintain the local population everywhere in the Army area in such a way that the military operations of the fighting troops were not impeded. Naturally the maintenance of security, food, water and health among civilians and their dispersal and possible removal from operational areas were primary objectives. Rest assured that every other conceivable problem arose - generally unexpectedly! Infinite compassion, unlimited resourcefulness and unshakeable strength of mind were the qualities most needed in a Civil Affairs Officer.

Group Captain Con Benson DSO, was the Senior Civil Affairs Officer (SCAO) on General Montgomery's Staff and led AMG VIII Army from the landing in Sicily until the end of hostilities in 1945. He was the best SCAO in AMG - in fact in the Commission - a man in whom I had complete confidence always, a trust which was shared by both my Chief Commissioners, British and later American. He was quite unflappable, suspicious of interference in his planning and his execution of such plans, but was, when one knew him, very ready to comply with suggestions which he regarded as sensible. He was intensely loyal to an HQ (ACC) which, as a merchant banker, he must have found untidy - to say the least.

Since September he had led his AMG team with VIII Army from Reggio through Catanzaro and Cosenza Provinces to Potenza and Matera (where they joined the American Salerno forces) and thence northeast to Foggia and further. As the VIII Army advanced so too did the Spearhead Civil Affairs Officers of the CCAO - and this is roughly how we organised the continuity of military government during the whole of the campaign in Italy: the mobile Spearhead CAOs were soon replaced by static CAOs who in turn handed over to Italian officials and finally the whole province or region was taken over by the Italian Government. When military operations enabled the armies to move rapidly, it was often difficult to fill the gaps in time (eg. during the advance from Rome to the Gothic Line) and, of course, as time went on the Italian politicians in Government were always clamouring to take over whole Regions prematurely.

In fact VIII Army AMG had recently experienced a most difficult time in the initial stages of the occupation of Foggia. German destruction had been intense and in their anxiety to re-activate the important airfields there (bases for bombing southern Germany), the US Air Force had ridden completely roughshod over all and every civilian and AMG requirement and interest. "The US Bomber Commands proceeded immediately to requisition every habitable building - including the Municipio." Moreover refugees and demobilised Italian soldiers were streaming south while the former resident Italian population began to trickle back in ever increasing numbers from the mountains whither they had fled. The Italian populace on the move in their own country was always difficult to handle. Sometimes I think both Italians and Allies felt "the poor people are Italians, uprooted and distressed, and here are the Allies, strangers, telling them where to go and what to do in Italy - their own country."

We had three days hard going by car and on foot to the VIII Army area in Foggia, passing through lovely country in bleak wintry weather; we met a number of AMG Officers and their teams - very arduous work for them and their civilian populations in this wet and snowy weather. One (US) officer told me of a village surrounded by a German minefield.

MSL to DRL 30.12.43:

"We went as far forward as we could and found AMG functioning within one mile of the battle line and came under shell fire. I found a very good show here and am very happy about it, with the reservation that I could wish they would be the same after 1900 hours! I have the most awful problems - but I think that they will come right."

On the next day we continued the journey in snow and within four miles of the fighting attended, with the CAO,

"a perfect New Year's Day luncheon in the Italian Baron's castle, with a Signora most sweet, two daughters, one nice, the other naughty but most attractive. I suspect they underwent a quick change of heart and attitude - and who can blame them?"

I also had the luck to run into General Montgomery who, on 30 December, was handing over VIII Army to General Oliver Leese. Both took five minutes to be most welcoming, remembering Tripoli, and Oliver Leese asked me to stay with them in ten days' time, which I did.

Those few snowy days introduced me to my team in VIII Army and to a number of old friends in that Army whom I had known in Africa - Dennis Erskine, John Millard and many others. Those renewals, even on the eve of Montgomery's departure, were heartening and sent me back to Bari with new vigour.

My visit to V Army (US) was not so prolonged nor did it produce old friends. But I was determined to see my US SCAO in action and went up to V Army for two days to be given formally a polite but very "keep away please" reception from the SCAO Brigadier Hume. His subordinates were far more forthcoming and I returned thence having learnt much about the difference between the British and American meaning of loyalty.

British High Commissioner on the Allied Advisory Council and first Chief Commissioner ACC 18.1.43

Before describing the next series of events - the 1944 reorganisations of AMG and ACC - I must introduce two personalities who were to have greater and smaller influence in the future of Italy during 1944-46, and with whom I was to work extremely closely: Harold Macmillan, British Minister of State, and Lieutenant General Noel Mason-MacFarlane, the first Chief Commissioner of ACC.

Harold Macmillan

Harold Macmillan was appointed by Churchill in January 1943 as British Minister Resident at Allied Headquarters, North Africa; as such he was British Political Adviser to General Eisenhower at AFHQ, Algiers. He and Bob Murphy, his American counterpart, did magnificent work together over the French imbroglio in North Africa and the final settlement with General de Gaulle in such matters.

When the Italian Armistice was first mooted, Macmillan was of course called in to advise and with Murphy was at General Alexander's side over the final negotiations. Macmillan was even under orders to take part in a divisional airborne assault on Rome by the Allies as soon as the declaration of the Armistice was announced. The rapid occupation of Rome by the Germans prevented this, but Macmillan was one of the first to greet King Victor Emmanuel and Badoglio in Brindisi after their precipitous flight from Rome. He and Murphy were, with Lieutenant General Mason-MacFarlane, the Head of the British Military Mission appointed to secure Italy's adherence to the Armistice terms and it was they who agreed to "King's Italy", the small part of the heel of Italy where the writ of the King and not the ACC would run.

Harold Macmillan had no hand in the planning or formation of the ACC in Algiers but he was appointed British High Commissioner of the Allied Advisory Council formed to supervise on behalf of the Allies the future of Italy. It was in this capacity that he had come to Ravello in January 1944, where I was to have my first meeting (with him as Chairman) called to discuss the organisation of ACC. He afterwards lived in the Villa Carradoro on the Bay of Posilipo outside Naples when I quitted it for Rome.

Thereafter I had many instances of working with him and of establishing a relationship which gave me much confidence and understanding. For here was a man after my own heart - with a wide appreciation of politicians (his trade!), business (publishing was his profession) and administration. He was easy in conversation, very quick on the uptake, and had a smile and a good word for everyone. Moreover there was nothing which gave him greater pleasure than to go forward into the battle area and see the men - AMG Spearheads, fighting troops, the lot - at work destroying the enemy and helping those destroyed by them. He was intensely mobile in his Naples, Rome, London, Athens and Algiers peregrinations. We were not surprised to hear of his magnificent and courageous effort in quelling the communist rebellion in Athens in 1944.

We were proud and lucky to have him as Acting President of the Allied Commission even though matters of British state called him to London prematurely. Moreover he was a tremendous admirer of Alexander, - and we had no shame in expressing to each other our admiration for our Commander-in-Chief; I have much joy in remembering the great and enduring qualities of both Alexander and Macmillan.

Lieutenant General Sir Noel Mason-MacFarlane KCB DSO MC

Here was a very different type of man, very much a soldier, who after Rugby and "the Shop", had served in the Royal Artillery in a score of countries from South Africa at the end of the century, through India, World

War I, Mesopotamia, the Afghan War of 1929 to become a Staff Officer whence he became a diplomatic soldier in various embassies in Europe. He was a varied and brilliant linguist. His World War II service had begun as Director of Military Intelligence with the British Forces in France and Belgium and then as Head of a British Military Mission to Russia, after which he became Governor of Gibraltar with a KCB. He was the obvious man to head the Allied Military Mission to Italy after the Armistice of September 1943 and thereafter was earmarked to head the Allied Control Commission in Italy.

As Head of the Armistice Commission in September 1943 Mason-MacFarlane (with Macmillan and Murphy) met Badoglio and later the King in Brindisi. Macmillan in his book *Blast of War* wrote:

"We lunched with the King and his small staff .... to my regret Mason-MacFarlane took a very hostile attitude towards the King, which seemed to be strange for a British Officer .... Murphy and I managed to see the King alone without the jaundiced presence of General Mason-Macfarlane.

14 September 1943"

On the other hand Badoglio wrote in his book *Italy in the Second World War* (p 90), describing the same first arrival of the Allied Mission in Brindisi:

"I thus got to know General Mason-Macfarlane and worked with him on the most friendly terms for many months .... He was full of sympathy with our unhappy position and did everything in his power to overcome our difficulties."

To Harold Macmillan's eternal credit I must make it crystal clear that his initial feelings towards Mason-Macfarlane were never apparent during the General's short presence as Head of the Allied Commission and I, who was close to both of them, had no inkling of them. I did know that "MasonMac" had a soldier's not unusual apprehension of politicians as a whole, but I, at any rate, felt that we were extremely lucky in our Resident Minister of State and his USA counterpart

General Mason-MacFarlane took over control of the Allied Control Commission on 16 January 1944 and as described below on 18 January, General Alexander approved the "new look" of the ACC.

I liked "MasonMac". He was an excellent chief, and once he had confidence in a colleague he gave him full rein to exercise his plans. I found myself absolutely free to run my "show" in my own way and at my own pace. In fact, the General embarrassed me by consulting me on practically every subject outside my administrative functions. I consistently refused to be drawn in to the political arena, but just had to discuss his problems on the edge thereof. He had a sense of humour and a great sense of loyalty both to General Alexander and to his subordinates. I suppose he was in rank very nearly the most senior military officer in the theatre, excluding Generals Jumbo Wilson, Alexander and Mark Clark.

He suffered from constant pain, chiefly in the back; he put it down to polio and motor car crashes in the past; in the '40s the treatment of arthritis and spinal injury was primitive compared with that of 20 years later. He was particularly tickled by the daily belching of Vesuvius after the March eruption. It was hard to embark on personal or unofficial conversation with him - to tell the truth there was no time; and by the time we could return to normal conversation even if only at meal times, he only had one topic - broken by ill health. I missed him when he went - his understanding and sympathy and his generalship.

Reorganisation AMG - ACC; Ravello, January 1944

MSL to DRL 10.01.44:

"We had such a wonderful day today and ended up at Ravello; I am sure there is no need to block that name out, for it is near to nowhere. Did not Ruth paint a picture here and does it not hang in the drawing room? We came (from Bari) over the southern passes of the Appenines, through lots of snow and arrived at the coast at dusk, so I could not see much as we came along the 20 miles or so of Corniche road along the sea to Ravello. The road was, as you can imagine, just one long series of hairpins. We arrived in time for dinner at the Hotel Colombo. This morning I woke to the most glorious view - rather reminiscent of Como, but the land stretching down to the sea instead of the lake - the intervening hills are of a wonderful colour and wisps of smoke caused by the charcoal burning are stealing up the sides of the mountains, topped by the snow of the Appenines in the distance. The sun is trying to appear and the war might be thousands of miles away. I came over in my rather smart Fiat motor car given by some *Duchesa* to Francis Rennell. He took the line that it was not to be used but I take the line that I would rather wear out Italian than British tyres. I cannot describe the beauty and the peace of this place - we had two eggs for breakfast!"

I had crossed from east to west to attend a conference under the Chairmanship of Harold Macmillan, by now British Minister of State in the Mediterranean, and British representative on the Allied Advisory Council for Italy (British, US, French and Russian). When I had met him briefly with Harold Caccia in Bari, we had discussed the different approaches of the Americans and the British to the Italian nation and people, and the problem of government in Italy during present hostilities. Macmillan had been at the Italian Armistice negotiations and saw the divergence of outlook at that crucial time.

Briefly, as Harold Macmillan afterwards wrote, the Americans took an interest in the Italians as friends and relations of a large and well-organised Italian population living and working in the USA. The British regarded Italians as individually pleasant, if indolent people; some of us remembered our Italian allies in WWI perhaps with the military proviso that an Italian military alliance was a hindrance and a menace (through inefficiency) to their Allies; but we all found it hard to forget the rape of Abyssinia, the stab in the back of 1940, and the many thousands of British casualties in North Africa where only a year before we had been fighting Italian troops. Britons found rather nauseating the habit of Italians of attempting to hide behind Mussolini's discredited petticoat tails.

As regards administrative policy, it was curious to find the Americans, who were persistent in their fear of our colonising ambitions, most consistent in their desire to exercise direct control over the Italian Administrative machine. In the end, the British (very colonial) policy of indirect control won the day, and Chuck Spofford, who more or less openly accused me of colonising ambitions with regard to Sicily, must have returned to his life in the USA in 1946, happy to leave the island independent!

I had discussed the future at length with my staff, and had their full agreement, I hoped, with what I was about to say at this conference at Ravello called I suppose by General Joyce, at which officers of ACC and AMG (MSL) were to discuss under the Chairmanship of Harold Macmillan, future plans for the government of Italy.

I went to this meeting invigorated by the loveliness of the surroundings at Ravello; invigorated by the experience I had enjoyed with AMG Spearheads of V and VIII Armies. Harold Macmillan had dispersed other members of the Advisory Council for Italy to have "a look-see" at parts of Italy - Naples (especially) - and as he wrote in *Blast of War*:

"…. took the opportunity to discuss with those concerned, some of the organisational problems; this was done during a whole day in general discussion, over which I (HM) was asked to override both AMG and ACC representatives. Some useful agreements were reached."

I, as CCAO, had an opportunity to speak; I had not been in the country more than a month, but I had four territories and two years of military government behind me. I proposed, quite simply, the complete merger of AMG and ACC into one body; and a very rigorous pruning of the present establishment set up by AFHQ. I proposed the merger with the rider that there should be one branch of the organisation which, under the Chief Commissioner and General Alexander, and no-one else, should have the responsibility of creating, supervising if necessary, and maintaining every form of Allied administration of the peoples of Italy, whether it be direct Allied Military Government in the combat areas, indirect mixed Allied and Italian Government in the areas adjacent to the forward areas, areas reserved for special treatment (ie. King's Italy) or areas handed back to the Italian Government. I spoke strongly of the object of the Allied presence in co-belligerent Italy - the defeat of the German Army; I spoke of the paramount object of all administration in Italy, be it under Allied Military or Italian Government, as the success of the Allied Military Forces, including Italian Forces, in this military victory over the common enemy. I assured the meeting and its Chairman that such an administrative organisation should not and would not become involved in politics. It would become the Civil Service, divorced from politics - and I admitted that I was speaking as a Briton, who believed that a nation's Civil Service was divorced from the politics of the day. This Allied Civil Service would serve the Chief Commissioner in the total sphere of administration throughout Italy and would help the Italian nation to provide its own service. This section of ACC and indeed the whole of ACC would be asked to serve (through the Chief Commissioner) one chief and one only - the Military Governor of Italy - General Alexander. I tried to eliminate the dead hand of SACMED Staff at Algiers.

I did not know my audience well enough to assess the effect my recommendation had made. Macmillan liked it well enough and MasonMac when he arrived a few days later in Naples and arranged for me to meet Macmillan, himself accepted the proposal of a completely separate branch of the new formation devoted to administration.

He and Macmillan were even more ready to accept the proposal when after earnest discussion with my AMG staff, I told them that if my plans were adopted, I was prepared to merge AMGOT with ACC and surrendering my appointment as CCAO, become part of the Headquarters of ACC. I did not disguise the fact that after three years of running my own show it was not going to be an easy change!

The rest of January 1944 was consumed with planning a workable Allied Commission - Harold Macmillan, Mason-MacFarlane and I putting our heads together. AMG, of which I was head, was not part of the original Commission. It had been clear to me, since my arrival, that it should be, and I told the other two so. They were grateful and we created a new section under myself as Executive Commissioner in charge of the entire administration, "all control work in the field". It meant surrendering my independent status under General Alexander (a fact which was appreciated) but it made for sense and cohesion and was clearly the proper solution. The plan is spelt out in the following paragraph. It had the full approval of my senior staff and that of the two Army AMGs. And so I ceased to be CCAO of AMGOT and became Executive Commissioner and a Vice-President of this new venture - Allied Control Commission - reborn January 1944.

Allied Military Administration of Italy 1943 - 45, CRS Harris:

"The Army AMGs, while still remaining operationally under the Commanders of the V and VIII Armies, were placed under the technical control of a new Section of the Allied Control Commission which took under its charge the whole of AMG, both in the forward and the static areas. This Section called the Regional Control and Military Government Section, was placed under Brigadier Lush, who was given the title of Executive Commissioner with the status of Vice-President. It was made responsible for all control work in the field including, besides the technical direction and administration of the Army AMGs, the Command of all Regional Officers, not only in territory subject to Military Government, but also those in Regions which had been restored to the Administration of the Italian Government. The Section was also made responsible for many of the duties which had hitherto been performed by the Chief of Staff of the Commission, whose post was abolished."

Here was a job worth doing and I was abundantly happy to try my hand at it. Macmillan and Mason-MacFarlane seemed very satisfied with the scheme and it had General Alexander's full blessing. All three recommended that the post of Executive Commissioner should carry the rank of Major General, a recommendation which was repeated many times with out any result! The Minister of State finally cabled:

"I presume that even in the British Army, merit has some place in decisions about promotion."

I never discovered why my promotion was refused. There was some argument about an equal balance between British and American Officers of the Commission. I shall not refer to it again nor did it in any way diminish the satisfaction and joy I experienced in doing my job; the hundreds of officers under me in the Regional Government Branch were apparently perfectly happy to be commanded by a British Brigadier! They proved that many of us were out to make this Anglo-American administration a success.

Let me say now that with all the disappointments about promotion I think that the job of Executive Commissioner, Allied Control Commission, which I held for nearly three years, was the most exacting, the most exciting and the most enthralling job I have ever held - particularly during 1944-45. During those years we held the administration - the government of Italy - firmly in good hands, Italian and Allied, and I learnt much of the ways of Americans.

I had a wonderful Commander-in-Chief - Alexander - who once assured me of his support ".... because you are a first class administrator."

Harold Macmillan took me greatly in to his confidence over Commission affairs. Mason-MacFarlane gave me, as he had promised initially, a completely free hand during the seven months of his leadership, and Ellery Stone, who succeeded him, was, I think, only too glad to allow me to concentrate on the rough work of administration while he played politics (hand-in-hand mostly with Macmillan and *Duchesas*!).

I found great help and consistent loyalty from my senior colleagues in the Commission, British and American; Bernard Fiske, my American Deputy; Evan Talbot and Guy Shippe, my Chiefs of Staff, one of whom later became Governor of the National Bank of Southern Rhodesia; Gerald Upjohn, Head of Legal Affairs, who became Lord Upjohn, Lord of Appeal; Tom Bergin, the academic American, who became the Commission's Public Relations Officer; Colonel Charles Poletti, lately Lieutenant Governor of New York State and certainly my best Regional Commissioner; US Colonel Montfort who was the first AMG Officer ever to function in Italy (on Pantellaria) and in Trieste. My Senior Staff Officers were some of the very splendid colleagues and friends, without whose support and loyalty I should have achieved nothing. They all served a hard task master; we had a lot to live down - inexperience, superabundance of officers, lack of support from London and Washington - especially in a Presidential election year; a difficult race to administer; a bi-national team recruited from scratch and hastily trained, was not the easiest machine to maintain in working order. But they were - by and large - a splendid team of men and women whom I was very proud to lead and who gave me wonderful loyalty and service.

The picture of the Commission, as it looked on paper, early in 1944, and as it changed in 1945, are shown in the charts following.

General Alexander approved the framework of the Macmillan-Macfarlane-Lush ACC. Now MasonMac and I had to create the body which in the forward areas would ensure neither obstruction nor hindrance by the civil population to the fighting forces of the Allies, and in the rearward static areas would keep the country on a steady course and ensure that the maximum of Italy's resources, both in manpower and material, were devoted to the Allied war effort.

In January 1944, MasonMac and I had our offices and billets in Naples and began immediately to create HQ ACC. I fitted most of my late, small AMG HQ into the new concern - a few voluntarily went home or to other theatres. MasonMac disposed of a Chief of Staff ACC, and I went at once to Salerno where the bulk of the ACC Personnel were situated, all rather biting their nails in the dismal state of inaction and uncertainty. I again met Captain Ellery Stone, US Navy, and all the Senior Officers, British and American. I spent two days preaching the revised organisation to them, *en masse* and privately. I stressed the equality of the Vice Presidents and their direct access to the Chief Commissioner. Some were suspicious, some encouraging and helpful; all declared that anything was better than sitting on their behinds in Salerno! And I believe that we all had one aim in mind - to make this Anglo-American Administration a success.

So we soon had a reasonable element of all the Sections working in Naples where our first and urgent preparations had to be made for the move to Rome (soon we hoped) of both the Italian Government and the Commission. Here, for me, was the opportunity to test my deputy, an American Colonel Fiske. I knew that the US Army would take Rome and the Spearhead AMG V Army was under Colonel Hume, US Army. What better than a combined plan for the eventual civilian administration of Rome. But this was a long way off. The consultations and decisions leading up to the new face of the ACC under General Mason-Macfarlane and the building of the new formation could not be allowed to keep the Executive Commissioner and other Senior Officers from visiting the various forms of administration now actually working in the field.

I had, as Head of AMG, seen the Spearhead AMG in action, and I had another occasion to see front line military government at work when I visited the beachhead enclave at Anzio, about a week or two after the landing (22 January 1944). The seaborne landings at Anzio were conceived as an alternative to forcing the winter line by frontal attack. The port lay 30 miles south of Rome and more than 70 miles behind the right flank of the German army. The operation had not been the military success intended, chiefly due to lack of foresight on the part of the American Military Commander in not taking advantage of the surprise factor and not pushing forward at once with every available unit. The situation had become static; all the more work for AMG. But the AMG party had done well. The official description shows that all the typical problems had been met and dealt with efficiently; appointment of Italian officials; distribution of food rations (luckily Anzio was a food producing area and most civilians had a small store tucked away); hospitals (fighting was fierce and civilian casualties considerable); and lastly, evacuation. The military "froze" all movement of civilians at the outset but as the position became more static evacuation of civilians to Naples was permitted and well organised at the rate of about 200 per diem. On my first visit (in a Royal Naval destroyer) I found the military situation confused and was not impressed by the military commander (who was afterwards removed).

Harris in his book *Military Government in Italy* writes that the Anzio operation provided in miniature all the typical problems facing the Spearhead AMGs. Tabulated, they were:

1 Selection of local Italian Officials and their supervision;
2 Provision of funds to meet extra communal expense;
3 Distribution of food rations;
4 Rescue of civilians trapped in ruins - or in minefields;
5 Enforcement of security measures - eg. curfew;
6 Procurement of civilian labour for the military;
7 Evacuation of civilians;

The towns of Anzio and Nettuno were under fairly steady shell fire and life was uncomfortable. My second visit in March found a more peaceful scene - but the military object of the expedition had failed. On both occasions, however, I was more than pleased with the work of AMG, firstly under shelf fire and thereafter in more static conditions. It was fun to have to wear a steel helmet again and to scramble for cover for a moment or two; it took me back a generation to guess *which* shell - that or this - was going to explode. It was also most interesting and reminiscent of Madagascar to be in the hands of the Royal Navy again for transport hither and thither; it was not pleasant being shelled at sea. The young AMG officers did appreciate a visit from a red tab!

The military situation produced orders and counter-orders concerning evacuation. The actual problem was to evacuate by sea to Naples 19,000 people. I was well satisfied with what AMG had done in a disappointing military effort.

During January 1944 we had moved Headquarters from Bari to Naples where Ian Carr had been busy house hunting while I visited forward AMGs. We found a temporary house in the outskirts of Naples, the owner of which greeted us with a bunch of flowers. But Ian Carr (whose comments on our Allies' scandalous methods of commandeering accommodation were worth hearing) had something up his sleeve and early in February we moved in to our new Villa Carradoro:

> MSL to DRL:
>
> ".... which is really rather a dream; built overlooking the Bay (in Posilipo), by a retired Milanese industrialist who was also clearly a mariner .... everything is nautical .... the tiles in the ground floor rooms are sea green; the ceilings portray the heavens; the walls portray the Hesperides; the bannisters are of white nautical rope; the lights are marine lanterns and my bedroom, besides having a wide open verandah, has three portholes above the bed, which, when lit, illumine fishy creatures! The house sleeps seven with three bathrooms. It has a fine terraced garden with an aviary containing a few birds .... The lower floors are just one complete suntrap - every inch is a window; we face east with a most lovely view of the Bay and the mountains in the distance are quite beautiful."

We were a long way from our ACC Headquarters office, but the motor cycle outriders of the US Army would escort my one staff car on most occasions, clearing the traffic and proceeding at a prodigious speed. The terrace garden contained a small aviary and I left a tame duck, relic of our Christmas dinner, who would meet me at the garden gate and waddle before me to the front door and inside. Not once or twice only, but on every occasion he mistook the sea green tiles of the living room for water, and spreading his wings plunged in - to be brought up sharply by the reality of a stony landing. This did not deter him from his daily breakfast of toast soaked in tea. We had many happy evenings in that lovely villa and when we moved to Rome we were very happy to hand over the Villa Carradoro to Harold Macmillan and Lady Barbara in July 1944.

In the early months of 1944 we continued to build our Allied Commission and I managed to pay short visits both to the "front" and also to the coast road where I found a serious problem festering with regard to refugees and displaced persons. Refugees was the term generally applied to Italians and of course they were a great problem to the Spearhead AMGs, particularly opposite VIII Army and in the Anzio beachhead. DPs (Displaced Persons) were foreign refugees who came south with the Italians. Many DPs came from Yugoslavia. The Spearhead AMG had coped well with these people - some 8,500 but their numbers were steadily increasing. [The terms 'Refugees' and 'DP' were redefined, with reverse meaning, by the 1951 Convention on Refugees - Ed] The Italian officials in King's Italy did not seem capable of dealing with them, and as the DP Commission came directly under me, I spent several days learning about and sometimes directing the organisation, and left a very competent Colonel Fothergill in charge.

In the body of the Allied Control Commission, as it now was, in addition to my own executive branch, there were three other main branches. Lord Stansgate headed the Administrative Branch which dealt with Medical, Legal, Education and Fine Arts. I seldom saw Lord Stansgate, who disappeared in his Puss-in-Boots topboots that he always wore, but I had a great deal to do with Gerald Upjohn (on legal matters) and with Grafftey Smith who, as Head of Finance and in the absence of the Vice-President of the Economic Section, did much to help us on the economic side.

MasonMac and I were thoroughly dissatisfied and extremely anxious about Washington's attitude towards our Economic Section. Harold Macmillan in his *Blast of War* wrote (p 545):

"…. our only trouble (in the ACC) was that the Economic Section was not well treated by Washington …. The Economic Section has never had a chance. First Grady came from America - stayed five weeks, then returned to the USA and was absent nearly five months. He returned for a month - and then retired. After him came Brigadier General O'Dwyear, a New York lawyer, and a purely political appointment; the second Antolini is another political appointment. The politicians came as brigadier-generals, saw for a few weeks and went back to conquer in the wards of the vital states, especially New York."

Luckily we had good heads of sub-commissions in the Economic Section such as Grafftey Smith in Finance, Colonel Legge in Food, and Colonel Braine in Labour who knew their business and acted independently, referring to me or the Chief Commissioner if necessary.

The three military sub-commissions - Navy, Army and Air Force - were in a way detached from the work of the Commission, but nevertheless were very loyal to the general aims and often attended our working meetings. Admiral Warren, General Browning and A V M Foster were very welcome and seemed to enjoy hearing the news.

The French and Russian Sub-Commissions weaved their own webs in and out of the ACC but we saw little of them. They were much more the eyes and ears of the French and Russian members of the Advisory Council, restricting personal contacts to a few social events - which at the Palazzo of the Russian Commission became (this was later in Rome) perfectly dreadful luncheon parties in which vodka and whisky played no small part. But finding the Executive Commissioner non-political, they did not invite him often! We all firmly believed that one of them regularly examined my confidential files!

The Advisory Council consisting of representatives of Great Britain, USA, Russia and France, was established late in 1943 to advise the Supreme Allied Commander "in his task of administering the policy of the United Nations towards Italy". It had no powers to issue orders of any kind to the Commander-in-Chief, nor did it concern itself with military affairs. At the outset of its existence the members consisted of Macmillan (UK), Murphy (USA) and Vyshinski (USSR); the latter was soon replaced by Bogomolov. Greece and Yugoslavia joined the council at a later date.

The Advisory Council was very active during the first few months of 1944; equally so were the Italian politicians, and co-equally so was the King of Italy and his Prime Minister. I was occasionally asked to explain the work of the ACC to the Council.

The King, after much cajoling by Macmillan and Murphy, finally put an end to his doubts and those of the Italians and the Advisory Council, by announcing his coming withdrawal from public affairs in favour of his son Prince Umberto of Piedmont who would become Lieutenant General of the (Italian) Realm, the appointment to become effective on the day on which Allied troops should enter Rome.

This statement, approved by the Advisory Council, was made public and met with approval from the Italian politicians who thereafter agreed to join Badoglio in forming a broad based Government. The five most prominent political leaders became Ministers without Portfolio: Croce, Sforzo, Rodino, Mancini and Togliatti (the Communist only recently returned from Moscow). All this happened in Salerno.

The Government under Badoglio, was required firstly to accept all obligations towards Allies undertaken by previous Governments, and also to pledge not to open the constitutional question until Italian people were free universally to express their views. By the end of April 1944, both the Italians and the Allies were well under way with their new administrations.

I had not met, by any means, all the Italian "personalities". I knew the King and Badoglio, Prunas (Secretary of Foreign Ministry) and several of the non-ministerial officers, but all seemed ready to assist or to be assisted in the dual form of administration, and I left the politics to MasonMac and the Political Sub-Commissioner.

Our first administrative duty after, or even during, our reorganisation was to rectify our position vis-a-vis the Italian Government (Badoglio) regarding the areas of Sicily and Italy which now (March 1944) lay within our respective jurisdiction. We had from the beginning allowed Italian rule in Apulia (Bari, Brindisi, Torento and Lecce) known as King's Italy where the Civil Affairs Officers of AMG and the ACC merely gave advice - eg. on food distribution, finance and transport; this had worked well since mid-September 1943. By 1 April 1944 we had turned over to Italian Government rule the whole of Sicily, Calabria, Lucania and Campania (without Naples, which remained under AMG). The territory administered by AMG was thus greatly reduced. Throughout liberated Italy a new regime of advisory control was inaugurated by which the Italian Government and Regional Commissioners were informed by ACC of general policy and the Regional Commissioners, by advice, ensured that the local Italian authorities were following this policy. It was not indirect rule; or let us say it was not intended to be indirect rule, rather indirect insurance. My answers to the critics of ACC who noted and in some quarters complained that the 'C' of Control rarely disappeared from ACC was, and still is, that the British Army was fighting with considerable vigour to drive the Germans out of Italy and that the Allied Army was suffering enormous casualties in so doing; the whole of Italy was committed to aiding the Allies in their life and death struggle on and away from the battlefield; Italy was a co-belligerent with the Allies and, therefore, at war with Germany. The discipline of a nation's life was bound to be more rigorous in war than in peace; it was vital to preserve the discipline needed in wartime *throughout Italy*; the disciplines which the Allies required were not the political disciplines of Fascism - they were the day-to-day rigours of life, which we expected the Italians to accept just as the Allied populations were accepting them at home; that was the kind of control I expected the Italian Government to exercise, and which I required the Regional Officers in Italian Government, Italy, also to require. I shall return to this when I discuss the "New Deal" for Italy which was introduced later.

In March 1944 we held our first Regional Commissioners' Meeting in Naples under the Chairmanship of our Chief Commissioner, General Mason-MacFarlane. The two Spearheads, V Army (USA) and VIII Army (British), under their doughty leaders Brigadier General Hume and Group Captain Benson attended, together with the Commissioners of Sicily, the Southern part of Italy and then of territory covering a narrow strip stretching across the country from Naples to the east coast. The rest of the country we were in the process of handing or had already handed back to the Italian Government, now based in Salerno. This did not mean withdrawal of all Regional Commissioners or staff from the provinces handed back; it meant that Allied Government was superseded by Italian Government with Allied control. ACC Staff, as I have pointed out, became guardians or controllers and advisers, instead of Governors, and the Italian Government "published in their Official Gazette substantially the contents of AMG Proclamations and Orders". The Commission's Officers in their liberated areas, which now covered all Southern Italy, Sicily and Sardinia, had nearly as much on their advisory plates as there was on their gubernatorial dishes; and far more indigenous staff! We must have numbered nearly 50 officers at that first RCs' Meeting.

All this was discussed at the Regional Meeting, the first of many which I held in many varying places throughout Italy in the next 18 months. I, and I am quite sure many of the men and women attending these meetings, found them invaluable. We often had political figures like Harold Macmillan and an American statesman or two. I believe one of our French commissioners came to an RC Meeting in Rome but we never saw a Russian member.

We discussed, especially at first, everything which appertained to administration; frank speaking was encouraged and people let their hair down. Wherever we held them, Naples, Rome, Sienna, Milan or elsewhere, I am sure that they were worth the tremendous effort required in organising them (members of my staff were first class planners, not only as regards the agenda, but also the billets, feeding and social side). They were truly cementing meetings between Allies, and I, personally, found them great fun.

In the same month, March 1944, the Allied Control Commission gave birth to a weekly Bulletin of news, political, administrative, general and personal. The first edition told us of Prime Minister Badoglio's tour of Sicily, and the arrival in Naples of Togliatti, the leader of the Italian Communist Party. It told us that Brigadier Dunlop had been appointed Regional Commissioner of Region IV, the eastern area of AMG behind VIII Army, while Brigadier Carr had taken over Sardinia.

Ceilings of ACC personnel, up to the Rimini-Pisa line, were envisaged at 291 for Headquarters with 900-odd in the field. The shipment of some 100 surplus officers to the UK (for Military Government of W Europe) was effected.

The eruption of Vesuvius on 22 March 1944 was reported and we learnt of the activities of Colonel Kincaid, Provincial Commissioner, and Colonel Charles Poletti, Regional Commissioner, in respect of this grave civilian emergency which, thank God, placed little or no impediment to military advance.

There were reports on the Black Market and convictions in the courts for offenses connected therewith; a drive by Colonel Poletti against dumping of garbage in Naples and the promise of "no smell in Naples this summer" (only a Lieutenant Governor of New York could have dared so to prophesy), cheered our hearts and noses. We learnt that an expert librarian had arrived from USA "to advise on archives", (would he consign them to the gallant colonel's refuse carts?)

The editor of this Bulletin, which I found sometimes useful and amusing, sometimes maddeningly hyper-political, was one Lionel Fielden, a distinguished broadcaster and Head of the Talks Department in the London BBC (1930), whence he moved to become Head of the BBC, India, until the outbreak of World War II. He was an amusing, somewhat dilettante Etonian, whom I must have infuriated at times, for I noted that his post war entry in *Who's Who* read, under recreation: "trying to avoid being organised". He retired to, and died in Florence, a notable member of ACC and a most able man. I was really very grateful to him for bringing us all down to earth - sometimes.

He was succeeded by an American Professor Tom

Bergin, who was, 20 years later, described by the then President of Yale University as "a wise, whimsical, even a chuckly man". He became one of my greatest friends and joined my household in Rome. He had married an English girl and in Rome missed his family even more than his academic career; the years of war must have been an inevitable waste of time and learning to a man of his intellect and literary prowess. He returned to his academic career after the war, serving as Professor in Ithaca University, and terminating his academic but by no means his literary career as Master of Timothy Dwight College, Yale University. After retirement he remained and flourished in the literary world as an expert on Dante. Luckily for me we exchanged visits in the '70s and our visitors' book contains his signature with the letters PLOS after it - if you can bear to read the latter chapters of these memories you will learn the meaning of that. He was a great addition to the Commission, and Diana and I value the friendship of Tom and Florence Bergin to this day.

I visited Anzio beachhead for the second time in March and found AMG work satisfactory. Another more peaceful visit was paid to Sicily and began with a night in Tunis, North Africa.

MSL to DRL 3.4.44:

"…. The most absurd thing happened. We tried to land here at Palermo on Saturday, but there was a howling gale on and so we had to fly on and spend the night in Africa! (Tunis) It is so very near. I don't wonder the convoys before 1943 had a bad time …."

We returned to Palermo the next day (Sunday) and

"…. had an afternoon of indescribable pleasure. There are some real gems here (Palermo). The Palazzo Reale has a wonderful royal Chapel done entirely in mosaics …."

I described also San Giovanni, the Cathedral at Mon Reale which:

"…. from top to bottom tells the bible story in super life-size figures - all done in mosaics …. after a marvellous dinner we listened to a first class pianist. Today I am seeing all the ACC officers here, and then go by train (!) to Messina and across to Reggio where I hope to find my car - and so home!"

A fact I remember on this tour is that I also paid (by car) my one and only visit to Calabria and the southern parts of Italy which I found extremely primitive, both as regards the rocky mountainous country and the inhabitants thereof. They seemed to be, as in many parts of Italy, extremely short of food, but as most of them were peasants rather than townspeople, one hoped that there was a little reserve tucked away in the ramshackle houses in which they existed - that is a habit of peasants the world over and I was not deceived.

The month of March saw two disasters which tragically affected the civilian population in Southern Italy, but luckily had no effect on Allied military matters. Unfortunately, the first accident cost nearly 500 Italian lives. All Italian railway engines burnt Sardinian coal which is extremely sulphurous. A train was travelling across Southern Italy, as usual heavily overloaded, and stopped as it attempted to pass through a tunnel in the South Apennines near Potenza. It was night and the passengers realised they were stuck but feared no evil consequences and were not advised otherwise by the railway staff. The fires were not extinguished in the engine or engines; the tunnel filled with the Sardinian coal smoke and became a deadly gas-filled trap; 500 Italian passengers were suffocated and died in their carriages or on the track (mercifully without pain). The only survivors were the railway officials and a few passengers who had left the train and walked towards the tunnel entrance to communicate with the nearest railway office or station.

On hearing of the tragedy which took place in Italian Government territory, I motored to the tunnel myself, but soon realised that nothing further could be done to save lives and sadly left the terrible scene to the tender and distracted care of the Italian officials and the ACC Liaison Regional Commissioner who arrived an hour or two after me.

I remember calling on the Prime Minister, Badoglio, and his Under Secretary for Communications next day to express my condolences. (That was the kind of diplomatic courtesy so necessary.) The whole tragic incident was one of the traumas which war brought to Italy. The Italians, at the same time, had no conception that a similar death toll might easily be a *nightly* occurrence in the air bombings of London.

Our next tragedy was the eruption of Vesuvius which took place on 18 March 1944. Thanks be, the Italians suffered no fatalities and the Allies suffered little from this physical phenomenon which I shall describe fully below.

Between the meetings of AMG and ACC officers in Naples in March and May, we were able somehow to accommodate more of our key staff in Naples and arrange for the machinery of administration to function. We, at the top, were beginning to understand each others' minds and the way they worked. Most of the Senior Officers and Heads of Sub-Commissions were able to journey northwards towards Spearhead AMG and southwards towards Stationary AMG and Italian administered territory. I suppose that the main problem which confronted many of us from the Commander-in-Chief downwards was food for the civilian population. Whether they were under the Spearhead AMG or the Italian Government, 15,000,000 Italians in the occupied part of Italy in April 1944 required FOOD - not on paper but in their mouths and stomachs. Naturally this problem was the first preoccupation of AMG Spearheads and many were the hindrances to distribution, even if the flour was available - devastation, minefields, destruction of mills, lack of transportation, battle conditions and failure in organising on the part of the Italians. In Naples there is no doubt that

"arrangements which had been made to procure food

stuffs from the United States broke down badly owing to mishandling by the Military Government Section at Allied Forces HQ in Algiers of calling forward required stocks."

Luckily an unexpected consignment arrived from the Middle East, but did not fill the gap completely. We at ACC HQ knew that the men in front (and behind too) had FOOD written on their hearts as top priority, and we did our best to see that the bulk would be forthcoming from outside, whenever it could not be produced from the countryside. The Military Authorities were splendid in their support; the leading figure there was General Brian Robertson, in charge of the port of Naples, and all that came through that port; he, by his exertions of good sense and sympathy, and great power of organisation, saved Neapolitans - and a good many other mouths too - from starvation. He and I had worked together in Tripoli where he always told me that there would not be any grain on the ships for my Arabs - and always managed to squeeze some out! In Naples he did the same and though we sparred mightily for two years in Italy, he asking why the Sicilians couldn't grow their own grain, I telling him (and the conference) the historical and social and agricultural reasons why not, he always came to our aid. A wonderful friend and helper.

FOOD and then MEDICAL SUPPLIES. In this field we had no words except praise for the Allied Medical Services and the Allied Red Cross for the quite wonderful work they did for the Italian population. British and American Red Cross personnel were not far behind AMG Spearhead Units, and did yeoman work in caring for the sick and refugees, mothers and children, in supplying medicines and welfare needs - in truth the official necessities of life.

MasonMac and I encouraged plain speaking at these Regional Meetings and we had plenty of it - plain but without enmity - and most of us came away refreshed by the ideas and criticisms which were given and taken by HQ and Field Officers. I, personally, found them invigorating and there never existed any rank consciousness and there was plenty of genial intolerance of the fleshpotters of Rome on the part of the field - and yet one's advice and rulings were willingly accepted - that was worth a great deal.

Our Villa Carradoro at Posilipo was a very happy place. I had with me Colonel Tony Grafftey Smith, Head of Finance; Colonel Dr Cheyne, Head of the Medical Services, and my PA, Ian Carr, who handed over to Major Arthur Stewart, when I sent him (Carr) home for posting to a fighting unit. Ian had served me magnificently for a year or more and I was never in want for any necessity or comfort, be it in the office, on the road or in our Mess, and seldom without good advice on many subjects. I was extremely indebted to and fond of a man who could with sympathy and forethought secure so many of the needs and desires of his chief in mind, body and estate - and crack a good joke at the expense of all and sundry.

As winter, rather slowly, turned into spring, our villa and its terraced garden proved a great haven of peace; we had innumerable guests, as many as we could collect from the Commission itself and especially "travelling firemen" from other parts of Italy and from abroad. Our neighbour, General Brian Robertson, occupied the Villa Hamilton, where Nelson and Lady Hamilton had made love and, more recently, where Goering had stayed. We often had the overflows from big missions to the General.

I had the great pleasure of entertaining Major John Fletcher RE (son of Cyril and Stella Fletcher and Diana's cousin) who twice came as an invalid from hospital, once with a poisoned leg, and very shortly afterwards as the result of stepping on a mine at Anzio. "Such a nice boy" is my description of him to Diana. We all liked him and he accompanied me to the Observatory, half way up the mountain of Vesuvius when that volcano blew its top and belched out lava and stones in a most frightening way.

Notable too was a Miss Patricia Russell, lately from the office of the Private Secretary to HM King George VI before becoming PA to the Middle East Commissioner of Red Cross and St John's War Organisation in Cairo whom some authority in Cairo had sent to the ACC to investigate our needs for women secretaries. Of course, the Cairo people could not have sent a better ambassadress and our needs were numerous and almost infinite if more Patricia Russells could join us. To cut a long and lovely story short, Patricia came, and accepted the post of PA to the Executive Commissioner; she entered Rome with me and not only looked after my office and myself officially but ran my house for 16 months.

She was a most admirable PA. "Nemo Lush impune lacessit" was very much her motto and many were the hours of interviews which she saved me by preventing through her own charm, callers from calling on me, or if they became insistent, from staying too long. Many were the times when, deeming that my caller had overstayed his time, she would enter most demurely, and explain that I was wanted on "the other telephone". They trained PAs very well in "Buck House" in those days and I was a very lucky man. Patricia also had the knack or ability to take shorthand while travelling in the back of an Army limousine. At the villa she ran a very efficient household, would stand no nonsense from members of staff and made us all, members and guests, thoroughly happy. Patricia joined me in July 1944 and her sympathy and charm, her efficiency and unceasing good will and cheerfulness, made a great difference in the lives of us all in the office or the house during those 16 happy months.

During April and May, all eyes and minds were turned towards Rome - I must admit rather despairingly. General Alexander had let it be known that he wanted the Americans to enter and occupy the city and for AMG that meant Hume and his AMG. In truth, he had been preparing for it during the last few months, if not before, and had even asked for a team of technicians to prepare themselves in Algiers. He was a great individualist and a lover of the limelight was our C-in-C! However, I was content, so long as I knew what was on his planning sheets - and I found out!

In Salerno, the Italian politicians under Badoglio had enlarged their Government to include all parties (not without misgivings on the American part, concerning Togliatti, the Communist, and the British concerning Sforza, whom Churchill could not stand!) The "Junta" as it was called, worked hard and produced some good laws though it was not easy for them - no offices, no civil service, knowing that their life was short for they were few and far from home; the real politicians were still in Rome and they in Salerno were hopelessly detached. MasonMac had at last persuaded the King to stand down, as soon as Rome fell, and to hand over to the Prince of Piedmont - Umberto. It was not quite an abdication, but the King was prevented, by Allied advice, from re-entering his capital from which he had fled in September - and he and his wife later retired to Cairo. I met and dined with Umberto before he went to Rome and found him pleasant and sensible; but he was never allowed to become the ruler of Italy.

During their six weeks of rule in Salerno, the Badoglio Government did especially good work in connection with the *Ammassi or Granai del Popolo*, the centralization of grain (and other produce) reserves for controlled distribution - quite the most important measures which affected the whole of civilian Italy south of the battle line.

Incidentally, they accepted all the obligations towards the Allies by the previous, and first post-armistice Government and also gave a definite pledge *not* to reopen the constitutional question until such time as the whole Italian population was in a position freely to express their views. Both these undertakings were required from and given by all the succeeding Italian Governments on taking office before the conclusion of hostilities.

The new Government almost at once tackled *Granai del Popolo* in Italian Government territory, just as the Agriculture Sub-Commission "is letting no grain ripen underfoot in its effort to exploit the present favourable situation." South of Rome a bumper crop was expected and everyone concerned, Italian Government, ACC and the Communes were reputed to be striving to arrange for the maximum amount to be turned in for general sale and consumption. Posters and decrees had been printed in order that each farmer should know the amount he might retain for his own use (consumption, seed etc) and a scheme was in hand to distribute widely a film on the subject.

The Minister of Justice pointed out in an interview that the immediate task of his Ministry was to remove existing Fascist legislation which impeded recovery.

At the same time, the Chief Commissioner issued a directive governing the treatment of Fascist Officials during the present advance, showing three categories: (a) arrest and internment; (b) arrest and hand over to the Italian Government; and (c) dismissal but retention of liberty; they called the whole process 'epuration'.

V Army was by now clearly all set for Rome. We had done all that we could in the Commission to support Hume and I sent my deputy to Rome - not to intervene or assert, but to help if necessary.

But the capture of Rome did not mean the capture of the rest of Italy, nor the destruction of the German Army facing General Alexander. He was planning ahead and we too, his Civil Service, had to plan also - which meant planning a "leap frog" system of administrative units for the onward advance.

Military Situation leading up to Monte Cassino and Rome

One cannot tell the story fully without explaining the strategy and tactics. So, here is a synopsis of the Military Situation leading up to the capture of Rome; Monte Cassino, of course, was the stumbling block - Alexander wrote of it in 1962:

> ".... Monte Cassino is one of the strongest natural defensive positions in the whole of Europe, and it hardly seems credible that we ultimately overcame it."

Thanks to General Oliver Leese who was by now (February 1944) Commanding VIII Army, I witnessed one attack (from a British artillery battery position).

We have seen that the landing at Anzio, though successful, was not followed up. In January 1944, two attempts were made to force a passage north through Cassino: they had no success. In February, attempts to break out from the Anzio perimeter also failed, as did further attacks on Cassino town and Monastery (in spite of an air bombardment of the building by 285 heavy and medium bombers on 15 February). Alexander wrote:

> ".... the aching struggle for an entry into the Liri Valley (in which lay Highways 6 and 7 to Rome) was not to reopen until 11 May. VIII Army took over the task of clearing the path to Rome - the Polish Corps took the Monastery with great gallantry while Canadian and Indian Divisions went forward on the south; the US V Army fought their way out of Anzio and finally, on 4 June, US II Corps entered Rome."

The foregoing summary by Alexander covers initial fruitless attacks on Cassino town and Monastery Hill with resulting very heavy casualties, the bombing of the Monastery itself on 14 February (1,100 tons of bombs), and "the all obliterating bombing of Cassino town on 14 March", all without success but again with a high casualty rate. The town and the Monastery, and indeed, the resulting almost hand-to-hand fighting, reminded one of the destruction in World War I. At the same time, the Germans were delivering a series of heavy and fruitless counter attacks on the Anzio bridgehead.

It was not until 18 May the XIII British Corps renewed the attack on the rubble of Cassino town and after four days of bitter fighting, reached the highways south of Cassino, while the Polish Division raised their standard on the Monastery itself. At the same time "after four months the Anzio bridgehead was to pay off, and by 22 May a composite force of British and American divisions attacked. By 24 May the German defence broke, enabling the Allied troops to join with British troops (and a French Division of African troops) coming along from the south."

All along the Liri Valley from Cassino northwards, the Germans employed a scorched earth policy in their retreat. Cassino fell on 18 May and the Germans fell back causing devastation and destruction along the whole front. Many villages were entirely devastated, others suffered less, but practically none escaped. The German demolitions were systematic and nothing which could be of use to the Allied Army or to the civilian population escaped destructive attention. In one village, the corpses of dead German soldiers had mines attached to them; the furnishings of churches were wantonly destroyed; flour mills, water installations, everything of use to man or beast, body or soul was destroyed. Five villages on the VIII Army front, entered on one day, were reported flat. Another would be found unscathed (the *podesta* of the village had probably given his wife to the German Commander for his pleasure). One never knew - but by and large, German policy in retreat was scorched earth - if there was time to scorch it! This was one of the penalties which Italy paid for her entry into the War in 1940.

Such devastation - and it was to be repeated throughout central Italy - added greatly to the task of the AMG Spearheads in restoring the necessities of life - food, water, even roofs for houses, sewage repaired, mines to be removed, security.

Lionel Fielden's excellent weekly Bulletin issued 27 May, reported that in 13 villages occupied by V Army US during the week, having a normal population of 63,000, nearly all the inhabitants had fled, leaving only 6,000; four villages were quite empty - and probably uninhabitable. The peasants, however, soon began to return and AMG policy was to allow a minimum number to become refugees, but to restore the people and as many of the villages as possible to some form of communal life. "Food supplies were made difficult by the lack of ovens". In two days biscuits were running out. The Food Sub-Commission, however, was able to despatch 40 tons on 20 May and by 24 May, bakeries were being started in newly constructed ovens.

"At Gaeta, the harbour having been cleared of mines, a warehouse was supplied with food shipped thither on a schooner." "Numbers of sick and wounded were treated at AMG tented hospitals."

On the east of the line, the French African troops (Gouins) had caused, and continued to cause very serious and terrible trouble, for though they fought magnificently and endured to the end, they pillaged consistently and raped every woman they could find. To escape death or violation at the hands of the Germans and then suffer violation at the hands of savage Allies was the ultimate degradation. I, myself, had dealt personally with similar outrages perpetrated by African troops in Madagascar, and knew that the inherent sense of conquest carried such practices in the minds of such races.

I see that, after visiting the US AMG, I reported that the refugees from the Pontine Marshes were the most pitiable refugees I had ever seen - they had not tasted bread for nine months (under Italian Fascist rule).

The officers of the Monuments and Fine Arts Sub-Commission were in the remains of the Cassino Monastery within 24 hours of its capture, reporting briefly on the effects of the bombardments.

Following are a few extracts from work done by AMG Spearheads and taken over by the less mobile provincial administration very soon after. The pace was nothing to the rate of progress after the occupation of Rome:

> "Health is generally good in the villages taken over; some, untouched by devastation, have hospitals; serious shortage of doctors, equipment and transport - especially transport; public security satisfactory; Finance Officers have visited 31 communes and two million lire has been advanced .... In Norma, AMG found a bus line running normally and a restaurant still open .... things are moving fast."

ACC HQ : 30 May 1944

Back in Naples, we had held a Regional Commissioners' Meeting on 30 and 31 May. I see from the Bulletin that we finished our business in two days and the morning was devoted to the Regional Commissioners Brigadier Carr from Sardinia, Colonel Hancock from Sicily and Colonel Dunlop from the Southern Region. Captain Benson gave us a first rate (and first hand) account of the work of the Spearhead VIII Army AMGs - noone from the US Spearhead was present. The Americans by that date were completely obsessed with the imminent capture of Rome. Benson told us that he had taken over 29 towns; one AMG alone had handled 11,000 refugees.

Although health was generally good, there was a shortage of doctors. All banks had been found demolished or closed. The coordination between the Spearhead AMG and the "follow-up" Static Administration had been good. Forty million lire-worth of forged notes had been discovered in Sicily. We, naturally, had a long session on the grain harvest, the collection thereof, and the ensuing distribution. Colonel Legge, our chief Food Officer, who ran a first class organisation, (we were by now feeding over 18 million Italians) urged that we reduced the number of ration card holders in order to enable us to increase the amount of the ration. The debate on food seems to have ended on the note that the reduction of the number of ration card holders "must somehow" be effected. Colonel Legge's assistant hoped that some better solution might be found when the olive oil harvest was "reaped". The Chief Commissioner quoted the Commander-in-Chief as referring to the ACC as his "Third Army".

Reference was made to a directive (May 1944) issued by the Chief Commissioner governing the treatment of

Fascist Officials now serving in German occupied Italy or Republican Fascist Italy, ie serving the rescued Mussolini. Lists had been prepared and smuggled down south by various means and the rules were simple (they had been drawn up in consultation with the Italian Government). The list showed Fascist Officials to be dealt with under the epuration rules. In fact, it was found by the AMG Spearheads as they advanced north, that the Partisans (CLNAI) had generally dealt with such officials far more drastically than the Allied directive laid down.

I was very content with our second Regional Commissioners' Meeting, for it was then made clear to me that we could, and indeed did, work as a team; and that AMG Spearheads plus AMG Rear, together with the ACC Liaison Commissioners left in the Italian Regions, could receive and seek direction from one Headquarters. I was particularly pleased with the very great assistance which the Spearheads were giving to the fighting troops. It was on the Cassino plain and in the advance on Rome that AMG had its first taste of devastation. Nevertheless, they met the challenge well and earned high praise. I believed that we had the confidence of Benson and Hume - the Spearheads - about our future plans to support them.

Next day (1 June 1944) I attended a full dress meeting of Army Chiefs at Caserta with MasonMac and Macmillan when it was decided that:

1 There should be no formal entry into Rome, the capture of which should be treated as a military matter by US troops;
2 A US general would act as Governor with Hume and AMG Spearhead under him (the Spearhead force had been greatly augmented for the purpose). AMG Rear would eventually take over. (I had earmarked Poletti as SCAO after Hume.)
3 MasonMac told us that he had arranged for Prince Umberto and Badoglio to go to Rome a day or two after its capture. Macmillan tells us "MasonMac had at last dissuaded the King from wriggling out of his commitment to abdicate". But Macmillan apparently was not at all happy at my Chief Commissioner's (MasonMac) handling of the whole affair.

VESUVIUS: 20-23 MARCH 1944

I shall begin this section by quoting from a letter written by the Younger Pliny to the Roman historian Tacitus describing the eruption of Vesuvius in AD 79. His uncle, Admiral of the Roman fleet in Naples, sailed from Misenum (Capo di Miseno) on the western extremity of Naples Bay to Castellamare on the southern side in an attempt to rescue the Romans living in that neighbourhood, nearest to the volcano and obviously in grave danger. He died at Castellamare in the attempt; asthmatic as he was, the ash and dry pumice choked him. We know, of course, that the death toll from that eruption was heavy (eg. Pompeii) and conditions were plainly far worse than in 1944.

Translation of a letter from Pliny the Younger to Tacitus, the historian, describing the death of Pliny the Elder during the eruption of Vesuvius in AD 79 (Bk 6.16)

".... My uncle was at Misenum (at the western extremity of the Bay of Naples) in command of the fleet. On the 24th August (AD 70), at about one o'clock, my mother pointed to a cloud of unusual size and shape. My uncle had had a sun-bath and a cold plunge and now, after dining, he was sitting reading. He called for his shoes and climbed to where he could get a better view of the phenomenon. A cloud - from that distance it was not clear from which mountain, though we learnt afterwards it was from Vesuvius - had sprung up, which I can best describe as shaped like a pine tree. A long stem stretched upwards and then spread out like branches, because at first I imagine it was carried upwards by the rush of hot air and then, as this weakened and failed and the weight of the cloud took effect, it spread laterally. It was now white and now black and dirty as it threw up earth and ash. My uncle, a scientist, felt this was remarkable and deserved closer study. He ordered a light galley to be prepared.

"What had started as a scientific trip now became an errand of mercy. He ordered out several *quadriremes* and went aboard to bring help not only to Rectina but to the many other inhabitants of this popular coast-line. While others fled he steered straight into danger, with such a complete absence of fear that all the while he was dictating and making notes on every change and shape of the phenomenon. Soon ash began to fall on the ships, and the nearer they got, the hotter and heavier it grew, followed then by fragments of pumice and stones blackened and cracked by the heat, and finally by unexpected shallows where the debris of the mountain was blocking the shore. He hesitated for a moment whether to return, and then, when the helmsman strongly advised this course, he said "Fortune favours the brave. Let's find Pomponianus." Pomponianus was at Stabia (Castellamare di Stabia), cut off on the other side of the bay (the shore here curves right round to enclose the bay). At first the danger had seemed remote though obvious, but then as it grew greater and nearer, Pomponianus had had his baggage carried down to the boats, to ensure his escape if only the contrary wind should drop. This wind was favourable on the other hand to my uncle, who arrived and greeted the trembling Pomponianus and told him to cheer up, and then to encourage the others, had himself carried off to his bath. After bathing he rested and dined in very good cheer - or at least (which was just as good) with all the appearance of good spirits. Meanwhile in several places sheets of fire and flame were appearing from Vesuvius, all the brighter by contrast with the darkness of the night. My uncle, to keep up their spirits, said they were fires of the local farmers who had fled in panic and left their farms burning. Then he retired and was soon sound asleep - he was rather stout and his snores were clearly audible to those without. Meanwhile, however, the courtyard into which the bedroom opened had become buried so deep in ash and pumice that it would soon have been impossible to get out. He was awakened and joined Pomponianus and the others who had stayed awake outside. They discussed whether to stay within doors or in the open for the house was being shaken by frequent tremors and was rocking to and fro on its foundations. On the other hand the rain of pumice although it was light and burnt out was something to be reckoned with. However, the latter seemed the preferable to the two evils. They bound pillows on their heads with cords as a protection against burns. By now it was day elsewhere, but there a night blacker and thicker than any ordinary night, pierced only by many torches and flickering lights. He decided to go down to the shore and see from close to whether the sea was yet favourable. This still seemed rough and contrary so he lay down on a mattress and asked for and drank a glass of cold water and then another. Soon after a strong smell of sulphur gave warning of approaching fire. The others fled and he awoke, and leaning on two slaves rose to his feet and promptly collapsed. As I understand his throat was choked with the thick atmosphere, for he was naturally troubled that way and suffered from asthma.

"When day came (the third since he had last seen daylight) they found his body untouched and unhurt and clad as he had been. He looked asleep, not dead. Meanwhile my mother and I were at Misenum - but that is another story."

Next can be read the very matter-of-fact official account of the eruption which Lionel Fielden, Director of Public Relations in the Allied Control Commission included in the very first Bulletin published on 1 April 1944:

Headquarters Allied Control Commission Public Relations Branch;

ACC Weekly Bulletin No 1 : 26 March - 1 April

"Vesuvius

.... On 3 March 1944 the cone of Mount Vesuvius caved in, activity stopped and there was hardly any smoke until the exceptional eruptive activity at 16.30 hours on 18 March. The lava stream started to flow down the northwest slope. At 10.00 hours 19 March the lava stream was heading towards Cercola, 12ft high, 500ft wide, moving at 12ft an hour and building up quite a head. At 11.00 hours 20 March the lava stream had increased its speed, reached a precipitous slope about 115ft high above San Sebastiano and was literally pouring over this spot like a cataract of fire. Civilians were alarmed and were told by ACC officers on the spot that San Sebastiano and Cercola would be evacuated before lives were imperilled. Civilians living in the lava path were told to start moving household effects to nearby homes of friends.

"Lieutenant Colonel James Kincaid, Naples Provincial Commissioner, in personal charge of the emergency, telephoned Naples from the field to send all available trucks, his Public Safety Chief and a detachment of *Carabinieri*. At 12.45, 20 March, the men reported for duty and at 15.00 trucks began evacuation work, as the lava stream had struck the outskirts of San Sebastiano and was within 1/2 a mile of the main street. Lieutenant Colonel Charles Poletti, Regional Commissioner, ordered evacuation of civilians from Cercola, to start at 06.00 on 21 March. At 03.30, 21 March, the main lava stream had crossed the main street of San Sebastiano; by that time the town had been completely evacuated.

"At 06.00 evacuation of Cercola began. At this time the lava was within 2,000 metres of the town. A large detachment of Military Police from PBS (Peninsula Base Section) were clogged with trucks, donkey carts and pedestrians loaded with personal effects.

"About 500 persons from Massa and 2,000 from San Sebastiano were moved out of the area to the homes of relatives or friends; 125 were quartered in the movie theatre at San Giorgio.

"At 11.00 hours, 21 March, an advanced HQ of Naples Province was opened in the *Municipio* at Cercola, from where Colonel Kincaid directed operations. Food arrived in trucks and was given to ration card holders. By 12.00 hours, 22 March, the lava movement became frozen, with the points of the two prongs, one 1,450 metres from the main street of Cercola and the other about 150 metres from the *Municipio* at San Sebastiano, and a salient between them running up the mountain for some distance.

"PBS, 57 Area and other Allied Units cooperated fully providing equipment and manpower. Feeding of refugee civilians was continued through 23 March but further evacuation was halted. After that period comparative quiet prevailed. There was at no time any looting.

"A great dust bowl has been created round the towns of San Giuseppe, Terzigno and Pugliano. Traffic is handicapped, fields covered (drifts of ash are in some places 5' high) and Region III has undertaken a relief programme. Forage for livestock, candles for homes (electric power in those areas is off) and trucks and bulldozers for highway clearance have been brought in. Region III Officers are working with civilian agencies on a place to procure fresh vegetables and other foodstuffs for the dustbowl area.

"A maximum of 77 officers, enlisted men and other ranks was used during the emergency. Other units demonstrated fine cooperation - the 57th Area loaned 300 trucks, PBS provided 200 Military Police and the Red Cross set up soup kitchens.

"Colonel Kincaid in a report to ACC praised the work of officers and men, but added that in the future, in such emergency operations, officers assigned to tasks should report with complete kits and be prepared to remain on duty until relieved. Too many officers, he said, appeared to have just come out from town to see the sights and many asked to return almost at once for changes of clothing, a shave, their kits, etc. Each officer so assigned to an emergency, should, Colonel Kincaid recommended, carry at least two days' rations."

The flow of lava rendered homeless nearly 3,000 inhabitants of two villages, San Sebastiano and Cercola. Charles Poletti, as Regional Commissioner and Colonel Kincaid, the Provincial Commissioner for Naples, with 77 officers, had the whole problem of the care and maintenance of the civilian population, and the refugees, if any, very firmly in their hands. They also had the local USA Military resources behind them; so I knew from the beginning that the entirely novel exercise in the life of American Political Officers would be well handled, as indeed it was.

Of course, it was minimal compared with the care and maintenance called for in Great Britain after a big bombing raid! But for newcomers to civilian disaster they could not have done better, nor more silently. They fully earned the praise which Harold Macmillan gave them later.

My next contribution is from my letter written at that time conveying my own feelings of an event which I had never before experienced:

MSL (Naples) to DRL (UK) 25.3.44
HQ Allied Control Commission

"…. Today is Thursday. On Tuesday afternoon I was standing in a sizeable farmhouse sheltering from a deluge of hail (as usual I had left my mackintosh behind). The house was empty and showed all the signs of a hurried removal of furniture. Then came a burly farmer who touched his hat as he entered. He was obviously a farmer and I asked him if the house belonged to him. "Yes" he said; "The house is mine and all the fields round here; the wheat over there and the beans and the oranges up yonder and the young almond trees in the dip." And then he burst into tears. And so, nearly, did I, because the fields weren't there, the orange trees couldn't be seen, the almond trees were standing but into the dip the spearhead of the most relentless, horrible thing I have ever seen was slowly, inexorably advancing - a wall of red hot lava, burning at molten red heat, moving slowly forward at then, probably a foot a minute - 40ft high and 100 yards wide at the tip and half a mile to a mile wide at its broadest.

"Behind was a village - all that stood out of the mass of black clinker was the church tower which miraculously had stood up to the most powerful thing on earth. The village simply did not exist - it will never be seen again! On Saturday night I had stood in its square and with several thousand of its inhabitants had watched the lava rolling slowly down the mountain side into the valley above. On Monday the first houses disappeared, rolled, flattened; on Tuesday the village had gone and the several thousand people were homeless, and not only homeless but without occupation because their fields are now covered with this awful mass of burning rock - billions of tons of it. Noone will ever plant there again. I have dealt with locusts and grass and forest fires in the Sudan, but I have never imagined anything so appalling as the results of a really big volcanic eruption.

"It all began on Saturday - although the Professor of the Vesuvius Observatory knew there was danger five days before when some guides told him that a fall of rock had taken place in the cone. The volcano became calmer and calmer and that worried the expert; for he sensed that those rocks had fallen down the funnel; he was right! On Friday night and Saturday no smoke came out at all; the funnel was choked and there was no escape for the gas. On Saturday evening off went the lid with a tremendous spout of lava which went high up to heaven (about 200-300ft) like a red rocket and then just bubbled over the mountainside. From a distance it looked as though there were a forest fire all round the summit. By Sunday night one stream of lava about 500 yards wide had travelled 3 miles; by Monday it had reached the outskirts of the village San Sebastiano and then flattened out, widening its path but reducing its speed. Another stream started down the south apex of the mountain and the volcano became more and more angry. By Monday it was obvious that several villages were threatened and we organised their evacuation all afternoon.

"The first to go was San Sebastiano. The stream of red hot clinkers (for that is what it looked like) hit the first houses early on Tuesday morning. I say hit wrongly, for it is more like a slow-moving caterpillar, or in a way, a host of hopper locusts. It piles up against the house, burning it of course, and sending up spouts of steam from drains and sewers and pipes which are boiled about 100 yards in advance of the stream until the poor scorched house just crumples up and on goes the lava, destroying everything and *covering* everything; that is the horror of it. A fire or flood or wind destroys - but it passes on and you can reconstruct - lava remains for ever. It looks just like the lava we saw at Kawash in Ethiopia and it is, in fact, clinker, red hot and molten. You can stand within ten yards of it as it advances.

"Tuesday I spent on the slope of the mountain evacuating the first village and preparing the three others. At 5.00 pm there was the most almighty rumble and up from the summit rose the biggest, blackest and most terrifying belch of smoke I had ever seen until that moment. It went up, filling in volume and eddying and turning like the most terrific explosion you can imagine and it rose about 12,000ft in the air.

"It was completely black and we all said 'Rain of ashes' (which destroyed Pompeii in AD 74). The wind was very slight and well - I had to know one way or the other what was going to happen and to try to warn people. So I jumped into a jeep and drove like mad to the observatory about 1,000ft from the top where the intrepid Italian professor who is the expert on Vesuvius had his instruments and books. We reached there at dusk and having inspected the needles (seismographic) which wiggled this way and that, I asked him - 'What next?' He hedged - but was definitely against ashes - and thought lava was the trouble for the next few days. I was comforted and then went out onto his terrace and looked at a perfect river of red hot lava two or three hundred feet below and thought of my villages down there.

"That was Tuesday. I got back here (Naples) to dinner at 10.30 pm, picked up John Fletcher and set out again for my condemned villages at midnight. The lava at night was even more terrifying than by day. We stood, warm, watching the stream - which was then moving more slowly. (I had marked off distances on the road.) Back to the municipal buildings where all day we had been issuing food and arranging for lorries for the people who had been made homeless or about to be evacuated. At 2.00 am the volcano went up in another cloud of smoke and a most almighty shake and bang. The village - till then asleep - suddenly came to frightened life. We calmed them and I got to bed at 3.00 am.

"Next day, Wednesday (yesterday), the flow on one side had quietened but a valley on the upper slopes had filled with lava and might overflow at any moment. Moreover, the volcano had been emitting the most awful smoke and gas all day. Early in the morning came reports of lava dust falling and of big pebbles from the sky. Well the truth is that the lava "dust" is as big as the bits enclosed and it falls with some velocity - crops are destroyed, windscreens broken and the whole country goes brown. The road was 6ins deep in this awful kind of grit, which goes muddy when wet by rain. Roofs fall in because it is mighty heavy. Luckily, so far it has fallen cool, but it has done a lot of damage. The cloud of cinders and lapillae belched up from the volcano like this (illustration) and then when the wind hits it, it blows away and down fall the bits of rock kept in the cloud. Some are small but some larger pieces come down and a tin hat is necessary. You know what the volcano did to Pompeii. Everything south of Pompeii was thick in dust.

"They tell me that bigger stuff came down and, in fact, MasonMac and I went out yesterday morning and encountered masses of large stuff fallen - a donkey and one or two animals had been killed, but I hope no man or woman. That night (Wednesday) I spent here, but tonight the old volcano was tremendously active and was spouting up flames many hundreds of feet - and all around was the most marvellous electrical storm with shafts of lightning meeting the flames. It rained a lot yesterday which made evacuation work pathetic. Imagine carting all the furniture out into one lorry - in the rain.

"Today the General and I attempted to go to Salerno by car - the road was choked with lava "dust" or lapillae, so we went a round about way through the hills. One hour out we ran into a *blizzard* of snow *white* to look at - but when it hit you and the car it turned completely *black*. It was frozen ashes. Never have I had such a trip. We turned back after an hour and got home to lunch: Vesuvius then gave the biggest belch of all time. It began at 12.30 pm and was going strong at 7.00 pm. It poured upwards masses of black eddying smoke full of lava dust and cinders. We had motored all down the western slope and went up (tin hat please) as far as we could. We established one good thing - the flow of lava had (perhaps temporarily) stopped. The rain of dust has only really begun and much harm has been and may still be done! 10,000 people have been rendered homeless by the lava stream. All have been evacuated and cared for by us. The dust will continue and at any moment the cone may be burst off by the appalling pressure from within. If so a catastrophe may occur.

"Tonight, the first cloud of red hot cinders has appeared and may fall. I have warned everyone. I can see the old devil from where I write and he is being quiet tonight. But he may be active again. I have 75 officers looking after the mess he has started and he is a nuisance. But the marvellous cloud and light scenes he has created I shall never forget. A wall of lava about to destroy a house, red hot, inexorable, noiseless at 2.00 am in the night is a wonderful, hateful sight. The cloud belched out at intervals of 6 hours is appalling and full of grit - but very wonderful. I hope this eruption which beats everything as far back as 1789 may soon cease. It is taking far too much of my time and that of many other folk. Everyone has behaved most courageously but most helpfully. I am very short of sleep! ...."

I had no official business to visit the area during the eruption for the upheaval of civilians was in very good hands. Yet I had never experienced a volcanic eruption on my own doorstep and the curiosity into the ways of nature or if you like it, God in nature, excited me; moreover I became British rather than Allied and wanted to see how the US part of our Allied Commission would tackle an emergency. I knew that they could do so; I wondered how. I was abundantly satisfied. Moreover, it was no bad thing for a "high-up" to be about when there was trouble.

To be faced with some of the extremities of behaviour in our earthly system is good for the soul; one had visions of the terrestrial turmoil of this planet during these two or three days.

Before, in Ethiopia, I had experienced other afflictions to the Italian citizens - eg. refugees from Addis Ababa to Berbera in the Mercy ships; in Italy itself, I knew that suffering and death among civilians was very present in Naples itself and would be even more present as the fighting progressed.

I knew that these peasants round Vesuvius lived tax-free because they were essentially at permanent risk from destruction; yet the relentless destruction caused by nature affected me deeply. I think the eternal destruction of living crops and the very soil moved me more than anything I have seen in the way of disasters.

It was well known and brought to the knowledge of the general public that the advance of a procession bearing the banner of the sacred San Sebastian of Cercola, together with the banner of the Virgin, stopped the flow of lava before the Municipio of Sebastiano and the village of Cercola. I can well believe it.

I, and my military friends, were most thankful that very little military damage was done to Allied commitments and one or two of them thanked God that the wind was west to east and not south to north. The messages received from ash-covered Bari were not complimentary.

Finally, I append an aerial, in more ways than one, view of the whole affair by Harold Macmillan and a typical Churchillian epitaph:

Blast of War by Harold Macmillan; pages 485-486;

"…. About this time an exciting physical phenomenon engaged our attention. On the evening of 10 March, after dining with General Alexander in his train at Caserta, John and I got back to Naples about 11.30 pm. I went out on the balcony of our villa and saw to our amazement, Mount Vesuvius, instead of crowned by the customary small glow like the end of a cigar, apparently in full eruption. We got a splendid view of the volcano across the bay.

"…. great flames shooting out and hot lava running in two red-hot streams down the mountainside. It was clearly a …. large eruption and I kept getting up during the night to watch it. All the sea was glowing red from the reflection of the lava and flames from the cone ….

"The next day the volcano was belching out rocks, stones and ash. It gave the appearance, so great was the volume being emitted, of an hour-glass. The dense smoke and flames and ash appeared to be almost as high in the air as the mountain itself. The eruption continued for several weeks and did great damage.

"On 25 March flying back to Naples from Algiers, I had a strange experience.

"The last 1,000 miles of flying was very curious. We dropped from 7,000' to about 100' and were just over the water underneath a thick cloud of smoke which was billowing out to sea from Vesuvius. The last 100 miles were almost completely obscured by this immense pall - a very strange phenomenon. The volcano had in fact, somewhat reduced its activities, that is to say, there were no longer so many flames or rocks being thrown into the air, but there was an immense belching forth of smoke of a thick oily character like a factory chimney in the north of England. The smoke practically obscured the whole Bay of Naples. In fact the wind has been so strong away from the town so that most of the ash has fallen on the villages either south of the volcano or right away as far as Sorrento. When the wind one day changed to the west some of the ash was carried as far as Bari right across the Apennines on the Adriatic coast.

"Some weeks later there was a characteristic sequel. By some error on the first occupation of Naples several brash officers had been able to seize the observatory in which a distinguished Italian professor and his wife lived, half-way up the mountain. They occupied it as a comfortable billet. When this was discovered, and the eruption was over, the professor was put back and General Alexander expressed a desire to go up the mountain and make his apologies. This he did with his inimitable charm. I shall not forget his saying in his best French, "Monsieur le Professeur, je vous felicite de votre eruption. C'etait magnifique." The professor bowed and appeared deeply gratified by this tribute. The General's courtesy fully compensated him for his earlier disturbance."

Churchill - *World War II; Closing the Ring* pages 443-444:

"Naples port and the Cassino front - Supplies:

"A few days later Vesuvius was in violent eruption. For several days traffic from the Naples airfield was partially interrupted, but the work in the ports went on. On 24 March a report of the Naval Commander to the Chief of Staff:

'The Naval Group of Ports is now discharging at the rate of twelve million tons a year, while Vesuvius is estimated to be doing thirty millions a day. We can but admire the gesture of the gods.'"

ROME

The Allies entered Rome on 4 June 1944. Early on 5 June, General Mark Clark, GOC US V Army, and Brigadier Hume, CCAO AMG, met the Italian General Bencivenga (who had been Italian "Liaison" with the Germans) at the Capitol where they set up the HQ of the Rome Area Command and the HQ of AMG Spearhead.

MSL (Naples) to DRL 6.6.44:

"…. Well! Rome is ours …. I shall not go into the city yet awhile. Our team of little more than a hundred men are there - administrators, policemen, judges, financiers, bankers, engineers, food suppliers, educationalists, and monument and fine arts preservers. I have talked to them and done my best with them, and now we must see what kind of job they make of it. They are under an American Brigadier and my deputy, Hume, an American too, has gone there. MM (MasonMac) did his stuff with the "Four Foot Six" (as we call the little man) and you will have heard that he (the King) handed over his powers yesterday …."

MSL to DRL 7.6.44:

"…. I haven't many reports from Rome yet, but from what we hear the place is better than we had expected. I have enough food up there to look after them, provided I can get the lorries to move it in and distribute it. I shall leave the team to do their best or worst for a week before I move in for a visit. I shall probably not move house for some little time .... Of course I would have liked to be at the surrender of what would have been my fourth capital occupied by British troops! But they weren't British troops and Alex wouldn't be there and one would have felt (and been) very much "de trop" in what was deliberately a fully American business - decreed as such by Alexander. But it was good to know that we held Rome and that we could now sweep away the nasty smell of German rule from the Holy City!"

Besides, I had my very nice villa in Naples - a suitable retreat in which to plan ahead.

Not a bit of it! I was called to Rome within days, to hold the hands of the US authorities on the question of the Lord Mayor and - even more urgently - on the "leapfrog" system ahead. Alexander was waging war against the German army; the Holy City and Capitol did not deter him from immediate pursuit once the enemy had shown his back. That involved swift movement by AMG and long leaps for AMG frogs.

Hume, in his own words, found that "Rome was little hurt. It had a two-day supply of food when we came in" (the population was estimated at two million people swelled slightly by refugees, of a better class, however, than in Naples). He reported little sabotage of essential installations, light, power and water - though much in this line were in short supply. "Rome" he added "Welcomed us as liberators!"

On the public security side, disarming of neo-fascist police was effected in 6 hours; there was some trouble in disarming the *partigani* (partisans), the first time (but by no means the last) on which we had found them in considerable numbers. The *Carabinieri* came up to scratch, their number being swelled by 3,000 ex-*carabinieri* who now came out of hiding. The quantity of arms not handed in by the *partigani* and others, was, however, for long a considerable menace in the city. By and large public security was quickly restored in Rome.

There was some delay (a few days) in the choice for the Head of Civil Administration in Rome. The Americans were clearly turning towards the wrong man - someone told me it was Aldo Castellani, a well-known Italian in London medical circles. As soon as I heard of this, I realised (and other British political advisors agreed) that I had better join the Roman party and press for the British point of view. I did so, and all parties, US and British, finally chose a most suitable and renowned Italian - Prince Doria Pamphili - a Cambridge rowing man, the richest man in Italy at that time. He married his Scottish hospital nurse, Margaret, who bore him a daughter, Orietta; one of the few aristocrats who openly opposed Mussolini, he was interned during the war with the Allies, after submitting to the King a denunciation of the declaration thereof by Mussolini. He escaped when Mussolini fell and returned to Rome, but during the German occupation of the city, after the Armistice, he was sought by the Gestapo; he escaped detection and arrest by going "underground"; there were plenty of good Italian patriots to protect him; he simulated very well a bad limp and remained undetected, as did Margaret and Orietta who also "disappeared" from society during the German occupation of Rome. But now here he was in June 1944, proposed by the Prime Minister of Italy and warmly supported by the Italians, to say nothing of the British, about to be installed in the Capitol as *Sindaco* of Rome, and I was most happy to be among the first to greet him and congratulate him. We met often during the next 18 months and became visiting friends with his wife and daughter - a splendid girl of 18-20 who was hard at work helping her own destitutes and refugees. It was about that time that Orietta met the English Naval Officer - who visited her Roman home and her parents, and whom she married nine years later, and with whom she lives with their two children - conservators of a glorious Roman Palazzo, filled with priceless treasures of art, and of their country estates and their own people. I am proud to have known her courageous parents and herself.

This was 13 June 1944 and it was one of my first visits to Rome. I was almost immediately afterwards summoned there by either MasonMac or, more probably, by US Army AMG who were becoming anxious about the rapid advance of both Allied armies north of Rome and of their successors in the city.

We were well-prepared; Colonel Charles Poletti was moved from Naples to Rome and Colonel A E Young took over the administration of the police. The transfer from Spearhead to Static AMG went very smoothly and effectively and Brigadier Hume was enabled to continue his operational administration in the field, while I was very happy to have Charlie Poletti to run Rome.

So much for administration. On the political side, my chief, MasonMac, had undergone a really rough time. As Head of the Allied Commission, it was his duty to ensure that the King handed over his authority to Prince Umberto as soon as the Allies entered Rome. The King had shown signs of ratting on this undertaking and Macmillan had advised MasonMac to take forcible measures (exile to Kenya) if this hesitation proved actual recalcitrance. However, the King complied and Prince Umberto became Lieutenant General of the Realm.

There then occurred a contretemps which noone appears to have expected, and which engendered great heat in Allied political circles, particularly in London. It appears to me as unreasonable, now recorded historically, as it did at the time - and I must own that during that time I thanked my stars that my personal job had to do with administration and eschewed politics!

MasonMac, as Chief Commissioner of the Allied Commission, arranged for Prince Umberto, the Lieutenant General to go to Rome with him, together with the Prime Minister (Marshall Badoglio) and the leaders of the parties represented in his Government (at Salerno). In Rome, Badoglio rightly and constitutionally, handed his resignation to the new ruler, Prince Umberto, who asked him to form a new government which would include some of the party leaders just liberated in Rome. On their arrival in Rome, MasonMac addressed them on the subject of unity but they demanded that a new Government should be formed not by Badoglio but by Bonomi (Labour Democrat).

The Lieutenant General, Prince Umberto, according to the historical record, "gave way to their demand" and MasonMac, the Chief Commissioner "took no steps to tell them that they could not act as they had done without obtaining the consent of the Allies" ie. the Advisory Council. I still ask myself whether it was his duty to do so.

The news of this change of Government in Rome provoked a series of violent telegrams from Churchill himself to Macmillan, to Noel Charles and to MasonMac. Churchill hated losing a sturdy old warrior like Badoglio, but had he forgotten words used, some months before, about the Italian people making their own choice? Macmillan, who received a similar rocket from the Prime Minister had not, in fact, been present in Rome, but was always nervous of what MasonMac might do, and did not trust him. Noel Charles, not yet Ambassador, had been forbidden by the US General Clark to go to Rome and did not appeal to London; noone in the Foreign Office in London had the foresight to imagine that Badoglio might be replaced.

MasoMac embroiled himself still further, this time with Washington, by telling Bonomi that Count Sforza would not be *persona grata* to the Allies as Foreign Secretary. At this news, Roosevelt and his State Department "flew off the handle" and denied the allegation! (Sforza was "good" for the Italian vote in the 1946 US election.) What the political advisors in the Political Sub-Commission were doing I just don't know. They were not at hand to advise their Chief Commissioner.

The whole matter was quickly and easily made clear and smooth by the Advisory Council who approved Bonomi's leadership and assumption of Foreign Affairs. In fact, most people, including the British War Cabinet "considered that there might be something to be said for a change of Government in Italy at this stage".

But the effect on MasonMac was serious. He had been suffering from back trouble and other ailments - the legacy of motor and polo accidents in his life - and he just couldn't take the hammering which he had received, together with the knowledge that Macmillan had little use for him.

He had a long talk with me, of course, but there was clearly only one course for him - sick leave; and on sick leave he went (in June 1944) - never, alas, to return. But he never forgave Churchill and Macmillan and notable among victorious candidates in the 1945 election in England was General Mason-MacFarlane, MP for Paddington North - Labour.

His departure did not do the Allied Commission any good. The Allied Governments could not make up their minds about his successor and his Deputy, Admiral Ellery Stone, US, acted as Chief Commissioner for at least six months before confirmation.

The change made little difference to me except by adding a load of responsibility and work - which I accepted willingly - only too thankful to remain Head of the Allied Civil Service in Italy (my adopted title) rather than assuming political responsibility. I soon became Chief of Staff and continued to run my administration.

There were, of course, minor difficulties in serving an American Acting Chief Commissioner, who, though easy in approach and almost ultra pro-British, did not really know or care about administration - his eyes, like practically all Americans, were fixed on the Italian political scene. The state of the harvest left him unmoved, though feeding the Italian population was of importance to him; the process of de-fascistisation or epuration was of little interest to him, though he was all for the principle. But he was very loyal to his British Deputy whose English bothered him. He begged me to Americanise the reports and despatches which I would prepare for him to sign (he abhorred putting pen to paper). "Maurice" he would beg "For Mike's sake, throw a few split infinitives and "gottens" into our reports and cut right out that Oxford English."

A Personal Tragedy

My initial months in Italy had been exciting in quite another way by news from Diana just before I left Tripoli that she was pregnant with a babe due to be born in April 1944. Had it not been for my Italian appointment I should have tried my utmost to obtain compassionate leave in April 1944 and this resolve would have been strengthened by serious and grave news about the health of Ruth, Diana's mother who became extremely ill round the New Year. Diana's pregnancy went well, in spite of worries about her mother, who enjoyed a brief recovery in March. Luckily, mails, which had been very bad when I first came to Europe, became more rapid in transit and we kept in comparatively close touch. Moreover, kind friends in England kept me well posted about Diana's health and that of her mother. I had little fear of difficulties surrounding the new baby's birth for Diana had always found childbirth an easy process. We had the usual parental interchange of choices of names and in the end seem to have decided mutually on Adrian or Nicola.

MSL to DRL 20.4.44

"…. Last evening a worried American Staff Officer who had just flown from the other side of the Med. came in with a telegram which he had brought. He couldn't make out what it was all about so he brought it to me, personally. I gravely thanked him and told him it was a financial matter of some importance - and then just hugged myself at the thought of our new baby …."

I was delighted at the thought of four children and saw a happy picture of the little family at home - also overjoyed at the new arrival. It was not until 25 April 1944 that I received DRL's "concessionary" cable (there had been a clamp down on mails and telegrams) telling me of our third daughter, Nicola's, arrival on 6 April and that all was well and happy, the baby having arrived between lunch and tea, with no difficulty. [DRL had moved to a private nursing home at Rudgwick run by Joan Boxall, where she remained throughout these events.]

And then the tragedy occurred. Julian was sent home from Prep School (Highfield, Liphook) where cases of whooping cough had occurred before the end of term. Julian, poor boy, developed the disease himself; Diana contracted it within a short time and passed it on to our new born babe. Nicola and her mother, with every assistance possible from doctors and nurses, put up a great fight; but the little girl died on 9 June aged 8 weeks. A great sorrow - a great tragedy and strain to Diana who must have suffered terribly - as no-one can really imagine. A friend who lived nearby wrote that:

> "Diana is the finest example of courage and bravery I have known .... a complete inspiration to others."

Another faithful friend and ally, Roy Piggott, wrote:

> "Apart from Dr Miller and the nurse and Di herself, there is an extraordinary atmosphere of happiness and serenity and *goodness* in that little house."

Never have I felt so utterly incapable of comforting or helping Diana in a time of deep mental and physical anguish.

Rome

Although I paid many visits to Rome after occupation in June 1944, staying in the Grand Hotel where MasonMac, Stone and I had very nice suites reserved for us, I did not close my beloved Villa Carradoro in Naples until early July 1945, when the whole of ACC moved in to the building known as the Ministero dei Corporazioni in the Via Veneto, Rome.

This was an enormous building: utterly fascist in design, outrageous in the scheme of decoration, quite different from the lovely ancient buildings of Rome among which it stood; inside, every design and decoration was ostentatious and one really felt quite ashamed, as one walked up the imposing staircase to work, in surroundings so different from the natural beauty of the city. Working in the Eternal City should have given one an aura of beauty: but in the Ministry of Corporations one was literally oppressed by the ostentatious vulgarity of the building.

We were, however, comfortably installed and especially on the first floor where MasonMac (and later Stone) and I had our offices; nothing was missing - including private bedrooms and bathing facilities! The Chief Commissioner sat in an enormous room, behind a cast mahogany desk and, in Admiral Stone's time, two large national flags hung motionless behind his chair.

I, myself, surrendered my large office to my private staff and for the use of visiting firemen, and was most comfortably installed in a smaller room which was just big enough to house my daily meeting of Heads of Sub-Commissions and other senior officers, a most useful half hour or so at the beginning of the day. My policy and practice was to trust to verbal communication - for the life of the Commission was short and we were at war. I tried hard to reduce inter-departmental writing to the absolute minimum and, although my confidential clerk did once complain that I had dictated to him on one subject, without referring to notes, for three solid hours of a hot summers' afternoon, I tried to reduce correspondence, even to Regional Commissioners, to a minimum and between internal offices to nil. How the author of *Allied Military Administration in Italy 1943-45* found sufficient records to fill nearly 600 pages I cannot conceive - it is a remarkable fund of information.

Well, here we were, in the city of Rome, whither the new Italian Government under the premiership of Bonomi moved simultaneously. The military scene had slipped north very rapidly and the AMG V Army handed over to Static AMG after a week or ten days, when I brought Colonel Poletti up from Naples to become Regional Commissioner, Rome. It was fitting that a Lieutenant Governor of New York State should govern Rome, though I am not sure that the patricians of the city relished the thought of an American-Italian who had "made good in the United States" as their immediate ruler.

However, Prince Doria Pamphili quickly restored Roman authority and, indeed, ACC handed over to the Italian Government the administration of Rome (and all Italy south thereof excepting Naples) six weeks after the city's occupation. I felt quite happy about initiating and carrying out this very considerable transfer of territory to the Italian Government. In fact, the military situation was now moving with such rapidity that it was of vital importance to release ACC/AMG officers, administrative as well as technical, from the south to take charge of really vast areas including many towns of considerable size which were falling into Allied hands with great regularity. I spent many days in the forward areas in the warm days of June and July planning (with great haste), moving (with no less rapidity) many Regional and Provincial Headquarters and teams from south to north in order to ensure that civil problems did not delay or interfere with the progress of our troops. These transfers of administrative officials affected not only Allied personnel but Italian officials as well. For many communes and cities would be found by the Army AMGs devoid of suitable Italian officials, many of whom had been Fascists and had either disappeared as their territory was occupied by the Allies, or had suffered removal by Spearhead AMG in the very necessary process of instant de-fascistisation. In fact, in agreement with the Italian Government, we set up in Rome pools of suitable national officials who could be sent north on call by AMG for posting to communes in need of Italian Government Officials to work under AMG Spearhead or Static.

On 7 June General Alexander ordered an advance to the Arno with all possible speed. I quote a paragraph from Harris (*Allied Military Administration of Italy* pages 175-6):

"…. During the retreat of the Germans from the Tiber to the Arno, the Army AMG had to take over a very large amount of territory in a few weeks. Rome had been entered on 4 June …. Orvieto (50 miles from Rome) and Terni (60 miles from Rome) were captured on 14 June and Chiusi on 20 June; Siena (140 miles) was taken on 3 July, Volterra on 9 July and Arezzo (150 miles) on 16 July. On the Adriatic Coast movement was equally quick. Pescara and Chieti (150 miles) were taken by 12 July, Ancona (130 miles) on 18 July, the same day as Leghorn (200 miles) in the west. One result of this rapid advance was that several of the towns south of the line Arezzo-Leghorn were not severely damaged (and so more easily administered), much less than those in the Cassino plain south of Rome. But just south of the River Arno German resistance stiffened. The southern half of Florence (180 miles) was not entered until 4 August and it took a fortnight to clear the Germans from the north of the city. Pisa (212 miles) was not entered until 1 September."

Quite apart from the administration of these areas which added some eight million extra Italians to our every day work - there were added eight million extra mouths and stomachs - the ACC had to ensure that food could be found and brought to those eight million. Their number was probably swollen by thousands of Italian refugees driven south by the destruction of their towns and villages by the retreating German forces whose next defensive position was the "Gothic Line" which ran from Pesaro in the east to south of La Spezia in the west - a line which they held during the winter of 1944-45.

Food was in good supply in the south of these new areas, north of Rome and the southern parts of Tuscany; indeed a surplus there helped to feed Rome. But further north the destruction of every town and every installation (hydro-electric, etc) made life impossible for the Italian population, north and south of the Gothic Line, and hungry refugees poured south from Lombardy and the Po Valley, adding seriously to our food problem and, of course, to the problem of housing and shelter.

Just at that time, Alexander was denuded of several divisions destined for Western Europe and the resulting chaos on the roads passed the imagination. This last factor made many of us realise that capture of the Po Valley and Lombardy north of the Gothic Line was doomed to postponement.

It was in the spring of 1944 that Alexander's plan of a right swing through northeast Italy, the occupation of Austria and the advance by an Anglo-American force into southeastern Germany, a plan warmly backed by Churchill, was turned down by the Americans and the Combined Chiefs of Staff who wanted and took more of Alexander's army to support an Allied landing in southeastern France - "Anvil" it was called. Anvil was backed against Alexander's plan to invade Austria.

"…. Thus were sown the seeds of the partition of Europe and the tragic divisions which were to dominate all political and strategic thinking for a generation and more …."

Thus wrote Macmillan - and how right he was!

But so far as this story goes, the loss of three or four divisions meant for Alexander and his troops a winter on the Gothic Line or a little north thereof, and postponement of final victory until May 1945.

In the meantime, the historian (Harris) continues:

"…. Under these conditions, the administrative arrangements of the Allied Commission were put to a severe test …."

True enough - a test which we overcame thanks to the courage and skill on the part of the AMG Rear Officers and tremendous hard work and again, imagination on the part of all concerned at ACC HQ in Rome. We knew what might be coming; we planned, and the Heads of Sub-Commissions all came up to scratch during those summer months of 1944. Noone had met an administrative problem of this magnitude before; noone shirked the possible results, nor the efforts required to ensure success. However, for the writer of *Allied Military Administration of Italy* to write on page 176 of his otherwise admirable history:

"…. It is not difficult to imagine the chaos that might have resulted had the Commission been forced to assume the Military Government of northern Italy in the autumn of 1944 …."

is quite wrong and shows a lack of appreciation of the characters who formed that Commission from top to bottom and the planning which was always in the background. I know, even now, that we should have fulfilled our task of protecting the fighting troops from undue civil disturbance, etc. had this been required of us north of the Gothic Line.

I cannot remember any period during that war in which I was so profoundly submerged in problems affecting my job, which I knew must be overcome, in loyalty to my chiefs - Alexander above all men, Macmillan who in MasonMac's absence consulted me more and more, and Stone who, somehow, overcame the then American average industrialist's suspicion, if not disdain, of Britons, and not only gave me some (not all) of his trust but listened to some (again not all) of my opinions on ACC strategy; never, however, on politics.

One day in July 1944, I was summoned to Alexander's HQ.

"Hallo Lush" he said "Thunder clouds round your head! The Pentagon say that you have been very severe on an American high ranking officer, thus showing your dislike of Americans. They want you to be removed. I have no intention of removing you; you are a first class administrator and you will stay under my command. What happened?"

"It's so ridiculous, Sir," I said. "My American deputy reported to me that a high ranking US officer had been drawing horse allowance of ___ per diem for six months and had never owned or looked at a horse. Send him to an urban appointment, I told my deputy. He did so. However, his cousin is a Senator."

"Take my advice, Lush" said Alexander "and never give an order to an American. I never do. It takes much longer to get across but it saves a lot of trouble. I have never given an order to an American General since North Africa - I always talk to them in such a way that finally they think that my wish is theirs."

Royal Visit

A week later, a message came from General Alexander's ADC:

"The General would be glad if you would dine with him at advanced HQ on Sunday evening next, to meet General Lion. Please bring with you US Admiral Stone who has also been invited."

Well, General Lion was the code name for HM King George VI who, I knew, was due to visit Italy that week. I must say that I was very thrilled at the invitation and so was my American Admiral Stone. Great was the cleaning and pressing of uniforms and the polishing of buttons. Many were the queries from my American chief on behaviour, address, etc. On Friday came a curt signal from GHQ -

"Dress tomorrow evening - shirtsleeves."

"Maurice", said my Admiral, "I will *not* sit down with your King in *shirtsleeves*!"

"You sure will", I replied.

On Saturday evening we set out from Rome at about 5.00 pm and headed north along the Via Cassia, a hot dusty ride, through Viterbo, an old fortified town which had been badly damaged by bombs, to Lake Bolsena. Here were grouped the caravans and tents of General Alexander's Forward HQ. There were not many and they were well hidden under trees on a gentle slope which went down to the lakeside. A sizeable tent-marquee had been erected with the west side open; through this the setting sun shone strongly. We had a wash after that dusty ride - rolled up our shirtsleeves and went into the marquee where we met two of HM's staff and General Brian Robertson whom I knew well. Alex appeared, was very hospitable and friendly and soon after, the Monarch entered - literally shaking with laughter; we were presented and he then, still laughing, said:

"General Alex, I have just listened to one of the funniest strategic conversations I have ever heard. General Oliver Leese (Commander VIII Army) and General Anders (Commander Polish Corps) were obviously not seeing eye to eye about some tactical problem. The discussion was in French and terminated with General Oliver exclaiming, with his best Parisian accent, 'Mais mon General, cela n'est pas ma tasse du thé du tout.'"

Soon after the two Generals came in obviously happy with their discussion. It was a most lively, friendly evening. HM sat down next to my Admiral and the most junior officer in the room. I sat opposite HM and either at dinner or afterwards had a long but light-hearted talk about the future from the Italian point of view.

MSL to DRL 31.7.44

"…. HM was obviously enjoying himself and the rest of the party was *so* friendly and helpful - we all came away about 11.00 feeling thoroughly happy. I had driven Stone and another American (General) there. They were just so tickled at HM (no tie or rank badges) and at Alex putting a captain next to the King while generals sat down the table. And HM was *good* with the Americans. A real highlight, quite unforgettable! The Americans, on the way home, talked to me about our Empire, and told me how gradually they began to understand how it held together. 'That guy in there means more to you than we can possibly understand - and sure, he means a hell of a lot to us too.' Nice! …. Had a most interesting talk with Harold Macmillan who has taken my villa in Naples."

That gesture of General Alexander in summoning me to dinner to meet my sovereign did me a power of good. I *did* write my thanks!

Villa on Monte Parioli

By the end of July 1944, the Allied Commission's accommodation officer (one Captain Drage, in civilian life the head of a large American Department store at $20,000 pa!) and my Military PA (Arthur Stewart) had secured a villa for me - the highest house in Rome, on top of Monte Parioli; not very beautiful but commodious and with a surround which passed as a garden. We allowed the old *"padrone"* and his female housekeeper to retain a room or two, and she was quite useful at times. In it we installed Tony Grafftey Smith, Head of Finance, Guy Hannaford of the Legal Sub-Commission, Evan Talbot, Chief of my own Staff, Patricia Russell, my PA, and Arthur Stewart. Tom Bergin, the American Public Relations officer who succeeded Lionel Fielden, joined us later and we had many semi-permanent residents from time to time for the next 12 months.

It was an imposing house, with two large rooms downstairs for sitting and eating: a very good dining room whose table would easily seat 16, and often did. The ground floor contained the vast kitchen and all ancillary rooms and cupboards and slept 17 of our personal staff! I always had my car and jeep handy and two drivers who were members of the downstairs household. We retained "Giulio" the owner's cook and ate the best pasta in Rome - rolled out daily on our own marble slab. I had a very commodious bedroom and bathroom en suite, also my own study. There was, high up on the roof, a tower with a glass room from which one had the most superb view of Rome. It was an ugly but happy house and finally became "home" to the Lush family when Diana joined me very soon after D Day in 1945 and later our children joined us in 1946.

It was good to get into a house; writing to DRL on 21.07.44 I had exclaimed:

"…. I hate this hotel, hate the food, hate the Romans in it (tarnished dowagers and men who may have been gigolos, but certainly nothing better) and long for home …."

I had however fallen in love with Rome, though I foresaw that I should never succeed in really knowing the city. It grew on me gradually and, of course, we saw the city in ideal conditions, when motor traffic was at a minimum and consisted of mostly Allied military vehicles and hooting was at a minimum. I was lucky in combing the mounted *Carabinieri* and finding that they stabled some very lovely horses. Early morning riding soon became the routine and we would find a really beautiful horse called Cairo waiting for me with others for my staff and driver and someone's batman - cavalry trained. The Borghese Gardens made excellent hacking and adjacent was the Gallopatoia with a schooling portion and some excellent jumps of all descriptions, the ace of which was a stone water trough. My horse, Cairo (was he named as a possible charger on which a fascist officer would ride through the capital of Egypt?) was a fine jumper and would sail over any obstacle in that arena - followed by Pluto, my bull-mastiff. One morning, all three of us, Cairo, Pluto and self, were doing just that when to my horror I saw below us, lying on the ground, a man's body tucked into the bottom of the jump. He saw us simultaneously and leapt to his unsteady feet. He fled, precipitately, followed by Pluto who luckily, responded to a vigorous shout from me. The sleeper ran like a hare, and I don't think he chose a jump for a bed shelter a second time!

Pluto

It should be explained that Pluto was a bull mastiff who came to be very much a part of MSL's household in Rome, later adored by all the Lush family. He came from Mason-MacFarlane on his departure from Italy in June 1944.

MSL recounted that MasonMac, a dog-lover, had acquired Pluto in the first place following instructions to London to procure a good dog to replace an unsatisfactory Italian one, "…. for I cannot go on travelling up and down this ruddy peninsula with a dog that only knows QUI." Pluto was thus acquired, fully trained, from the Police Force. On arrival in Italy, at the airport was a car for "Mr Pluto".

One early morning when MSL was leaving his villa on Monte Parioli to go riding, he saw an unfortunate Italian bicycling down the hill. "Go for him" he murmured misguidedly: instant response - Pluto bounded playfully after the cyclist, but with no intention of harm. The cyclist was not to know this, of course, and with a yell of "Mama-mia!" partly dismounted and completed the entire descent cowering on one pedal, on the opposite side from Pluto.

On the beach at Frigene, Pluto suffered miserably from headaches in the intense sunshine; he found relief by wearing sunglasses and a hat. He enjoyed swimming in the sea but could only do so by carrying a log of wood to support his head.

In the villa, he would attend family meals, sitting and resting his jowls on the table - a perfect height - drooling at the food. Pluto could be incited into racing the length of the basement, towing one of the children on roller skates; he enjoyed obstacle races, lured by a bowl of spaghetti at the finish.

[On the Lush family's final departure from Italy, Pluto was entrusted to the Mess of the Royal Air Force Sub-Commission which took over the villa - Ed.]

Administration

Let us return, after a good breakfast, to the ever moving, ever growing problem of administering the new territories, the new towns, the eight million inhabitants and the large number of refugees. The HQ of the Commission had completed their move to Rome by early July and here I was, established officially in the brash but extensive building in the Via Veneto which housed us as a body; my villa on top of Monte Parioli was a good mile away. In these buildings we were to remain officially and personally, for nearly two years - always remembering that until the end of the war, the Executive Commissioner (myself) generally succeeded in spending 40% of his time in the Regions. My Chief Commissioner, after MasonMac's departure, was not a great traveller, a habit which suited me admirably but earned a criticism from Harold Macmillan who loved nothing more than to be with the forward troops.

I must admit that we all found great advantages in being housed in one office building. It eliminated, at my insistence, all question of written memoranda between the many Sub-Commissions and Departments. Officers were finally convinced, not without difficulty, that a war at General Alexander's pace could not be conducted on the minuting system. I helped to overcome this by holding an "Ex-Com" daily meeting at 9 am which 15-20 Heads of Departments attended, and corresponded by word of mouth, expressing problems and solving them verbally in one hour or less. These daily conferences were invaluable and became very popular - top generals, visitors, French and Russian, occasionally attended or came by mistake and stayed for "Ex-Com's 9 o'clock". The paper which they saved us and, I hoped, the misunderstandings made right, were legion. Not until the end of the Commission - long after the war - were they made weekly.

Again, at these meetings, our main subjects were unchanged - support for our Spearhead AMGs, food, public security, Partisans and Refugees - as our main objects of discussion and decision - and I underlined the importance of the latter state and tried to live up to my reputation of decisiveness, for better or for worse. Our opening was a two minute on the political situation by Lionel Fielden.

In the following pages I am going to pick out a few illustrations from our daily bulletin between July and December 1944 of matters which were discussed, a decision taken or a direction given.

Remember, O reader, we in the Executive Commissioner branch were not to be concerned with politics.

Of course, the foregoing statement is incorrect for we were bound to be influenced by the political situation and, for instance, our thoughts and planning in the higher strata of the Commission's work were motivated very strongly by directions from Washington and London about the New Deal which was to drop the "middle C" in the name and function of the Allied Control Commission.

Moreover, one of our most important functions was to advise the Advisory Council on the handing back of Italian territory from the Commission to Italian administration. The Italian Government never ceased to press for this and it also released experienced officers for the forward regions which were falling to Allied troops and Forward AMG with great rapidity.

The formation of teams staffed with both Allied and Italians for immediate service in recently conquered areas was in a constant state of progress, and throughout the summer of 1944 we were forming teams ready to administer not only Tuscany and Emilia (which they reached before the winter) but Liguria, the Po valley, Lombardy and Piedmont in Northern Italy, which fell in the New year. When it is considered that these northern regions were the most heavily industrialised and the most densely populated in Italy, it can be realised what immense care had to be taken by the Regional Commissioners during that summer and autumn, in the training of teams, consisting not only of Allied officers, but Italian civil servants and technical experts, and in keeping them in a state of efficiency. This process of leap frogging began with the swift advance of the Armies after the fall of Rome, and the experience in Tuscany and Umbria taught us a great deal for the final great advance in 1945. The choosing of the Regional Commissioners was no easy task, for we had by now a number of fine administrators (for the task in hand) out of whom we had to choose the best. I think we succeeded: quite apart from Hume and Benson who led the Army AMGs from Sicily to the northern frontier, men like Dunlop, Miller, Bowman, Carr, Hancock and, of course, the best known of the lot, Poletti, were magnificent leaders.

Concomitant with this came the harvest, the reaping, the *amasso* into Government stores, it's transport thereto and therefrom to the consuming areas - all these were ever present problems, the successful solving of which was of paramount importance, and which naturally attracted the strongest and bitterest criticism. The Regional ACC Officers concerned were really magnificent; one of the most senior and experienced reported that in Italy there existed 62 different ways of avoiding sending the prescribed amount of grain to the Government store. Without doubt some areas suffered considerable shortage and I am sure that mistakes were made. We had every assistance from "Q" at Allied Forces HQ (General Brian Robertson) but help from overseas was not so successfully provided. But to feed the 45 million people of Italy in the most appalling circumstances of "scorched earth" warfare was no mean feat. One of our most senior Food Officers was Colonel Legge who after the war ran the International Lawn Tennis at Wimbledon.

We had many conferences on the thorny question of Italian partisans who did magnificent and dangerous work before the Germans left an area, but therefore were apt, fully armed as they were (by the Allies), to be an embarrassment to AMG procedure. However, more often than not, the AMG officers persuaded them to surrender their arms before they did too much damage (summary execution of Fascists was their chief sport) or assumed too much authority. The arms so surrendered were flown to other patriots behind German lines. We had a magnificent officer, Colonel Spicer, who was the Commission's expert on these brave and sometimes unruly young men.

During this summer of 1944 the USA (whose representative on the economic side of the Commission had been remarkable for his absence from Italy) replaced their economic nominee by two very smart performers, a Colonel O'Dwyer and a civilian named Antolini. They certainly began to move the economy along somewhat - and, as we thought, only just in time. We also thought that their arrival and activities were not far removed from thoughts of the 1946 Presidential election and the large Italian speaking vote in America! For whereas the American officers on the job in the Allied Commission were loyal to the military presence of the Commission and it's undoubted value in helping Alexander and Mark Clark lead their armies to victory, it was perfectly clear to any of us that US policy as formulated in, and dictated from, Washington was that the long term status of Italy was a European and, therefore, a British rather than an American affair. BUT the short term welfare and goodwill of Italy was of vital importance in the approaching US Presidential election; every effort therefore, must be made to create quickly, even on a short term basis a happy, well fed, if alien, population who would tell their kinsfolk in America to vote for Roosevelt.

The Italian Government's power to suppress rioting was badly shaken (and British and American respect for that power) when an Italian ex-prison governor in the Regina Coali prison in Rome was lynched by an Italian mob. The mob had broken into the magistrate's court in Rome, intending to lynch the chief accused, Caruso, a former Chief of Rome Police during the German occupation. Failing to find Caruso, the rioters set on the ex-Governor and killed him with great brutality. The matter was an entirely Italian affair, they being in charge of security and administration of Rome, but it was widely advertised in the Italian and Allied press and made a very bad impression in Rome, London and Washington.

I heard, about that time, of an extremely courageous act on the part of Colonel Poletti, the Regional Commissioner in Rome. He walked unarmed, escorted only by two British police officers, into the prison mentioned above, and quelled a particularly nasty riot by just talking to the prisoners. I must own that being "talked at" by Charles Poletti was an experience. The same British officers, Colonels Pollock and Coxhead, later alone and unarmed quelled a riot near the Spanish steps - partisans versus politicians, ie. Communists against the Right.

Nor were the troubles of the Monuments and Fine Arts Commission forgotten. Quite apart from the treasures in Rome, we heard of the vast amount of loot removed from the city; of the steps taken to find some of it and restore treasures; more terrible were the tales of destruction, generally wanton, in many of the cities of the north, but I must confirm that the Italians, private persons and officials, seemed to do their utmost to restore the results of vandalism.

I have mentioned refugees before - they (Italians) were an ever-present problem and were admirably handled by the AMG Forward officers in the first place, and the Sub-Commission's Officers when they reached the war areas, including officers of the Italian High Commission for Refugees established, probably before but certainly as soon as we occupied Rome. Reception centres were established in many places; the condition of refugees always gave cause for anxiety as regards health, epidemics etc. As operations continued, northwards, there were sudden surges, firstly from German occupied territory southward to the Allied lines; thereafter as territory was liberated from the Germans, a return surge northwards, back home; but this was far more difficult to permit. The treatment of these wretched Italian people uprooted by battle, the flotsam and jetsam thrown overboard by the fighting troops of both sides, was a continuing operation demanding much skilful organisation, inexorable discipline and infinite sympathy. Luckily we had as Head of the Displaced Persons Sub-Commission, Col Fothergill, a man of great compassion and organising ability whose patience was never exhausted and who won the trust of his "patients".

In 1944, 155,487 refugees passed through his reception centres (many of which were at times under shellfire) of whom 150,880 were dispersed to homes, some indeed only temporary places, throughout Italy. In 1945, as Italians came streaming south from Germany, over the Brenner and other passes, this figure exceeded half a million. But that is another story. The Displaced Persons Commission had always been the Sub-Commission dearest to the sympathies of my heart - the victims of war were so helpless, so inoffensive, and I had been glad when, at the very outset of the Commission, it had been placed directly under my personal supervision. I don't suppose that my personal qualities had much to do with the work which Colonels Fothergill and Findlay and their men managed to accomplish; but, at any rate, they had direct access to the top and my heart was very much in their work. They deserved all the help which we could give them; and they taught me much of what I tried to do after leaving the Commission in 1946. In fact, they inspired me to follow in their footsteps.

I quote the following from the Commission Bulletin of 1 October 1944. Lionel Fielden wrote under the title *The Road Back*:

"…. The road back to Italy for thousands upon thousands of Italians, now stranded in enemy areas, will lead through some of the 10 or 20 or 30 camps that Colonel C Findlay, Director of the newly amalgamated Displaced Persons and Repatriations Sub-Commission, is contemplating - Colonel Findlay admits it will be a whopper of a task. There may be half a million Italians under forced labour in Germany, perhaps 200,000 in the Balkans. Austria is known to be the crossroads of Europe for displaced persons and entry into Italy from Central Europe will certainly be a problem to handle. Italians will be used to handle Italian refugees coming home, and Allied personnel will tackle Allied refugees. In the meantime, the Colonel is looking forward to the taking over by UNRRA of over four camps in Southern Italy, mostly inhabited by Yugoslavs. He hopes that UNRRA will undertake with money and food some of the commitments made at Quebec."

We must return to the military situation in the summer of 1944.

General Alexander states:

"…. On 7 June I ordered an advance to the River Arno with all possible speed."

Leghorn was entered on 18 July; Florence by early August. The line ran eastwards towards Pesaro on the Adriatic; on 25 August it was 200 miles north of Rome; another seven million mouths to feed, a further seven million to administer - and our second real meeting with the *partigani* - the CLNAI. Moreover, the armies were not stopping there - fighting and advances continued thought the early winter and, as Macmillan observes in his book *Blast of War*, Alexander failed by a cat's whisker only to break into the Lombardy plain and the Po valley in 1944. As I have noted, I think we should have coped, but I cannot conceal that the respite from Christmas 1944 until the early spring, disappointing from a purely military point of view, rendered the next and final stage possible - untidy as it was.

Our plan - simple on paper - was to choose our Regional Commissioners and their Deputies, supply them with sufficient staff, Civil Affairs officers, security men, Carabinieri, finance, food, industrial experts and give them a region already occupied in which to train; then to see that they did not become stale and to send them forward at the right moment (generally on the call of the Senior Civil Affairs Officer of the Army Spearheads) to the correct region.

So simple to write down a directive on each line; not quite so easy to choose the cast or put them in their places! So simple for regions as far north as the Gothic Line - Tuscany, Marche, Umbria, Lazio; but supposing they break through that line and debouch into the real north - some seven large, heavily populated, industrialised provinces, filled with *partigani*, highly communist - how could we cope then? Well, we had three Regional teams in being, another four in reserve; we were being ordered to hand more regions over to the Italian Government; we knew what we were about, and, always relying on the personnel of AMG Spearhead and the ACC in the rear regions to say nothing of a redundancy of staff at the Commission's HQ (whom I warned as the days went on), I knew we should fill the bill.

It was very necessary to impart this confidence into the Regional teams already in Army AMGs and the immediate rear thereof, and I started, that summer, a series of Regional Commissioners' Conferences at Siena (once we had invested the place) and in that lovely city we had several frank, outspoken, noisy conferences in which I explained the plan, won the confidence of the field men concerned, and also some of those outside the ACC - eg. a fighting general or two, an Advisory Council member, a visitor from UK or USA, etc.

Harold Macmillan was no stranger at these Regional Conferences at Siena. Ellery Stone, mercifully and wisely left the planning, the directives and the agenda for the conferences to me but sometimes looked in or attended. I often had a "fighting" soldier there - a Brigade or even a Divisional Commander. They were tremendous fun and really useful. Many of the Regional teams and others were leaders of men in industry or finance in civil life, and military rank was often quite forgotten in discussion - but complete loyalty took the place of the discipline of rank.

I used to spend a night or two in Liszt's house opposite the Cathedral and was always enchanted by the beauty of Siena. We always seemed to motor back to Rome by night, picnicking in some Tuscan countryside, sometimes seeing the dawn rise before we sought our beds. Patricia, Tony Grafftey Smith, Evan Talbot and others of my staff were tremendous props during the hot summer in that lovely war-scarred country.

Well, in due course, a "cat's whisker" preventing Alexander and Clark from breaking the Gothic Line, we had a few more months in which to breathe. When the break did come, how proud I was! All my Regional Commissioners and some of their staff reached their objective - and, I may tell you now, that I was not far behind them. But of all that, anon. Into Rome re-entered Harold Macmillan, wise as always, debonair as ever, charged with a good look in to the Allied Control Commission. Also entered Noel Charles, now British Ambassador (and Alexander Kirk his USA opposite).

Winston Churchill

Then came Winston Churchill to have a look at the whole scene and, typically, to have mercy on the Italian people who were the first Europeans to lose their war. Were we, the British race, doing the right thing by them? A little compassion had entered his soul for these misled people.

During August 1944, Winston Churchill visited Italy where

"…. many questions could be more easily settled on the spot than by corresponding."

He left the UK at the end of the attacks thereon by the V1 (doodle-bugs) which was defeated after three months, having caused civilian casualties of 6,184 dead, and 17,981 seriously wounded. His first duty was to see Marshal Tito of Yugoslavia whom he met in Naples - a successful meeting.

Churchill's second duty was to watch from a British destroyer the Allied landing on the south coast of France between Cannes and Hyeres. Their objective was to defeat such German forces as were in SE France and join with the Normandy landing force in the centre of the country. This they did. The 45,000 Germans:

"…. isolated remnants of the German First Army willingly gave themselves up"

This landing, named "Anvil" (later Dragon) was the cause of the most formidable split in the Allied strategy, in which Churchill and the British Chiefs of Staff were forced to give way to Roosevelt's and Eisenhower's insistence on reducing the strength of Alexander's force in Italy in order to make the landing in France numerically possible. British strategy was to make such a landing at the north end of the *Adriatic* after Alexander's forces had broken into the valley of the Po, and then advance by Trieste and the Ljubliana Gap to Vienna. Eisenhower demanded the diversion of about 100,000 men from Allied forces in Italy to ensure the success of "Anvil", the operation in France.

Churchill and the British Chiefs of Staff, greatly against their will, deemed it necessary to give way. Churchill foresaw the immense benefit to international relations that would arise if the British could capture Vienna before the arrival of the Russians, and even in August 1944, maintained the forlorn hope that Alexander might achieve this:

"…. I have told Alexander to be ready for a dash with armoured cars."

Naturally, this was Churchill's first concern in Rome and therefore his first visits were to the military forces and in his inimitable way, he went right up to the front, which caused every man on the spot to exert himself to the limit so that Churchill could see and learn the whole and every part of the matter. The PM, with Generals Alexander, Leese and US Mark Clark, was in the front line at the opening of the attack on the Gothic Line. Chapter VI of Churchill's book *Triumph and Tragedy* (Volume VI of *The Second World War*) is a magnificent description of his visit through minefields to within a thousand yards or so of the front line combat. But he wrote bitterly about the robbing of Alexander's armies to support the Allied landing which he had watched in SE France:

"…. Here (in Italy) was this splendid army, equivalent to 25 Divisions, of which a quarter were American, reduced till it was just not strong enough to produce decisive results."

Dinner at the Embassy 22 August 1944; (written at the request of Martin Gilbert for the 7th Volume of the Biography of Winston Churchill)

"My word it *was* a hot day! August is the worst weather month in central Italy and in peace time no sensible Roman, who could afford to move, remained in Rome. I lived in the highest house on the summit of Monte Parioli, with some of my Anglo-American staff and there was never the whisper of a breeze. I nearly disgraced the British Army by wearing shorts in the Eternal City; my Chief Commissioner, Captain Ellery Stone US Navy (in private life of Bell Telephones USA, never having walked the deck of any ship in his life) certainly pulled out his "whites". He and I (Executive Commissioner) were trying to run the Allied Control Commission in Italy - the Anglo-American unit, some 1,000 officers strong, whose job it was to keep the Italian population fed, housed, orderly, healthy and useful while General Alexander and his armies drove the Germans out of Italy; we, Alexander's III Army as he styled us, aimed to replace Fascism by democracy.

"Winston Churchill, who was on a visit, primarily to the army in Italy, looked in on Rome for a couple of days to acquaint himself with the Yugoslavian and Greek problems and especially the Italian situation. On one of the hottest days in the year, he saw, as Harold Macmillan relates, 'all forms of power in Italy - spiritual, regal, governmental and the fourth estate of the Realm'.

"My American Commissioner and I had been asked to a small dinner party that evening to meet the PM who was staying at the Embassy. I knew Sir Noel and Lady Charles well and had the privilege of counting them among my best friends in Rome. I felt extremely sympathetic towards Noel Charles, who had been sent out by the Foreign Office to Italy, early in 1944 as Ambassador elect to the King and Government of Italy - but the King had handed over his powers to a Lieutenant Governor, his son Umberto, and the Bonomi Government was provisional. So Charles could not be appointed as Ambassador proper. The Russians and also the Americans were not so finicky and just gave their men full Ambassadorial rank - exequatur or not! Noel Charles was left in mid-air and to add to his discomfort, Winston Churchill sent Harold Macmillan as Resident Minister to Italy and was about to appoint him or have him appointed President of the Allied Commission, the sole recognised link between the Allies and the Italian Government. Macmillan (*War Diaries*) wrote that on the afternoon of 22 August, Charles had exclaimed to the PM and Macmillan 'But what am I to do?' Churchill countered by asking 'What do Ambassadors do?'

"Lady Charles was made of sterner stuff but was equally charming and lived up to her Christian name of Grace. She disliked the Embassy building which they took over in July 1944 - it really was not a building fit for an Ambassador; she would have loved to entertain Churchill in the Palazzo d'Orsini which became the British Embassy in 1945, and was worthy of all her charm and efficiency …. But even in the 1944 house she was a splendid hostess.

"In addition to the PM and Macmillan, who had spent a gruelling afternoon discussing the future of Italy and the Allied Commission therein, the Charles's had invited Stone, myself, leaders of the Commission, and Brigadier Low who looked after all the British troops in Rome (no easy task), also Myron Taylor, American Ambassador to the Holy See, who fitted Macmillan's description of him "old, rich and charming"; he certainly charmed Churchill who was due to have an audience with the Pope the next day. At dinner Churchill reminisced on his last audience in 1926, during the Fascist regime; this led me to tell of my first visit to Italy, travelling by train to Venice in 1922, on the day on which Mussolini marched on Rome. The cold champagne was extremely refreshing on the stifling evening and I envied Churchill who drank his from a large crystal beaker! I cannot quite remember how we sat at table but I have a hazy recollection of Grace Charles between the PM and Myron Taylor and the Ambassador between Stone and myself, with Macmillan between the two Americans. We sat long at table and afterwards Churchill took the American Ambassador to his room. At about midnight he and Macmillan and staff received and sent telegrams, and at 1.00 am the PM sent for me!

"In that curious building the best approach to the sanctum allotted to him was down an iron spiral staircase. One arrived in his presence, therefore, in a state of incipient vertigo. However, this was soon alleviated by a glass of brandy and a very interesting conversation followed. I reminded Churchill of our last meeting when we had lunched *al fresco* in a field well outside Tripoli, with Generals Alexander, Montgomery, Leese and Alan Brooke, soon after the capture of the city in 1943. The PM remembered that, en route to the lunch, members of Italian colonists had cheered him lustily. We then discussed the state of affairs in Italy, the role of the Allied Control Commission and the slackening of our control. I knew that Churchill was most anxious to effect this "muting of the 'C'" (London Times). I told him that we, in the Commission, were also most anxious to effect this, not only from our desire to effect freedom of thought and action in Italy, but because we needed the Allied personnel, now engaged in mid and southern Italy, for operational administration as soon as the north fell. We needed every Allied and Italian administrative officer to be ready to move north as soon as the advance began. There was, however, a grave shortage of capable and experienced Italian administrators available who had not been trained in Fascist ways. I also asked the PM to believe me that, whenever we moved an Allied administrative officer to give way to an Italian, there was a howl from the local Italian councils and populations, and in some cases politicians, at the consequent lack of efficiency. I assured him that I would do my utmost to silence the 'C' in ACC and make Harold Macmillan's job easier, always remembering that General Alexander's Army had priority, and that their well-being and success must not be jeopardised by deficiencies in law and order, feeding and health of the civilian population caused for political reasons. I begged him to ensure that Harold Macmillan became President of the ACC. We had great faith in him.

"We then went on to discuss the role of the Allied Military Government and the Allied Control Commission when, as we hoped, we broke through that autumn into the Po valley and the north. I told him of our plans and assured him of their efficiency. He nodded and became cheerful for he was, next day, continuing his participation in the battle, with Alex and his men. He hoped so much to take part in the first stages of the autumnal break-through in Italy, which would have enabled Alexander to swing to the right - overcome Austria and so alter history. He gave me a cheerful "Goodnight" at 2.00 am. That ended my last interview with that great man."

The offensive of which he had seen the opening, just failed to break through:

".... A very little more - and we could have broken in to the valley of the Po in 1944 with all the gleaming possibilities and prizes which lay open towards Vienna."

So far as Civil Affairs were concerned, Churchill came to Rome to discuss the future of Italy with Macmillan, Noel Charles, the Ambassador (with whom he was staying), Roger Makins, Bob Dixon of the Foreign Office and, no doubt, others including myself. As recounted above, following the dinner party, I had been summoned at 1.00 am to meet him privately. His appreciation of the problems of administration in Italy was, as I expected, accurate and positive - and full of sympathy for the administration. He asked pertinent questions relating to relaxation in our methods of administration and our domination in Italy. I told him that there was a distinction between domination and control, and that our Political Officers were taught always to control rather than to rule, and generally were good at muting the middle 'C' of ACC; but I warned the PM that so long as Alexander's forces were fighting in Italy against large German forces, so long as the civil population in the north was ruled by a quasi-fascist Italian Government with a large number of partisans run by communists in opposition to any such German backed government, we could only mute the middle 'C' by varying degrees, eg. more in Siena, less in Naples or Bologna, when we captured the latter place. I warned the PM that Italy was at the moment very short of non-fascist trained men who could control anything, and in certain aspects of administration a modicum of control by somebody was essential. I also asked him to consider the ability of the existing Italian ministers - all of a certain age and out of practice (I put the matter of age very tactfully for my listener was just under 70). Would they be able to cope with the young *partigani* of the north?

Once the hostilities had ceased we should have no hand in the administration of any part of the country, and yet I knew that the Italians would need and be glad of help in the restoration of their technical structure. I told him that the Americans in their election year would wish to go further than their allies in handing over in toto to the Italians, and I warned him that we might have to watch and listen to vote-catching actions and words. On the other hand, I, for one, hoped that the proximity of the elections might quicken American activities on the economic side, which had been very dead. I also told him that our need for men to control, with a big C, the north on liberation, would automatically mute some of the C in the rest of Italy. I did not think that either of us was filled with inspiration between 1 and 2 am that morning, after a pretty gruelling day, both for WSC and MSL, but I hoped that I left him with the impression that our view of the hard facts of the administration of the Italians, as he wrote, "for whom I have always had, except when we were actually fighting, a great regard" was sympathetic.

That was my second and last personal interview with the great man and I felt proud that he should have wished to hear my views.

He left the next day still hugging a forlorn hope that Alexander's troops might still, by a miracle, reach and hold Vienna before our allies, the Russians, entered from the north east. Such is the course of war when three or more countries are allies!

MSL to DRL 01.09.44:

".... In the last fortnight, practically every member of the British Cabinet has been out here, and that has meant long visits to the office and long memoranda to be dictated (and thought out!) and then long dinner parties in the evening. Noel Charles (who is "Ambassador to be") has been very good and has had me along to all the dinners. I met and talked at length (at 1.00 am) with the PM (Winston Churchill) and met all the other Cabinet ministers. Our own particular minister (Macmillan) spent the morning with me and we liked each other (I hope!). They are all discussing the future of this Commission and the Head thereof, until I am a little tired of it all! In the meantime, Stone and I carry on as if we were in complete charge. I had a long talk too with General Wilson who also came to our conferences and he was illuminating and sympathetic - I am planning ahead most days. We had a very successful Regional Commissioners' meeting, 156 present. Then the Advisory Council in Italy asked me to talk about the Commission and we did so in the Palazzo Feranese, one of the most beautiful palaces in Rome ...."

I cannot remember my address to the Advisory Council referred to in that letter, though I do remember a similar address which I gave in Rome at about that time to an American Commission of Enquiry into the activities of the Allied Control Commission.

Harold Macmillan as President of ACC

One of the main results of Churchill's visit, so far as it affected the Allied Commission, was his proposal to appoint or have appointed Harold Macmillan as Head of the Commission. This was good news for the Commission, for Italy and for myself personally. Here was a leader who, in my experience, had an understanding not only of politics but also of administration, had been in at the reorganisation of the ACC and, although he disliked MasonMac, had faith in the work of the Commission and seemed to like some of the men. Some of my staff did not hold him in such esteem and dubbed him "a good actor".

Macmillan was a man of intense interest and vigour, and I found that if he believed in what one was doing, he did not interfere. He was also a man of action; a searcher of knowledge; a man who liked to go to the forefront to find out, not necessarily to rule or dictate. He was never so happy as when with Alexander in the front line; he admired Alexander immensely and his presence with him did both Alex and Macmillan a power of good.

He was a politician, par excellence, saw good in most people, including your humble servant, gave his confidence to such people and let them get on with the job. He was discreet but sometimes deliberately indiscreet, if he wanted something done. When he did not know the art or means of doing or making something, he discovered who did, trusted him, prompted him and found he accomplished the job.

He was good to me; he trusted me, as I hope, and my endeavours and allowed me freedom of action.

The changing role of ACC

When therefore, in due course, ie. November 1944, Macmillan became our Acting President to be, I knew that I could proceed tranquilly with the two main projects which faced the ACC: the muting of the middle 'C' ("Control") and the preparation of a military government in northern Italy which would do its job for Alexander. Together, the muting of the 'C' and the elimination of appointments held by Allied officers and thereby their release for other appointments made the two problems apparently more easy.

We began by our build up for the future, for northern Italy, AMG. I appointed a staff officer in charge of the establishment of the Regions of northern Italy - he told me that north of the Gothic Line lay the thickly populated provinces of Veneto, Emilia, Lombardia, Piedmont, Liguria. We also had a staff officer in charge of the liquidation of Allied Commission posts in the remaining Regions of Italy. The Chief of Staff of the Italian Government regarded, perhaps, the second appointment as the more important. It was not. Our main task in the Commission was to ensure that the operations of fighting troops were given every assistance possible in the field of civil affairs. Our secondary task was to give a New Deal to Italy.

Taking our cue from the "leap frogging" which took place during the rapid advance from Rome to the Gothic Line in the summer of 1944, we prepared similar plans to be made on a much larger scale for the northern Regions.

The Regional Commissioners were appointed. They were authorised to plan and fill the vital posts of the Regions (Provincial Commissioners and all Technical Heads) on paper, in conjunction with my Staff Officer Forward Regions; after approval, they then had to find them temporary Regional HQs in the regions already occupied. The existing Regional or Provincial Staff in those areas had orders to accommodate them in every way, and the Regional Civil Affairs Officer thereupon began his training of teams topographically, economically, industrially - in every way.

The fact that the New Deal required us to remove ACC Officers from rear Regions, gave us a certain but not adequate number of officers from which to obtain our northern regional staff.

All this took immense thought and effort, but everyone in the commission seemed to understand the plan of having this reserve of what Alexander had truly called his "Third Army". To tell the truth we were a trifle worried at the thought of a complete break through the Gothic Line during the coming winter: we were ready - just - for that, but we were more ready in the spring.

The British and American Governments prefaced the muting of the 'C' or the New Deal for Italy by issuing a joint statement, after the meeting in Quebec between Churchill and Roosevelt, called "The Hyde Park Declaration". In short it stated quite vaguely that in view of the Italians' attitude towards freedom and the Allies' cause, an increasing measure of control would be gradually handed over to the Italian Government. The Allies would continue to help and the Italians were expected to respond. Everyone looked forward to freedom and free elections.

The muting of 'Control', like all destructive or despoiling policies, was not so easy to achieve without a ruthlessness which was abhorrent to us all and horribly impolite to the Americans in election year. The fact was that having regard to the temperament and the lack of training of non-fascist Italians, there were not in existence sufficient people who had the courage and experience to take up the Commission's muted 'C' and play it loud and clear.

The Italian politicians wanted the earth, and the Italian Government according to Macmillan, sent a memorandum demanding alterations in the whole system of the Commission, including the introduction of Italian representatives to the Commission itself.

Macmillan, with our help, prepared draft proposals which he sent to London and Washington where they were sat on for two months. I had tried to look at the future from the point of view of the men and women in the villages and small towns I had seen - not the Neapolitans, who we knew were extremely political, but the people in the south, the Sienese and the Florentines.

Italy in late 1944

The Italian people were in a bad state physically, mentally and morally. I am now referring to the great bulk of the population, particulary in the centre and south, and I am omitting the *partigani* and the more virile (and Communist-minded) people of the industrial north.

Fascism had painted a veneer of discipline over the Italians and even that could not dispel weariness of war and hard work; they longed for peace and the life which their lovely country allowed them to live; the disciplines imposed by Mussolini had been tolerable in peace time, but when he brought their country to the horrors of war, a costly war which lost them their "Empire" and countless thousands of lives, they broke down. They surrendered; they offered to fight against their former allies; they found themselves fighting their own people; they found that the war in their own beloved and beautiful country, far from ceasing, had intensified; their cities and villages suffered destruction and ravage at the hands of their new friends and allies as well as those of their former; even when the battle had moved away from their towns and villages, the mines remained and killed countless people; food was short - "Why should we starve at the hands of our new allies?" they asked.

We were, in truth, dealing in the southern and central areas with a very demoralized people, and, as in many similar cases, the people themselves had rather a perverse hankering to be controlled by foreigners. There were reports in our Bulletins of riots in Sicily (none against occupying forces, all against Italian rule); of 25 murders per mensem in a southeastern province; of 55 suicides in Brindisi - all these in already de-controlled Italy. There was no question of the *people* yearning to throw off the shackle of control. The de-control cries came from the politicians and allies, who, being free people, thought that the Italians would find control irksome and degrading; the Americans had in mind their own candidates at the hustings in the USA. I do not suppose that the Russian member of the Advisory Council demanded the muting of 'Control'; he had demanded the execution of the Fascist leader ab initio! And I am certain that the French would have wished their neighbours to be driven with a very tight Allied rein.

The British politicians led by Churchill brought on to the stage our inevitable national emotion in favour of the beaten and we administrators in the Commission needed every Allied Civil Affairs Officer on whom we could lay our hands. So we loyally carried out the policy of our governments and the Hyde Park Declaration.

No one, and I am ashamed to say, not even myself, sufficiently made the point that in effect the middle 'C' would, in due course, disappear of its own volition as the administration of the Allied civil affairs through Italian officials progressed - that was the inevitable result of what was a natural sequence.

I think The Times had it nicely put in their article of 27 September 1944:

> *Muting the middle 'C' in Control Commission.*
> "The Allied Control Commission will drop the word 'Control' from its title though doubtless not the reality in so far as control may still be required."

One of our Vice Presidents broke into verse (with apologies to John Masefield):

'C' Fever
We must go down to one 'C' again
For the other 'C' must die;
All that's left is the hardship
With no star to steer her by.
For without control
The ship will roll
Despite the crew a-trying.
But we'll hear "What a mess!"
From the CCS
Through CASERTA cry....ing.

APGS
27 October 1944

We in Italy had received no official information of this change in the score reported by The Times, but such 'non sighting' was quite customary even in those days. "Let the press have the story and tell the men in charge when it suits us, politically" is almost an historic policy of governments.

Reorganisation as Allied Commission

I sat often as Chairman of the Manpower and Reorganisation Committee of the Commission in Rome, and I see that we pruned HQ by 200 officers, rolled up several Sub-Commissions, and streamlined HQ by turning over some functions to the Italian Government - as we were continually practising. We established the office of the Chief of Staff (myself) directly under the Chief Commissioner and directly in charge of the rest of the Commission: in fact, regularising what I had been doing for six months and making the job easier title-wise.

The Bulletin wrote:

"…. Regional Commissioners and SCAOs of armies, together with HQ Staff met under the Chief of Staff at Siena in an atmosphere of intense airing of difficulties, mutual exchanges of views and on the spot solutions which again proved the value of these exchanges. Caccia explained the political situation; two Regional Commissioners who were forming skeleton and more than skeleton Regional Staff or Northern Regions such as Piedmont and Liguria, complained of raiding of their carefully chosen staff in Province A by others with equally urgent difficulties in Province B, just occupied. The names of splendid officers and administrators such as Poletti, Mayne, Kirkwood and Marshall, all fighting like fury for their particular "babies", all content to accept the usual compromise - good naturedly, as for example, Brigadier Hume, facing, as he put it, "fluid conditions" of expansion and contraction in accordance with tactical changes, insisted on "no withdrawal of personnel from Army area". Colonel Wayne, his most able, British second-in-command, complained of unrealistic directives (from ACC Rome!) on patriots - but accepted with resignation that every patriot incident had different origins. Colonel Ames defended lustily the accusation that the people in Rome were fed better than those in the forward areas, and that he was in the habit of removing grain from rural areas to feed the cities. (He was a splendid amasser of grain, was Col Ames.) Mr Antolini, our civilian Economic Director, did not come off very well in defence of the lack of supplies currently shipped from USA to Italy (why not to Great Britain? asked MSL) but hoped that Colonel Legge (British) now in Washington, would turn their hearts. Brigadier Upjohn spoke of eleven Italian prefects who formed a pool of Italian municipal leaders ready to take over towns in the north …."

The Bulletin ended:

"…. satisfied that, however bad things look and the real bad news about conditions in town, there was the determination and potential to work things out. The meeting broke up early, to repair to the recuperative values of Tuscan wine and Colonel Kirkwood's hospitality."

I have mentioned prison troubles in Rome above. The courageous Colonel Pollock who had been largely responsible for quelling a riot in the Rome prisons, after writing his recommendations for prison reforms by the Italian Government, added:

"…. It is all very well to say that it is the responsibility of the Italian Government, but, if things had gone badly, it would have been a reflection on us because the Italian people, whatever is said to the contrary, look to us for help, guidance and support."

This was a reasonable comment on muting the 'C', borne out by a statement in the House of Commons by Winston Churchill to the effect that the lynching in Rome of the Italians (fascist) prison governor:

"…. was the responsibility not only of the Italian Government but also of the Allied Military Authorities."

I, myself, certainly agreed with Churchill. So long as we were present as an Allied Commission, we were responsible to General Alexander for maintaining the elements of public order.

Shortly after, it was reported, correctly, that industry of any value left in Italy was in the hands of the Allied Military Authorities, who employed about 300,000 workers in machine shops, cement and brick factories; this of course, was before the capture of the vast industrial areas in the Po Valley and Liguria. It was evidence of the Allied control still extant in the country.

Also, at his time, the Commission submitted to the Advisory Council Brigadier Upjohn's extensive Report on Epuration. This was a wise, clearly stated report on the action (practically wholly Italian) being taken to punish Fascists: to purge the administration of Fascists, to dispose of the profits made by them and to confiscate their property. This was the kind of action and report which the Advisory Council found valuable in their estimate of the Commission's work! Colonel Fothergill continued his unremitting and often unreported work on Displaced Persons and Refugees.

So much for the Bulletin.

In the autumn of 1944, I had a message from Sir d'Arcy Osborne, British Minister to the Vatican, and a good friend, that His Holiness, Pope Pius XII, would be glad if I could attend a private audience as he wanted both to meet me and learn about his flock in countries where I had recently served.

Audience with Pope Pius XII

During the autumn I was privileged to have an audience with Pope Pius XII in his study at The Vatican. He had, it was told to me, wanted to see me because I had recently administered countries whose European population had been mainly Roman Catholic - in fact Italian.

At 10.45 am I arrived at the visitor's door of the Papal residence and was greeted by a Guard of Honour of Swiss Guards. A Guard of Honour is a high honour and requires meticulous acknowledgement; all went well outside; inside the building I was taken by lift to the Papal floor - and being inside a building removed my red hat; as I stepped out of the lift, there stood a Guard of Honour - the Noble Guard; a hatless Brigadier at once dressed himself properly and acknowledged the courtesy. I was escorted by a high cleric towards the inner rooms in which, blow me, if they had not stationed a third G of H - the Papal Guard - but I was too quick for them, having spotted the formation through a glass door. Hat on this time ab initio - we were becoming Latinised already. Here the military reception ended and I entered a hushed atmosphere as I approached the private Papal apartments. Cardinal Mancini, destined to be the next Pope, emerged - greeted me warmly and put me greatly at ease. He was Cardinal Secretary of State and I was in close touch with him over a number of official matters. I found him charming and most efficient. We chatted until out came a (clerical) Private Secretary on duty and ushered me into the presence of Pope Pius XII who was sitting at his office table - a very lovely oak knee hole desk in his study - a room of no great size and dimly lit.

His Holiness rose, shook me by the hand and greeted me warmly; how did I enjoy the beauty of Rome? what were my impressions of Italy? He had heard much of me, he said at once, from his Bishops and clergy and some of his flock returning home from or in Ethiopia, Tripolitania and Madagascar. He thanked me warmly for all that I had done for the unhappy Italian Roman Catholics in Ethiopia and Tripolitania where the impartiality and sympathy shown by the British administration and the justice done to all would long be remembered by him and the members of his flock. I was moved by his genuine friendliness and still more by his obvious appreciation of the situation in the various countries which we discussed quite fully. He then said:

"But now General, I want to hear your frank opinion of my Bishops whom you found in those countries."

I told him frankly, how, sad to say, his Bishop in Addis Ababa had transgressed the laws inherent in the Anglo-Ethiopian proclamations - and I thought in his loyalty to his church - by harbouring in his house, after the surrender of Addis Ababa, both arms and ammunition and a wireless outfit which could be, and was, in use for communication with the enemies of the Ethiopians and the occupying power, the British. I had no option but to have him treated as a military prisoner of war but I hoped he had returned to Italy in one of the Mercy ships sent to Somaliland for the evacuation of civilian Italians in 1941-42. I took the opportunity of thanking His Holiness for all that he and the Vatican had done in the arrangements for the supply and sailing of these vessels. I assured him that we had done our best to alleviate the sufferings of the Italian women and children who had made that ghastly journey from Addis Ababa across Somaliland to Berbera.

I asked His Holiness to remember with thankfulness the forbearance shown by the Ethiopian population towards the Italians in Ethiopia, after the defeat of the Italian armies and the return of the Emperor.

We skirted over Madagascar where I told his Holiness that I hardly knew the Roman Catholic clergy or congregation as distinct from the general population. Nor was he very interested in the French island.

I told him that in Tripolitania our name for the Bishop was "The Old Fox". He kept his flock in good order, they had little to fear and had suffered but lightly; but we never knew where we should find the Bishop next, or what he would be saying. His sermons were always very correct, but, I was told, they often approached a degree of naughtiness surprising on the lips of the spiritual leader of a congregation whose military leaders had suffered a crushing defeat! I told him that I could have wished to find more charity extended to the several thousand Jews taken from Benghazi to the hinterland of Tripolitania where we found them in a pitiable state.

The Pope was clearly interested; he told me that he had shown his displeasure towards the Bishop of Ethiopia and chuckled aloud at the title bestowed on Monsignor from Tripoli. We discussed Ethiopia at some length.

He then asked me about myself and my own family, sent a rosary and a cross to each member thereof and thanked me for what we were doing for the Italians - gave me his Papal blessing (I think I omitted to kneel) and the audience ended. I was moved by the warmth of his words and the time which he had given to listening to me.

Diana and I were honoured with a second audience in 1945.

Let us return to more bland affairs, continuing with extracts from letters.

MSL to DRL 10.9.44

"…. I think the greatest piece of war news is a lifting or partial lifting of the blackout over the UK. It is the first tangible sign of complete victory and it is right that it should give, however small, a benefit to the "home front" and to all of you in England who have borne yourselves so completely heroically. This sounds perhaps artificial - it isn't. It does represent what all of us feel and you ought to know! …. I went up to Siena and spent the night there in the museum! Mine host (an American Colonel) slept with a Botticelli (a lovely Madonna and Child) and I with Liszt's piano. It was a lovely place and Siena is quite the most lovely town that I have seen in Italy.

"…. Had a 10-hour conference: a difficult one; four very controversial subjects and a volcanic atmosphere; anyone likely to go over the boil at any moment. However, we held them and got a lot of good out of the meeting. They all, as usual, wanted another one (Regional Commissioners' Conference) in 15 days' time …."

MSL to DRL 14.9.44

"…. You cannot imagine what it is like to work in an Allied "machine" during election year in the States. Poor chaps - it is no blame on them but everything in this country, in this Commission is subservient to the ELECTION …."

MSL to DRL 18.9.44

"…. I was summoned by "the powers" (in Casserta Allied Forces HQ) and told I was wanted to plan for the next country (Austria). I retorted that I would do so if I were to go as No 1 in Civil Affairs, but that I would not go as No 2 …. I feel so justly and strongly about it. It would be great fun and my fifth country, so it is worth fighting for …."

MSL to DRL 19.9.44

"…. I had told Macmillan what I felt about the

country next door. He felt strongly that I should not go as No 2 and advised me to express my views in writing - and in fact dictated a letter for me! (Not often one has a Cabinet Minister to dictate one's letters!) I feel that I have done all I can - and if nothing happens, I shall be very happy to sit back and stay here ...."

I can now record that the powers that were did not choose me as No 1 but sent an unemployed Major General to learn from me in Rome. The origin of the order "to plan for Vienna" lay in a forlorn hope that Alexander might succeed in breaking the Gothic Line in 1944 and having won access to the valley of the Po might be able to do a right hook for Vienna before the Russians could reach the city. It was not to be. Churchill writes in *Triumph and Tragedy* Vol VI p440:

> ".... Our chance of forestalling the Russians in this ancient capital had been abandoned .... when Alexander's forces in Italy had been stripped for the sake of landing in the south of France ...."

The Russians invaded Vienna which was later divided into three zones - Soviet, British and American. I think I was better off in Rome!

About this time (September 1944) a combined party of British and American trade union leaders came out to Rome. I met them at the British Embassy where I was told that, between them, they drank 12 bottles of whisky in 21 minutes. Macmillan reported that, of course, the British could speak no Italian whereas the American Trade Unionists whose names were Belzoni and Antolini could hardly speak any English but were very fluent in Italian; they imputed (to the press) the worst charges against the Commission, alleging that the British were trying to turn Italy into a colony.

MSL to DRL 2.10 44

".... I am getting very disillusioned about the good faith and honesty of anyone in high places. You and I have lived too long in the shelter of the Sudan, which , whatever it faults, was pretty free from intrigue. I realise why the bigger Colonial Service, the Foreign Office and our handling of matters like Civil Affairs are so bad - because personal ambition, place hunting and place giving to the hunters comes first ...."

MSL to DRL 6.10.44

".... I wrote a long letter to Harold Macmillan exposing the abominable way in which the ACC and MM, Stone and myself have been treated. I think he will read it and be interested ...."

This referred to a violent attack on the Commission by the American press.

".... The weather is pretty foul and as the BBC will tell you has hampered operations and everyone is feeling a bit frustrated. I have all the teams prepared for the north - wanting to get in and get to work .... we had the Charles' (Embassy) to dinner and the Therons, a most charming couple of whom I am fond; he was PS to Smuts and is now his representative in Cairo, Athens and Rome ...."

MSL to DRL 7.10 44

".... I have staying here a Mrs Angus, Kenya Red Cross, who used to be one of my evacuation women in Ethiopia ...."

MSL to DRL 22.10.44

".... First of all I am going to talk about the Allied Control Commission. There is, as you will have heard, talk about dropping the "Control" out of the title; in fact our leading statesmen have declared for this. But, and this is no secret, we have received no instructions yet; typical of the way this Commission has been dealt with for some time past. Ellery Stone, now a Commodore (= Brigadier) is, and has been since MasonMac went, the Acting Chief Commissioner. The reorganisation that we made recently changed my position from that of equality with the Heads of the Administrative, Economic and Political Section to that of superiority. As Executive Commissioner I was nominally equal with the others and could give them no orders - result: no coordination. This was MM's idea; in fact he was forced to do so because Stansgate (Admin) and Henry Grady (American Econ) were political appointments and he did not want to put me *over* them - though the work I did as Ex-Com was in fact getting *them* to do things! When Stansgate went and Grady was replaced, we could put our house in order. I am now Chief of Staff or Chief Secretary or Business Manager: they are all Deputy Chiefs of Staff. I now hold staff meetings twice a week and we settle policy and execution then. I see that it is carried out not only at HQ but in the regions whose Commander I still am. It is one hell of a job! But it is already working and I do think the Commission works better already. The President of the Commission is General Wilson, Supreme Allied Commander: he is only titular and the Chief Commissioner, or now Acting CC, Ellery Stone, is Deputy President and runs the show. Harold Macmillan is Political Adviser to General Wilson and Resident Minister in the Mediterranean (not only Italy). Stone made me Chief of Staff with Wilson's approval. La Guardia's possible appointment is, I think, all part of the American election campaign; he *might* come across as Economic Deputy Chief of Staff, but I doubt it. I don't think he will come as Chief Commissioner but they may play with the idea in America for the purpose of the election, in order to get more Italo-American votes. Practically all business in USA will cease now until the election is over. They may take it very seriously so we shall probably get no answer to the appointment of the new CC until the election November 6 - then I think La Guardia's name will drop out. I very much hope that the man to whom I wrote the letter may become the CC. I stayed with him the other night and had the most interesting and sympathetic 2½ hours' talk. He had already written a short but very charming (but non-committal) reply. We came to the above conclusions. In the meantime we carry on. I am firmly interested in the Commission. People do come to me because they get decisions and the main difficulty is to keep the Anglo-American balance. They (the American press) all say Stone is in the pockets of the British; we try very hard. HM showed my letter to his boss, I think. But everything is really subordinate to the USA elections and we shall be a political football until that date. All quite wrong; all very difficult; all very democratic; and therefore we must be very tolerant.

I have now a magnificent staff - my two PAs, Stewart and Patricia, who are splendid and selfless and a tower of strength and sympathy; Guy Shippe and Evan Talbot, my main pillars in the main office. In this main office we also have two American officers, a junior British Captain and his first class ATS officers. One has just married a Czech - the other engaged to a POW. They do all my work and from start to finish try to prevent work having to come to me - and yet keep me in the picture. All are, I say in all humility, devoted. Guy Shippe, Talbot, Stewart and Patricia all live in the house. The latter housekeeps very efficiently and selflessly. Well, so much for the old ACC. It will still have as many critics in the future as it has had in the past. We shall have more riots in Rome and Palermo; you can't disrupt people and keep them on short rations without a flare up now and then. I am not unduly anxious. I refuse to be allergic to the newspapers. The tripe written therein, especially, I regret to say, in the USA, just makes one laugh. But we have, for the most part, enabled Generals Alexander and Oliver Leese to fight their battles and win them without having to look over their shoulders and be concerned with the plight of 25 million Italians behind their armies. We look after them and, as I said before, it is one hell of a job! I love it - I get despondent at stupid things: I wonder why I can't be made a Major General. But we are constructive; we are helping a liberated people; we are not, believe me, doing too badly. We do it largely by making them (the Italians) do the work; by making *them* take responsibility - and Sudan training comes in well. I am trying hard to get home to tell the War Office a lot of this - and other ministries. We had a succession of very interesting meetings this week (we had 7 in one day!) and a lad called Morris of the Foreign Office was pretty helpful. But until we know the future of the Commission, you mustn't expect me home. Moreover I am the Senior British officer on the Commission and I have a responsibility to the other 800 British Officers to see that all is well until that time comes! So much for the ACC. I wanted you to know all I think and some of what others think and what we do ...."

MSL to DRL 22.10.44

".... I played four chukkahs of polo today. It was wet and we played on the smaller ground - standard not high - mostly Italians - ponies good; it was the greatest fun ...."

We played polo on boarded grounds which was new to me but very entertaining. We had to abandon the habit of playing because we found that the Italian owners of the ponies and some of the players were non-epurated Fascists and were screening themselves and their misdeeds behind their alleged popularity with the top executives in the Allied Commission. I played once more on Christmas Eve.

Those were the last games of polo I have ever played and I cursed politics and Fascists and war for blotting out of my life the one game at which I had, in any slight way, excelled. Of course, it does not suit impecunious brigadiers to play expensive games but I am always proud to have gained a 3 handicap in the fastest polo ever played - that is, at Omdurman!

10 days Leave in England

Having warned Diana in my letter of 22 October 1944, that while the future of the Allied Commission was in flux, I could not get home, I seized a sudden offer by Anthony Eden of an air lift to London and on Saturday 4 November.

".... breakfasted in Italy, lunched in midair, and was met by DRL at Ockley station - supper at Westlands. Thus home again on the spur of the moment after 18 months' absence."

I remember landing at Northolt where as senior officer I was wafted through Customs etc - and looking back finding my Ambassador in Rome and host of many evenings being led into the Immigration and Customs officials' den. Anthony Eden had gone out leaving rather scurvily his Ambassador to the Immigration hounds. However I was able to disperse the pack of civil servants and free my friend Noel Charles - and how wonderfully, next year, he remembered and repaid me! I myself telephoned home to learn that Diana was at Liphook, bringing home Julian for half-term - which did not deter her from meeting me at our local railway station - whereupon began a halcyon ten days with Diana and all the family - my mother, Diana's mother Ruth, all our children and many from Brookside, the Sandford and Lush house in the next field - so to speak. We had an Armistice Day Service in Ewhurst. Alan Hill and the sailor, Richard, appeared for tea and supper; we had a wonderful day in London with Julian (1/2 term holiday for him too) lunching at a London club with grandfather Charles Hill (Diana's father). A day for me followed at the War Office and the BBC, then a tremendous get together party minus children. "Julian in bed" says the diary. "Slept at Alan Hill's house, saw and heard my first 'doodle-bug'." I met my brother Cecil and Marjorie in London. We had a lovely birthday party for my youngest daughter Meriel - she was 5. After more family parties, all children went back to school and finally I left Paddington on the 4.12 and was home for lunch in Rome on 16 November.

That heavenly leave of ten days gave me the gracious and last opportunity of seeing Ruth Hill, Diana's mother, alive. Apart from my own mother, who was 20 years older than Ruth, there was no one in the world of her age whom I loved and admired more than Ruth Hill. From the very first days, when Diana and I knew that we wanted to share life together, her mother was of the same mind, and took little pains to disguise it from one of the principal parties. In fact she was the chief conspirator and it was a very wonderful power for me to know that I had her, Ruth's love, to bind Diana and myself together. What she did for us two before and after our marriage, I cannot describe, except to say that it was completely selfless love which prompted her to do so many things in pursuit of our happiness, our comfort, our success. She suffered greatly herself from ailments which were due to an internal ulcer and was very near to death (in the same maisonette) when Julian, our first born, arrived. But she survived and was nursed back to health and miraculously to a return of her great artistic talent; her great human standby then was Ursula Jarrett - a trained nurse - who not only gave all her knowledge and deep affection to Ruth as a 'case' but persuaded her, while still bed-ridden, to return to her youthful occupation - painting. We have that first endeavour of her return - a spray of leaves on the mantlepiece of her sick room: one of her finest artistic endeavours. She delighted us by joining our family party in Cairo in 1935/36 and achieved some lovely paintings of Egypt and of Wadi Halfa in the Sudan. I think those were happy days for her too and she made a number of friends. She and my father-in-law had by then given up the family home in 32 Queens Gate Terrace (from which Diana and I had been married) and Ruth bought or rented several houses or flats in the country (eg. at Mortimer, Berks) or London (219 Knightsbridge) to which Diana and I and our family were always welcome - nay more, they were home for us all during the six months' leave which the family took from Cairo or the Sudan, and the three months which I enjoyed. Her care for Diana and the little family, and also for her two bachelor sons, Richard and Alan, was the great spur to her partial recovery before the war; her lease of Westlands, Ewhurst, Surrey in July 1939 was a masterpiece of imagination and forward planning. There, bless her, was a haven, and a lovely haven, for Diana and the family, next door (a field or two away) to the house Brookside, which my sister and brother had rented for the larger Sandford family and my mother. Ewhurst with the Sandford and Hill-Lush families adjacent to each other - in the country but not so far from London - made a wonderful rendezvous for many, many people, young and old. Here, in Ewhurst, Ruth continued her painting and we have memorials, her own memorials, of two homes which she had adored and made happy by her presence. Ruth had rare (if expensive) taste: she filled Westlands not only with her radiant happiness and skilful taste, but with some of her lovely furniture. No son-in-law could have been more spoilt or rendered happier by his mother-in-law than I. She wrote splendid letters during the war - the horror and bestiality of which she found very hard to bear. She was ill for two years and caused great anxiety to Diana who, in spite of her own family concerns and the tragedy of Nicola, nursed Ruth devotedly. Ruth died on 30 January 1945: peacefully, without pain. At the end of my letter to Diana, I wrote then:

> ".... Ruth will go over to that world of beauty and light and happiness and love, the four things which made life for her, leaving with us the radiance of her unselfishness, her glorious, infectious, loveable impetuousness and she will be received as one who on earth was beautiful and lovely, who gave out love and beauty, who has enriched the lives of others with her selfless love - and her own handiwork ...."

Rome again

Returning to Rome in mid-November 1944, I was able to see Harold Macmillan and help Ellery Stone to install him as our Acting President and then had a midnight, almost Churchillian meeting, in his bedroom. He was, as always, helpful to me personally - extremely so. He went to London en route to Washington; he never reached the USA but was diverted back to the Levant to deal with the crisis in Greece where he remained for a month.

His plan for muting the 'C' submitted to London in November, had not yet received approval either from London or Washington. He wrote in January 1945 that the Allied Commission was a large and rather uncoordinated organisation, nervous about criticism and rather uncreative. Had he remained in Italy and seen what administration was created in the north, I do not think he would have written those words.

I would have rejected this criticism in part. Economically we had been uncreative due to the lack of stimulus from the Americans who led that side of the Commission; administratively we had governed the area of Italy occupied to date and were fully prepared to administer Northern Italy, when occupied. We had handed over vast areas of occupied Italy, successfully, to the Italian Government, in such a way that the military forces of the Allies were not impeded. The Italians always, the Allied Governments generally, and our Acting President, Macmillan, on this occasion, were apt to forget that all Italy was a battle ground.

However, Macmillan summed it all up when he wrote on 1 January 1945 that:

> " ..... the team here is pretty good on the administrative side, but very weak on the economic side ....."

He also referred to the astonishing accusations against British policy and administrators emanating from Washington - even in high press circles in the USA. He writes that in spite of all this nastiness (and the smears left a nasty feeling):

"…. the splendid standard of Allied cooperation, set by Eisenhower, was maintained until the end …."

Of that I can be a strong witness. One of my closest and best American colleagues in the Commission wrote, long after the campaign when I expressed my frustration about something that hadn't gone right:

"…. you know, we Americans have really only two important missions here, in Italy. The first is to manage things in such a way that after we have gone, the Italians will think kindly of us. And the second, is to learn to work with the British …."

A few years ago, in the 1980s, he wrote of meeting an Italian:

"…. on a station platform in Brindisi; when learning that I had been a member of Allied Military Government (40 years ago) his eyes lighted up and he treated me as a long lost friend …."

Duty No 1 accomplished! My very dear American correspondent ends his letter:

"…. blessings on you dear friend …."

Clearly Duty No 2 fulfilled!

Macmillan at once pleased my heart by getting up to the front as soon as possible, and working with AMG Officers in the liberation of the north - "That's how I like to see my Acting President act", I told Admiral Stone. In all his visits forward - and now he was concentrating on seeing Allied Military Government at work, rather than the fighting forces - he gave our civil affairs and military government officers a real shot in the arm. Moreover, to see a British Minister of State in civilian clothes right up in the primary operational areas impressed the Italians mightily.

On 12 December 1944, Alexander succeeded Jumbo Wilson as Supreme Allied Commander Mediterranean and, more important to us his troops, had been promoted to Field Marshall with seniority as from the capture of Rome in June 1944, thus preserving his seniority above Montgomery. General Mark Clark (US) moved from Commander of V Army USA to Commander of XV Army Group - but Alexander who had planned the strategy and led the fight, retained his strategic and almost tactical command over the Allied armies in Italy.

He moved from Forward Headquarters to Casserta but fought the Italian battle from there. Earlier, in the autumn he had decided, owing to the ever decreasing number of his troops to reduce the offensive in 1944 to give his armies a rest and start again in early 1945. We all knew that when this battle did start Alexander was out for the kill.

In the meantime we worked at our dual purpose, firstly to have everything ready when 'the balloon went up' in the north; secondly to cooperate with the Italian Government in carrying out the terms of the New Deal. I may say that, co-incident with the Government's demand that we should hand over to Italian adminstration nearly all the regions, came the plea, especially from technical ministries, not to remove Allied Commission officers from such areas. It was a great tug-of-war. We required all our officers, administrative as well as technical, for the northern industrial regions. The Italians wanted adherence to the letter but deviation from the practice of the New Deal. However, despite much criticism in some parts of the Italian and quite often the American press, we found a modus operandi - even if tempers rose!

In the Allied Commission's Review produced in 1945 by the Public Relations Officer it was written:

"Looking forward to its job in the north the Commission re-emphasised that AMG should work wholeheartedly with the Committees of Liberation for the north, when the time came, using them in an advisory capacity only and insisting that Il Comitato di Liberazione Nazionale turn over to the Military Government any power and authority assumed by them. Fifty American Officers from combat units were detailed by higher command to attend an indoctrination course at the Allied Commission for possible later assignment to AMG in the north. Plans were made for closing the frontiers both for security purposes against war criminals and to avert an uncontrolled inrush of refugees from Central Europe. Food stocks were stacked at Ancona (southeast) and Leghorn in the west, to move into the north. 20,000 *Carabinieri* were alerted for northern duty."

Christmastide 1944

Christmastide was a busy social time for the senior British officers in Military Administration.

On Christmas Eve, after four chukkas of polo in the afternoon, I went to a carol service at our Anglican Church, All Saints (temporarily in the charge of a Military Chaplain) where I worshipped most Sundays and sang lustily for an hour. I dined early and went on to the Sergeants' Dance - about three or four hundred; they all seemed to be enjoying themselves - lots of girls, WAAF and WACs and nurses! At 10.30 I left the dance, picked up Admiral Stone at his house and off we went to attend Christmas Eve Mass at St Peter's to be celebrated by Pope Pius XII - Pontifical Mass 1944. We arrived at 10.30 pm by a back entrance to the Cathedral and were taken to special seats in a separate box with "prie dieu" reserved for VIP Allied officers. There were eight choirs, each in a separate part of the building (some in the galleries). They sang, sometimes separately, at other times together. They had begun singing as we found our way to our seats and they continued for four hours, except during the celebration of the mass by the Pope himself.

The effect was quite wonderful and one felt exalted long before the beginning of the Mass. St Peter's was filling rapidly and from where we sat - very near the high altar - it did not seem as if another person could enter - let alone the Papal procession. But at 11.30 the Holy Father was borne in on his Papal Chair, held high aloft, preceded by his Papal Halberdiers with their battle axes and a section of almost armoured soldiers with swords who all reminded one of British Lifeguards! "Bravo Papa! Papa! Papa!" shouted the congregation as he was carried in his litter, shoulder high, by clerical strong men up the steps and along the aisles of the not very well lit Cathedral. He was finally set down at the foot of the high altar where, assisted by high dignitaries of the church, and acolytes with much incense, and I noticed with shock that he was aided or accompanied by two military looking guards in shining armour who stepped forward, noisily, when he proceeded, and stepped back when he receded.

The celebration was accompanied by the most lovely singing from the choir, and the atmosphere should have reached its climax when he raised the Host for public gaze - but the clink of the two guards adjacent to the altar robbed, for me, that wonderful climax of nearly all spirituality! It seemed so far distant, so foreign from the upper room where the Christ, the Pope's Christ as well as mine, had so humbly, so modestly, displayed His love to the Twelve. I have been to many services of Communion at Roman Catholic altars before 1944 and since and always found more grace therein. And yet the showing of the Sacrament was a very moving instant - chiefly due to the reverence and adoration of the congregation in St Peter's - and that belief, after all, was the spiritual intent. Most of us found places in the seats set apart for the Corps Diplomatique and VIPs to receive the Sacrament from the Pope - a notable moment for most Roman Catholics. On - on - in ever increasing beauty, if in decreasing volume, the choirs sang - music of all tongues and nations, but of one intent: "Glory to God in the Highest".

I came away with the sense and realisation of the wonderful power of the Roman Catholic Church, of its appeal to the worship of God among countless nations and peoples. I prayed: "for mine own soul's salvation grant me the simplicity of a midnight communion service in a small parish at home!"

I felt most privileged to have been part of that devout and devoted congregation in St Peter's. Of course, I longed to be with Diana at Ewhurst Parish Church!

Christmas Day 1944

We returned from St Peters at 03.30 am and by 07.15 am I had to be at All Saints Church again for Anglican Communion.

MSL to DRL 27.12.44

".... A lovely service in a beautifully decorated church with a great deal of Royal Naval silver on the altar. Back to breakfast and "family" presents at 8.15 and then a rush to get to the 9.00 am service for our "other ranks", which we held in their Mess Room. I played hymns and carols for them and read the lesson. At 10.00 we changed and on to the football ground - "Officers v Men". I played back. A good game and I emerged without being ill or hurt; a bit stiff next day. Back to the house and change and down to the men's Mess again to see the Christmas Dinner. Speeches, etc. They did very well - 60 turkeys! Back to our lunch - a little talkative as speeches were accompanied by toasts! After lunch walked to the office to go round the Duty Officers. There are seven floors and it meant about 24 visits. Back to the house to take Patricia to a cocktail party. Returned in time to change for a very quiet Christmas Dinner. Just ourselves, Tony Grafftey Smith, Guy Shippe, Evan Talbot and Patricia, and we had invited the Earl of Ranfurly (one of our best young officers - an escaped POW) and his sister-in-law, Daphne Llewellyn, Tony Quayle who is a young playwright and actor and now ADC to Admiral Stone, also a young ATS Officer, Peggy Mason, who is engaged to a POW in Germany. Patricia had arranged a lovely table centre. After dinner you won't be surprised to hear that we all settled down in a warm room we always call Pont Street .... I am going tonight to a party given by Christopher Lumby of the "The Times". He lives with the Reuters people, Spriggs .... My social life is pretty restricted so far as Italians are concerned, not only because of work but because I cannot bear to see these Romans behaving as if nothing had happened and the war was won, and I won't go to their houses. They always ask me (as a Briton) to take over the country and govern - as they are incapable."

That was my last letter to DRL written in 1944. The next year was to see great changes which at that time of writing simply did not seem possible: victory in Italy; the dream of a family reunion in Rome; the end of separation; the beginning of a new life together, and often together as a family. But we had six months of immensely hard work before that dream could come true.

The editor of our Allied Commission Bulletin ended his 1944 Christmas number as follows:

".... A chosen few among us will remember 1944 for the hysterical joy of welcome given us on our entry into Rome - even a night spent on the ground in the Villa Borghese was a small price to pay. And for all of us there will be satisfaction in recalling the warmth of the Roman summer - with all too infrequent excursions to Frigene and Ostia - and the sense of victory on the way and contact again with the life of a capital and a city unmarred by war. Winter comes again now and we shall again be cold and cough and sneeze, and it is a long way from where most of us would like to be, but in retrospect 1944 has had its points. We haven't solved all our problems; some of them even grow greater with time and even from the humble - or lower echelon - point of view the headaches are still with us and the aspirin is running out. But we have come a long way together since the gloomy days of the Internazionale and some of it has been pleasant. There is a proverb in this country: *"Buono compagnia mezza la via."* One could wish 1945 may shorten the way but however long it may be we can only be grateful for the company. *E a tutti buon capo d'anno!"*

1945

I had a pleasant surprise for the New Year, a CB [Companion of the Order of the Bath] in the Honours List, for which MasonMac had recommended me to Alexander before he left. I first heard of it by catching Patricia telephoning to our stores "My Brigadier has a CB - please send up some ribbons *quick*!" I was very grateful and doubly so because CBs are generally not awarded to officers under the rank of General. But it was even more encouraging to hear the very nice comments of my staff - and to receive a cable form Oliver Leese in Burma! The Bath is the highest order of chivalry next to the Garter and Thistle group, and Diana and I have been regular attenders of their functions and services in Westminster Abbey where the Prayer for The Order is recited daily and where the Grand Cross banners are hung in the Chapel of King Henry VII behind the High Altar.

I was beginning to see some of the lovely buildings in Rome and in a letter to Diana I describe a walk home via the Forum, the Tarpeian Rock, the Venus de Milo, the dying Gladiator - and a little later was thrilled to find some spring flowers (mimosa, azaleas, etc) heralding the warmer months ahead - for it was cold; all the hills round the city were snow clad and not one of our heating appliances in office or house was a regular performer - we had to buy "Pig" stoves for the house and office and I bought a greatcoat! It was, of course, nothing to the wintry weather at home and I was very anxious about Westlands, Ewhurst, which did not boast of central heating.

In January 1945 I carried out a tour of inspection in "the north" (our northern boundary was at that time slowly but constantly moving forward north of the Gothic Line); December and January were months of continued fighting and penetration until as Alexander wrote "sheer exhaustion" brought operations to a stand still. Our line ran roughly from a point on the Ligurian Sea (west coast), 20 miles north of Leghorn to Ravenna on the east coast, passing through a point some 20 miles from Bologna -a key town for entry to the Po Valley.

My week's tour in took me to Siena (my favourite city) and Florence where I was in the hands of Colonel Montfort, a fine and very able, understanding American, and his British deputy, Colonel Friend James, who was later Mayor of Brighton, Sussex and had been very good to me in Naples. Florence had not really recovered from the fighting there in the autumn but good progress was being made in civil affairs. Pistoia and the lovely town of Lucca were next on our programme: Lucca, the walled city, on the walls of which one used to drive horse-drawn carriages; Pisa with its leaning tower and Leghorn badly damaged; then home via Florence once more and Areggio - lunch on Lake Trasimene - the attractive old town of Perugia - and so to Rome.

It had been a good tour and I was satisfied with the results of the two purposes of my visit: firstly to see the AMG Rear in Tuscany, Umbria and the whole territory between Rome and the Gothic Line; secondly to see the AMGs in reserve for the real north - they had the most difficult task of keeping on their toes with nothing special to do; and thirdly a quick visit not of inspection but of encouragement to the Spearheads.

In December, for instance, the AMG entered Faenza just in time to relieve from starvation some 6,000 citizens hiding in cellars in the town. People were grinding grain in coffee mills. The town had been devastated - every tower that might have been used as an observation post by the Allies was destroyed by the Germans before they left. The food situation was not bad - some had been hidden, AMG produced the rest. The sick and wounded were taken from the old hospital which the Germans had used as a machine gun post into the AMG hospital. The partisans had helped considerably. Doctors, nurses, technicians from the waterworks were being allowed back to the shattered town and orderly life was slowly being restored. Half the priceless and famous exhibition of Faenza ceramics were saved - the rest lay under a heap of rubble and might be preserved. *Carabinieri* came back quickly to support the one brave man who stayed. The *partigani* had been helpful and cooperative - arms had been handed in to AMG and the *Sindaco* of pre-Mussolini days had returned to office. I was very impressed by the demeanour of all the Italians in their stricken town.

At Forli, a largish town, further east, life had not been so easy for the AMG team. There had been demonstrations against requisitioning by Allied troops and the troops themselves, having borrowed 150 chairs from the Italians for Christmas, duly returned them: but not one chair was useable. A bad or careless military unit could spell a mint of trouble for AMG.

As always, the Military Government teams, Spearhead and Forward, were immensely hospitable. I always hoped (and believed) that my visits had given support and done good. It was always good to be out and about with these men and on return to Rome and its comforts (sometimes) one inevitably repented of plans gone astray, efforts disappointed, envy at being merely the chief paper producer, not having borne the brunt of battle. But that was inevitable. One could try, not only to put right a few wrongs, but to guide and support many who were complete amateurs - but very good amateurs - in the game of looking after a civilian population in such a way that they acquired the art of looking after themselves.

The early months of 1945 spelt busy times at HQ in Rome and Ellery Stone was suffering from some strained vertebrae, due to washing so he said, so that a good deal of the semi-political problems came my way. However, Harold Macmillan was about and I saw a great deal of him and learned even more, for he had a happy way of going straight to the summing up of a case without undue talking. Alexander and he dined at our villa - a signal honour and were "terribly nice and friendly". Then suddenly Macmillan would shoot off to Athens! He had been more than helpful in trying to achieve my promotion, of which both he and Alexander were valiant prosecutors - failing before the dead hand of the Civil Affairs Department of the War Office. The impression we gained was that there were so many Generals out of jobs in London that they dare not make any more promotions.

In the meantime publication appeared in American and British papers of the New Deal for Italy, spelling out, for all to read, the policy which we had, without publicity, pursued since the Allied Commission came into real being a year previously. The New Deal had a mixed reception from the Italian Government and press; for the Allied Commission and its officials, as I wrote to Diana it meant:

> "…. not much less work for us; as we pull out of the south we shall probably take on more in the north - and northern Italy with its twenty five million people is going to be a real problem …."

Regional Commissioners' Meeting March 1945

The first Regional Commissioners' Meeting since August 1944 was held on 8-9 March in Rome with full attendance of all the dignitaries from the field and the resident ones at HQ. Our Acting President, Harold Macmillan, presided and met the Commissioners en masse for the first time; in the evening he gave us all a cocktail party.

Unfortunately, Ellery Stone was still away "sick" so I had to take the Chair. It was indeed a very interesting meeting after a fine start by Harold Macmillan, who spoke on the New Deal and the Allied Commissions' role vis a vis the Italian Government as a consequence of the new status for Italy. He confirmed that the Allied Commission's objectives were still:

1 to facilitate military operations;
2 to assist in the immediate rehabilitation of the Italian population;
3 to prepare for the transfer of territory and administrative functions to the Italians.

He predicted that the new populations of the north would have an invigorating effect on the Military Government/Allied Commission operations but he warned us that, should hostilities cease, there would be no collapse of the Allied Commission's functions but rather an intensification and a continuation of activity so long as Allied troops remained in Italy.

Indeed we had already begun seriously to think of the next problems after the one before us - which had not even yet come to a head. By "we" I mean the top flight in the Commission and at Alexander's Headquarters.

I told the meeting that we had, under the New Deal, withdrawn all officers form southern regions except 66, of whom seven remained in Sicily, two in Sardinia to look after the coal mines, 24 in Italian Government territory (chiefly supply, finance, transportation men) and 33 in the commune of Naples which still remained entirely under AMG. I foresaw 1,000 officers being stationed in the northern provinces. I see that my two stalwarts Lombardy and Dunlop, whose region would be Venezia, pleaded strongly for appointments to be left to the men on the spot and not superimposed either by Italian or Commission Headquarters. This was a constant worry especially with the Italian Ministers who would replace Italian officials in the Forward areas with men of their own choice. I ruled out any idea of an Advanced Commission Headquarters in the north unless it was called for by Regional Commissioners, though the Chief Commissioner might have a Forward Liaison Officer in order to keep us au fait with any operations undertaken by the Italian Government. It was, I declared, our intention to hand over to the Italian Government at the earliest possible moment.

Henry Hopkinson, our Political Adviser, spoke strongly on the use of Italian Personnel in the northern regions and emphasised that the policy should be to use the personnel of the Committees of National Liberation.

Colonel W J Legge, our splendid Director of Food appearing for nearly the last time, gave an excellent description and prognosis of the food situation in the south, centre (including Rome) and north (when we reached it) of the country.

Mr Braine, one of the few British civilians in the Commission, seconded, I think from the Ministry of Labour, gave "one of the most interesting and lucid expositions". The keynote of our Labour policy would be encouragement to accredited organisations and a sympathetic approach by Military Government. No deportation of agitators - they would only go elsewhere. The Italian Central Labour Authorities (CGIL) would hold a conference as soon as possible.

Preparation for holding local elections was also considered with Ralph Temple, a very good American officer on Gerald Upjohn's staff. Finally, Stewart Brown, Director of our Public Relations, told of his plans to produce worthwhile stories of achievement.

Harold Macmillan wound us up with some very encouraging remarks and it was clear that everyone was really on tip top form ready to get down to the job in the north and that we were all keyed up with excitement of what was to come.

This was destined to be our last Regional Commissioners' Conference of the war - and it was a good meeting. I think Harold Macmillan inhaled a better understanding of the planning and coordination which lay behind the work of the AMG Spearhead and follow-up work which he had seen in the field. We all enjoyed a very happy party as his guests that evening.

Leave March - April 1945

Then I was offered a month's leave - special concession to Senior Officers who had foregone leave in the past two or three years. Grafftey Smith went very quickly but I was forced to stay because of Ellery Stone's vertebrae, but got away at last and spent nearly five very happy weeks with the family - or families, because my mother, then aged 84, and sundry Sandfords lived next door. I had dreamt of and proposed a fortnight's holiday a deux for Diana and myself, but Easter and the school holidays most conveniently occurred during those five weeks and we fell to the temptation of a real family party at home for the whole five weeks. I arrived at the end of March and for a few days Diana and I were able to devote the time to each other and see a good deal of my mother, brother Cecil and various Sandford children. Also many friends in Ewhurst who had been so good to Diana and the family when Nicola had died in June 1944 and Ruth, my mother-in-law, died in January 1945. We visited London; I certainly went to the War Office in search of promotion - unavailing - but we saw a host of friends and relations. When the three children came back from school we had four good weeks at home - with excursions, one of which was to Winchester to finalise Julian's acceptance into Colin Hunter's House, provided he achieved the scholastic standard (which he did), and Sylvia and Meriel's entry into St Swithun's, Winchester.

I cannot remember any doodle bugs about, even in London; in fact they had been laid to rest some months before, but the memory of the V2 bomb was not so far away and although, by March, Holland was bearing the brunt of their attack, an occasional bomb would reach England.

Those five weeks in the last spring of the war were full of happiness.

Return to Italy

I returned to Italy on 24 April 1945 and, as I wrote, judging from the war map which I studied on arrival in Caserta and news from the north next day in Rome, arrived in the nick of time for things were quite definitely on the move.

The offensive which had begun on 5 April while I was at home had developed during the month and V Army (US) had entered Bologna on 21 April to find the Polish Division of the VIII Army (British) already there! This was the beginning of the last phase which carried the Allied armies from the Apennines to the Alps in a little over a year.

On 22 and 23 April we had crossed the River Po. By 29 April Venice had fallen in the east and we had driven through Genoa on the west to reach Savoie and the French border on the west at Menton; Milan fell on 30 April and Turin on the west and Trieste on the east fell on 2 May.

General Alexander wrote:

"…. The last battle in Italy was a text book military operation which by first enveloping the enemy's left wing in a classical outflanking manoeuvre and then breaking through, with a sudden blow, his weakened centre, drove him against the River Po where he was annihilated. By 2 May an army of half a million men had been destroyed and on that day all the enemy forces in Italy and Austria laid down their arms in unconditional surrender …."

Harold Macmillan paid AMG the compliment of visiting Spearhead Units of VIII and V Armies during the advance at the end of April. He wrote:

"…. Colonel Benson had laid on an excellent programme of AMG activities …."

Macmillan visited seven towns just captured under the guidance of our Regional Commissioner, Colonel Al Bowman, US, a first class man; the next day he was in Ravenna and Rimini and then met Brigadier Hume, V Army, who had established himself in Bologna, just captured; on they went to Modena, the occupation of which town he took his part, for he entered it before the final surrender.

"…. The leader of the partisans kissed me on both cheeks on being told that I was the famous Harold Macmillan …."

He was formally enroled as a partisan with armlet!

On his return south Macmillan went to Assisi - to be out of the way at the moment of German surrender. He caused me and Patricia a rough midnight excursion thereby for on the night of the surrender a "Most-urgent-operational-immediate" cypher telegram was brought to my house for urgent transmission to Acting President Allied Commission resting in Assisi. Patricia was dragged out of bed, also my driver, and swiftly we went to our office and despatched the news to Macmillan - it was of course the news that General Morgan, Chief of Staff to Alexander, had accepted the surrender of the German General Vietinghoff, and terms agreed. This was 29 April but it was 2 May before we knew that the terms of the surrender would be honoured by the German Commander who had changed since 29 April! Macmillan records his delight that Alexander obtained his surrender before the unconditional surrender of all German forces in Europe was signed on 7 May. So were we his "Third Army" proud of our Field Marshall.

There followed 8 May VE Day on which we all attended a religious Service in the Mussolini Stadium. A disappointing affair; no imagination and dreadful surroundings.

My feelings about VE Day were summed up in my letter to DRL written that day.

MSL to DRL 8.5.45

"…. Listening to the PM's (Churchill) announcement this afternoon, I thought, as I suppose many of us did, of the years between. Long years: for some, packed with interest and novelty, and business in its true sense; for others, made longer by the dull routine of life; for all of us, more full of sorrow and unhappiness than of joy.

"And now they have gone. The endless years of separation are over. The separation that affected countless millions.

"Because, horrible as is destruction in war, of physical and material bodies, I think the separation of husbands and wives and children and families is the most horrible thing brought about by war. For millions it brings final, irrevocable parting, at any rate on this earth, and for many more like ourselves it is a temporary but terrible break in family life. When one thinks of the millions of slave labourers who are now walking in every direction in Europe - we think that we shall have a million such to deal with -Italians, French and Jews - one is appalled by the bestiality of mankind ...."

MSL to DRL 9.5.45

".... I have thought so much of you yesterday and today. My mind went back to August 1939, when we drove to Reading West - of the way I heard of the outbreak of war, in Glasgow on board Montcalm; of my listening to the news of the invasion of France in May 1940; of Mussolini's alliance with Germany in June 1940 and his stab in our back; after my devastating attempts to come on leave from the Sudan - and then that long wait until 1943 - three and a half years. For with all the interest and excitement which I have had, the being without you has been the overriding beastliness.

"However, let me tell you, straight away, that Lady Charles (I dined at the Embassy this evening) suggested that they should ask for you to come out with them when they, the Charles', return from England. They hope to go on leave this month for six weeks. One must not hope too much because we still have to get military leave to get you out - that is going ahead - but ....

"Yesterday, 8th, we took as a holiday but I don't know that it was for me, for we have (a) a political crisis here (in Rome); the liberation of the north has set free the most virile and intelligent of the Italians; (b) Trieste and the Yugoslavs - the most delicate problem the solution of which I cannot see, though I am deeply involved; and (c) the French, on the west, who are infiltrating the Piedmont and doing very much what the Yugs are doing in the east ...." Our Allied VE Day Service (unimaginative) had been followed (for me representing the Allied Commission) by a most beautiful Memorial Service in memory of the sister of the Italian Regent (Umberto) held in the Chapel Royal at the Quirinale. A very Royal, Corps Diplomatique affair .... but a really lovely hour in the beautiful chapel with wonderful music - an unaccompanied Requiem Mass ...."

That brought me back to what should have been the spirit of our VE Day Service in the Stadium.

In the meantime, although hostilities had ceased, administration had to be maintained. Let me recapitulate what the final Allied advance had meant from the point of view of the Italian population and the Allied Military Government and Commission.

On 20 April Bologna had fallen - with Allied-trained Italian Army troops having the honour of participating in the liberation of one of their chief cities for the first time. In swift thrusts the Allied Armies had swept into the Po Valley and up to the Alps. The great cities of the north - Milan, Genoa, Venice and Turin - all were liberated by patriots before the Allied army forces moved in. Everywhere valiant patriot forces had saved industrial plants and power installations from German destruction, preserved order and executed Fascists, including the former Duce, Benito Mussolini.

The north was virtually intact and full of energy, although fuel and raw materials were lacking as the Nazis in Italy surrendered unconditionally on 1 May 1945. The Allied Commission was entering the last phase of its mission.

Neither the Italian population, south and north, nor the Italian Government nor the *Partigani* - the CNLA - were in a condition stable enough to face the future of Italy in the coming times of peace. The danger from the common enemies (note the plural), Fascism and Germany, having been defeated by arms (chiefly of wholly present Allies and quondam enemies), some influence had to prevent the existing militant portion of the civilian population, ie. the *Partigani* (mostly heavily armed) from becoming an obstacle to the return of democratic life and government. This they might do by imposing post-war militant government, supported by an armed ally from outside Italy. It was vital to the Allies, to the United Nations and all that we stood for, that democracy should be established in Italy.

And so the Chief of Staff of the Allied Commission and AMG with the Rear Commission regions behind them entered the Italian world of politics! Not by discussions with or agreements with the party politicians of the Italian Government who were so anxious to go to the north and show their power, but by slow and gentle but relentless persuasion of the *Partigani* (CLNA) that government by armed men was bad government, that mortal destruction of one's political leaders was neither necessary or *comme-il-faut*; that Italy free from the fear of firearms would be a better and happier Italy than one controlled by the bullet, and that the *Partigani* would have their recompense in the final democratic state of Italy.

In these weeks and months the Allied Commission through its Forward officers, probably achieved their finest services to the Italian nation. They followed no text-book, no political instruction; they played every scene of the drama as it was presented to them, relying on the general principles which we had discussed, on various Regional Conferences when the early experience of *Partigani* was encountered - and these principles proved correct.

There was at Headquarters of the Commission in Rome an almost general desire to go north and see what was happening. I was very happy to remain en poste and did not leave Rome, staying at the end of the information line until a month had elapsed. We had not encouraged the Italian Government in Rome to send their Ministers to the north early, although several went and were encouraged by our Regional Commissioners to cooperate; but we wanted the *Partigani* and Military Government confrontations to settle down.

There was no doubt about it that, whereas in the south provision of food was our main problem, in the north the maintenance of public security took priority - and some notable breaches of security did take place, mostly before the arrival of Allied troops or Military Government. There occurred a vacuum between the Fascist Republican regime aided by German arms (and Blackshirt *Carabinieri*) and the arrival of American or British troops with AMG. In that vacuum the CLN or CLNAI took rapid and rigorous action. Their first action was to exterminate their Fascist opponents and oppressors - and this they did rigorously. Figures of executions of Fascists or Neo-Fascists during the vacuum were difficult to asses with any credibility, but there is little doubt that executions of these unfortunate people with or without proper trial between 25 April and 5 May, numbered between five and ten thousand. The arrival of Military Government put a stop to mass executions but inevitably, in the early days of AMG, murders continued until the *Partigani* could be brought to order - which they quickly were. The Italian Government did their utmost to assist the Military Government units, for they realised they were the only authority which could save the north from civil war. Moderation and expediency, however, gradually prevailed.

Eventually even the purge of the Italian Civil Service and the professions, which was meant only to penalise Fascists active and influential before liberation, was gradually diminished and by 1946 only a few of the 800,000 Civil Servants serving had been removed.

Returning to Rome, the capital received a visit early in May by a body of northern CLN *Partigani* who called on the Italian Prime Minister and Government, on Admiral Stone in the Allied Commission and on the Embassies. It was interesting to meet them.

And then the problem of Trieste and Venezia Giulia descended on us. It was to remain a problem throughout 1945 and 1946 but during 1945 we found a peaceful solution which led to a temporary agreement with the Allied Military Government established there.

It was about this time that I had a look at the north myself (the Chief Commissioner and others had all been there), and so with Tony Grafftey Smith and Patricia and my stenographer Staff Sergeant Gilliland who had never stirred from Rome for months, we set out. A good arrival in Bologna when we arrived just in time to attend Colonel Al Bowman's Regional Conference.

MSL to DRL 29.5.45

"…. Through the Gothic Line and the Futa Pass; lovely country, windy roads, lots of streams; but villages terribly smashed by shells and bombs. In future noone in Italy will live on a main road, near a bridge or near a railway station! If they do - and indeed if any one in Europe does so - it will be evident that war will be no more …. We dined and had a look at Bowman's sumptuous villa overlooking Bologna. Bologna sausages are not made here but at Modena close by and were not made at all during this war until some 500 horses arrived the other day from Austria …. Slept in honeymoon suite of hotel but Tony and I were kept awake all night by the most awful clatter in the main street. Changed rooms. Conference all next day. That evening from the hill above Bologna, among fireflies in the air and glow-worms on the ground, looked at Partisans and Poles still celebrating victory by firing green, white and red rockets. Next morning in my cold bath (new bathroom) brought my head up sharply against the tap and filled bath and room with blood, only staunched by pouring whole new tin of talcum powder on to the top of my skull - tottered out leaving bathroom scented as no respectable bedroom should and a pyramid of TP on top of my head!

"…. We crossed the River Po and passed many columns of filthy Germans - all coming south. Reached Padua and after three hours talk were wafted off to Venice by Brigadier Dunlop, my British Regional Commissioner, about 25 miles away. It was packed with Allied troops. The Grand Canal was a mass of gondolas, motor boats and "Ducks". The last had been introduced to break a strike of gondoliers demanding higher fares. A marvellous sight! We pulled up at the villa of Lady Castelrosse (now in the States) which had been requisitioned by the Regional Commissioner. An erotic villa full of white satin and mirrors; I discovered a button by the bedside which opened the back gate of the villa leading on to a small canal - dear Lady Castelrosse! We dined at the Grand Hotel - a very good dinner - and then went on to some other villa for a glass of port and so to bed. A lovely evening …. we will do the trip together yet! Next morning I set off feeling very piano (too much port?) and we motored to the edge of the Dolomites, from Padua to Belluno, passing through Vittoria Veneto. We lunched in the square of Belluno where from four lamp posts hang wreaths bearing the names of four *Partigani* whose bodies had been found by our troops on entry, hanging from the lamp posts. Back to Padua, where we had dinner, and a conference on the future of the Commission with Henry Hopkinson (Embassy), Grafftey Smith and Dunlop. Next day to VIII Army HQ to meet Benson near Udine and a long discussion on the Trieste situation - Benson was also in charge of the British area occupied in Austria and in the evening drove up through a vivid and graphic thunderstorm. Next day to Vittoria Veneto and then started on the most perfect day's motoring through the Dolomites. One town, Cortina, was a very large hospital centre for German prisoners and Germans were walking about the town and occupying the best hotels, blast them. Such was the POW situation - the proper collection and centralisation into concentration camps of some prisoners took weeks. We lunched in the valley outside Cortina - perfect skiing country -

and finally came down the valley to Bolzano, all through German speaking country, which, of course, the Germans hoped to annex after winning the war! Just outside Bolzano, after dinner, we saw the most amazing view. Overlooking the town is a great triangular massif of the Dolomites - about 40 miles away - snow clad. The setting sun had just caught it and it became a mass of flaming pink."

We had a late conference that night on how to deal with the mass of Italian plant, tools, immense stocks of clothing, silks, pictures and art treasures looted by the Germans:

"…. We are keeping a number of Germans in Bolzano to make an inventory, under Allied Supervision, and to help unravel the enormous mass of shear wanton loot. We make them walk two miles from their camp to the listing centre each day …."

I had to own to my companions that having served in four countries looking after Civil Affairs I had never experienced such horror at the crime of looting as by these bestial Nazi Germans.

Next morning I visited a refugee camp. Two thousand entries clocked in on that morning:

"…. We are moving between 10,000 and 20,000 refugees every day in *every direction* - north, south, east and west; a superhuman task but all is going well. There are representatives of every nationality in the camp: Italian, Russian, Yugoslav, Pole, Greek, Jew, Chinese. I had a long talk with the officer running the camp and running it well - a young American. A talk with the Provincial Commissioner, one Colonel Dusty Miller, and then for the south - destination Milan.

"We were blocked for two hours all down the first valley by an endless convoy of German transport (and men) going south; buses, lorries, horse-drawn carts, all carrying German prisoners who had perpetrated the damage and loot in this lovely country and now, thank God, were *hors de combat*.

"We reached Lake Garda and motored for 25 miles along its west bank passing through 57 tunnels all of which were filled with lathes and every kind of machine for making aeroplane engines. The Germans had removed all the machinery from factories in the plains below, together with the factory hands, and carried on the work on the side of the lake in perfect safety. In a lovely villa on the lakeside (not so beautiful as Cadennabia on Lake Como of 1932) we had a long and useful talk with AMG V Army USA (always a difficult approach!). We sent Patricia forward to forewarn of our arrival in Milan, dined at a lakeside restaurant (Grafftey Smith and I) and set forth for Milan, 100 miles to the west at 8.30 pm. Tyre trouble postponed our arrival in Milan until past midnight. Next morning we had a wonderful reception from Charlie Poletti - in his element. He had arrived in Milan before the Spearhead AMG of V Army (who had ordered him out!) and I believe, though he never confessed to it, he saw the bodies of Mussolini and his mistress hanging there in that city. I never knew officially. I knew I could leave Milan safely in the hands of Poletti, so after a morning's discussion I left for Turin. Had lunch there and a very good talk with the Regional Commissioner. Motored back to Milan through the villages on a festive Italian Sunday afternoon, all the villagers on bicycles! My driver and I decided that double contraception - human and bicycles was called for. A great man, my driver Holden, a street bookie in peace time. Had a most peaceful dinner in Milan with Tony Grafftey Smith, Charlie Poletti, Arthur Hancock and Patricia. Strawberries and whipped tin cream! Discussed and voted against setting up of HQ Allied Commission in Milan to which we were all opposed. But Admiral Stone may have committed himself and I flew off quickly next day to Rome to have any such suggestion quashed! I trusted Charlie Poletti more than one hundred of Allied Commission HQ. I won! Back to Milan to join my small party whom I found had not wasted their time. Grafftey Smith had long wanted to tie together the Roman and northern strings and to inculcate into the industrial financiers of the north, some of the Allied art of international financial thinking. Henry Hopkinson flew with me from Rome to Milan where he was ensconced as Northern Political Adviser to the Embassy (no longer did ACC officially have such men!) and I think he had a lot of problems to place before his Ambassador. On the whole, however, whether it was due to the influence of the Italian Government (who claimed that honour) or the political tactful handling by the AMG officers (which I most definitely claimed) or whether as always, it was a mixture of the two was debateable, but in the majority of cases the *Partigani* (CLN) had given way to disciplined forces of law and order."

From Milan we went to Turin, a pleasant city where I found the Regional Commissioner in good heart - Colonel Marshall (USA). A very pleasant dinner at a village outside Turin and next day a further conference in the city after which we went south.

"…. Arrived in Alessandria after lunch in a poppy field. Found it full of beastly grey uniforms and even greyer policemen ordering us about. Patricia in her most exporative mood began to spit and called them German pigs and I told them to get the hell out of it - and then we found they were our brave Brazilian allies! The descent to Genoa is lovely and we found Brigadier Carr ensconced in office in one of the big shipping offices. Genoa is a bit battered - bombs and naval bombardment. We found the harbour extensively mined …. Arrived in Rome next day at 3.00 am. Staff Conference at 9.00 am. Found a mountain of work and then arrived Sir Desmond Morton, PA to Winston Churchill. Had a long discussion on future of the Commission …."

I found Sir Desmond more interesting and amusing

than sound in his views but we got on very well together and, of course, he was full of delightful stories about Churchill; a bit nebulous and not always right on the facts.

Our principle problems at HQ in June 1945, now circled round the stupid and very offensive behaviour of the French in the Val d'Aosta where they had sent troops over the border and put on an air of intransigence, and in Trieste where Tito's Yugoslav troops were threatening to occupy the town in violation of agreements made with Field Marshall Alexander in 1944.

At the start of the following letter I had written to Diana that the Executive Commissioner of the Allied Commission "the Head of Alexander's Civil Service" (MSL) had turned political and had written a despatch entitled "The future of Italy" which started "Italy is at the parting of the ways" and continued somewhere ".... allowing her to emerge from defeat through co-belligerency to a more healthy state of partnership ...." I was trying, as I told Diana, to extract some firm policy - our respective Governments then having no policy. One, USA, being in the throes of a domestic election, was doing its best to divest itself of responsibility and of the necessity of declaring a policy.

MSL to DRL 25.6.45

> ".... I fear that the coordination and cooperation which brought USA and UK through this war is fast disappearing and unilateral action, nationalistic approaches and suspicion are all making their appearance .... Desmond Morton comes out and wants to form a British Mission .... The US Government in the meantime, suddenly *publishes* to the world that Admiral Stone is to be succeeded by a civilian "Colonel James Douglas". No word to the Allied Commission nor to the British Government .... In the meantime, with Stone tearing his hair and the wires hot with protests and counter accusations (chiefly American) we have to endeavour to administer Allied Military Government in northern Italy, to say nothing of Venezia Giulia (Trieste). In the former the people are very jumpy, and we have not yet been able to establish the "fourth freedom" - freedom from fear - because so many people are still armed and so little difference lies between Fascist tyranny and Communist tyranny. Both still have nasty habits of lynching their enemies. In Venezia Giulia it is fair to say that the Yugoslavs are doing their utmost to sabotage any agreement we may have!"

Such was the administrative and political situation when our first post-war Regional Commissioners' Meeting met in Rome on 27/28 June 1945 of which more in a moment.

In the meantime, I had been in close touch with that splendid and lovely person Grace Charles, the Ambassador's wife, who had worked hard on my behalf "as the senior British officer in the Allied Commission" with my Commander in Chief Field Marshall Alexander. She had encouraged him to say that he would countenance my wife's arrival in Rome. The day before the conference I went to Casserta to see Alexander's Chief of Staff who had the authority to write the letter to the War Office in London. I saw the Field Marshall himself also: "Let her dress up in some kind of uniform!" he said as he gave his blessing. I returned to Rome armed with a very precious document conveying my Commander-in-Chief's authority for Mrs D R Lush to enter his zone of Command. Knowing my Civil Affairs Branch in London I had every suspicion that they would, in some way, block even this issue and I determined to produce the letter, even to the Secretary of State himself - after my Regional Commissioners' Meetings.

Of course, my own future, as well as that of the Commission was in doubt. The Civil Affairs Section in the War Office had, in their concern for Military Government in Germany and the Far East, lost all interest, all enthusiasm, all concern for the British Component of the Allied Commission in Italy - 600 British Officers. When General Anderson the Head of the Section visited Italy, I was away in the north, unaware of his advent. He came and went leaving no message of encouragement or hope for the future of any British Officer in the Commission. From May 1945 the Civil Affairs Section of the War Office apparently washed their hands of us as a Commission and as a British unit for which they were responsible. Not that I had ever nurtured any regard for the Section, either for business or for any sympathetic regard to any of the British officers in the Commission and, perhaps, least of all to myself. Their efforts at assisting families or their counterparts in Italy were deplorable. They could not even ensure that mail from or to England reached its destination by the shortest possible route and in quick time. We in Italy had the feeling that the Civil Affairs Section did not really care for people.

Thus at the end of June 1945 we held a Regional Commissioners' Conference in Rome - probably the last, we thought, in the history of the Allied Commission. We were all light hearted in the knowledge of a good job done.

All the northern barons attended: Brigadier Hume of V Army US, greatly decorated by said US Army; Con Benson, his usual urbane self, now thinking perhaps more of Austria, parts of which he was governing; the valiant Charlie Poletti from Lombardy, which, from Milan, he ruled perhaps a little more sedately than his beloved Palermo in days gone by - Charlie came to our meeting in Rome half an hour late, explaining that the southern heat of Rome had caused him to oversleep, but Admiral Stone and all of us waited for him - was it not election year, and was he not bound to be in New York again before Polling Day? Brigadier Dunlop, the wise "old" man from Venezia cautioned much care in the matter of Trieste, the hot spot to the east of his Venezia region: he was due to leave us soon for Hamburg where he earned glory; Al Bowman celebrating his first annual birthday in charge of the southern province of Emilia; Colonel Marshal of Piedmont, with Turin as his capital, and the French invading Val d'Aosta; and finally Brigadier Carr from his port of Genoa - all well administratively, but death to ships, owing to thousands of mines in the harbour. All were presided over by Admiral Stone, the Chief Commissioner - "cool, imposing and decorative in one of those Navy uniforms" as Tom Bergin wrote of him. We had too some Italian Ministers and Civil Servants with us who listened a good deal but who also spoke urging more Italian say in some project or other. Admiral Stone spoke of the need to strengthen the cultural aspects of democracy with a big D and promised the arrival of The United States Information Service and the British Council. Were they strong enough, I asked myself, to prevent the Communist *Partigani* from preaching Communism? For the war against Fascism having been won we were now faced with the menace not of fascism resurgent but imminent Communism. And suddenly one began to care - to realise that we were out of the Fascist frying pan and into the red flames of the Russian flag! Russian domination of Europe was now blatant and intense; the American leadership having prevented Alexander from his strategic right hook and his pre-emptive (to the Russians) entry into Austria, were now sending the USIS and Attlee of the British Council to prevent the power of Russia from dominating Europe - or at any rate the south west thereof! So when Admiral Stone touched on the possible states of Italy and advocated full aid, I saw a reason for further help to Italy and to Europe. I remembered Macmillan's warnings and realised that there might be more useful work to be done in this part of the world.

The Conference went on to debate free elections in Italy, "a consummation devoutly to be wished but in the consensus of the moment, somewhat dubious of execution" - a beautiful Berginese epigram! Gerald Upjohn, about to return to the majesty of British Courts of Justice and high standing therein, handed over to the local government expert (and Director) of the Allied Commission, Colonel Cripps - a wise, realistic administrator. He pointed out the difficulties of organising free elections throughout Italy; he would need one hundred days of preparation. The Chief Commissioner, Admiral Stone, with Italian Ministers present, ordered Cripps to put the work in hand at once (by 15 July). It was agreed by the Conference that it was an Allied responsibility to see that Italy had a free and honest-to-goodness election and it was further stressed that the use of Allied troops would be necessary and desirable to ensure free voting without fear. "Guys have died for democracy here in Italy" Charlie Poletti exclaimed; "We can't walk out now and leave chaos". So the Allied Commission was committed to arrange free elections with Allied troops present at the polling booths. In fact, political elections together with a referendum on the monarchy were held in June 1946 and although there were still Allied troops in the country I cannot recollect that their definite employment was involved. The elections were Italian but very peaceful.

Public security, of course, took an important place in discussion and whereas Regional Commissioners at first spoke optimistically of public safety, and the disarmament of partisans, when it came to robbing their regions of police to help Venezia Giulia, where public security was clearly about to count very high in the problem book, the northern barons were loath to divest themselves of a single police officer! I could not blame them, for the *Partigani* were a very volatile lot of Communists.

We all noted with great satisfaction that our two peripatetic (Italy - London - Washington) American economic chiefs were prophesying that, on this side of the changing picture, Italy was turning the first corner even a month or two after hostilities had ceased. "One solid fact buttresses this thesis, namely that the critical deficiency in coal will be met!" Keystone of this partial recovery was the planned partial recovery of the steel industry - up to one million tons per annum. The future of the Italian power situation seemed more hopeful than we could have dreamed. They told us, and we could hardly believe it, that the north, where hostilities had only recently ceased, would supply power to the centre of Italy and the centre would help the south. It seemed an upside-down prophesy, but it was true, and when one looked at the figures one began to understand how terribly the centre of Italy had suffered from the ravages of battle in the early and summer months of 1945. An important industry such as textiles was expected to reach 50% of full production by the autumn of 1945.

I listened with amusement to the American Head of our Economic Section at Rome, recently joined, detached as they all were in that section from the Commission as an entity, discussing the economic future of the north with Charlie Poletti, who, centred on Milan, regarded himself as the economic and certainly the industrial king of liberated Italy. Of course, our Charlie won the day and economic centralisation in the north came about - fostered not by the Commission but by the Italian Government itself. Nor could I quite credit that "there had been no ports open for the delivery, recently, of 40,000 tons of coal in June". The destruction of Germany was brought home to one on learning that the Ruhr coal mines were working at 3% capacity!

Mercifully food supplies in the north were reported satisfactory, and transport was better than expected. Military units about to be disbanded soon would hand over their trucks to civilian truck units - Allied or Italian. That was a wonderful gesture on the part of the Military units.

We had invited a number of Italians to this Allied Meeting, including the Minister of Reconstruction and the Minister of Transportation. The report ran:

> "the two Ministers came through in good enough shape despite some pretty straight cross-examination from the Regional Commissioners. Their proposal for the appointment of a Minister for the North did not find favour."

And so closed one of our final full Regional Commissioners' meetings in Rome. One could not but look back; just over 15 months ago we were hardly an integral cohesive Commission. Now we had achieved what we set out to do and what was expected of us. The laurels went to Benson of VIII Army, and Hume of V Army who never let us down. Only just behind were the others - Dunlop, Marshal, Carr, Bowman, Montfort, Hancock and the HQ men Grafftey Smith, Fiske, Upjohn, Legge, Shippe, Talbot, Braine, Fothergill, Wellor, and my personal staff of Patricia Russell, Staff Sergeant Gilleland, Drivers Preston and Holden.

Together we had helped Field Marshall Alexander to exact from the Germans unconditional surrender. We had not fired a shot, but these men round the table had never let him down.

We had received unsparing assistance, moral and material, from the fighting forces in Italy; once convinced of our needs, the leaders from Eisenhower, Wilson, Alexander and Robertson downwards, had seldom withheld help and ready help, whether by way of orders to the troops about treatment of the civil population, provision of flour for that population or the sparing of works of art in captured towns. Alexander's allusion to us as his "Third Army" was a thank you good enough for us. I wish I could record the same gratitude to the Civil Affairs section of our Governments in London or Washington. They maintained no personal touch and were invariably late in providing help: invariably dumb in appreciation of things done.

DRL to Italy July 1945

A week later I found myself in an aircraft en route for London. In my pocket was my Commander-in-Chief's permission for Diana to join me in Italy. It was up to me to convert that into a military permit issued in London by the Allied Forces Headquarters. I can remember little of those ten days which involved firstly acquainting Diana of the plan and arranging with her the disposal of our goods and the chattels of Westlands in Ewhurst. Luckily the owners of the house had arrived home from Kenya and were prepared to live in the house, as our sub-tenants, and look after the furniture and said goods and chattels; secondly, we had to plan for the physical guardianship of our three children (a) for the summer holidays in 1945 about to commence; (b) for the Michaelmas Term; (c) for Christmas holidays and their passage to Italy by sea sometime during those holidays. Thirdly, and curiously, lastly, we had to make an honest worker of Diana by enroling her in some relief organisation to take up duty in Italy: "Get her into some kind of uniform" were Alexander's words. Fourthly, we had to obtain the military permit and arrange with Sir Noel and Lady Charles, together with the Foreign Office, for Diana to fly with them to Italy under Foreign Office auspices at the end of Sir Noel's leave any day after 20 July.

To cut short a long story of seven intensive days of telephoning, meetings - much sympathetic and ready help from many people - the ready assent of Diana and the three children themselves to their desertion for six months; a willing acceptance by Sir Charles Emerson, Chief of the InterGovernmental Committee on Refugees (IGCR) to enrol Diana as a member of staff and a very warm invitation to Diana from the Charles's to join them on their return flight to Italy in about a week; finally the promise of a permit for Diana to that end by the Permit Office of Allied Forces HQ.

I have spelt out in some detail one of the most moving (in more senses than one) weeks in my busy life. As always, for Diana especially and indeed for both of us, the wonderful expectation of life together again entailed sorrow at separation from the children, especially during the first summer holidays of a peaceful England - a period which Meriel especially, at five and a half years old had never known. But I, and I think and hoped Diana also, was persuaded that for her, after five and a half years of war in England, a respite from close family anxieties and chores, a life quite different from the routine of family duties in UK would bring strength and health to a mind and body which had suffered much.

At any rate, on 23 July Diana left Northolt with her charming hosts, Sir Noel and Lady Charles (to whom Diana was recorded as Personal Assistant) and after a night in Paris arrived at Rome airport on the late morning of 25 July 1945 nearly six years after I had left UK (31.8.39) and life together for us both began again - to remain unbroken for over 40 wonderfully happy years.

The arrival of the aircraft carrying the British Ambassador and Lady Charles - and to me someone far more precious - was not without anxious moments: the fire engines raced on to the tarmac; "Why?" I asked. "Trouble with fire in mid-air" came the laconic reply from the landing staff. However, down they glided without sign of trouble, and out stepped His Excellency and His Lady to be greeted, according to protocol, by the Foreign Minister (or his Deputy). But HE and Lady Charles were good enough to stay the official proceedings until Lady Charles' "Personal Assistant" should have disembarked and been decorously but rapturously welcomed by MSL! Off moved the official cavalcade - remained DRL and MSL and the lowly staff who dealt with luggage. Among this was a fair sized cabin trunk which was about to be loaded into the Embassy truck. "Hi" said Diana "That's mine!" and disclosed that her host and hostess, en plein air, had not only carried her, but this largest piece of luggage of the whole party which Diana, her mind back to the 1930s, had thought would go by sea. How we were grateful to the charming Ambassador and his wife - always remembering that it was she who persuaded my Commander-in-Chief to issue a private permission.

A splendid remembrance of that flight still remains in the Foreign Office index (1945) kept in the Public Records Office at Kew for all posterity to read. In this Red Index, 1945, lodged between "Italian Government resigns" and "Italian Government reformed" comes the laconic item "Lush: expenses of Mrs Lush's flight to Rome". No papers are now available - but the facts and the dire financial debt remains!

Diana came to Italy as a working officer on the staff of the InterGovernmental Committee on Refugees, about which more anon; we had therefore determined that on arrival we would maintain my Headquarters Mess - we used to call it the ExCom's household, but that was slightly snob - rather than set up a *maison a deux or trois* and so Diana became a member of the Mess, for whom we drew rations, and Patricia, my PA, continued to run the household. It all worked very well and the only changes made were invitations to fill the places of men (or women) who had left. Although for two of us Life began again with a large and happy L we hoped that for the other very good friends, we made it possible for them to share in that happiness. Certainly the house never ceased to overflow with visitors and friends of both sexes, and our gallant staff never ceased to care for us in every way. I think, with Diana's arrival, our feminine guests increased, for now it was surely permitted for female members of the most disciplined units of the forces to visit and even stay at Brigadier and Mrs Lush's house! So we continued to be known, I hope, as a gay and welcoming household who welcomed guests from every quarter and were sometimes inundated with Civil Servants from Whitehall, Generals from Cairo, politicians, Red Cross luminaries, General's wives looking for their husbands, and others.

Diana with IGCR

Diana was soon in action with IGCR working for the Committee's representative in Rome - Colonel Julian Tomlin, whom we had known and liked greatly when he was Director of Post and Telegraphs in the Sudan Government stationed, of course, in Khartoum. He and his wife had visited us in Damer and I was delighted to have him in Rome, not as a member of the Allied Commission but working closely as the head of our Displaced Persons Section.

The InterGovernmental Committee on Refugees (IGCR) was created in 1938 by Roosevelt primarily to try to persuade the countries of Europe and indeed the world to succour the victims of Nazi persecution in Germany. Sir Herbert Emerson, an eminent retired Governor (Punjab) of the Indian Civil Service, was Director from creation of the Committee until it handed over to the International Refugee Organisation (IRO) in 1947. The IGCR's main work had been diplomatic, persuading nations to have pity, give temporary help and permanent asylum, and helping to coordinate the work of voluntary societies in their care of refugees. During the Second World War the Committee's scope was much enlarged and it became semi-operational: 'semi' because the Civil Affairs branches of the Armies assumed the operational care of Refugees and Displaced Persons when it was discovered what a harmful factor uncontrolled refugees could create to combat troops; thus sub-commissions of the Allied Commission took steps to control the refugee movement. IGCR could be, as we discovered in Italy, most helpful in marrying the operations of the state and the military forces, and Colonel Tomlin was IGCR's representative in Rome, working hand in hand with Colonel Fothergil of Displaced Persons, Allied Commission and bringing to bear a civil and international viewpoint on to our military aspect. IGCR had also in its care some of the pre-war refugees in Rome and Italy whom we military chaps could not touch - and who had gradually lost all hope when Italian voluntary societies faded out. To Diana, Colonel Tomlin handed these particular cases: they became her most precious duties.

DRL to SRL 8.9.45

"…. I work hard to try and [sic!] help poor people who are far away from their homes and find themselves with no way of earning money or buying food or clothes. I have seen many families who are living in what was an unfinished new building, without doors or windows, where they are sleeping with their blankets on the stairs and floor, sometimes without mattresses and without bedsteads. For chairs they put bricks together and cover them with newspapers to make a stool to sit upon. They are so grateful for anything one can do to help them. It seems wonderful that they can smile and laugh. To see them makes me very thankful for the good things *we* have. The more one sees of other countries the more we realise how lucky we are to be English …."

Diana was writing about White Russians - a number of whom found asylum in Italy during and after the Russian Revolution of 1917.

I shall have more to tell about IGCR in the next chapter for I joined myself in mid-1946 and Diana and I both served Refugees for four years after leaving the Allied Commission.

Our household in Rome in the latter half of 1945 consisted of Diana and myself with Patricia, Tony Grafftey Smith, Guy Hannaford (a lawyer who knew Rome and Romans well) and Tom Bergin. There were many others who came and went, not only as visitors but as temporary residents.

The end of the war by no means meant the end of the Allied Commission nor the cessation of work - but it did reduce the pace and the tension which military operations, the outcome of which was never absolutely certain, must always create. Now we were back to politics in peacetime, no less uncertain (I must own) and administration, still slightly at the mercy of the *Partigani's* armed ebullience, but in an atmosphere of, shall we say, conditional friendship - or a state which was improving daily.

Life in the Headquarters of the Commission went on at a *tempo moderato* with occasional *prestos* when Italian politicians or the American press were more than usually tiresome - or when Tito and his Yugoslavians pushed their intransigence too far.

Venezia Giulia

I should at this point try to summarise the situation in Trieste and the neighbourhood where Tito had at first shown great intransigence towards the Allies by occupying Trieste and setting up a Yugoslav administration there from the date of the German surrender until 21 May (just under a month). On 21 May 1945, Tito (probably on Russian insistence) announced a reversal of that policy and agreed to the introduction of Allied Military Government in Trieste - with Yugoslav participation. The three weeks of Yugoslav rule in Trieste had seen some very bloody executions of Italians and other harsh repressive measures. Allied Military Government had been set up, however, on 21 May under a very capable and courageous American Senior Civil Affairs Officer, Colonel Monfort who had been Colonel Benson's right hand man. He took with him an equally capable British Police officer Colonel Richardson, a member of the Metropolitan Police in London. These two men handled a particularly tricky state of affairs with great skill and courage; and when Monfort left the theatre early in July (demobilised) his successor Colonel Al Bowman, who had administered Emilia for twelve months, followed worthily in his footsteps. The administration of Trieste and neighbourhood (called Venezia Giulia) was the Spearhead AMG of General John Harding Commanding VIII Corps (British) with Headquarters at Udine, and in the particular and highly tricky international situation in the area, my Chief Commissioner agreed that Headquarters XIII Corps would deal direct with Allied Forces HQ (Field Marshall Alexander and then General Morgan) on AMG matters - circumventing Allied Commission Headquarters in Rome. We showed great foresight in this for the Allied Commission dissolved in 1946-1947, whereas Military Government in Venezia Giulia continued until 1954. In fact I knew General John Harding well (from Tripolitanian days where I was standing near when he was wounded) and he allowed me to visit Colonel Al Bowman from time to time in 1945 and '46, and give general and sometimes particular advice to both himself and the Regional Commissioner.

RC's Conference, August 1945

In early August we held a short Regional Commissioners' Conference in Rome with the object of setting a date for the final hand back of the Northern Regions to the Italian Government. Our Bulletin styled it "Turnover Huddle". We decided that, administratively and economically, all the Regions could be handed back at any time, but public security - or the lack of - made it another matter. Much depended on the presence of the Allied troops; no-one knew their precise movements. The Italian Army had been handed back to the Italian Government, but AMG relying on Italian troops did not make sense. The question was - would Italian elections on the question of the Monarchy and the Constitution make sense without the presence of Allied troops? However, although a firm date for the turnover was lacking the general opinion of the meeting pointed to 30 September 1945.

Tour of northern Italy

It was time that I had a look at the north and helped, if possible, to tie up final loose ends. Diana in the meantime had settled down in Rome's hot weather, without too much hay fever, and was tackling her job under Colonel Tomlin, Head of IGCR. He, however, wanted information about refugees and gladly released her to accompany me. Her presence must have distracted me for I can remember but little of our first tour together, except that Patricia came with us and that after a night in Florence we visited Brigadier Dunlop who, of course, insisted on an 'inspection' of Venice. Venice was very much *en fete* - packed with allied soldiery and the *Prefetto*, excusing himself from joining in festivities at a time of tragedy for Italy, offered us the hospitality of his enormous official gondola - a black craft painted with gold and furnished with red cushions, his *gondolieri* wearing exciting black uniforms. It really was a wonderful evening and Dunlop took his honoured guests back to the Danielli Hotel for the night.

Thence we went north - avoiding the trouble area, Venezia Giulia and Trieste, still the subject of international inter-play - to Bolzano, near the Brenner Pass where Colonel Dusty Miller was Senior Civil Affairs Officer and a very good host. I know we went through Cortina d'Ampezzo. We had penetrated the passes of the Dolomites in most lovely country; we were seeing skiing slopes in full summer; and finally we reached Milan - but spending en route a long time in the wonderful workshops which the Germans had fashioned in the tunnels along Lake Garda. We had been right up to the Alps and were now coming slowly south.

The country was returning to peace time conditions and I was glad to see Milan looking so normal. Diana and I had seen it in 1932 and Charles Poletti could not have been more welcoming on our arrival 13 years later. He certainly laid on everything he could for Diana to whom he was especially welcoming. We had a happy day and night there and then motored back to Rome. It was a wonderful tour for both of us with obvious welcome and friendship shown by Commission staff who must have envied their Ex-Com with his wife.

I thought it worthwhile to have a summary of my report on that tour published in the AC Bulletin, 24 November 1945:

> **"Allied Military Government in the North**
>
> "AMG in Northern Italy is being carried on by literally a handful of officers, and it is a remarkable achievement on the part of these officers that the ten million odd people are being governed adequately. This is due to a number of factors.
>
> "In the first place the policy laid down in the Chief Commissioner's memorandum of 1 May 1945 has been followed from the outset. Even when Regional Staffs were more plentiful, indirect administration was definitely the order of the day and the local government admnistration has been set well into operation from the beginning. The difficulties caused

by the clashing interests of the CLNs [partisans] still remain but in a reduced form, and recently Regional and Provincial Commissioners have shown the CLNs and the public that Allied Military, and consequently Italian local, Government can be the only executive authority, and that the CLNs must abide by their agreement to assume an advisory capacity only. Not all have acquiesced in this policy but public opinion has recently shown signs of helping the local government in this respect.

"Secondly, the economic situation, although serious, is showing sign of a certain degree of recovery to which the arrival of coal and other raw materials has given a remarkable psychological fillip.

"Thirdly. the staff that are left have tackled their multiple jobs with remarkable determination and selflessness. There are a good many cases in the north of officers voluntarily foregoing their LIAP in order that the work can be carried on. The impression that one gathers is definitely that AMG may have lost quantity but that it has definitely retained the quality.

"The uncertainty as to the date of restoration of this territory has, of course, had an unsettling effect on the population and the administration."

Allied Commission, late 1945

We came back to find that one of our stalwarts, Gerald Upjohn, Head of the Legal Sub-Commission and thereafter Vice President of the Civil Affairs Section was leaving. I had always entertained a great regard for Gerald and his legal advice to the Allied Commission was impeccable. He maintained a legal outlook, but we had many outlooks in common, and he was a great supporter of the Allied Commission as we fashioned it. He left us for much greater spheres in the world of law in England and died a Lord of Appeal and a well-known member of the Judiciary. How he must have enjoyed the tidy sanity and order of British justice and British courts after three years of the untidiness which prevailed in the judicial circles in Italy!

Diana returned to her IGCR work and I found the pressure markedly less with the two remaining problems, the Venezia Giulia question and public security in the north (and elsewhere), requiring very careful reconnaissance and thought. I also had a new question regarding all the British personnel under my command: namely, their future - in the Italian theatre, outside Italy, on demobilisation - with all the peace accompaniments, viz wives and families, local and home leave. This was indeed one of the problems of peace.

Everyone knew that I had taken my leave and now had my wife with me. What about Colonel X, Major Y and Sgt Major Z? The fighting military units were already on the move - some to Germany, some to the Far and Middle East, some to the UK. Luckily I had an excellent establishment officer and staff and they kept me fully versed on regulations and private worries. Military regulations on army or personal matters always seemed to me far removed from humane thought. One would have thought that an officer whose unit was about to move either to UK or some combat zone would be less eligible to have wife and family in Italy than an officer in the Commission prepared to stay a year or so at his job in Italy. But such was not the ruling, the basis of which was fixed on points. I should shortly have to expound some probable plan to my people on their futures.

Cultural contact with Italians was being urged upon me by the Education Sub-Commission who had already made widespread plans in this direction. There had been a substantial import of cultural literature. The AC Bulletin declared that we wanted to instil a

> "greater understanding by the Italian people of the free institutions of the USA and the UK, where elections of almost revolutionary portent can take place without the recrimination and blood letting that sometimes occurs in other lands."

That did seem, to my private mind, a failure to distinguish between the blood pressure of those who lived in temperate climes and those whose country stretched south nearer to the tropic zone. Moreover, having lived through an American year before Presidential election when business stood still for nearly twelve months, to my certain personal experience, and a British general election in which the electorate rid themselves of one of the greatest men in British history who brought them to victory in World War II, I was chary of quoting either country.

In the months to come, living a more normal and indeed perfectly lovely existence with Diana by my side, in a happy and most friendly household, we both had time and took opportunity to get to know and understand the Italian people. Administration now changed from the (successful) effort of restraining the Italians from interfering with the military achievements of the Allied Armies, to a more constructive sense of what American and British democracy meant - as Churchill had said in August.

It was about this time that a committee of Congressmen from Washington put in an appearance and wanted to learn what had been going on in Italy. Representatives from a number of institutions within and without the Allied Commission were invited (not summoned) before this group of questioners who said that they had no purpose in their questioning except to learn and possibly help. They really did not know enough about the picture nor the plan to make one's appearance before them worthwhile - a rather typical visit which left behind a feeling of irritation and pity! Visitors from our own country were on their way though not so many came.

On the home front we had found bathing at our usual beach or sand was becoming a trifle too hot (August and September) and bad for tender skins, but one of our personal staff, I am sure it was Patricia, found an ideal summer resort in the shape of a house at Anticoli, way up in the Alban Hills, about 40 miles from Rome; whether we rented it (I suspect) or sequestered it (in a co-belligerent country, our ally) I do not know, but it was the answer to hot weather in Rome in August and throughout the autumn. We could relax, utterly, there, walk in the hills, eat *al fresco* and sleep deeply in the fresh air. So it was a popular resort for our household and I made it clear that others had access to it. We used it right into the early winter when there were vestiges of snow on the hills above.

I remember that this village of Anticoli was a well-known resort for artists, and some Italian friend in Rome had begged Diana and me to call on one of them - I think she was the Brazilian wife of an Italian. We went round to the house, knocked - and the door was opened by a lady who was clearly artistic. Surprised, she nevertheless was hospitable and asked us in. We stepped in and then I, at any rate, automatically stopped, for there on the blue wall, facing us 15 feet away was a life size, or even larger, as it seemed, portrait of our hostess (now uttering words of welcome) completely nude and in nudity not as beautiful as she appeared covered. It was a most embarrassing visit to a charming and vivacious hostess. It was such an almost brutal nude, and I defy anyone male or female to behave without shifting eyes and likewise thoughts in such circumstances. Somehow one would have felt less embarrassed had the wall been blank and the hostess nude.

Diana and I visited Naples - I expect I had a conference at Caserta and managed to fit in a matinee of the Barber of Seville in the Opera there. I was able to show her nostalgically the Villa Carradora where we as a bachelor Mess had such a very happy six months.

The captains and the kings were indeed departing. Here is an extract from the Supreme Commander Field Marshal Alexander's farewell address to his Armies at the end of September 1945:

> "…. The Allied Commission under the capable direction of Admiral Stone has been a very cornerstone in our whole Allied set-up, and I owe him an immense debt of gratitude for his extremely efficient handling of affairs, and for the close and friendly relations we have always enjoyed …."

A few weeks before, Diana had attended the memorable Service of Memorial for the Polish soldiers who had died at Casino and elsewhere in Italy, when General Anders and the Field Marshal rode together on white chargers at the head of a remarkable assembly of all races.

In October one of the stalwarts of the Allied Commission, Director of Finance Tony Grafftey Smith left us and the army to take up a business appointment in the financial world. He was one of my best friends and advisers in the Commission and I was very sorry to see him go. At the same time my faithful PA, Patricia Russell, decided that Royalty had more need of her than the Allied Commission and returned to Buckingham Palace. She was a wonderful PA and a great favourite in and out of the Commission and I was to miss her sadly.

We decided to give a dance at the Villa, in honour of Diana's arrival and Grafftey Smith's and Patricia's departure. We entertained 120 guests from the British Ambassador and Lady Charles downwards with quite a number of British Embassy and Allied Military staff with their ladies. There were even more ladies than we had hoped for including Princess Galizine, Orietta Doria, Jacqueline Theron. Of the very polyglot names of men I notice Air Marshal Bomber Harris, General le Couteaux de Caumont and Major Petre (against whose name there is a note "won the Grand National in '46 on Lovely Cottage!"). It was a splendid evening, superbly arranged by Patricia, her last lovely gift to our household.

Diana and I made two other tours in the north based on Milan. We very nearly lost our lives when we encountered a live electric power cable hanging across the road (to Turin) and only some alarming but consummate tricks of good driving by Preston, my driver, saved us. I think it was on this same tour that the Director of La Scala in Milan invited Diana and me, with Charlie Poletti, to occupy the Royal Box at the opening night, but I cannot remember which opera we heard, superbly rendered.

I have used the reports in the weekly Bulletin (7 January 1946) to tell of the results of that tour, the decision totally to turn over northern Italy (excepting Venezia Giulia, ie. Trieste) to the Italian Government by the end of year 1945 and the well-deserved letter of thanks from the Chief Commissioner (drafted by MSL) to the Spearhead AMGs and their successors in the north. I could have wished to add some expression of gratitude uttered by the Italian Government - but other than some awards to American officers I could find none. I cannot remember any approach having been made by the Italian Government to decorate British personnel. Perhaps it was obvious that no Briton would have dreamt of accepting such an award.

I have at this point, however, included two more extracts from the Bulletin describing the award of the KBE to the Chief Commissioner Admiral Stone and the Legion of Merit to myself. I wrote the Citation for Ellery Stone, whom the existing Commander-in-Chief, Ben Morgan hardly knew. I, myself, was pleased and proud to wear an American honour, and much appreciated the kind words uttered.

15 December 1945

BRIGADIER LUSH HONOURED

In an impressive ceremony at AC HQ today,

Brigadier Maurice S Lush, Executive Commissioner of the Allied Commission since the amalgamation of all Allied Military Government agencies in Italy in January 1944, was presented the Legion of Merit, Degree of Officer, by Rear Admiral Ellery W Stone, USNR, the Chief Commissioner.

The citation accompanying the award was signed by the President of the United States, Harry S Truman, and reads as follows:

"Brigadier Maurice S Lush, British Army, as Executive Commissioner of the Allied Commission in Italy from January 1944 to July 1945, was responsible for the implementation of high policy and coordination of the work of the four sections and the independent sub-commissions of the Commission. Under his expert guidance plans for the rehabilitation of Liberated Italy were successfully carried out. His tact and consideration were of great value in the efficient co-functioning of the British and American members of the Allied Commission. Overcoming many obstacles by his unceasing effort, unusual executive ability and faithful perseverence, Brigadier Lush made a valuable contribution to the successful rehabilitation of Italy."

7 January 1946

ADMIRAL STONE K.B.E

All hands in the Allied Commission will join us, we know, in offering congratulations to our Chief Commissioner, Rear Admiral Ellery W Stone, USNR, on his award of the Knight Commander of the British Empire to which "His Majesty King George VI has been graciously pleased to appoint him".
The citation ran:

"Rear Admiral Ellery Wheeler Stone has achieved outstanding work for the Allied cause in Italy. As Director of the Telecommunications Section in the Allied Control Commission he laid the foundations of effective co-operatioon between the Italian Government and technical authorities and the Allied Forces in the field of communications. Appointed Deputy Chief Commissioner to Lt General Sir Noel Mason-MacFarlane in January 1944 he played a principal part in the re-organization of the Allied Control Commission, in the planning and execution of Allied Military Government in Italy, in establishing the closest relations between the Allied authorities and the Italian Government in the most difficult circumstances after the Armistice and in the critical days of the formation of the first representative Italian Government after the occupation of Rome by Allied troops. On the departure of General Mason-MacFarlane, Admiral Stone was appointed Acting Chief Commissioner and later confirmed as Chief Commissioner. In this capacity he helped to establish confidence in the new Italian Government and effectively carried out military government as the Allied Armies advanced northwards through Italy thereby ensuring the maintenance of law and order and the establishment of military government in the newly liberated territories and the maintenance therein on adequate supplies of food and medicines. As head of the first Commission to undertake the administration and guidance of the first liberated country in Europe, Admiral Stone has shown himself a great Allied leader."

Franco-Italian Frontier Problems 1945

One problem had arisen in the northwest, even before our advance in April: that of French penetration into Italy, especially in Val d'Aosta - the province which contained the Little St Bernard Pass over the Alps. Here, for military reasons it had been found wise for Allied Forces HQ or Supreme Commander Alexander to ask Eisenhower for help in supplying food to Italian Partisan forces who had crossed into French territory, and as part of this plan French forces had been allowed to penetrate Italian territory for about 20 km. This indeed was quite natural as all that part was French speaking. Moreover, the French presence fortified the *partigani* and were probably holding down two German divisions in the area. When the German surrender took place, the French, of course, took advantage of their position and ordered their troops to penetrate deeply into Italy and to resist establishment of Allied Military Government in a number of areas - even at the point of the bayonet. Very sharp words were exchanged between the French and Allied Generals on the spot, but wisely our AMG officers took a placid line and retreated before the angry French - reporting to us in Rome. We, at AFHQ thought likewise, but, reporting to the Supreme Commander, insisted that the matter be prosecuted at governmental level. For once the Foreign Office were quick to helpful action:

"A strong personal message was sent by President Truman to General de Gaulle that unless French penetration into Italy ceased, the supply of all materials to the French Forces, except rations, would cease."

This had immediate effect. General Juin, who was commanding the French forces in that area, was sent to Alexander's Headquarters; French penetration ceased and all was well. I wished I had known General Juin was going to Caserta - we could have talked about Madagascar!

The problem on the eastern side of Northern Italy, Venezia Giulia was not settled until 1954 and in 1945 we had many problems in that very live and busy Military Government territory, administered by Colonel Al Bowman.

So ended 1945 - surely the most momentous year of the first half of the 20th Century.

Let us recapitulate some of those momentous happenings: in Italy the year 1945 had begun quietly on land due to weather conditions; but Allied bombing especially on German lines of communication had been relentless. In Northern Europe Eisenhower's and Montgomery's troops crossed the Rhine in March and thereafter their advance was spectacular.

In the first four months of the year the Russians made a rapid and most victorious movement westwards and had entered and occupied the capital cities of Warsaw, Prague, Berlin and Vienna. Then:

9 April 1945 — Alexander's attack on Germans in Po Valley and Northern Italy began.

12 April 1945 — F D Roosevelt, President of USA, died; the friend and confidant of former naval person was no more.

1 May 1945 — The German Army in Northern Italy surrendered to Alexander; "There have been few campaigns with a finer culmination." (Churchill); AMG continued uneventful administration of 24,000,000 Italians.

2 May 1945 — Berlin surrendered to Russian Army.

7 May 1945 — Germans made final capitulation to Eisenhower.

8 May 1945 — VE Day.

12 May 1945 — Churchill to Truman: "I am profoundly concerned about the European situation. An Iron Curtain is drawn down upon their front."

13 May 1945 — Churchill's victory speech broadcast.

18 July 1945 — Potsdam meeting: Churchill (Attlee), Truman, Stalin.

26 July 1945 — General Election Great Britain results in Labour landslide with a majority of 200 seats: Attlee supplants Churchill as Prime Minister.

6-8 August 1945 — Atom bombs dropped on Hiroshima and Nagasaki.

2 September 1945 — Japan capitulated.

September/October 1945 — Churchill stays on holiday on Lake Como, Italy, in complete secrecy at invitation of Alexander in villa requisitioned for him and guarded by detachment of four Foot Hussars - his old regiment.

October 1945 — Field Marshal Alexander left Italy to become Governor General of Canada.

Alexander's departure from Italy was a great personal loss to me. I could not claim that he was a personal friend but he had shown to me understanding and appreciation in Tripolitania, Middle East and especially in Italy. I shall never forget his greeting to me when I arrived in Bari, to take over from Francis Rennell in 1943 and his kindness to me in inviting me to dinner at Lake Bolsena in 1944 to meet King George VI. I saw little of him during 1945 and had or perhaps took no opportunity to say goodbye to him before he left. But Alexander was the man in Italy for whom I worked - and there seemed to be an empty space in the High Command when he went.

1946

Diana opens her diary for this first year of peace with a list of members of our household in the Villa belonging to Gr. Uff. Zenardo (ex Tita Ruffo), 11 Via del Sassoferrato, Monte Parioli:

Jnr Cmdr Jo Carlisle ATS (PA to myself); Madge Angus, IGCR; Julian Tomlin, IGCR; Lt Col Guy Hannaford, Legal Sub Commission, AC; Lt Col Tom Bergin, Public Relations, AC.

Brigadier J K Dunlop who had been Regional Commissioner of Apulia was staying. We generally had a guest or two in that capacious house. He took us to an "excellent performance" of the Marriage of Figaro at the Opera House!

1946 was to be a family year for the Lush family and late in December I flew to England to arrange (among other matters of state) for the journey to Naples of Sylvia and Meriel and physically to put them on board the good ship Georgic which sailed from Liverpool for Naples with British soldiers, Italian prisoners and a number of British forces families (Operation Stork). Sylvia was an experienced traveller (pre war) and I had no qualms about them.

I also saw the Civil Affairs Department of the War Office who had little to say (and nothing to offer) and then spent three anxious days trying to coax our aircraft bound for Italy into the air. We arrived in Naples simultaneously with the good ship Georgic - which Diana and I met in Naples harbour in the morning. We were all home in the villa at Rome that evening - nearly the whole family but we still awaited Julian to come in the Easter holidays - for which I had made another plan.

The order of disembarkation of this 'Stork' ship at Naples, was very British and, we thought, very praiseworthy. First came the Italian prisoners of war - now almost regarded as Allies returning home after years of captivity. They were met by reception parties of Italian and Allied ladies, given a large packet of sandwiches and some cigarettes, receiving more or less VIP treatment!

Next came about 500 British troops, replacements for those demobilised or about to move, whose papers directed them to such and such a base camp - lucky if they found transport thither. No sandwiches for them! Lastly came the chattels: wives and children of British Army personnel whose relatives were not allowed on board - my exalted rank overcame that veto - and were waiting impatiently while the soldiers disembarked; after all she was a troop ship.

It was just as well that the parents of the Misses Lush were permitted to search for their children; there were no little hands waving from the deck, nor through a porthole; distracted parents, we found them snugly in the laps of two young British ship's officers to whom they were bestowing their last kisses. Unashamedly they greeted their mother and father while they extracted themselves and sorrowfully, as it seemed, left the ship. And so when we reached Rome that evening my dream of six and a half years came nearly true and all that was missing was Julian about to take his entrance exam into Winchester. The girls soon forgot their *patrons de voyage* and gave their love with great and immediate abundance to Pluto, from whom they became inseparable.

In my absence Diana and Madge Angus had carried out a very successful tour of Displaced Persons in the north and had, for this purpose, visited Florence, Lucca, Pisa, via Reggio, Spezia, Rapalla to Santa Margherita and then Portofino. Thereupon they went to Genoa and discussed the problem with AMG and the French Consul. After two nights they went into France and visited an Allied National's Camp and next day with full French approval continued to Nice where at the Hotel Negresco they found Diana's Aunt Mary (her father's sister) widow of Henri Soeters, a Dutch rubber merchant in the Dutch East Indies. He had died during the war, in exile in Nice and Tante Marie had stayed on, as a Dutch national, in the Negresco. Diana and Angus stayed the night there - masquerading as American GIs. Tante Marie could not disguise her disgust at the behaviour of the GIs compared with the exemplary manners of their predecessors, the Germans. The two voyagers returned to Rome after ten excellent and useful days of touring in the north and in two days Diana was in Naples when I arrived by air and we both met Operation Stork - described above.

Order of Merit of the Knights of Malta

On the very next day Admiral Stone and I went by appointment to the Palazzo Condotti, the house of His Highness Prince Chigi, Grand Master of the Order of Merit of the Knights of Malta, for our investiture by him of the Order which, with the blessing of the Pope, or maybe at his direction, was to be bestowed upon us - a signal honour which I much appreciated. We donned our No 1 dress and presented ourselves to the address in Rome, were met by an official of the household (in formal civilian frock-coat) and taken into the presence of Prince Chigi, who was sitting in his easy chair by a table; we were also asked to sit with the Prince and a desultory and not uninteresting conversation took place. We were offered Italian vermouth to drink; the Prince then casually remarked:

"Admiral, there is your decoration" (handing him a case) and "General, may I hand you *your* case."

We took the cases, somewhat taken aback at the lack of ceremony, and after some conversation, said our goodbyes and thanks - and left. The insignia of the Order is a white cross bearing the (abbreviated) inscription "Military Order of the Knights of Malta: bene merenti". The ribbon is black with a red band at each end. It is relatively unknown among British experts and I had Messrs Spink guessing when I asked them to produce a miniature. I wear the ribbon with my other insignia and occasionally used to wear the cross itself when preaching an Armistice Day sermon in our Protestant parish church. Thirty years after bestowal of the Order I noticed that there was a British Association of the Knights of Malta which seemed to me well known and had social meetings - always mentioned in Court Circular page of The Times. I called at their Headquarters - a small office in St James' Street and met the Secretary who was gracious and asked me to make my application to join in writing. I did so and received a very stiff reply from Lord Furness, the Secretary General, who told me straightly that the membership of the Association was confined to Roman Catholics having, inter alia, the necessary guarantees from their Bishop and "is entirely separate from your lowly Order of Merit". The question of my membership of the Association did not therefore arise. WOW! However I did receive from the Chancery of the Order in Rome a warrant of the Order!

We had determined before the arrival of our two daughters in Rome that they should continue some kind of education in Italy during what would be term time in England and I see from Diana's diary that less than 48 hours after their arrival they were introduced to the Convent of the Angeli del Sacro Cuore di Gesú on the Via del Monte Parioli. Our landlord Zenardo took Diana and the children round there and next morning they began to learn Italian in an attempt to equip them a little for lessons which began in earnest during the following week. Sylvia was very ready to go but her sister, who after all was only six and a half, found it very hard to enter those iron gates of the Convent. However, she (or others?) overcame her hesitation and the two girls were usefully taught at the Convent throughout their stay in Rome (excepting holiday times). They were the only British children in the school there; naturally, Italian was the sole language.

Diana and I soon called on and then were bidden to lunch with Prince and Princess Doria Pamphili (he the Mayor of Rome) who were not only then, but always, quite charming; he also full of tactful advice on British action in Rome.

The girls' education was not confined to the three R's (in Italian the three L's) for within a day or two we went down to the riding school of the mounted *Carabinieri* whose senior riding master took them in hand for instruction. Sylvia remembers to this day the facts recorded in Diana's diary:

".... S fell off, landed on her head; rode again and jumped."

A brutal father insisted on the almost immediate remounting and second attempt.

I was most grateful to the Italian police riding master for the lessons which he gave to all of us in that riding school. They laid the foundation of good seats and great confidence in the girls - and did no harm in reviving a few principles of riding in their parents.

At week ends we generally went *en famille* to Anticoli and walked in the hills - Jo Carlisle, my PA, was a first class organiser, was much beloved by the family and I hope enjoyed her last few weeks of service in the

Commission.

Here I must add another kind of lesson arranged for our daughters. Entry in the diary 11.2.46:

"…. Signora Loredana Franceschini arrived for first piano lessons …."

"Arrivederci Tom Bergin"

At the beginning of February Tom Bergin left our household and the Commission to return to academic life in USA. I wrote an official appreciation in the Bulletin "Arrivederci Tom" (as follows). I have written earlier my private appreciation of him.

"…. (Editor's note: the following piece has been sent to us by the powers that be. We personally and heartily say "amen *and* amen" and could say much more ….)

"The Director of the Public Relations Branch will have left us when this number of the Bulletin appears. Though not always Director of the Branch, he has, however, for many months since the Naples days, contributed to the weekly publication of the AC with his brilliant prose. Lieut Col T G Bergin managed to put in his columns on the Italian political situation his deep and humanitarian understanding of the Italian people while his perfect knowledge of the language has enabled him to read the daily papers himself, and therefore to grasp many points that might escape a non-Italian reader. Whoever will, after this week, be writing the "Political" is undertaking a heavy task and a great responsibility. May we say - we who would never be able to write so accurately and so wittily at the same time on a subject so dull and serious as policy - how much we have enjoyed reading Col Bergin's articles? The Bulletin's readers will certainly miss the sparkling columns of this young Professor of Romance Languages from Cornell University. The whole staff of the Public Relations Branch - and we are sure the numerous friends he has made among the British and American officers of the AC - will miss the *camaraderie* and the kindness with which he treated everybody. Our *auguri di buon viaggio* will accompany him across the ocean."

He was the best American friend I had in the whole Commission. He remained one of my best friends on earth, whose friendship in the 1940s was invaluable and whose abiding friendship as we both grew older was even more precious. Diana and I looked forward to his valued missives and had often those jewels of speech, prose and verse which appear in "Masterpieces". I only wish that my intellect could absorb and appreciate his academic prowess. I just love his personal messages. As I have mentioned before, we kept in touch with Tom and his charming wife Florence. Not one Christmas has gone by without an exchange of greetings; we have stayed with them on both our journeys to USA in the 70s and have entertained them at home when we lived in Sussex; on one occasion they sat on our lawn for two days putting the last touchstone on to his Concordance. Tom has entertained us to a view of American football (of which he is a great exponent) in the Bowl at Yale University and we have lunched with him in Hall at Timothy Dwight College, Yale, of which he was Master for five years.

Roman Catholic Consistory held by Pope XII

Staying with us at this time was Dick Stokes, a British MP and the senior Roman Catholic MP in Parliament. He took his religious position seriously and had come to Rome to see the Cardinal Archbishop in London receive his biretta.

Diana's diary for 21 February 1946 records:

"…. MSL No 1 uniform but Dick Stokes in evening tail coat, white tie, black waist coat and Olive (Moore) and D in long black dresses and black veils *(mantillas)*, arrived at St Peters at 8.30 am to attend the Consistory Session. Pope and all Cardinals, Guard Nobile, Swiss Guards, etc …."

This morning's Ceremony was the finale of a series of (to me) complicated and secret sessions of the Sacred College in the Vatican. The College had met in the Sala Consistotiale at the beginning of the week. The Pope had told members of the college (existing Cardinals and other high dignitaries) that the War had prevented him from creating Cardinals; that he now proposed to create 32 new cardinals. All this in Latin. *"Quid vobis videtur"* he asked, to which their Eminences signified their assent by raising their red skull caps. Whereupon the Pope nominated 32 saying (all in Latin) that it was his pleasure to decorate with the majesty of the Roman purple men who had merited greatly of the Catholic (sic) Church and of their own fatherlands.

The next stage was to give the *"biglietti"* or written notices of elevation to groups of couriers (officials and existing Cardinals) who would convey the news to the new Monsignori. The new British Cardinals received their *"biglietti"* in the English College of the Vatican where another courier informed the Rector of the College when the biretta would be conferred on the Cardinals. The new British Cardinals were Monsignors McGuigan of Canada (the senior), Gillroy of Sydney, Australia, and Griffin who was now Cardinal Archbishop of Westminster, London. He gave the address at the Venerable English College at which d'Arcy Osbourne, the British Minister to the Holy See, our guest Dick Stokes MP representing Roman Catholic members of the British Parliament and many Roman Catholic chaplains to the British Forces swelled the numerous Roman Catholic members of those forces present. The new American Cardinals included Mons Spellman whom I had met in Tripoli and who had been tipped for the next Pope!

The ceremony to which we had come was the final and public ceremony of the new appointments. Here is the official report:

"The ceremonies of the public Consistory commenced this morning at 0900 hours in St Peter's Basilica.

To a fanfare of trumpets, His Holiness the Pope was carried in from the back of the cathedral, up the aisle past the crowds of people who had been arriving since 0700 hours, to a raised dais and throne.

The newly elected Cardinals later arrived in procession and one by one went before the Pope.

Afterwards the Pope was carried round the altar and then back down the aisle, and away from the Cathedral.

The new Cardinals then went to the inner or High Altar to prostrate themselves, finally leaving in procession down the aisle. This brought the ceremonies to an end."

My own description continues:

"We had VIP seats (of which there were not many) in the nave of St Peter's, in which a vast crowd had assembled, all eyes turned on the elevated papal throne erected under the dome. We arrived to watch the last touches being put to the ceremony and listened to the beautiful music sung by several choirs. The Pope was duly carried in on his litter and established on his throne - to the acclamation of the wonderfully disciplined congregation. Then one by one the newly elected Cardinals entered from the west door and one by one at quite long intervals walked up the long aisle of the nave, preceded, each one, by his private priest and followed by someone who appeared to be his chancellor. Thirty two of these groups of three walked slowly up the aisle, made their obeisance to the Holy Father and remained in a group beneath the throne. I cannot be sure that the biretta was bestowed then or privately later."

It was a most impressive Service of Loyalty by the new Cardinals to the Holy Father: Cardinals from all the five continents in the world. It gave one an impression of the great influence of the church throughout the world. It also gave the impression of the desire to magnify the omnipotence of God (there were helmeted soldiers bearing swords on each side of the Pope); the only instance of humility was in the simple priest who preceded each Cardinal and, I suppose, the black dresses and *mantillas* worn by the women in the congregation. One could not but reflect that the power of the great church in which we stood had not yet been able to stem the satanic evils - the Jewish holocaust to name one - which had been manifested in the country in which three of the Cardinals ministered.

In the same context on 26 February 1946 Diana wrote in her diary:

"…. After lunch dressed into pale blue long evening dress with long sleeves, white small hat, gloves and fur cape; collected Maurice from office - he in uniform - and drove to a reception *"nel Reale Palazzo del Quirinale, d'ordinie di sua Altessa Reale il Principe di Piemonte, Luogotenente Generale del Regno"*, attended by 50 Cardinals and numerous guests."

This was the lay or royal sequel to the religious consistory of last week and was a brilliant affair - one of the few international parties given by the Lieutenant of the Reale, Umberto, who had been titular ruler in the place of his father since the occupation of Rome and was so soon to lose his position by the will of the people. It was certainly the first Royal party I had heard of or attended, and it was most interesting to meet members of the Government and a member of the Prelates (not, of course, the Pope) and then to see the enormous oval table prepared for the 50 Cardinals, old and new, at which they were to sit with a few members of Royalty. The floral decorations on the table were massed red roses, all the Cardinals wore their red robes and their enormous red hats were already hanging on the back of their chairs. As Diana wrote, it was a great sight. Of course the array of lay guests was very different from receptions at the Quirinale before 1944, for today there was not (it was to be hoped) a single Fascist. We missed a party to meet Cardinal Griffin of Westminster but had our own Roman Catholic dinner party that evening for Dick Stokes, the other guests including a Benedictine Abbot Philip Langdon (of the Vatican Staff).

A day or two later Diana and Dick Stokes had an interesting morning at the *Carabinieri* training barracks seeing recruits on foot and in their riding school (fanfare of trumpets, exhibition of riding and jumping by recruits and experts) on the whole a most impressive performance, arranged for the British MP.

Italian Elections

It was about this time (early 1946) that Allied Military Government folded up completely in Northern Italy and the administrative side of the Allied Commission therefore ended. Harris writes, in *Allied Military Administration*, that thereafter the only Allied political object of paramount importance was to ensure that adequate arrangements were made to give the Italian people the opportunity of deciding by a free vote the form and constitution of its future government. In the months leading up to the elections, the Civil Affairs Officers left in the regions took an extraordinarily careful interest in this last aspect of freedom committed to their care.

We had, of course, two first class experts in our Local Government Sub-Commission, Colonels Cripps (British) and Tomlin (American). These two had, from the beginning, studied and worked for the final plan of holding free elections as the first step towards the rebirth of democracy in Italy. As our Bulletin rightly wrote, free elections involved electoral lists, to be made by various agencies (eg. in Great Britain by the Parishes); these agencies need local officials to guide and supervise. After years of Fascism all this had been forgotten and had to be created - and the wanton hand of Communism was about ready to supplant Fascism and rout Democracy. Cripps and Tomlin, nevertheless, never weakened their endeavours, their determination to foster the idea "to build up the machinery to ensure freedom of choice". Let me quote a paragraph in our Bulletin of 7 July 1945 *First Steps*:

> "The immediate step in the North is to insure that every one of the 4083 communes in the 40 provinces .... have proper officials, from prefect to *Sondaco* and communal secretary. Sub-Commission officers will visit every province .... to advise both on getting local officials into office, which means chiefly clearing CLN appointees with AMG, and to give pointers on starting electoral lists themselves. Why this job is one of the most difficult confronting AMG can easily be appreciated from the fact that there has not been a so-called free election in Italy since 1925 in a commune nor since 1933 in the nation, and that even the last going to the polls - in 1939 - was merely one of the Mussolini calls for a rigged vote of confidence. Plainly, hardly any officials exist who are familiar with the techniques of the duties involved. Extant are no electoral lists which might have been revised. Records of all kinds are in a parlous state - lost, burned, destroyed, scattered. And the amount of record-checking involved is appalling, as will be explained later. Let us not speak of the difficulty of communications with the outlying communes, the perennial lack of transport, or even the scarcity of paper and of wood and glass to make the ballot boxes themselves.

By March 1946 "tentative battle formations" were being formed as our Bulletin put it, for the coming elections. It had been decided to hold local elections in March followed in June by those for the *Constituente* together with the referendum on Monarchy and Republic. The first local elections (and they were the first for 25 years) were successful and were carried out without disorder which augured well for the June elections. These too enjoyed the same freedom from trouble.

Venezia Giulia

At the beginning of March the AC Bulletin was able to publish a very comprehensive and, on the whole, encouraging report compiled under the direction of Colonel Al Bowman, Senior Civil Affairs Officer of AMG under the direct orders of Lieutenant General John Harding, Commanding XIII Corps with HQ at Udine. Every help possible had been given to the SCAO by the various Sub-Commissions in Rome, but I had been careful to ensure that the authority stemmed not from the Commission in Rome but from XIII Corps: in fact from the local military HQ. But our help was needed and given as I have noted before: General John Harding knew me and was very content to allow this form of help to continue.

The situation had not been easy but gradually the firm hand of Allied Military Government had given to the Italians courage and to the Slovenes a perhaps unwilling appreciation of firm and abundantly just handling.

The Legal Division had perhaps had the most difficult technical problem. All legislation enacted after September 1943, either by Slovenes or Italians was invalid! By 1946 a host of proclamations, orders and notices had been drawn up and appointments of officials had been legalised. Courts of Law were established and functioned well.

Food and agriculture had been organised; 40,000 tons of food had been imported in the last six months of 1945. Agriculture had been re-established and increased; rebuilding of demolished villages had begun. The port of Trieste was restored; on my first visit in 1945 it had seemed, to my landsman's eye, inoperable. Perhaps I had forgotten the speed of reparation accomplished in Tripoli, Libya. But very soon Trieste was functioning as a live port.

Refugees had been dealt with by the Displaced Persons Division who were tackling not only Italians returning to the Province but Slovenes returning home from Germany in their thousands and Germans going north from Yugoslavia. Public Health was now satisfactory - there had been few but extraordinary problems here. The Education Officers were faced with the demand for Italian and Slovene schools with differing curricula; but this was allowed only in a few cases.

The creation of a Police Force presented a most difficult problem in a territory so divided by nationals who were at each others' throats. It was decided to disband completely all existing police forces and to set up a completely new AMG Force based on American and British Police principles. By January 1946 this was in full and most successful operation.

In Colonel Bowman's absence on leave, Colonel Robertson (British), the Acting SCAO, was able to present to the international Allied Investigating Commission (British, American, French and Russian) a territory in which law and order ruled, and administration was completely impartial. I am sure that General Harding was proud of it: I was!

Having seen Al Bowman established in his very difficult job of administering Military Government for two mutually opposing nationalities, one of which was there unlawfully but was tolerated for international reasons; having found him running this odd administration very well and to the liking of his British Military Commander, I left him alone and went to Trieste only on call. My last visit was just before I left the Commission in October 1946 and he remained there for some time after that. In fact, Venezia Giulia was under Allied Military Government until 1954. The Great Powers made a terrible muddle of the whole question, but that was no matter for the Allied Commission which had disappeared by 1947.

Family Life

We were settling down by now to family life in the villa - our two daughters went daily to the Italian Convent in the morning and had their riding lessons almost daily before breakfast or after lunch, with piano lessons once or twice weekly. But I fear the social life which was very much part of my job as senior British officer in the Commission did create a good deal of havoc in their young lives. We tried hard to keep weekends at Anticoli or some other rural outing, and later sea bathing, sacred for the family. Visitors like Dick Stokes however, were demanding. Moreover, the social life of Rome, or shall I say the Allied Diplomatic and Forces in Rome, was demanding. Sir Noel and Lady Charles were extremely good to us and made us welcome at any party of note; Alexander Kirk, the American Ambassador, was not so open hearted but always pleased to see us; the French and Netherlands Ambassadors held open house to us, and Sir d'Arcy Osbourne at the Vatican (and his staff including David Utley and Brian de Salis) was a welcome host and guest. Our contacts with the Vatican seem to have grown as a result of our hosting Dick Stokes. He himself became a great friend. All these, our hosts and friends, came often to the villa as our guests. I see names of Italians mentioned in Diana's diary and there is no doubt that her presence encouraged friendly exchanges between her and many Roman hostesses who admired her work among the White Russian refugees and others - and themselves helped. Again an entry of Lady Symes' (Sudan days) niece, Contessa Orietta di Gropello Figarolo, tells of a request made from UK and reminds me of a request to me cabled from the Lampsons, in the Embassy in Cairo, to see that the Castellanis came to no harm. I never saw them in Italy but made it my business to ensure their safety from harassment. Diana was able, on several occasions, to take Sylvia and Meriel to musical concerts given in Rome by Italian (and White Prussian) composers and players, including a boy prodigy, Pierino Gamba. We were also able to introduce Sylvia, and later Julian and Meriel, to opera both at the Rome opera house and at the famous summer opera in the open air at the Baths of Caracalla.

Change of PAs

In March 1946 I lost my loyal and very competent PA Jo Carlisle, who had served me and all of us in the villa so admirably since Patricia's departure. The word "sterling" is most apt in describing Jo's qualities and after 40 years I can still remember and appreciate the very real quality of her help and service to me, both official and personal. She went home to be demobilised and married a fine soldier from the Sudan Defense Force, Billikin Cornish. We missed her great efficiency greatly.

I had foreseen Jo Carlisle's departure and, when in England during January, had persuaded a great friend of all of us, Olive Moore, to come out as my PA. We had known her in Cairo in 1935: she was now living alone with her three children and had been a marvellous hostess to our three youngsters over Christmas 1945. The thought of a break from England with the chance of her children joining her for the school holidays was enough to lure her to work in Rome. I believe she had to face a board of Senior Officers before acquiring permission to come to Rome; but as she was, then, the wife of a well known and gallant Brigadier in the Grenadier Guards she had little trouble; moreover she had great personal charm and luckily flew out with Admiral Stone who had been to London to receive his KBE from the King. Olive was very good looking and the Admiral sank like a stone before her, so that no questions were asked as to her right to use Government aircraft! She was, again, a good organiser, and arranged the journey to Rome at Easter not only for her own three children but for Julian our son - which entailed a hard railway journey from England to Rome which they all endured and arrived blackened by Sardinian coal. Olive met her second husband under our roof.

In the meantime we entered March 1946 with snow in the Alban Hills and cherry blossom in the Borghese Gardens. We went to Sir d'Arcy Osbourne in the Vatican for a tea party to the British cardinals and we met John and Margaret Ward Perkins, the newly appointed Director of the British School at Rome (Art, Archaeology and Classics) at dinner with Mr Bottrell, Head of the British Council in Rome. John had organised military government's Department of Antiquities in Tripolitania. Suffice it to say that the Allied Commission had something to do with relieving him from his duties with us and having him appointed to the British School.

All this time Madge Angus had been with us in the villa (her job was with refugees) but she went to Kenya for a spell - she will return!

We held a splendid children's party at the villa, 21 children, 17 adults and films. A pathetic last sentence in Diana's diary:

"…. all went to film in evening - *Rhapsody in Blue* (George Gershwin); DRL slept …."

Another late afternoon at the opera *La Traviata* followed a motor trip to Caserta where in the morning the women saw the renowned gardens and waterfalls while I saw the Commanding Officer; we picnicked at our old Villa Carradoro and visited Monte Cassino on return.

We saw General Scobie on his return to UK from his command in Greece and went to a farewell dinner to Henry and Alys Hopkinson (Minister in the British Embassy) after which Diana records "after dinner a gambling game called BINGO."

In mid-March, Diana and I, with Olive Moore, began a northern tour. We left our daughters with friends in Rome and set off to visit Siena and stayed at Florence. Next day we lunched at Bologna with two British police officers (seconded from the London Metropolitan Police) and others; we crossed the Po and reached Milan for dinner with the British Civil Affairs Officer, Col Arthur Hancock.

Next day, 19 March, after lunch, we drove to the Villa Lucertola between Lezzano and Bellagio: memories of 1932 for the Lushes, but no access to the Villa where Diana had stayed. On we went to Bracciano and dined on the way home to Milan. This was a really lovely drive and I wonder now, 40 years later, whether Alexander had acquired the Villa for Churchill and so made it incommunicado!

Next day we visited Turin where I spent the late morning and lunch with a Colonel Ross, the AC Liaison Officer; leaving him we enjoyed the hospitality of Arthur Hancock who had arranged a cocktail party for the Mayor of Milan and his wife to greet Diana and self.

We travelled eastwards through Brescia and eventually reached Bolzano for dinner with Colonel Dusty Miller and his officers late due to a puncture en route. Our hosts increased their hunger by hiring a local professional yodeller who curdled our food and drink, but wisely followed dinner with a film shown by a deaf photographer who had some wonderful slides of the Dolomites.

Dusty Miller had very "personal" liaison in the region: the Prefect of Bolzano obviously liked him and worked hand-in-hand with him. Dusty was, together with his obvious efficiency, a very charming person in whom the Italians delighted. We spent a happy, useful day having a look at education in the region and then spent the evening dining at the Hotel with the Prefect as our host.

We flew from Bergano to Rome where I attended an UNRRA dinner for ex-President Hoover. Next day we went to the opera: Wagner sung in Italian with excellent scenic effects. Nor were we content with that for, two or three days later, we heard Beethoven's Eighth and Ninth symphonies consecutively in one evening. No wonder I commented that the Ninth outshone the preceding symphony.

In April Olive Moore went to Lausanne to meet up with her three children plus our Julian, and to continue by train. They arrived in Rome quite black from the train journey but made a wonderfully happy Villa. I see a DRL entry:

"…. High tea before much bathing! Trimmed and washed Julian's hair and cut toe nails." (He was under 13!)

Thereafter we spent a lovely whole family Easter holiday. Julian and Meriel heard their first opera, Carmen, in a big box for twelve filled by Lush and Moore families.

We still had our social duties and I see that we entertained the Commander-in-Chief (Alexander's successor, General Morgan) to lunch with suitable Commission Staff, British and American. My Chief Commissioner was on leave in USA and I was in charge. I never came to know General Morgan well but we exchanged courtesies officially and unofficially. I then notice in the diary a much more interesting dinner party *chez nous*. Lord Stansgate (Secretary of State for Air), an old boy of the Allied Commission, Sir Kinahan Cornwallis, Chairman of the Middle East Committee in the Foreign Office, A V M Fogarty, Air Marshal Commanding RAF Mediterranean and other locals. With all those high sounding guests Diana writes: "Men talked about the Sudan after dinner!"

We met the same team at the Embassy next evening plus the Comptroller of Overseas Trade and a Labour MP, Harold Laski and his wife "he a great pillar of the Labour Party". I spoke to all these Labour politicians and discussed Italy, but I was at a loss to discover their aim in visiting the country or their intentions towards Italy, nor whether they had any great political interest in or personal knowledge of it.

The Lush-Moore families Easter holiday expedition of 1946 was to Aquila in the Abruzzi Mountains where a tremendous holiday festival had been arranged (probably NAAFI helping) in the chief hotels. We rode and walked and roller-skated on the roof, explored the country and came home to entertain Harold Macmillan at the Villa (I suspect he had been visiting Churchill on Lake Como). Sir Quentin Hill lunched with us - Director of Overseas Trade - and I see that we went to hear *Aida* at the opera (six children in our party).

No-one could say that we or any British (or Allied) troops and their families were without entertainment, and good entertainment in Rome during 1946. The Italian operas were becoming excellent; Italian musicians were reviving good music after a quarter of a century of imposed music; ENSA plays were multiple and well performed; the film library was well stocked and improving mightily in technique. We lived in a most beautiful city and in a lovely country. When war had ceased, and the stress thereof and our families were with us, we had few complaints and not much work. I only wish that during those last few months I had learnt to speak and read the Italian language; that failure was a great loss, a great blot in my life.

One Signorina Anna Lelli came greatly to the aid of all of us in exploring Rome - the Palatine and Quirinale Hills, the Tiber and Capitoline Hill, Campidoglio, Pantheon, Piazza Navona, Trevi Fountain, The Aurelian Walls. Such treasures she pointed out and visited with our families the Baths of Caracalla, the churches of St Peter-in-Chains and Santa Maria Maggiore, and the catacombs to quote but a few.

Practically every morning we rode early - such a wonderful opportunity for our young and ourselves.

A great occasion was a family visit to the Palazzo Doria Pamphilia near the Janiculum Hill - a personal tour with Prince Doria. Another occasion was our family's first ballet *Coppelia*.

Alas, on 5 May Julian flew to UK (in the cockpit of the aircraft) for his last term at Highfield.

The diary entry on 17 May: "saw some most excellent jumping at the Concorso Ippico" reminds me that it included jumping by an Italian Colonel who had suffered an amputation of both legs just above the knee, and was strapped on to his horse. His horse jumped well and he was as good as his horse.

Indeed there was no lack of things to do in Rome for children and grown ups, and we, who were lucky enough to have a large house and many interesting friends both in Italy and from overseas, made the most of those happy months of early 1946.

2 June 1946 - The Admiral's Stone

More seriously we found our Chief Commissioner, Admiral Stone ill in hospital and I was glad to be back to take his place.

Apparently he had suddenly experienced dire, serious pain about his middle; this became agonising before he retired to bed and he had his ADC, Anthony Quaile, summon the doctor. He was by now suffering severe pains in abdomen and thereabouts. By American regulation only an American Naval doctor should attend a Naval person. Our Naval Sub-Commission put their American staff to finding a US Medical Officer in the city, and they found a Lieutenant Pearson, attached to the American Hospital. Anthony Quaile explained the Admiral's symptoms on the telephone and summoned him without delay. The young "lootenant" listened carefully and said "I will be with the Admiral in half an hour" He was as good as his word. He nervously entered the Admiral's room and made a manual examination of the writhing patient; he asked questions and wrote down answers; finally he closed his notebook, put away his stethoscope and in a sepulchral, convinced manner asked: "Admiral, do you have a sensation of impending doom?" At this point the Admiral, whose impatience and pain had reached the maximum, leapt out of bed and chased the unfortunate officer out of his house. But Medical Lieutenant Pearson was correct. He had determined that the symptoms led to one diagnosis only and the paragraph in Gray's Anatomy or Brown's Diseases of the Kidneys and Urinary Tract contained one confirmatory final symptom "the patient has a sense of impending doom". The bruised Lieutenant Pearson explained this to Anthony Quaile and between them (and the Commander of the Naval Sub-Commission) they moved the now groaning and thoroughly shaken Chief Commissioner to hospital. When I visited him next day he was his old, and delighted self, saying:

"See Maurice, I've passed the biggest rock ever known - and here it is. That ..... medico boy was right after all!"

He really was proud of his stone which adorned his desk for a week or so!

Election and Referendum

As the Italian elections came near, the Italian Government showed some anxiety and twice in Stone's absence (sick) I went to see de Gasperi, the Prime Minister. I have no record of our conversation, but I am certain that I repeated my assurance that Allied Officers would be conspicuous by their absence from all polling booths and meetings, and that the Commission had good reports on the security situation.

In the event the elections and the referendum passed quietly on 2 June - an event which I celebrated by yet another visit to de Gasperi, the Prime Minister, to congratulate him. He incidentally returned to office in July as head of a government which, as well as Christian Democrats, included Communists and Socialists.

The result of the elections gave the Christian Democrats eight million votes with four million (plus) to Socialists and Communists alike. But almost more important was the referendum on the monarchical system: King or Republic?.

The referendum produced twelve and a half million votes for a Republic and ten and a half million for the Monarchy. Prince Umberto was unwilling to accept the verdict, based on such a small majority and demanded a further referendum. This caused a good deal of tension and rioting in which the Commission almost inevitably became involved. We had to advise Umberto to accept the vote of the people. In the event, the Prince yielded to pressure and left Italy on 13 June never to return, even though he prayed to be allowed to die in his native land in 1984.

Life in Rome

The British Ambassador and Lady Charles celebrated the King's Birthday on 13 June 1946 with a Garden Party at the Embassy to which all of Rome was invited. It was a notable occasion: the first such celebration since the war but the sun, somehow, forgot to shine. "Horribly cold wind, shivered with arms like goose flesh" wrote Diana in her diary. It was odd weather for Rome in June and a bad augury for next evening when 140 guests came to a dance at our Villa from 9.00 pm until fried eggs and bacon at 3.30 am. "Sylvia watched from staircase until about 11.00 pm." It was a happy evening and enabled Diana and me to say thank you to many people for their kindness and to say farewell to Guy Hannaford who was leaving the Commission to join the British Embassy. I am not sure that Olive Moore, my PA, was not behind the idea. She was about to marry her second husband, Dick Stokes, and left Rome a week later. She was an expert in flower arrangement and certainly did the flowers that evening.

The day before the dance an entry in Diana's diary runs:

"…. Mr Sarell, friend and colleague of Aubrey Halford, arrives to stay *en route* from Addis Ababa …."

The last three months of the Lush family in Rome and in the Allied Commission were the happiest we had known. The three next paragraphs tell the prologue of part of that happy story.

In May a letter had been dispatched by Diana to Pamela Crowther Smith suggesting that on demobilisation from the WRENS she might care to come to Rome as my PA for what might be a short-term engagement but would give me great help (badly needed) and the whole Lush family much pleasure. Pam arrived to the great joy of the whole said family on 28 June.

On 29 June the Lush family with my new PA, Pam, went to the opening night of the opera season at the *Termi di Caracalla*. The opera was *The Forces of Destiny* (La Forza del Destino) by Giuseppi Verdi.

We had also taken Rod Sarell and Admiral and Mrs Warren. This opening night was the best summer evening entertainment in Rome and gave the most wonderful presentation of Italian opera that I have ever seen.

The site was in the ancient Roman Baths of Caracalla, two millenia old and now, of course, in partial ruins. The proscenium was immense and could accommodate 800 players, a bull ring, a carriage and fair; the back stage must have been immense. The auditorium too was an immense rectangle with 100 wooden benches (with low back rests) which could each accommodate 100 people and they were invariably packed. Each row was slightly higher than the row immediately in front; one could hear equally well from, say, row 99, as from 3, for the acoustics (in complete open air) were perfect.

The season ran from the end of June until the end of August. The audience, which, even in the days of Allied occupation, was mainly Italian, knew every word, every note of all the operas: Aida, Pagliacci, Carmen, La Forza del Destino, Tosca, La Boheme, Mephistofele, and many more.

We saw and heard them all, some of them twice, generally *en famille* (Meriel then aged 6, can still remember them) and it certainly was the best way of hearing Italian opera that I can ever imagine. When an audience of 10,000 hangs on every note and nuance, the singers give of their very best - and the atmosphere of this *al fresco* feast was ideal. If we and our children gathered nothing else from our stay in Rome, those evenings gave us not only the utmost pleasure, but an insight into some of the character of the Italian people - concentrated happiness in the romantic setting and rendering of Italian opera!

We were now (June 1946) in full summer and visits to the Tyrrhenian sea coast were in great demand; we could reach Frigene in 40 minutes and would often snatch an evening bathe and be home in time for dinner; there was also St George's Tennis Club which had the additional joy of a swimming pool; here Julian (when present) and Sylvia had their first lessons in lawn tennis and showed promise, and also learnt the rudiments of diving, an art in which Sylvia, especially, has excelled.

Diana and I spent the evening of our sixteenth wedding anniversary "dining together in sunshine on the terrace of Casina Valadier" and then we went onto a delightful orchestral concert with chorus and four soloists. We listened to Berlioz, Cesar Franck, Maurice Ravel. The night before we had listened to an orchestral performance of Verdi's *Requiem* in the Basilica de Massengio, "the ancient remains making an open air amphitheatre in beautiful surroundings. Lovely warm night. View of Colosseum floodlit."

Sir Quentin Hill and his daughter Elizabeth had come to stay. He was taking up a post as Economic Counsellor to our Embassy and his daughter nobly filled a gap as PA to me between Olive Moore and Pam Crowther Smith.

Practically every day of the diary begins "BB (before breakfast) MSL rode" with members of the family and household. That early morning ride was an absolute benison to me and I was so delighted that Diana and the children often came too.

As far back as May 1944 Diana had, in these southern climes, shown symptoms of hay fever - the really terrible condition which had threatened to spoil so many of her summers, but which she had courageously fought. Someone told her of a 'wizard' Italian, Doctor Assennato, who with electric needles could and did cure this allergy. I accompanied her to the first visit to this Dottore Pericle Assennato, via del Tempio 3. The front door was opened to us by a Sherlock Homes looking figure, swathed in purple dressing gown. I was glad I had accompanied my wife! He ushered us in to his consulting/operation room where he explained that he had learnt to give the Chinese cure for hay fever by inserting needles into the patient. He proceeded to explain further. On the next assignment he inserted needles into toes, legs and ankles; two days later insertions were made into Diana's shoulder blades. Always at these seances Dr Assenato would implore Diana "Signora, when I say "INSPIRE" kindly inspire, and when I say "EXPIRE" please expire." Two days later Diana called for treatment. Here is her diary entry:

> ".... Dr Assennato gave me 25,000 volts to breathe in from ten points hanging in front of my face. One terminal actually touched my nose. Also two needles in legs and one in chest; the next visit was for electrically charged air and two needles."

The fifth treatment was needles only. That evening a very small cat gave Diana a severe bout of hay fever! Nevertheless she continued: electrical breathing and two needles in arms near elbows; next week six needles and no *inisiagione*. Diana fell into a doze during this session and her head fell forward until her nose was within an ace of the high voltage terminal. I fear that all the man's needles and all his brave talk did nothing to relieve Diana of hay fever allergy in Italy.

It was on 11 June that Frank Theron, the South African Minister, and his wife paid us the high compliment of inviting us to their Legation to meet Field Marshal Jan Smuts. Diana had not met him before. It was good to remind him of my stay at Liberty House, Pretoria, in 1943, when he had asked me to help him draft a telegram to Churchill about the South African division lost at Tobruk. He remembered and we thanked God for victory and mercy since then. He told me of the high regard he had for Frank Theron.

That meeting was a great comfort and a refresher to me. Regardless of what the present was or what the future held for us, it was good to have met men like Smuts - probably the greatest thinking British statesman in the Empire; greatest because he could remain detached from the appalling minutiae of every day problems and could see the wood in spite of the trees. In the last three years I had met men like Smuts and Churchill, Alexander and Macmillan, Eisenhower and Robertson, and learnt much from their outlook, their courage and their faith.

On 2 July the Lush household rose early and motored to Siena, 143 miles, to watch the Palio (the traditional horse race round the Piazza of the city). Siena was in full fete and Rod Sarell and I, after a wash and brush up in the Albergo Excelsior, called on the Prefect who was charming and pleased to see us. We then lunched at the Ristorante Cannon d'Oro where "local Garibaldini and wounded ex-soldiers were lunching and making speeches." The Communists were very much masters of the ceremonies. Diana, who had been very plucky to come, for she was suffering much from bodily sunburn, found what rest there was in the car (every building was packed with people). We others rather cruelly left her and visited the Duomo and then returned to the Circolo where we waited on the verandahs in most oppressive heat (a storm was brewing but never burst) from 6 - 8 pm. The Piazza, except for the racetrack round the edge thereof, was now packed to a standstill with people.

The Palio is so named because before the race a procession marches round the track in which the insignia of the various quarters of the city are worn by costumed men who wind and wave and throw giant flags most attractively, miraculously and scientifically, each flag preceding the horse of the quarter which is about to compete, as the mount is led round by his jockey accompanied by a knight in armour. The Palio or flag exercise is a most exhilarating sight which somehow increases the excitement of the crowd at every window and door round the Piazza to fever pitch - the massed bodies in the central enclosure are too tightly squeezed to breathe. The horses are mounted, the jockeys riding bare back, the horse having bridles only. The jockeys carry whips which can be used on his own horse, the horse or body of an opposing rider or any object which attracts the jockey's fancy. The race is started by the firing of a very loud maroon. On this occasion the noise of the explosion caused one of the horses to leap right over the rails of the race course and into the massed crowds in the centre. From our verandah one could see the whole mass of some thousands of people sway visibly to our left. The horse and jockey were retrieved unhurt; the casualties in the crowd were presumably healed or removed to hospital or mortuary (in addition an old gentleman immediately below us was removed in the throes of heart attack). A false start having been declared the horses were realigned, a second maroon overcame the noisy scene and this time they were "off". Four times these courageous horses galloped *ventre a terre* round the sanded piazza, round the people sardined in the centre. The whips were put to use right early; the noise rose to more than a crescendo; one closed one's eyes from watching the most dangerous corner; miraculously no horse fell; no jockey was dismounted nor lassoed by the leather whips. One horse easily came first past the winning post opposite the Prefect and ourselves; there were mighty cheers from part of the crowd, and at this moment we slipped away. Preston, my ever gallant driver, led us to the Humber which he had parked for a quick getaway and we sped southwards through the failing light, stopping only to devour a little supper and vino before dark, and thereafter Preston and I drove a gallant trio of passengers to a 2.30 am arrival in Rome.

That same month, July 1946, Colonel Dusty Miller, Regional Commissioner of Bolzano and the north, came to say with us and on 9 July departed for his Bolzano bearing with him our daughters, Sylvia and Meriel, and Iride, the Italian maid, to look after them. They flew from Rome to Venice whence they went by car to the highlands of Bolzano. They stayed with their generous and hospitable host for over a fortnight, away from the heat of Rome in the lovely mountain region, and most thoroughly enjoyed themselves eating peaches.

We (Diana, Rod, Pam and various guests) left Rome towards the end of July for my last tour of the north: some (Pam and I) by car and others (Diana and Rod) by air. Let us face facts: the journey was designed to join pleasure with duty.

We joined forces at Venice where we entered the general merriment of the Fiesta (The Feast of the Redemption) and spent two days in Venice, went on to Udine where I had a meeting with many AMG officers and also met General John Harding (on the polo ground). I then went on alone to Trieste for my last visit to Al Bowman and AMG there, while Diana and Pam stayed at Aiello with John Fletcher (Diana's cousin) who had recovered from his two wounds and was in command of a Royal Engineer Unit with his wife, Cecily, alongside. I had a most satisfactory meeting with Colonel Al Bowman whom I noticed was becoming somewhat regal but seemed to have the Trieste situation in hand. I then returned to Aiello and we all drove to Bolzano to stay with Dusty Miller, the Regional Commissioner (or was he by now a Chief Liaison Officer?) and rejoin our two daughters. Dusty of course, had been immeasurably kind and the country, in which the lovely villa Boscaverda was situated, just outside Bolzano, was very beautiful. I remember being much impressed by the atmosphere of the Displaced Persons camp in the barracks of Bolzano and we all enjoyed a rattling good entertainment of folklore (with Tyrolean costumes, songs and dances) which the Camp Commandant, a Captain Dawson, had put on for us.

I flew on to Milan to spend a busy day there and was joined by Diana, Sylvia, Meriel and Pam and we all dined with the British Liaison Officer Colonel and Mrs Gardner and had a cheerful evening. From Milan I went with Pam to Turin and the French frontier, and then to Genoa leaving Diana and the family and others to fly to Rome. We all came together again after a day or two and celebrated Diana's birthday quietly in Rome.

By this time Major General Edward Goulburn, Head of the British Military Mission to the Italian Army, had appeared on the scene. He was an old Sudan Defence Force officer and we started a friendship which was to last long after Rome and the war, and to include some delightful visits in the '60s and '70s and '80s to Bridgenorth, Shropshire where his hospitality was always abundant.

The beginning of August brought the "Bing Boys" to stay with us at the Villa, viz. Julian Snow MP and Geoffrey Bing MP (the latter a near Communist) but both very good house guests who enjoyed their stay in Rome *chez moi*. They were given every honour and opportunity by the Italian government, especially the left wingers, and this gave us a lot of fun. *Very* curious politicians came to see Geoffrey Bing.

In July 1946 Julian, having been extracted from the train in the small hours by my late PA, Arthur Stewart, who gave him an excellent day and night in Venice, arrived by air in Rome. Our Bing Boys had gone to Greece.

I note an early entry which shows Diana acting as hostess for Sir Noel Charles at the British Embassy to entertain to dinner General Auchinleck, General Godwin Austen, Brigadier Desmond Young and Eddie Goulburn.

Somebody crept into the bedroom that night and ecstatically told us the great news for herself and for us; we greatly rejoiced to know that Pam Crowther Smith and Rod Sarell were engaged to be married!

The diary entry reads:

"…. Great were our family and villa celebrations next day, and after dinner we all went down to the sea at Frigene and swam; and swim we did next day (it was a very hot Sunday) before going to the opera Mephistophele - Bing Boys and all."

Two days later the Bing Boys took us, after a day's bathing, to *Aida* at the Baths of Caracalla. Then, honour heaped on honour, we sat down fourteen to lunch to welcome back to the fold Judge Governor Charlie Poletti from New York State with Arthur Hancock, his old "buddy" from Palermo and Milan, and the British Bing Boys. That *was* a party at which, we thought, Charlie Poletti was extremely interested to meet Julian Snow and Geoffrey Bing, two notable back benchers in the Labour Government in London. I think it was Charlie's night!

In mid-August the said Bing Boys took Diana and Julian for a three-day tour in Tuscany. They travelled in a leisurely manner and extracts from the diary read:

"…. stopped at Foligno to fill up (petrol and of course vino); Assisi for ices, church and wine; left Perugia (lunch) and bathed in Lake Trasimene (very hot shallow water), drinks at San Giovanni, Val d'Arno, Provincia d'Arezzo; arrived in Florence (Excelsior Hotel) and after dinner all five walked to Ponte Vecchio and round Florence …."

They were shown some of the treasures of Florence next morning, including Michelangelo's David, and went up the hill to San Miniata Church whence a wonderful view is had of all Florence. They reached Siena in the afternoon and watched another Pallio, from the Club verandah with the Prefect. They left Siena early next morning and some miles down the road had a grand breakfast of fried potatoes, tomatoes and two eggs each with coffee and wine, reaching Rome at 3.30 pm glad to tuck into a cold lunch. That evening there was opera and ballet at Termi di Caracala: I Pagliacci di Ruggero Leonearalla and I Pini di Roma di Ottorina Respighli: the first performance of this tuneful ballet. Not a bad three days for a boy of thirteen!

Angela Sarell, Rod's sister arrived the next day and remained until the wedding day. For Pam and Rod had opted (with our "gracious permission"!) to be married from our villa in mid-September. This unfortunately precluded the presence of many relatives. Diana and I had the (pleasant) but strenuous task of writing to Pam's parents, telling them all about Rod Sarell (or as much as we knew, which was all good) and now we wrote another series saying what a splendid sister he had. Pam's sisters and brothers, meanwhile, had sent us a questionnaire about Pam's intended: Did he eat his porridge (or pasta) in a gentlemanly manner? Did he snore? Did he wear a bow tie?

Pam had sweetly asked Sylvia and Meriel to be bridesmaids and, of course, we asked whether we could hold the reception, *in loco parentis*, at the villa.

All this was agreed both by Pam and Rod, by Pam's parents and by Angela his sister, and thenceforth the private lives of the inmates of the villa were joyously concentrated on the happy celebration of that wedding. First the civil authorities must be involved, the British Consul and the Italian office of Prince Doria; then the Priest-in-Charge of the Protestant Church. Finally all was arranged and the wedding set for 14 September 1946.

MSL's future

As late as 7 September I took the decision to quit the Allied Commission and the Army and to accept Sir Herbert Emerson's invitation to join the InterGovernmental Committee on Refugees of which he was Chairman and to spend a year or two working for them. Diana was already a member of the organisation. I had been impressed by the Chairman whom I had met in London. In one way, I suppose, it was a *faute d'mieux* for someone who had aimed higher - I had asked the Colonial Office if they had any Governorships to spare. In spite of the lunch which Shell had given me, they had not made any offer of employment and I was chary of a direct approach; and in truth, the one problem which seemed to me to need a solution or aid towards a solution was the desperate plight of refugees, the flotsam and jetsam of war, of which I had experienced ample proof in the last four years. I had most thoroughly enjoyed my experience in administering Allied Military Government in four countries during the war and I decided to continue, during the next two or three years, the task of trying to help some of those hapless people rendered homeless by war; to enter into the empty territory of the homeless man, this time, thanks be, in company with Diana. Neither of us regretted our decision, which was mutual, at any time during the next four or five years, during which we travelled over much new ground and some old, made many new friends and were able to fulfil our determination (at any rate during school holidays) of living a family life.

So I gave my notice to Ellery Stone and cabled the IGCR in London.

Rome's maximum temperature then was 103°F so it was not surprising that the whole Lush family, Guy Hannaford (who had become a very integral and beloved member of the family), the Sarells, brother and sister, Pam, Madge Angus (who was to become a very close part of our new life), Marion Planner von Plann, Pluto and Preston all went off after church to the beach, where the stream runs into the sea; there we spent the afternoon. We probably slept a good deal in 100°F, but I have no doubt that four of us, at least, had happy visions of the new life to which we were now committed - and were contentedly apprehensive of what was to come! Only four days left before Pam and Rod's wedding, six days before Diana and I left by air for UK.

We still rode each morning and I had a morning to effect a temporary handover to my successor. On 14 September Rod and Pam's wedding took place.

Extract from Diary 16 September 1946:

> "Met in MSL's office at 11.45 am and proceeded, with Guy Hannaford, to the *campidoglio* where the Mayor of Rome, Prince Doria Pamphili joined us. Pam, Rod and Angela arrived for the Italian Civil Marriage Service. Prince Doria took the service in Italian and translated into English; he was wearing the sash of the Italian Tricolour .... Guy took Rod out to lunch for his stag party; 4.00 pm wedding service in All Saints Church. Maurice gave Pam away; Guy was best man; Sylvia and Meriel were bridesmaids - dressed in blue - and Julian an usher."

We held a reception in the Villa that afternoon after the wedding. There was a throng present, a happy, friendly party of which Diana wrote "Angus was the mainstay of the party".

With only one day intervening, Diana and I handed over the three children to Madge Angus who entrained them at Rome station to face a three-day rail journey to London. The same morning we flew by empty Dakota via Ystres (near Marseilles) where we had engine trouble and burst a tyre taking off, before reaching Blackbush. Then began a hectic three days. The bride's parents, the Crowther Smiths were given a full description of the bridegroom and of the wedding. Then we met the three young and by now very dirty and weary travellers, who, however, had time and energy to see their maternal grandfather Charles Hill at the Carlton Club before bath and bed. Next day we deposited our two daughters at St Swithun's School, Winchester where Sylvia rose to be Headgirl in 1953/4 and where Meriel was to continue for eleven years (surely a record for a boarder), and Julian at Morshead's, Winchester College.

After a few busy days during which I paid farewell calls to the War Office and Civil Affairs and also started work at IGCR Headquarters in Hill Street, spending off time hours with my mother and brother and some Sandfords at Brookside, I flew back to Rome where I was still on duty.

In Rome it took some time to put ***finis*** to a number of questions and matters and to hand fully over to my successor Brigadier Carr, a Regional Commissioner of long standing and sureness, and also a good friend. There was the question of honours and awards to the British officers and men who fully deserved them and had not been included, for lack of priority. The Villa was handed over to A V M Brodie of the Air Force Sub-Commission and questions of compensation to be ventilated, if not settled. I said goodbye to my friends in Caserta, who were good enough to give me a farewell luncheon and finally I placed Pluto, our family Pluto, in the good hands of A V M Brodie and his staff at the Villa. (We were to see Rome and many of our friends and Pluto once more when we passed through as civilians at the beginning of November 1946.)

In fact, I did not return to London for ten days, just in time to go with Diana to Judith Lush's wedding with Tom Minta, a young engineer, at Tamerton Foliot near Plymouth. This gave us a good opportunity for discussing the future with Cecil and my mother.

On 10 October, 1946, I was demobilised at a demobilisation centre in Guildford. I was duly given my papers, my journey money and a not too bad suit of clothes in which I drove away - like many of the other men and women of all ranks re-entering civilian life again. I had ranked as an officer in His Majesty's Army for almost exactly 30 years, ten of which as a serving soldier in World Wars I and II and twenty in the Regular Army Reserve of Officers. I write the next sentence with humility but this is a record of my life. During those ten years I was awarded the Military Cross and Bar in World War I and made a Commander of the British Empire in 1943 and a Companion of the Bath in 1945; I was also mentioned in despatches Madagascar, Tripolitania and Italy four times.

Now all our efforts were concentrated in the new beginnings which our three children were to make at school in Winchester, and the new mission which Diana and I had deliberately chosen for ourselves. Once we, or perhaps I myself, had decided to quit the Army and Civil Affairs, we felt relieved and enthusiastic to begin a new life in which we, as lucky survivors, were charged with the relief and future happiness of those who had suffered far more than we could imagine.

Finis Italiae

ROME 1946

Together again, Rome, 1945

MSL, DRL, Sylvia, Meriel and Pluto at Rome Airport, 1946

Meriel with ever-helpful Pluto

The Sarell wedding in Rome, 16 September 1945

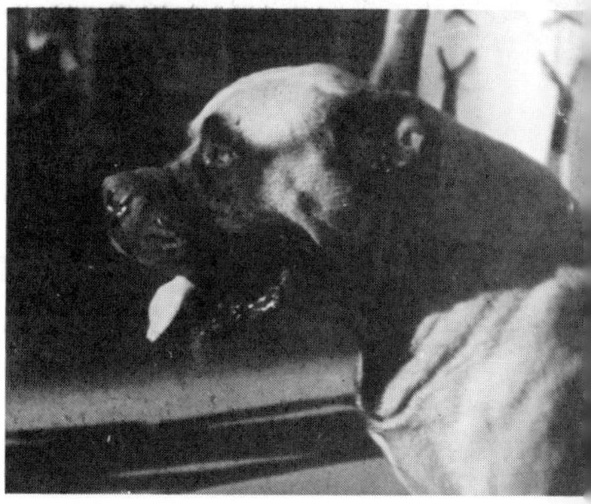

Pluto, above, and below, in sunglasses

GERMANY 1947

Ann Bowman, MSL, Madge Angus and Temnomeroff, 1947

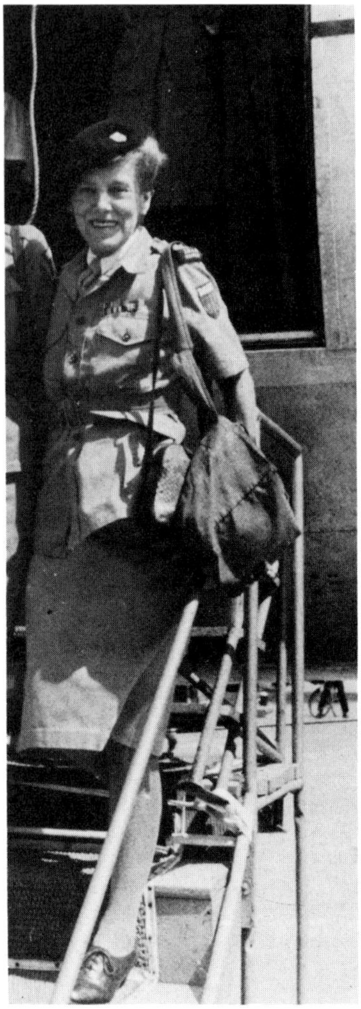

Madge Angus

Alan Hill, Temnomeroff, MSL and others in IGCR, 1947

Alan Hill with refugees for resettlement, 1947

Post-War: International Service

CHAPTER 14

IGCR and IRO 1946-51

14.1 - Resident Representative for Germany/Austria, IGCR: Oct 1946 - Aug 1947

I had followed Diana into the service of the Inter-Governmental Committee on Refugees (IGCR). The IGCR had been established in 1938, at the instance of President Roosevelt, to meet the problem arising out of

"the tragic impasse of many thousand victims of Nazi intolerance who could find no permanent asylum outside Germany because of the impact of economic depression in many countries both in Europe and overseas ...."

The IGCR's funds, provided mainly from British and American Government sources, were spent almost entirely on internal administration. It relied on diplomatic pressure with extraneous financial support to effect the movement of refugees.

The outbreak of war in 1939, and its immediate effects, underlined the inadequacy of the whole structure of IGCR, manfully as its members had committed themselves to the task. But the intergovernmental efforts had served usefully to coordinate the work of voluntary societies in every nation, and had introduced the significant concept of PLANNED MIGRATION.

The IGCR had been empowered by the League of Nations to consider the planned movement of Jews out of Germany as well as the problem of German Jews outside Germany and it was at this time that the conception of planned migration was introduced.

During World War II the importance of the *military* control of the displaced persons (DP) problem had become apparent to the British Army in the German advance into Belgium and France in 1940 and when Supreme Headquarters Allied Expeditionary Force (SHAEF) came into being in 1943, the Displaced Persons Branch under SHAEF (and as we had seen, in Italy, under SACMED) became an integral part of the Army. Plans drafted by this branch became part of instructions to Army group commanders. In liberated countries (eg. France, Belgium, Netherlands) the care of DPs was the responsibility of the Allied Governments (Britain, Canada, America, etc) assisted by the Supreme Military HQ; in occupied enemy territory they were the direct responsibility of the defeated enemy (German and Austrian) authorities supervised by Allied Military Government.

The repatriation of DPs to and from France, Belgium, Luxembourg and The Netherlands, although difficult, was relatively easy compared with the task which confronted the Allied military authorities and their successors in Germany, Austria and Italy.

At the end of the war there were more than 11 million displaced non-German people in Europe; most of these were in the occupied countries of Germany, Austria and Italy - occupied by the Western Allies and the Soviet Army.

The collaboration between SHAEF and the European Allied Governments was admirable and repatriation of six and a half million people was carried out successfully by the military components of SHAEF with the assistance of United Nations Relief and Rehabilitation Agency (UNRRA). The military authorities, through their Refugees and Displaced Persons Sections of Civil Affairs Departments, took responsibility for all basic supplies, movements and provision of transport together with security etc. UNRRA took charge of administration of assembly centres including the work of voluntary agencies in such centres; the operation of the Central Tracing Bureau (a vitally important factor in all refugee work) and coordination with the Military and Governmental authorities in arranging the movement and repatriation of DPs. UNRRA was expected to participate both in planning and operations concerning DPs acting under the orders of SHAEF and through military channels.

So far so good as regards repatriation of those who were repatriable and willing to go home. It was a complicated and difficult task of maintaining and caring for those who had been separated from the countries to which they belonged, who regarded those countries as ultimate home and wanted to go home.

But there existed a class of DPs who were "non repatriable": Sir Herbert Emerson, Director of IGCR, described them (October 1944) as

> ".... persons who are stateless - lacking in law or in fact the protection of any Government - as a result of racial, religious or political policy adopted by their former countries. This class includes persons of German or Austrian origin, principally but not exclusively Jewish by religion, most of whom have suffered 'denationalisation'."

Some Austrian Jews, although denationalised, were still in Austria or had returned from temporary absence.

There were also many thousands of Poles, Lithuanians, Estonians and others from the Baltic group who would not voluntarily return to their places of origin owing to the seizure of their countries (Poland, Lithuania, Latvia and Estonia) by the Soviet Union and the establishment therein of Communism.

It was such people scattered over Europe, Middle East, Africa and even India, which came under the aegis of IGCR and it was this problem that Sir Herbert Emerson asked me to help him solve "as a colleague", working as Chief of Mission of IGCR in Germany and Austria.

In September 1946 I took the decision to accept and cabled Sir Herbert accordingly. I was proud that having administered the civilian victims of war for five years it was compatible to continue that mission among those who had suffered terribly as a result of war - far more than any who, so far, had come within my ken. I never regretted my decision and I hope that, together, we brought some hope, some happiness to men and women and their children who had no place, no country, no well remembered town, hamlet or house to which they could return; who by their own decision, forced on themselves by the behaviour of others and their own conscience or pride, found life in new and strange lands where freedom reigned.

We experienced in these next five years (1946-51) both compassion for those who were not repatriable, and immense respect and gratitude towards the countries and their peoples who received this homeless multitude. Diana and I travelled through many countries in the Middle East and Africa during the next few years and experienced some moving instances of help and sympathy extended to these victims of war by the arrogance and cruelty of political regimes.

From that day in September 1946 in Rome, the tempo of our lives moved fast. We left Rome by air, two days after the Sarell wedding, condemning our three children to a journey by train across Europe (see below) where, on arrival, they proceeded, one and all, to new schools: Julian to Winchester College, Sylvia and Meriel to St Swithun's, Winchester. Diana and I had an adventurous flight via Ystres, but eventually landed a little late to find a noble Mervyn Hill waiting with our car at Blackbush, near Camberley.

We saw the parents of Pamela Sarell and talked of the wedding and bride and bridegroom; we visited our two daughters in St Swithun's School, met my mother and brother Cecil in Devon and various Sandfords in Surrey; I flew back to Rome officially to wind up my military office while Diana visited Julian at Winchester and rejoined a few family and other links. I managed to arrive in England just in time for my goddaughter and niece's wedding in Tamerton Foliot church in Devon - Judith Lush married Tom Minta - before my demobilisation on 10 October.

I interviewed and took on my PA, Anne Brymer Jones (Bowman) in the House of Commons, we bought a Vauxhall car and I spent a good many hours studying at IGCR, 17 Hill Street, where Emerson and his staff (whom I met severally and en masse) were most welcoming.

My first duty for the remainder of October was to learn my job in IGCR. My appointment was Chief of Mission IGCR in Germany and Austria and my Director (Sir Herbert) told me that he was appointing an American General John Wood, as my Deputy. I insisted on the expression "colleague" rather than "Deputy" and indeed John Wood, who turned out to be one of the salt of the American earth, worked as a loyal colleague throughout my service in IGCR.

In London I had the privilege of discussions with Emerson and members of his staff who were charming and I very soon felt more than content, indeed very happy, in my choice of service for refugees.

Care of and especially resettlement of the non-repatriable was very much the kernel of our discussions and programmes, and it soon became apparent that John Wood and I would find our early days in Austria and Germany explaining to all the authorities on the continent both Military (British, American and French) and UNRRA our plans of selection, care and maintenance, movement in Europe and finally actual voyages to resettlement.

As I explained above, the general care and movement of all refugees was shared between the military authorities (who had the first and final say) and UNRRA: and here we of IGCR came as a third party. I knew that UNRRA was not particularly beloved in military circles

- I had been a soldier myself! It would need much care to achieve full acceptance of our plans from both the Military and UNRRA and the situation was not made easier vis à vis the generals by the knowledge that both IGCR and UNRRA would disappear within a year, giving way to "another ruddy international body" called the International Refugee Organisation, a child of the United Nations; "God knows what good can come of the UN - just remember the League of Nations and their pitiable performance before the last war" must have been the thoughts of the occupying military powers.

All this I was absorbing in London together with one other vital factor. A resettlement plan was very much in the wind and in fact the Deputy Director (Malin) was now in the receiving country, Brazil, dotting i's and crossing t's regarding the personal and legal status of the DP migrants on their arrival, while a Brazilian team was in Europe taking a good look at their future citizens as they began preliminary tours of the refugees prior to individual selections. In fact, just before we were due to leave *en mission* I went on a 48-hour visit to a spot in Germany to meet Brazilians (and John Wood).

I thoroughly enjoyed my initiation into IGCR and found the staff thoroughly versed in the main job and only too ready to impart knowledge. I liked Emerson immensely and, although he was the older man, we had much in common professionally.

All this time, from 17 September until 4 November, we were living in 73 Fortune Green Road, West Hampstead, kindly lent to us for those six weeks by Pam Sarell's parents, the Crowther Smiths. It was, in fact, one of their London houses which Molly and other daughters used - Sheila and Tim lived next door. It was a wonderful haven for us during those busy weeks, though we were seldom there, except to sleep, during the week. Our waking hours were spent in London where our social centre was always the Conservative Club (at the bottom of St James's Street). I had been a member since 1922 when Alec Douglas Home, Consul in Abyssinia, proposed me, and a great number of Sudan Political friends joined at about the same time or after. It was, in fact, the Sudan social centre for many years - conveniently situated near the Sudan Government Office at Wellington House just across St James's Park. Moreover, in 1920, I found that my father-in-law and all his sons were staunch members. During that autumn of 1946 we ate and drank our fill in that hospitable friendly building - with its ladies entrance in Little St James's Street. Pruniers was next door and for special occasions we would take our friends thither.

We saw a lot of the Crowther Smiths and Angela Sarell at the beginning of our visit to London (Rod and Pam Sarell were now *en poste* in Bucharest) and of course, my father-in-law, Charles Hill "CAH", with Richard, Mervyn and Alan Hill. CAH was not at all well - very shaky and wobbly on his feet, but his humour had not left him and he was genuinely delighted to see Diana and the three children.

Here let me confess to a parental sin of much gravity - for which I blame myself - suffering as I was in Rome from a military sense of instant duty: on Monday of the week of 16 September, the day Diana and I left Rome, we had handed over our three children aged 13, 10 and 6 to Madge Angus, be she never so kind, to entrain next day in a children's return railway journey Rome-London, 1200 miles! They travelled in two parties, boys and girls apart. Not until Thursday 19 September at 5pm did that party of young travellers arrive at Waterloo Station, having travelled for two and a half days.

Other friends and relatives whom we saw included my mother (aged 86) who was holding the Sandford fort at Brookside, a few younger Sandfords, including Dick, now recovered from his wounds received in Burma and about to enter Oxford; Dora Carson Roberts nearing 80, in her hospitable house in Mallord Street; the Campbell Taylors still in Ewhurst, and a number of Sudan friends many of whom were returning to Africa after leave. Sir Stewart and Lady Symes asked us to a party and we dined at the House of Commons with the "Bing Boys" (Julian Snow and Geoffrey Bing). As always in Winchester we stayed with the ever-hospitable Matthews and from their Sandpits made forays to St Swithun's to catch a glimpse of our two very precious daughters. Of Julian we saw less but heard that he was settling down in Mr Hunter's house.

Incidentally, it was at this juncture in our career that I told our three children that I had accepted this job with IGCR, that it would entail service and living abroad but I assured them (and ourselves) that wherever we were stationed our home would be their home and that they would spend the holidays with us without fail. We lived up to that assurance throughout their school and university careers and in fact until 1960 when we came back to the UK to roost.

Let us return to November 1946. At the beginning of our stay in the UK we had bought a Vauxhall 4-seater car for our private use in the UK. The IGCR kindly provided us with a V8 Ford, a dark brown tourer 22HP which was always a bad starter but did us proud on our many journeys first London to Rome, thence to Vienna, Munich and the north, and on countless rapid journeys to the North Sea coast. For Sir Herbert had stressed, from the start, his preference for personal visits (a week each month) to correspondence.

After my 48-hour visit to Brazilians in Brussels we finally left the UK, Diana, Anne Bowman and myself, by car for Rome on 5 November. I was determined not to make this a rushed journey, nor were there facilities, eg. at Folkestone, where we spent our last night in England, for anything more than a leisurely loading of the car (by crane on to the quarter deck) and a leisurely unloading at Calais. We met at lunch on board no other than ex-Lieutenant Commander Simpson Jones RNVR who had so curiously emerged from the French side when they surrendered to us at Tananarive. He was also en route for Rome (on what intent we did not enquire). We spent our first night at Arras, thence to Besançon and on the third day crossed the Swiss frontier (433 miles from Calais). It was good to journey though Switzerland, clean and beautiful, no trace of war; having lunched at Lausanne, we passed Château de Chillon and climbed to Martigny whence we crossed the Grand St Bernard Pass. We reached the snow-line and very icy roads at sunset and the summit (all road surface snow) in full moonlight. How they allowed us to attempt the crossing at that hour on that date I never discovered (we were probably the last private car to tackle the pass that year). I emerged from the car at the "Sommet" notice and fell flat on my face in the frozen snow. We thought it was wise not to tarry and began our 22-mile descent to Aosta to find the Swiss and the Italian customs closed! But thank goodness not so shut that they could not let us through with clicks and clucks and warnings not to attempt such a thing again. We slept thankfully at the Hotel de la Couronne - but found no hot water - a bad omission after the Grand St Bernard Pass under snow in moonlight. Outside Aosta we called on old friends of last year, Cecile and Edmond Howard and then drove on to Turin. We continued as far as Genoa where we found good hot baths at last. I made my number with the British and Brazilian Consulates while Diana and Anne searched for petrol, finally finding help from one of the few relics of the Allied Commission, a British Liaison Unit. Diana "pulled out my name" etc. and so 30 litres became ours. On through Rapallo and La Spezia and through the Italian marble quarries, Forte del Marmi - little known, and worthy of a full day's visit. Called on the Contessa di Gropello and left a parcel from Viola Symes (herself an Italian); ended the day with a good dinner at my favourite walled city of Italy, Lucca, and a drive round that city *on* the walls - admiring the loveliness of the placid November evening under a full moon. Again *"niente corrrente"* and so *"niente aqua calda"*.

It was raining next day at Pisa but I took my PA, Anne, up the leaning tower (always rather a disappointment to me - in war or peace), remembering my first visit when Pisa was under shell fire.

We reached Rome in the evening and dined at the Casino Valadier after several of their well known Alexander cocktails, then acquainted Mrs Angus of our presence and finally reached Hotel Flora and slept the sleep of the just in the very hotel (but not the special suite) where I had first stayed in June and July 1944.

It was good to have driven a car 1,000 miles, as a civilian, and to feel unattached in Rome - much as we had loved our villa and its beloved occupants. It was now, I suppose, that I began to realise the full gravity of the task of IGCR had taken on and asked me to do, viz. the finding of new homes in unknown countries for some thousands of unhappy people who just could not go home. It was such a terrible outlook for them, such a serious task for us - so necessary to judge aright both seekers and recipients.

I thought it right to enlist the Vatican's assistance. I wrote to IGCR on 15.11.46:

".... I had a private audience with the Pope this morning when I gave him a picture of the work of IGCR and I am seeing the Senior Cardinal in the Secretariat of State tomorrow."

The Vatican was tackling the refugee problem but, as d'Arcy Osborne (still HBM Minister in The Holy See) warned me, in a truly Curial manner - ardent in intent, archaic in practice. D'Arcy Osborne was, as usual, helpful and wise in his advice, and at any rate I had introduced IGCR to the Holy Father and found out the names of his useful prelates in Austria and Germany. I knew a number of them from Allied Commission times especially Mantini, destined to be the next Pope, then Cardinal Secretary of State.

I also met Neiva, of the Brazilian resettlement mission, to whose country we much hoped to send our first batches of refugees.

It was, I repeat, good to be in Italy again, and the transition from Chief of Staff of the Allied Commission to civilian rank seemed to make little difference for we had so many friends - even among hotel staff! Of course we had to do more for ourselves (permits, petrol, food and stores) and that is why I continued to carry a PA who tackled all such problems. Diana and I both realised at once how much we had loved the city and all our friends therein and in other parts of Italy. There was much to do both for IGCR and as relics of the Allied Commission.

Diana spent many hours, and I not a few, at the Villa Zenardo, Via del Sassoferrato sorting out possessions, packing some and disposing of others. She was aided by our former maid, Iride, who had been so good to the children, and the quartermaster of the Allied Commission, Major Tim Scully, who came loyally to the rescue. We said a final sad farewell to the staff of the Villa which was now the Mess of the Royal Air Force Sub-Commission into whose care our beloved Pluto had passed - apparently very happily.

Many friends welcomed us and said goodbye especially the Dorias, d'Arcy Osborne, the Therons at the South African Legation, Ian Brodie, John and Margaret Ward Perkins, whose appointment I had sponsored as Director of the British School in Rome and whose guests we were to be some 15 years later. Finally Prince and Princess Doria asked a few of our Italian friends including their daughter Orietta, Princess Borromeo, together with the Olivers to meet us at a final dinner.

On 20 November Diana and I, with Anne and Madge Angus (in her tiny Topolino), and a lorry with a great deal of our Rome luggage

".... left the Hotel Flora, called at Trevi fountain where we threw coins into the water, set out on the Via Flaminia ...."

We headed north to Rimini. Next day "we crossed the Rubicon" and reached Udine where John and Cecily Fletcher and Betty Moreton joined the party for lunch. We crossed the Austrian frontier whence we worked our way to Hans Heindall Velden near Dellach on the southern shores of the Worthe Sea where Diana and I were to stay with Brigadier and Lady Katherine Armitage - he Head of the British Red Cross in Austria (and Germany) - a lovely job with this attractive house on the lake.

Bavaria

So began our IGCR work in Austria and Germany. The Committee had already notified all authorities (military, civil affairs and UNRRA) of our mission regarding refugees: we had assumed responsibility for the resettlement of refugees who for political, religious or racial reason were not repatriable and therefore stateless, in law or in fact. UNRRA had assumed the care of DPs still in enemy territory who did not wish to return or did not wish to return immediately.

In order to implement our duties IGCR had to trace such non-repatriable refugees, and counsel them regarding: (a) a possible change of mind towards their homeland; (b) choice and selection of a country in which they would like to make their home; (c) movement to their chosen home. IGCR also had the duty of persuading such countries to receive them.

As Head of the IGCR Mission in Austria and Germany, it was my job to explain our mission to the Allied military authorities and to UNRRA. As regards the military authorities, who themselves had repatriated about 12 million DPs returning voluntarily to their homelands, SHAEF had been, most naturally, inclined to believe that once the fighting was over, practically all the DPs would be eager to return to their former homes to participate in the painful reconstruction of their countries.

It was now apparent that this did not apply to all refugees and that there would be left a large group of unrepatriable persons of Estonian, Latvian, Lithuanian and particularly Polish origin, from Yugoslavia and other south eastern European countries, and of course, a large number of Jews. IGCR had already begun dealing with these groups both inside the camps by training and counselling, and abroad by consultation with receiving countries; we had men and women in Austria and Germany and would have more. I, with John Wood, directed the operations in the Allied zones of occupation while London was dealing with the receiving countries. London had recruited another General, Walter Wood, and suggested that we three carried out a tour of all the authorities concerned in Germany and Austria in order to acquaint them fully of our presence and intentions and to ask for such administrative and residential aid as they could spare for us - always in the hope that the more they, the authorities, helped us, the sooner the task would be completed.

Leaving Diana in Klagenfurt I went on with Angus to Vienna where the others joined us (we squeezed in two Acts of Tannhauser at the Volks Opera House), the others being Generals John Wood and Walter Wood - the latter late Quartermaster General in the US War Department, ie. an expert on movement, etc. We hired a railway saloon coach wherein we three men established ourselves very comfortably and carried out a quick but comprehensive rail tour of the Allied Occupation Zones of Germany and Austria, including Berlin, seeking out all the authorities from the Commanders-in-Chief downward and telling them what we were up to. It was very interesting. We three got on very well together and between us we knew, personally, most of the military in charge and the UNRRA people who by now were running the camps. We were known as "Operation Timber". The railway authorities (under military direction) did us very well and we had a most successful week. We were a fairly high-powered mission!

Our only signal failure was to persuade the C-in-C US Forces to allow the establishment of my own (and John Wood's) Headquarters at Frankfurt. Even my two stalwart American Generals could not move the gallant C-in-C. The American authorities longed to be quit of DPs, especially the "hard core" as they described our particular unfortunates, but, as always they were suspicious of civilian organisations in their midst. I must say that I, remembering my feelings as Executive Commissioner in Rome, felt slightly sympathetic with them! But it was a local setback. John Wood and I went off to Paris and London to talk about Operation Timber, leaving Diana to find us a temporary HQ for Christmas in the US Zone near Munich: I had loose ends to tie up in our own organisation in that zone before moving north. Angus and Anne were apparently summoned to London leaving Diana alone, but with several willing and efficient IGCR men (Temnomeroff, Van de Bogaert) to find, furnish and provision our house for winter quarters near Munich - a house at Feldafing on the Lake Starnberg, 25 miles south of Munich. Diana's diary tells the story of her successful efforts to have a house ready for all of us (including our three children) at Christmas. She also achieved, solo, a very good relationship with all the IGCR workers both in Munich and Starnberg, the town nearest to Feldafing. Moreover, winter had set in with a vengence. On her way from Austria to Munich Diana had first encountered snow and her diary entry on 15 December ends a busy day with ".... snowing all the time."

There was quite a number of IGCR men and women at Munich and there occur the names of Ives de Vernoy, the French representative (who had plans for resettlement in Morocco and Tunis) and Otto E Abrecht, Alexander van de Bogaert, Tom Burr, Francois Avendt and many other good friends.

John Wood, Angus, Anne and I met in Paris to discuss plans with the most efficient Paris IGCR office. Our journeys on to London were, for Angus and me, full of incident. In Paris we had been offered an airlift (for two only) in a US Dakota - which I gladly accepted for Angus and myself, telling Anne to make her way by sea.

We left Paris before noon on a sunny morning but crossing the Channel I noticed the ominous yellow mist which promised fog (it was December). The US pilot was aiming at a certain airport just north of London. It was very foggy but he saw a gap in the cloud and dropped to land but before the wheels were unleashed I heard him say "Christ, I can't do it!" and up we zoomed into the sun (2,000ft) above the fog. He knew of no other aerodrome in the UK and sent for me to give advice - Northolt and Croydon were "out" and I advised Bournemouth (Gatwick and Heathrow did not then exist). He could not find Bournemouth and by now the UK was definitely fogbound and our only course of action was to make a quick dash for Paris: he had just enough "gas" for Paris, he said. In mid-Channel, believe it or not, we became thoroughly embroiled in a thunderstorm (more alarming than dangerous) and we touched down at Paris Airport (US) thanking our stars that peasoupers were an English delicacy. Madge Angus and I had consumed half a bottle of cognac in that flight! Anne Bowman arrived in sunshine in London just before the blackout. Angus and I devoured a very pleasant and expensive langouste thermidor that evening, and flew over in the same Dakota and perfect sunshine the next day.

John Wood was with us on our second flight and gave Angus and me dinner at the Berkeley the next evening. In the middle of the meal the waiter announced that there was another regular "peasouper" outside. "Peasoupers!" exclaimed John "I must see one" and up he leapt, dragging me out with him into the worst fog I have ever experienced. Every piece of traffic was halted and one stopped in one's tracks trying to avoid colliding with obstacles - hopefully only human obstacles smaller than oneself, and not lampposts or taxis. There was no noise - just beastly, pungent, clammy yellow moisture - very cold. Half an hour was enough for John Wood who was really shocked - and even more so when it took us nearly an hour to find our way from the bottom of St James's Street to the Berkeley, then in Dover Street. "Maurice" he said "You guys have surely gotten something on us with your climate."

Angus, Anne and I returned to Munich by the Orient Express just before Christmas, home late because of ice and snow; for the worst winter in living memory had gripped Europe in 1946-47.

As I have explained, Diana had been hard at work in obtaining the house for our accommodation (4-6 adults and 3 children) but also furnished and victualled against Christmas. Diana procured a great supply of food and drink from the American PX and the US Commissary who gave us everything we needed.

Our London and Paris offices (IGCR) had, in the meantime, persuaded the Brazilian Government to accept a number of refugees as immigrants "after inspection of applicants" and simultaneous with all our Christmas preparations there arrived the Brazilian reception emissary to make plans with us and have a look at some of the Poles. My Orient Express from Paris was late and I saw little of them at work though I managed to have a good outspoken conference at which I convinced them of our readiness and which led, eventually, to action by them.

Christmas and New Year at Feldafing, Bavaria.

The house was called Haus Seepunkt, in the village of Feldafing on the Starnberg See. The mountains and good skiing country lay close by: there were indeed small skiing slopes in the garden. Oberammergau was not far away. The house belonged to Fraulein Evelyn Freis and there were already accommodated in the house another German family called Shayek (all on the top floor). We had fairly cramped but comfortable quarters and the two German ladies cooked and looked after us all. We were five Lushes, Anne and Angus and always a guest; we drew American army rations - very plenteous.

There remained the problem of the children's detrainment from a British military train at Munich in the US Zone. Diana roused most of the transport officers, British and US, on the line between Ostend and Munich to ensure that the children travelled in the portion of the train due to stop at Munich. They had joined the British Army section of the Allied Children's Holiday Train at Ostend. This portion was bound for Vienna or some such city further on. No British child, under pain of death, was allowed to go into the US portion of the train nor to disembark in the US Zone - in which we were living. Then by luck Diana and I met, in Munich, an American officer wishing to join the Christmas train at Trudering, the nearest station to Feldafing, a few miles beyond Munich. Thither we took him and persuaded the stationmaster to telephone the Christmas train then at Karlsruhe. I managed to persuade the British Officer in Command of the British train, on the grounds that we were international, to take our three to the US section and disembark them at Trudering where we would meet them at his estimated ETA - midnight. Mercifully he agreed. Trudering "station" was a goods siding and the stationmaster went home at midnight leaving the signal man in a hut on the line. There we waited until 3am and then leaving cake and coffee for the travellers went home to be woken up at 5.30am by three frozen and rather cross children on the telephone, whom we collected at 7am. However no harm done. [Ed. Nonsense! It took hours to persuade an objectionable American junior officer to make the call, recipient and number unknown: it was 9 am by the time M & D arrived.]

My word it was cold! The coldest we had ever experienced but Diana had done wonders with our Haus Seepunkt and we had a happy, well provisioned Christmas with our own family service (hymns and cards) in the morning and a very jolly international party in the evening with 15-20 in all. "Soup, turkey, mince pies ...." The children did the famous Lush bottle trick with cork, matches and forks. Then our Temnomeroff, a charming person, began and of course continued his conjuring tricks - and he was very good. The diary ends:

"... Party broke up at midnight - children very happy and good."

How we thanked God that at last we could have them

with us (perhaps forgetting the perils and discomfort of reaching such family unions!) Nor did we forget the Shayek family, in whose house we were so happy for we had them all with us on Boxing Day.

Then comes a momentous entry in Diana's diary:

"…. On our return from Munich (where MSL had entrained for Frankfurt on some ploy) stopped at Starnberg to collect skis and ski boots for the children."

Follow other entries:

"…. Children all out with their skis …. Julian and Sylvia on skis to the railway line …. After lunch out on skis again - stayed out till dusk 5.20pm …. Sylvia, D, Angus and Meriel skied - lovely sunshine; clear blue skies …."

In fact Diana had realised from the beginning that the garden at Haus Seepunkt had ski slopes, so she had most splendidly and in a thoroughly professional manner taught our three children to ski - in a week! Skiing had always been one of the joys of her life and she was an expert herself from the age of 14. I fear marriage to a *ful-Sudani* put an end to that joyous display of her grace and art, but here in Feldafing in 1946 she had taken the first opportunity to teach and communicate her skill to our children - who were quick to learn and who, as they grew older, gave full proof of Diana's skill in those first lessons; for they became and remain devoted to the art of skiing and are fine performers - Julian won a half Blue at Cambridge in 1956.

Nor was it all milk and honey for Diana. On Epiphany 1947 she came in from the nursery slopes "…. suddenly felt sick and faint with cold; revived by Bovril and HWB ….". However the next day but one "…. D,J,S and Meriel skiing. Meriel good straight running; other three over small jumps …."
"

In mid-January 1947 I was deserted by my family who spent a day in Paris and were home mid-month and back to school. I joined Diana in London at the end of the month to discuss finalities of the Brazilian settlement with IGCR, and also the take-over by IRO. Our car was stolen for four days but little had been taken from it when found by police. Diana and I returned via Paris where we were, as always, most hospitably entertained and even cossetted by French IGCR. On this occasion we met the British Consul General and the Commander of British Troops in Paris (what a lovely job!). We trained back to Frankfurt and met General John Wood, put our finishing touches to the selection of and the gathering together of the Brazilian Settlement Poles and talked of the take-over by the International Refugee Organisation (IRO).

Lemgo, Lande Lippe

We then had a month of almost unbroken life in Lemgo, Lande Lippe in central Germany, where I had decided to transfer my base of activities. We visited nearby office and camps but not moving far (for the first time since November 1946). We met Air Marshal Sholto Douglas at lunch, Head of the Allied Commission, a contemporary of mine (and classical scholar) at Tonbridge; also the Bishops, he Head of Civil Affairs. We visited John Wood in March and stayed at Hanover and at the end of the month I was Chairman of an IGCR meeting in Frankfurt where discussion on resettlement in England and France (50,000) took place. Then we were joined by Sir Herbert Emerson from London, whom we brought back to Lemgo where we entertained him and caused him to meet nearly all our staff and General Fanshawe of UNRRA and Colonel Todd of the Displaced Persons Division of the British Forces in Germany.

At the beginning of April 1947 our three children joined us in Lemgo for the Easter holidays - their last holiday in Europe for two years.

On their first day "Operation Timber" came to tea in Lemgo and John Wood demolished the family's marmalade ration for one month in one sitting - eating this new (to him) delicacy with a spoon direct from the pot. Family faces fell - revived by a present of 12 pots of CREAM!

Alan Hill had appeared on the scene from somewhere, welcome guest, though one spots entries in DRL's diary of "…. very late home coming AWH …. peculiar noises 2.30am …."

The children went in a party to see the Pied Piper's village of Hameln and by the end of April the first trainload of Polish resettlement candidates had arrived at Buckholz Camp near Lemgo.

Life for the children had not been dull at Lemgo for nearby there were British Army institutions with a squash court and other young people; they rode a little but I cannot be certain whether any of us did bathe in the swimming pool in our garden. We had a pleasant but very commodious house and a resident young German couple of whom the man worked elsewhere and the wife cooked and "did" for us, not very well. These two infuriated me by stealing the children's sweets! In fact, the general impression which I was forming of the Germans, a beaten people in a devastated country (although we lived in areas which had not suffered badly), was of a people who at that moment in their national lives - as an occupied people, unnatural and fettered - really did not care very much about any ideals in life.

I myself was extremely busy ensuring that the final stages of our first resettlement movement went well, that is the resettlement to and in Brazil - and also that the more extensive (and more popular) resettlement plans in Great Britain and France were being shaped on the right lines. I was in close touch with the British Ministry of Labour officials who visited the British Occupational Zone, in which we lived, and persuaded them to accept my amendments to the leaflet which they intended to distribute among non-repatriable refugees. The Ministry's first approach was to attract workers on temporary work, with or without dependents, with the right to opt for permanent settlement elsewhere, at a later stage, if they so wished. The question of citizenship was not mentioned though subjection to British Law, National Insurance and Income Tax was naturally included. I found myself in Vienna, whither the British delegation had gone during April, tying up loose ends of the first movements of Brazilian resettlers and also trying to find out what the underhand movement in the French Zone (definitely anti IGCR with a shade of Soviet policy about it) was achieving.

On my return I found our resettlement camp filling up and still we could not extract a decision from the US HQ at Frankfurt on the use of Bremen (British zone) as port of embarkation for our resettlers. The US military authorities (in Germany) were terribly 'national' and sometimes forgot the word 'international'. For the third member of "Operation Timber" had not been idle and there were rumours of converted liberty ships coming across from US ports to collect resettlers - that was one reason for our 'final' camp at Buckholz filling up rapidly. We just *had* to be ready.

At the end of April Diana went to England and put the three children to school; I joined her in mid-May but not before the first Liberty ship, mentioned above, had sailed from Bremerhaven for Brazil with 800 resettlers and without a hitch. John Wood and I motored like demons from Lemgo to Bremerhaven as soon as we had news of the ship's arrival only in time to see her slip away from the quay. All, apparently, had gone very well as a letter to London shows:

".... everyone spoke highly of the fine quality of the Displaced Persons selected .... they compared favourably with 'the scum of the earth', the phrase applied to those going to the States under the Truman Scheme."

My report also contains the following paragraph:

".... Let me add that the port authorities demanded a four months pregnancy ban but that, on my earlier insistence, broke down. There was a good deal of "I told you so" on their part when one woman, on putting her foot on the deck, immediately began a premature delivery."

In June 1947, Diana and I watched the embarkation of 861 refugees of mixed nationalities, chiefly Poles, with a mixture of Estonians, Latvians and Lithuanians, on board the second ship sent to take refugees to Brazil. It was most successful and very moving. I quote the last paragraphs of my dispatch to IGCR, London:

".... They were pretty dazed and even after boarding the ship they could not (as they told us) really believe that they were leaving Europe, their life of wandering, their sojourn in camps without future, and without work. But they soon settled down and were only disturbed by finding husbands separated from wives and all the complications connected with personal luggage that must ensue therefrom. The accommodation on board is all that could be desired. The lucky ones, perhaps, are those mothers with small children who have three berth cabins plus cot with running water and a shower, and a dining room with tables and chairs for feeding. 'At last' said one such 'We have reached civilisation' and she did not know that ice cream was on the menu! The others sleep in dormitories in swing beds - all with blankets and mattresses and the women between sheets. The latter alone must seem like heaven to most of them. The cafeteria feeding (at any rate in calm weather) looks most efficient and having seen the first meal under preparation I have no qualms on that score except complications from over feeding - a problem which is very carefully watched.

"The ship's officers and staff on board were warm in their sympathy for DPs and enthusiastic in their desire to do all they could to help them and IGCR in this (by far the most comfortable) period of migration, and one had the feeling from Captain Donoghue, the ship's most charming Master, downwards, that every one in the ship was determined to do his or her best for the passengers. The Transport Command Officer (who speaks Russian among several languages) and his staff regards his duties as a mission and DPs in the Heintaleman are in very capable and sympathetic hands."

I have watched many movements of DPs in many countries and they have always brought a lump to my throat. But I have never felt so moved as on that day, watching those young families moving up the gangway, dumping their luggage in their berths or by their bunks, sitting in the sunlight on the deck looking towards the sea, and finally when mistaking me for a DP who had strayed "off limits" a kindly US Transport Sergeant, speaking fluent Polish, led me in a gentle and most fatherly manner to the men's dormitories, explaining I suppose, that that was where I belonged.

We owe a great debt to the US Army authorities and to General Walter Wood for making all this possible. The DPs owe a similar debt to Brazil and the IGCR. I think they will repay their debt to Brazil.

Change to IRO

Before Diana and I joined IGCR we knew that the International Refugee Organisation, a child of the United Nations, would come into being during 1947, replacing IGCR and UNRRA. Our Director had sent out a fully explanatory circular to that effect: it contained the warning that "when IRO comes into operation IGCR will cease to exist". The Preparatory Commission of the IRO was formed in January 1947 with Arthur Altmeyer (US) as its Director. He began to examine the take-over of IGCR and UNRRA which was to take effect in June 1947. John Wood and I met Altmayer (with Hall his assistant) in Frankfurt at the end of May but ".... found them oyster-like as regards plans and frankly uninspiring." However I had already opted to go over to IRO ".... to help in this great human problem which

IRO had to tackle" but only after much pressure.

This acceptance, though I did not know it then, meant cutting adrift entirely from IGCR links in London and Europe and devoting ourselves to the refugee problem in Africa and the Middle East.

Diana and I met in London during May and crossed to Ostend whence we came via Brussels and Liege to Lemgo. In mid-June Diana and I, with Angus, motored to Linz in Austria to say farewell to our Austrian team. In a few days we were back in Ostend and again we were in London and Winchester. Thence I flew to Paris and met Diana in Ostend whence we made Lemgo, driving all night. On 7 July I flew to Geneva and, as I wrote in the diary, saw Altmayer and Hall of IRO at the Palais des Nations. I accepted, after much pressure, to go to the Middle East provided my family could go with me. Altmayer was willing and gave orders for our journeys to be arranged - he was very forthcoming. I had another morning in the Palais des Nations fixing details and then home to Lemgo. On 12 July Diana and I again lunched with Sholto Douglas, the Air Vice Marshall and C-in-C. Sholto announced at luncheon that he was a Christian Communist! I left Lemgo mid-July for London but returned after two days to see the departure of the first flight of refugees for Venezuela - "Babes in the Air" we called it.

We finally left Lemgo in a blaze of glory(!) champagne and the VIP coach on the railway on 22 July for England.

I had enjoyed my nine months with IGCR principally because Diana and I were able to achieve or attempt a combined operation not only in our mental and thoughtful attitude to the very human problem before us but in the practical approach. We shared the driving over many thousands of kilometres of European roads and saw a great deal of Europe from our cars and from railway carriages. We had interests and vital work not only in the capital cities of London, Paris, Vienna, Brussels but also in the vast area of Germany and Austria - and we met on the staff of IGCR and the various delegations who visited us, a varied mixture of many nationalities. We encountered on our own staff on the continent of Europe a type of man and woman somewhat unfamiliar to us, although Diana had seen the fringe of their sort in Italy. We found they were more numerous and more international than, perhaps, we realised at the time, with a novel approach, more emotional than that adopted by our British colleagues (and less definitive). But we enjoyed from all with whom we worked, a loyalty which was most encouraging.

They were nine months of rapid and almost ceaseless movement wherein, had we remained in Europe, I would have said that we sowed the seeds of much work among the non-repatriable refugees in the coming years, (statistics show that refugees were moved from Austria, Germany, Italy and the Netherlands in the next three years), and had indoctrinated staff in sufficient numbers to make an effective mark. I can only hope that John Wood and Peter Gibson who became IRO Chiefs of Mission in Austria, and General Evelyn Fanshawe (late UNRRA) who was Chief in Germany, agreed with me. I left them 33,000 refugees in Austria and 604,000 in Germany in 1947 which they reduced to 2,000 in Austria and 60,000 in Germany by 1950.

I would pay a very loyal tribute to Sir Herbert Emerson who began the whole business and was the most efficient, sympathetic and constructive leader under whom to work. We both admired and appreciated highly his leadership, his patience with our impatience, his great courtesy and kindness. To our shame we did not keep in touch with him after we left IRO in 1950.

Our last days in the UK before leaving IGCR and England, as recorded in Diana's diary, were a miracle of well-organised buying and packing, bidding farewell in London and the country; gathering children in London and Winchester where we spent our last night en famille with all three and with my ever-resourceful brother Cecil who managed to combine a birthday dinner for Diana in Winchester with a midnight carousal on a shipmate's yacht in Beaulieu, before depositing us in our hotel in Winchester at long past midnight. We made Southampton by afternoon on 1 August 1947 after delivering our beloved Vauxhall car to be driven to London and garaged. Thus we embarked on P&O SS Strathmore at Southampton on 1 August, a full family complete plus Anne Moreton whom we were taking as a surprise present to her parents Group Captain Noel and Betty Moreton in Ismailia, great friends from 1935 days. In the same ship there travelled Rev Leighton Thomson who 17 years later married Julian to Sarah in Chelsea Old Church.

Our departure and our break with that particular episode in our lives, November 1946 to July 1947 was made very memorable by an enormous and very lovely bouquet of flowers in Diana's cabin from Julian Snow. They made me homesick for England until Gibraltar.

14.2 - Chief of Mission, Middle East & Africa, IRO, Cairo: Aug 1947 - Mar 1949

It was good to slip away - as every good liner does - on the evening tide of 1 August 1947; to know that we were to be at sea undisturbed until 9 August; a heaven-sent holiday, which, after covering most of Europe by car, train and air for the last eight months, we greatly needed. More than that, the joy of being en famille for this trek to the Middle East was a success in my scheme of things: *"Nihil nos seperabit"*. The addition of Anne Moreton to the family was a great joy.

The sea journey was uneventful but very enjoyable. The children appreciated the bathing and the deck tennis, and we arrived in Port Said in good order. Here, no less than three officials from IRO office (late UNRRA) in Cairo met us together with Betty and Noel Moreton so that women and children could see the famous Simon Artz shop (full of rubbish) while the men dealt with the Egyptian customs. We lunched with the Moretons at Ismailia and were able to watch various ships coming north through the canal. Finally we reached the Mayfair Pension in Sharia Aziz Osman, Zamalek, Cairo, where we had only just time to settle in before Ted Fouracres of the Sudan Agency and Archdeacon Frank Johnston with Gladys his wife, called to welcome us. And strange though it was to be in a pension, a stone's throw from our old flat of 1935 days, it was as if the 11 years since 1935 had just rolled away. Nor did we find that the change of status from the well-known position of Sudan Agent to that of Head of Mission in a United Nations Organisation made much difference in the attitude of the Egyptians or other officials. The Prime Minister and other ministers on whom I called knew that my job was to remove the 700 refugees from the camp at el Shatt near Suez and, though I cannot remember any promise of help or actual help itself, the attitude of the Egyptian officials was invariably friendly. One fairly senior official indeed did give notice that he expected me to leave a small bribe for his help in permitting a Jew (I cannot remember his other nationality) to leave the country but there was only one such instance of an approach to corruption.

It was in the pension that Meriel, seeking a drink of cold water, went to the frig in the living room in which water was kept in old gin bottles, but, due to a confusion of new with old, helped herself to a large and unwanton swig of the real thing - finding it "awfully strong".

We left the Pension Mayfair early in October and for two months were the guests of John Hamilton, absent on leave. Diana had undertaken to oversee the interior decoration of his flat which it badly needed - but the result made discomfort for her - my absence on journeys to Palestine and East Africa saved me from sharing the chaos which only Egyptian decorators can cause.

Soon, however, it was suggested to us by Archdeacon Frank Johnston that, on his transfer to Alexandria and in the absence of any other priestly candidate, the Bishop might allow us to occupy the archidiaconal house in the Cathedral Close; this was almost too good to be true for it was a lovely house, well equipped and furnished. Then additions of our own furnishings and some of our Sudan furniture which we expected to retrieve from Khartoum would make it an ideal family house in the holidays and the large number of official guests which we expected in the months to come. The Cathedral authorities were not allowed to rent the building but I naturally promised to pay an ample and not too regular sum into the Cathedral Appeal Fund. The Bishop gave his permission and we entered residence of that lovely home on the eastern bank of the Nile in the shadow of the Cathedral early in December 1947. Just in time for the children's holidays - for I had promised them regular family life every holiday. They spent four holiday periods in Cairo and we ourselves made the fullest use of the house for the 15 months of our stay in Egypt. We could not have been more comfortable nor better placed and throughout our second (and final) tour of duty in Egypt we gave much thanks in our hearts to Bishop Allan and his wife Madeleine, and to Frank and Gladys Johnston for their wonderful gift to us of a real house. Moreover, having a real house we felt empowered to suggest to our old Sudan *suffragi*, Abder Rahman, that he join our service once more in Cairo. This he did, God bless him, travelling on the instant from Khartoum. Our old cook, Mohammed Dhahab, hearing of our return, had also turned up on the third day in the pension to offer his services again. Thus life was nearly perfect.

I must admit to a near disaster during our stay in that admirable house, opposite to the Bishop's house with which it was identical in shape and form, colour and general aspect, but on the other side of the entrance of the Close. In November 1948 we had staying with us two young, very competent and most charming guests - one a late Wing Commander RAF, employed by Airwork, a well-known British Air Transport firm; the other a member of a financial firm in the City of London. These two guests had been touring East Africa and Egypt with me and others, working extremely hard on an operation called "Airlift" about which I shall write anon. Our two young guests had not had an evening off for weeks and on November 14 (the date is clearly in our memories for Prince Charles was born that night), they asked their host and hostess if they could have a key to the house for "they might be a little late". At 3.45am next morning they returned by taxi after a carousal on the town and proceeded to insert the latch key of the Archdeacon's house into the keyhole of the Bishop's neighbouring and identical house.

Luckily the departure of the Cairene taxi, never a silent performance, awoke Diana and me who were sleeping lightly in expectation of news about our Queen's firstborn. I heard suspicious noises and looking out of our bedroom window saw to my horror the attempt to open Bishop Allan's front door, now made perhaps easier by the action of a friendly Egyptian policeman who was unfixing the bayonet from his rifle in order to insert the weapon into the edge of the door.

Our two visitors who were both swaying slightly were delighted with their unexpected aid to house-entering by authority - but it was, mercifully, a long process and I managed to don a dressing gown and race to the scene of the crime. Laying my hand on the shoulder of the happy Wing Commander I hissed "You are at the wrong house!". Seldom have I seen two unsteady mortals stiffen and regain full consciousness so quickly. *"Malaish"* I said to the friendly disappointed policeman and we tiptoed in the now approaching dawn to the Archdeacon's house. Diana's entry in her diary of the morning in question begins: ".... Geoffrey Ford sleeps late".

Cairo, in fact Egypt as a whole, seemed not dissimilar from the country that we knew so well before the war. The Egyptians certainly had not changed and the European and western population seemed as large and with the same characteristics as before. Entertainment seemed to be on a similar scale and one wore a black tie if one dined at one's host's private house. The clubs, Mohammed Ali and the Turf Club, were very much the same and it was not until we had visited the Gezira Sporting Club a few times that we appreciated the complete absence of the British Army. And then one realised that they had disappeared from the city. A British uniform, of course, was never seen - they were forbidden, just as they would be in Baghdad or Damascus. The polo and races were run by Egyptians; Kasr el Nil Barracks had been destroyed (and we hoped all the bugs therein) and Abbassia contained Egyptian cavalry (or tanks). The anti-aircraft shells which we heard and saw in the Arab Jewish war of 1948 were fired by Egyptian gunners. The British backbone of the Egyptian Civil Service - the Watsons, Keown Boyds and Russells - had disappeared and corruption had increased. Cairo was an Egyptian city, overcrowded, just as noisy, with more motor transport on the dirty roads making more noise with their klaxons and with no diminution of camels, sheep and goats in the streets; the traffic was as badly controlled as before by inefficient but friendly Egyptian police. But we both enjoyed our sojourn in that muddled city. We found many old friends - the Beslys, Marie Pearson, the Ayres and old Prince Mohammed Ali. The British Ambassador, Sir Ronald Campbell, and his staff were most helpful officially and privately hospitable as were the Pinckney Tucks, he the American Ambassador (brother of my Chief of IRO in Geneva). Indeed the several diplomatic missions with whom we had to deal readily gave advice and help and showed sympathy with the perplexities of my mission. I made it my duty to call on Embassies who were actually or likely to be involved, eg. Canada, Australia, South Africa, France, Brazil and Venezuela and met some old acquaintances - the Therons - and made some new friends. The British Ambassador threw a party soon after our arrival in honour of the Dominion status for India and Pakistan which gave us the opportunity of meeting the diplomats en masse. It was good to be in the Embassy gardens again and remember with affection Miles and Jacqueline Lampson.

So much for initial personal activities, surroundings and friends. I must describe the reason for our residence in Cairo.

What was IRO's mission in the Middle East? I quote from *The History of the IRO*:

> "After Germany attacked Russia in June 1941, the Soviet Government came into the war on the side of the Allies and consequently on that of Poland. A Polish Army was formed in Soviet territory consisting of former deportees who were returning to their country on the heels of the retreating German armies. Under an agreement concluded by the Polish Marshal Sikorski and Stalin, approximately 112,000 persons (72,000 military personnel and 40,000 civilians) were released from Russia and went to Iran in 1942 where [the military] formed the so-called 'Anders Army', joining part of the Second Corps which had gone to the Near East, and later fighting in Italy and participating in the Normandy landings. The civilians were received in various countries of temporary asylum, and were dispersed in a way probably never before seen in history. Four thousand were sent to India whence half left for Mexico; 7,000 were divided between Lebanon, Palestine and Egypt; no less than 16,000 were taken over by the British Government in East Africa while 3,000 went to Rhodesia."

The historian does not mention that the reception administration in Persia and the evacuation from Persia of these Poles to the various countries of asylum was carried out in 1942-43 by the Middle East Relief and Refugee Administration (MERRA) set up by the British Minister of State in Cairo. An account of the remarkable operation of mercy and compassion carried out by a handful of British officers is told in the appendix to this sub-chapter.

Between 1943 and 1947 UNRRA's success in repatriating several thousand, combined with other reasons for wastage had reduced the numbers to 28,000 distributed as follows:

Palestine	3,332
Lebanon	3,617
India	4,200
British East Africa Kenya Colony	349
Uganda Protectorate	5,149
Tanganyika	6,029
Rhodesia (S & N)	4,368
Poles	27,044
Yugoslavs	875

In the Middle East proper, as I wrote in 1949, not one of the governments, Turkish, Egyptian, Arab or Lebanese was a member of IRO or was prepared to recognise the Organisation officially. Letters of introduction therefore from my HQ which were so useful elsewhere and opened many doors, were no passport to assistance in the Arab areas. Egypt and the Arab states were openly suspicious of an organisation one of whose aims was to resettle Jews in Palestine. The results of this were that IRO staff received no official status and during the Arab-Jewish hostilities were subject to drastic security investigation. Nevertheless, working on a purely personal basis, IRO staff managed to overcome the official obstruction and suspicion and received, for the most part, consideration and sympathy for the task they had to complete. In countries where inefficient bureaucracy, made worse by blatant corruption and refusal, point blank, to accept responsibility for refugees seeking asylum with them, our staff found that the Gordian knot of obstruction could be loosened or even cut by patience and sympathy - never by corruption - but it was a long process.

In East Africa the reverse was the case. There one needed no introduction for the 17,000 Poles who had been received with compassion and maintained with mercy and understanding. The Colonial Authorities had HMG's word that their guests would be moved and they welcomed with open arms and gave every assistance possible to anyone who could remove the refugees in due, and not too distant, course. Here it was a matter of impressing on the host countries that the IRO meant business in their removal.

In addition to our regular and registered clientele the HQ of IRO Mission in Cairo had fired at them questions on refugees in countries such as New Zealand, Malay States, Seychelles, Madagascar, South Africa, Portuguese East Africa, Belgian Congo, Syria and Transjordan, Iran and Iraq, Greece, Eritrea, Libya and Ethiopia. Indeed on one occasion an enquirer into a refugee problem in Gambia (West Africa) was referred to the Mission in Cairo as being able to investigate the case "on the spot".

The first task of the Mission seemed to me to instill into the minds of the refugees and of the Governments and authorities concerned with them that IRO was determined to fulfil the assurance of HMG made in 1943 that the refugees would not remain in their territories after the end of the war and that repatriation (already accomplished by UNRRA) or status quo were not the only alternatives.

With this object, a statement was prepared, in conjunction with heads of IRO in the field, for circulation to authorities and refugees alike based on the possibilities of resettlement, individual or en bloc, and ending with the statement: "The status quo cannot continue".

The field officers concerned were Arnold Curtis, Head of IRO in Nairobi and East Africa, Dr Hans Wilbrandt, a splendid German defector from Nazism in Turkey, Michal Tyszkiewicz, a Pole in the Lebanon, Miss Elizabeth Brown, a Canadian in Palestine, and David Stephens, the Australian Commandant of El Shatt Camp in Egypt.

There followed a period of gestation of this policy by the refugees and their camp authorities and of great efforts on the part of IRO to bring into execution plans to fulfil the policy.

We found one splendid ally in HMG who had instituted a scheme to reunite the relatives abroad of the members of the Polish Armed Forces at present in the United Kingdom. The scheme was merciful and natural - and HMG carried it out with alacrity and complete success. The scheme was known as "Polejump". The reunions were carried out in fulfilment of assurances given to members of the Polish Armed Forces; the scheme was implemented with liberality in application and efficiency in execution; no trouble was spared to investigate claims. Over 15,000 from the Middle East theatre and East Africa were resettled by this truly British operation in 1947 onwards. The relief of finding some means of permanent homes for our refugees was of course enhanced by the wonderful thought that we were to bring families together after years of separation - in battle for the men in Europe, and continual uncertainty and privation, sometimes in inhospitable countries, with no chance of normal family life for the women. As soon as London gave the word 'Go' and we had received the forms (it was very necessary to see that wife joined husband) our staff started work with the papers and preparation for the move at the same time, especially in the north, eg. Palestine and India where from the political point of view urgent evacuation of refugees seemed essential. Other schemes of resettlement were proposed and some applied at a later date, but Polejump was the first and because of the political urgency we snatched at it and worked at an early application in the two countries.

Palestine

In Palestine we had over three thousand Polish relatives, some Jews but mostly Christians. They were probably some of the lucky ones who managed to remain in the north after leaving Persia and so were near their menfolk training in Iraq. They lived in Polish settlements or communities scattered all over Palestine - some in Jewish land, some in Arab. Even in the autumn of 1947 when I first got there it was difficult to pass from Arab settlements to Jewish and there were Poles in both. However the High Commissioner and Chief Secretary who welcomed me as an answer to prayer for the removal of all Poles, encouraged me to instruct Elizabeth Brown, my representative in Palestine and a truly courageous and efficient member of IRO, to make immediate plans for the registration of all Poles worthy of Polejump and for their removal to Great Britain; also for the very early removal of all other Poles to the Lebanon. I then summoned the Polish Committee and in her presence and that of a British member of the Administration explained the necessity of rapid evacuation, of the application of Polejump and the possible necessity of withdrawing IRO assistance from Poles who delayed their departure from Palestine. On my return to Cairo I sent my No 2, Percy Ball, to Palestine to give Elizabeth Brown and her stalwart staff a helping hand with a whiff of authority.

This is how the IRO History described the evacuation of Poles:

"Palestine was still under the British Mandate when IRO began its operation. The problem of Polish refugees in Palestine eligible for IRO assistance was obviously a matter of increasing concern, even before the announcement of the partition of Palestine on 30 November 1947 intensified the situation. Some of these were Jews but the majority were not, and as their position was increasingly dangerous their evacuation from Palestine was arranged."

"Conditions under which preparations for this evacuation and the evacuation itself, were carried out seemed completely unreal in retrospect. In Jerusalem where the IRO office was located, conditions were extremely unstable; security, mail, telephone and transport were almost non-existent. Arab and Jewish convoys were attacked by the opposing side on roads connecting the two spheres of influence. IRO officials attempting to make contact with widely scattered settlements and individuals did so at great personal risk.

"An IRO official from the Middle East was sent to Jerusalem in order to arrange an early evacuation from Palestine of all eligible refugees. In conjunction with the Polish Committee of the Palestine Government the IRO decided to inform all refugees that it would no longer be possible to afford them cash assistance after 1 January 1948. They would have to choose between repatriation, the Polish Resettlement Corps (if eligible under its criteria), absorption into Palestine or they could remain under IRO's care and be evacuated in the near future. The joint convoy of nearly 500 refugees finally left El Shatt camp in Egypt with the permission of the Egyptian Government. The French zone of Germany was their destination until they could be established elsewhere.

"The removal of Poles of Jewish faith by boat from Haifa entailed even greater difficulties than the evacuation of Christians as any appearance of forcing these Polish Jews to leave had to be avoided. Embarkation on two ships was finally completed and the rest of the refugees were ultimately evacuated over land to the Lebanon."

On 8 March 1948 two months before the end of the Mandate when security in Palestine appeared from reports to be at a pretty low ebb, I flew to Jerusalem to see for myself that all had been done to remove Polish refugees and to thank my really very gallant staff for the enduring effort which they had made to carry out IRO's purpose. I went by invitation to Government House: my host was none other than General Sir Alan Cunningham with whom I had experienced the surrender of Addis Ababa in April 1941. It was good to see him again and to be told that he was equally glad to see me. "But where is your wife, Maurice?" he asked. I explained my impression that women visitors in these days of insecurity might be an embarrassment. This cut no ice with the High Commissioner. I quote form DRL's diary (in Cairo) of that day:

".... Telephone call from Jerusalem and invitation to Government House; ADC asked whether I could catch the next plane .... I told him it took off in 10 minutes but I would book on the one after, 7am next morning, which I did .... flew in a Beachcraft plane to Lydda. MSL drove from Jerusalem to meet me at Lydda airport where had breakfast. Returned to Jerusalem in the Government House Rolls with armed escort in a military car. Our military orderly in the front seat carried a loaded rifle across his knee .... we passed through several Arab and Jewish road blocks - all blockers armed to the teeth!"

Next morning Diana came with me to the IRO office in a building which we shared with the Spanish Vice Consul. His Chief, the Consul General had been killed when the King David Hotel was blown up some months before. While we were working there was a tremendous explosion in the vicinity. Diana joined the Spanish Vice Consul in an immediate rush to the roof whence Diana took a photograph snapshot of the smoke arising from the destruction of the Jewish Agency by Arabs. I cannot remember whether there was a great loss of life and such terrorism was regarded as an every day affair by Government House when we returned to lunch.

That afternoon our host, the High Commissioner, sent us out to have a look at Jerusalem. This was our first visit to the holy places and included the Mount of Olives, the lovely Church of the Ascension and then a visit to the Museum where the Director, Hamilton, who turned out to be an Old Wykehamist and knew many mutual friends of Diana, joined the Rolls and took us to Bethlehem. En route we had an alarming holdup between road blocks when an Arab with rifle at the ready, pointed at us, came running down the road in a most offensive manner. "Keep your heads and bodies down!" snapped our Corporal orderly in the front seat to us, as he shouted to the Arab to stop and showed that we were armed and came from the *hakouma*. Then we had a peaceful and most interesting hour in Bethlehem under the guidance of the Director, especially of course in the Church of the Nativity which we saw practically deserted - except for the priests. Palestine was no tourist attraction in those troubled times. In Jerusalem itself the shops had all their shutters down to within a foot from the ground and though entry was possible, one crawled through the gap at ground level.

But the dinner party at Government House that evening was a gay affair - we met the Colonial Secretary, Henry Gurney and his lady wife and others from the Secretariat with, quotes the diary, ".... the Hamburgers of The King David Hotel."

That morning early, I had watched the departure of a road convoy of Polish refugees to the Lebanon which was one of the last to leave. Alan Cunningham and his Colonial Secretary were well pleased with IRO's work of evacuation; the Poles whom we met later in Brumana, Lebanon, in their curious impersonal way, were, I think, not ungrateful to be away from the Arab-Israeli War in Palestine which began immediately after the end of the

British Mandate.

I have jumped several months from the end of 1947 and must retrace to recount adventures in other lands.

Lebanon

We also had 3,600 Poles in Lebanon; they had come from Persia like the others. Lebanon recognised the Polish Government in exile in London and there was a Polish Ambassador of that Government in Beirut who administered these Poles through our very good supervisor, Tyskiewicz, and was financed by the British Consul General. We found these Poles in houses and buildings scattered over a group of Lebanese villages near Beirut. The Polish Committee were quite determined against repatriation and resisted all our encouragement to seek other countries of resettlement. The British operation Polejump affected some of them but otherwise it was a case of *"j'y suis, j'y reste"*. We will return to Lebanon after India and East Africa for it was obvious that here was a group of politically minded Poles and not until we were rid of the intransigent Polish Government in exile and took over control of the administration of those Poles in 1949 did IRO make any advance in reducing their numbers.

India

In India we had 6,000 refugees. They were in camp at Kohlepur about 400 miles south of Bombay. I cannot imagine at this distance of time why I did not fly to Kohlepur almost immediately after arrival in Cairo in July 1947 before Independence and the partitioning of India into two States - Pakistan under Jinnah and India under Pandit Nehru. I had a good Director of the camp and either he or some friend in the last remnants of the Vice Regal Government must have advised me or my Director in IRO Geneva not to visit India at that particular crisis, for failure to do so left the problem with Pat Nolan, the Camp Director and IRO representative to whom I sent all directions by mail, including Polejump correspondence. This failure to visit a vital problem now seems strange to me and against my nature, as in fact I did not visit India until 1948 when, thanks to Polejump, all but 1,000 Poles had sailed for UK and the remainder were booked for Mombasa within a month. I see that I wrote (in 1949):

> "…. India took the line 'either come here in force and deal with our seven million Indian refugees or remove your few thousand Europeans'."

We carried out the latter recommendation and over 800 Poles went to Mombasa.

I went to India in March 1948 and confirmed that all was well thanks to the excellent work of Pat Nolan and the great help and advice tendered by the British High Commission in Delhi, General Neame and his Deputy Frank Roberts (whose best man I had been at his marriage in Cairo in 1938).

A not very significant number of refugees, mostly of Balkan origin, existed in Turkey. Their representative on IRO staff was Dr Hans Wilbrandt, a most intelligent German who had defected from Nazism to join the Turkish Government and settle in Turkey as Director of Agriculture. I was happy to leave the refugees in his competent and sympathetic hands. They were individual cases rather than mass problems and I asked him to use his own discretion, in the knowledge that he had IRO backing, until I should be free to help him personally in the coming year.

East and Southern Africa

The main problem confronting IRO was in East Africa, which, for the purpose of this account, meant the British territories of Kenya Colony, Uganda Protectorate, Tanganyika (British Mandated) Territory, Northern and Southern Rhodesia. In these territories were approximately 16,500 Poles sent by MERRA from Persia in 1942-44, augmented by approximately 1,000 Poles from India (see my paragraph above) - 17,500 Poles in all.

The Governments of these territories had willingly accepted and maintained these refugees most excellently; they relied most fundamentally on the assurance of the British Government given in 1943 that the refugees accepted then and thereafter, at the instance of the British Government, would be removed after the war in toto by the British Government.

The Poles had lived, since 1943, in ten camps distributed throughout the territories mentioned above. The camps were administered by the governments of those five territories, coordinated by the East African Refugee Administration (EARA) who had maintained a very high order of management throughout the 10 camps, generally under the aegis of a retired British officer or official who became "father of his people" (sometimes perhaps a trifle too paternal) and was responsible for health, security and good order. Each camp had a Polish Committee responsible to the Commandant for all Polish affairs including for instance education of the young: this the Poles maintained at a very high standard. Each territory had a main Polish hospital in the larger camp and Tongeru Camp in Tanganyika had an orphanage containing 26 children. About half their number had been brought as an entity from Russia by one Polish woman, a Mrs Grozicko.

As a general pattern the camps consisted of a number of circular mud huts with conical grass thatched roofs - communal rooms were large rectangular mud buildings also with (very well) thatched roofs. All huts had wooden doors and glass or talc windows. During their three or four years sojourn the Poles had managed to make them comfortable buildings and had established, in most camps, agricultural and horticultural plots. The majority of the camps were really most attractive places and those in the highlands of Tanganyika near Arusha (Tongeru Camp), on the shores of Lake Victoria and near Lake Tanganyika were really beautiful sites. On the other hand Gatooma camp in Southern Rhodesia consisted of a series of low mud rooms with corrugated iron roofs and was one of the grimmest encampments imaginable.

On arrival in Cairo in 1947 I had appointed Arnold Curtis a very fine educational official and an "international" in Kenya Colony as head of the IRO team in East Africa. I and Geneva had sent him adequate staff in addition to any he appointed himself whom he described "as good a team as I could ever wish to work with". Their job was "to remove all Polish refugees from East Africa Territory in the shortest possible time by repatriation or resettlement." He and his staff succeeded by November 1950 - a very fine achievement in which after 1948 Curtis was in sole charge as Chief of East Africa Mission.

Let us return to 1947 when I spent the month of October in this large area, met all the British Heads of Government with several of whom I stayed. I discussed the problem with Curtis and my own people and with the East African Refugee Administration, paid a brief visit to the South African Government and the British High Commissioner in Pretoria, visited all 10 camps in East Africa and the Rhodesias (entailing journeys by air totalling 6,000 miles) and met many Polish refugees and those who looked after them.

Personally I was met with kindness hospitality and understanding wherever I was sent, I was well armed with official letters of introduction but only in a few cases were these necessary because, in many of the countries concerned, I met old friends or was personally well known - credits which were of infinite value when travelling. Not once during my first or other visits to East or even South Africa did I stay in a hotel - and life in colonial Government House was extremely pleasant and filled with unforgettable kindness and service. Everyone whom I met - except later in South Africa - showed and gave sympathy with my task in Africa even if they could not absorb my refugees.

In Nairobi I had a warm welcome, as always, from the Governor, Sir Philip Mitchell, my old chief in OETA and at the outset in Madagascar. I met his charming wife for the first time who was equally kind - and I met once more in his stables my old and devoted pony "Wilbury" of Damer (1935-40) days whom Mitchell had moved to Addis Ababa and made an honorary companion of his stud. Wilbury had always carried Mitchell on his many visits to the Legation in Addis Ababa and died, full of years and well being, in the Nairobi Government House stables some years after.

When the Mitchells were away I had a standing invitation which I accepted often to stay with General Dimoline - the Dimmy with whom I had entered Tananarive, Madagascar in 1942. Nairobi was full of old friends. I found that the Head of East African Refugee Administration, Belper, who had administered all our Poles, had been the head of my Italian refugee staff in Abyssinia: so he knew me for good or for bad. I liked him immensely and much admired his work and the compassion with which he approached our problem in Addis Ababa and now in Nairobi.

Curtis had arranged several meetings with Belper and his EARA team and I began, in earnest, to air my Directorate's (Geneva) very natural (to them) idea of solving the Polish refugee problem in Africa - by absorption into the African colonies and South Africa of all Poles who wouldn't be repatriated, thereby eliminating the necessity of finding other countries of resettlement, the visits of selection teams, and the expense and trouble of further movement.

My Director David Morse and his deputy Sir Arthur Rucker were extremely anxious that I should try to persuade the African Governments to extend their welcome to the Poles and their wonderful maintenance of them by just one further step. Great Britain they argued, was doing more than her duty in applying Polejump to families of Polish troops in UK. Let her Colonies respond by an equal act of kindness and self sacrifice by absorbing into the admittedly wide spaces of Africa the remaining 5,000-7,000.

I had told Geneva personally and in writing that of course I would sound the colonial authorities on this proposal but that, with my knowledge of African Government, I did not think that the idea would find favour. I talked it over privately with Mitchell and his Colonial Secretary and found little basis for hope. However I persevered as my report shows but EARA and the Governments were "totally opposed", I wrote. In Africa a concerted approach was made to the governments of six Colonial and Mandatory administrations and to the South African Government to absorb those Poles who would remain after the conclusion of Polejump and repatriation and so solve the African problem in Africa. This appeared the logical solution to IRO, Geneva. It implied taking the bad with the good on a basis of good will rather than economy. In 1947 the Chief of Mission wrote:

"…. on the face of it the absorption of 5,000 refugees in the wide open spaces of Africa would seem a simple problem. It is far from simple. British colonial policy in Africa does not embrace the settlement of many Europeans, least of all those who may be regarded as "poor whites". Employment of European labour is but a temporary phase pending the development of the indigenous population and the eventual full participation of the African in all enterprises. As temporary labour, the refugee is welcome, for he fills a gap in the present economy, but as a permanent settler he presents a problem."

As a result of discussions with EARA I let it be known that full scope would be given to (a) repatriation, (b) Polejump, or (c) any other possible form of resettlement.

Notwithstanding our approach IRO would fulfil the undertaking made by HMG for the total removal (even by absorption) of the Polish refugees. I believe that they trusted me. Certainly Arnold Curtis won their confidence.

Before I left on my camp tour the remnants of OETA Headquarters (who had moved to Nairobi from Cairo in

1942-43) did me the honour of giving me an OETA luncheon at the Nairobi Club. A very friendly get-together though I knew few of them. I let it be known quite specifically that I knew and accepted fully that IRO had a duty and a responsibility to accept the undertaking of eventual repatriation or resettlement of all refugees in East Africa.

After these preliminary but full and frank discussions among people whom one recognised as friends but who were aiming at a complete clearance of refugees in the near future, whereas IRO hoped for some local absorption and knew that final clearance was a year or two in the future, and after gaining mutual confidence, Curtis and I left on my 6,000 mile tour of the ten refugee camps.

For this purpose we had hired a twin-engined Anson aircraft from a local firm of Noon and Peace. The latter came as one of our pilots and Macdonald as his co-pilot. They were good pilots and engineers and I enjoyed flying with them. The engines were reluctant starters but never faltered in mid air. Our pilots flew well but did not wholly know the country. Approaching Bathurst in a violent pre-dusk thunderstorm our navigator shouted back to his disconcerted passengers "Anyone got a map of this place?". We did also approach Johannesburg from the SW rather than the NE but "we still had two gallons of petrol in our tanks" explained the pilots. We had various other adventures when their skill saved us from discomfort and we all thoroughly enjoyed the journeying that fortnight.

My first sight of a refugee camp was Koja in Uganda. MSL to DRL 7.11.47:

"…. Koja is one of the camps with a perfect setting almost on the shores of Lake Victoria. Hundreds of native huts mud and thatch, all very well built; gardens with a profusion of flowers and a charming bamboo church on the top of a hill. We talked a good deal with the Poles and their leaders. We lunched with the Chief Secretary at Government House, Entebbe (in the absence of the Governor) and discussed the Polish future. I gathered the message from him was "No resettlement in Uganda!" Another smaller camp in the Protectorate was not so attractive but obviously filled with refugees contented with existence …."

Our next visit was to Tongeru Camp near Arusha on the southern part of the mountain range which is capped by the volcano of Kilimanjaro at 19,000ft, visible at times from the vicinity of the camp. I quote again from a letter to DRL on 3.11.47:

"…. Tongeru Camp.

It is really a large township of white thatched *tukls* covering 1,000 acres (on the most beautiful slopes of the approaches to Kilimanjaro). There are roads, hedges, 300 acres of vegetable garden and a dairy herd of 250 cows. The camp contains 3,800 Poles, 75% of them women and children (the men mostly over or under military age), who have been here for four years and are, I have no doubt, quite content to stay for the conditions are magnificent. The Camp Commandant, Colonel Minnery, (a retired British Officer) is the father and mother of them all whose heart will break when the camp breaks up. And IRO is here to preach disruption!"

I spent two days in that efficiently but most extravagantly run camp and during my visit spoke to many of the staff and to the Polish inhabitants in an attempt to cause them to think of a permanent life in more static conditions. There were of course many children in the camp and I begged the elders to think of their future.

I saw the Colonial Secretary in Tanganyika and my old Chief of Staff in Ethiopia, Guy Shippe. I saw the Polish TB Sanatorium in Loliondo (Northern Tanganyika) and then flew south to Salisbury in Southern Rhodesia where I visited Gatooma refugee camp where there lived a number of Poles in conditions as different as chalk from cheese from those in the northern camps. The camp was merely a collection of tin huts on the outskirts of the town of Gatooma. They were clean and furnished but oh so different from the northern camps from which I had come: a suburban outrage in a lovely country. I don't think the resident Poles minded. They were inhabited by the same type of Polish refugee as I had seen on the north but their mentality appeared to be the same: *"J'y suis; j'y reste"*.

Incidentally as I left Gatooma Camp I said goodbye and thank you to the British Commandant. "How long had you been here?" I asked. "Forty seven years, covering three major wars. Came out for the Boer War!" he replied. Speechless I returned to Salisbury.

I found the Governor of Southern Rhodesia, Sir John Kennedy, (a gunner himself who had been Director of Military Operations during the war and knew me by name from Ethiopian days) and his wife with whom I stayed in the bungalow of Government House. Life in Southern Rhodesia was still pleasant and peaceful in 1947. The Governor, holder of a Polish Decoration for valour, told them that he would arrange to settle several hundred Polish refugees in his territory, if his Government would agree. I saw his Chief Secretary and other members of the said Government and they definitely did not agree. A compromise was the final solution as you will read hereafter.

After Southern Rhodesia I slipped south to Johannesburg and Pretoria hoping to see General Smuts - now a Field Marshall - who was rather a king-pin in my hopes for help from his country. I hoped that he would accept some refugees and at any rate join the IRO. But Smuts was unexpectedly away, and he was out of office on my next visit.

I picked up Curtis again in Lusaka in Northern Rhodesia where we spent a day in Lusaka Camp. After two visits to other camps which were all of the same rural type, well managed but with the same hall mark of eternity on them, we spent a night and a day looking for a camp that did not exist at Livingstone. Here I saw the Victoria Falls for the first time. I will describe them and our reactions when I came to the combined visit by Diana and myself in 1959.

I had now seen nine camps (I have not described them all) because they subscribed too much to one pattern - peace, comfort so far as Africa can give comfort, health and complete assurance of good food and security. I would underline "so far as Africa can give comfort" for these were not dwellings in Polish surroundings but the very best which British people could provide to a European community for whose sufferings they had great compassion and whose future they viewed with great sympathy - based on the knowledge, and I repeat the certainty based on experience, that Africa was not the best settlement area for any except a small minority. For those who were allowed to stay and made good, the Britons and (so far as they could be concerned) the Africans also gave full support. For the majority, resettlement out of Africa had to be the solution.

The last camp on our list was at Abercorn (now Mbala in Zambia), the northernmost town of Northern Rhodesia near the southern shores of Lake Tanganyika. We flew in there early in the afternoon of Thursday 20 November 1947, the wedding day in London of Princess Elizabeth with Prince Philip, Duke of Edinburgh. We noticed with some astonishment and no little concern that the aerodrome was deserted - not even a policeman or guardian was present and transport ordered for us and our pilot (who had agents here) was absent. After half an hour a Ford T car drove along the road from the bush and gave me lift to the hotel. Here I found not a man or boy sober. Most were incapable; a few were roaring and dangerously drunk. The receptionist told us that we could have the "whole bloody hotel". We borrowed a further lift from the Ford driver and went to the agent of the air company and the purveyor of petrol for the aircraft. The Agent was missing - we guessed asleep. The petrol store was guarded by his brother, a policeman in the South African Police, on leave. He had in his hand a short rifle - loaded, as he said he would shoot the sanguinary guts out of any one who stepped forward towards this petrol store! We did not, luckily for our lives and our dignity. At that moment arrived a car driven by a sober and white driver. He was Curtis' agent, British, who had been in the refugee camp some 10 miles out and because of the general intoxication of the town had not been aware of our arrival. He was stone cold sober and I forgave him all. We left our pilot and a sober friend of the IRO staff to defend the plane and then drove some miles out to the camp - to spend a very pleasant and interesting afternoon and evening. Here was a second Tengera Camp - an African home from Polish steppe home; a first class Commandant - one of the "dug-outs" which the colonies had discovered and to whom they had given great joy by employing. They were good - too good of course - because they turned the appalling conditions of camps in Russia and Persia into garden cities where the sun was warm and the earth gave forth its fullness in food and flowers. Our commandant had done so in Abercorn and in so doing unwittingly had made IRO's task more difficult: *"Ici on reste."* We discovered this, Curtis and I in those hours in Abercorn Camp - our last visit. It put the seal on our thoughts of difficulties ahead - particularly if we could attract no Selection Committee for a resettlement country to visit East Africa. We dined with the Commandant discussing thoughts.

As I left with words of thanks to the British Colonel in charge, I asked: "What, Colonel, is your chief worry here?" "Lions, Sir!" he said "they even jump or climb over the *zariba* and steal my animals and poultry."

We aeronauts slept for safety in one room, crept out at dawn, refuelled our Anson tanks through chamois leather and took off unheeded and unmolested. Only anxious as to whether we should surmount the high mountains which separate the Lake from our direct route to Nairobi. Never before or since have I seen a townful of people intoxicated in toto. Thus they loyally celebrated the Royal Wedding in what was once Abercorn.

Curtis and I had three or four days in Nairobi signing up and planning. Representatives in the camps were to educate the largely feminine and not very stable adults to recognise the grim facts of life after war. Polejump did not come into operation until 1948 but preparations had to be made therefor and these, of course, aroused thought which was born of the wish to be admitted to Great Britain. In fact, and naturally, all eyes looked towards Great Britain where the bulk of Polish manhood still alive and not in Poland, was now enjoying demobilisation and citizenship if they so wished.

I had seen and learnt all I could in East Africa and so returned to the north to tackle Poles in Lebanon and Palestine. I left Curtis and his team with the hard task of trying to make the Poles face the facts of life; of encouraging repatriation; of interesting the refugees in any possible facet of resettlement that might come their way; of seeking out all possible outlets for resettlement both locally and outside Africa; of finding life in some other part of the world and becoming citizens rather than parasites. But how could one blame the Poles for longing to be left alone - albeit in peaceful distress? For me it had a been a most interesting trip and I had met with friendship and sympathy everywhere. But it was a grim outlook for the Poles.

1948

I spent ten days in Geneva at IRO Headquarters in January 1948, giving my HQ a picture of Poles in the Middle East and particularly in East Africa. My object and duty was to attract more resettling governments to send selective teams to seek out people and to give my own people a personal picture of what IRO Middle East faced. Curtis met me on my return to Cairo.

I did not return to East Africa until June 1948 when I went with Sir Arthur Rucker, the Deputy Director of IRO Geneva who paid with me a visit to Lebanon (of this anon) and Cairo and then south to East Africa.

For in 1948 movement had begun from the camps. Polejump had started operations directed by the British War Office. Curtis reported that he had repatriated

1,800 Poles but continued: "Significant repatriation movement ceased about the time when the Communist Party in Poland was silencing all opposition."

As the reader can imagine the figure of orphans in this tragic group of Poles stood high, although IRO East Africa had been able to reunite many families - by careful tracing to the Polish refugee camps, some by repatriation. The figure was 300. Many of these children owed their lives to Mrs Grozicko, a heroine who formed the orphanage in Russia and brought it intact to Tanganyika in East Africa. Nearly all the girls of this orphanage were eventually claimed by a British Selection Mission from England, placing them in domestic and other essential services in Lancashire and Staffordshire.

I quote a paragraph from Curtis' final report, which relates to a process of local absorption started in 1948 - local marriage:

> "One of our best means of resettlement has been local marriage. There has been an impressive record of local marriages - about 300. For instance in Southern Rhodesia lonely prospectors would write to a camp proposing marriage to any suitable girl prepared to share his life. These proposals were posted without comment on the Camp Notice Board and a number of successful cases of resettlement followed ...."

Numbers in East Africa Camps were obviously falling and there was annotated in Sir Arthur Rucker's paper before the Rucker-Lush visit in June 1948:

> "The whole object of the visit is to persuade the African colonies to absorb the Polish Refugees now in African camps, 500 each in the Colonies, 5,000 in South Africa who would join IRO."

Arthur Rucker, whom I joined in Lebanon, had an opportunity of seeing the Poles in Lebanon (the most intransigent of all) and my staff and many diplomats and others in Cairo. He stayed with us, had two official parties and one international. He had every chance of 'doing his stuff' in a Cairo where he had been Secretary to the British Minister of State in 1944.

We spent two or three days in Cairo now and then flew to Nairobi. There were by now fewer than 10,000 Poles in East Africa and our plan was to try by hook or by crook to let Africa absorb them all, half in East Africa and half in South Africa. We then tackled Nairobi (EARA) and East African Government (Mitchell was away) and saw Tongeru Camp and another (Koja in Uganda). Rucker posed his proposition to the East African Governments who were impressed but did not depart from their negative response. We then went on to South Africa. Arthur Rucker failed to meet the new Prime Minister or any politicians. He saw Evelyn Baring, the British High Commissioner, but the omens were not good in Pretoria. Arthur Rucker flew home to Geneva leaving me to see the South African Prime Minister and his Ministers which I did after a week's interval. Incidentally during this interval I watched some 300 Poles leave Mombasa on repatriation to Poland. I had become by now more amenable to the idea of absorption of some Poles by Africa to be able to write to DRL in June 1948:

> ".... I am striving hard to get Africa to absorb the (Polish) African refugees. If we fail I feel convinced that we shall have to upheave them - for they are dug in too deeply and too complacently. If we drastically closed the camps we should ipso facto increase our repatriation. The group I saw off yesterday were all thoroughly happy ...."

So I returned to Pretoria convinced that South Africa had a duty as a British Dominion to help the British Government fulfil her obligation to remove the Poles from the small African colonies and to absorb 5,000 Poles into the Union. I knew that South Africa needed more white workers - we had them on her doorstep. To allow them to resettle in South Africa would be an act of mercy and of international cooperation for which the United Nations was pleading.

Such was my approach, which I rehearsed to the High Commissioner, Sir Evelyn Baring, with whom I stayed on my second visit to the Union in July 1948. What a charming person he was!

Here was I in Pretoria again with a meeting arranged with Mr Dongwes, the Minister for the Interior and then with Dr Malan, the new Prime Minister who had just succeeded Jan Smut's coalition of United and Labour Parties which was defeated by the Nationalist Afrikaner bloc, standing on an 'apartheid' platform. The new government had been in power just one month when I saw these two men.

I had been informed by cable from Geneva that the representatives of four countries had been instructed to represent to the new South African Government the desirability of joining IRO.

I saw Dongwes, Minister of Interior first. Baring had not met him but had warned me that they were all very different from Jan Smut's regime. Dongwes was not an imposing man - nor did he show any signs of affability towards me, still less sympathy with what I had to say. But he listened and when I had finished he said quite bluntly:

> "Mr Lush, we do need immigrants but we need people selected by us; we are not prepared to receive even selected Poles; our immigrants have already been selected and are on their way here by sea; they are German citizens and they are the skilled people whom we need. We cannot consider taking any Poles."

I was astonished at their choice of Germans and said so - they were importing into the Union, German nationals who had fought against South African troops and our Polish Allies at Tobruk - allowing thousands of Poles to remain as unemployed refugees. Dongwes was not impressed and repeated his preference for German nationals to Polish refugees. My abrasive host bade me farewell - more or less abruptly. In the afternoon I was received by Dr Daniel F Malan - a very different man - more gentle, probably more intelligent and certainly more polished than my morning host. We discussed the question of South Africa joining the IRO and Malan (who may also have been Minister of Foreign Affairs) told me politely that it would not be in the interests of his Government to join IRO. He said that it might have been a popular move internationally but they could not receive refugees and therefore joining IRO would be useless.

"You will have understood" he said "from Mr Dongwes that we cannot accept Polish refugees. I have to be guided by my Ministers."

He did say that he was sorry to refuse me all my requests and then ended the interview, rising, shaking me by the hand and saying, as I understood it then and remember it now, "I advise you to leave the Union within the next 48 hours."

Could I have heard aright? I may have been *mouvemente* by the two interviews - but that was unlike me. I may have misheard the Prime Minister; in any case I was due to leave within 48 hours and having reported "failure of a mission" to Evelyn Baring (he had foreseen the same) I stuck to my programme and left with the prescribed limit (if there ever was one!)

A letter to my brother Cecil dated 5 July 1948 describes my journey in brief:

MSL to CHL 5.7.48

"…. As you will see I am on my travels once again - this is my second visit to Pretoria (within a month) in an unsuccessful attempt to get this (new South African) Government to accept refugees. I started this tour in Istanbul, came south to Cairo (our home) via Lebanon. Had a hectic five days in Cairo and then went on to Kenya, Tanganyika, Southern Rhodesia to South Africa and then back to East Africa for a spell. I hope to reach Cairo again this week and possibly find Diana there. She went to the Sea of Marmora to spend a restful month on one of the Princes' Islands - Borgas - I expect you know it …. I must say that South Africa is a lovely country - a mid-winter climate in which you can spend six hours a day in shirt sleeves suits me!"

I shed the dust of Pretoria form my heels and spent 24 hours in Nairobi, leaving Curtis and his noble men to do their utmost working on the minds of the refugees and their hosts while I promised to breathe heavily down the necks of officials in Geneva and London, for it became more and more obvious that the Power who planted the Poles in East Africa would in the end, have to bear the brunt of receiving more and more of their saplings - short of food, housing and money as Great Britain was in 1949-50. I felt particularly bitter about the uncompromising selfish refusal of the South African Government - until I remembered the look on Jan Smut's face as he came down the staircase in Liberty House that morning in 1943 bearing the terrible news of the loss of the South African division at Tobruk - the flower of the youth of a small country. His political opponents never forgave him, nor the British, for their country's participation in the European War.

I also told Curtis that I should be clearing the IRO Mission in Cairo by the end of the year and that he would become head of East African Mission directly responsible to Geneva HQ. It was not however to be my last visit to East Africa that year for I paid a whirlwind visit thither on the abortive Mission Air Sea Lift which I shall describe briefly later.

I flew north and after greeting briefly DRL, back from her month's holiday in Turkey, I flew to Geneva, London and Rome with the urgent plea that resettlement havens be found for the Poles whom South Africa would not receive. In the end Curtis and his team achieved remarkable success and when he wrote his final report he was able to state that only 266 really hardcore refugees remained.

Great Britain, of course, had taken the bulk of the Poles, 11,200 in Polejump and Westward Ho! (a scheme initiated to fill a labour gap in UK), Australia and Canada some 2,000 between them, local marriage already described absorbed 300, mostly into Southern Rhodesia which also took a further 120 (the colonial territories took up to 1% of their white settler population).

The IRO history described the operation as "almost a complete success".

I enjoyed my two missions in East Africa. The individuals like Curtis and his staff who undertook the job of moving these unhappy people (who longed to remain in status quo) fulfilled their task with such devotion and compassion. The Governments with whom we worked were, with one exception, so generously sympathetic, that one felt inspired throughout the work and grateful for such inspiring help. Curtis made it, like his final report, a tidy job and I was proud to have been associated with them all.

The Airwork Scheme for Immigration to Australia

I mention this abortive scheme for moving British immigrants and European migrants (refugees) from Europe to Australia via Nairobi, Mombasa, Asmara and Massawa in which I became involved during the autumn of 1948 at the insistance of IRO Geneva.

I formed a reconnaissance mission to examine the project consisting of Wing Commander G E Ford of Airwork Ltd London (to cover air movement), D E Holmes of the Refugee Movement Division, IRO Geneva (port facilities, Mombasa), Dr James Petrie from the Division of Health IRO Geneva (inspection of Camps); D C Stephens, my Camp Commandant, and G A Christie, a young financial advisor to Airwork, accompanied the Mission. We held discussions in Cairo and then carried out a detailed reconnaissance in Nairobi, Mombasa, Asmara and Massawa lasting a hectic week at the beginning of November 1948. A Viking aircraft belonging to Airwork, fully equipped with staff, flew us in great comfort throughout the week and we were given every facility and encouragement by the East African and Eritrean Authorities.

We worked like anything and produced a voluminous report; we became a very happy team and were much impressed by the efficiency and hospitality of Airwork who finally flew us all (including Diana) in their Viking back to London (via Geneva).

Briefly, the idea was to avoid the expensive and unhealthy sea voyage through the Suez Canal (very high fees per capita and per ton) and the Red Sea (many casualties from heat). British migrants would fly from UK to Nairobi, Kenton Road Camp, at the rate of 63 per diem, there move to English Point Camp, Mombasa where numbers would build up to be reduced by scheduled embarkation on passenger ships from and to Australia. European refugees would fly from Nice to a camp at Ghindi, Eritrea which would be subject to regularly emptying by similar scheduled arrivals of ships at Massawa. I was quite prepared to supervise from the Asmara Camp the refugee movement.

The Airwork scheme was an interesting experience and showed me how a thrusting airline was prepared to work (and how they insisted on acquiring full knowledge of the last details before engaging their valuable aircraft). I was much impressed by Wyatt, the Head of their London Office (and one of the Chief Executives in the company) and less impressed by the young and rather brash finance expert whom the firm providing the money had sent out on the reconnaissance. These were the days before computers and he was extremely able and quick with figures - and, as I thought, a trifle too slick. I remember him asking Diana during lunch in our house in Cairo, whether he could speak to his wife. Diana, of course, acquiesced and only after the young man was heard speaking in French did she realise that the call was Cairo to Paris - and a lengthy one at that; we were not in those days accustomed to global conversations - nor able to afford them.

The last scene of the expedition was a flight - Cairo to Geneva - where most of us deplaned but Diana and the young financier continued by night to Blackbush (Airwork's British Terminal).

At this time the Airwork Scheme was quite viable and after confirming IRO's (Geneva) approval we others followed to London. There we tied up final loose ends with HMG, Australia and British Refugee authorities, and Airwork. I note that on my 52nd birthday, I went to a large cocktail party given by Airwork, of whom I was ordained to become an employee, and I naturally took note of my future fellow workers. "Terribly nice people running the company - but spending money like water" was my impression then. But I was much impressed by the Chief Executive.

I have no record of the date but in early December I returned to Geneva and it must have been there that we learnt, to our chagrin, the news that the Australian Government, who by now had examined our report, were unwilling to provide the necessary finance. So all our great work had been in vain.

This was a great disappointment to IRO, Airwork and all connected with the scheme. For ourselves, Diana and I, were not too down hearted especially as IRO had indicated that they had work for me based at Geneva for at least another year.

Lebanon

Although I had visited Lebanon soon after arrival in Cairo I had not seriously tackled the problem of the resettlement of the 4,000 Poles in the country - indeed I increased their numbers by sending some 2,000 Poles from Pakistan just before the British Mandate ceased. I found the situation in Lebanon did not call for immediate IRO action though I promised to the British Legation rapid action after the East African problems had been solved.

The political situation of these Poles was different from other groups. They came, mostly, from the British/Polish Army HQ in Baghdad and so became eligible for the British scheme made available for relatives of Polish soldiers in the UK. The remainder adopted a disinterested attitude towards repatriation and resettlement; this was due to the accepted presence in Beirut of an official Ambassador (representing the Polish Government in exile in London) accredited to the Lebanese government who had never recognised the Soviet Polish Government. The Polish refugees were settled in villages and given maintenance allowances administered by the British Legation and a strong local Polish organisation headed by the most charming and also efficient Pole, "Mish" Tyszkiewicz and aided by Madame Isa Maria de Landsberger.

Diana and I paid our first visit to the Lebanon in March 1948 when we had a very warm welcome both at the aerodrome where we were met by HBM Consul and then by the British Minister, W E Houston Boswell CMG MC and his wife with whom we stayed and who were the kindest hosts imaginable and entertained us royally, ensuring that we met at his residence all the "interested parties" including the Lebanese Minister for Foreign Affairs, the Polish Minister Plenipotentiary, the President's ADC, etc. His wife, Margaret, was equally charming and saw to it that Diana visited the right places in Beirut. Hoosty Boosty as he was called was a lighthearted jovial diplomat who preferred the personal rather than the hyper-official approach to problems and appeared to have great sympathy with IRO and our concerns. He begged me to rid the Lebanon of my Poles and gave me all the official help possible. Lebanon was a peaceful country then and notwithstanding undercurrents of tension one lived a normal life without fear. The British held a strong position (of neutrality) and the British Church and Club of St George were much in evidence.

Diana and I visited the village of Ghazi one cold Sunday accompanied by Tyszkiewicz, the Polish refugee leader, Madame de Landsberger, a charming Dutch girl Jetske van Lennep and our splendid IRO representative Harold Griggs. We drove thither through Nahr el Kelb and saw inscription of all the armies who had fought in that pass throughout the ages - ancient Egyptians,

Assyrians, Darius, the Crusaders and the French, first under Napoleon III and recently in 1910 and 1941.

On the way to this village which was the centre of the Polish settlements which had been these 4 years, I remember asking Tyszkiewicz "I presume most of your Poles speak Arabic now?" "Oh no" he replied "the Lebanese have learnt to speak Polish!" That gave one a clue to the Polish attitude to their hosts. And it was this attitude which we had to overcome. We met a number of their leaders on this exceedingly cold hillside and I spoke to them bluntly but I hope not without sympathy on the transient nature of their stay in Lebanon. Of course many of them had already left for UK on the British Westward Ho! schemes for relatives of Polish forces demobilised in the UK, but I found a very cold reception to any suggestions for considering alternative resettlement schemes, both on that day and during the following few days. These were enlivened by a luncheon given by the Polish Minister (or Ambassador) Zawadowski and an IRO luncheon given by Diana and myself in return at the Lucullus Restaurant which the Houston Boswells were good enough to attend. I was appalled to find that whisky was a pre-luncheon drink at £L14 a tot!

Sandwiched in between these IRO functions was what should have been a pleasant interlude when we were invited to visit the Middle Eastern Centre for Arab Studies and there to deliver a lecture. Our host was Bertram Thomas, the Warden and Director, an eminent Arabist and Middle Eastern expert and the first Briton or European to have crossed the Rub' el Khali in Southern Arabia. Thanking heaven that the lecture was to be in English I faced 30 or 40 young Arabists - Ambassadors-to-be, budding Directors of oil companies - in an icy lecture room with one stove round which *they* all crowded, and told them either about governing a province in the Sudan, administering Ethiopia, Madagascar and Tripolitania or, more likely, how to resettle refugees. The future specialists on the Middle East were interested and kind, and Bertram Thomas, when he flew back to Cairo with us next day, asked me whether he could recommend me as his successor to direct MECAS. I told him of the comment of the Sheikh in the Northern Province on my Arabic and thought of the icy blast blowing through the Centre and declined. However the Lush connection with MECAS was not severed - Julian went there as a student with Shell in 1958-9 and thus became an Arabist. I paid several further visits to Beirut, once with Sir Arthur Rucker, once with Diana. Gradually the rump of immobile Poles was reduced and the official history records "by persuasion and by the efforts of the Australian and Canadian Selection Missions, most of the Poles were found new homes by the end of 1950." The balance went to Argentina or was accepted by the British Government - please note the final and accurate conclusion.

Turkey

Turkey was not originally in my bailiwick for the Turkish Government in the early days was in the import business of refugees, particularly, of course, the reception of Muslims, and IRO HQ in Geneva preferred to deal with that question direct. However I was drawn into the Turkish problem somehow and so visited Istanbul in March 1948, there to meet the man who was acting for the Turkish Government with the IRO. He was Dr Hans Wilbrandt, a German, who with his wife and family had fled from Nazi Germany in the 1930s and found not only a home in Turkey but a responsible occupation in the Department of Agriculture of the Turkish Government. He and his wife were a devoted couple with three young children who had made a niche for themselves in the cosmopolitan population of Turkey before and during the war (I never enquired into his wartime work - undoubtedly pro-Ally), and with his wife devoted himself to the refugee problems. I fell for them at once and within three months Diana was spending a halcyon month as their guest on a remote island in the Sea of Marmara. I visited Wilbrandt on two other occasions while I was in Cairo.

By 1949 Turkey had welcomed as immigrants some 2,000 Moslems from many countries in Europe. There were no restrictions of age, profession or health; the only criterion was profession of the Moslem faith. The acquisition of Turkish nationality by the immigrants immediately secured for them full rights of work, and a new law enabled them to live anywhere in the Turkish Republic. The Turks had enacted the sympathetic law granting citizenship to refugees which we in IRO struggled so often to exact from other would-be host countries. When I paid another visit in 1951 at the invitation of the Turkish Government the Wilbrandts had returned to Germany where, in a new country, he soon found that his talents were recognised and he secured a good appointment in the new West German Agricultural world. We had become good friends and he came during the '60s to stay with us in Sussex.

There follows Diana's letter to my mother on her holiday on the island of Burgaz, the holiday home of the Wilbrandts in the Sea of Marmara:

DRL to FEL (UK) 28.6.48

"About a month ago Maurice was in Istanbul with Sir Arthur Rucker and Dr Wilbrandt invited me (unseen!) to stay with his family in their summer quarters in a fishers' dwelling on the Island of Burgaz, one of the Prince's islands in the Sea of Marmara, near Istanbul. These islands are quite lovely, and rival any of the beauty spots of Italian or French Riviera. I expect Cecil knows them. Tomorrow I hope to go on expedition by steamer through the Bosphorous to the Black Sea. I have been sight-seeing in Istanbul, and thoroughly enjoying myself. The boys (Hansi 17 and Rupi 13) have a boat which occupies much of their time and energy: soaking, cleaning, scraping, painting and varnishing it. We spent a heavenly morning in it, rowing over to Heybati, the next island, and bathing from it. Then a Greek friend with a motor boat picked us up at Heybati and towed us back to Burgaz.

It was a dream of loveliness. But alas, my skin was not prepared for the heat of the sun, and I am now paying for my over-exposure with a very red and sore body! One day we went by steamer to Prinkipo, the principal of this group of islands, and drove round that in an old-fashioned two-horse carriage with a sun-canopy. The islands are green with pine forests and have innumerable attractive coves. There is not such a thing as a motor car at all, and on this island not even a horse-carriage. The paths are steep and rough.

"Life here is as different from Cairo as it is possible to imagine. In Cairo recently we were living a very full busy and rather diplomatic life. For Sir Arthur Rucker's benefit we gave two cocktail parties, inviting all the Ambassadors and representatives of all countries. Shortly before I came away I was dining and dancing on the roof of the Semiramis Hotel with the British Ambassador. The thermometer bumped up to about 112° in the shade and I was having three or four baths a day. Into an aeroplane (Cyprus Airways), one night in Nicosia, on via Ankara to Istanbul and by paddlesteamer to this heavenly island, and into another world. *Degrees* cooler but warm enough to have all our meals al fresco and to bathe in the sea. This is a good thing, because there is no bath in the house! At first I felt lost with out one but now I can achieve wonders in my little enamel basin. The Wilbrandts (a devoted Derby and Joan couple and Christians in every sense) and I walked up to the summit of the island to look at the view by full moonlight. It was like an Edmond Dulce illustration to a fairy story, with the islands and Istanbul and Anatolia picked out by myriads of twinkling lights and the full moon making a brilliant pathway and turning the sea to silver. A voice addressed us in French. This was a Greek priest who invited us to see the remains of an ancient church built there about eleven hundred years ago. We could see the old walls and capitals of old columns half covered by long grass. He brought us sweet water to drink which he took from a Byzantine cistern which he cleared out himself, he said. It seemed like a fantastic dream that I should be on top of an island in the Sea of Marmara, with Germans, listening to a Greek priest telling us Byzantine history in French, by the light of the full moon ...."

Wind-up in Cairo

Diana had, of course, been of the greatest help during our sojourn in Egypt and our travels in Palestine, Lebanon and Turkey. She was after all the first of the Lush couple to learn the job of IGCR and IRO, was full of compassion for the refugees themselves and in great sympathy with the IRO staff and any others who tried to help them. My IRO staff had a great regard for her, not only by reason of her experience with refugees but because of her abundant knowledge of the Middle East and the common language, Arabic, just as during our service in Cairo as Sudan Agent she was well known among the people of all nationalities who were our neighbours, hosts and guests. She was tough, ready to face with equanimity the cholera scare, the puny air raids and unreasonable restrictions imposed by governments and enforced by officials and police. Once when we were motoring from Cairo to Suez, Diana, who was tired and under the weather, was stretched out sleeping in the back seat. At a police check point I was immediately suspected and accused of carrying a cholera patient or even a corpse from the city to some country place. Out she had to come, pull herself together, and face interrogation in the stifling police hut. She laughed the suspicious officials to scorn, performed a few gymnastic gestures and then asked in Arabic whether they still thought she was a corpse or moribund. *"T'fadl ya sitt"* exclaimed the police ("Please proceed, my lady") and we continued our journey with Diana again asleep in the back of the car. In Jerusalem when the Jewish Agency was blown sky high a few hundred yards away, it was she who ran up to the roof and took snapshots while I retired (I must admit, according to orders) under the office table. I will admit that Diana did sink to the floor of the Government House Rolls Royce at the urgent request of the military orderly alongside the driver when several gunmen outside the Hebrew University in Jerusalem levelled their rifles directly on the car as we approached the entrance. She was the moving spirit when at Port Said one afternoon she and I persuaded a friendly BOAC pilot to embark the wife of the British Ambassador to Greece who, having played truant in the morning from her embassy to attend a luncheon in Cairo, had missed her scheduled connection home to Athens where she *had* to be hostess at an official dinner that evening.

Of course for Diana the school holidays were the months which brought most joy. We maintained our vow made in 1945 that wherever we might be there would be home for the children. Our lovely, spacious Archdeacon's house in Cairo close to the Gezira Club, where every kind of sport was available, became just such a house.

I returned from Geneva to wind up the IRO Mission office in Cairo and Diana with the three children joined me just before Christmas 1948 which we spent in the Cathedral house - our last Christmas, as we thought in North Africa. But as the reader will see, the gods had willed otherwise.

While in London we had persuaded Dora Carson Roberts, our hostess in Mallord Street, to accompany Diana and the family to Cairo. She was a very old friend to whom the Hill family had been devoted for many years. She was born out of England, to a Mrs Noble (who later married secondly a Lindeman) in about 1874. She, Dora, celebrated, soto voce, her 100th birthday in the mid 1970s but no recognition was made. Her brother-in-law, Bertie Davidson was a great friend of C A Hill my father-in-law, and with him, as leaders of the Portland Club (the Senior or Supreme British Bridge Club) he journeyed to USA, there to change the

American Laws of Bridge to Contract Bridge. He died in the 1950s.

Dora and Bertie Davidson had made prodigious journeys to countries far and near. She was a fund of knowledge especially on matters botanical, and a great leader in the musical world. I have told of her friendship with Pouishnoff, the celebrated pianist and John Vallier (originally Jean, from France) was a well-known protégé of hers. She was devoted to Ruth my mother-in-law and also to Diana and therefore accepted me! Both Diana and I owe much to her both for hospitality (we stayed at 20 Mallord Street on many occasions) and for housing our luggage and packing cases.

So it was a multiple delight to us when she accepted our invitation to come to Cairo for Christmas and a week or two afterwards. I was very glad that en route the BOAC aircraft spent nine or ten hours in Castel Benito Airport, Tripoli, whence Travers Blackley, still Chief Administrator, snatched them from the airport and gave them all baths and dinner in the Villa Volpi before their dawn continuation. So Diana saw the house which I had occupied five years previously. I met them in Cairo and there we spent a really lovely 'last' holiday in Africa. I think it was the best which we had spent in Cairo. The elder children were old enough (15 and 12) to play tennis and squash and enjoy evening parties; they met many others and Julian rode often. Not even the assassination of Nokraski Pasha, the Prime Minister, nor my allowing the bath shower to ruin Diana's newly coiffured hair, really damped our happiness. Dora C R was as gay as any of us and this was by no means her first visit to Cairo. The names of Searight, Elgood, Marshall Cornwall, Hamilton, Bewsher, Crawford and Haselden, Troutbeck, Bishop Allan and beloved Frank Johnston feature in Diana's diary, with David Hoare and Pamela, Marie Devonshire, the Havers, the Rowlatts, Geoffrey Parker, Atiyeh Bey, "Solomon" and Hope Wise, Gilbert Inglefield, Gerald Kenyon Slaney, Eve and Henry Ayres, Frank and Audrey Theron.

Dora Carson Roberts became part of our happy family party and stayed for six full weeks: a most wonderful gifted guest. Diana wrote in her diary of 1 February:

"…. M & D to supper before the fire; first meal together alone at home since last October!"

So far as IRO was concerned I was engaged in winding up the Cairo office. We made our final IRO staff party when Russell Ball, my number two who had held the fort for me on so many, many occasions and achieved innumerable tasks unnoticed, left to join Arnold Curtis in Nairobi.

Russell Ball was a New Zealander. I forget his background if indeed I ever knew it. He was unassuming, not at all social and puzzled many of us by adopting a young waif and stray Egyptian girl and taking her quite legally into his bachelor house. She was well under six but he went to endless trouble with a successful conclusion, to have her adoption approved by the nearest relatives and legalised by the Egyptian Courts and finally took the child as his adopted daughter with him to Nairobi and eventually to New Zealand. I heard from him once later that all was going well and that Roheyr, the Egyptian girl - or young woman - had been accepted by his family.

I spent half of February 1949 in Beirut and Geneva where in Beirut, I continued my battle with the Lebanese refugees, and in Geneva agreed to remain in IRO a further year or two and rented (in a blizzard) a house for the family.

Finally we found ourselves, not without many sad partings, out of Cairo, spent a few days sightseeing in Baalbek (Lebanon) and Syria - we had always wanted to walk along the "Street which is called Straight" in Damascus and then, after a final Polish cocktail party given for those who had become "settled" in Lebanon, and a farewell lunch at the Embassy, flew to our beloved Rome. Here we were met by Colonel Fothergill, now IRO, and then had a great meeting not only with the Therons (South African Embassy) but also with Viola and Stewart Symes. We met them all again at dinner with Prince and Princess Doria at the Palazzo Doria. On the morrow, having cabled Diana's Aunt Mary at Nice (now a widow) we met her on the aerodrome there en route Rome-Geneva, and then flew into our home town, Geneva, to be met by Winton Lane of IRO HQ and Isa Maria de Landesberger. She had booked us at the Eden Hotel whence we soon moved to our new home, Les Marguerites, a sizeable house in the village of Veyrier, about three miles north of Geneva city to which it was connected by a rickety Swiss tram which we all used regularly. This ended our work in the Middle East.

APPENDIX TO 14.2
THE POLES IN PERSIA 1942-43

Their reception from Russia; their administration in Teheran and Isfahan; their evacuation via Ahwaz and Khorramshar.

While on the job in Cairo and East Africa I had often wondered how the Poles fared in Persia: who administered and maintained them and finally who and by what means were they moved to their temporary destinations in Africa, India and the Lebanon - their penultimate resting grounds.

To my shame I never really pursued my questioning thoughts until I began to write down their story. Now with the aid of Chatham House and the Army Museum I can describe briefly what happened and shall devote this appendix to this story. General Anders' book *An Army in Exile*, a type-written document of 1943 discovered deep in the archives of Chatham House, is my main source.

General Anders in his book tells a harrowing and true story of the Polish deportations to Russia in 1940 and 1941. The MERRA report estimated that at the end of 1943, after the evacuation of 112,000 Poles from Russia to Persia, and excluding 221,000 who had died in exile, there were still in Russia 647,000 Poles detained against their will.

After Germany attacked Russia in June 1941, the Soviet Government came into the war on the side of the Allies, and consequently on that of Poland. Under an agreement between the Polish Marshall Sikorski and Stalin, approximately 112,000 persons (72,000 military and 40,000 civilians) were released from Russia and went to Persia in early 1942. The Polish military personnel - the Anders Army - transferred into the British Middle East Force, joining part of the Second Corps, and later fought in Italy and participated in the Normandy landings. The civilians were received in Persia and various other countries of temporary asylum, subsequently to be dispersed in a way probably never before seen in history. 4,000 were sent to India whence half left for Mexico; 7,000 were divided between Lebanon, Palestine and Egypt; no less than 16,000 were taken over by the British Government in East Africa, while 3,000 went to Rhodesia.

However, in early 1942, when the movement from the southern provinces of Russia began, a British formation called the Polish Evacuation Staff was sent to Pahlevi, the Persian port of the Caspian Sea whither the Poles would come by sea transport from Krasnovodsk in Russia. Colonel A Ross OBE, in command of Polish Evacuation Staff, had Polish elements attached to him. When he arrived he found Pahlevi thickly carpeted with snow and the first transport carrying 1,387 evacuees, already lying off the harbour.

In the first eight days over 29,000 evacuees arrived. The ships came without warning at all hours of the day and night, one carrying as many as five thousand. The cargoes were much mixed. The soldiers, although underfed, were properly clothed in British battledress sent into Russia through Archangel, and had British equipment. The civilians wore old overcoats and shapeless trousers, torn shawls and faded gaberdines, boots falling to bits, nondescript wrappings of greasy flannel and tattered linen. Forty in every hundred were infested with lice. Some of the women were advanced in pregnancy and among the children were seventy orphans from three to twelve years old. This variegated multitude, unloaded on to the wharf, spilt over on to the beach and stood there in crowded groups or stopped in the roadway and sat down in the soiled snow, where curious Persian children gathered around them. Many were silent, others voluble. Some excited by freedom and loaded with typhus wandered off into the town. A few lay down and died.

A military "Area" under Brigadier Crampton had also moved to Teheran to take charge of the Poles - military and civilian camp sites were allotted to both movements - on the fringes of Teheran whither all refugees military and civilian were moved by road along the "Shah's Road" from Pahlevi to the capital. Polish authorities, especially the Polish Delegation, were brought into the administration of the Poles. The Delegation was part of the extensive adjunct to the Polish Embassy in Tehran. Moreover as the future of the Polish civilian refugees became under discussion, every authority including the Foreign and Colonial Offices, the War Office and Controller of Shipping, the Conference of East African Governors and the Government of India - the lot - all became, no doubt sometimes hysterically, involved and the Minister of State in Cairo, whose writ ran in Persia, wisely put MERRA (Middle East Relief and Refugee Administration) in charge and obviously a good man in command. MERRA took over everything connected with Polish civilian refugees from their entry into Persia at Pahlevi through the camps in Teheran and Ahwaz as far as embarkation on ship to India and East Africa or by lorry to the Middle East. And very well they received, administered and discharged their Poles. It was the usual British way of three good men and a boy given a freehand and moving (Polish) mountains. They used all the agencies enumerated above with one directing mind and force - and with compassion.

Somehow they made plans with the Government of India to receive and maintain some 10,000 refugees in camp not far from Bombay and with the East African Administration to receive 30,000 via Mombasa. Others, clearly linked to the military personnel who went to Khanaqin near Baghdad, were routed by road to Palestine and Lebanon where there was already a nucleus of Poles in a village near Beirut.

In Teheran MERRA and the Polish authorities, aided greatly by Persian cooperation, had established camps, some with solid buildings, for the refugees. Here was their first rest after two or three years of Soviet oppression and cruelty, under a power which they began to realise was merciful, compassionate and kind.

The physical state of the Poles was not good. Here was a microcosm, as the report states, of the whole

Polish structure: aristocrats, intellectuals, officer-class, technicians, and business men, but most of all peasants and small holders, uprooted from their land, divorced from their way of life, mixed with equal proportions of the less fortunate classes of life - criminals, prostitutes. All suffered terribly during their years of exile and brutality: undernourishment near to starvation, complete lack of medical treatment - all the evils which the Soviet Russians, impervious to natural compassion, could inflict on captive people were inflicted mercilessly on these Poles. Starvation, cruelty, indifference to suffering and hatred for the brave but beaten enemy produced a pitiable physical state among them. Perhaps their captors were determined on their extermination - they exerted no measures to prevent such an end.

But the Poles - men, women and children - were and are a tough breed of Europeans and though they arrived in Pahlevi in a really terrible state of exhaustion - to say nothing of mental aberration - a state which prompted General Anders to predict an immediate death rate of 25%, they soon took heart; compassion combined with good food resuscitated them in the camps in Teheran, even before they had to move on to yet more distant continents, and before they could think of home in their own or some foreign land five years away.

In fact the death rate of Poles in Persia was only 5% (2,119 to the end of 1943) - a testimony to their resilience and the great and successful efforts made by the medical staff (chiefly Poles themselves), greatly aided of course by MERRA.

In the MERRA report much appreciation was recorded of the help given by the first Secretary of the British Legation (himself a Polish linguist) and one can imagine the whole of the Legation staff, under R M Hankey, now Lord, especially perhaps the women, pouring their help and compassion into the Polish camps.

MERRA soon had the civilian camps in Teheran and Isfahan (120 miles to the south) in working order. Maintenance of order was not easy at first, but with the help of Polish and Persian authorities disturbances were avoided.

The negotiations with the authorities in India, East Africa and the Middle East must have been well conducted at both ends and no doubt the British Legation played an important part therein. Extensions to the existing transit camps in Southern Persia at Ahwaz and Khorramshar (for actual embarkation) were rapidly made and the first movements by sea to Bombay and Mombasa began in August 1942, four months after the refugees first entry into Persia and by the end of 1943 no less than 24,000 Poles had left for India (and on to Mexico) and Mombasa, East Africa and 7,000 by road for Palestine and the Lebanon.

One of the bizarre stories in MERRA's report told of the popularity among the Poles of Ahwaz camp where the summer temperature rose as high as 128°F. Several refugees absconded from the embarkation batches preferring to remain in this warm paradise! This was especially true in the summer of 1943 when preferences for life in Ahwaz caused great difficulty in filling the final sailings of ships.

The average complement of refugees on each ship was 830. Medical staff accompanied every sailing. No mention is made of the type of ship carrying the Poles nor their ultimate destination nor have we any information about enemy attacks en route. We can presume there was none and indeed the Indian Ocean and Red Sea were tolerably safe at that time. I myself engaged in the Madagascan affair from April-November 1942.

The writer of the MERRRA report speaks highly of the devotion of the indefatigable medical staff in all the camps. Understaffed and poorly equipped, they performed a wonderful job among men, women and children who came in poor physical condition and often needed constant and careful medical attention. Malnutrition made all the Poles ready subjects for the diseases which accompany undernourishment.

Important steps were taken in Teheran and Isfahan camps to institute and increase educational facilities among Polish children. By the end of 1943 (after 18 months sojourn, often very transitory) 32 schools had been established and nearly 4,000 children had received some form of education. The representatives of the Polish Government in Exile took a leading part in this side of Polish life.

By the end of 1943 this unique and successful movement of 40,000 civilian Poles from Russia and Persia was over and MERRA in the person of Colonel A Ross OBE, Highland Light Infantry, had accomplished with compassion and success a unique movement.

14.3 - Special Representative Middle East, IRO, Geneva: Mar 1949 - 1951

Les Marguerites, Veyrier

Veyrier was a Swiss frontier village; in fact the boundary between France and Switzerland ran along the wall at the bottom of our garden.

Les Marguerites was an old house but had a number of sizeable rooms on three storeys, and we could sleep 6 - 8. The big hall or dining room had odd carved furniture therein, including one high chair the back of which was carved in the likeness of a lady's torso - the points of her bosom impinged sharply into father's head if he threw it back too quickly. The drawing room had wine coloured velvet for wall covering, a beautiful Spanish silver mirror, a bronze satire with a tail and a 6" hole in the floor which peeped into the *cave* or cellar. The breakfast room could seat 8 and had a most enchanting chandelier about 3 feet in diameter composed of a circular band of brass on which antlered deer perpetually chased each other. Our parson's (C of E) wife once earned SFr 100 by impaling on one of those antlers, high above the table, a piece of cheese sprung from the end of her knife. The furnishings had indeed originated from an Austrian *schloss*, and were in keeping with such a style.

Les Marguerites had a large garden: the chief features were (1) the lawn, which consisted entirely of dandelions: these on Thursday would be a sea of yellow but after a good mow on Friday gave us a really green sward for the weekend; (2) a large cedar tree, at the foot of which were the graves of a previous owner's dozen pet dogs (behind railings and quite sacrosanct) and half way up the trunk of which was a hornets nets - not so funny; Julian's plucky effort, one day, to smoke out the nest, set fire to the whole tree and failed to dislodge the hornets who, the fire extinguished, remained with us and the dead dogs; (3) the vegetable garden; this presented a further problem, for the potatoes were riddled with Colorado beetle than which, of course, there is nothing more obnoxious and pestilential, except perhaps rabies. We had lovely fruit trees and a greenhouse of a sort, the side door of which opened onto a most luscious green meadow on which, very often, there grazed a dozen or more of those immense dun coloured Swiss cows whose udders drip Nestle's milk. By opening that door I once silenced even the revered Said Abder Rahman el Mahdi, the well known Sudanese leader who was in Switzerland for some cure. He came to tea with his two sons, and after fullsome compliments on the house, the garden, the tea party, and the fruit, asked: *"Wa andak beheim?"* ("and your cattle?"). I showed him through that garden door and he found himself gazing at these gorgeous, stunning animals whose yield was probably 20 times greater than any Sudani kine: he was most duly impressed!

Les Marguerites had garages for two large cars and dog kennels - wire cages which were the abode of two elderly and rather disagreeable mongrels, remnants of the previous owner's assembly of creatures saved, the children imagined, from the vivisectionist's knife (see below).

Les Marguerites also contained Christine, our cook, a Swiss girl, espoused to an Italian but kept asunder by the Roman Catholic priest who would not part with Christine's savings devoutly handed into his care. We lived in Les Marguerites for over two years and loved it. The house and garden were just adequate for our needs and enjoyment.

Writing of Christine reminds me of where she worked and where she lived. The kitchen at Les Marguerites was as old as the house and had never suffered from any modernisation. It was dark and the cupboards were smitten with the very clean and respectable dirtiness which one always associates with old kitchens. There was no 'frig - but there were two larders, one above ground, the other in the magnificent rock hewn stone cold *cave*, rat free and so far as one could sense, quite clean. Many were the meals I stored there (for in good time I became cook) until my young family and friends found the way to the stone shelves. The *pièce de résistance* in the kitchen was the gas stove (whence came the gas G.O.K.) which illuminated on top - i.e. on the hob, but the oven of which required the application of a strong naked flame at the very bottom rear, an effort which impelled the cook or lighter to lie prone and outstretched on the floor in order to bring the flame adjacent to the gas, the said application requiring several attempts during which the gas was 'on' at full strength: the gas bar awoke to flame with a roar which drove the illuminator sharply backward on his or her stomach, carrying some of last night's over-cooked meal with him. It is small wonder that since our return to U.K. and civilization we have always insisted on the installation of a waist-high oven.

Mention of Christine also reminds me that there was a second upper storey to Les Marguerites - indeed, a long *grenier* under the roof. For the first was full of main and guest bedrooms as well as a playroom for the young, and their sleeping quarters. The staircase leading to the first storey contained on its wall a life size painting of a lecherous satire advancing on an unclad female. In order to avoid lingering on the stairs at bed time and questions such as: "What is he going to do Daddy" I had the portrait removed to some obscure room, only to find that childish assemblies invariably chose that room. It was then put back on the stairs.

Another painting not quite so large hung over the front door of the house - this portrayed Lida and her Swan in the most amatory pose - really quite well painted but hung in such a way that full tribute could not be paid to it as a work of art, often obscured as it was, (and possibly quite tactfully so) by the front door curtain.

To whom did this rather exciting house belong? The house agents, Bernard Naef & Cie who appeared to have been in existence since the Stone Age, rented us the property *composé de 10 pièces meublées, avec salle de bain, chauffage central, et garage*, for one year 1949/50 at an annual rent of Fr.9000. We also had the run of the garden, fruit and vegetables.

The house had been the property of Mademoiselle Lind af Hageby, a Swedish lady of some note, described in Who's Who (1948) as Speaker and Writer with two addresses in London (Regent's Park and St James's Place) and one in France. She occupied 74 lines in that great work of reference and was, in fact, the founder (in 1906) of the Animal Defence and Anti-Vivisectionist Society and used Les Marguerites in conjunction with Nina, Duchess of Hamilton and Madame Mordant of Geneva. The Dowager Duchess was President of the said Society. Madame Mordant, the lady involved, lived in Geneva and was the senior Swiss member of the Animal Defence League and, for us, the local representative. For through Mademoiselle Lind af Hageby the house belonged to the Animal Defence League and was used by them as the League's HQ after our departure. We saw Madame Mordant often and were good friends. Her Society's office in Geneva was a place of morbid fascination, containing gruesome evidence and examples of vivisectional practice. I knew she appreciated our care of the property, especially the work which we devoted to the garden, which improved beyond all expectation from the hard work which was bestowed. *La pelouse* at Les Marguerites was well known among our foreign friends and a worthy joke among our English acquaintances!

Our entry into our new residence, our first family home in Europe, was nearly marred by what might have been a real tragedy. We brought no furniture from the Sudan via Egypt but we had 14 packing cases containing our *'penates'*, pictures, rugs and silver which consisted, of course, of wedding presents and a few nice pieces of Sudan silver. These were exported from Egypt and imported into Switzerland under our semi-diplomatic visa and we had little trouble with customs. As a precaution however I sent my personal assistant, one Sonia Sandaljian, an Armenian girl who wanted to migrate to Europe, on the ship from Alexandria carrying the 14 packing cases to Genoa. She had orders to oversee the loading and unloading of the cases and almost to sleep with them on board ship. So she did and they duly arrived at the house in Veyrier, all 14 cases plainly marked.

Diana and I joyfully welcomed them at Les Marguerites on our first day in Geneva, but on close inspection there seemed something peculiar about case 13 which should contain our silver. Sure enough when opened it was found to contain a brick and bundles of papers of no value relating to el Shatt Camp in Egypt - clearly a case of fraudulent substitution in place of our silver. Of course the unfortunate Sonia came under silent suspicion but, at the same time, we cabled the Master of the ship which had left for Marseilles. 48 hours elapsed without reply and then came the surprise of our lives "Lush Case 13 on board returning Genoa today." Well, we recovered the silver intact and enjoyed it in Geneva, Tripoli, Karachi and for 15 years in England - where it suffered the fate which it had avoided in five other not so civilised countries - loss by burglary.

In the meantime Diana had achieved the first of her or our "quick trips" to U.K., this time to reclaim our Vauxhall car and render ourselves mobile in a civilised Europe. She took the sleeper from Lausanne on Saturday, at 9 p.m., and was in London, very comfortably, next afternoon; spent three days in UK, collecting Julian, the Vauxhall, licenses etc., and drove across France to Geneva by Friday. Sylvia and Meriel arrived a day or two later.

We spent a really wonderful first 6 months in Geneva getting to know the Headquarters form, revelling in our first European home to which came the three children Julian, Sylvia and Meriel every holidays of the two years we spent in Veyrier, sometimes by road with one or more parents driving to meet them off the cross channel boat at Calais, and returning across France, sometimes by train. Holidays included, of course, the invaluable winter and early spring weeks when they made day trips to the snow slopes and learnt really to ski instructed without stint by their expert and indefatigable mother - the nursery slopes at Feldafing had not been forgotten.

Many of our family and friends came to that hospitable house to stay a week or so, beginning with my mother and brother Cecil (the eldest guests) then David Fletcher, Shirley Whittaker, Giles Constable, Ursula Jarrett, Angela Sarell. We were scarcely ever alone there and the house seemed to enjoy the crowd and the fun and youth (and the old 'uns too). Ian Skeet came for a few days during an Oxford vacation but stayed, a welcome adjunct to the family, for 6 weeks. Meriel lived at home for a year and attended, daily, the Ecole Privat in Geneva and thus learned French.

We met many people of all nationalities. Of those many, the personalities of C J Edmonds and later his wife Phyllis, Paul and Jean Guinness of the YMCA, Dick and Alison Hansen, the Vicar of Holy Trinity, Geneva, and Stanley Pope, the conductor.

Of course the country was lovely, the climate very good - we had a good car, sometimes two, and were determined to take every advantage of our good luck in serving there, and to forget the hard times of war and separation.

IRO, Geneva

From the career point of view I recognised that I found myself in a backwater - my days of leadership were over. They had begun in the Northern Province of the Sudan, continued during the war and ended when we left Cairo in March 1949: and a very fulfilling period it had been, covering just over ten years. In Geneva I became just one of the IRO Headquarters staff, ready (I hoped) to do what was asked and expected of me, but without the sense of responsibility which I had felt as Head of Mission. It was really quite a relief to sit back, enjoy a fairly lengthy period of irresponsibility and take things moderately calmly with the family - but there was just something missing: independence!

I had a room (B519) in the Palais des Nations, where

my PA, Sonia Sandaljian, was established on the HQ staff and we found enough to keep us busy, firstly with the preparation of a history of IRO Middle East and also dealing with odd problems connected therewith which the Middle East Committee produced for solution. I made closer contact with Tuck, the Director, and Arthur Rucker, his Deputy, and made personal contact with the various heads of Sections at Headquarters.

I do not think that I earned my salary in 1949, certainly not to the extent that I had done previously. I wound up the hard core in Lebanon and other countries in the Middle East, through the generosity of Great Britain, whose good feelings and sympathy I exploited shamelessly at various meetings, particularly at the final session of whatever Committee dealt with refugees. I spoke to them all, as one who had been with the Poles for 2 - 3 years, and won their hearts: most of the Poles still left in East Africa and the Middle East came to Great Britain. It also fell to me to begin to wind down the 180 missions in the Middle East.

I also used my several visits to London to further the cause of my own future, but it soon became quite clear that at 53 I was really not in the market for any job under HMG or sponsored by the various Departments of Government. Moreover, Macmillan, who would have helped me, was in the wilderness and my Labour friends (Julian Snow etc) did not seem to have much 'pull'.

Thus, I was by no means idle though I missed the joys and sorrows of leadership which I had enjoyed for so many years, and winding up a Mission thousands of miles away from the scene of action was an unnatural task. I remember how infuriated I became when I found it necessary to discuss every problem of mass or even individual future of Middle Eastern refugees with the Heads and members of four Departments - Welfare, Resettlement, Legal Protection and Administration, and I begged the Director of IRO, as missions began to decrease in numbers, to create Theatre Committees who could view area problems as a whole instead of departmentalising every question.

During 1949 IRO in Geneva had been realising that one particularly difficult hard core among refugees was the not inconsiderable number of professional men - doctors, engineers, teachers and academics - for whom, in post-war years, there must be a demand in many countries especially nations recently made independent in what we now call the third world. A scheme was therefore evolved to offer such highly educated persons to various Governments of countries short of qualified people.

So, with great labour and enthusiasm, lists were prepared and plans were made to publicise the 'goods' at our disposal - a work in which I assisted - and to send out high powered members of IRC to persuade Governments to accept the candidates which we had to offer on the terms which IRO maintained for every resettled refugee - permanent settlement with full citizenship in the receiving country. Of course it was a very one sided offer and demanded great compassion on the part of the receiving country and great courage on the part of the candidate.

I was asked to take on the job of 'selling' these professional people to Governments in the Eastern and Middle Eastern hemispheres as Special Representative of IRO. I accepted and by good fortune found that the first country on the list was apparently anxious to investigate and experiment with the scheme. The Government of Ceylon had heard of our proposals, knew that they were woefully short of educated professional men and invited me to come out to Colombo to discuss the whole matter - as a guest of the Ceylon Government.

Ceylon Dec 1949

My career as Special Representative Middle East (MESR) had begun and off I went to Ceylon. In those days (the 1940s) the quickest route from Geneva to Ceylon was via London, Rome, Cairo and Bahrain with a night stop at each of these cities. However on arrival at Colombo airport I found a very kind reception committee from the Ministry of Foreign Affairs and Education and the whole of the Ceylon Press. I was moved and highly gratified by their enthusiasm though one of the Press boys asked: "Are you planning to send refugees to take the bread out of the mouths of our Ceylonese educated classes?" to which I riposted that I thought the Ceylonese ate rice. As a fact that riposte was far more apt that I had intended, as the next few weeks and months were to show.

They had given me a very comfortable suite at the Belle Face Hotel (I never discovered the origin of the name) and were very good hosts to me - although I well remember with dismay the heat of the curry at my first luncheon as guest of the Minister of Education. It was stronger than the dish at the Charterhouse Hotel which in 1909 had destroyed my chances of a scholarship at Charterhouse!

Let me remind the reader that Ceylon was a Crown Colony with a British Governor General (Lord Soulbury about to retire as such), who did not govern but left everything to the Ceylonese Parliament under the Prime Minister, Mr Bandaranaike. This fine old man had been Prime Minister for a dozen years or more; highly respected and very wise, he knew a great deal about his country and the Ceylonese - in fact he was the wise old man of an island state which had never known war and had avoided the political changes which war must bring about. I paid my respects to the Governor General, Lord Soulbury, a politician who had just been translated to the House of Lords after a lifetime in education; he, Soulbury was a figurehead, pleasant, wise, witty but a stop-gap Governor General with no experience at all of colonial rule. The Prime Minister ruled. I spent four days really trying to gauge the receptivity of Ceylon to Polish refugees. I found myself in a country and a community, Ceylonese and British, which had no experience of war or upheaval of society caused by war. The Head of the YMCA, as nearly always, had the soundest conception of introducing lowly paid Europeans into this insular society; the very British members of the

Colombo Club (most generous to me personally) had no doubt that if white refugees were introduced they must be paid a sufficiency to preserve the superiority of the white races: enough to own a car. I myself was most sternly entreated not to travel anywhere by the very good British made London buses. The Ceylonese Government officials wanted to raise the standard of efficiency by the introduction of educated professional and technical men and women on the same wage structure and level as the Ceylonese. Everyone would have been happy to have the Europeans at a higher rate of pay than the Ceylonese for a short period of years on contract. But the grant of permanent citizenship appalled the Kwai Hais of the Colombo Club, was not received well by the Ceylonese Government (though not rejected), and was utterly rejected by the P.M. I tried to persuade one and all that there existed Europeans who did not require the high standards of the representatives of the white subjects of the British Raj; that there had been successful Dutch burghers in Ceylon who had become assimilated; that there were white people ready to eschew the superior status imposed by the East India Company and the British traders who followed in their wake. In a country where the cost of living was as high as in Geneva this may have been spurious, but I had the Ceylonese Civil Service behind me and a hundred dossiers or more had portrayed the very people they required NOW; but when it became FOR EVER - then there was hesitancy, sharpened by the completely negative attitude of the Prime Minister who would have no truck with citizenship and would rather delay the educational and professional advance of his country than dilute Ceylonese indigenous structure with a strain of Europeans - be they never so cultured.

During my second weekend I went up country to study conditions there; of course I found the climate much better and conditions more primitive. Again I found that the predominance of the British cult and ideals about 'whites' was still a danger for the future. The idea of bringing 'poor whites' into the hallowed Golf Club society in the hills was condemned. Poverty among the Ceylonese could be excused - they and poverty were native to the country - but to introduce a European pauper would be disastrous to British and Ceylonese.

I had three glorious hours during that weekend in which rich and poor, British and Ceylonese people, played no part. First, I had my first view of trained elephants (Indian) at work lifting and stacking, moving and putting in order, heavy lengths of timber: the most fascinating sight of work done with highly disciplined and well-trained endeavour, noiselessly (the humans spoke scarcely a word) and successfully. Suddenly, so it seemed, the several elephants silently laid down their last load and padded or rather sloped down to the river for their prolonged post meridiem bathe followed by rest and food and then sleep. Elephants left their task (they were building a country bridge), as I was told, precisely on the tick of 2.30 p.m. daily. Nothing would make them move after that hour.

The second delight was a visit at 8 a.m. to the Peredeniya Botanical Gardens outside Candy. Here on a lovely Sabbath morn (I had been to the local church for Communion) I saw hibisci and bougainvillaeas of every hue - 70 different species of the former, 20 of the latter, glistening with the night rain, radiant in the sunshine - a breath-taking sight. Lucky the refugee to give play to horticultural education in these, the Peredeniya Botanical Gardens. I never returned to see a vision of floral beauty which left me speechless. I wonder if any Pole attained to the job of gardener in Peredeniya.

I learnt that in the New Year a conference of British Imperial Ministers was due in Colombo. Bandaranaike encouraged me to leave my proposals and my dossiers with his Government and entreated me to go home to my family for Christmas and return after his people had digested my proposals in their entirety - and as I said "Au revoir in the New Year" replied "I suppose you haven't a good cook among those refugees?"

I sent a telegram to Geneva "Expect 2 elephants with keeper on 24th".

During my first visit to Ceylon I could not fathom a sense of Sudan memories whenever I saw or entered Public Buildings - and then I remembered: the first members of the Sudan P.W.D. (Public Works Department) had built all our buildings in the Sudan on the Indian pattern; I was seeing the originals of provincial and central Government buildings in El Dueim, and Damer and Khartoum here in Colombo (climatically more like Port Sudan).

Well the two elephants (ivory miniatures) and their keeper landed at Geneva on Christmas Eve and we had a heavenly family Christmas (1949). Moreover I was able to discuss Ceylon as a home for refugees with those who would select them and send them thither. I have copies of our copious discussions on the despatch of Europeans to this island at the foot of India. I can read now my own doubts and uncertainties. It was desperately important to solve, correctly and humanly, the problem of sending Europeans of good professional qualifications but with absolutely no financial foundations to live and breed and terminate their lives in a country where the climate, the background, the emoluments were almost totally in their disfavour - nay to their detriment. Could Poles and nationals of northern or middle Europe establish for themselves a position and a life in Ceylon (and the Indian sub-continent) as successfully as the Greeks and Levantines had done in Egypt, the Sudan and other Middle Eastern countries?

Having seen the Poles in East Africa, and realising the vast differences, climatic and circumstantial, I thought they could - just! Or were we introducing to Ceylon a stratum of poor whites who would never weather the vast differences of climate and environment which would kill them off or produce a permanent problem to the host countries. The same doubts presented themselves all over the Indian sub-continent and in India itself there was even more resistance from the Indians themselves and such British as were left. At any rate we went ahead, with Geneva's blessing and Bandaranaike's doubtful approval (he gained a Polish pastry cook plus husband as part of the deal) and a batch of some 40 Poles were listed to reach Colombo in the later summer of 1950.

In Ceylon however, there was sufficient local support for resettlement of a few specialists, including the Prime Minister, who was eventually won over, that when I paid my second visit in February 1950 I was able to write:

"I hope that I have achieved a modicum of success in Ceylon .... Owing to illness I have not been able to see him and consequently have been unable to present him with the temptation of accepting the late Mr Masaryk's pastry cook (with her husband) into his own household .... It is perfectly true that the production of this dossier, as a final trump card, secured his grudging approval for the immigration of D.P.'s."

I also managed to find a retired British official who had decided to remain in Ceylon for the rest of his life to serve as IRO representative in Ceylon. Mr Morrison was invaluable and a keen supporter of the IRO scheme. To him I handed over the dossiers for final selection, the actual arrivals later in July and their initial dispositions. By then 4 educationalists, 6 agricultural and 5 irrigation experts with some 20 or 30 engineers, architects and civil engineers were up for selection. In July of the same year I was congratulating him on his success, referring to dates of sailing, and comparing Ceylon most favourably with the rest of the sub-continent where interest had been shown but action had proved practically non-existent.

This was abundantly true. Six months of intensive travelling and hard endeavours to seek the professional refugees as permanent citizens elsewhere led to no success with the exception of fifty medical Poles about whom General Faruki, head of the Pakistan military medical services was already in treaty with Dr Cologny and others in Geneva. I completed the local details of the acceptance into the Pakistan Army and resettlement in the country of these 50 doctors whose service to Pakistan was valuable and for whom a new life as Pakistanis seemed tolerable. In fact I found some of them still serving when I returned to work in Pakistan some six years later.

Before describing my adventures in India and Pakistan let me tell of the conference of the International Labour Organisation held in Mysore in January 1950 to which I was IRO's delegate.

ILO - Mysore January 1950

ILO had been from the very beginning of IGCR and IRO most interested in the refugee problem, particularly where skilled personal and vocational training were concerned. The Organisation kept, or pretended to keep, a close eye on the balance of labour markets, and the sudden shifting of large numbers from one part of the globe to the other upset these markets. I knew precious little about ILO before I went to the conference; I learnt a little during the sessions. I tried to make IRO's point about absorption of specialists and avoided, as instructed by Geneva, involvement in contentious arguments. I was told that a Communist strain ran through the Organisation and I found confirmation, albeit slight, of this suspicion. I met several pleasant members of ILO - we were mostly staying in a very pleasant hotel called Krishnarajsagar, 14 miles or more from Mysore on the shores of a lake which had been dammed; our hotel was obviously a State guest house and had beautiful gardens, illuminated by night and comfortable mods and cons. There, or in the conference, I made several acquaintances but cannot remember the name of one.

Our nearest airport was Bangalore (90 miles) whence I took a car in order to be present at the opening ceremony by the Maharajah of Mysore, Sir Sri Jaya Chamaraja Wadiya Bahadur GCB, GGSI, who since 1940 had ruled the State of Mysore; 30,000 square miles with over 7 million inhabitants. He was highly educated, a charming character, spoke perfect English and I discovered later, was an extremely gifted pianist. I sought out his Comptroller of the Household, a British officer whose name I forget, who was devoted to him.

I arrived only just in time and, in fact, shocked the ILO organising secretary by changing from travel to No 1 clothes in his office. The Maharajah arrived in rather a dingy hall where about 100 ILO delegates were assembled.

MSL to SRL 6.1.50

"Then there was a fanfare of trumpets and the Maharajah of Mysore came in preceded by his macebearer and also a man who appeared to be carrying a large red, gold and green feather duster. The Maharajah wore white jodpurs and a long white coat buttoned up to his neck. On his head he wore an enormous turban of green and gold. As he sat down his mace-bearer began, as I thought, to clear his throat very, very loudly but apparently it was some formula telling us to sit down, which we did but only for a moment because the band struck up the Indian National Anthem - a sad tune - and then the Mysore anthem.

"The Maharajah opened the meeting speaking perfect English and after dutiful replies by our Chairman (Mr Morse, an American, who spoke very second class English!) we all went off to the local gymkhana for tea and then to a vast concourse of about 10,000 people and a primitive cinema - tableaux entertainment, depicting the victory of Right over Wrong! The evening ended with very good fireworks and then suddenly the whole Palace of Mysore with its 6 white domes became a blaze of light as 500,000 lights were switched on."

The discussions of the ILO were prolonged (three days) and, for me, dull. I said my piece about refugees but the presence of Russians inhibited much talk of Poles and I found the sessions tedious. The one bright interlude was a long talk with the Maharajah whose help I besought on behalf of refugee musicians. He was charming and I discovered that his munificence was directed in a big way toward helping musicians in Great Britain and Europe. He promised help for refugees, but we did not in fact take advantage of his generous offer.

The ILO meeting was indeed a drab affair, well organised but with no scope for any effusion or even spark of real humanity. We were gathered together, it seemed, in order to ensure the moral preponderance and influence of the workers, indeed of the proletariat. There was no eloquence - indeed it was hard to find subjects on which anyone could wax eloquent and it seemed to me that the spirit of man was completely subdued during our discussions by the importance, in the eyes of the majority, of the status of man. My appeal for mercy to be shown to refugees, the story of IRO's successes and failures, was heard without emotion, almost without comment. I came across one Briton who seemed to have a love of countryside; his name and association I cannot remember.

India and Pakistan - 1950

As a preface to my several and very intense visits to both India and Pakistan, I am about to quote almost *in extenso* a letter I wrote to the Dutch Chief of IRO (who had been in touch with the Indian authorities) in July 1950. It sums up my views after 7 months' work as MESR.

MSL (Karachi) to Dr Sark, The Hague, Holland - 16.7.50

"There is no doubt that there exists a real need for specialists in India in common with all the countries in the Middle East. There is also no doubt that many of our refugees have the necessary qualifications and experience to meet that need, but there are many difficulties to overcome before we can persuade the Governments to accept our people. The chief stumbling block is that oriental Governments demand very high academic qualifications from their employees, pay little attention to the value of experience and offer totally inadequate rates of pay; even their own nationals are sorely underpaid. Other factors are ignorance of continental European institutions: the authorities here cannot gauge the comparative standards of the various universities, of some of which they have never heard. There is also a certain amount of xenophobia born of jealousy among Government servants who are fearful that they may lose promotion. But really the chief difficulty is that our proposal is something new, something which is partly political, partly economic and partly social. It takes these people a long time in their adolescent state to take hold of new ideas (especially those which stem from the west) then make rapid decisions thereon. We must remember that so far as India and Pakistan are concerned we are asking them to accept a Western proposition; to receive into their not too wealthy economy a group of Western people having different religions, different upbringing and a different outlook on life, to fill appointments which they must publicly admit cannot be filled by their own nationals and to fill them not merely as temporary experts but as permanent residents and maybe citizens. Finally, we are asking them to take compassion on this group of refugees, although the whole proposition is one of mutual advantage, when they have between them twelve million Indian and Pakistan refugees displaced within the last three years. We cannot be surprised that the reaction is not rapid. Nevertheless, Pakistan has come forward with a very helpful approach and already business is brisk, far more so than in India where Government held back, except the medical authorities, and where demand was limited to industrial concerns. Government Departments on the educational side insist on academic qualifications which none of our refugees have. Generally speaking, it is fair to say that the oriental Governments aim too high and we, the IRO, rather overstated our case in the 'Forgotten Elite'."

India - Jan 1950

During my first visit to Delhi in January 1950, I stayed with the Deputy High Commissioner, Frank Roberts, and his quite charming wife, Celeste, both of whom we had known well in Cairo in 1935. Through their kindness and that of Gen Sir Archibald Nye, Great Britain's first High Commissioner to the new independent Dominion of India, who had been a Governor of Madras, I had instant contact with the Indian Government at a high level. The Secretary for Foreign Affairs gave me the entrée to many Government Ministries and Departments and I had instant success with the Ministry of Health who were in urgent need of medical teachers. I also found myself talking for an hour to the International Rotary Club of Delhi and was afforded office accommodation in the Headquarters of the United Nations Information Office.

It was in the Department of Health that I found most openings - they were crying out for ordinary doctors, of whom we had many, to go to the Rural Areas whither no Indian Doctor would venture; the reason: "No money". The lady Minister herself told me that she had 2,000 or 20,000 vacancies in the countryside of India which she could not fill - nor did she expect to fill these from refugees who must expect to make money. "Our country villages are suitable for missionaries only who are fed by God" she said - and how right she was. Nevertheless on my first visit I sent home urgent demands for the dossiers of doctors and nurses.

I failed utterly to find an agent in Delhi or any person who, on a voluntary basis, would take over some of the work which I should leave behind - to establish some link with Geneva. But as in Pakistan, no native of the country could bring himself to work for European refugees with 7 million Indians displaced from the Punjab and elsewhere sitting on his own doorstep.

The British High Commissioner, Archibald Nye, gave me much help and advice. But, as I wrote at the time,

General Nye gave me the strongest warning against the introduction of Europeans into more than a few selected cities in India. He drew a grim picture of a country without any social welfare system, suffering from a deplorable lack of sanitary and hygienic measures, full of disease and with a negligible number of hospitals and medical staff. He warned me that if the displaced persons came to India they must expect absolutely nothing in the way of welfare or medical, social or moral aid if they fell on evil days. I agreed and realised that in a city like Delhi, the capital, if a displaced person needed urgent hospitalisation, it would be extremely difficult to find any hospital for himself or his family.

All the cards were stacked against successful infiltration, let alone immigration, of European refugees and yet the country was crying out for trained men in the medical, educational, agricultural, engineering and industrial interests in the country and I felt sure that a visit to the fourteen States of the country would more than absorb the dossiers of professional men whom we had in Geneva! I had made myself most unpopular in the Headquarters of IRO by advising industrialists to apply directly for suitable men and women. They were overwhelmed - and I had not yet recommended firmly to my people that India was a suitable country for permanent settlement.

Pakistan - Jan 1950

I am not sure why I left Delhi so abruptly for Karachi in January 1950 - I may have been asked to do so by Geneva who were about to send some Polish doctors to Pakistan - a move arranged between the Pakistan Army and the Health Division in Geneva direct - of which I knew. But I began a most interesting visit to that country in mid January and found the Pakistani response far more favourable and firm than the Indian.

Pakistan, on Partition, became (so Whitakers informed us) the largest Islamic State in the world. It covered 1.3 million square miles (compared with India's 1.5 million) and contained a population of 70 million people compared with India's 389 million. No wonder the problem seemed easier of solution. Yet 5-7 million Pakistani refugees were very present - more visible in the smaller areas whose towns had their main roads converted into shanti dwellings for refugees. It is true that the Pakistani Army seemed highly disciplined and their headquarters far seeing: one remembered that the standards at the Staff College at Quetta were second only to the Staff College in Camberley, GB, the finest in the world. The leaders and officials of the Civil Service seemed quicker off the mark and more ready to grasp the nettles of misfortune and tragedy. They were, it is true, obsessed by the alleged treachery on the part of HMG and the then Indian Government concerning Kashmir, a territory they most ardently required.

The Pakistanis seemed to realise the immense difficulties attached to accepting as citizens (not just employing) European refugees. They had already accepted 40 or 50 European refugees into their Army Medical Service; these Poles were in fact beginning to arrive at the start of my visit and proved initially a success in the Medical Corps. Quite apart from that I found discussions and negotiations with the Pakistanis - of all types - easier than with the Indians.

I flew to Karachi - the new capital of this Muslim territory. I found that it was the political capital in that the President and Prime Minister, with most of the other Ministers, lived and functioned therein. It was, of course, the one and only port of the country and therefore the chief business centre. But it really was a terrible place! Mangrove swamps lay on each side of the harbour which in itself was a dirty affair, and the smells on the western outskirts of the town were unbearable. The main hotel kept a permanent Pakistani medical whose sole duty was to administer antidotes to the weekly attacks of 'Karachi tummy' which regularly assailed all visitors; it was a dreadful hostelry. (The Beach Luxury Hotel which was in course of erection in 1950, was sited on the edge of a mangrove swamp which at low tide was malodorous: it had no beach, no luxury and barely counted as a hostelry.)

However, I started business in Karachi, had a good hour with Liaqat Ali Khan, Prime Minister, and we engendered a mutual liking for each other. We talked for an hour after which he gave a cordial blessing to my mission and then asked me to tell him on my return from the north of anything wrong with the Administration! I met his equally charming wife at the Governor's luncheon table next day where she gave me a voluble and graphic description of the proper way to take off and then enrobe herself in the really beautiful blue and silver saree which adorned her comely figure: it was a faultless performance, beautifully given. From Karachi where I seemed to have had a good start, I took train to Peshawar, capital of the North West Frontier Province where, as I wrote:

> "it freezes in winter and goes up to 120°F in summer; where the men are 6ft high, pretty wild in the eye and loose on the trigger. My train journey thither which lasted from Saturday evening until Monday morning ..."

Travel in Pakistan is no luxury trip and as I wrote:

> "You would have laughed to see the Special Representative eating the dinner of cold curry standing up in a First Class compartment lately occupied by indigenous passengers who had strewn everything from oranges to liver, from soup to betel nut (mixed with saliva) all over the floor and finally lit a fire in the lavatory."

This was in the second train which took me from Lahore to Peshawar, 250 miles - a night journey which landed me, to my great embarrassment, half an hour early at Peshawar station where there awaited me, on that chilly morning, a group of officials from the Chief Secretary's office who found me only half dressed!

My first impressions of the North West Frontier Province were similar to those in Karachi: friendliness, admission of shortage of professional men and women, readiness to accept help from IRO, but was it not adding Pelion to Ossa if they accept European refugees in addition to their own millions? The Chief Secretary, who was charming but practical, turned me over, as if to prove his doubts, to his wife, a stout hearted, plain speaking Begum who gave me a charming but forthright reception and at once questioned the rightness of our adding to the insoluble problem already facing Pakistan with her 7 million workless, landless, penniless Pakistani refugees by sending more European refugees who did not even belong to the country and had the rest of the world in which to settle. My reply, of course, was that the European refugees whom we would send were professional people of whom Pakistan was woefully short and who would, because they would be given citizenship in her country, be more ready to help the refugees they found. I instanced the arrival of the Polish doctors in the Army. She was not convinced (was I?) but showed me an excellent Pakistan rehabilitation centre of which IRO could have been proud. I also saw some of these Polish doctors and met the Commander in Chief of the Pakistan Army and a number of his staff at a party in Rawlpindi whither I travelled by car after a coupled of days in Peshawar. I longed to go up the Khyber Pass, but on my way to visit the big Pakistan public school, run by a Briton on British school principles (and his lady wife who ran an equally successful girls' school), I saw a little of the surrounding country. The Headmaster even wanted refugee staff because he required teachers with the necessary training!

On my way down to the coast I spent some days at Lahore, the centre of administrative Government, just as it had been when capital of the Punjab. It was a far more official capital and far better equipped materially from the point of view of personnel than Karachi. I found the now customary acceptance *"en principe"* of European refugees and a very encouraging list of actual demands from the Registrar of the Lahore University.

After my return to Karachi and a couple of days in which, inter alia, I tested the Beach Luxury Hotel, I found a willing and delightful assistant in a Mrs Alington, wife of a British accountant of some note, who was prepared to help and could type. I then took to the air and flew 900 miles by Pakistan Airlines preceded by a kind introduction from the High Commissioner's office to his Deputy in Dacca.

The British High Commissioner in Karachi turned out to be Sir Laurence Grafftey Smith, my former colleague in the administrative mess in Madagascar caused by the insistence of the Foreign Office in taking a premature hand in the Administration. He had been appointed High Commissioner for Pakistan at the time of Partition in 1947. Chapter 3 of his book *Hands to Play* (Routledge and Kegan Paul 1975) gives to my mind a brilliant description of the days immediately preceding Partition and the events of the next four years. He became a great friend of the Pakistan Prime Minister and an ardent but necessarily silent supporter of Kashmir's adherence to Pakistan. The High Commission was staffed with ex-Indian Civil Servants recently ejected, or, more politely or truthfully, retired from the Government of India, still with many or few years to go for pension and all (or nearly all) anxious to ensure that the dedicated work of their service, the Corps d'Elites of British Civil Services, was not thrown overboard in the immense transshipment of power which took place in 1947. Grafftey Smith spoke highly of their loyalty to him as High Commissioner and to the country which they were still serving - with a difference. I must admit that to the travelling seeker after truth, like myself, some of the advice they gave was invaluable - even to the bed roll etc I should hire and the providers (Thos Cook).

I was of course intensely interested visiting the Pakistan Administration and had a rare opportunity of examining the refugees' homeland-to-be, observing their schemes, noting the very serious number of vacancies to be filled for which Pakistan had no source on which to draw (many posts had been held by Indians). I with my lists (and some dossiers) appeared heaven-sent by many of the Pakistan Civil Service and many senior civil servants would have engaged some of my paper candidates on the spot. Others were more canny and realised the immense difficulties in granting rights of citizenship and sufficient emoluments to complete foreigners, unable to speak even English. I began to have a gnawing feeling that this was no country for poor European immigrants in the long term. Then I could but think of the conditions which had been endured by many of the Poles on my description sheets. Might they not snatch at any offer which gave them a future in which their abilities could be used, in which they could start life again despite the certainty that any compassion due to refugee status and real homelessness would be most certainly lavished on 5 - 7 million Pakistan refugees rather than on them? Moreover the dossiers I held and others yet to come from Geneva were not all those of Poles.

I declared my belief in a despatch that "there was some scope for European refugees in Pakistan; but they will come to a hard life: anyone coming in the next few years must come with a pioneering spirit."

I have left descriptions of the country and towns in Pakistan until a later chapter when I shall be describing our family life in the country where we spent three happy years from 1956 - 1959. I propose therefore to close this section by quoting a paragraph from Grafftey Smith's *Hands to Play*.

> "(Karachi's) selection as the first capital of Pakistan was natural only because there was no alternative .... Before Partition a clean little provincial town with a population of under half a million. It had importance as a port .... but it lay out of the mainstream of Indian political life on the perimeter of a backwater province (Sind). Within a matter of a week (after Partition) it was invaded by nearly a million unhappy refugees, over a hundred thousand of whom were for years to have no home except the pavement."

East Pakistan - Feb 1950

MSL, Dacca, 4.2.50 to SRL and Lush family, Geneva and UK.

"It was rather a milestone in one's life yesterday when the pilot of the aircraft, who had been asked to look after me, came up and quietly said, pointing out of the window: "That is Mt Everest". We were flying from Karachi to Dacca via Delhi and had come into view of the Himalaya Mountain Range 280 miles (one hour's flying) east of Delhi. The massif of Mt Everest was quite visible and I felt a thrill to have seen the highest thing in the world. Our aircraft was a Convair, very fast and absolutely crammed including another Brigadier (War Graves Commission), rather a grave-yardy man and STONE deaf. MSL shouts: "Do you see Everest?" Reply: "No, I never sleep after lunch". Silence.

"After Everest the flight became tame but we did follow the rivers of northern India until they became the Ganges which we crossed and them came on to the Brahmaputra on which Dacca, capital of East Pakistan (1950) lies. The whole area over which we flew is very reminiscent of the north of Italy."

I was taken to the Circuit House in the Cantonment of Dacca well away from the town. Sir Frederick Bourne, the ex-British Governor, was still in residence and was extremely kind and hospitable - he told me of a TB hospital recently built by a rich Bengali which required a full staff and he, Sir Frederick, could think of no one better than refugees to do the whole job. I found the Bengali (Pakistani) officials more suspicious than their western counterparts and found little hope in that quarter - indeed I wrote off Dacca and the southern part of the Province as quite unsuitable climatically. Chittagong was somehow different and I recommended an immediate visit from a medical representative from Geneva. The only communications between Dacca and Chittagong, the port of Bengal, were by air or train. I elected the train (metre gauge) and had an excellent night journey but was met by a host of medical men and women who thought I was International Red Cross and just melted away when they discovered their mistake. The port was in a miserable state of unpreparedness for being the port of a large Province.

Ceylon - Feb 1950

I left by air for Calcutta, a city which filled me with dismay and having no business there I flew to Bombay to be greeted by my niece Judith Minta and her splendid husband Tom who were most hospitable; thence to Delhi where I stayed with Frank and Celeste Roberts, found a disappointing reaction among Indians, all round, and so flew off to Colombo in Ceylon where, in a week, I was able to persuade the PM to accept some refugees for whose reception I made preliminary arrangements previously and found a retired British couple to act as IRO representative, Mr and Mrs J T Morrison. I had a very comforting week in Colombo, and left feeling quite satisfied that there was a future for Displaced Persons in the Island: I had persuaded the Prime Minister on the same lines and set in motion the whole process of selection by the Ceylonese, firm commitment on granting status of citizenship (no easy task this) and (in the hands of my Representative) steps towards ear-marking residential quarters. The Morrisons also promised to prepare Ceylonese and British society for coming of these new Europeans whose arrival could now be expected. I left for the north without misgivings on our policy - my feelings were apparent in a letter to IRO at the end of my visit which read:

"I have just seen the Prime Minister of Ceylon. He is convinced we are on to a mutual benefit scheme. He is convinced that we will not sell him pups and, because he was hesitant at first, he is determined that those D.P.'s who do come shall be properly housed."

India - Feb 1950

A second visit to India, staying at the Deputy High Commissioner's house in Delhi produced nothing except an even stronger warning from Archibald Nye, the High Commissioner, against bringing "poor whites to India". Nor did I obtain any help from the Indian Government officials.

The commercial and industrial community seemed very ready to employ Displaced Persons but they could not or would not produce a body to act as IRO agent; so I told them to apply direct to IRO Geneva - who were not amused. I myself 'went on the air' and had a Press conference but to no avail. India was a dead duck and I left for Karachi intending to clear up the Tuberculosis Hospital staffing at Chittagong (a really wonderful opportunity) and to visit Iraq.

C.H. Lush

On arrival in Karachi, however, I found a cable from Diana giving me the tragic news of the sudden death of my brother Cecil in London on Friday 17 March 1950. Within an hour I had cleared with IRO and booked a passage to London where two days later I was in Plymouth with Diana arriving the day before Cecil's funeral.

Luckily Cecil's godson, Bill Ross Smith, a young gunner Major happened to be in London and had made most efficient arrangements for all concerned.

Cecil's funeral service was at the very lovely church at Tamerton Foliot where he and Marjorie had worshipped. A number of Naval officers were present with the Deputy Lord Mayor of Plymouth where Cecil had, as King's Harbour Master, made a name for himself in civic circles. The Rural Dean took the service and Last Post was sounded by Royal Marines as his coffin was taken to the Committal Chapel at the Cemetery whither Marjorie, his widow and I followed. Both his children were abroad - Ted in Australia, Judith had just left

Bombay. Our mother who suffered most on that day and whose protector at the end of her life had suddenly gone, was with Diana - close by - who became her supporter and comforter until the end of her life.

Cecil was only 60 when he died - his grave illness as a midshipman and a bad accident on his last commission at sea probably brought about the heart condition from which he died; but let me add that the 2nd World War undoubtedly aggravated what might have been checked, and his complete lack of care for himself - a habit which we were all powerless to improve - undoubtedly took years off his life.

I think, of all the three children, Cecil missed the influence of a father more than anyone. Whereas we both turned to him, he became the arbiter and adviser to both Christine and myself - who adored him as our hero and our friend. I know that my mother turned to him for advice which normally she would have received from a husband. He alone had no adviser to whom he could turn until he and Marjorie married during the first World War. Not only did he become chief adviser to the family but from the time he drew pay as a Royal Naval officer, he helped our mother financially - an assistance, a very necessary assistance, which he and I shared from 1915 onwards. He was devoted to the Royal Navy and won high academic honours at Dartmouth and as a young Navigator. He was Navigator of the Royal Oak at the age of 36, no small honour. He was devoted to his family, and the death in Malta of Pamela, his elder daughter aged 7, the result of careless doctoring, nearly broke his heart. He was a great countryman, walking and bicycling, and my own knowledge of the Sussex downs and Dartmoor was culled from him. He had a great love of music and played the piano with a better touch than our sister Christine who was the outstanding musician of the family. He was a most sympathetic accompanyist. His health prevented his final promotion to Captain - a rank he attained only on retirement after five arduous years during World War II at the home end of the Western Approaches and at Gibraltar, from which his health finally cracked and he realised, though he told no one, that his heart had been affected. This Naval silence about himself was undoubtedly a contributory cause of his early death. I attributed it at the time to his anxiety lest our mother should worry at the sight of an invalid son, but I think now that he knew that he was nearer to death than we all realised. His death came as a grievous shock especially to my mother who, after the anxieties of the second War, had broken her hip. She was full of courage but naturally saw no future happiness - her home, which had been assured with Cecil and Marjorie, was no more.

Diana and I spent a few days in Crowborough while I, as Executor, sorted Cecil's papers (in apple pie order) and wrote to Judith and Chris.

Veyrier

Then Diana and I flew back to Geneva without so much as a brief view of our children. Within a week I flew to Northolt, met my mother and companion, whom Marjorie handed over to me and next morning we were joined by Julian and Sylvia, flew to Geneva and so all arrived at Veyrier where my mother lived with us for just over a year.

My mother thoroughly enjoyed her stay at Les Marguerites, where she arrived with one companion, Miss Maunders, engaged another, Miss Dorothy Spencer, and left with Miss Osborne who was her constant companion for two years or more. They then went to Brookside until September 1951 when my sister Christine, who had come on a European visit, took her and Miss Osborne to Addis Ababa.

The climate of Veyrier agreed with my mother; only her calliper, which the doctor in England had insisted on her wearing for the rest of her life, irked her. One morning she asked Diana "What good does my calliper do?" "No good" said Diana. "Then throw it out of the window" said my mother - and never wore it again.

My mother was devoted to Diana who, indeed, deserved that devotion in Switzerland and in the years to come. 'Granny' I must say was great fun and joined in all our childish games. Holiday time, when the children came out, was, of course, her great delight.

I.R.O.

Back in Les Marguerites, where Pam and Rod Sarrell had held the fort and looked after Meriel, at the end of March 1950 I had to turn my attention to refugees and was soon off again on my travels.

In the spring Arthur Rucker and I tried to clear up a forgotten Albanian "mess" in Damascus - and succeeded. I paid a quick trip to Karachi, found the Pakistan Government still wrestling with doubts and IRO dossiers of useful people. A short visit to Baghdad before Easter did not prevent my being home for the family gathering at Les Marguerites for Easter holidays: for Julian the last holidays before his School Certificate. My mother appeared to be settling in and the young had a good deal of skiing - Diana's brother Mervyn and Kitty stayed a few days.

I see that the apple blossom and wisteria were "quite remarkably lovely" in May and in the middle of that month I left for a 10 week tour which embraced Pakistan, India and Ceylon, Iraq and Iran. I was able to finalise nothing in Pakistan nor India. I made progress in East Pakistan with the scheme of staffing the Tuberculosis Hospital entirely with Poles, but I do not think that this ambitious scheme came to anything. India I wrote off and though we all (IRO Geneva and self) made strenuous efforts to put Iraq into the category of receiving countries, it finally proved impossible: the climate was extreme and the Iraqi administration so backward on matters of housing and health, and indeed of understanding of the whole problem, that it would have been criminal to send refugees thither.

Iraq - June 1950

I wrote on 20.6.50:

"A week in Baghdad, an excursion to Babylon, 50 miles away and a flight to Basrah have given me a sight and sound picture in which I can trace no beauty and no dignity. The country around Baghdad is featureless, the Tigris has no character whatever, not even a sailing craft. Baghdad is the most disappointing of all the many cities which I have visited in the Middle East, and is a ragged, crowded, noisy, undignified town. Basrah smells .... The worst drawback to my mind is the apparent absence of any good country, health resort or recreation centre accessible to the ordinary poor citizen. The mountains exist but they are unlike the hills of Lebanon. The sea coast is to be avoided. Baghdad enjoys no beauty and it is pathetic to see the citizens thereof, on a warm evening, jostling each other on the only and very small river walk .... There is undoubted need for first class experts and specialists and for second class technical professional men and women .... Lack of decision in the administration of Government make it doubtful whether any government department may take really effective steps to engage the latter."

I continued:

"The largest employer of labour outside Government, is closed to IRO. The Iraq Petroleum Company is bound by contract to train Iraqi nationals."

No one had shown me any desire to consider Displaced Persons except as a source of cheap labour.

I returned once more to Baghdad later in the year but found no reason to change my advice. R.I.P. Iraq.

Iran - June 1950

I approached Iran with higher hopes. It had, as I thought, at any rate in some places, a less arid climate than Iraq. Polish refugees had experienced a short sojourn there. I thought that the government would be more approachable, more effective. How wrong I was!

I decided to see a small slice of the country and to travel by road from Baghdad to Teheran - a distance of some 600 miles. Having taken expert local advice in Baghdad, I hired a car and driver from Thos Cook in Baghdad and made plans for food en route. At the last moment Thos Cook asked me whether I would share the car with an Egyptian gentleman who wanted to drive to Teheran via Kermanshah buying carpets en route. Of course I agreed: it halved the cost (already less than air travel) and would provide me with an excellent guide and companion - it also gave me an added sense of security to have two people aboard who knew the country and the (Persian) language.

The driver, a Turk, by name of Mohommed Bashir (his Iraqi name) gave a fine performance of driving and car upkeep - for the roads were not good, no maintenance having been applied. He bestowed money handsomely to officials and also to every beggar we met - their presence was legion on the roads in Iran. He explained his generosity by "there, but for the Will of Allah, go I": but I had no doubt that it was a wise precaution to ensure safe passage.

My co-passenger was Mr Aziz Atla of 37 Sharia Malika el Ferida, Cairo. He was buying for several merchants in the Muski, the Cairo suq, and knew, by name, a number of our European friends from Egypt and the Sudan who had bought carpets in the Muski. I learnt a great deal about carpets from Aziz Atla, who told me the difference between a Khamshar, a Hamadan, a Qazvin and a Bokhara. I did not accompany him on his visits of purchase in the towns and villages.

The journey was without incident but not without interest. One hundred miles of "khallo sakit" as I called it (flat space), Iraq at its worst; sleepy customs and police frontiers; little traffic, if any. Then in Persia the steady rise to the hills - quite soon, at 150 miles, running water, trees, more people. Our driver gave more alms - we crossed a low pass, then one higher; finally one at 9000 feet, under snow during winter; wheat appeared in the fields, even fruit trees; water from *qanats* (underground tunnels); very dirty villages; signs of British and American occupation (until 1945) until we reached Hamadan at 6 p.m. after 350 miles.

"A large town with very wide streets - water rushing down the gutters of the streets and feeding the houses. The Iran hotel (at Hamadan) is not luxurious; clean as to the rooms but the sanitary services left a lot to be desired."

My carpet companion and I dined together and then I left him to order his carpets - which I presume he did all night. I slept and at 4 am we left in silence going northeast along a barren road, or so it seemed in the twilight of the dawn when we again began to climb and then found ourselves running along the base of the Elborz Mountains with a wide and potentially fertile plain on our southern flank. The road became worse and showed little sign of any maintenance but we finally entered Teheran before noon.

Well, I had seen 600 miles of rural Persia and, bar the fact that it was not desert such as Iraq and that temperate crops grew in the plains and in the valleys, I could detect little from that quick look through the car windows that belied the report which I had read to the effect that

"food and housing are meagre and the standard of living among the farming families is commonly low due to primitive production methods, absentee landlords, lack of education."

Most tree life had been destroyed without any sign of regeneration. Erosion had been allowed to wreak its terrible damage unchecked. Cattle were small, a sign of bad husbandry. Menfolk appeared inert, in tatters (they wore the trouser, generally in tatters); beggars swarmed. The only article of clothing that earned a mention was the cloth cap which was very common. "The cap is worn in Persia" was one of my first comments.

The towns were not much better. The streets had been laid out well - wide and spacious, but they bore few signs of maintenance. "The cities and towns are still without sanitary water supplies or sewerage systems." The water bubbled up, in most residential streets, at the highest point from a *qanat* and ran down the two sides of the street in the open gutters gathering up any garbage, dung or carcass that happened to be in its path; each householder had an entry canal or sluice down which the water was allowed to flow until his domestic tank was full. The said householder would probably bribe the municipal water man to give him more than his due if necessary. 'Thunder boxes' were used for night soil. "Ice is made in the cities from polluted water and distributed without adequate sanitary precautions. Food is neither dispersed nor kept under sanitary conditions." The priority given to ice in this excerpt proves that this report emanated from American sources as indeed I learnt on first arrival in Teheran.

On my initial reconnaissance in the Chancelleries and Embassies of Teheran as a member of IRO, United Nations, I received much help, freely given. The Counsellor at the British Embassy, an Indian Army officer seconded to the F.O., was my chief adviser; I think the Ambassador was on leave. The U.S. Embassy were helpful and I must again stress what great advantages emanated from advice given by diplomatic and other officials on service in the country. It was through them that I gained entrée to Persian Government officials with whom I was able to discuss their needs and the possible help which IRO could give.

I found a plan for the future all ready to be implemented: it was the work of Overseas Consultants Inc., an American organisation with a directorate and a large staff of American consultants all ready to launch the plan on to the rural and urban areas of Iran, if only they could find an Iranian Government ready to crack the bottle across the good ship's bows.

I wrote:

"The new Government which, headed by the late Chief of Staff of the Army, came into power two days after my arrival (mid June 1950), is reputed to have the intention and the vigour to pull the country out of the morass of inefficiency, bankruptcy and apathy into which it has fallen and to set the Seven Year Plan of Development in motion."

Of the need for specialists and skilled workers, of whom I had a number of dossiers, I had no doubt. But whether the Iranians would ask for them, give them citizenship, suitable pay and conditions - whether they would live up to any assurances - were all imponderable. My view written in this, my first report, was that the Iranians would ask for specialist refugees but too late; that they would probably fail to fulfil their obligations to such new citizens but would never turn away any family once accepted into their country.

On general conditions I wrote:

"I will not enlarge on primitive conditions. The erosion of the soil, due to man's improvidence, seems to have had the same effect on the Persian mentality. Persia has stood still while time marched on. The gardens for which Persia is so justly famous were the gardens of 1,000 years ago. The water system of qanats (conduits) must have been one of the finest in the world - 1,000 years ago; it has remained and is not dubbed insanitary."

"Village baths spread infection" says the report, but I wagered they were the first village baths in history.

I added that I was not much impressed by the accounts of primitive conditions for I thought that conditions in some of the countries of our refugees were not so first class themselves. I was, however, worried by the almost complete absence of education.

I did succeed in making contact with a number of Iranian Government officials and some ministers. I had meetings with many of them; I addressed a letter to the Prime Minister, and I received assurances that all my demands would have careful consideration. I was not impressed with the new Government nor the officials but I was just convinced that there was a need for the very men which IRO could provide. I was equally certain that it would be a miracle if we sent them there.

However I succeeded in one important move: I found a Briton who agreed wholeheartedly to become representative for IRO in Iran - H J Underwood, a military attache to the British Embassy. I am pretty certain that Underwood did "other" things in Teheran besides commerce and, no doubt, the IRO hat made excellent extra cover for him.

I left Teheran for Baghdad satisfied that here at last was a country whose climate and topography might be suitable for European refugees - of all types - if the propinquity of USSR, and the lack of what we knew as civilised amenities, could be forgotten (especially by the highly civilised staff of IRO) and which was known to many thousands of Polish refugees who had made sojourns there.

This was in June 1950. I returned to Iran in November of the same year for my last visit. I have, alas, no records of that short stay in a very different state of affairs. I had been in Karachi for a week and thence flew, for my sins, in an Iranian aircraft, controlled from Teheran but piloted by a Greek aeronaut with a French co-pilot. When we landed at the Persian frontier the usual formality papers were exchanged but there was commotion; something had changed: no longer sleepy officials but life, movement, orders snapped out. The long and short of it was that two Iranian military officers were intending to fly from the frontier to Teheran - "we have orders from Government" - and in reply to cries that the aircraft was full "either passengers or heavy luggage must be unloaded and abandoned!" The officers would "strap hang" if there were no seats. The co-pilot at once abandoned the aircraft unwilling to break all international rules of flying. I wondered for a moment, whether as an official of the United Nations, I too should abandon aircraft. A case or two of my most attractive refugees (on paper) were already on the ground and I decided that my own presence in this God-forsaken frontier post would not dissuade the Iranian officers, by now up the aircraft steps. So on we flew with two extra passengers, violating every International Air Safety regulation and making the mountainous terrain over which we flew even more terrifying to the pit of the stomach! The silence of quite deep fear descended on the craft and when we landed safely at Isfahan there was an audible sigh of thanksgiving. But our troubles were not over. We shed some weight and passengers at Isfahan but as the lightened aircraft attempted to take off in the dusk we appeared to be taxying all the way back to Pakistan without taking off and escaped disaster only by quick and mercifully successful brake action by the pilot in the field adjacent to the aerodrome. It was dark when we reached the aerodrome again and the decision was made to fly no more that night. I shared a motor car with another passenger or two and covered the 120 miles to Teheran by 10 pm.

There we learnt the reason for the rough orders and decisions at the frontier: Moussadeq was in power, not yet Prime Minister but with authority to "get things going".

All was well; my dossiers of refugees unloaded at the frontier, arrived after a few days and I myself was granted an interview by Moussadeq to find him in pyjamas on his truckle bed in some Government office at 7.30 a.m. He listened patiently to my explanation and suggestions and received my aide memoire, but it was clear that the man, if he thought of our project at all, would not put the note at the top of his tray.

Moussadeq failed entirely to impress me either by his early matutinal meeting, nor his night attire - as I wrote "the pyjamas had been slept in". I left after a week's preparation of the mind of the good hearted H J Underwood.

I think the political events of 1952 in Persia put an end to any positive action - I lost sight of the acceptance of refuges in Iran, when reflecting on the maelstrom of Iranian politics and their chaotic path.

My aerial adventures were not quite over; on my departure from Teheran I was one of very few passengers flying in a British aircraft, en route for Bombay. One of the crew approached me quite normally and asked whether I had such a thing as a screwdriver. I regretted that I had not and asked whether an integral part of the machine had fallen off, and was it not the habit of the cockpit crew, where all the instruments appeared to be screwed into the dashboard, to carry a set of useful tools? I received a negative answer to both questions and learnt that the pilot had a private wireless receiver which he wished to repair en route.

I returned to Geneva via Delhi and Bombay fairly exhausted, according to Diana's diary, with suspected malaria.

I found the little household at Les Marguerites in fine fettle in spite of a very wet November: the diary entry read "MSL landed in first sunshine for nearly a month". But my mother seemed to have borne it well and having discarded her iron calliper clamped to her leg was far more mobile. By now she was a well known figure in the little lunch cafeteria of the Palais des Nations and was game for any excursion by car into the country. She had made many friends who were good enough to pay frequent visits to Les Marguerites.

Turkey 1951

My final foreign visit took place early in 1951 when I went as a member of a three man IRO Mission to Turkey. The Turkish Government asked for advice or help or both (I never saw the terms of reference) regarding the Turkish Moslem minority in Bulgaria. The formation of Bulgaria as one of the Balkan States after World War I left a number of Turkish residents (Moslem) in Bulgaria and non-Muslim Bulgarians in Turkey. A Convention allowed a regular annual exchange of nationals by means of ordinary emigration and this had worked very well until August 1950 when the Bulgarians demanded the repatriation of a quarter of a million Turkish Moslems within three months. They later agreed to accept 80 per diem. The Turkish Government asked us as experts to advise on their administration of this problem and to provide "technical assistance" for the reception and settlement of these large numbers. We in IRO believed that the Turks wanted financial assistance as well, and this was borne out by press reports while the Mission was in Turkey that IRO was providing a large sum of money in addition to their advice.

The Mission consisted of Myer Cohen, the Deputy Director General (American), Dr Coigny, Head of the Medical side of IRO, and myself: a high powered collection of experts who were given a warm reception by the Turkish Government from the President downwards, and the Press, and afforded every facility by all concerned - the difficulties and setbacks which we suffered were due to a national weakness in administration which resulted in muddles and postponements. We visited the reception centres on the Bulgarian frontier, notably at Edirne and elsewhere, the staging camps where the immigrants stayed on arrival, and the settlement programmes in the Provinces which finally received them as citizens.

The success (for us) of the whole mission was assured by Dr Hans Wilbrandt, the IRO representative in Turkey whom I knew well.

We reported to our hosts that in all the preliminary stages we were impressed by the spirit of sympathy and understanding shown by everyone toward these new and obviously happy people returning to their own country. This was indeed the truth: here were welcome Turks returning home; they found food, housing, fuel and often pocket money. This however was but an initial welcome and we found that further plans, to say nothing of permanent employment, were lacking. We really were telling the Turks that they were acting truly in accordance with their character.

It was, indeed, a very happy picture of real home

coming, and could not be compared with the uncertain future which faced refugees entering a foreign land on resettlement. But we warned our hosts that "The present conditions of temporary care cannot be perpetuated and that further considerations for permanent settlement were necessary."

We added in our report a short homily on the duty of the Government to make a comprehensive plan including roads, canals, railroad extensions and housing plans in this, apparently promising, area and to resist leaving this most important foundation to local authorities.

We ended:

> "It seems to the Mission that a programme based on expansion and development of small communities already in existence is the solution. It is not merely a question of finding a solution to an immediate refugee or immigrant problem: rather it is the arrival of the immigrants which can serve as a stimulus to the realisation of larger needs in Turkey, at the same time disposing of the relatively small but important problem created by the group itself."

I could hear the Prime Minister, or whoever invited the Mission exclaiming:

> "But where is the money - the three million which they were supposed to supply?"

My own views were expressed in a letter dated 29.7.1951 to Sir Desmond Morton who with Commander King Hall (a well known 'broadsheet' publisher) was, I understood, interested in the emigration of the Turkish minority from Bulgaria.

On the whole the Mission was great fun in spite of the characteristic muddles which the Turkish officials created for us and for themselves. We visited quite a large area of Turkey and found politeness and help on every side although on some occasions it stopped at politeness and the help was never really effected. Strong words of protest at quite obvious failures were deprecated by Myer Cohen but often on my lips - with effect. I complained privately in my letters to Diana that Cohen and Coigny spent far too much time in bed - never arising until 8.30 a.m., and often taking a long siesta! But we bore each other's idiosyncrasies well. The British Embassy entertained us royally - I found Noel and Grace Charles en poste and as usual, quite charming. "Grace" I wrote to Diana "looks as beautiful as ever, only her hair is now yellow (golden) not blue, but very beautiful." As is usual the Embassy staff (whom I tackled on first arrival) were full of knowledge and good advice. The French diplomats were also hospitable; the Americans, represented by the Economic Consultant's Administration, had strong views, some sound - some not so good.

For me the most enjoyable and interesting visit was when, as a guest of the Turkish Governor, I visited Smyrna (Izmir), sat with his Provincial Council and then accompanied him on a gubernatorial tour of part of Smyrna province. I might have been back in the Sudan even to the presence of petition writers!

Ed. Foreseeing the end of his service with the IRO on 30 April 1951, MSL spent much of that year in correspondence in his search for future employment. He applied to UNRWA and the Council of Europe in the hope of continuing with refugee work; he contacted the UN in New York; he registered with the Ministry of Labour and National Service expressing interest in overseas work with British missions or international organizations and the Foreign Office suggested the post of Technical Assistance Officer, Lebanon; but all to no avail. At the same time, he was wrestling with the question of whether to seek ordination in the Church and in communication with certain Bishops and the Dean of Windsor (see below). The family remained on in Geneva for some months in mid 1951 before returning to London.

CAIRO

Left top:
The Archdeacon's house, Anglican Cathedral, Cairo, 1947

Left centre:
Julian, Sylvia and Meriel with Abdul Rahman, Mohammed Dhahab; Cairo, 1947

Left bottom:
After the explosion in the Jewish Agency, Jerusalem, taken by DRL from IRO office, 11 March 1948

Archdeacon Frank Johnston with the three children, 1947

On the summit of the Great Pyramid, 1947

Right: MSL with his three children, Les Marguerites, April 1949

Below: MSL, Alan and Meriel in the garden of Les Marguerites, Veyrier, Geneva, May 1950

GENEVA

The family in the garden of Les Marguerites with Granny Lush and Garth ap Rees

Meriel, Sylvia, Julian and Philippa skiing at Megeve, with MSL, 1949

CHAPTER 15

Shell: Libya 1952-56 (Qatar 1952)
Representative, Anglo-Saxon Petroleum Company

Tripoli, Libya

1st January 1952 found the Lush family at Alan Hill's house, 4 Cumberland Gardens, WC1, which Alan had most kindly put at our disposal, and we were very grateful to be so comfortably quartered in London. The house was small but contained us and London was the best place for finding a job for myself. Here I was at the age of 55, fit in body and mind but with no prospect of earning sufficient money to support my family of whom all three children were still on the ladder of education - of which every rung cost money. I had been well paid by IRO but there was no pension, not even a gratuity attached to my service therein, and the school bills would soon arrive and continue for at least 5 years. Moreover the only future which was apparently open to me was service in the Church whither I had made, I hope, humble approaches through the Bishop of Derby and Canon Vidler of Windsor. But no income which a Church appointment could provide, after a year or two, would fill the bill for education, and though Diana showed no visible sign of anxiety and said not a word of opposition, I knew that anxiety was her fellow, day and night. Frank Johnston, Bishop in Egypt, our dearest friend in such matters during that time of grave anxiety and doubt gave me this advice: "If, Maurice, you should find a barrier dropped in your present path of seeking service in the Church, take great heed thereof."

The two elder children were approaching critical years in their educational lives - and let me state here and now they both weathered those years and emerged with flying colours from Cambridge and Oxford - at any rate a good Second was then recorded as a pretty good start on the first rung of the ladder in life. But in 1952 there was no little anxiety as to the educational future.

Julian had left Winchester with, if not distinction, at any rate a good mark not only in his School Certificate but in his mark as a Wykehamist, for he was asked to stay on in Morshead's as Head of House to assist the new and perhaps temporary Housemaster, who had been summoned to run the House during the absence, through illness, of the Housemaster (Colin Hunter). I was glad of this for it gave Julian a sense of responsibility and self esteem which is so satisfactory, nay essential, in a boy of 17, wherever he may find himself.

Since 1950 I had been in correspondence with various educational authorities in Winchester, Colin Hunter, Cambridge (C L G Pratt Senior Tutor of Christ's) and others. In the final event we had won the good will of Pratt who wrote that he would like to have Julian not because he would ever be an eminent scholar but because he was a "good egg". From that date onwards (1950) it was clear to me that Julian's future lay in Christ's College, Cambridge, and after some doubts as to academic path, thither he went in 1954.

In the meantime life for him meant National Service. The early days of army training in 1952 and later as a 2/Lieut. in 5th Royal Horse Artillery in Germany rapidly opened with great happiness and dedication to his Regiment on Julian's part and clearly a very satisfactory response from his senior officers. His letters were full of laughter at the apparent foolishness of, but the real necessity for, rigid discipline and gradually loyalty to his Battery and his Regiment becomes manifest as he writes first of 6 horses in this (Horse Artillery) Regiment kept in the town, of hunting on one of them, of running the Regimental football team and of the Regimental yacht club and skiing team. He served a happy and successful two years in the Horse Gunners and arrived in Tripoli in January 1954 and almost immediately signed a six months contract with the Libyan Development Agency to undertake a field survey of the ancient Roman water cisterns in Tripolitania, with a view to their resuscitation and re-use as part of a UN Development Programme for the country. He worked enthusiastically at that job - he was provided with a jeep, driver and cook - and I think his results were good; he certainly showed his family one interesting ruin in the desert on the borders of the Fezzan which held a human skeleton - date of death unknown. He also learnt the basis of the Arabic language which has blossomed throughout his life. He finally left Libya for Christ's College, Cambridge, in September 1954, whither Pratt, still Senior Tutor, welcomed him, provided he did not read Mechanical Engineering but did play football - which in fact he omitted to do.

I remember discussing with Pratt, before Julian's arrival, what he should read. The conversation ended by

Pratt's question to Diana and myself: "But - may I ask frankly what the hell this has to do with you, his parents? This must be Julian's choice." Julian chose Law not with any intention of entering the legal profession but as a background of intellectual attainment. I myself found Pratt a delightful person and was always grateful to him for his unswerving decision to have Julian as a member of Christ's College, almost "come what may". It was he, I believe, who spotted that Julian was neither fitted to have taken the Mechanical Sciences Qualifying Examination nor in truth a suitable candidate for an Engineering degree, for which he had destined until Pratt discovered the real working of his mind. At any rate, as his senior tutor, Pratt refused to consider him as a prospective Engineering student, and so Julian turned his mind to Law, in which subject he gained a IInd class honours degree.

Sylvia was in her last year at St Swithun's and apparently doing very well, though I remember a serious disagreement, to say the least of it, with Miss Watt, the Headmistress who, in Sylvia's presence, entirely misled me during a discussion as to what Sylvia should take for her A levels: she recommended a course to which I agreed, but with which the school teachers were in total disagreement! Result - a terse letter and an even more difficult interview at 9 a.m. (I had driven down to Winchester from London at dawn). All was eventually settled amicably and successfully for Sylvia who remained for a further year as Head Girl of the school under Phyllis Evans, a notable Headmistress, who, thanks be, succeeded Miss Watt and transformed St Swithun's into a fine school with a very high academic record. Sylvia did extremely well both as a scholar and Head Girl and left finally in the spring of 1954 for a six month's course before sitting for a scholarship at Oxford: she was *"promine accessit"* and entered Lady Margaret Hall (then a College for young ladies only) in 1955. There she gained a IInd in P.P.E. in 1957.

Meriel remained happily, or shall we say, inescapably at St Swithun's before finding comparative freedom and much happiness at the University at Aix en Provence whence she emerged bi-lingual (she had endured a year at l'Ecole Privat in Geneva during 1949) and the owner of a 'Diplome'.

The above retrospective paragraphs touching the lives of our three children could not have been written had I entered the Church, for purely financial reasons. I realised in 1952 that I was jeopardizing the educational future of our young family, to say nothing of the manner of life, if not the livelihood of Diana and myself.

My approaches to the Bishops and the Dean of Windsor (Canon Vidler) continued in spite of the knowledge that life would take a very different course for everyone of us if I were found acceptable as a probationer in God's service.

Of course Diana and I discussed this bleak future for our economic life but I am not sure that either of us fully realised what it would mean for all of us. I know Diana was still hoping, praying that something would turn up. I suppose that my hopes of real service to God and man, and the exigencies which would arise therefrom might be changed to some service which would demand less sacrifice. Both Diana and I were still smarting from the apparent refusal formally to recognise my service to HMG during the war, especially my service in Italy where recognition was denied to me by a department in the War Office who firstly had sent to supplant me, whom General Eisenhower had chosen to lead AMG in Sicily and Italy, a self seeker from HMG, and secondly, had denied me promotion, recommended by my C-in-C, Alexander, and the Minister of State. Was that bureaucratic action to hinder progress for the rest of my career life?

Quite soon the barrier fell.

On a Friday evening, 11th January 1952 one John Gaynor, a member of Shell's Anglo-Saxon Petroleum Company, a major component of the Shell Group, whom I had met in Ethiopia and Rome, telephoned me and asked me if I was still unemployed and if service in Shell would interest me. I had no hesitation in saying "Yes" whereupon he asked me to visit Anglo Saxon, Floor 4, St Helen's Court on Monday where I would meet members of the company who had been present at the luncheon given to me some years ago and would like to see me. On Monday 15th off I went to St Helen's Court and there found an atmosphere in which I could breathe freely and people who talked the same language and were loyally devoted to one object.

I met Geoffrey Tait and Geoffrey Stokes who were Coordinator and Assistant in the Middle East Department of Shell Exploration and it was in that area that they thought my experience and knowledge of Arabic might be useful to Shell. They put a proposition before me, asked me to consider it and to meet them again next week. I liked that interview in which they were obviously exploring me and expecting me to consider their tentative offer before replying.

During the weekend Diana and I considered the Shell proposition. It ran thuswise. The presence of oil in Libya had been suspected for some years: the suspicion was confirmed by (secret) seismic soundings at the end of the British Administration under Travers Blackley, who had taken over Tripolitania from me in 1943. During that Administration, however, he and HMG were prevented, by International Law, from allowing any prospecting or searching for minerals in the Territory and although Shell had submitted a request through HMG to prospect, it had been refused, filed and handed over to the Libyan Government when Independence came to them on 24th December 1951 under King Idris. At that time no one had seriously prospected for oil in Libya.

Shell's optimum hope was that the official request made before Independence should be considered by the Libyan Government as one with top priority and, with diplomatic handling, would be granted. Shell would then have priority in prospecting and hopefully in drilling the first oil wells in locations of their choice in Libya. The Directors, as I knew from the luncheon given to me after the war, knew of me and of my knowledge of Arabic and Libya and therefore asked me whether I would join the company and go to Tripolitania quite soon to explore the political ground, make the proposal to the Libyan Government that the application on the files should now be considered and that a Prospecting Licence should be granted. Shell were not at all sanguine about immediate success but they thought no harm could be done in an attempt, and I appeared to be singularly fitted to make trial of the proposal.

If I should be met with a refusal of immediate grant of licence or permission to explore then the Directors wanted me to represent them in Libya and build a position for Shell in Libya second to none so that when negotiations started with full Government approval, Shell would be well known to all concerned and receive consideration from the Libyans as *primus inter pares*: and I was warned that there would soon be many *"pares"*. I was asked to come back in a week's time with my reply.

It was, of course, a wonderful offer and there was really no question of refusing it. But consideration had to be given to family problems. Did Diana and the family really want another period of no home in U.K? Were they prepared to live or spend their holidays abroad? Could I fulfil my commitments to my mother? Was this the hurdle that Frank Johnston had predicted? Could I pull my weight in helping a company make more money? Discussions were many. I made my peace with the Bishops and the Dean of Windsor. I knew Tripoli well enough to recommend it as a home for my mother. After a wintry month or two in her brother's house in London, Diana (and the family) were all for the shores of North Africa.

So, of course, I accepted, and accepted with gratitude the good salary offered, little knowing the extent of Shell's generous treatment of their employees and their families.

I accepted the job on 24 January. Diana and I then spent a month's indoctrination into the oil industry: the Thames Refinery, a week in Holland visiting oil wells, seeing "yes - nodders", the silent, almost perpetually swinging beam pumps at Utrecht, Amesford, Groningen, and the laboratories at Amsterdam, Wittenberg and Grevenhage. At home we packed and stored furniture.

On 24 February DRL and I flew to Malta where we spent two days further indoctrination in Shell marketing under Jimmy Gubbins, Chief of Shell Marketing in the Mediterranean including Tripoli, and Mrs Gubbins, a charming couple and he was a tremendous help and a close friend.

We arrived in Tripoli on 26 February and found that Victor Merceica, Shell Marketing Libya, had booked us a suite of rooms in the Waddan Hotel which became our headquarters for 9 months. "Waddan" is the local Arabic name for the Mountain Ibex (Capra Nubrana) which is the national animal of Libya. Specimens used to be kept (alive) at the Agricultural Farm (Government) near Tripoli.

Diana and I set about looking for a Shell House almost at once. St Helen's Court approved of our resolution to be housed within 3 months, but did not favour, as a general principle, purchase of a house. In the event we found house-hunting most ill rewarding for there were still many Western officials about: advisors to the Libyan Government, United Nations officials, bankers and other commercial interests established before Independence and not so eager to quit. I was wafted away for months on end and the whole matter of housing fell on Diana who achieved marvels although she also was away from Tripoli a great deal herself, in Benghazi, UK and elsewhere. She did in fact find a suitable residence and, once Shell had, to our delight, agreed to the purchase, achieved all the local legal matters and arranged all the necessary building changes and furnishing by Christmas time 1952.

However many events and much travelling outside Tripoli and Africa took place during 1952 especially for myself. The early months in Libya itself were interesting enough and it was perhaps lucky that we were based in the Waddan Hotel, the best at that time, for the 9 months, building our foundations elsewhere but enjoying the not too uncongenial hotel life even during the girls' holidays in April and July - September, two periods when we were lucky enough to be together. We were absent for many periods long enough to lighten the monotony of repetition and entertainment of large numbers could easily be arranged at short notice. This last convenience was valuable for one of our chief duties was to make the name of Shell not only well known but pleasurably known and connected.

Of the Libyans in high places I really knew only the Prime Minister, Mahmud Muntasser, whom I had appointed as the foremost Libyan with whom I dealt under the British Administration in 1943. I was thankful in 1952 that Native Administration had taken prior place in our policy from the beginning of British Military Administration in 1943, and was glad to find that Mahmud Muntasser had survived the nine years of British rule and was the first Prime Minister of Independent Libya. The other Ministers, Fethi Kekhia (Justice), Mansur Kadara (Finance), Mohammed Osman (Health), Ibrahim Shaaban (Communications and Works), Mohammed Saquisbi (Education) and even Ali Bey Gerba (Defence). Frankly though, I could not remember several of them and some hundreds of other Libyans (especially Tripolitanians) who vowed personal dealings under my administration. All were, traditionally and, I thought, sincerely glad to see me - someone who reminded them of the happy honeymoon sensations during their first days of freedom. Scores of ordinary citizens would embarrass me by reciting incidents or happy favours experienced in those early days. By and large, however, I never found my previous incarnation in Tripoli inconvenient with my presence as Representative of Shell - and here let me emphasise that my official title in Libya was Representative of the Anglo Saxon Petroleum Company (to whom the Concessions were eventually granted).

I missed the 20,000 Jews whom I had found in the Old City in 1943 - Zionism had taken its toll of that long established part of Tripoli's population.

It must be remembered that my job covered all Libya, and that Cyrenaica was very much part of Libya, a part of which I had no personal knowledge but where King Idris, whom I had never met, resided and whose capital was shortly (1954) to share with Tripoli the privilege of becoming the seat of Government for 6 months in every year.

I found the two personalities with whom I must make immediate contact on arrival in Libya, the Prime Minister and the British Minister, Sir Alec Kirkbride, were absent in Benghazi on our arrival in February. This gave me time, after signing our names in their books, to take stock of some of the other personalities before divulging the request of my Company for immediate recognition of our claim to search for oil in Libya.

My first Libyan contact was Ali bey Gerba, the Minister for Defence who was, in fact, brought along by one of our first British visitors - Colonel Peter Wreford Brown - head of the British Military Mission in Libya. Ali bey Gerba was a firm Anglophile from the very beginning and told me, very diplomatically, a number of interesting facts, not about his fellow Libyans (he was far too loyal) but about other *feranges* (foreigners) in his country - and therewith a good deal about his country.

I called on the Adviser to the Prime Minister, a Briton with Palestinian administrative experience who had been Travers Blackley's Chief of Staff - the Earl of Oxford and Asquith (Julian as he became known to us) with his wife Anne. He was very welcoming though non-committal in every sense - I think that he was not very fully briefed Libyan-wise and we exchanged little but courtesies.

Julian Asquith's No 2, as he was called, was Philip Bradburne, an extrovert who became and remained one of our close friends. Even now I don't know how he came to Libya and we first met him at a Church Service (Anglican) in the Pigeon Club in the Marina of Tripoli Harbour. On Sundays he played the piano to a motley and regular Anglican congregation. He had served with Blackley and knew Arabic well (he practised it in HMG until 1984). I see that I have catalogued him as Economic Planner so he may have had more to do with oil than politics. But his local knowledge was widespread and he was ready to share it with people who cared about the country. Later he went to Sudan (after Independence) to instruct the Sudanese on Parliamentary procedure. He was extremely kind to my mother when, later, she came to live with us and, at the end of my service in Libya, he and one Hugh Cruddas lived in our house for over two months looking after the old lady and two companions during our absence in England, preparing to go to another country and arranging for an English home for my mother who could not accompany us. Thirty years later Philip was still among our best friends - debonair and looking scarcely a year older.

Another, and very important Adviser to the Libyan Government was one E. Pitt Hardacre, the British Adviser to the Minister of Finance. I think that he was an efficient and very necessary Adviser to the Libyan Government on all financial and many economic affairs. I found him perfectly correct but entirely unsympathetic to the representative of a British oil firm ready to spend a million or two prospecting for and perhaps producing oil in Libya. No doubt, when it came, he made full benefits for the Libyans from the oil; however there was no doubt at all that he did not help representatives of oil companies in their task. I do not blame him - Libya was besieged by thirsty oil companies before her economy was ready for them - and I was the first.

Among a good many other Advisers and remnants from the British Administration were several ex-Sudan officials who, after yeomen work under Blackley in British Military Administration, remained on in a country which they had learned to like, to steady the first steps of independent toddlers.

C.A.E. Lea, Sheikh Lea as we always called him in the Sudan, and Mrs Lea were the first to take us under their wing, and this they did the third night of our arrival when they showed us much kindness and painted a very fair picture of the state of affairs in Libya. Lea himself had served in Cyrenaica in O.E.T.A. during the war under de Candole and was a most useful narrator of the life of King Idris during the early days after his return to Libya.

Percy and Kay Coriatt were two other Sudani's who were most hospitable and helpful from the very beginning. We had known Cori well in the Upper Nile Province in 1934 and he had spent all his service (since 1922) in the Southern Sudan. He joined the S.D.F. in 1946 and went to join Blackley in Tripolitania, where he stayed becoming Director of the Interior in the British Administration and Adviser to the Minister of the Interior after Independence. He was a sure fount of information, certainly about Tripolitania, and was most helpful throughout the first two years. He left to become Commander of the Muscat and Oman Field Force in 1953. His wife was a very good painter and they became close friends while we were together in Tripoli.

Wreford Brown, as I have written above, became a very firm friend and adviser and was by and large our closest friend throughout our residence in Libya.

My first business call in Tripoli was on Charles Tilney Bassett, Manager of Barclays Bank, who with his most charming Swiss wife became life-long friends but he an exceedingly wise and helpful counsellor on financial affairs.

Diana's diary, for our first month in Tripoli, reads like a very busy debutante in the days of old. We never refused a party nor an invitation. We spent fourteen days in a complete and almost uninterrupted spate of official and social exchanges and meetings. We had no permanent transport but because we had many friends in Libyan society, and because that same international society was attempting, in the infancy of Independence, to assert itself, we found ourselves wafted from house to house, from party to party, some ceremonious, some just social and friendly until Diana's diary has an entry: March 4th "DRL day in bed" and full rightly had she earned it! A full social round in a strange (to Diana) country when one is dependent on other people's transport is quite lovely but most exhausting. But withal we were doing our duty by Shell.

Call on Prime Minister

During the first fortnight of March, Diana and I had met a good hundred new people each one of whom might be useful to Shell and our guests. On 13th March I saw Mahmud Muntasser, the Prime Minister, and was greeted cordially with every sign and gesture of a friendship regained. That relationship never changed. We spent a warm reminiscent half hour of good memories going back to Montgomery's hand-over to me of the administration of Tripolitania, the lean but happy days which followed, then the final gradual gain of Independence by Libya and all that it meant.

"I have come, Mr Prime Minister, to claim one result of that period of peaceful administration and reconstruction - the early, favourable consideration of a request put forward before Independence by a British company, Shell, for rights to explore and if successful, to drill for oil in this your country." I reminded him that during the British Administration no company or individual, regardless of nationality, had been allowed to prospect for oil and that Shell had abided by that rule but had taken the step of making a formal application, knowing that Independence would come. Shell had carried out no exploration on the ground and was prepared, naturally, to abide by any rules or terms be they enacted now or during the future by the Libyan Government. Shell would abide, of course, by any legislation to be enacted in the future governing the exploration and production of oil from Libya. At the moment there was no legislation but there was now in the Prime Minister's office the representative of an oil company ready to start exploration almost at once, ready to abide by laws and regulations as soon as they were made and ready to bring to Libya the extraordinary practical and financial benefits which would accompany the very presence of an oil company at work. It would raise the financial status and prestige of the country to a high level - very necessary for a young country.

Mahmud Muntasser was interested - he saw the picture of early success in the finding of oil and the beneficial effect it would have but, of course, he had to insist on a slow beginning, a legal cover for every step in allowing the exploitation of his country's natural resources and he gently but firmly insisted that there must be established a legal framework which would cover the search for oil and any mineral wealth in the country. A Mineral Law was already in the process of being drafted and he would be grateful if Shell or any expert company or individual would help in preparing such legislation and bring their past experience to the aid of a new country in the first months of life.

He was grateful to think that so large concern as Shell should have shown optimistic and friendly interest and sufficient faith in Libya to suggest immediate exploration and to send me to plead their case; he would do his best to advance the pace of producing legislation to safeguard the interests of his country and of those who had enough faith to wish to explore for unknown natural resources in these early days. He looked forward to a happy and successful outcome of any exploration. He would consult his Government and hoped for a rapid result from our first conversation.

We talked about a number of other matters naturally and I learnt from him much of what I had suspected, and in a month's visit noticed and recognised, namely the remarkable atmosphere of joyful and peaceful transition, after centuries of suffering the domination of other powers, which was apparent, at any rate in Tripolitania - what a remarkable job Blackley had done in building up this small country into an entity which could accept Independence rightly granted to her, with tranquility and dignity. True it was a poor country with vast stretches of desert - true such agriculture as existed was still done by traditional methods (other than the plantations of the Italian colonists), but one had reason to be optimistic.

I ended the now overlong but very cordial interview by telling the Prime Minister that, in the making of legislation to admit oil companies and to administer the finding and exporting of oil, I on the instructions of my company, Shell, and, of course, much by my own wish, would do my utmost to help him and his Government to produce quickly the best oil laws and regulations possible so that exploration could begin without delay; once exploration could start the Libyan Government and people together with the oil companies could work one with another, having confidence that each party had a fair deal.

I came away from this first and extremely cordial meeting with an old friend knowing where we stood as regards the main purpose of my mission and determined now to carry out the second part of my instructions from Shell. They had told me, in St Helen's Court, that they wanted me to establish Anglo Saxon as the leading company in Libya, both in Libyan and international esteem.

This would not, it seemed to me, be a very difficult task in spite of the fact that I was a newcomer to Shell and to industry as a whole. I certainly knew the people in a way which no other European knew them and my name was known to a great many Libyans. But the first necessity was to find a house in which to live.

Immediately after the declaration of Libyan Independence, the British Government established a diplomatic mission in the country and appointed Sir Alec Kirkbride as the first diplomatic representative with the rank of Minister, with Charles Gault, who had been Political Adviser and Deputy to Travers Blackley in BMA, as his Counsellor. Kirkbride was a Middle Eastern expert with over 30 years service in Palestine and Transjordan ending as British Resident in Transjordania in 1939 and the first British Minister to King Abdulla with whom he established a close relationship. On King Abdulla's death and the succession in Aman, what better post to offer Kirkbride, who was by then approaching the end of his career, than Minister to the court of King Mohammed Idris Al Mahdi Al Senussi, the constitutional King of Libya.

On my second visit to Alec Kirkbride (my first had been brief and an official matter of courtesy) I explained my position as representative of Anglo Saxon Petroleum Company and the desire of my parent company to seek to fulfil the objects set out in a petition lodged with the British Military Administration. I received his official blessing and good wishes for success, but I had the impression that this was the first the Minister had heard of transactions dealing with oil exploration and that diplomacy and politics were his chief interest rather than oil exploration. Both he and his staff were always ready to help but naturally found themselves unable to do more than support requests and suggestions made by myself. The days were yet to come when British diplomats were trained in commercial matters and, to tell the truth, Libya in 1952 needed men with sound political foresight, experienced in building the political and administrative side of its Government and Constitution even more than the country's trade. I always found ready help and true friendship from the Kirkbrides during their 3 years in the Legation which became an Embassy and he Ambassador in 1954, the year of his retirement. But it was help based on the political situation and having regard to political issues in Libya rather than advice to the Libyan Government and myself which could be used as ammunition to defeat the demands of a rival, e.g. an American oil company contra Shell. The latter, after all, was the reason for my own presence in the country. I do not wish, in any way, to belittle the help given to Shell or myself by our Legation, which was always readily forthcoming, especially when legal issues were at stake, (emanating from the legal expert later appointed to the Legation).

I, for one, always found it difficult to realise that Libya was a state having a hereditary monarchy, and that the people of the three Provinces, Cyrenaica, Tripolitania and Fezzan had formed the United Kingdom of Libya and that King Mohammed Idris Al Mahdi Al Senussi was the constitutional King of Libya. The Senussi movement began about the same time as our Queen Victoria ascended the British throne, and was founded by King Idris's grandfather who moved from Morocco to the east where he set up an ascetic Beduin faith and brotherhood in the attractive countryside of Cyrenaica. It was purely religious but when the Italians invaded Libya in 1911 the sect became a rallying point for Libyan patriots.

I myself had visited Barce during the war when Idris lived in exile in Egypt but, as Administrator of Tripolitania only, had no touch with him in 1943.

It was now my obvious duty to visit him and in March 1952 Diana and I flew to Benghazi where I arranged a call on the King and Queen with one Alexander their British Adviser. We found Benghazi very much the alternative capital of Libya, even if not so prosperous as Tripoli. We were entertained by the Area Commander and his wife and called on the Wali before going on to Barce where we stayed with Cecily and John Fletcher, Diana's cousin who had stayed with us in Naples when wounded.

Next morning we drove from Barce to Lethe the Royal Residence and were received by King Idris and his Queen respectively and in separate parts of their palace.

I can remember but little of the interview with the King who was courteous and grateful to the British Military Administration which I had instituted in 1943. He asked a few questions about oil exploration and showed that he had been well briefed as regards my request for immediate attention to Shell's application. His mind, however, was not attuned to discussion of oil matters or any matters of interest in the industrial future of his country. I clearly was not versed in the history of the Senussi movement or its future and the interview was not prolonged. That was the only private audience I had with King Idris which I have since regretted for his personal interest was one which I should have sought more often and more strongly - even if only to have his *baraka* on my company's future.

Shell's Marketing Company had, of course, important interests in Cyrenaica and Boustani, their representative in Benghazi, then and always was at great pains to make my visit easy and successful on that and all other occasions. One other old friend from the Sudan whom we met in Benghazi was Major Eric Evans, Galloper Evans, as he was known in the Sudan. He lived out along the coast where he kept bees.

Soon after our return from Cyrenaica Shell cabled me to see them in London about a small, high-powered mission which they wished to send to Qatar in the Persian Gulf to negotiate terms for off-shore exploration. They wanted me to go as Arab Adviser. In London I received the details and the scope of my role with the mission which I shall describe separately and which took me away from Tripoli for two months in the summer of 1952 and 6 weeks in the autumn. Luckily it did not interfere with school holidays which the two daughters spent happily enough in Tripoli rather enjoying life in and out of the Waddan Hotel, the novelty of which had rather worn off in respect of their parents. There was a great deal of bathing and tennis and the bathing cum sightseeing expeditions to Leptis Magna and Sabratha were a constant delight.

Moreover by midsummer Diana had, at last, spotted a possible bungalow which, when finished and converted to our liking seemed to be the answer. It was in the last stages of construction as a pair of bungalow apartments - but we liked it well enough to enter into negotiations for certain modifications to be made which would convert it into a single bungalow for the Lush family; the existence of a reasonable piece of flat ground which could easily be made into a small garden convinced us that it was worth the very high sum demanded by the Maltese owners who saw, no doubt, the chance of extracting a very good sum from the Shell Company. I must admit that I thought St Helen's Court were very generous in giving their blessing to the deal and convinced me that the policy of insisting that their staff were well housed even at great expense, was to be applied in Libya as in the rest of the world. Negotiations took many weeks and I was glad to be handy at the critical times to help Diana on to whose shoulders the final decisions would fall in my absence.

There was no doubt, so far as I see, that Shell House should be established in the Piazza Medaglie d'Oro, almost the centre of the residential area of Tripoli, thus following my Directors' instructions to make Anglo Saxon Company the leading one in Tripoli. With Shell's hearty encouragement both verbal and financial this was not too difficult.

Diana arranged transport from UK of our *penates* and a Daneman grandpiano which I had bought at Harrods. She engaged the house staff and had our Christmas cards printed and in great part despatched (by Christmas) almost single handed. It was a wonderful work of dogged perseverance coupled with the knack of enlisting the help of everyone whom she needed - qualities of courage, endurance and charm which Diana has always displayed, and which, led us as a family, to spend a happy family Christmas (1952) in a capacious house in the Piazza Medaglia d'Oro and to live there most happily until 1956.

Here I shall leave Libya for the rest of 1952 during which, in my absence, more than half of the time Diana (who herself spent many weeks in UK and elsewhere) managed to install us as a family in the house. Luckily, and partly by good management of timings in my secondary task, I was able to be present in Tripoli during the Easter and summer holidays when Sylvia and Meriel arrived from Winchester: Julian missed the Easter break but joined us in August having passed out of Mons Officer Cadet School, Aldershot on 7 August 1952 (after 8 months service) and was now 2/Lieut, posted to 5 RHA in Germany.

Qatar (1952)

The negotiations which led me to the Persian Gulf during four or five visits in 1952 had, as their aim, the grant of an exploration licence to Shell by the Ruler of Qatar (a small peninsular adjacent Bahrain) where a branch of the Iraq Petroleum Company was already producing oil (on-shore) at a very steady rate.

Shell's geologists had spotted further good areas off-shore in the waters of the Qatar peninsula and the Directors had determined to send a small mission to visit the Ruler of Qatar (in Doha, the capital) to negotiate a concession for off-shore exploration and production.

The Shell mission consisted of Bill Higgins, who had reached retiring age in Shell service in which he had risen to the position of General Manager in one of the South American oil fields; Tony Miller, a man of long experience in the London office (with an immense fund of knowledge of detail) and myself, the "Arabist".

Qatar was one of the seven independent Arab Sheikdoms in the Persian Gulf, bound by Treaty (1920) with the United Kingdom who was responsible for external affairs and who kept British Political Officers in each State. These States (Kuwait, Bahrain, Qatar, Abu Dhabi, Dubai, Sharjah and Ras Al Khaimah) had real or potential oil wealth, and Bahrain in 1952 maintained the senior British Political Resident and was regarded as the "Capital" of the seven States. The Political Agent in Qatar looked to Political Resident Bahrain for orders and it was to Bahrain that we, in the Shell mission, went as our jumping off place. Bahrain boasted a good aerodrome, moderate hotels, a club. The Residency was not outstanding but it was undoubtedly a good centre from which to work and in Bahrain we finally established the Shell mission's headquarters in a remarkably well found building once owned (and well stocked) by an American oil company who had given up the search for concessions both in or around Qatar and neighbourhood.

Reverting to more accurate details we were met in Bahrain on 6 May 1952 and housed in the Iraq Petroleum Company (IPC) rest home. We found hospitality, by way of a sundowner, with Robert Hay, Political Agent, and here I found my first ex-Sudan friend, Eddie Thomas - and well met he was. I was to repeat this kind of meeting of Sudan friendship all over the Gulf and it was invaluable. In Bahrain we met Dalrymple Belgrave who with his lady wife had lived there for over 20 years as Adviser to the Ruler - and the founder of a most lovely garden! In Bahrain "Sudan Political" was a sure passport for friendship and I found much in common with them both, and learned a great deal.

Next day we chartered an Anson (my mind went back to refugee days in East Africa) and flew round the peninsular of Qatar landing, finally, at the airstrip outside Doha.

Extract from letter MSL to DRL 7.5.1952

"The peninsular of Qatar looked, from the air, to be what it really is: plain and horrible hard baked surface without a single redeeming feature. The town of Doha outside of which we landed is a collection of wretched houses bordering on the sea with the Ruler's palace on a slight eminence. The building, with obvious signs of the simplest form of drainage - evacuation from the windows - is a dreadful dirty white pile. Doha is an appalling place.

"We were met by the Political Officer, Michael Weir, who took us directly to see Shaikh Ali bin Abdalla Al Thani, son of the Ruler. We were then introduced to the Ruler and the usual greetings were exchanged - the Political Officer and I interpreting for my colleagues. The Political Officer ventured to suggest that the Ruler might have heard of the British Company called Shell and its international reputation. *"Abadan"* said the Ruler - or was he referring to the big refinery in the west of Iran? Neither Weir nor I could guess. I still think that he denied all knowledge of Shell and meant the riposte as a diplomatic snub! He receives £3 million per annum from oil already exported from his peninsular and, so far, has done nothing towards the benefit of his people or the country."

We returned to Bahrain to make many and various plans for a longer stay including the hire of a small launch on which to live and so avoid the heat and dirt of Doha. I stayed a few times with the Political Officer in Doha but found the quarters lacked assured electricity and were useless for a business party like ourselves.

We returned to Doha en bloc after a few days and lunched with the Ruler. The Ruler was all smiles and bonhommie: the hallway decked in crimson curtains and be-cushioned chairs: various "wicked uncles" were present - as one could tell by their unrestricted belching: the sheep were well cooked and swimming in their greasy fat: the Ruler revelled in the amount of meat and rice to the obvious discomfort of his guests, or some of them, in this, to us, revolting feast. I personally have often partaken of Arab feasts in Egypt and the Sudan in places just as remote as Qatar. But never had I experienced such primitive lack of cleanliness or order as in the "Palace" of Sheikh Abdalla bin Qasim Al Thani whose annual income from oil was, as stated, at least £3 million. The Palace and the luncheon were typical of the rest of Sheikh Abdalla's capital and, with the exception of that part occupied by the oil company in the north west corner, the whole of the territory on Qatar Peninsula under his rule.

I spent several days on my own in Doha staying with Michael Weir, then a young Foreign Office official who was taking the place of Ewart Biggs, one of my bright young administrators in Tripolitania, (1943), who had done well there under myself and Blackley and who, when he returned from leave to Doha in 1952, met us and it was obvious he was a man of ability and "guts" for he showed great enthusiasm even in Qatar.

Michael Weir served for a number of years in the Trucial States and became Political Resident in Bahrain and ultimately British Ambassador in Cairo. Ewart Biggs had a distinguished career in the Diplomatic Service ending as British Ambassador in Dublin where he was murdered in 1976 by the IRA.

I had little good to say of Qatar or indeed of any place or country in the Gulf.

MSL to DRL 9.5.1952

"Kuwait is just about the end. We did not see the town which I believe is beyond anything! Bahrain is perfectly revoltingly ugly - the island is just a flat piece of mud, dirty at the edge - the town is both dirty and smelly and there is no redeeming feature.

"As I have already told you, the peninsula of Qatar looks, from the air, just what it is - quite horrible expanse without a single redeeming feature of trees, greenery or water. The town of Doha, described earlier, is a collection of wretched houses on the sea which seems to evaporate in the heat as the waves break on the shore. It is a quite appalling place without a vestige of green (except the well of the British Agent's "Garden"). The town boasts two cows, one of which eats the flotsam and the other the jetsam."

I who had seen villages or towns in Lower Egypt, Palestine and Syria, thought that Qatar was the most barren piece of inhabited country that I had ever seen and Doha the filthiest, most wretched town. In the next paragraph I shall describe my delight and amazement at what could be done by people with a large amount of money to be spent on providing the most comfortable accommodation and living conditions for highly paid, well educated and skilled employees. It should also be remembered that when I left the Sudan in 1940 there was no air-conditioning installed in any buildings in Damer, headquarters of the Northern Province; electric light had only recently been installed in the Governor's house. So I viewed IPC's accomplishments with the green eye of jealousy emanating from an ex-Governor of a Province in which the State budget (1940) balanced at about £14,000.

MSL to DRL 16.5.52:

"Next day we flew over to the western side of the peninsula where a conglomeration of companies comprising the Iraq Petroleum Company - Shell, Compagnie Francaise de Petroles, Anglo Iranian (BP), two American companies and one, Mr Gulbenkian, had been running a land-based oil field for a number of years and had found and were producing oil which brought a large revenue to Shaikh Abdulla bin Qasim Al Thani and his wicked uncles."

Here we found a very different scene. We were met on the airstrip by the Manager who drove us in his large Buick to the IPC Company settlement at Dukhan and stopped at the Guest House - very large, all air-conditioned; each guest had a room with private bathroom.

"We spent the morning going round the commissariat - the help-yourself grocery (stocked for 375 Europeans), the laundry and the general welfare store (so important to women and families). We saw the butchery and cold meat store and it was quite clear that good feeding and good maintenance were essential. We went to the nearest "field" (no oil visible, all piped). We saw a drill pipe being removed from a drilling well; all sorts of technical drilling engineering details were explained to us. We then went back to change for a cocktail party and dinner. Very convivial but T.G. bed early. Next day the others fished while I motored the 60 miles back to Doha and more talks with the Political Adviser and the Political Officer. Back westward towards sunset and the best bathe of all time".

Next day we had a full day at an oil rig and I really did learn a lot about the marvellous technical skill which the riggers and tool pushers displayed. Here in the oil field there were prefabricated houses for all the western workers - beautifully fitted with kitchens for the wives who were encouraged to join their husbands even near the centre of operations. I must own that women and their mates had a hard time near the rigs and wells -

everything smelt of and was saturated with oil - and its permeating substance. Later that evening I talked with some of the very competent sensible and charming men and women at the headquarters of the Company as we sat at dinner in their air-conditioned mess eating excellent food, well cooked and served in a temperate atmosphere. I asked them whether they ever went to Doha and visited the British Adviser to the Ruler and his wife, and the Political Officer and his wife, and realised how comparatively squalid were the quarters in which they (British Government servants) lived and what a vast contrast existed between their conditions.

It must be remembered that I was, in 1952, at the very beginning of life in an international company after 35 years in a service. I now had to learn that, whereas I was accustomed to serving either my country or the Sudanese, in Shell the word service meant service at all levels: by the top management towards the company's employees (in order to ensure good work), by the employees themselves or the company's service to the public in order to recoup good revenue for good value. I was astounded at the service given by the Directorate to their employees (which clearly gave outstanding results), and equally astonished at the payments or gifts given to our hosts - e.g. the Ruler of Qatar and his followers, in addition to the agreed bargain sum. Let me stress that these gifts were paid as goodwill after the agreement was signed. I am writing, of course, of the days (1952) when the resources of the oil companies and prices for oil and the terms under which they sought for it were all very different from today.

Writing about gifts reminds me that over lunch the Ruler had expressed a wish for some mobile water tankers, as owned by the IPC company, and we had promised him 3 as soon as we could deliver them.

We finally extracted ourselves from Qatar and Bahrain two days before Ramadan when all real business ceases. We arranged for negotiations in Doha to continue with the Ruler's negotiator, Abdulla Darwish, a Pearl merchant of some wealth and esteem. In October I had discovered that the British Adviser to the Ruler was about to be succeeded by a good ex-Sudan friend of mine, Geoffrey Hancock, which was excellent news. We arranged for the hire of a 30 foot seismic launch with air-conditioned cabins, fully staffed and provisioned for October as accommodation, and then we all flew to London and thence to The Hague to report conditions and progress. This was at the end of May.

I found Diana in London and we spent a month together, I attending St Helen's Court often but not always, and succeeded in getting a good English translation of the Libyan Oil Laws done by a Sudanese student. We saw our two daughters at St Swithun's, remembering that it was examination time and we managed to see a good deal of Julian who was based in Aldershot at Mons Officer Cadet School. We stayed with the Moberlys in Henry II Tower of Windsor Castle and experienced the discomfort of round walls and a circular iron staircase. But it was a great experience and we took Communion and went to Matins in St George's, Windsor where, but for Shell, I might well have been ordained. We had a splendid month together in U.K., but I left for Tripoli alone on 7 July. Diana and the two daughters joined me a month later having motored from UK via Marseille to Tunis (where I met them) arriving Tripoli on 8 August where 2/Lt A J M Lush, arrived by air. We were still at the Waddan Hotel and the family had a wonderful month. I was chiefly concerned with discussion on Libyan mineral laws and negotiations for our house in the Piazza Medaglie d'Oro. On 14 September I left with the children for UK leaving Diana with a temperature in the hotel (Diary next day reported All Well). I then concentrated on the Qatar Concession for three months leaving Diana the complicated final business of the house.

Tony Miller and I went to Qatar at the end of September and presented the water tankers to the Ruler. I remember the trouble I took to obtain a good Arabic word for a mobile 1000 gallon water tanker, only to find that the Ruler called them tankers. We presented them only to be told that they were half the required size! However the Ruler was all smiles and affable on the next occasion which he celebrated by asking for a motor car for Abdulla Darwish, the negotiator. Granted!

We made final arrangements for our full meeting in October -found our launch and land accommodation in Bahrain satisfactorily arranged by a Shell storeman sent out for the purpose and repaired to London.

I had long sessions in the Foreign Office (I was the party's link with the F.O.) and should have been discussing our oil problems with Rod Sarell. He however was busily engaged in dealing with Moussadek's (Persia) latest ultimatum and so I had to be content with his No. 2. It was fun working in Whitehall again and I find that one letter to Diana was written from the F.O. during a spare moment. I also was in long correspondence with Geoffrey Hancock who, with his wife Honor, was going out as the new Adviser to the Ruler Sheikh Abdulla. We gave him a "private room" luncheon in the Savoy and told him our Shell tale before the poor man had even left England; but the Savoy did the trick and Geoffrey Hancock was our firm supporter when we met the next week in Qatar. We had drafted our Concession Terms in English, had the agreement of the Shell legal boys thereto, and then I had them translated into Arabic by a young Sudanese from Khartoum and typed in Arabic by an Egyptian in the BBC - 30 pages including the Arabic for "spring tide" and "neap tide": it needed all the Arabic at my poor command to explain to the translator what the difference was. I finally persuaded the Egyptian from the BBC to accompany the Shell party to Bahrain where he spent a week in complete luxury with no work until he was our salvation when he and I typed the final text in one long night.

On the whole I found my weeks in London, on this mission, as full and hectic as the days in Doha were burdensome and hot. However I seem to have bought the Daneman grand piano (new) for £246 at Harrods and arranged for the packing cases in the Army and Navy Store at Turnham Green containing our 'penates' to be shipped for arrival in Tripoli during November.

I escaped from London for a blessed week to have a look at my Tripoli scene, to say nothing of a week with Diana whom I found successfully immersed in the house and yet sufficiently extricated to be able to enjoy life. I returned to London just in time to join my Qatar party now consisting of Bill Higgins and Tony Miller, as before, but with the addition of Charles Saville, a Shell Lawyer and Fuad Khalil Gemie, our quite charming Egyptian translator. We were travelling with various IPC oil men returning to Lebanon, Kirkuk (Iraq, the HQ of IPC) and Qatar. We motored to Blackbush near Camberley, well known to me and Diana in wartime and post war flights. I was by now the joke of my Shell party as the man who could never travel incognito and sure enough we were met at Blackbush airport by one Edwards who recognised me and telephoned his superintendent of Station, W/Cdr Ford who both Diana and I knew well coming and going into Blackbush in 1947-48. Complete VIP treatment by both (chuckles from my Shell companions) and off we went to Rome where it was then the custom to night stop, and where I was met by Anne Moreton from the British Embassy (renewed sniggers) whom I eventually took away with her flat mate and our Egyptian Fuad to a Ristorante where we spent a happy evening, getting lost in the nether parts of Trastevere. Next day we flew to Tripoli, Lebanon, where we all went to a drinks party given by Rylands, the I.P.C. General Manager of the Pipeline and DC in the Sudan around 1930 and whom we had met at Pao in 1932. At dinner which followed, I was hailed vigorously by one Hope Dixon and another Tenet, both of my Administration in Ethiopia, now in IPC (loud hoots from my Shell team). A tremendous IPC Pipeline cum Kirkuk "dinner for 30 and we are being called at 4.15 am!" as I wrote next day 21.10.52; "arrived last evening very tired after dark. Lunching the Navy today!" Incidentally we had, en route Tripoli to Bahrain, diverted slightly and flown over Adaban, Persia. Arrived in Bahrain and lodged in our spacious comfortable flats, we established touch with Abdulla Darwish in Doha and arranged to start talking in 48 hours. We then sent our launch "Povaco V" round to drop anchor in the roads off Doha. Thither we flew and established ourselves on board in air-conditioned cabins, stocked for 14 days food and drink and a bit more. Let me say that with the noon temperature running at 105 degrees or more, with a heavy dew at night we lived as comfortable a life as possible on the water half a mile from shore. There was always a breeze blowing out there and the air-conditioning worked well except on one night when Bill Higgins and I woke to find icycles hanging in our cabin - the result of over exertion by the air-conditioning. We were rowed into shore each day at 7.30 and negotiated until noon or later in Abdulla Darwish's air-conditioned parlour. He was always agreeable, plied us with cool drinks one of which was a very sweet coagulated pineapple beverage which, especially when not fully iced, created a most dreadful traffic jam in the mouth, throat and then stomach. He preserved that particular poison for occasions of 'impasse' when he would leave us perhaps for a quarter of an hour, writhing in torture, while he relieved himself, or quite often, bargained with local traders for a particularly valuable pearl - he was the Ruler's principle pearl buyer. The negotiations had, of course, a simple issue: Shell wanted to search for, and hopefully drill for, oil under the sea in a specific area some 15 miles from Doha and to lay a pipeline, if necessary to the shores of Qatar. My Arabic sufficed for Abdulla knew English well. A brief spell in London intervened to report progress.

So began the last and final lap of negotiations which we all wanted to terminate on our own terms. We had a hard week of give and take, of bluff and hard faces, of shrugged shoulders. Life was more pleasant on the launch than anywhere else, but was not very varied: we rose at sunrise and negotiations started early onshore. Abdulla Darwish gave us lunch on occasions and one day we ate a very good bustard brought down by one of the Ruler's falcons (a change from curried goat, oh, so hot) with greasy rice followed by a green blancmange. The days were generally punctuated by code telegrams to and from London. (No decoding clerks on our liner!) However after 10 days negotiations had almost reached finality except for a tremendous amount of writing, translation into written Arabic and final presentation. The Ruler wanted a week's respite - and so did Abdulla Darwish. So we sailed back to Bahrein (150 miles) and then it began to blow; how that small craft did pitch, roll, corkscrew and disappear below the sea for a time. I retired to my bed on the bridge and had a first class view of it all without unpleasant sensations or much water. At about 3 a.m. the weather moderated and it was then that our small fishing launch (which we towed) broke away and drifted helplessly. We turned to salvage her but at that moment one of our engines broke down and we noticed an 18,000 ton tanker bearing down on us - this caused us to abandon the small craft and she sank before our eyes, all £5,000 worth of her.

I managed to snatch a week in Tripoli and found Diana had done wonders with and in the house. They were a busy 7 days including attendance at a Royal Opening of Parliament by King Idris, a longish interview with the Prime Minister and the completion of 200 Christmas Cards in the evenings. At the opening of Parliament I handed my card to the (Libyan) Usher who called out in a stentorian voice "Mister Lush, our first Governor". No little embarrassment "but rather nice" as I wrote to the family.

On 15 November I flew back to my negotiating party, the sole passenger on a freighter aircraft - not much fun. We were soon afloat again and entering the penultimate phase of our negotiations. Six days of hard horse trading enabled me to write to Diana on 21.11.52 "Well - verbally - we have achieved a success at a lower price than we had estimated and very much quicker than we had hoped: we are now in the throes of minor Articles and still have the mechanical processes of final translation and typing in two languages with which to pass the time!"

By November 23 Fuad, our Egyptian translator, and I, after intense checking of English and Arabic script, were able to begin the mammoth task of typing the whole Concession Agreement accurately and legibly - each sheet containing two columns of script, one English and the other Arabic. It had taken 48 hours (in our air-conditioned flats in Bahrain) to have the Agreement written in manuscript, and I remember sitting down at about 9 p.m. to achieve the task of typing in English (MSL) and Arabic (Fuad) the final pages. No errors or visible corrections were permitted and the night, punctuated by relays of hot coffee and sandwiches reminded me of my first night in the Legation at Addis Ababa in October 1919! I had sent the rest of the party to bed and Fuad and I worked in separate rooms. "At 10 p.m." (MSL to DRL 24.11.52) "it seemed a 4 hour job: at 1 a.m. only 8 out of 80 Articles done, it seemed quite hopeless: but at 4 a.m. we had broken the back of it and at 7 a.m. I was able to give the 120th sheet (foolscap) in English to our excellent Fuad to be typed in Arabic on the right hand side of the same page! I drank nothing except plain pink gin before dinner and I did not feel the least bit tired or sleepy." It involved an enormous amount of concentration and I was delighted to know that on my 56th birthday I could still achieve the job and put in a full day's work checking the results next day.

We had six more days off and in Doha of final intensive haggling: (MSL to DRL): "We had a hard week; very tricky negotiations which threatened to break down at the very last moment. The situation was saved by a compromise (suggested by MSL) and so, having spent most of Friday night retyping and re-translating large blocks of the final Concession Agreement, we took the document to the Ruler's Palace on Saturday morning and with a Parker Pen (gold £38) the Ruler deposited an enormous blot on the final page of that precious document - that however we cleared away and he signed the document which Bill Higgins also signed." Geoffrey Hancock and Christopher Ewart Biggs were both present - the former having only recently arrived. Then came the exchange of presents. The Ruler presented each member of the Shell party with a golden handled "khanjar" or dagger and Abdulla Darwish gave us each a golden bracelet studded with pearls for our wives. The ceremony was terminated quite abruptly by Abdulla Darwish saying: "On Saturday mornings His Highness the Ruler always goes to join his youngest wife - so we must excuse ourselves." We did. The Ruler unabashed (we were a male party!) said: "Yes, Wallahi, and I still have two even younger girls to obtain."

But the most important part of the drama was not yet enacted. One of the Clauses just signed in the Palace was financial and part of that Clause mentioned the payment on signature by Shell to the Ruler of 1 million Rupees (or more) - I cannot remember the exact figure. We all (including the Political Agent and the Adviser) imagined that Bill Higgins would hand the Ruler a draft for Rs 1m on the spot. We were quite wrong - and here we Arabists were caught out! The Ruler required the money to be paid in cash in notes of Rs 10. Moreover he required the money to be delivered to the Palace at dead of night - otherwise the wicked uncles would hear of it and get hold of their wrongly imagined due. Luckily there was in Doha a young member of the British Bank of the Middle East about to return to Bahrain. We sent him off in our Anson, with a letter to his Bank Manager and a quantity of cabin trunks and suitcases. The Bank took our request on trust, raised the money from their own vaults and also from merchants in the suq, and the young Bank official was back with us with a great quantity of luggage by evening. It took us 6 hours in Christopher Ewart Biggs's compound to check the boodle and repack the notes. We then (this was my job) removed the luggage after dark to the British Adviser's house where they were placed under his quite adequate Qatari police guard. Geoffrey Hancock then nobly undertook to convey the boodle to his Ruler chief at the appointed hour. He having reported to us, at dawn, of the safe deposit in the Palace of the money, we recovered such pieces of luggage as belonged to us, said fond farewell to Doha and Qatar, and flew to Bahrain and thence to London to report to the Production Department, and to our Directors (Stephens and Loudon) who were apparently delighted.

I regret now that I did not keep closely in touch with Production Department in Shell as to the developments in the Concession which we had achieved. For it was an achievement in which I admired immensely the knowledge, the patience and the foresight of my colleagues, Bill Higgins, Tony Miller and later Charles Saville, our legal expert, and the professional and scientific knowledge shared by them and St Helen's Court which made quick decisions during negotiations so much easier and therefore more successful. Throughout our discussions with Abdulla Darwish, I had the sure feeling that Higgins and Miller had a knowledge and competence which gave them, and all of us, great confidence to maintain our line of argument or give and take. Cables of interrogation from St Helen's Court were always couched in the atmosphere that we were probably right and were never critical. This gave our two leaders, and all of us, the sense that we had the confidence of Shell - and so felt stronger when the next dose of coagulated pineapple juice came along. I was glad to have been chosen to accompany the party and, in fact, my acquaintance with so many Britons, and others, in the Middle East and the Gulf was of great advantage and gave the whole party, myself included, the assurance that we were not without friends - even outside the oil circle - whereas my knowledge of Arabic, such as it was, oiled many wheels in our ordinary lives. It was a very pleasant and unusual shock to hear London indicate a Christmas present of £500.

I was happy to hear 30 years later that Shell did very well from the off shore wells which they had found and produced as a result of our labours; Shell was thereby involved in Qatar for about 40 years.

15.3 - Tripoli

On 9 December 1952 I flew to Tripoli and life in Shell House Piazza Medaglie d'Oro began in earnest and with the Christmas spirit in the air.

Diana had done *wonders*; in fact, single handed she had produced a house in which we, as a family, plus my mother later, lived for three happy years. Our young came readily and, we hoped, willingly. Their presence, besides building up the morale of their parents added considerably to the quality and the gaiety of the house. Julian was absent (Christmas 1952) but joined his sisters in January 1954 on completion of National Service.

It is a curious fact that we never gave the house a name nor displayed Anglo-Saxon Petroleum on a name plate: it was always well known as the house in the Piazza Medaglie d'Oro (what "gold medal" that square signified I never knew) but I have heard it described as the house with daffodils and flowers in pots on the walls; we were rightly proud of that description.

The house and our lives therein were organised so that it was open to all comers: to Libyan Arabs or Berbers from the Prime Minister to a Sheikh from a small village 100 miles S.W. of Garian; to the diplomats and representatives of all nations - both in Libya itself and passers by to all and every seeker after oil; in fact to all and sundry. That, at any rate, was the message which we intended to give at our house warming party on 5 January 1953 to which 120 guests came, representing all the above and gave to us a wonderfully warm welcome as residents in Tripoli. "A happy return to our country" said the Prime Minister who came with a number of colleagues; there were many too from the Municipality of Tripoli of happy memories; there were most of the dips and a host of our friends. We had two bars - one "dry" in our drawing room, the other less conspicuous but wet in the dining room - and it soon became amusingly clear that the Mufti and the Khadi were doomed to splendid isolation in the drawing room unless a change in beverage took place. As a family we, and our close friends, found our first party at home to be the greatest fun. It was the first of many such *azoomas* in that house which, in itself, was never empty of guests.

I wanted to tell all and sundry that Anglo Saxon was here on a permanent basis, hopefully as a pillar in the industrial palace of Libya. I must own here that my natural emphasis was on Tripolitania, because we lived there, and I never threw such a party in Benghazi - where much of the oil might be. As a fact a vast amount of the oil was found finally in Fezzan and God forbid that we should have to throw parties in that bleak desert.

Quite apart from the house, I was very anxious to develop our small garden, small as it was - we could entertain double the number of guests at a party al fresco - and for our every day enjoyment of life, a garden with a lawn was a necessity. The local agricultural and horticultural experts lived and worked at Sidi Mesri, the Agricultural Centre outside Tripoli. Thither I went to discuss "lawns", the possibility of obtaining stipes of the "Uganda grass" which we used for our lawns in Khartoum. This Uganda grass had the unique quality of growing well under a hot sun and spreading remarkably quickly and well and, if well irrigated, of retaining its bright green colour even in tropical sun/heat. We used it extensively in the Sudan in places where perennial water was available - e.g. on the banks of the Nile and it proved hardy enough to make the excellent tennis courts in Khartoum and Damer which I have described. I had often seen Sudani gardeners planting these small grass roots - we called it stippling - but had never done so myself. The horticultural authorities in Khartoum were kind enough to send me 2000 "stipes" or roots of this grass and I prepared the main "lawn" with excellent soil from good friends at Sidi Mesri. When this was ready and thoroughly damp I spent an exhausting day stippling the roots therein - not more than 3" apart. To our great joy our faith was fulfilled - the stipes took and within 6 weeks (I may be exaggerating) we had the semblance of a lawn and in 2 months I was using a hand mowing machine - which had greatly puzzled the customs when I brought it out by air.

It was the first lawn of its kind ever seen in Tripolitania and we held all our tea and cocktail parties between the spring and autumn solstices in our garden. For Tripoli soil, when properly tended, was wonderfully kind to flowers, and Diana and I knew from experience what a Sudan garden could produce, roses, begonias, petunia, dahlias, citrus trees, bougainvillaea, hibisci and so on. With temerity which was crowned with success we embarked on daffodils and hydrangea, tulips and the like, sweetpeas in profusion and aubretia in the walls - the ubiquitous geranium could always be relied upon to fill in gaps and we had great fun with the creeping water plants.

We were very proud of our daffodils which were planted in large 18" red flower pots, some score of which adorned the top of our high white wall which constituted the front of the property: "the house in the Piazza Medaglie d'Oro with the flower pots." Not many were stolen!

Our love of gardening and the surprising results did a great deal to 'establish' us in Tripoli. One American resident was heard to say "The Lushes always lay down a brand new green lawn whenever they hold a drinks party."

While we were finding our feet as residents with a home rather than as visitors in the Waddan Hotel our happiness was much enhanced by the arrival of my mother - which I briefly mentioned earlier.

My Mother, F E Lush

Since my brother Cecil's death in 1949, my mother had lived first with us in Les Marguerites, Geneva, then for a few months in Brookside, Ewhurst, Surrey, before flying with my sister Christine and Miss K T Stephenson to Addis Ababa, Ethiopia in September 1951.

In Ethiopia she lived for the most part at Mulu, about 40 miles north of Addis Ababa where Dan and Chris

Sandford had, by now, a flourishing farm with 300 cattle, 200 acres of barley, 61 acres of strawberries and fruit trees - plums and apples; 2000 ft below Mulu (whither my mother never penetrated) were coffee trees, oranges and other sub-tropical fruits. There my mother lived a quiet family life in the country, at an altitude lower than Addis Ababa (8000 ft) with a garden full of English flowers, excellent fresh farm food, and every servant at her beck and call. At weekends Chris and Dan held court to up to 100 visitors of every race who came out from Addis Ababa for a day in the country with the two most popular Sandfords. Three or four times in the year the Sandfords would take my mother into Addis Ababa for some Ethiopian or British festival, e.g. the investiture of Chris with her CBE. (Both Sandfords and all three Lushes, CHL, CS, MSL, received that honour).

My mother also saw her granddaughter who, with her husband, were Headmaster and Deputy of the English School in Addis Ababa (700 pupils of 29 nationalities and a waiting list of 200).

After two years my mother showed signs of strain due to height and refined air and it was decided in February 1953 that she would accept our warm invitation to join us on the Mediterranean coast.

So along she came at the age of 92 - by air. In those days it had just become possible to fly direct from Addis Ababa to Cairo, so my mother and her companion Miss Osborne had only one change, at Cairo, where beloved Bishop Frank and Gladys Johnston saw them comfortably rested at the airport before starting them on the three hour flight across the desert. At Castel Benito, Tripoli, Dick Coles the Manager of BOAC, and by now a good friend of ours (Shell, after all was a good customer of the airline as we had already shown) gave a really wonderful reception. FEL (as I shall describe her in future) was very much "all there" and emerged looking well and almost alert when she recognised us, and we soon had her before a friendly fire in our new drawing room in a proper house and furnished room which she at once noticed and appreciated. She contrasted it with the countryfied sitting room at Mulu, which might be peaceful at one moment and then full of strawberry baskets, farm hands and the like the next, when Chris, my sister, was conducting the bearing of the fruit into Addis Ababa or the delivery of a calf or tomorrow's garden programme, all in Amharic which FEL described as "an outlandish language". She was delighted with her bedroom and that of Miss Osborne's next door, and when both of them saw the *"scalda bagno"* or (electric) geyser in their bathroom they whooped with joy. No more waiting for the petrol tin to be carried from the Mulu cookhouse, 30 yards away, and emptied in the very pimply bath, lit by one candle and resting on a mud floor covered by a rush mat! Here I must confess that the installation of the said *scalda bagno* had been achieved with complete avoidance of the first and most simple rule of electric installations in private dwellings. The engineer pointed out with pride to Diana that the electric switch controlling the geyser could be operated comfortably while lying in the bath!

The joy and comfort of living in what Miss Osborne called "a civilised house" drove away all feelings of fatigue after a 3000 mile journey and a drop from 8000 ft to sea level. She came into dinner that evening and was very gracious to the two young men who came to take the ladies to a reel party.

My mother did not realise until the morrow that Tripoli was a seaside resort and then her joy was unbounded, for she was back in Brighton again. Within 48 hours we took her to the dedication of our British Garrison Church which created a double happy thought - a civilised Church again (I must say the soldiers and our civilian congregation had made the Church look very English and very homely) where my mother could worship; it was dedicated by the Bishop of Croydon in Surrey. It all took her straight home - and Miss Osborne felt much the same - delighted to see a number of British faces and to sing British hymns. Let me quote an entry in DRL's diary on the fifth day of FEL's arrival: "M and D around to fetch 9 carnation plants and 12 seabins. Lunched in the garden. Lovely sunshine ... Dinner party here (8 including FEL). Others came in afterwards to listen to Flavia Marsh play the piano. Bed about 2 a.m." I hope my mother made an early retirement before then. She fitted exceedingly well into our family life; she loved to see the garden in the throes of creation and had her special jobs therein.

We ourselves, while exploring the joys of a new house and the creation of a garden, indulged in many expeditions: primarily, of course, to the famous and exciting sites of the Roman cities Leptis Magna and Sabratha, both on the sea, both demanding, and with ample reward, not a few but many visits, and both the bourne of our many visitors who came, mostly to work, but could not be allowed to go without the 70 miles to Leptis Magna or the 35 miles to Sabratha, with a picnic and a bathe thrown in.

Diana and I had the good fortune of personal introduction to those cities by famous archaeologists; Ward Perkins, who was then the Director of the British School at Rome, Olwen Brogan, an eminent archaeologist specialising on Libya, and finally Max Mallowan who had been part of my administration in 1942 and came back in 1953 and 54 with his wife Agatha Christie.

My mother was soon introduced to what we called our private bathing beach; it was and remained entirely free of others for a full three years, 30 miles from Tripoli on the Misurata road, going east and within easy reach. The last few yards were not of easy access - a 50 foot scramble down an almost perpendicular slope but my mother was manhandled down, and up again, and adored the sand and the fresh water stream emerging from a little hollow in the cliff. We and our visitors loved the clear sea water and the Roman columns clustered on the sea bed, the blue of the water and the solitude after a busy week in Tripoli. We had countless bathing parties in that cove and were never molested by Libyans or bathers. But always, whenever she came with us, my mother, after 2 or 3 hours on that lovely beach, would exclaim: "Well Maurice, we had better be moving up, the tide will soon be coming in." She could not understand that the Mediterranean, unlike the Channel, was tideless. Agatha Christie, however, her proportions matching her renown, held no such faith "My friends" said she "I am about to enter the water; a tidal wave in Nice may be expected this evening."

We bathed many times at Leptis Magna by the ancient customs office, and at Sabratha where it was always fresh, breezy and sometimes to be avoided when the water was badly blood splattered by the tuna fishing.

Other excursions were to the hills - Garian - or to the Italian colony in Tarhuna, and once or twice Diana and I with Julian went further towards Fezzan and also to Ghadames. My mother did not accompany us on the longer trips but was always game for a picnic, almost anywhere, and I cannot remember any occasion when anyone of us, our children included, felt that Granny was an encumbrance on an outing. Diana, of course, was wonderful to her mother-in-law and gave her great devotion.

One evening our great friend, Wreford Brown, who was always in and out of the villa, brought to see us the Minister whom we knew best of all in the Libyan Government. My mother was in the drawing room reading the Life of King George V - she read a certain amount and always liked to have a book with her. Peter Wreford Brown introduced Ali Bey Gerba to my mother, adding "He is the Minister for War in Libya, Granny". "How do you do" retorted my mother a trifle fiercely "Minister for War are you? Then what are you doing about this War" she asked pointing to the Chapter in her book "Britain declares War on Germany, 4th August 1914". Ali Bey was not put out. "We are finishing it very successfully for you, Mrs Lush" he replied and then skilfully led the conversation round. My mother had a habit of dubbing our Ambassador's wife, Lady Kirkbride, who was quite a quarter of a century younger, "That old Lady" - a remark which was hopefully smothered when the lady was within earshot. The sobriquet was created one evening when Diana, my mother and I called at the Embassy, fairly thirsty, to be met by His Excellency, alone, who after a few thirsty moments said: "I'm afraid I cannot offer you a drink - my wife is out with the keys of the wine cupboard!"

I was very proud of my mother at the dinner party in full dress with decorations which was organised by the British community to celebrate the Coronation of Queen Elizabeth. Diana was in England at the time watching the Coronation procession - on that wet day - in the Sudan Government stalls at Hyde Park inner corner. My mother was hostess at my table and earned a full burst of applause as she came in looking every inch a Queen Mother. "A very pleasant dinner party" she said as she retired to bed.

She was very gracious at our big parties and vivacious when the young were about. She loved her game of backgammon or bezique after dinner, but even more so the many evenings when we had music - our Daneman grand piano had stood the journey well: we had several quite competent pianists and singers, male and female, so that our house became quite a venue for live music and, of course, with two large rooms, a much favoured focus for Scottish reels. Diana with her love of rhythm and her lightness of tread was very much the leader in these reels; a clear proof of her descent, as we discovered 10 years later from the Robertsons of the Clan Donnachaidh.

As the Beach Club comfort and service progressed, FEL was often there and much enjoyed being hostess at meals.

On 1 September 1954 the diary shows "FEL 94; Granny received presents and flowers in plenty all morning and later afternoon. All prepared for tea party 5 p.m. MSL mowed the lawn. There arrived 24 adults, 8 juniors and 1 infant. Hassan produced a birthday cake on which stood 94 lighted candles. Ice cream, Pimms No. 1 after the tea party." My mother enjoyed every moment of it and, as it is recorded, extinguished the candles with one puff. I must interpose here that Miss Osborne, after 3 or more years of faithful, patient and devoted service to Granny who, outwardly, was by no means patient with her subordinates and maintained the Victorian view of "class" - but withal felt love and sympathy towards her fellow creatures - had left us to succour her own mother in England.

My mother's next birthday was celebrated by a similar and probably much larger party at Mulu, Ethiopia, for early in 1955 she, with her comparatively new companion Miss Veronica Huthwaite, flew from Tripoli to Addis Ababa to join Chris and her many Sandford grandchildren (and not a few "great granders") in Ethiopia. The intrepid old lady had a rough journey to Cairo, sleeping on a trucklebed in Benghazi, where there was an enforced stop. It must be remembered once more that commercial flying, especially in North Africa, often failed to provide the smooth travel we all expected and which BOAC, manfully attempted to provide. But by this time Granny Lush was a wellknown passenger of BOAC, with a high reputation as our oldest passenger and with Veronica Huthwaite as companion we knew that Granny was travelling on the best airline in the world with a very resourceful, caring person at her side. We never knew the full story of Veronica's life but always remembered that at one period in her career, not so long ago, she had served in the film business as a stand-in for a prominent actress who, as heroine, was called upon to perform some highly dangerous feat, such as leaping across a precipice or through a raging torrent to avoid the would-be assassin at her heels. She had thoroughly enjoyed these horrendous scenes and was only disappointed when she found that the hero who saved her in the end was not the Paul Temple of the story but some stooge like herself. We understood that she had opted for service abroad with a nonagenarian in order to enjoy a period of quiet, if monotonous, service. Little did she know that within a few months she would be asked to be responsible for the safety and comfort of the said patient by air from North Africa to Ethiopia. But Veronica did not flinch and took my mother to Addis Ababa, back to the very rural and often primitive life of Mulu.

Granny thoroughly enjoyed that last visit to the Sandford family in 1955. After 9 months at 8000 feet that courageous heart again showed signs of strain and the doctors in Ethiopia recommended a "breath of sea air" as my mother explained and so she returned to her Tripoli by the sea and her garden and young Meriel's rabbits. There she remained, much to our delight, and was often alone in our house save for Veronica Huthwaite and our staff of servants, but nobly guarded, supported and entertained by two of her most ardent admirers, Philip Bradburne and Hugh Cruddas, who gave her most devoted friendship and care and enabled Diana and myself to leave the country and arrange for Granny's future in UK, on our transfer, in Shell, away from Libya.

At the beginning of 1956 we found a Home, Crieff House, 282 Kingston Road, Teddington, for old people where my mother's younger sister, Grace, was a resident. After much deliberation we decided that our next Shell appointment, to Pakistan, was to a country most unsuitable for my mother. So we left her in Teddington and by the time we had left England she seemed thoroughly comfortable, if a little bereft and lonely after the social days in Libya. We saw her whenever possible and took her to some of the places she had known when young - her home at Cross Deep, Twickenham, a mile or two away, to Richmond Park, Hampton Court via Bushey Park at the gates of which lived her cousins, Kate and Mary Cope. We both visited her on our trips to UK from Karachi and I was lucky enough to be in London during her last few days of life and was by her side when she died peacefully on 12 July 1957. Christine, my sister, was also in England and was able to join a small family gathering at Kingston Cemetery for my mother's funeral.

Such were the last years of a wonderful person who spent her life in the service of others: as a girl, as was expected, in the service of her parents; after early marriage in the service of her husband to whom she bore 4 children (one died in infancy) before he left for 15 years in Canada looking for employment, leaving her to bring the three remaining young through childhood to manhood, to see to their education, not only at school but as Christians: a task for which she herself had no training, only a deeply abiding faith in the help of God and the strength of friends. During those years she and her little family lived in a small house and I can vouch for the fact that she never took a holiday except to stay during her children's three school holidays in *her* mother's more capacious house in Twickenham. To her children, she was a wonderful source of inspiration and a sure refuge when required. When my Father returned and her children were fending for themselves and in some ways helping her, she then spent the next 30 years of her life caring for him - restoring some of the comfort and peace which his wandering middle life had missed. We were glad, my brother, sister and I that we were, on my Father's death, able to give our mother not perhaps the peaceful home she had foreseen, but homes with all the comfort and love we could bestow. It was a pitiful return for the self sacrifice she had demanded of herself and given to us all during our childhood.

Tripoli - 1953

Diana entered fully into the policy of making our house a centre of social attraction and entertainment both for Libyans and for the international population which was by now beginning to increase almost daily - particularly seekers after oil. On the national side Diana joined the committees of two Libyan institutions connected with children which involved her in weekly meetings. The Tripoli School Welfare Committee was one, the Boys Reformatory another where Diana worked in the clinic, and the Women's Teacher's Training College. One diary entry records "Miss Khouri and Miss Sophie Lubast brought 7 school girls to tea: Miss Rosemary Irvine also to tea" (later to become Headmistress of North Foreland Girls' School). A few days later we find a cocktail party, *chez nous* for 82 people, international, to meet the Bishop in Egypt, our beloved Frank Johnston (Meriel's Godfather) who was staying with us. Dora Carson Roberts aged 85 from London was also our guest during the school holidays of our two daughters. Our guests to stay were "legion" and we seldom had a bedroom in the house empty until Sylvia and Meriel went back to school.

At the end of May 1953 Diana flew to London where she stayed until July. With Sylvia and Meriel she witnessed the Queen's Coronation from the Sudan Government stand in Hyde Park and afterwards joined the serge to Buckingham Palace. She then stayed at Windsor Castle with Sir Walter and Lady Moberly who were Grace and Favour tenants of the Queen while Sir Walter was head of Cumberland College in Windsor Great Park. I managed to visit UK soon after the Coronation in order to help my Shell Directors - John Loudon and Stephens - entertain the Libyan Prime Minister to lunch at the Dorchester. Mahmud Muntasser was an easy guest and the occasion was uneventful.

On 16 June Diana and I had a most memorable day, attending the Naval Review at Spithead as guests of Capt Geoffrey Whittaker RN and his wife Monica, on board a frigate, HMS Launceston. HM the Queen, on board her Royal Yacht, led a procession in review of almost the entire fleet of the Royal Navy - an enormous Armada of every conceivable type and size of warship, drawn up in 10 lines over an area of some 25 square miles. Ahead was the Flagship, the battleship HMS Vanguard, followed by aircraft carriers and the remainder in perfect line and order - an unforgettable experience.

We were all back in Tripoli by the end of July 1953 when Sylvia and Meriel joined us for their summer holidays which were filled with tennis and sailing, a good visit to Leptis Magna. We also went en famille to Nalut, 230 miles south of Tripoli. We met a good many Mudirs and Sheikhs, some of whom remembered the British Wali who visited them in 1943 and, mirabile dictu spoke Arabic.

August was also famous for the arrival of Anne Skeet who had come to work as secretary in the Shell Marketing Company and live chez nous. (Incidentally her brother Ian Skeet joined Shell in London on 5th October 1953 and remained with the company until 1985).

Life continued busy both from the oil business and the domestic point of view throughout the rest of 1953 and well into 1954. The Beach Club of which I had been elected chairman was now becoming the centre of recreational if not social activity in Tripoli. We had a strong committee with Libyan members and made vast improvements to the accommodation, the catering, the bathing facilities, tennis courts and gardens. I spent no Shell money on the centre but I gave a tremendous amount of my own and my family's time doing the spade work myself of tennis courts, their surroundings and especially the gardens. We grew grass lawns in the Club grounds and finally we made Sadiq Muntasser, Wali of Tripoli, President of the Club and persuaded him to use it or at any rate to preside at our dinners and sporting events and become one of us. It was not always plain sailing and I remember him walking out of one dinner party because of his deemed insult as to the place he was asked to occupy!

Meanwhile in 1953 and 1954 world interest in the possibility of oil in Libya had grown as was shown by the steady influx of oil companies into the country. The Libyan Government became concerned about legislation to protect its subterranean wealth. Representatives of the oil companies in the country, including myself, knew of its preparation and I naturally consulted London, often by personal visits to obtain the views of Shell which I passed on to the Libyan Government either to the Government officials or their British advisers, sometimes direct to the Prime Minister or through the British Embassy. Charles Saville, one of the legal advisers in Shell, was my chief source of advice in London and it was then that we devised the idea of persuading the Libyans to have a Petroleum Adviser of their own whom Shell "magnanimously" produced.

The Mineral Law was enacted by Government in August 1953 and after declaring the Libyan Government to be the owner of all minerals including hydrocarbons, prohibited exploration, extraction or exploiting of such minerals without a permit. It provided for the issue of permits for exploration etc and regulations for their implementation.

> "The purpose of the law was to attract international oil companies to invest in oil exploration ... to discover the country's oil position as soon as possible."

Nine companies took out permits under this law - Mobiloil; Standard Oil of New Jersey; Anglo Saxon (Shell); Compagnie Francaise des Petroles; D'Arcy Exploration (BP); American Overseas; Oasis Oil; Nelson Bunker Hunt; Libyan American Oil.

Exploration began and soon there were geologists and small exploration parties roaming about the country. They were more in evidence in Cyrenaica than in the western province. Shell sent only a small party because the geologists in the Hague had already determined the areas which they thought to be favourable.

In the meantime two appointments were made by the Libyan Government in 1954: Anis Qasim, a lawyer from Palestine was appointed legal adviser to the Ministry of Finance with especial reference to petroleum legislation. It was he who organised the drafting of the Petroleum Law and for all oil companies represented in Libya to sit in conference to discuss the draft and produce an agreed document for presentation to the Libyan Government for enactment as the Libyan Petroleum Law. Anis Qasim was a competent and, as most of the oil companies representatives thought, an honest collaborator in this joint enterprise. I personally came to know him well and respected his apparent honesty but we naturally confined our relations to official contacts.

The other appointment was that of Mr Hogenhuis, a retired Shell Dutchman, as mining expert, firstly to the Ministry of National Economy and then to the Ministry of Finance. Hogenhuis' appointment was the result of my prosecuting a request by the Libyan Government for an oil expert to St Helen's Court, whereupon Shell found a recently retired employee in Holland. This of course was made quite clear to the Libyan Government whose British official advisers handled the appointment - but his Dutch nationality screened him from the suspicion of being inspired by Shell in his advice to the Libyans. He was, in fact, a splendid person completely devoted to his new Libyan masters - and even the most suspicious of the oil companies accepted his integrity - and was invaluable to us all, Libyans and oilmen.

The first meeting of the Oil Law Committee took place on 1 November 1954. Shell had sent Charles Saville, their Legal Adviser, to keep me on the right lines. On the proposal of Anis Qasim I was elected, nem con, as permanent chairman and representative of the oil companies for the Arabic tent. The Libyans were extremely conscientious on this matter and I spent many hours with Government scribes working out amendments to the Arabic. For I must explain that at our first meeting a draft text in English and Arabic was produced with the Libyan Government request that the Oil Law Committee should study and discuss the document clause by clause. This we did intently over a period of some 10 months.

The Libyan draft had been carefully prepared (Hogenhuis's advice was available just in time to ensure this) and although we went through the document with a tooth comb and some important alterations in wording were made together with a few addenda, even the most critical oil company (and I seem to remember this was Compagnie Francaise des Petroles) could find nothing fundamentally wrong with the Libyan draft; moreover, the oil companies found them very ready to make amendments of detail, particularly when points of inter-company competition were concerned. Of course all those present knew that Shell had made application for a concession both before and immediately after the declaration of Libyan Independence and great importance was attached to the clause in the draft law which laid down that only applications for concessions made *after* the enactment of the Petroleum Law would be considered: of course Shell expected this and the Chairman (myself) had to smile a wry smile at the unanimity of the meeting on this point. Of course we were discussing the English draft of the Law. The accuracy of the Arabic version was left to Anis Qasim in conference with me. I insisted on the inclusion of Philip Bradburne, a fluent scholar of Arabic employed by Mobiloil, to assist.

The meetings of this committee, sometimes daily, sometimes at longer intervals, often heated (especially in the hot weather) enabled, nay compelled, us representatives of the oil companies to know the intentions of the Libyan Government and their own competitors. As will be seen the Government were the first to offend!

In May the areas in which Concessions would be offered to the oil companies were circulated to us by the Libyan Government; this was the first real step towards the search for oil in Libya. I sent these at once to London for determination by the geology department in London and the Hague as to our general preferences.

After the information about areas there was of course a great deal of discussion between companies and a general interchange of views on selected localities. It was very apparent that secrecy and even hostility between oil companies seemed already to be fading away while we waited for the final areas to be allotted. We met a lot of new faces and life took on a more business-like turn.

The end of the year 1955 was a remarkably busy season. Quite apart from the comings and goings of the company representatives on oil business, I made several visits to London and the Hague, and was thankful that my Headquarters were in Europe and not across the Atlantic. On one of these visits I learned that as soon as the Anglo Saxon Concessions had been granted, my place in Libya would be taken by a technical General Manager, but that Shell had something up their sleeve to keep me in their employment! They proposed to send out a temporary replacement for me in Libya in the person of Noel Yule, a charming person who paid a visit in December 1955 involving a short trip to Cyrenaica.

Returning to the matter of oil, the Libyan Government handed to Noel Yule and me the details of the concessions allotted to the Anglo Saxon Petroleum Company on 11 January 1956. They conformed with our requests in number, size and locality - we should not, in fact did not, take them all up, but were satisfied with the Libyan Government's response to our requests. But we had heard, early on the same morning, of a blatant departure from the law and practice which we had all so patiently discussed for the past year. There was a particular anticline in Cyrenaica (an anticline is a geological feature, generally apparent on the surface under which the presence of oil is quite probable). The anticline in question was well known and had been the subject of discussion at our conference, as a result of which it had been decided unanimously that it should be excluded from the first distribution of concessionary areas, after which four or six small triangular areas should be delineated, leaving the centre of the anticline's surface as the peak, and that the four or six areas should be allotted by a public lottery among such oil companies as cared to compete. In the event the areas had been allotted to four oil companies, who shall be nameless, who so the story went, had been prepared to pay £40,000 for the prize. Whether money passed or not was not confirmed, but the allotment was so blatantly unjust and contrary to the whole spirit of our combined deliberations and agreements that, after confirmation that the allotment had indeed been made in this manner, I could see no prospect of the future performance of the Libyan Government regarding oil. Thus I cabled Shell *en clair*: "Strongly advise you to withdraw from all negotiations with the Libyan Government concerning oil".

Shell London took the cable very well but not my advice - they told me that, while they understood well the basic reasoning of my advice, they could not afford to withdraw from exploration and exploitation in a country where the presence of oil seemed so certain. In the event all Shell's concessionary areas produced dry wells and they were forced to buy their way into partnership with other successful companies.

My disingenuous advice made no difference to the directors' wishes to offer me further employment which turned out to be, much to my surprise and delight, Managing Director of Pakistan Shell Oil Company, an exploration company already in process of formation to search for oil in Pakistan.

I must complete the Libyan story before sailing for Karachi.

Noel Yule and I received our concessionary areas on 11 January 1956 and I made no bones about my personal disgust at the anticline business both to Anis Qasim with whom I had worked so closely and the Prime Minister, Mustafa bin Halim, who had succeeded Mahmud Muntasser, who was undoubtedly involved in the disreputable deal. Let me add here that the companies who paid the bribes gained nothing: no portion of the anticline produced oil.

I had let it be known that my job in Libya with Anglo Saxon Petroleum Company would come to an end as soon as we began exploration. I resigned as Chairman of the Tripoli Beach Club and later arrived at the Club as Father Christmas mounted on a camel to start the children's 1955 Christmas party and received a charming farewell gift from the committee (on my desk as I write these words). Noel Yule, my temporary replacement, had arrived and taken over after farewells to Prime Minister and Anis Qasim. There was a spate of farewell dinner and cocktail parties. Diana, Julian, Sylvia and I gave our farewell drinks party for 118 people to include all our official and personal friends. We paid a farewell visit to Leptis Magna where Julian, Anne Skeet and I traced the Roman fresh water aqueduct (underground) from Wadi Caw to Leptis, an interesting discovery walk of 15 miles. After a final assault on the locust swarms then attacking the Tripoli countryside Julian and Sylvia ended their farewell to Libya en route to England - Julian to Cambridge where he had been in residence at Christ's College since October 1954, Sylvia to Lady Margaret Hall, Oxford where she had spent one term, and Meriel still to St Swithun's School, Winchester.

I found that the house was not required until March for my successor, the technical Managing Director Evangoulof was not due until then. I so deferred my final departure and procured Shell's permission to keep the house in my name and as a splendid winter residence for my mother whom we left in the caring hands of her companion, Veronica Huthwaite, with Philip Bradburne and Hugh Cruddas, both of whom were houseless, as guardians. They were delighted, my mother had a wonderful winter residence and two devoted young men as guardians (and Philip was an excellent and ardent pianist, and Shell paid the rent!) Diana, Anne Skeet and I motored home in our private car from Rome via Siena and Luca in Italy and thence to the Loire where, even in winter, the chateaux and the country were good to see. In UK I went to hospital for a successful and not unpleasant hernia operation by Sir Arthur Porritt (who later became Governor General of New Zealand - one of my great claims to fame!). The "great freeze snow" of 1956 coincided with my internment in King Edward VII hospital but this did not prevent Diana from her usual busy social life in London: she saw a great deal of her elder brother Richard (who was reporting squash racquets competitions for the Times).

It was not until early March 1956 that Diana and I returned to Tripoli the very last time. We found my mother and Veronica Huthwaite in excellent health (glad to have avoided the great freeze in UK). Noel Yule had guarded Anglo Saxon interests well and had made all preparations for the arrival of George Evangoulof who arrived on 19 March to direct the Exploration and, hopefully, Development, company. I and Noel Yule spent a week introducing him to the Libyan Government and the oil companies. Noel Yule arranged a large cocktail party at the Waddan Hotel to introduce him socially and we felt that the future of Shell Libya was in good hands - as indeed proved to be the case.

Diana and I had a bad 48 hours packing our furniture (especially the piano!) but finally left in two instalments, Granny flying through the night and arriving in Teddington restless and shaken but quick to recover, and I following next morning to be with her and her two sisters, Aunt Mat and Aunt Grace, in Crieff House who, bless them, saw to it that her surroundings should seem familiar by their presence (both had reached the age of 90!). For the next two weeks Diana and I visited Crieff House almost daily and found my mother quickly accommodating her 96 years to their new and very English surroundings.

I had spent most of my mornings at St Helen's Court learning about the job in Pakistan and on 4 April flew to Karachi.

The theatre, Sabratha, 1952

Visiting troglodyte dwelling with Mudir of Cabao, 1953

The family with Granny Lush, summer 1954

The family with Anne Skeet and Miss Osborne, Piazza Medaglie d'Oro, 1953

LIBYA

Above: MSL with Prime Minister of Libya, Mustafa ben Halim, 1955

Left: Granny Lush in 1953

Baharistan, on arrival, 1956

Baharistan, with garden matured

Above:
Surveying by air in the East Wing, 1959

PAKISTAN

Right:
Giandari drilling site, 1958

Below:
Family Sunday at the beach hut, with Anne Skeet, Douglas Bader, Ann Leslie and others, 1959

CHAPTER 16

PAKISTAN
Managing Director, Pakistan Shell Oil Company
July 1956 - May 1959

My first personal contact with Pakistan Shell Oil Company was in April 1956 when I flew to Karachi to find Bill Higgins, an old friend from Qatar days in 1952, and his wife staying in the Hotel Metropole where I joined them for 10 days. Bill Higgins was Shell's diplomatic expert who was putting finishing touches to negotiations for exploration licences with the Pakistan Government. Negotiations had been continuing for two years and the Concession Agreement was signed in May 1956.

I myself did not take part even in the final stages of the negotiations and left before the signing of the Agreement - after all my very appointment depended on that Agreement. But I was able to learn from Bill Higgins the story of the last stages of the negotiations and the general attitude of the Pakistan negotiators. Although there existed one oilfield in Western Pakistan (Attock) this had come to production during imperial times and the Pakistan Government had no experience of post war oil production; but the pre-Partition oil legislation had effect and was probably the basis of Pakistani thought.

Higgins was also able and very ready to make introductions of both myself and Charles Mackay who as Technical Manager elect was also in Karachi, very busy with operational planning. We both met at various meetings and parties organised by Higgins and his lady wife, all the people who mattered among whom I was delighted to find a few friends from my visits for IRO in 1950. I quote from a letter MSL 8.4.56 to DRL. "Bill & Helen Higgins have been amazingly kind but, my word, what a life they lead! I was spun into the local night club two hours after arrival. One dines at 10 and beds at about 3." I did not mention the inevitable "horse's neck" (or two) with which those two invariably broke their fast, even in the temperatures of Karachi. I wrote encouragingly about the Hotel Metropole where "Bill has very kindly booked me into a room with air-conditioning which was pleasant but which I have turned off."

I formed a very good impression of Charles Mackay, (Technical Manager) who had come ahead of final agreement to make initial and very necessary arrangements for the various work parties who were to arrive in Pakistan following an Agreement. In this field Mackay had made excellent progress and had found good flats and houses - including one for his Managing Director.

I was able to see it and the owner thereof - the wife of the Pakistani Ambassador to the Shah of Persia - Begum Raga. She was a most charming person and willing to convert a building constructed as two flats into one mansion, for the sake of enticing the Shell Company as tenant. Of course it *was* a mansion but we took the house; Begum Raga played the game over house and garden, and we spent 3 very happy years in "Baharistan".

Photographs of the house and garden taken before occupation give the impression of a property requiring some years of residence before the possibility of becoming home-like. The snapshot of the garden, however, one year later in 1957 shows a lawn, abundance of flowers and trees with shrubs and creepers hiding the rather stark stucco walls. We were comfortable and happy in the house and were able easily to accommodate our family of 5 (at times) and Anne Skeet who had consented to come to Pakistan with us as my PA, for all 3 of our children spent quite lengthy periods with us fulfilling what I had always promised them - and warned my employers - that wherever we found ourselves overseas, there would be their home. Moreover it was the policy of Shell to see that their senior staff were comfortably housed especially in inclement climates, and Karachi certainly attained a full measure of discomfort.

We departed wholly, however, from Shell practice in the way of travel for we had chosen to journey to Karachi by sea. Both Diana and I needed a period of enforced immobility and we both loved sea travel - memories of journeys to and from the Sudan had ingrained in us a liking for ocean liners. We persuaded Anne Skeet to come with us by holding out the carrot of seeing *en route* her brother, Ian, then in Shell Cairo - for her, the only bright 24 hours in a horribly dull 18 days on RMS Circassia of the Anchor Line. In that good ship we sailed from Liverpool on 16 June 1956 having dined and spent the previous evening at the Royal Festival Hall whence we took a rather surprised but very charming American couple all round the City of London, rising but not yet risen from the ashes of the war. We packed, sorted and tidied all night; after hot baths I cooked breakfast and Julian, Alan and Betty Moreton helping with 3 cars, drove to Euston with 33 pieces of luggage en-route for Liverpool where we embarked. An uneventful voyage except for Anne who, after my impassioned plea to the Captain over the dinner table, was allowed to leave ship at Port Said, see Ian and rejoin her at Suez. We arrived at Karachi port in early July and were met by Charles Mackay; all our gear including grand piano, Standard car and countless cases were processed through customs and we were driven to the Hotel Metropole where we had an air-conditioned suite. Noon temperature was a damp 103 degrees but monsoon rain sometimes brought it down to 90 degrees. There we lived for 4 weeks during which Sylvia joined us after 5 days and helped Diana mightily in the move to our house - Baharistan - interspersed with several introductory parties, official for us both and feminine for Diana to meet wives. We found in those 4 weeks immense kindness and hospitality, official and private, Pakistani and western, which gave us great confidence.

Our first month in Karachi cannot be ranked among the happiest of times of our career. The monsoon brought rain, heat, humidity and discomfort. Life in an hotel is always monotonous and in the drab Metropole of Karachi, so different from the smart Waddan of sunny Tripoli, the monotony was too often broken only by "Karachi tummy" from which only Diana escaped. The Pakistani bearer was somehow different from our Arab servants and we did not speak the language. Karachi was an untidy muddle.

July 1956

Here I was in Karachi, Pakistan, Managing Director of Pakistan Shell Oil Co., at the head of a very live and busy exploration company in a country where oil was already being produced in small quantities and in one locality. Why? I quote from a subsequent handbook "First Steps in the Search for Oil" given to visitors to our first rig:

> "Assessment of the general geology of Pakistan had been carried out by the Royal Dutch Shell Group before they decided to start negotiations with the Pakistan Government for an Agreement mutually satisfactory to the authorities and the Company. Negotiations continued for two years and an Agreement was signed in May 1956 under which the Company was granted exploration licences over four areas, each of 5000 sq. miles - two in West and two in East Pakistan."

A group of Pakistan private investors needed to be found to invest in and form the Board of the local holding company to be established under the terms of the Agreement (Petroleum Development Pakistan). The Board of the operating company (Pakistan Shell Oil Company) was established with six Directors representing Shell interests 75% and two Directors from P D P representing 25%.

Management and technical staff began to arrive in June 1956 and, directed from two rooms in the Hotel Metropole, Karachi, the venture was soon under way.

My first job after arriving in Karachi was to find that group of Pakistani private investors and an extremely hard task I found it. I forget how many lakhs of rupees I hoped to collect but wringing water from a stone was easy compared with persuading a Pakistani statesman or businessman to stretch for his cheque book. I naturally went for advice to Norman Leslie of Burmah Shell and Forsyth of the Chartered Bank: both were, of course, helpful but held out little hope of my collecting much. Forsyth called a meeting of industrialists and financiers at his Bank at which I did my best to interest them in the venture but to no avail or, shall we say, to little avail for I eventually managed to persuade 4 influential Pakistanis including Wajid Ali and Feroz Khan Noon, to invest. It was one of the most unpleasant and unsuccessful duties I ever had to perform for Shell and it spread itself all through my first year. The Pakistani's point of view was clear enough. "Shell wants our money. We want Shell's oil. When Shell produces the oil we will gladly invest - but money is too short, our country needs it for so many other projects that we do not feel that it is reasonable to ask us to provide large sums for a gamble at this time."

The last 5 months of 1956 saw us digging in both as a company and as a family. As a company, regional (i.e. Pakistani) staff were recruited; office, staff houses, garages and materials yards were rented and by October 1956, geological, seismic and gravity survey parties were operating in the field both in West and East Pakistan. Geological surveys explored and mapped the exposed surface of the ground in the areas allotted to us. They also collect fossils for study by palaeontologists; later we had a palaeontological section at work in Karachi. Seismic surveys explored and mapped the underground geological structures - a fascinating process based on the principles of radar and echo sounding. I made it my business to visit some of these survey parties at work but was careful not to delay the urgency of their very technical work.

All this preliminary survey work in itself demanded a large amount of transport and materials all of which was imported through Karachi and Chittagong. Areas and go-downs had to be found or erected to house the materials. At one point a Shell helicopter arrived by ship and required assembling near the quays. I remember shuddering at the apparently diminutive size of the bolts and nuts which secured the rotar blades, but I flew happily in her later. We needed one at our rig site in West Pakistan and I think there was a second in operation in the Eastern sector. (I will write about our operations in the Bay of Bengal and Chittagong later).

Our brochure had these paragraphs:

> "The large bulk of the specialised equipment used directly or indirectly in the search has to be imported - from geological hammers to the huge 26" diameter drilling bit - all has to be brought into the country.
>
> "The materials department has the responsibility for seeing that equipment and spares are ordered, received, guided through the thorny path of licences

and customs and finally delivered to the party concerned exactly on schedule. Oil exploration brooks no delay."

Mackay seldom came to see me for assistance at high levels, though there were occasional incidents when Ministerial intervention was needed at the port or on the question of wages and conditions of our very numerous Pakistani staff. It was not difficult to approach the Ministers but their inefficiency was grotesque and one was compelled to find a senior civil servant who could really achieve some results. But we must go back to 1956 and our earlier days in Karachi. I naturally called on the President, Iskander Merza, and had a most friendly and interesting interview in which we talked about practically everything except Pakistan and oil. Those two subjects were left to a second and perhaps more serious conversation. We discovered that both of us had started life as soldiers in the UK, I at the "Shop" in 1915, he at Sandhurst five years later. He, in fact, was the first Sandhurst cadet from the continent of India to be gazetted into the British Army when he joined the Cameronians in Poona in 1921. He joined the Indian Political service five years later and served in many places, including Peshawar and Khyber Pass, for 20 years when he joined the Indian Ministry of Defence in which he served until Partition when he, of course, came to Pakistan and became Acting Governor General in 1955 and the first President of the Federal Republic of Pakistan in 1956. I found him a very agreeable man, I judged him to be a first class administrator (I did not then know his full record). He listened carefully to my dissertation on the search for oil and promised all possible help from his Government. Pleasant rather than powerful, a good leader in times of peace, yet he was uncertain in the face of a political crisis needing wisdom and power.

Within a week of my interview (DRL diary 31.8.56) "MSL, DRL, Julian, Sylvia and Meriel attended a luncheon party for 12 in the President's house - present President Iskander Merza, his son aged 28 married to an American girl (she not present), the Governor of W Pakistan; Ghurmani, Minister of Communications Frontier Regions, Dr Khan Sahib, Minister of Finance, Sirdar Abder Rashid, General Mohammed Ayub Khan, Commander in Chief, Charles Mackay and a Naval ADC. Left at 3 p.m." It was a most friendly, almost family party for the Lushes to whom the Pakistan guests were also most affable - an attitude he always adopted to us during his Presidency. General Ayub was very forthcoming and told me that the President and he had returned from Baghdad only that morning where they had been "trying to mend the Baghdad Pact after the b.... mess caused by the British action at Suez".

I had, of course, called on the Prime Minister from September 1956, Hussain Shaheed Suhrawaddy, a Bengali Muslim of 54, a prominent Muslim leader in undivided India, educated in Calcutta and Oxford; organiser and President of the Awami League in Pakistan. Officially I had little to do with him, but one met the little man at every party organised in Karachi especially if there were any chance of dancing. He was very fond of good music and I remember him coming to the dress rehearsal of a piano recital in our house given by one Shanti Seldon, a fine pianist; Suhrawaddy refused an invitation to the piano recital "because he had Canadian guests" but asked to attend the dress rehearsal; we therefore had asked an audience of young friends and our three staying in the house. He was a perfect guest and when Shanti Seldon had closed the piano he asked Diana "if we could roll up the carpet to have some dancing" and we and our guests danced until 2 a.m. Next evening, while Shanti Seldon was playing the first movement of a Beethoven Sonata I heard, to my horror, the wail of the Police siren approaching our house - the worst happened. The Prime Minister with his Canadian guests appeared and said that they had finished an early dinner in order to attend the piano recital. One does not refuse the Prime Minister of one's host country however *outre* may be his social demand, but I refused to let him go upstairs until the Sonata had been completed. He then more or less burst into our drawing room with many apologies to Diana, a tribute to the pianist who, after half-an-hour, continued her very excellent performance. Suhrawaddy really enjoyed her playing and sent her flowers next day. But when she had left our house - more or less exhausted - the Prime Minister turned to Diana with almost a leer and taking off his dinner jacket, displaying thereby a beautifully embroidered waistcoat, he said to her: "Now, my dear lady, may we roll up the carpet." And so we and our more elderly musical friends were compelled to accede to the preposterous demand and danced again, this time until 3 a.m. Luckily we had a houseful of young people - and we allowed the sage and elderly to slip away.

To Diana's and my intense relief Suhrawaddy was dismissed from office soon after and replaced by Malik Feroz Khan Noon, a Pakistan aristocrat, whose family had owned property near Lahore for generations He described himself as a lawyer and a politician and had been in Punjab and Indian politics since he came down from Wadham, Oxford in 1917. But he had filled many important official posts in undivided India. He was High Commissioner for India 1936-41, on the Viceroy's Council 1941-45; Indian member of the British War Cabinet 1944-45; he was extremely shocked by Partition but became a member of the Pakistan Constituent Assembly and was appointed Governor of East Pakistan in 1950, a post he had just vacated when I first met him. I persuaded him to take shares in Pakistan Shell in which he forthwith always showed a great interest, although he devolved the interest in oil onto his son, Nur Khan Noon, who had spent his early youth on the farm. He was a member of various international bodies such as the International Labour Organisation and had published several books (in English). Diana and I with Meriel and Anne visited the extensive family property at Noorpurnoon, Tahsil Bhalwal, Sarghoda District, whither we were taken from Lahore for a very happy 24 hours on New Year's Day 1958. Here was a large estate owned by the Noon family where we met Malik Feroz Khan Noon's first wife, a most charming (old) lady and many of the family that evening. We slept in the guest rooms of the family home and were wonderfully entertained by Noor. Next morning we had log fires in our bedroom and a splendid country dinner in this farm centre; we saw cotton cultivation, the ginnery and lastly were given a large case of grapefruit.

Another good friend of ours, who always gave us the hospitality of his house at Nasheman, Lahore, was Said Muratib Ali who was a Knight of the British Realm, a leading industrialist, also a Director of the State Bank of Pakistan and Director of countless industrial concerns. He put no money into Pakistan Shell but he was uncommonly generous to their Managing Director and his staff. Not an easy man in conversation, but very direct and helpful in advice.

Wajid Ali, another industrialist, was also a Director of various industries including Pakistan Shell, was most friendly and helpful in every way. I remember at one of our Board meetings the rupee salaries of our top staff came under review: our financial member had made allowance for Pakistani income tax which was very high and thus increased our estimates for staff salaries to almost astronomical figures. "I cannot think" interposed Wajid Ali at one point "why we are so concerned with Income Tax - I never pay it."

The family whose friendship I renewed from my earlier visits to Pakistan and who maintained that friendship ever since was the Cowasjee family headed by Rustom Cowasjee.

Rustom Cowasjee was one of the first industrialists whom I approached with the invitation to take up shares in Pakistan Shell. He was the head, indeed the founder, of the Pakistan Shipping Line whose ships ran an important and regular freight service from Karachi to Dacca and Chittagong in East Pakistan. He listened with interest to my persuasions to join the company financially but I failed to attract his money (he nevertheless invested subsequently in the Refinery which was erected after my time). But his failure to invest in my company did not reduce his friendship and hospitality.

This was one family who gave to all of us, young and old, friendship and hospitality, warm and generous, which brought great happiness to us during our service in Pakistan and continued throughout the many years since we left Pakistan. In 1950 when I first visited Karachi on behalf of IRO, I had received great kindness from the three sons of Rustom Cowasjee; they always chided me for sleeping throughout a cinema film to which they had taken me.

The brothers were Ardeshir, who managed the shipping part of his father's family business. Ardeshir was a highly educated, very competent man, artistic and a lover of beauty, as was his charming wife, Nancy, a doctor, who had given him two children. Their house in Mary Road was full of exquisite things, typical of their ideals. The second son of the family was Cowajee R F Cowasjee, generally known as John, who lived alone separated from his first wife; he later married Vera, an archaeologist. He had been educated in England at Repton School and had adored his years there and English ways in general; he was neither slow nor silent in expressing his admiration for most things English and he was, by nature, most generous hearted. This quality seemed to bubble over in his kindness to our family, and our three children and Anne seemed to be the particular objects of his kindness - sailing, fishing, hunting, and parties were organised by him for their delight, and he was full of help and good advice to their parents.

Cyrus, the youngest son, looked after the local interests of the family business and though we did not see so much of him, we liked him immensely. Mrs Cowasjee was kind enough to accept us into her Parsee family and many were the luncheons which we attended - meeting the numerous members, especially the women, of that large and generous hearted family.

It was of course extremely pleasant to find that the Pakistanis with whom we had to deal not only spoke the same language, in a domestic as well as in a linguistic way, and were able to mix and did mix perfectly naturally with Europeans in their houses. So far as dress was concerned, the Pakistani womenfolk in their beautiful saris, worn with great elegance, added a touch - nay more, a flood - of beauty to any party. A sari is a unique form of dress which can, and probably should be, worn with almost total abandon, thus rendering it to appear the most simple and perfect covering to the wearer's figure. And most Pakistani women knew perfectly the degree of abandonment to adopt. Some saris were most beautifully decorated with jewels, others with embroidery skilfully interwoven. Pakistani memsahibs were generally very talented and ready to add their knowledge and charm to the general wheal and no party was allowed to be dull when they were present. I think Diana and I - and especially our young family and their friends - seldom came away from a Pakistani evening or closed one of our entertainments where Pakistani couples had been present without the sincere comment "what a good party".

Sir Laurence Grafftey Smith, the first British High Commissioner for Pakistan wrote (*Houses to Play*, 1975): "Before Partition Karachi was a clean little provincial town, with a population of under half a million. It had importance as a port serving a prosperous agricultural hinterland, but it lay out of the mainstream of life on the perimeter of a backwater province. Within a matter of weeks, it was invaded by nearly a million unhappy refugees, over a hundred thousand of whom were for years to have no home except the pavement." The refugees were certainly there in 1956, increased in numbers, and their shacks now occupied large settlement areas and even the central division of any dual carriageway in or near the town. The smell was often unbearable especially in the neighbourhood of a creek connected with the harbour where twice daily the sewage was pushed to and fro by the high tide and swirled around the dwellings. The main mode of transport for goods from the harbour consisted of low carts with rubber tyres pulled by camels - not the sweetest smelling animal itself. It was the common belief that Pakistan refused to alter their rule of the road from left to right because it was known that the camels would never conform thereto.

In the ten years since Partition a greater effort had been made both by the Government and industry to enlarge the areas in and around the original town both for industry for the accommodation of the thousands who poured into the place on governmental and other business, and for military families (never forgetting that the army might be called out at any moment to deal with a most unstable political and civil situation). Some of the old hands e.g. the Standard Bank, retained pre-Pakistan offices, but a good deal of rather haphazard new building had been completed in the main part of the city with apparently little coordinated town planning. The ever increasing Diplomatic Corps and the Government and municipal employees had a special area set aside for their accommodation called the Public Employees Corporate Housing Society in which certain large foreign firms were also allotted either land on which to build or dwelling houses which they could inhabit. Thus Charles Mackay had secured for our European staff several blocks of flats in this area - which was well outside the city itself, on high ground leading to the Karachi International Airport. The flats were habitable with drains and water systems already established but as can be imagined, the organisation was by no means stable: our piped fresh water supply for instance generally petered out long before the tanks were filled but we seldom had to wait long - a couple of hours or so - before an enormous water tank would arrive to finish the job. I was sometimes rather ashamed at the priority given to Managing Directors over the employees in P E C H S. We maintained a permanent electric cable which could be connected with our closest neighbours - and there was a good deal of illicit neighbourly sharing.

One of the reasons for our most favoured nation treatment was due to our landlady, Begum Reza. The Begum herself was a very intelligent and (financially) ambitious woman. She was delighted to think that Shell of London could be her tenant and from the beginning did everything in her power to see that the Managing Director was made comfortable and was satisfied. She might be sitting on a wonderful income from her house for years to come if oil were found. We therefore found that she herself or her brother or agents were constant visitors and willing helpers in the first few months of our tenancy and indeed throughout our stay in Karachi; when she found what I was prepared to do for her garden, her joy was overwhelming and her cooperation unbounded.

Baharistan

What kind of house was this - Baharistan - which I had agreed to rent from Begum Reza for 3 years, with a possible second contract on behalf of Shell?

My first description to DRL written in April 1956 ran "There is no doubt that it is a lovely house situated on high ground with no possibility of further building at the back. The house itself is a mansion." (7 bedrooms, 6 bathrooms, 2 reception rooms over 50 feet in length and covering 950 sq. feet).

The house which indeed looked large was built in three blocks having its frontage on a wide arc of a circle, built as two large apartments one above the other. The southern and narrowest block contained the front door, vestibule and wide marble staircase. (It was terrifying to watch the Chinese removal men lifting the grand piano up this flight of stairs with a 180 degree turn!) At the back were large kitchen, pantry and laundry rooms extensively fitted with sinks and concrete slabs and shelves. On the west side were two smallish rooms (fitted bathrooms) which became my study and Anne's room.

In the centre, slightly set back were two very large rooms 54' x 19' feet, one on each floor. Each room had a large window at the west end, and contained 25 electric points. Shell furnishing department thought nothing of the size of the rooms and provided two splendid movable curtains to divide the lower room into a breakfast room and dining room, and the upstairs room into a splendid cool and serviceable drawing room, with a secluded portion behind this lovely curtain containing the grand piano. Neither the instrument nor the music were normally seen or heard - but with the curtain parted a very adequate reception or recital room was formed. It was very satisfying to find that our furniture was adequate for this large wall and floor space, and that the room on a normal night was almost cosy and for a reception or recital quite admirable.

To the north of both these large central rooms were 2 double and 4 single (often converted into double) bedrooms each with its bathroom and closet. Every bedroom had windows on west and east sides providing a courant d'air, for air conditioning was by no means available nor considered necessary in the 1950s!

On the west of these six bedrooms was a magnificent sun veranda 30' long. It was fitted with louvre windows and could be used either as an extension to the big central rooms or by the occupants of the bedrooms. In addition the two principal bedrooms had their own private sun parlour on the east of the building.

Very adequate servants quarters and garages (3) were provided in the wide space to the east of the house where there was also adequate room for a flower nursery, a space for motor vehicles and clothes lines.

The garden of a quarter to half an acre was bereft of any soil when we took the house. It was clear from the beginning that more soil was essential and the number of large lorries containing both soil and water for the garden was legion. Our landlady had already begun by planting a small tree or a bougainvillaea here and there. Diana, Anne and I really got to work on the job: we resurfaced the whole area, we planted 600 seedlings in pots in the back yard and 6000 in the new beds and Diana must have wearied entering into her diary the daily message "MSL gardened p.m." Tennis and squash were available at the Sind Club and elsewhere for the young, but I spent most of my spare time in that half acre in front of Baharistan.

Sylvia and Meriel had joined us in the Hotel during July and they joined Diana in the most hectic month of designing, ordering, purchasing and installing furniture, soft furnishings and the lighting system (the 22 rooms absorbed 150 bulbs) and engaging servants in monsoon weather. We moved into Baharistan on 4 August 1956 and had our first dinner party (for 10!) there within 7 weeks of our arrival in Karachi. It is true that 6 of those ten were the Lush family plus Anne, for Julian had arrived having trekked overland from Beirut by bus to Teheran. We had a very happy family month of September with all six, ending with a large party for Meriel at which half the young element were extremely charming Pakistanis. Just before her departure Meriel was able to watch, with us, the extraordinary sight of scores of female turtles emerging from the sea on a moonlight night, scrambling at a deliberate gait across the beach to a stretch of hot sand, there unhurriedly digging shallow depressions in the sand and almost immobile, laying their scores of eggs and carefully covering them before, this time, making a rather hurried return to the sea.

We also had a largish cocktail party to meet Group Captain Douglas Bader and Thelma his courageous wife who were staying with us. He had flown himself his Shell light aircraft from London, continuing further east. Diana always tells the story that last thing at night, outside the Bader's bedroom door stood his shoes *and* legs for cleaning. They were both charming on this and their second visit in 1958. Of course he had many calls on his time, with which he was most generous paying especial attention to the young Pakistani Clubs and Associations.

In the meantime Pakistan Shell had moved into a newly (and badly) built high rise office near the harbour called Qamar House and here I finally made my own office and the Board Room. For gradually a few Pakistanis were prepared to risk their money in an oil venture and I became more satisfied that our initial outlay on the social side was bearing fruit.

Karachi - 1956

Karachi of course became of necessity our home town and Baharistan, therein, the centre of our existence. Once we had established ourselves in the house and garden, that centre became a very gay and cheerful place generally filled with guests and for much of the time young people - our own three who, bless them, gave us practically the whole of their school holidays or university vacations and bringing with them their friends. Sarah Campbell Taylor, Jane Catterall, Celia Hensman, Winifred Borthwick - to mention only a few of our lovely young visitors who gave enormous pleasure and added greatly to the fame of Baharistan. Nor can one ever forget their guide, their adviser and confessor, the organiser not only of innumerable official Shell parties, but of so many meetings and expeditions, Anne Skeet, my quite imperturbable PA who herself found her future happiness in the person of one of the nicest collection of hard working young Britons I have ever met in a foreign community, Bill Lindsell. Normally Diana and I would have kept our entertainment to the senior stratum of official or commercial communities: having for a great part of our sojourn in Pakistan some of our young family with us, they encouraged us to invite, in addition, the younger members of Pakistan and western society - and what an attractive addition they formed! Nowhere in very personal entries in Diana's diaries covering those 3 years in Baharistan can I remember any comment other than delight at these young people.

Of course in addition to social gatherings there were more serious outlets to our spare time: there were various British and Pakistan societies and hospital work; the British Council and the Pakistan University organised lectures and debates. The Sind Club provided the usual athletic amenities and a few interesting meetings but was not the centre of social gaiety to which we had transformed our Beach Club in Tripoli. The Dramatic Society was a flourishing concern: Diana took part in several productions and proved that she had not lost the dramatic art which had earned her high honours at the Royal Academy of Dramatic Art before our marriage. She excelled particularly in almost her first performance in Karachi by carrying a play to a successful "curtain" when the chief male actor quite failed to learn his part (which Diana spoke for him!) Her appearance as Lady Elizabeth in the "Confidential Clerk" earned from the critics "The most difficult role in the whole play is that of Lady Elizabeth and Mrs Diana Lush lives up to it with admirable versatility. In this delightful study, we were irresistibly reminded of Miss Edith Evans." She next appeared as Alicia in Black Chiffon the notice of which read: "Black Chiffon - a triumph for Mrs Diana Lush in a very difficult part."

The Karachi Yacht Club was the great centre for, I would dare say, the majority of Karachi families of all nationalities and our young people used it with great enjoyment. We owned a sailing dingy "Mistral" which, though she did not distinguish herself greatly in the innumerable races in which Anne Skeet and our children and young guests sailed her, gave good account of herself and afforded tremendous fun. I myself am not a keen sailor for I have always found the endless racing and competitive spirit not to my taste: moreover, in Karachi I was completely wedded to that garden at Baharistan in which I dug and planted and mowed to my heart's content. Diana and Anne and indeed all the family, when present, gave me ungrudging support with the result that a number of our social parties took place in our garden amongst some lovely young flowering trees, bushes and creepers (five varieties of bougainvillaeas) against the walls to say nothing of an avenue of tomatoes leading up to the front door! I admit I was lavish with money to lay the foundations of the garden by the purchase of permanent shrubs and trees, but the rest of the garden was grown at my expense. I even purchased, myself, 600 flower pots in which my seedlings started life - which, at certain seasons, had all to be moved into or out of the sun, twice daily!

We were all regular attendants at Holy Trinity Church in Karachi at both services in the morning (H.C. and Matins). The vicar, Rev Crouch, was well known to us but never became a close friend. He and his wife were a self-effacing couple; Crouch himself was a sick man: he had trouble in his throat which rendered him nearly speechless, especially when he tried to intone. Soon after our arrival in Karachi, having listened to a good deal of sympathetic criticism from other members of the congregation who were honestly trying to raise our Sunday worship to something better, I and the organist suggested that I should intone firstly the response and then the office prayers, leaving Crouch to preach the sermon: this gave him the opportunity of facing his congregation with a clear, if not strong, voice. This explains the weekly entry in DRL's diary "MSL took Matins". I cannot remember ever preaching a sermon in Karachi - that was a penance which I reserved for life in retirement in England.

I realised during those three years in Karachi how greatly the British professional or businessman (and woman) appreciated the continuing background, once a week, of an ordinary Christian form of worship and how much they were prepared to give, of themselves and their charity, to maintain this. In Libya the Church had been organised by the British soldiers on military lines and, there, some British (by no means the majority) were grateful and happy to partake. Here in Karachi I think a remnant of the spirit of the British Raj made that help more significant - and the Moslem leaders and population were well aware of it.

1957

By the beginning of 1957 work was going well ahead in the preliminary stages of Pakistan Shell Oil's activities. Naturally many of the uninitiated thought that after 6 months in the country any respectable oil company would have a rig in operation: they had a great deal to learn about the intense exploration necessary over wide areas before that stage could be considered. There was little realisation, even among the Government officials, of the careful and patient research and co-relation of all the data from geological, geophysical and palaeontological studies which are essential preliminaries and that teams of scientific personnel must spend months in the field and in laboratories in order to arrive at an accurate determination of the best spot in which to drill for oil. Since September 1956 such parties, headed by the geologists, had been at work in the very inhospitable waterless desert in which our area in western Pakistan was situated (roughly the immense triangle having as its northern base an imaginary line joining Multan and Quetta and its sides the railway line Sukkur-Quetta and Sukkur-Multan). The geologists studied the exposed rock strata, described the different rock types and their structural position and collected fossils in the areas for examination. Their main task was a geological map. Pakistani geologists had also to be trained in this highly technical branch of field work. The geologists' results were studied by the seismic and palaeontology experts before the former could carry out seismic exploration to detect where the oil might be trapped - thousands of feet below the surface. In seismic prospecting energy waves were created by exploding a charge of dynamite at the bottom of a hole in the ground. The sound waves thus created travel downward and are reflected back to the surface by successive beds of rock and are detected by instruments. The magnified and amplified sound waves are recorded photographically and the results interpreted. Maps of the underground formations are constructed wherefrom possible subterranean formations can be detected which may or may not contain oil which has been trapped for millions of years: the certainty of the presence of oil can only be proved by drilling down to these formations. Throughout the hot season of 1956 these stalwart scientists prosecuted their quest in the grim surroundings of the desert south of Dera Ghazi Khan until they could with clear and scientific knowledge point to a place - a point in the stark treeless desert - in which they estimated oil might reasonably be found by drilling.

Well site - Giandari

Our experts finally decided that our first deep test well should be at a place called Giandari, a most barren and God-forsaken spot in the Suleiman Range of hills; it was 80 miles from Railhead Kashmor, end of a branch line to Multan about 200 miles away. The first and most important problem was that of access: how indeed were Mackay and his team to get to this desolate spot? How to transport the several thousand tons of material, including the rig itself, the hundreds of drilling pipes, the operating engine, to say nothing of living accommodation for some 40 men? "After careful reconnaissance" runs the brochure "a beginning was made in constructing the access road in November 1957. The road, 86 miles in length, was completed in February 1958, a great tribute to our contractors, the South Eastern Asia Drilling Company who also undertook this work." A large amount of heavy road building equipment was assembled for the work: heavy bulldozers, graders and water trucks were used and large gangs of men from the local Mazari tribe assisted by building stone river crossings and in conditioning the road. The Drilling Company did a magnificent job on this road and found themselves up against a particularly odious Collector (District Commissioner) in the area who, because of some accident where a Government telegraph pole was damaged, stopped all work on the road until a large sum of money was paid - a clear bid for a bribe. Luckily this was reported to me and I managed to have the work resumed at once and the Collector removed; a visit to the Governor at Multan was necessary. Having built the 83 miles of road they had to prepare a landing strip 12 miles from the location and a road thence to the rig. Our troubles were by no means over even then for although there was a water spring near to the rig, the water was found to be salt and useless for drilling purposes (a rig consumes about 120 tons daily); it was therefore necessary to lay a pipe line 33 miles from the nearest irrigation canal, fed by the Indus. We had great trouble during the operations at Giandari with the constant tapping of this water line by the local Mazari tribe whose women persuaded their menfolk to save them many miles of trudging through the sand to the distant wells, their normal fount of supply. The treatment of that pipe line reminded me of the British Army's petrol line through central Italy: leaks were deliberately made and we lost 10-20% en route! I must admit that I formed a very poor opinion of Pakistan's administration in those parts.

Thanks to the excellent work of the drilling company, we were able to "spud in" the Giandari well on 26 February 1958, a month ahead of schedule. Owing to the extremely difficult access even for aircraft, Charles Mackay did not arrange a spudding-in party but both Diana and I flew to the site together on 1 March 1958 to visit the camp, see the drill at work and meet the amazing men who form the drilling team who hired themselves out to oil companies all over the world. Rough lives they lived and loved (apparently), and they worked without ceasing, strong and wiry, apparently regardless but really very conscious of danger which they avoided by constant regard to the discipline of drilling routine. They lived hard: no alcohol on a rig site. They ate prodigiously and well and they stuck to their drill. What they did on their one week's leave every month nobody enquired - but we certainly had no complaints from the authorities.

Our official story runs:-

"A complete transformation has taken place in the location as the geologists left it. In a barren valley there has sprung up a village with a dozen air conditioned caravans and buildings comprising the offices, messing rooms, sleeping quarters and shower rooms of the drilling teams of expatriates and Pakistanis. Here you will see the store rooms and the storage tanks for fuel and water - and the mud and chemicals required for drilling.

"Here at last you will see the rig. It is an Oilwell 96" outfit, one of the best and most modern rigs yet devised by the oil industry. You will see but may not recognise the derrick and the ginpole, the hoisting winch, the draw works and the kelly, the casing head and the casing rack. You will be in the good hands of the tool pusher of the South Western Asia Drilling Company who are under contract to drill the hole for us.

"We had aimed at spudding in Giandari well by 1 April 1958, but have been able to improve on this by fully a month. This deep test will be drilled to between 10,000 and 12,000 feet and will explore formations not previously tested in this country."

I had visited the drilling site but this was my first visit to our drill at work. It was certainly not my last - I took out various parties of VIPs including the President Iskander Merza and various Pakistani notables, as well as my own High Commissioner and various members of his staff - and, it goes without saying, all the members of my family and important house guests.

I had little to do with the considerable organisation which all the above activity required and I must say I envied Charles Mackay and his very capable staff and longed to give more practical help. However that would have been quite wrong and I had to confine myself to being to hand when needed - e.g. a word to the Minister or Under Secretary involved when the Pakistan administrative wheel failed to revolve; to give an impression that Shell was dependable, knowledgeable, shrewd, capable and entirely honest as a company, by whom straight dealing was expected and returned; moreover a company whose leaders were experienced and capable but young in spirit - young and compassionate enough to understand the problems of a young country. For whereas most of the Pakistanis with whom I had to deal were in their last years of service after long careers in the British service in India, there were many young people in the field who were working with our young technical staff.

Karachi - 1957

Returning to the beginning of 1957, Diana and I had more or less settled into Baharistan and Diana had with great resolve and courage resolved to endure the haphazard, undisciplined and uncaring behaviour of our domestic staff who took every opportunity to avoid work and really had little loyalty to the house or household, but whose efforts just passed muster when we had guests especially when such people as the President or Prime Minister came to the house.

I have already described our first experience of entertaining the Prime Minister on two consecutive nights: by February we felt ready to entertain the President Iskander Mirza and his wife. Diana's diary for that day begins: "Pretty average hell of a day preparing for dinner party for President of Pakistan." It must be admitted that the first ten lines of that entry are concerned with hair coiffeurs of DRL and MSL and the assistance of a Mr Snodgrass who must have come as Master of Ceremonies for he borrowed my white dinner jacket. We had asked the Ambassador of the Netherlands (remembering Shell's dual Nationality), the Italian Ambassador and Signora Calisse (great friends), Amir Ali Faney (representative in Pakistan of the Aga Khan's 'takria'), two Pakistani industrialists, the technical and financial managers of Pakistan Shell, Charles Mackay and Bill Rivers and their wives, Anne Skeet who as usual had been the backbone of our assistance and Tony Hampshire of Metal Box, our chosen young friend. The President and his Begum with ADC and Lady in Waiting completed the tally of 26 people at table - and oh how grateful we were to the furnishing department of Shell who had insisted on our choosing two dozen plates of the most attractive Wedgwood turquoise dinner service and to the readiness of our chief guest in sipping our champagne. My memory of the evening is that our guests enjoyed themselves among friends but that we breathed a sigh (inaudible) of relief when (as Diana enters in her diary) Begum Mirza prevented her husband from playing bridge.

Diana records on the very next day that we held a cocktail party for 65 guests, of all nationalities, at which 3 Shell films were shown - "The Changing Earth", "The Search for Oil" and "The Rival World".

It was now time to turn my attention to other parts of western Pakistan. Our first visit was to Lahore where I have already described our visit to Feroz Khan Noon's estate. We were always the guests of either the Noon's or Sir Muratib Ali or Sayed Wajid Ali in Lahore and very wonderful hosts we found them. Lahore itself was a most refreshing place in which to stay; the climate was cool (sometimes cold) and dry, the people were lively and Lahore en fete always during the February Horse Show.

In February 1957 Diana and I with Anne Skeet accepted the invitation of Sir Muratib Ali to stay with him and his wife at Nasheman his estate to attend our first Lahore Horse Show. We decided to travel by car via Sukkur, where we spent two nights in the Circuit House, thanks to the Company of the Executive Engineer who arranged for "boiling hot water" for baths and made us most comfortable for two nights. In the intervening day we visited the ancient City of Mohenjadaro which lies 100 km from Sukkur and where we found the Curator of the Archaeological Department with whom we spent the whole day exploring the ancient city dating back to the Indus Civilization of 2500 BC. It was obviously a well planned city whose citizens had reached an advanced stage of learning with terra cotta covered drains and soak pits for sewage disposal. The West first heard of it in 1924 and since then Sir Mortimer Wheeler's many books on the Indus Civilization are the great authority. It had a language with 400 signs some of which are still to be deciphered. Shems el Haj el Tishti, the Curator, gave us his whole day and showed us the Museum as well as the City.

We set out next morning over the Lloyd Barrage, lunched on the Canal bank near Rahim ya khan and on to the Rest House at Khanewal. We slept in the Canal Rest House after cooking our own supper and next morning visited Harappa, a city which flourished in 3rd Century BC.

Next day we received a warm welcome from our host Sir Muratib Ali who with his wife and son were perfect hosts who not only gave us the hospitality of their house at Nasheman, 4 Farman Christian College, Gulberg, Lahore, but also introduced us to the Lahore Horse Show and the leaders thereof and took us to the many scenes of hospitality, luncheons, buffet suppers, receptions and even dances which were the concomitants of this annual festival.

First day	Large luncheon party given by Pakistani friends. Reception and films by Chief of BOAC. Dinner and dance at the famous Faletti's Hotel.
Second day	Official opening of Horse Show by C in C. Massed Pipe Bands: animal parades & jumping (animals included horses, bulls and camels). The bulls took part in the jumping! Large buffet luncheon by Muratib Ali. Polo matches - India v Pakistan. Dinner by C in C Police West Pakistan, President chief guest.
Third day	Prime Minister Suhrawaddy arrived in state; welcomed by massed bands. President & Prince Ali Khan at Horse Show. Large buffet luncheon by Gens Mohd Azam and Ayam Khan. Prince Ali Khan & MSL meet (first time since Libya 1943) Races. Buffet dinner party by Quizilbushi's and Gymkhana Club Dance.
Fourth day	MSL judged Children's hacks at Horse Show. Buffet luncheon party: Polo India v Pakistan 6 - 6 (pony died on the field). Dinner dance at Pakistan Officers Club. Dancing through the fire with P Ali Khan.

On the 5th day we were seen off at the aerodrome by our host and took off in the Dove. After an hour's flying southwards the starboard engine cut out and we force landed at Sui, HQs of Sui Gas where B H Watts, in charge of Pakistan Petroleum Ltd, telephoned Karachi and gave us much hospitality. We used the morning returning literary thanks to Lahore and took off p.m. arriving home half an hour before our own dinner party to say farewell to friends leaving Pakistan.

Such was our first experience of Lahore Horse Show. We attended two more and found the welcome from our friends and the hospitality not one whit less: indeed the presence of some of our family increased the enjoyment.

In April we visited Beach hut No 129 in an area of the coast known as Little Cornwall. After another visit we bought the hut in which thereafter we spent practically every weekend. The hut could sleep up to about 6 people, had a paraffin fridge and fresh water laid on. There was a system of watchmen and we lost but little. Many happy hours were spent and many family letters were written and typed in that hut which was near enough to Karachi: e.g. to enable us to drive in for early Church service on a Sunday, stay for Matins and be back at the hut for a bathe and lunch. We had some wonderfully happy and peaceful parties over 2 years in that commodious, ramshackle hut.

I notice an entry in the Diary for 23 April 1957: "Queen's Birthday Reception for 900 at High Commissioner's House." Alec Symon (and his wife Dodo) had been British High Commissioner for Pakistan for nearly 2 years when we arrived in Karachi. He had had a wholly Indian career since 1921 either in the sub-continent, where he was Deputy High Commissioner Delhi 1946-49, India, later Commonwealth Office where he was Deputy under Secretary of State 1952-54. We liked them well enough but never knew them intimately. I gained the impression that he was not interested in the search for oil. He failed to join our Shell Gala flight to the Giandari Rig in 1958. They both had bad luck at the two receptions which we attended: in 1957 (Queen's Birthday) it was blowing sand all along the coast and Runnymede their residence, was not large enough to contain the 900 guests even on the finest of evenings. At another Royal reception organised by the Symons with marquees and tentage, a freak rainstorm wrecked the marquee intended for the reception and spoilt a number of ladies' evening gowns especially ordered for the occasion.

On the other hand we found Bob Fowler who arrived in 1957 as Deputy High Commissioner with his charming wife most attractive and interested in Pakistan Shell Oil: they became very good friends and would often come to our beach hut parties - a sign of intimacy! He was particularly fascinated by his visits to the oil rig at Giandari.

The political shambles in Pakistan and the Baghdad Pact countries during and after the Suez crisis of 1956 must have produced problems in the minds of any Representatives of the UK during the ensuing years.

Generally speaking we found the High Commission staff always ready to help on any occasion but far more interested, naturally, in the political situation (always dicey) than in the industrial future of Pakistan. We knew and entertained all the young men and found them not very exciting and certainly on one occasion dismally quiet and devoid of enterprise.

Eastertide of 1957 was the first holiday period since 1952 in which the family were separated. None of our three children visited us. The main reason of course was the short period involved and the great expense of air travel to and from Pakistan compared with the short flight to Tripoli, Libya. Julian was in his last year at Christ's College, Cambridge, and gave notice of working during the Easter vacation at his law studies. Sylvia had a week in hospital at LMH, Oxford, for removal of a wisdom tooth and, like her brother, promised herself a week or two studies at PPE. Meriel facing her last holidays from St Swithun's had a round of visits.

London - Summer 1957

I myself spent 5 weeks in London during that very hot June of 1957. Shell wanted me at home to help entertain Prime Minister Suhrawaddy and other Pakistanis to lunch. I wanted to discuss the Pakistan Government proposals for future oil legislation with St Helen's Court. I personally also wanted to define the relations Managing Director, Technical Director and Finance Director with Nuttall in Shell. I was also rightly anxious about my mother about whom reports were disturbing. Lastly my sister Christine was due to arrive in England from Ethiopia to visit her younger son, Stephen, who had suffered from a severe attack of meningitis in Oxford - an attack defeated, so it was reported, by the intervention of Christine, his sister, herself a practising doctor.

Before I describe the luncheon let me record that I found full support from St Helen's Court over my reaction to Pakistani Government's amendments to the oil legislation, and that they approved my ideas on internal reorganisation of Pakistan Shell Oil Company. I also elicited from Nuttall (and my Directors) a firm assurance that they wanted me to stay in Karachi and that I had their full support. Lastly and sad to report, I found the news of my mother only too true and she died, aged 96, very peacefully, in her sleep on 12 July 1957. Christine and I were at her funeral and cremation at Kingston Cemetery and her ashes were sprinkled over rose trees which we had caused to be planted there. So ended, in peace, the long life of a very wonderful mother and a very courageous lady.

During the first week in July the Directors of Shell had invited the Prime Minister of Pakistan, H S Suhrawaddy to lunch at the Dorchester. In the morning I briefed the Managing Director, John Loudon, and three other Directors whom I also knew - Platt and Stephens and a new man Berham. Two members of the staff, Geoffrey Taitt, the Staff Manager for Pakistan, with Wilfred Nuttall, (geologist and palaeontologist by profession but my particular adviser and chief) were there and for an amusing hour I briefed them on the Pakistan situation and the Prime Minister in particular, his not very stable Government, his strong points and his foibles. When I met Suhrawaddy to take them up to lunch I found that in addition to our second guest, Mohammed Ilkramullah, the Pakistan High Commissioner in London, and Malik Feroz Khan Noon, the Foreign Secretary had 'gate crashed'. He was the last person whom I would have suggested to accompany the P.M. for he was a Pakistani patrician landowner and quite different in birth, upbringing, career and outlook from Suhrawaddy. However he had put several lakhs of rupees into Pakistan Shell so up he came with us to the Pent House and I spent a busy few minutes explaining him away to the Shell hosts. The party went well enough - the Directors had no little experience of foreign potentates. Feroz Khan Noon who had a distinguished career in the British Indian Government Service pre-Partition spoke intimately of Viceroys and their ways and was shot down continually by his Prime Minister - the political lawyer and demagogue. But this was all grist to the conversational mill, no less than Ilkramullah's views on the Eton and Harrow match at Lords. The only possible pause in a lively flow of conversation occurred when Suhrawaddy picked up his Dorchester poussin with all ten fingers and demolished it by frontal dental attack. A few of us kept him company in this sensible form of mastication but I noticed that the Directors upheld civilization.

It was a very good party perfectly hosted by John Loudon. Suhrawaddy did put the question to him "Why are there no women at this charming party?" I forget the reply but he also confided to me going down in the lift: "A very nice lunch but I much prefer a quiet lunch with Mrs Lush." When I returned to join the Shell hosts Loudon remarked: "You have that little man taped", a compliment which predicted a further two years in Pakistan for Diana and myself.

The historian Herbert Feldman wrote that Suhrawaddy "was in office but not in power" and by the end of that same year (1957) he had been succeeded by Malik Feroz Khan Noon, whose uninvited but welcome presence that day had saved Shell another Dorchester lunch!

I had begun a letter describing the lunch by reminding Diana that 90 degrees F in England in just as warm as 90 degrees in Karachi but "in London there are no fans."

I returned to Karachi ten days later to find two of our children had arrived before me and that Meriel was expected at any time.

I must record here that during the years 1952 - 1958, when we visited London we found the most wonderful hospitality in three homes. 20 Mallord Street, the home of Dora Carson Roberts which we used in the early days of our Shell service, not only as a second home but as a depository for luggage and packing cases; our hostess having been a great traveller herself accepted the arrival of any article from a perambulator to a pair of skis with equal aplomb. Then Winifred Grant, a widow of Fred Grant (who had been Captain of 94 Siege Battery and in later life became Chairman of the British Steel Corporation) in her capacious house 12 Ladbroke Grove (later in an equally large flat in Melbury Court) was a wonderful hostess to Diana and our two daughters - especially when Meriel and Jane Catterall were presented to the Queen in 1958. Thirdly, in this short list of hosts, equally hospitable and tolerant, came Betty and Noel Moreton, in their lordly, small house in Donne Place whence for 14 years Noel drove 5 days weekly to Covent Garden at 4 a.m. to stock his green grocer's shops and Betty planted and tended hundreds of window boxes of business houses in the West End - and still had time nobly to entertain me on my flying visits. Those three fountains of hospitality brought peace and order and great happiness to our apparently hectic and disordered visits to London and elsewhere.

Karachi

My return to Karachi in July 1957 was marked by a noticeable resilience on the part of the Pakistani Oil Department of Government: what of the Dorchester lunch? I asked myself. It was not to last long but it made possible a fortnight of local leave and a visit to Kashmir, which I had always promised the family and also warned Shell on my appointment. What a shame that we could not cross the border near Lahore and treat it as a "duty" visit to learn more about Pakistan! As it was we had to obtain special visas from the Indian Consul in Karachi and approach out goal via Delhi and Indian Airways and railways. It was almost a tragedy when Julian, on the eve of our departure, was struck down by a slipped disk which rendered him bedridden under doctor's orders. Diana with our daughters were the first to go and flew to Delhi where Philip Wade of Burmah Shell, who had been our very popular guest in Karachi, not only arranged their accommodation but sent two of his staff to show them round the sights of Delhi and sent them off by air to Agra where they visited the Taj Mahal. Anne and I joined them in Delhi next day spending the time to visit the President's Headquarters and Residency, built by Lutyens for the Viceroy: the approach thereto, with its gentle rise, is one of the most imposing approaches (one mile in length) to any official Residence. "Viceroy's house had 340 rooms and one mile and a half of corridors and the Viceroy discovered that 7000 people were employed on his estate" wrote Graffety Smith who was a guest of the Mountbattens in those vital days which led to Partition. I had once during the last Viceroy's reign signed my name in the Vice Regal Visitors' Book and realised the immensity of the building and the intensity of life therein.

Driving up that wonderful mile with the family ten years later and walking up the steps of Presidential Headquarters, I remembered that some thousands of miles away in Africa, the Condominium Governments in which I had served for 20 years were planning the independence of the Anglo Egyptian Sudan, a country in area not much smaller than the Indian Sub-Continent, though in population infinitely inferior. And I was proud to belong to a country who had led the world and for whom the peoples of her far flung possessions had fought and laid down their lives to ensure the freedom of the people of her Empire; that my country should be ready to hand over the power of government to those who had been at first subjects of the Empire and later citizens of the Commonwealth we had aspired to create. Of course there were mistakes, naturally many of the countries concerned were immature - unready (but not unresolved) for independence: of course we the Rulers were sometimes hurried and forced by circumstances. But had we British people not understood the blessings of freedom, for which we ourselves had fought in 1914 and 1939 and subsequent years, we could not have been so ready - some would say, perhaps, so foolhardy - as to give that freedom to the peoples of the Empire. We may be proud, not perhaps of the results themselves, but of the spirit that passed that freedom on to those countries whom we had governed.

Kashmir

We all left Delhi for Srinagar - having heard that climatic conditions there were not too good: flooding was reported round about if not in the capital itself. In fact the early flight brought us to the "delicious clear atmosphere of Srinagar by 10 a.m. and having dumped our luggage at Nedon's Hotel we gathered from Mr Crabb of Lloyds Bank that three of the famous houseboats on Lake Dal still remained available for hire namely: St James' Palace, King's House and King's

Bench. We found the owner, saw the houseboat and arranged to stay in King's Bench for three or four days. The boats were old but had once been well fitted: there were holes in the deck but the cabins were clean and the cooks' galley free of cockroaches (by day at any rate); the blankets were old but clean - and the view across the lake and beyond the towpath, where we moored, was exquisite. Diana and the daughters refused to leave the craft in case any other "tourists" came to claim shelter so Anne and I hurried back to Nedon's Hotel (quite a way) and fetched our luggage to find our family already bathed in the lake and crying for the very good vegetable lunch which was first class. In the afternoon we all took a shikara or rowing boat across our Lake Nagin to the Shalimar gardens where "the flowers were wonderful". Enormous dahlias, chrysanthemums, every kind of flowering shrub and tree, giant zinnias, lilies, saffron - every kind of exotic plant and flower. That evening writes DRL "We saw the comet". We spent the next morning obtaining various permits to visit forests etc., and then back to an afternoon on the lake going by Shikara in the small boat from garden to garden. Meriel had a nasty accident which ended with a scalded foot and I was amazed to see our Gaffer, son of the owner, row fast to the shore, leap on to a bicycle (whose?) and return with the dispenser from the local village clinic on his handle bars bearing disinfectant vaseline to cover the scald. Meriel's scald remained clean and she was walking again in 2 days. On our third day Sylvia, Anne and I did a monumental climb up to Hyan Pass (3500 feet in three and a half hours) and came down to meet Diana and Meriel in the Shalimar gardens.

I must admit, or rather I admitted at the time, that the climb up to the top of the Pass, after an hour walking along the road because some river was running in spate, was nearly my undoing. I suppose I had forgotten that I was 61 and climbing from 5000 feet to 8500 feet, but about 500 feet from the summit (an approach through thick forest and fallen leaves) I thought that ignominy was ahead of me. However Anne (who was panting slightly herself) encouraged me and we were rewarded, not only by the view from the top but by the descent through a series of newly planted trees into the Shalimar gardens which were a perfect riot of flowers. We went from the gardens unwillingly at sunset and I notice "hot baths" in the Diary. I also note an entry that SRL not well in the night! We enjoyed a rough night with lightning striking the mountains, very beautiful, and rain on the lake. Our craft's roof did not leak much and it was fine by morning when Anne and I set off by taxi for Gulmarg while the others had a quiet day!

The word "marg" means a mountain meadow - and that is what Gulmarg is - a very beautiful area covered with these grass and flower laden meadows, the jewels, in the description of Kashmir some hundreds of years ago, as an "emerald set in pearls". Gulmarg, 28 miles from Srinagar and several thousand feet higher, is said to have been discovered in 1580 by Yusef Khan, a ruler who gave himself up to pleasure: it has remained so ever since, always a pleasure ground and a holiday resort which, as winter sports, introduced by the British, have taken hold on the young Indian population, has become extended from early spring until early winter. The interesting fact which hit me hard when I studied a map on my first visit is that Gulmarg is 50 miles and no more from the Pakistan border and 100 miles, no more, from Rawlpindi (now Islamabad, the capital of Pakistan). I do not intend to explain the terrible wounds suffered by the people of Pakistan by the omission of Kashmir as part of Pakistan in the division decreed at the time of Partition, and the futile attempt by an unauthorised body of Pakistanis to seize the state - after Partition.

Let us return to Gulmarg as we found it having ridden, Anne and I, the last 3 miles on ponies, our bags on donkeys. We found the Nidon Hotel a wooden structure and very suitable for the family who joined us next day. During the night a moderate earthquake woke us all: the whole wooden structure swayed and we thanked the Lord for pliable wood and asked our daughters not to pull the loo chain so abruptly next time; daughters not amused. In the morning we were up betimes and with ponies and the picnic lunch in a basket carried by a boy, we climbed to an altitude of 12,000ft, above the treeline, and sat to have lunch by a frozen lake. The altitude made us all feel odd: Anne began to throw stones at the party - quite harmlessly! We encountered a hail storm after lunch and descended in light rain to tea at our chalet and elastic hotel. Anne left next day to catch a train to Delhi and aircraft to Karachi. Family spent a fourth day notable for a wonderful early morning sight of Nanga Parbat - a very good experience: a pleasant day visiting Ninglemulla and Liangmarg. We returned to Srinagar for the night, thence by air to Delhi where Leila Kabir, a friend of Sylvia's, joined us for the evening before we flew to Karachi to be met by Julian (not quite recovered) and Anne.

East Pakistan

During 1957 both Charles Mackay and I had, naturally, turned our attention chiefly to Western Pakistan. Once it had been decided to drill the test well every effort had been made, successfully, to expedite the commencement of operations at the drilling site, Giandari. Our concession, however, gave us the right to explore and prospect for oil or gas in Eastern Pakistan. Let it be remembered that in those early days, Eastern Pakistan was part of the Islamic Republic of Pakistan.

While the prospects of finding oil appeared to be better in Western Pakistan, and the terrain easier for immediate exploration, we were in no mind to neglect the quite different and more difficult problem of the Eastern province, especially in the South Eastern corner and the waters in the Bay of Bengal. While, therefore, the exploration was more apparent and more advanced in the West we had been by no means idle in the Eastern province of the country. Let it be remembered that East Pakistan was much smaller in area than the Western Province, that Dacca lay 900 miles away from Karachi (4 - 5 hours flying in 1958), that the dominating physical characteristic there is the system of mighty rivers flowing southward towards the Bay of Bengal until they join the Ganges, whose immediate delta, known as the Sunderbam, stretches for a distance of some 300 miles along the coast. The rivers are the great channels of trade and communications and it was estimated by Feldman that they carried 300,000 country boats and nearly 500 mechanically operated passenger launches: altogether about 2,500 miles of waterway are navigable (in the monsoon 4500 miles). A watery province, it was an extremely difficult area in which to search for oil. The exception is the Chittagong Hill Tracks area in the South East corner of the Province, with the important port of Chittagong, on the eastern extremity of the Bay of Bengal. The Chittagong Hill Tracks have country with altitudes of 2000 feet. It was in this corner of East Pakistan and in the Bay of Bengal itself that the technical advisers of Shell in the Hague recommended that we explored for oil.

A seismic party was soon established in Chittagong and our Eastern Headquarters were set up in that area. I quote our Pakistan Shell brochure (1957):

> "First of all a gravity survey (much the same as a seismic survey) had to be made over the area, on land by landrover or helicopter, in the Bay by a Catalina aircraft. Seismic prospecting can also be carried out at sea, even in deep water, and this is being done by Shell in the Bay of Bengal. In marine work geophones are attached to a cable which is pulled through the water by a boat. Explosive charges are dropped in the water and set off by an electric impulse. Pakistan Shell have developed special equipment which enables this type of survey to be carried our from a Catalina amphibious aircraft. This flying boat takes off from its base every day, lands on the water, plays our the cable and goes into operation while taxying over the water. The use of these craft were extremely suitable in areas of shallow water and sudden storms - very common in the Bay."

I made several short visits to the Eastern Province during 1957, short because the teams were in the acts of settling in and starting their runs. I had the intensely interesting visit when the head of the survey gave me a quick rough introduction into the exploration surveys and I had several most interesting flights in the Catalina which the pilot and crew handled as if she were a light aircraft. I thoroughly examined Chittagong port and many of the people handling our unique imports - all with the longer view of exporting oil or gas. I suffered the rail journey, by night, from Dacca to Chittagong and enjoyed the warm hospitality of our own people in Chittagong and the many ship brokers, and I flew low over that appalling country which forms the land and water surface of the delta of the four great rivers which empty into the Bay of Bengal, the Jammu, the Bhahmaputra, the Meglina and the Ganges, each draining the snows of the Himalayas - the Ganges rising not far from the Eastern boundaries of Kashmir, and the Brahmaputra flowing from Tibet, through Assam and collecting annually 100 inches of rain during their final 500 miles to the coast.

The flight from Karachi was always slightly exciting for, if one had the luck to choose a flight arriving on a fine day, and a willing pilot who had the kindness and temerity to diverge a degree of two from his proper flight route, one could have, 150 miles to the North, a very good view of the Himalaya range containing Mt Everest. Through the kindness of willing pilots Diana (once) and I, several times, enjoyed this superb sight which, like that of Nanga Parbat, is quite unforgettable even after a period of thirty years.

It is difficult to describe Dacca where Pakistan Shell had no office or representative. But as Managing Director one had to know and be on speaking terms, if not en rapport, with the Governor and the Chief Minister and several of the other members of the Provincial Government, and the leading Bengali Civil Servants together with the British Deputy High Commissioner in order to keep them in touch with what we were doing in our exploratory manoeuvres in the Province. I must own that it was difficult to explain, as layman to Pakistan layman, what I was proposing to achieve as a passenger in our Catalina aircraft over the Bay of Bengal, or what purpose would be achieved by the three Decca Stations set up in three remote corners of the Province. However, I found Bengali Pakistanis most welcoming and helpful though I think I lost caste by travelling by night train from Dacca to Chittagong in order to save time. (It took 12 hours but with a reserved carriage, a supper packed at the hotel and a friendly guard one was in peace, not too warm, and very comfortable). I had learnt this mode of travel in 1940. Having fulfilled my official calls in Dacca to Narangytang Jute mills one hour up river on the Ganges (or was it the Brahmaputra?) always preceded by a dozen dolphins - the train journey in the dark was peaceful!

At Chittagong I met the exploration technicians, surveyors, seismologists, flying men of the Catalina flying boat and our helicopters, geologists and naval men of the seagoing launch with the gravity observers who sailed in her. They all lived in quite pleasant houses up the hill from Chittagong harbour and were as interesting a body of men (and some women) as one could find. I think they enjoyed a visit from a M D who was quite unscientific and was also ready to go out with them and try to learn their magic. They were especially hospitable and kind not only when Diana and I visited them but when in 1958 I managed to fly Sylvia, Meriel and Jane Catterall and threw ourselves on to their most friendly hospitality. (Sylvia once flew to Dacca as Air Hostess in Douglas Bader's aircraft).

Karachi

Let us return, after our Kashmir holiday, to Karachi and Baharistan where we found Julian better but still bedridden, and all five Lushes were once more together for a short time. Julian was soon recovered enough to join the social life at the Yacht Club, (where our boat,

Mistral, underwent a much needed paint at their hands) and a monumental gay life. I notice a sentence in Diana's diary which was to repeat itself several times. "We were the only other British there." This happened to be at the French Embassy to meet the French Foreign Minister but it was not uncommon at Pakistan parties - which meant that in that part of social activity we were following Shell directives to become part of the international life of a country.

We were not to remain en famille for long for Sylvia left in mid September for her last year at Lady Margaret Hall, Oxford. However, Alan Hill arrived in mid November and was part of the family for six months. The Medical Officer of Shell at St Helen's Court also came to stay and he and I paid a visit to Dacca, East Pakistan.

Sylvia spent her Christmas and Easter holidays in England working for her "finals" in which, in May and June, she scored a good Class II - she had worked extremely hard for her finals and we were all delighted and proud to have a son and daughter BA.

Another visitor who made herself a much loved member of our family was Jane Catterall, a school friend of Meriel's and daughter of Joy and Christopher Catterall, both in the medical profession: also brother of Anthony Catterall, later (and now) to become an eminent orthopaedic surgeon and, at the time of writing, consultant at the Royal National Orthopaedic Hospital London. Jane was with us for 6 months.

Julian returned to England where, in October 1957 he too chose to join the Shell Group; following an introductory course he moved to Beirut, his first assignment with Shell, during which he was due to attend the MECAS Arabic course at Shemlan.

Political changes in Pakistan did not pass unnoticed; at the time of our arrival in July 1956 Chowdry Mohammed Ali was Prime Minister, appointed in September 1955 at the time of the centralisation of the various provincial administrations of Western Pakistan. At the same time the existing Governor General resigned for reasons of health and was replaced by Major General Iskander Mirza. On 23 March 1956, just before our arrival, the Islamic Republic of Pakistan came into being as a member of the Commonwealth with Iskander Mirza as its President and Choudry Mohammed Ali as Prime Minister. Chowdry Mohammed Ali was an able man with a long and distinguished career as a Civil Servant. However, deserted by his party, the Muslim League, he was compelled to resign in September 1956, to be replaced by H S Suhrawaddy, an able Bengali lawyer and politician, organiser and convener of the Awami League. I naturally saw a lot of him officially and socially (as already recounted): he never appeared to me as a man of administrative ability and we, as a family, did not much appreciate his social habits! Chundriya of the Moslem League followed him. I called on him (at his house) but had no business for he lasted but two months to be followed by Malik Feroz Khan Noon, one of my first and best friends in Pakistan who gave me his confidence and help from the beginning and who, during his short period as Prime Minister, continued that help and friendship before he, too, disappeared from the scene. He assumed Office just before Christmas 1957 and when calling on him to congratulate him, I told him that at last we in the oil industry would have someone at the top who knew something about the industry. I was glad, too, that some of Shell in St Helen's Court had met him and that we had killed two birds with one stone in the Dorchester. I am glad to record, as I will relate in a page or two, that Feroz Khan Noon was as good as his word when he promised on that December morning of 1957 that he would do all in his power to help the oil industry in Pakistan make as much money as possible for his country. His second wife, Vicky Noon, was a lively, forceful lady. According to Who's Who, Feroz had married Elizabeth Rikh in 1945. We could never be sure of her country of origin but found her very friendly and forthcoming, a great help, we thought, to her husband as P.M. and a winner for extorting money out of "you rich oil magnates" (she spoke very fluent English) for her Charities. She was an ardent supporter of the Red Crescent and knew a great deal about gardens and flowers, and that's the way she wheedled money out of MSL.

Neither Sylvia nor Julian were with us for 1957 Christmas, Sylvia working for finals and Julian about to leave for the Lebanon. But we had Alan, Jane Catterall and Meriel to keep us alive, and the presence of one or two of H M ships kept the young people busy at the Yacht Club, our Beach Hut and Baharistan. Diana gave us all great pleasure by helping one Ronnie Ogden at British Council in his lecture on English poetry, by herself reading a number of poems. There were carols by candlelight; I found myself not taking Matins in Church but playing the organ! Diana notes "excellent singing" by our choir and YWCA at the Carol Service and next day we entertained in our garden all the Pakistan Shell children to a Christmas party. Father Christmas (myself) dressed in crimson, drove up in a camel cart - presents round an enormous tree and then a Pakistani conjuror, who was excellent.

On Christmas Day after two Church services, we drove out to our Beach Hut for a bathe and lunch. Alan, Anne and I returned early - Anne to prepare for our Christmas dinner party, Alan and I to attend the President's reception in honour of the Qaid-i-Ayam's (Jinnah, deceased) birthday. Back to dinner for 16 at Baharistan. On Boxing Day we visited Shell employees in hospital and we then entertained a number of Pakistan Shell wives and husbands to drinks and buffet dinner and dancing "including Rock'n'Roll". Bed about 2 a.m. Meriel, it is recorded slept all day and all night.

Diana had weathered the whole year in Pakistan and for a break she and Alan spent a week visiting Bombay and then flew to Aurangabad whither they motored to the famous Ajanta Caves, and next day to the Ellora Caves. They took excellent (colour) snapshots of these famous caves and then flew back to Bombay where Burmah Shell looked after them magnificently. They "did" the Victoria and Albert Museum, saw the famous Stone

Elephant and then with Mrs Lister, drove round the north of the island and through the National Park. In the evening they were entertained by the German Consul and "our" pianist Shanti Sheldon, whose whisky and champagne they swallowed before attending the gala dinner and dance at the Taj Mahal Hotel where they "saw in" the New Year and danced till 1 am. They flew home to Baharistan on New Year's Day 1958 and, undaunted, attended with Anne and me, and the President and Begum Iskander Mirza, the Celebration at Sudan's Independence Day - just two years ago that evening.

And so began our last full year in Pakistan. Throughout the latter part of 1957 John Cowasjee had been a constant and welcome visitor to Baharistan and was always infinitely kind to all of us - young and old. His family now seemed to like the company of the Lush family and we were often the only non-Parsee guests at their large family midday luncheon parties at which it seemed to us that every member of the Cowasjee clan must be present from grandmothers to the smallest additions. We were immensely touched by this very warm reception into the heart of the Cowasjee family whose generous welcome to their houses and hearts has never failed.

In January Diana and our household had the good fortune to be present, by invitation, at the Takht-Nishini ceremony of enthronement of the Aga Khan: there was a record crowd at this interesting ceremony. We had met the Aga Khan in the company of our own Prime Minister at the High Commissioner's house and though we made our bows to the great man, we had little or no conversation although I do believe that I mentioned that his son, Ali, had served in my administration in Africa - without creating any apparent interest in the Aga Khan.

In January 1958 the Rt Hon Harold Macmillan with Lady Dorothy Macmillan arrived in Karachi, the first British Prime Minister in office to visit Pakistan. Be sure that we were all at the airport to meet him though we had no opportunity to talk until next day after his address to the U.K. Association; after his speech Diana and I had a brief meeting with them and talked of Italy and Sussex, and we met them again at the Pakistan reception for them to which Feroz Khan Noon had us included. We took it that Macmillan was visiting Pakistan as a member of the Baghdad Pact in an attempt to explain away the Suez debacle of 1957.

At about this time our exploration experts advised that they had found a second site for a test well: Giandari was nearly ready for drilling and it was good to know that a second site was considered feasible. The Hague had approved the decision and I therefore informed the central Government in Karachi, beginning with the Oil Ministry there and then with the authorities in Lahore, the long task of receiving the approval and assistance necessary to start drilling at a second site when appropriate. The second site was at Kharampur near Multan and although the actual site was on the edge of a village, it was in an inhabited area. We and the Pakistanis knew that our seismologists had been carrying out a series of seismic tests round Kharampur and thus the site was no surprise; but the negotiations for occupation of the land and access thereto affected a number of people all of whom, from top to bottom, were about to exaggerate grossly the value of land and right of access. I started off in January with the head of the administration and the chief oil man (a civil servant) in Lahore; negotiations continued amicably - slowly but successfully - sofar as the provincial authorities were concerned, and, to cut a long story short, we had everything en train when at the end of the year we started drilling.

It was before this time, in fact in the autumn of 1957 that I became aware of a change in the attitude of the Pakistan Government with regard to the general principles of the terms under which our original acreage was granted in 1956, terms which had been agreed upon after 2 years of negotiations. The main point in dispute was the 50/50 principle which was the basis of all oil exploration in unknown areas. We had thrashed this out with the Libyan Government and our people had done the same in Karachi. Now the Pakistanis were warning us that the 50/50 principle would be changed for new acreage granted for exploration "Mind you", I wrote "the present arrangement stands unchanged for existing acreage, but we have found half of that devoid of geological structures and therefore not potentially petroliferous and we want to explore elsewhere under the original terms." (MSL to DRL 4.5.58).

I and the other oil companies had protested against this volteface with the Ministers of the three quick change Governments of 1957-58. The Ministers had made vague promises but found themselves up against their own civil servants who had called in a Canadian, a socialist ex-Minister from Saskatchewan whose high and mighty ideas might well apply in a country rich in oil such as Canada, but which were absurd and vexatious in a non-proven country like Pakistan. In the end, during the middle of Feroz Khan Noon's term of office, I persuaded Shell to send me an expert on concessions and out came a young man who knew his subject well. He and I tackled the permanent officials who in the kaleidoscopic state of the Pakistan Government had the Ministers in their hands. Finding them obdurate I did approach the P.M. Feroz Khan Noon who reached for his telephone and directed that discussions on oil agreements should come first on the Agenda at the next Cabinet meeting. It never appeared on the Agenda. However Feroz Khan Noon gave me an assurance that no decision would be taken before October 1958. He kept his word - and in October lost his job. But that is another story.

Our friends in the north had swamped us with invitations for the Lahore Horse Show in February and this year we decided to make an extended visit even further north to include the Khyber Pass. Diana, Jane and Meriel drove the whole way in our own private car and used the railway for the extra bodies - e.g. Anne and I met the car party at Lahore where our host, Bill Dyer of Burmah Shell, a delightful person, who took us to the opening of the Horse Show which we then left and spent the next night at Rawalpindi (H.Q. of the Pakistani Army) whence we visited Taxila. Here we saw proof of the historical fact that in the third century BC, the Hindu civilization of Asia was disturbed by the armies of Alexander the Great and the Hellenistic occupation had a profound influence on local architecture and sculpture, the remains of which were many and plain to see. It was a very extraordinary feeling to find Greek architecture and sculpture in this part of Gandhara (the ancient name of the North West Frontier Province and other neighbouring areas). How I wished that my education in Greek History (which stopped in 1914) had extended to this far flung occupation by Greeks. We had a splendid day in Taxila thanks to a Parsee friend of John Cowasjee, who gave us an excellent day historically. Alan and I took the train and luggage from Taxila to Peshawar while the family drove thither crossing the Indus and Kabul rivers via the Attock Bridge. They had a close shave for the road bridge closed at sunset. We all dined and slept at Dean's Hotel in Peshawar. I can do no better than quote DRL's entry for the next two days.

DRL Diary 25.2.86 Peshawar.

"MSL called on Harrison, Deputy High Commissioner: left Ahmed in Peshawar: other seven in Chevrolet drove through grounds of Islamic College and Peshawar University via Jamrud, where showed passes and deposited cameras, past Coke's and Jamrud Fort and the Khyber Rifles in Shagai Fort, all through the Khyber Pass to Torkham, the border of Pakistan and Afghanistan; 34 miles from Peshawar, 309 from Lahore, 1107 from Karachi, (165 miles from Kabul capital of Afghanistan). Picnic lunch on way up Kohat Pass. Stopped to watch workers in arms village Darra tribal arms factories. To Handyside gateway at Top of Kohat Pass. Tea and dinner at Dean's Hotel."

Shagai fortress is reputed to have accommodation for a battalion of troops and nearby on a large expanse of rock face are inscribed the insignia of the many Regiments which served in the Khyber Pass during British Rule. It was for all of us an historic drive through this really terrible country - some of it outside the ordinary administration of Pakistan and known as tribal country - easy to recognise for every other male over 12 carried a rifle.

While we were in Peshawar my mind was full of John Maffey who spent practically all his service with the Political Department of India, both in N.W. Province of Afghanistan (as Chief Political Officer) and as Chief Commission N.W.F.P. at Peshawar before he came as Governor General to the Sudan.

On next day we sent off Ahmed the driver with all our luggage by train to Lahore and six of us left Peshawar by car and returned via Nowshera (the road junction for Swat, whither Sylvia went later) and Attock (where Burmah Oil had found the only oil field in West Pakistan) to Rawalpindi where we turned North to visit Murree (7500 feet altitude); we arrived in a slight scurry of snow and there was old snow on the ground. We ate lunch beside a roasting fire in Pott's guest house before we left for Lahore. Murree was and still is a favourite hill retreat and had many of the marks of a popular resort for the well-to-do. I had been there in 1950 chasing the then Pakistan Government with whom I insisted on discussing refugees and remember well that the only consolation for an infuriating wait with nothing to do was a wonderful post dawn sight of Nanga Parbat. However in 1958 we returned to Lahore in time for a dinner party at Jim Dizer's house (our host) where we met Bingo Bais, famous as a great international polo player with a handicap of 10, and John Cowasjee from Karachi. We ended the day by attending the Police Tattoo - a midnight end! After two final days when we really did go to the Horse Show, we attended the Polo Ball (somewhat wild, writes the diarist). However it gave me the opportunity of a good talk with Alec Symon, British High Commissioner, away from Karachi. Finally we sent Alan off by car with the young ladies; Anne had already flown south leaving Diana and me to catch the Shell Dove and spend a day at Giandari to see our rig in action on the second day of its drilling (when they reached 112 feet) - a very exciting and interesting day when we were alone with the drilling party.

The road party arrived next day slightly demoralised by a piece of bad driving which caused their car to leave the road, slide down a bank and nearly overturn. Alan was naturally most disturbed. Mercifully only the car suffered and that damage was not irreparable.

Soon after our return from the Lahore Show Diana left with Meriel and Jane for Europe and in May they were all bidden to Buckingham Palace where Diana presented Meriel and Jane at the last Presentation of Debutantes to be held by Her Majesty on 19th March 1958. The two Debs made their curtsies to their Queen and enjoyed the occasion and Diana was proud of her protegees; they toured the Palace after the Royals had left and had a lovely party at the Savoy that evening. They both enjoyed their formal entry into society which exists no more - and Meriel helped to carry the cake at Queen Charlotte's Ball.

The following cables were exchanged between Karachi and London:

"Meriel Lush London Darling Double Daughters Dress Daintily Don't Descend Disjointedly Devastating Duke Desist Denigrating Decadence Dance Delirious Dallying Devotedly - Daddy."

"Lush Karachi Spring Sunshine Suffused Scene. Sweet Super Seventeens Saluting Sovereign Superb Setting. Salaams. Sweethearts."

Diana had arranged it all in conjunction with Winifred Grant. After the presentation and the dinner and dancing at the Savoy, there followed debutante balls and parties, theatres and concerts, and finally a cocktail party for 60 friends of Diana, Meriel and Jane in Winifred Grant's capacious flat in Melbury Court. Diana and Meriel went to Eton and Harrow, attended Trooping the

Colour (a great friend, General Sir Rodney Moore, Sylvia's godfather, was Commanding London District and arranged places); they then did a round of visits, sometimes together, including Margie Geddes in Jersey, and yet had time to discuss renting a Shell flat against my imminent leave in June.

Anne and Alan and I were left but not alone - a guest was with us and I spent 3 days in East Pakistan with him - and certainly not without problems. For the Pakistan Government unleashed their document amending the 50/50 agreement of 1956 for future exploration permits and, unlike the other oil companies who went directly to the Minister, I determined to have a go at the permanent civil service staff of the Department. We had two visitors from Shell to evaluate the whole position in Pakistan, one a senior financial expert.

Finding I was making little headway with the Pakistan Departments I requested and was sent the young concessions expert from Shell mentioned earlier: he was a novice in eastern ways and arrived with no thin clothes at all. But he knew a lot about concessions - the exact terms in Bolivia, Iceland and I expect the antarctic when it becomes petro-suspect. But he cut no ice with the Pakistani civil servants - they had, as I have said, the Canadian adviser sitting with them, with great assurance persuading them to apply the ever changing policy of petroliferous Canada to this very dry area of Pakistan.

I visited the East twice and made myself acquainted with the mysteries of gravity and seismic work in Catalinas. I became much better acquainted with the highly technical group of geologists, Decca surveyors and flying men attached to Shell Pakistan in Chittagong. I never quite discovered how Chittagong, well down the mainland eastern coast and almost in Burma, could have become the main port for seaborn vessels in East Pakistan.

Soon after I had returned from Dacca the most absurd and childish imbroglio occurred in the Government of Pakistan which was clear proof of the disastrous state of affairs in Pakistan politics - east and west. The Chief Minister started a bout of dismissals of Ministers from office which finally included himself and the Governor. It was all so ludicrous that I reduced the fact to ridiculous poetry. But it was a pointer to the gradual dissolution of good government that was to follow, leading to the imposition of Martial Law.

Anne and Bill Lindsell (who was now a resident in Baharistan), Alan and I with Jim Dizer, spent a happy and prolonged weekend in Quetta and thanks to ready help from Pakistani officers saw a great deal of the military in Quetta and also of the neighbouring countryside.

In Quetta we were shown the Staff College, a most impressive building, and even in 1958 steeped in British military tradition. The first thing which hits one in the entrance hall is the life size double portrait of Kitchener standing on top of a pass with a Bengal Lancer (a facsimile of the portrait which used to hang in the Palace, Khartoum). Every room was lavishly furnished, money apparently no object. The names of Kitchener (the first Commandant), Haig, Wavell, Auchinleck and Montgomery appeared in the list of many British generals. We were very impressed and it is indeed a little oasis of British tradition in this part of the world.

We had three or four days to celebrate the Eid after Ramadan. We all flew by 'Dove' to Giandari - had a good three or four hours there chatting to the experts. Our well at Giandari was drilling well but we had hit some extremely hard rock and had used no less than 17 drill bits! However the experts seemed optimistic and late in March I took a large party of diplomats and leading Pakistanis and some press to see the rig at Giandari in action: weather prevented half my party taking off the ground, and one stalwart (Pakistani) then did the arduous journey by road.

Indeed the period of Martial Law in 1958 brought few difficulties to me and other Westerners. Prices in the shops went down and the Pakistanis took full advantage of that and so stocks of necessities soon diminished and then disappeared, e.g. butter. Many provision shops opened for a few hours per diem. Whether the morality laws "teasing women in public" and "making water in the streets" were observed it was hard for me to say, but the order concerning the speed of buses and priority to women passengers was strictly enforced by the militant rank and file who were pretty rough with men who preceded women in a bus or sat while any woman stood. (The Pakistan Government was copying the courtesy to women practised in London in 1958!) My own opinion was "that Martial Law is being extremely well administered and that the honeymoon period still exists". We were all a little surprised at the rapid return to Cabinet Government when within two weeks I wrote "We are becoming quite respectable in Pakistan with a Cabinet and a Prime Minister". General Ayub Khan, the Martial Law administrator, became Prime Minister and there were several generals in the Cabinet. I also noted how "extremely detached" from the political scene were the Air Force and the Navy. But the cleaning up process was pursued with vigour. The car and driving license offices had queues of 3000 a day. Later, of course, the President, Iskander Mirza, was peacefully removed and Ayub Khan, the Prime Minister took his place. The country continued to be run, to all intents and purposes, by the Army and soldiery became more apparent though not everywhere nor in great numbers. We were sorry to lose the Mirzas who had been good friends and I regret to say that we did not renew our friendship when we returned to U.K. - for that matter we also lost touch with the exiled Crown Prince of Ethiopia in his house in Portland Place.

We continued our friendship with Suhrawaddy; "went out en famille to their ghastly house" - Suhrawaddy had toothache, danced a bit and then slumped in the middle of our family party. We apparently asked him back keeping the numbers to the Martial Law figure of 30 and "had a thoroughly good evening": drinks in the garden and a very good buffet run entirely by the four girls, Sylvia, Sarah Campbell Taylor, Winifred Borthwick and Anne Lawrence, the last an extremely good organiser:

she had arrived to replace Anne Skeet who had become engaged to marry Bill Lindsell.

The Pakistan Shell news wasn't so good - the Giandari well which had produced that incredible layer of almost imperturbable rock was abandoned at 12,000 feet as the following excerpt from Dawn, the English newspaper of Karachi, sadly related:

"Shell to start oil research near Multan: D G Khan well abandoned.

"Pakistan Shell Oil Company Ltd, abandoned the first exploration well in West Pakistan, the Giandari Well in Dera Ghazi Khan on Oct 16, 1958. This is the 26th dry exploration well drilled in West Pakistan by various oil companies since the beginning of 1955.

"The systematic testing was completed on Oct 14, the process being attended by a Government representative from the Department of Petroleum and Minerals. The exploration had reached a final depth of 12,007 feet. A test depth of about 6,000 ft showed the presence of both salt water and gas. The gas, composed of 54% methane and 46% nitrogen, was too small in amount to be of commercial value. All the other tests gave nothing but slightly salt water with traces of gas.

"Pakistan Shell will, however, continue their search for petroleum in West Pakistan. All drilling equipment will be moved as rapidly as possible to a second location at Karampur, in Multan district, with a view to drilling a second well. Exploration work in East Pakistan continues."

However we soon started our second well at Karampur near Multan which was to give us proof of the existence of oil at 7000 ft but unfortunately a million years or so too late - we extracted quite a long core of bitumen! Sadly it raised hopes among the Pakistanis, including the President (Ayub Khan) to whom I took a foot or so of the bitumen and it provoked suspicion, among many, that we had found oil but were not prepared to confess the find nor pursue it!

Here I must record a splendid day with the two Navies which Diana accomplished with Anne Lawrence and other girls while a VIP and I were in the North. Owing to misdirection they only narrowly caught the R N pinnace whose young Commander, spotting five lovely girls, turned back to pick up the late comers - DRL's diary continued (21/11/58).

"Splendid day on board HMS Loch Inch, joining in international naval exercises code name "Shop Window". HMS Albion, (Aircraft Carrier), Pakistan Navy Ship "Babur", frigates and destroyers demonstrating gunnery, flying off carrier and submarine diving. While others having g & t before lunch DRL saw large school of whales, also swordfish: told drinkers who came out to watch. Exercise carried out before President Ayub in P N S Babur."

Our three young ladies, Winifred Borthwick, Sarah Campbell Taylor and Sylvia left on 10 November for their northern tour to Lahore, Peshawar, the Khyber Pass, Malakand, Swat and Murree then back to Lahore where they would meet Diana and myself with our VIP guest, Geoffrey Tait. I must own that I was a trifle nervous of what they would find in Swat but the Deputy High Commissioner in Peshawar saw little risk of trouble there and had promised to keep an eye on them. They accomplished the first part of their journey, which was an immense success, by rail for they found this the most satisfactory mode of travel by which to see Pakistan scenery and way of life, but north of Peshawar they travelled by jeep.

Diana and I had travels to accomplish in the future with Geoffrey Taitt, head of the Production Department in Shell, London, who spent five hectic days with us visiting West and East Pakistan. He met a number of Shell staff at drinks and dinner in Baharistan (oh, how we blessed the garden, looking lovely under lights as a rendez vous for large parties), visited our second well at Khampur next day and "did" Lahore, seeing a number of notables. Next morning we took off in the Dove to Peshawar, were met by two police officers who had apparently been extremely kind to Sylvia and co. on their way to Swat a week before. They took us and our Dove pilots over the Khyber Pass to Afghanistan and back via the Durra arms factory for Taitt, and via Waisak Dam for MSL and the pilot, masquerading as Taitt (who was officially expected!)

The flight between Lahore and Peshawar was most impressive. The whole range of the western Himalayas were spread out before us looking quite wonderful in the evening sunset on our return. We tried in vain to spot the ice mass of Nanga Parbat.

We arrived from Peshawar at Lahore Airport simultaneously with the three Swatees (Sylvia, Sarah and Winifred) en route for Karachi after their visit to Swat "the Valley of the Hanging Chains". We had a splendid evening, very different from the day before when Taitt and I dined with the (Pakistani) Governor and Chief Secretary.

Next morning Diana and I with Taitt and our acting Technical Manager, John Carr, caught the morning aircraft from Lahore and flew within view of the eastern Himalayas most of the flight with Everest at the eastern end. I sent a message to the Pilot asking to be told when we had the best view of Everest: the reply came back "we are not landing at Everest today". In Dacca we attended a dinner that evening in our honour given by the Governor (Martial Law Administrator) and many others: all were quite charming as were the hosts next day in their offices. We had on arrival spent a pleasant hour watching the hundreds of river craft plying between Dacca and Narayanganj, a lovely sight in the sunset - there was no time to do the trip by river. Next day we spent the afternoon in one of our Catalinas and flew to Cox's Bazaar (on the frontier) and a few mock exercises at gravity work - Taitt then departed by air for Calcutta and Delhi.

The Shell and Decca Navigation staff, with whom we stayed, threw a tremendous party for us before dinner with the Watsons, our hosts, who were charming and de

Baars a visiting geologist from the Hague. Diana and I flew back to Dacca where we had more entertainment by charming people of the British Council and many Pakistanis. We were lent an old launch and steamed up and down the Ganges for an hour or two - one of the best trips on the river which is quite unforgettable.

Here is an extract of a letter about Taitt's second visit to Karachi:

> "Taitt returned from Delhi a week before Christmas and we really did get down to entertainment! We took him to the Fowler's (Deputy High Commissioner) farewell party: we gave a buffet lunch for 35 Shell-Pak staff and wives at the Beach Luxury Hotel and a buffet supper for 35 for the elites - Dutch Ambassador, the Fowlers again and some Pakistanis (for in these martial days many are asked but few come); the General Azam (Military Minister of Industry, Jane's Lahore admirer) came. Taitt saw a good cross section of the communities. He had 8 interviews, with the President Ayub Khan, who was charming, and the others with military folk in Industrial and other Ministries - especially the Department of Petroleum. Moreover Bill Lindsell arrived on his last morning and gave a very lucid account of the situation in Iraq, which interested Taitt and Fellowes greatly.

Perry Fellowes and I met at a meeting of ECAFE (Economic Council for Assistance in Far East) in Delhi which I had attended on behalf of Shell and found most interesting and well run: I brought Perry back to Baharistan for we were old friends since 1942 days in Addis Ababa where he was Public Relations and did not always agree with my policy.

Julian arrived from MECAS at Shemlan, Beirut but missed our Shell guests: he was just in time for the Christmas Children's party from which we excused him and let him go sailing in our boat "Mistral" which the girls seldom used. However Julian was in time to attend our dinner party for the Wali of Swat and Begum and other Pakistanis and their wives who had been kind to the three girls on their travels.

We had our usual conjurer for the Pakistan Shell children's party on Christmas Eve when Santa Claus (not MSL) drove up behind 6 gaily caparisoned donkeys - the same conjurer too for our Christmas dinner. Our big Christmas Buffet supper had to be split in two partly owing to Martial Law restrictions and we started with 35 each at Baharistan and the Mackay's house - in their absence our young people hosted the latter. Our two young guests, Winifred and Sarah, left before the New Year.

One grievous fault which Martial Law did not immediately put right was negligence and worse in the Pakistan postal service - both in and out. I think it was due chiefly to peculation. I made a habit when we visited our Beach Hut, which was almost a fixed weekly performance, to write or type a family letter with copies to any of our children, not present, and close friends like the Moretons and Anne Lindsell. At least 30% of these effusions failed to arrive and many letters from Meriel in Aix en Provence suffered the same fate.

That Beach Hut was a weekly salvation to us all; by the end of 1958 it had been refurbished and repainted. As many as 19 could and did comfortably bathe, eat and sleep there by day and I think we limited night accommodation to six: here is an extract from my Christmas letter of 25.XII.58 to 6 recipients. "A happy Christmas to you all! I am writing this at Aefata Beach Hut ... today is really lovely and we have bathed. I did not get off a Sunday letter because I just gardened all day. In fact we all gardened for it had rained cats and dogs for two days and on Sunday the garden smelt just like an English one in summer." Our garden had been a tremendous success and trees, bushes, sweet peas, carnations, bougainvillaeas grew apace and flowered prolifically. We certainly left our landlady a tremendous legacy of good soil and good plants - and a good measure of honest sweat! The garden was certainly my great joy in that ugly town Karachi.

We had, as I reported in letters, the most exhausting Christmas of the three spent in Karachi. Julian, Sylvia and our two young guests were wonderful in support: Sarah went home, much improved in health and spirits, and Winifred was about to quit for her tour of India. Bill Lindsell was still with us. We were at last getting regular mail from Meriel in Aix en Provence, Geneva, Paris, Spain, etc. She seemed well attuned to French University life. Bill Lindsell the bridegroom to be of our Anne next month, was our only worry. But the following telegram was finally despatched to the Skeet household in West Tytherley: *"Party Poured Into Panam Pretty Pickled - Pakpals"*.

Julian had visited our new rig-site at Karampur (Multan) with John Heaney who was the Pakistan Shell representative at the drilling site. I wrote on 3 January 1959 - "Douglas Bader and his wife Thelma ... arrived in the London Shell Dove - a very posh affair. He is intending to take two days to reach Calcutta via Delhi and Miss S R Lush has been signed on as an extra hostess. She will continue to Dacca and Chittagong with Winifred." We had a party for the Baders.

I flew back in January for 9 weeks to attend Anne Skeet and Bill Lindsell's wedding at East Tytherley Church and then the reception at Normancourt School near West Tytherley. It was a freezing cold day, a lovely wedding and a very cheerful reception at which I proposed the Bride, and was proud and happy to do so. I quoted:

> Round the next corner, in the next street,
> Adventure lies in wait for you
> Could life be anything but sweet
> When all is hazardous and new.
> Round the next corner in the next street
> Adventure lies in wait for you.

It was good to think that their next street would be Karachi - where they arrived in February - much to our joy. They and their lovely children have remained very much part of our family ever since.

I came back with detailed information about my

successor, his arrival, our departure which Taitt and Nuttall had been good enough to give me with their blessing and regrets that I could not accept an Ethiopian offer. H G Llewellyn, my successor, the Public Relations Officer in Lagos, was expected to arrive Pakistan in March 1959. We had another two months before the hand over and our departure in May.

The two months before hand over were full enough, both from a private and Shell point of view. Celia Hensman came to stay and later to accompany Sylvia on travels via East Africa to Lebanon. Dora Carson Roberts arrived by ship to stay with us and then with Iris Leghari, wife of Omar Leghari (Commissioner for Punjab in Pakistan) attended the Lahore Horse Show. The Economic Committee of the Baghdad Pact met in Karachi and caused a round of official receptions, they were followed by H.R.H. The Duke of Edinburgh to whom we were presented at the airport, met (and talked to) at various receptions before we went up to our last Horse Show. The Duke, of course, was there (as was also Prince Ali Khan) and was interested in the quest for oil. His arrival with the President at the official opening was a magnificent affair and the Army, with Martial Law behind them, showed us clearly who wielded the power in Pakistan. I managed to send Diana and Dora Carson Roberts south by our own Dove via the second rig at Karampur which was drilling away, and thenceforth the Dove did a panorama flight (e.g. Sukkur etc) to Karachi.

Shell policy in Pakistan was to seek more exploration acreage in West and East Pakistan. In the West we had scored two dry wells but were still anxious to ensure that, literally, no stone was unturned. In the East, we wanted to add to our exploration acreage before drilling. Negotiations proved relatively easy with the new regime who were not so much in the hands of the permanent staff as the politicians had been and our intransigence of 1957 and 1958 now bore fruit. I was glad to have a good record to produce to my successor on that subject. Shell also had agreed to join in an intercompany reconnaissance (arranged in Europe) to examine the possibility of a refinery in Western Pakistan and at about this time a party intent on that purpose arrived in Karachi. I naturally aided and abetted the party though I was not a member thereof - nor was I much consulted: perhaps my successor would be.

On Palm Sunday we had to visit our Holy Trinity Church, the Archbishop of Canterbury who with Mrs Ramsey had arrived by air at 3 a.m., and after a short Matins service for a congregation of 700 British, Pakistan and all nationalities, gave a wonderful address, entirely stimulating. One very significant remark was "Security is the greatest problem which faces Christianity."

We lunched in company with the Archbishop and his wife and Bishop Chandra Rae and his wife, with the Deputy High Commissioner. We had been able to introduce John Cowasjee, an old Reptonian to Dr Ramsey, his old Headmaster there.

Early on Easter Sunday Anne Lawrence and I collected two large bunches of tulips and daffodils ordered from London by Diana and myself, from BOAC, and arranged them in our Holy Trinity Church. They looked quite lovely and, so that they should not wilt unloved in Church we brought them all to Baharistan in the evening! I believe our landlady Begum Reza who was very perturbed at our impending departure, called to be reassured about Shell's intentions for Baharistan, and saw them.

My successor, Hugh Llewellyn arrived on 5 April and the process of a hand over began almost immediately (it was a Sunday) at the Beach Hut! In fact, because of the holidays occasioned by Id el Fitr, we spent several afternoons and one night at Aefata - returning to his evening parties for Hugh to meet Pakistan Shell staff and others. In 10 days we had met the President, U.K. High Commissioner and all the necessary leaders - and at least 100 others in our house. Diana and I then took Llewellyn to Lahore, Attock and the North, then Dacca and Chittagong (where the Shell party gave Diana and me a very warm farewell and a silver model of a Batialo Nanka boat), and so home to Karachi after a most successful heart warming trip, at the end of April. In Karachi many kind people gave us farewell parties including the whole staff of Pakistan Shell on the roof of Qamar House followed by a dinner party for 40 people given by John Cowasjee, including the High Commissioner and Lady Symon, the Deputy High Commissioner and Mrs Walsh Atkins and the Australian High Commissioner. A wonderful evening which only John Cowasjee could have organised.

We left next evening for Aden, Jibuti, Ethiopia and our "Swan Song" through Africa.

Brantridge Forest, 1961

From the lake

Cosmo's male lineage: MSL, Rodney Searight and Julian, 1970

MSL and Macmillan

Family gathering, September 1969

Golden Wedding party, 26 June 1980

Grandchildren's Orchestra, Golden Wedding party, June 1980

Maurice and Diana
at 3 Carlton Mansions

Postscript

My father, Maurice, was writing his memoirs up to the time of his stroke in May 1990; he entrusted me with their completion. For me, helped by Sylvia and Meriel, this has been the most moving and rewarding task, saddened of course by being unable to discuss it with him. Since his own account finishes at the end of his working career, this postscript is merely to round off the story with an outline of his years of retirement which undoubtedly provided some of the happiest he and Diana spent together.

Maurice and Diana's first venture at the start of their retirement in 1959, on their way home from Pakistan to UK, was to make their "Swan Song" trip through central and southern Africa. In Ethiopia they stayed with Chris and Dan Sandford and in Kenya, Rhodesia and South Africa they were thrilled by visits to a succession of wild-life parks, as guests of Arnold Curtis and other friends.

In England they rented a house called Stoneacre in Westerham for six months while scouring west Kent and Sussex for a permanent home. Eventually, some hundred houses seen and discarded, the ideal property was found and Brantridge Forest was bought. It was a large country house of 1904 vintage between Balcombe and Handcross, set in 23 acres of mixed garden and woodland with a slope running down to a lake and a fine view out over Sussex.

During this time, Diana's eldest brother, Richard, fell seriously ill with lung cancer and died at Stoneacre; this was a profound shock to her. Diana's youngest brother, Alan, was later to join Maurice and Diana in living at Brantridge Forest.

Brantridge Forest in 1960 became their home for twelve years - over twice as long as any previous residence. The house contained quaint features, such as the bizarre black and pink bathrooms, but the hall compensated with its fine oak linen-fold panelling. The gardens were gradually extended by hard labour by week-end guests and steadily reclaimed from many years of neglect. They revealed a wealth of rhododendrons and azaleas which thereafter thrived as a joy to the eye in early summer. The lawns accomodated tennis and croquet and involved a walk of several miles for a complete mowing. Without any doubt, it was here at Brantridge Forest that Maurice and Diana found the greatest happiness of their lives together and a perfect outlet for the very considerable energy they both still enjoyed.

In 1961 a huge marquee occupied the lawn for three weeks to accommodate the guests for the successive weddings of Sylvia to Patrick, Viscount Glentworth, now the Earl of Limerick, followed by Meriel to Ian Tegner. In 1963 Julian too, having been working in Oman, became engaged to Sarah Searight; their wedding took place in February 1964. In due time these unions produced for Maurice and Diana seven grandchildren who desported themselves as infants or youngsters at Brantridge Forest: Edmund, Alison and Adrian Pery, Kirstin and Luke Tegner and Louisiana and Cosmo Lush. It was, of course, a much favoured week-end retreat for all generations living in London (despite the exaction of arduous gardening dues) and all three families could be accomodated without difficulty for their regular reunions.

Maurice and Diana equally enjoyed welcoming to Brantridge Forest the many friends acquired over the years in so many parts of the world; new friends of all ages came too. Brantridge was also the venue for a regular annual concert in aid of the British Red Cross. The house contained two grand pianos, one in the drawing room and the other in the hall; Maurice would regularly sit down to play at one or other in the evening before dinner, exercising his lifelong ability to improvise or play by memory - moving moments of which no one ever tired. At the concerts, young pianists, singers and other instrument players came willingly to perform to audiences spilling up the staircase.

Maurice's personal activities were various: he was Treasurer to the British School at Rome; he was Chairman of the Overseas Committee of the British and Foreign Bible Society, involving him in at least one trip to Africa to visit BFBS representatives in several countries, and another to the USA; and, perhaps most demanding of all, at the instigation of Diana's cousin, Conrad Rawnsley, he became a very active Vice Chairman of Enterprise Neptune, the National Trust's campaign to save the coastline of Britain, on its inception in 1965. The start of the campaign was marked with much publicity and the lighting of a chain of beacons the length of the land; it achieved its target of £2 million within five years and saved 175 miles of coastline in perpetuity. It is still active today.

Maurice took part in parochial affairs in Balcombe and, inspired by his desire actively to perform in his service to God, began to preach the sermon at the Sunday service in church and became a lay reader.

In 1965 they made another visit to Ethiopia and there at last, after much preparation of the way, took place a reconciliation between Maurice and the Emperor Haile Selassie. A further visit followed in 1968. They were of course overjoyed to be with Dan and Chris Sandford once again at Mulu Farm.

Time, of course, could not be made to stand still, even for Maurice and Diana. During the 1960s Maurice had first one, then the other, hip replacement operations. By 1972 a combination of factors - the heavy physical and financial burden of the upkeep of the property itself when Maurice had turned 75, the reduced call on Brantridge as a haven by the younger generations and the increasing difficulty for their own friends to reach them in Sussex - convinced them that they should move to London where all three children had homes and where friends would be closer to hand.

Thus 3 Carlton Mansions was found - a ground floor flat in Kensington ("So easy for the undertakers" as Diana was fond of quoting) - and the great move made in 1972. Although they both missed the garden and tranquility of Sussex, the Holland Park Gardens tennis club gardens, visible from their bedrooms, became a substitute often frequented.

The move proved right in every way; the flat soon became a centre for all sorts of visitors, old and young, and activity with the sound of music remained at a high level; for the grandchildren it was a special focus where the grandparents became devoted friends and confidants to each and every one. Freed from the encumbrance of maintaining a large property, they embarked on further travels: first a round-the-world trip, largely by sea and including a stay with Julian and Sarah in New Zealand; later came an extensive tour of friends in the USA, a trip to Pakistan to attend the wedding of John and Vera Cowasjee and further visits to Julian and Sarah in Japan and Abu Dhabi, interspersed with innumerable ventures through England and Scotland.

During the 1970s the idea of writing these memoirs began to take root, but Maurice's first and essential preliminary task was the assembling and putting into order of all his papers, letters and other material, in particular Diana's comprehensive diaries; the writing came later.

While they became staunch supporters of their local church, St Barnabas, they would divide their allegiance with Holy Trinity Brompton, the church of their wedding in 1930. Active participation in the affairs of the Sudan Pensioners Association, the Sudan Church Association and the Egypt Diocesan Association claimed much of their attention too.

In 1979 disaster struck in the form of Diana's stroke. Suddenly and without warning, she collapsed with partial paralysis of her left side. She made a good initial recovery - she could still drive a car for some time and bravely continued with many activities - but gradually she declined. In due course she took to a wheel-chair and needed personal care. At this point, in 1983, Norma Forsyth came to them (from looking after Maurice's old Sudan colleague, Angus Gillan) to take on the house-keeping and caring for Diana; she remained faithfully and devotedly with them for nine years. This enabled Maurice to embark in earnest on the writing of the memoirs, and he remained doggedly at it, in his own hand and with deficient sight, until they were finally type-written and could be edited for publication.

They followed with immense interest the careers of their children and it was an event of great pride when Sylvia was appointed Chairman of the British Red Cross Society. Of all joys to them, they were able to attend the wedding of Kirstin Tegner to Matthew Neill - the first grandchild to be married; later Maurice also attended Edmund's to Emily Thomas but sadly Diana was unable to make the journey.

In May 1990 Maurice too was smitten by a stroke; this left him able to hear and understand but unable to speak, a condition of unutterable frustration to him. Mercifully, he died peacefully a fortnight later on Sunday 20 May, Diana at his side.

Diana, herself declining steadily, suffered greatly from his absence but amazingly clung on to life for another seven months before she too was released from her severe disabilities and died on Sunday 30 December of the same year, 1990.

A.J.M.L.
November 1992

APPENDIX 1

DECORATIONS

1916	**Military Cross**
1918	**Bar to Military Cross**
1938	**Order of the Nile, 3rd class**
1942	**Commander, Order of the British Empire (CBE)**
1944	**Commander, Order of the Bath (CB)**
1945	**Officer, Legion of Merit (USA)**
1946	**Commander, Order of the Knights of Malta**

APPENDIX II

Maurice Lush: Obituaries

The Times, May 29 1990

Brigadier Maurice Lush, CB, CBE, MC and Bar, who held important posts in the administration of territories liberated by the Allies during the Second World War, died aged 93 on May 20. He was born on November 23 1896.

Maurice Stanley Lush was educated at Tonbridge School and the RMA Woolwich. He went out to France with the Royal Artillery in 1915 and fought on the Western Front until the Armistice, winning the MC and Bar. On demobilization he joined the Sudan Political Service in 1919, being seconded to the Egyptian Army and serving as Sudan Secretary at the British Legation at Addis Ababa from 1919 to 1921. Thereafter he filled posts of increasing importance in the Sudan administration culminating in the Governorship of the Northern Province. Lush had been the oldest surviving member of the Sudan Political Service.

The outbreak of the Second World War brought Lush's recall to the Army where his wide administrative experience was soon to be put to good use. He first returned to Addis Ababa where he established the Occupied Enemy Territories Administration (OETA) in 1941 as Chief Political Officer. With the return to Addis Ababa that year of the Emperor Haile Selassie, Lush was caught in the crossfire of a sharp disagreement between Nairobi and London about the future administration of Ethiopia. The matter was resolved the following year with the return of the British Legation, the re-establishment of Haile Selassie's government and the withdrawal of OETA.

This episode was only the preliminary to Lush's most distinguished service to the Army's Civil Affairs branch as Military Administrator in Madagascar and then as Montgomery's Chief Civil Affairs Officer in the advance through Tripolitania in January 1943. He established there an administration replacing Italian rule which won friendship for the British. The culmination of this phase of Lush's military service, for which he was three times mentioned in dispatches, was the appointment in 1943 to be the British head, Executive Commissioner and Vice-President of the Anglo-American Allied Control Commission, later Allied Commission, for Italy. As such he virtually administered the liberated areas of Italy until a reconstituted Italian government could take over. He left Rome in 1946.

After demobilization Lush devoted himself for the next five years to the post-war problem of the resettlement of refugees, being Resident Representative for Germany and Austria of the Inter-Governmental Committee on Refugees (IGCR) in 1947, Chief of Mission in the Middle East for the International Refugee Organization (IRO) from 1947-49 and special representative for the Middle East, IRO, from 1949-51. In the work he travelled widely appealing for help to, amongst others, Jawaharlal Nehru. When Lush sought aid to resettle one million refugees India's Prime Minister replied that he was trying to resettle nine million.

On retiring from government service Lush represented the Royal Dutch Shell Group affiliates in Libya from 1952-56, from where he negotiated an offshore concession in Qatar, and in Pakistan from 1956-59. On returning to England he helped organize the National Trust's Enterprise Neptune of which he was Vice Chairman from 1965-68.

Lush was a strong churchman and a supporter of the British and Foreign Bible Society of which he became Vice President. Throughout his career and in retirement he supported the Anglican Church in Egypt and the Sudan. A man of great energy, a keen horseman and polo player in his younger days, he maintained to the end a clear head and a memory much prized by historians researching Sudanese affairs, drawing on his many years of experience.

The bluff and cheerful good humour which were so characteristic were no facade but reflected the warmth and kindness which he bestowed on all his many friends, young and old and of many races.

He was a great gentleman, one of the last of a group of men of judgement, integrity and courage who went out from Britain before, and after, the First World War and by their devotion to the country and its people brought peace and prosperity. In addition to the MC and Bar of his youth his subsequent war service was recognized by his appointment as CBE in 1942 and as CB in 1944. He held the Order of the Nile Third Class and received the US Legion of Merit. He was also appointed a Commander of the Order of the Knights of Malta.

In 1930 he married Diana Ruth, daughter of Charles Hill. He is survived by his wife, one son and two daughters.

The Daily Telegraph, May 28 1990

Brig. Maurice Lush, who has died aged 93, consolidated a formidable reputation as a political officer and administrator during the Second World War when he was charged with restoring a measure of law, order and recovery in the wake of the advancing Allies across Africa and Italy.

In 1941, after the British defeat of the Italians in Ethiopia, Lush became involved in controversial events attending the return of the exiled Emperor Haile Selassie. Brought in from Sudan, Lush found himself faced with the problem of balancing the requirements of the British arrival and occupation with the impatient desire of the Emperor to resume rule of his people.

In the ensuing conflict of interests there was political disagreement with the former Mayor of Addis Ababa and advisor to the Emperor, Brig. Dan Sandford, who happened to have been Lush's old battery commander on the Western Front in the First World War - and was also married to Lush's sister.

The Emperor sensed a whiff of the old colonial instinct, but Lush's priorities demanded firm action. One of his first duties was to disarm and evacuate some 30,000 Italians from Ethiopia.

During this task there was an incident which typified both Lush's sense of humour and his refusal to be deflected by jacks-in-office. On receiving a critical signal from Nairobi that two Italians had arrived armed with revolvers he was asked to send a 'full report' instantly. When he failed to reply the signal was repeated. Finally Lush responded: "Suggest pull trigger and report will follow."

Maurice Stanley Lush was born on 23rd November 1890, the son of a solicitor who emigrated to Canada. Young Maurice and his two siblings were brought up by his mother in somewhat reduced circumstances in Brighton; but he won a scholarship to Tonbridge, where he excelled in classics and music.

After the outbreak of the First World War he decided against a bible clerkship at All Souls College, Oxford, and proceeded instead to Woolwich, being commissioned into the Royal Artillery in 1915. Lush was posted to No. 94 Siege Battery - one of the first to be equipped with 9.2" Howitzers - and won a Military Cross in the Battle of Poziers Ridge in September 1916.

In 1918 he led volunteers into an exploding mêlée after an ammunition dump had been set ablaze, put out the fire and rescued ammunition from the dump. For this gallant act he received a Bar to his MC.

After the Armistice Lush heard that Dan Sandford's pre-war post as secretary to the Legation in Addis Ababa was available. Despite the lack of a university degree he landed the job and was accepted as a member of the Sudan Political Service (traditionally known as 'Blues ruling Blacks').

He served successfully as a District Commissioner; Assistant Civil Secretary of the Sudan Government; Private Secretary to the Governor General; Deputy Governor; Sudan Agent in Cairo; and, from 1938-41, was Governor of the Northern Province. Lush relished life in the Sudan, particularly the polo and the long hours in the saddle as he traversed the country in the course of his duties.

Towards the end of his time there he ruptured his bladder and sustained other serious injuries when a rogue railway engine ran him down on a bridge at Atbara. He endured much pain and frustration in hospital in Khartoum, but his characteristic determination carried him through.

In 1941 he was recalled from the Regular Army Reserve of Officers, promoted Brigadier and posted to Ethiopia as Deputy Chief Political Officer in the British Military Administration, later becoming Chief Political Officer.

On April 6th, as the British entered Addis Ababa, he was conducted to the Emperor's palace, then used by the Italian Viceroy, the Duke of Aosta, to participate in the formal surrender. When the Duke was taken prisoner he followed the old military custom of carrying out an inspection of the troops to whom he had surrendered - the last vanquished general ever to do so.

Lush noticed with satisfaction that the Italian police had already reinstated left-hand driving in Addis Ababa, a sign of their readiness to co-operate. The chief concern of the Italians was for the safety of the 50,000 civilian men, women and children.

This Lush organized, proceeding also to arrange the disarmament of Italian troops and their despatch to Kenya. At the end of the month he visited the Emperor who had been pressing for permission to return to his capital from the moment the British troops entered it.

After various vicissitudes Lush helped to organise the Emperor's triumphant return to the capital on 5th May 1941, five years to the day since the Italian occupation. The Emperor's entourage included the maverick Brig Orde Wingate, inspiration of the internal Patriotic Revolt, and leader of the Ethiopian and Sudanese irregulars - "Gideon Force" - who had contributed valiantly to victory.

In 1942 Lush moved on to the Indian Ocean island of Madagascar, where, after the surrender of the Vichy French, he again distinguished himself as an administrator. Later that year the occupation of Tripolitania required similar services and on the surrender of Tripoli he was appointed Chief Civil Affairs Officer in the British Military Administration.

Concerned that the 8th Army, after weeks of privation in the desert, would soon eat and drink the place out of macaroni and red wine, he went to see Montgomery and urged restriction to haversack rations only, save for tea and buns.

He was then posted to Italy, where he served as Executive Commissioner and Vice-President in the Allied Commission from 1943 to 1946, and worked closely and convivially with Harold Macmillan and Gen Mason-Macfarlane.

Lush subsequently described this as the "most exciting and enthralling" job he had ever had. His powers were such that privately he was acclaimed "Viceroy South of

Naples".

Next the plight of people rendered homeless by the war demanded Lush's expertise. He was appointed Resident Representative for Germany and Austria of the Inter-Governmental Committee on Refugees. He served as their Chief of Mission in the Middle East from 1947 to 1949 and Special Representative for that region from 1949 to 1951.

In 1952 his knowledge of the Middle East commended him to Shell. After four years as representative of its Anglo-Saxon Petroleum Company in Libya, he moved on to Pakistan where he was Managing Director of Pakistan Shell Oil from 1956 to 1959.

On returning home after years of dedicated overseas service, Lush devoted some of his immense energy to Enterprise Neptune, the National Trust's coastal preservation programme, of which he was Vice-Chairman from 1965 to 1968. But he still found time to entertain a steady stream of overseas visitors at the Athenaeum and to encourage young people throughout the years of his retirement.

He was also Vice-President of the British and Foreign Bible Society and a Fellow of the Royal Geographical Society. He was thrice mentioned in dispatches in the Second World War; was appointed CBE in 1942 and CB in 1944; he held the Order of the Nile and the US Legion of Merit, and was a Commander of the Order of the Knights of Malta.

He married, in 1930, Diana Ruth Hill; they had a son and two daughters, of whom the elder, the Countess of Limerick, is chairman of the British Red Cross Society.

The Sudan Church Association - Notes and Commentaries

Brigadier Maurice Lush, CB, CBE, MC and Bar

For the reconquest of the Sudan, Kitchener led an Anglo-Egyptian Army, many of whose officers came from the RMA Woolwich, in particular the Royal Engineers, mostly in their 20's. For the two decades until World War I came a score of its survivors, all highly decorated for courage, and of proven judgement and integrity, to form the cadre for the expansion of the Political Service. Among them, from the same 'Shop', Woolwich, still only in his early twenties, came Maurice Lush. Service in Ethiopia and Cairo, and as Private Secretary to the Governor-General in Khartoum, gave him unusually wide experience.

Added to his administrative duties in the Sudan, this formed a varied qualification for his later undertakings, all requiring the basics of good administration: law and order, human rights and food, leading in due course to shelter, health and education.

To all these challenges he was to bring his outstanding Christian faith, needing tact and steadfastness, particularly in the Anglo-Egyptian Sudan, where among the three groups of the 'People of the Book', attitudes towards human rights were to differ on occasion towards slavery, female circumcision and forced first-cousin marriage. His success as Governor of the Northern Province of the Sudan in the chaotic summer of 1940 made him the obvious choice to be the senior political officer in Ethiopia in 1941, helped by Dan Sandford, his brother-in-law. In Ethiopia, later in Madagascar, and later again in North Africa and Italy, he concentrated on the same three basic needs. Working myself from bases in Southern Italy in 1943-44, I could observe, and benefit from, his paramount authority among the Top Brass as a Professional among Politicians, few of whom had any deep knowledge of administration. 'South of Naples', once battle had passed by, became as calm as the Northern Province of Sudan in 1940. If ever the need arose, a call to Maurice, especially if spoken in Arabic, would bring a quick, reasoned reply, acceptable to all. His knowledge of, and standing with, both civil and military persons and procedures, was to support the fighting services well, with little call on troops for action. Those twenty-five years contained the achievements of several normal lifetimes. Yet in the forty-five years to follow he made so many substantial contributions - to commerce in the Middle East and to moral and material good works in the United Kingdom, to help the British and Foreign Bible Society and to protect the coastline of Britain among others. Throughout he was splendidly supported by Diana, for all but sixty years, and surrounded by a devoted family and numberless friends and admirers who shared his Christian belief that one day we will all be together again. Few have contributed so much to so many in so many different ways.

Sir D.D.P.

Sudan Church Association - Notes (2)

Brigadier Maurice Lush

For those who receive the SCA 'Notes and Commentaries' the excellent obituary will give some idea of the wide range of service of Maurice Lush, so here are just a few extracts from the address given by the Rev. Sandy Millar at his funeral.

Not only did Maurice Lush have a distinguished career in the Army, having joined up at the age of 17 in the First World War. He was awarded the MC and Bar for gallantry. After this he served in the Sudan Political Service and during the Second World War he took the formal surrender of Tripoli.

Maurice was a 'gent' of the old school. He loved life .... he was humble, courteous, courageous and very charming having a love especially for the young which was both attractive and infectious. He was a landmark rock of moral integrity but even more than this he had a great sense of fun. Mr Millar told how on Easter Sunday at Holy Trinity Brompton, at the end of the service he mused, "I can't help recalling an Easter service we went to - and I forget how many years ago it was - in the jungle. There were about 200 of us there, and I think that Diana and I were the only ones who had any clothes on at all. I was thinking," he added with a great grin, "of what a great contrast this has been today!"

His Christian faith was plain to all and he looked forward to crossing "the Horizon, which is the threshold of life eternal, realise fully the infinite love of God, and enter His service with that knowledge and in eternal service, to do His work, having met Him face to face."

The Tonbridgian

Brigadier Maurice Lush - Sc 1910-15

Brig. Maurice Lush, who has died aged 93, consolidated a formidable reputation as a political officer and administrator during the Second World War when he was charged with restoring a measure of law, order and recovery in the wake of the advancing Allies across Africa and Italy.

In 1941, after the British defeat of the Italians in Ethiopia, Lush became involved in controversial events attending the return of the exiled Emperor Haile Selassie.

Maurice Stanley Lush was born on Nov 23, 1896, the son of a solicitor who emigrated to Canada. Young Maurice and his two siblings were brought up by his mother in somewhat reduced circumstances in Brighton; but he won a scholarship to Tonbridge, where he excelled in classics and music.

After the outbreak of the First World War, he proceeded instead to Woolwich, being commissioned into the Royal Artillery in 1915, and winning a Military Cross in the battle of Poziers Ridge in September 1916.

In 1918, he led volunteers into an exploding melee after an ammunition dump had been set ablaze, put out the fire and rescued ammunition from the dump. For this gallant action he received a Bar to his MC.

When posted to Italy, he served as executive commissioner and vice-president to the Allied Commission from 1943 to 1946, and worked closely and convivially with Harold Macmillan and Gen. Mason-Macfarlane.

Lush subsequently described this as "the most exciting and enthralling job" he had ever had. His powers were such that privately he was acclaimed "Viceroy South of Naples."

On returning home after years of dedicated overseas service, Lush devoted some of his immense energy to Enterprise Neptune, the National Trust's coastal preservation programme, of which he was vice-chairman from 1965 to 1968.

He was also vice-president of the British and Foreign Bible Society and a Fellow of the Royal Geographical Society. He was thrice mentioned in despatches in the Second World War; was appointed CBE in 1942 and CB in 1944; held the Order of the Nile and the US Legion of Merit; and was a Commander of the Order of the Knights of Malta.

He married, in 1930, Diana Ruth Hill; they had a son and two daughters, of whom the elder, the Countess of Limerick, is chairman of the British Red Cross Society.

APPENDIX III

BIDDING PRAYERS
read at the funeral services

MAURICE'S funeral at St Barnabas Church on 29 May 1990

"We give thanks for the life of MAURICE LUSH, 1896 - 1990

For his courage, loyalty and achievements in a life of service.
For his boundless energy, generosity and hospitality.
For his abundant interest in the lives of others of all ages; for his warm sympathy and desire to share in their joys and successes, their worries and sorrows; for the inspiration of his wisdom and counsel. For the love and devotion he had for Diana and they both had for their children, grandchildren and wider family as well for their countless friends.
For his enthusiasm, cheerfulness and sense of fun; for his quest for understanding and, in a changing world, his perspicacity and optimism.
For his conviction of right and wrong and for the high standards he set by his example. For the joy of his music, the quality of his writing and the gardens he created.
For his enduring faith in, and witness to, the love of God which made him an irresistible power for good."

DIANA'S funeral at Golders Green Crematorium on 5 January 1991:

"We give thanks for the life of DIANA RUTH LUSH, 1908 - 1990

For her devotion to Maurice and all her family.
For her beauty and gaiety which enriched the lives of so many.
For her kindness, generosity and hospitality, and for her enchanting gift of friendship.
For her energy, common sense and fortitude
For achieving so much - in the nick of time.
For her lovable eccentricities and perfectionism, and for her sense of humour.
For her skill in acting and dancing; for her love of the English language and for her memory of poetry and rhyme.
For the record she left us through her diaries and photographs.
For her indomitable spirit in times of separation and in the last years of her life."

Index

94 Siege Battery, Royal Garrison Artillery (RGA) 13, 15, 17-20
Ababa Aregai, Ras 132, 133
Abder Rahman (sufragi) 91, 99, 106, 113
Abder Rahman, Sayed Sir, KBE, CVO 76, 97
Abdulla bin Qasim Al Thani 286
Abdulla Darwish 287-289
Abyssinian Corporation 28, 34, 35
Acland, Peter 152, 154, 160-162
Adams, Reginald 87, 90, 151
Adeane, Robert 147
Aga Khan 304, 311
Agatha Christie 291, 292
Alexander, Field Marshall Sir Harold (later Viscount) 159, 165, 167, 171-174, 176-179, 184, 185, 191, 192, 195-203, 205, 207, 208, 210, 212-214, 218-220, 222, 224, 225, 226, 231, 232, 235
Ali Bey Gerba 281, 282, 292
Ali Faney, Amir 304
Ali Khan, Prince 167, 305, 316
Ali Maher 105, 106
Allan, Bishop 248, 261
Anders, General 249, 262, 263
Anglo-Egyptian Treaty 68, 69, 72, 92, 93, 96, 112
Angus, Madge 207, 226, 227, 231, 237, 241-245, 247
Annet, Governor General 143, 144, 146, 149
Asquith, Julian/Anne 282
Atbara Bridge 40, 99, 108, 112
Atiyeh, Samuel Bey 66, 88, 89
Ayub Khan 299, 313-315
Badoglio, Marshall 171-174, 176, 177, 181-183, 185, 187, 192, 193
Bailey, Robin 46, 49
Ball, Russell 250, 261
Baring, Sir Evelyn 256, 257
Barker, Major "Pongo" 111
Barnett 143, 146
Barton, Sir Sydney 78, 95, 119
Bassett, Charles Tilney 282
Bath, Order of, Companion (CB) 212, 222, 223, 226, 227
Beamish, Colonel 157, 160
Begum Reza 301, 316
Belgrave, Dalrymple 285
Bell, Sir Humphrey 66, 67, 94
Benson, Gp Capt G C, "Con" 175, 182, 186, 187, 198, 214, 216, 218, 220, 222
Bentinck, Major Arthur 27
Bergin, Lt Col Tom 179, 183, 196, 219, 221, 226, 228
Besse, Antonin 26, 129
Bing, Geoffrey, MP 236
Blackley, Brigadier Travers 121-123, 129, 134, 137, 138, 152, 154, 160, 162, 168, 169, 261, 280, 282, 283, 286
Bolton, A R C, "Rollo" 58, 61
Boromeo, Princess Orietta
Borthwick, Winifred 302, 313, 314
Bowman, Anne 240, 241, 244
Bowman, Col Al 198, 214, 216, 218, 220, 222, 225, 230, 235
Boxall, Joan 194

Bradburne, Philip 282, 293, 295, 296
Bredin, G R F 58, 62
Brogan, Olwen 291
Brooke, General Sir Alan (later Lord Alanbrooke) 159, 167, 201
Brown, Elizabeth 241, 250
Browne, "Pull-through" 45, 49
Burgess Watson, Capt 140
Caccia, Harold 173, 177, 205
Calisse 304
Cambridge, Col Richard 160, 162
Campbell, Sir Ronald 241, 249
Campbell Taylor, Sarah 302, 313, 314
Cane, Sir Cyril 27, 33
Cantlie, Neil 52
Carlisle, Jo 226, 227, 231
Carr, Brigadier 182, 186, 217, 219, 237
Carr, Capt Ian 163-165, 167, 171, 172, 180, 184
Carson Roberts, Dora 62, 241, 260, 261, 293, 307, 316
Cassidy, Lt D M, "Mike" 14-17, 35
Catterall, Jane 302, 307, 309, 310
Cawood, WBC 7, 8, 9
CB (Companion of the Order of the Bath) 212
Chapman Andrews 119-122, 136, 137
Charles, Sir Noel/Grace 193, 200-202, 208, 218, 220, 236
Chowdry, Mohammed Ali 310
Churchill, Winston 120, 122, 136, 139, 143, 145, 158, 159, 172, 176, 185, 191, 193, 195, 200-205, 207, 214, 217, 218, 223, 226, 232, 234, 235
Claerebout, Colonel 141
Clark, Florence Emma (Mother; see also Lush, Florence) 1
Clark, General Mark 173, 177, 191, 198, 200, 210
Clark, Nell (aunt) 3, 4, 7, 8, 10, 25, 35
Clarke, Peter 56
Coates, Dinah 56, 57
Coles, Dick 291
Coningham, Maori 76, 83
Coriatt, Percy/Kay 282
Counter Battery, III Corps Heavy Artillery 20, 21
Courselette 16
Cowasjee, Ardeshir 300
Cowasjee, Cyrus 300
Cowasjee Dinshaw 26
Cowasjee, John 311, 312, 316
Cowasjee, Rustom 300
Craig, J D, "Sarah" 58
Crawford, Bill/Marjorie 63, 90, 99, 100, 102, 105, 106, 108, 109, 112, 121
Crowther Smith, Pamela (see also Sarell) 96-98, 100, 114, 233, 234, 236, 237
Crowther Smith 241
Cruddas, Hugh 282, 293, 296
Cummings, Duncan 122, 161
Cunningham, General Sir Alan 117, 118, 121-127, 129, 130, 132-137, 251
Curtis, Arnold 250, 253-257, 261
d'Arcy Osborne 242
Dallas, Lt Col 124, 125, 128
Dawson, Col Lionel 151, 157
de Coppet, Maurice 31
de Gaulle, General 139, 142, 143
de Guingand 158
de Landsberger, Isa Maria 258, 261
de Montfried 26, 31
di Pirajno, Alberto Denti 154

Dimoline, General 145-147, 253
Dizer, Jim 312, 313
Dodds, Major J Hugh 23, 25, 27-29, 32, 35, 78
Dongwes 256, 257
Doria, Orietta 192, 224
Doria Pamphili, Prince/Princess 192, 194, 227, 237, 242, 261
Douglas, Air Marshall Sholto 82, 245, 247
Dunlop, Brigadier 182, 186, 198, 213, 216, 218, 220, 222, 226
Dyce Sharp, Dr Neville 27, 33
Dyer, Bill 311
EARA (East African Refugee Administration) 252, 253, 256
Eden, Anthony 143
Edinburgh, Duke of 316
Eisenhower, General 166, 168, 171-173, 176, 200, 210, 220, 225, 226, 235
El Shatt camp 248, 250, 251, 265
Emerson, Sir Herbert 220, 221, 236, 240, 241, 245, 247
Erskine, Dennis 176
Evangoulof, George 296
Evans, Maj Eric, "Galloper" 284
Evans Prichard 80
Ewart Biggs, Christopher 166, 286, 289
Farrar, Lady Sydney 129
Fellowes, Peregrine 315
Festing, Brigadier Frank 141, 142, 144
Fielden, Lionel 182, 186, 188, 196, 198, 199
Fiske, Bernard 179, 220
Fletcher, Maj John/Cecily 184, 190, 235, 242, 265, 284
Fletcher, Norman/Nancy 64, 68
Forbes, Rosita 41
Fothergill, Colonel 181, 199, 205, 220, 261
Fouracres, C E, "Ted" 57, 248
Fowler, Bob 306, 315
Fuad Khalil Gemie 288
Gatacre, General 84
Gault, Charles 283
Gaynor, John 280
Geddes, Margie 313
Gelsthorpe, Bishop 102, 160
George VI, HM King 165, 184, 196, 225, 226
Giandari (well site) 303, 304, 306, 308, 311-314
Gibson 38, 97
Gillan, Angus/Margaret 85, 87, 89, 96, 102
Gordon, General Charles 1, 8, 40, 67, 68
Gordon, W M 9, 10
Goulburn, Maj Gen Edward 236
Grabham 37, 38
Grafftey Smith, Sir Lawrence 88, 143-147, 149, 172, 181, 184, 196, 200, 211, 213, 216, 217, 220, 221, 224, 307
Grant, Douglas 137, 139-142, 145, 146, 148, 160, 163
Grant, Winifred 302, 307, 312-315
Greyberg, General 159
Griggs, Harold 258
Grozicko, Mrs 252, 256
Gubbins, Jimmy 281
Gwynne, Bishop Llewellyn 39, 40, 60, 97, 98, 102
Haile Selassie, Emperor 50, 64, 105, 111, 112, 118-120, 132, 135, 136, 138
Halley's Comet 8
Hamilton, John de Courcy 39, 50, 87, 143, 248, 251, 261, 265
Hampshire, Tony 304
Hancock, Geoffrey 75, 77, 287, 289

Hannaford, Guy 196, 221, 226, 233, 237
Hansen, Dick/Alison 265
Hardacre, Pitt 282
Harding, Lt Gen Sir John 153, 173, 222, 230, 235
Harper, Rev B J, "Uncle" 39, 40, 58, 111
Harrison, Maxwell/Phyllis 103, 106, 109
Harrison, Rex 99
Haselden, "Kit" 46
Hay, Robert 285
Hayton, Colonel 128, 131
Headlam, "Tuppy" 63
Henderson, Dr Leigh/Diana 100, 109, 110, 112
Henshaw 160
Hensman, Celia 302, 316
Hewins, Ralph 66
Higgins, Bill/Helen 285, 288, 289, 297
Hill, Alan 62, 73, 241, 245, 279, 310
Hill, Charles Alexander, "CAH" 62-64, 96, 241, 260
Hill, Mervyn 240, 241
Hill, Richard 63, 209, 241
Hill, Ruth 62-64, 90, 98, 209, 214
Hodson, Arnold 34
Hogenhuis 294
Holden, Corporal 217, 220
Hopkinson, Henry (Lord Colyton) 87, 88, 213, 216, 217, 231
Horrocks, General 166
Howe, General 160
Howe, R 137
Huddleston, Maj Gen Sir Hubert 112, 113, 167
Huddleston, Sir Arthur 45, 61, 66
Hume, Brigadier General 174, 176, 179, 182, 184, 185, 187, 191, 192, 198, 205, 214, 218, 220
Humphries, Julian 35
Humphry, John/Mary 69, 76
Hunter, Colin 279
Huthwaite, Veronica 292, 293, 296
Idris, King Mohammed Al Senussi 280, 282, 284, 288
IGCR (InterGovernmental Committee on Refugees) 220-223, 226, 237, 239-247, 260, 268
Ingleson, Philip/Gwen 43, 52
Iride 242
IRO (International Refugee Organisation) 239, 245-261, 264-266, 268-277
Iskander Mirza 299, 304, 310, 311, 313
Jerusalem 260
Jews of Tripoli 151, 155-157, 161-163, 165, 169
Johnston, Bishop Frank/Gladys 97, 107, 248, 261, 279, 281, 293
Joyce, General 173, 174, 178
Julian 81, 84, 85, 90, 91, 100, 107, 108, 114, 115, 240, 241, 245, 247, 259, 261, 264-266, 273
Kassa, Ras 30, 31
Kelly, Sir David/Marie Noel 92, 96, 97
Kennedy Cooke 120-122, 135
Kennedy, Sir John 254
Kincaid, Colonel 182, 188, 189
Kirkbride, Sir Alec 282-284, 292
Knights of Malta 227
Knott, Peter 10, 11
Laidlaw 123, 129, 131
Lampson, Sir Miles/Jacqueline 65, 88-91, 93, 94
Lawrence, Anne 313, 314, 316
Lawrence, John 129
Lea, C A E 282
Leclerc, General 159, 162

Leese, General Sir Oliver 152, 153, 157-161, 173, 176, 185, 196, 200, 201, 208, 212
Legentilhomme, General 149
Legge, Colonel 181, 186, 198, 205, 213, 220
Leghari, Omar/Iris 316
Legion of Merit 224
Leighton Thomson, Rev 247
Lemgo 245-247
Leslie, Norman 298
Lij Yasu 30, 31, 33
Lille 21, 23
Lindsell, Bill/Anne 302, 313-315
Llewellyn, Hugh 316
Loraine, Sir Percy 65, 67, 71, 88
Loudon, John 289, 293, 306, 307
Lowry, Charles 9-12
Lugard, Lord 32, 34, 35, 44
Lush, Cecil Hubert (brother) 1-3, 7, 9, 14, 35, 51, 52, 62, 64, 90, 96, 98, 104, 146, 167, 240, 247, 257, 259, 265, 272, 273
Lush, Christine (see also Sandford, Christine) 1-3, 7-9, 13, 14, 21
Lush, Florence Emma (Clark, mother) "FEL" ii, 1-5, 7-9, 11, 13, 19, 23, 25, 26, 35, 153, 156, 166, 167, 281, 282, 290-293, 296, 306
Lush, Hubert Stanley (father) i, 1, 2, 19, 23, 35
Lush, Joseph (grandfather) 1
Lush, Josephine 1
Lush, Marjorie (Smithers) 63, 90, 108
Lyttleton 136
Mackay, Charles 297-299, 301, 303, 304, 308, 315
Maclean, Sister Fiona 91, 100, 111, 160
MacMichael, Sir Harold 57-61, 64, 66-69, 71-73, 85, 87, 93
Macmillan, Rt Hon Harold/Lady Dorothy 167, 173, 174, 176-182, 187, 189, 191-193, 195-197, 199-204, 206, 207, 209, 210, 212-214, 219, 232, 235, 311
Macphail, James 103, 105, 106, 108
Maertens, Capt de Vaiseau 141, 142
Maffey, Sir John/Lady Dorothy 56, 61-63, 65-69, 72, 73, 85, 88, 93, 96, 97, 312
Maji Commission 27, 34
Makins, Sir Roger 167, 173, 202
Makonnen, Dejazmatch 119, 124, 125, 129, 131
Malan, Dr Daniel 256, 257
Mallowan, Prof Max 165, 291
Mason-MacFarlane, General Sir Noel 172, 173, 176-180, 182, 193, 197, 225
Matthew, Rev Austen 78
Maurice, Jack, "JK" 83
Mayne, Dr 108-113
Menelik, Emperor 30, 33, 34
Merceica, Victor 281
Meriel 96, 103, 104, 108, 114, 166, 240, 245, 248, 265, 273
MERRA (Middle East Relief and Refugee Administration) 249, 252, 262, 263
Messines 17
Military Cross (MC) 17, 18
Miller, Col "Dusty" 194, 198, 217, 222, 232, 235
Miller, Tony 285, 289
Minta, Judith/Tom 240, 272
Mitchell, General Sir Philip 118, 120, 124, 129, 137, 139, 144, 145, 253, 256
Moberly, Sir Walter/Lady 287, 293
Mohammed Dhahab 56, 70, 71, 90, 91, 99, 113
Monteath, J Guthrie 40, 42, 48
Montgomery, General Bernard (Viscount of Alamein) 151-155, 157-160, 165, 166, 173, 175, 176, 201, 210, 226
Monypenny 167
Moore, Maj Gen Sir Rodney 313

Moore, Olive 228, 231-234
More, R E, "Dick" 65, 66, 87
Moreton, Anne 247, 248
Moreton, Gp Capt Noel/Betty 96, 242, 247, 248, 288, 297, 307
Morse, David 253, 268
Morton, Sir Desmond 217, 218
Munro, Pat 55, 56, 58
Muntasser, Mahmoud 281, 283, 293-295
Muratib Ali, Sir Sayed 300, 305
Murphy, Bob 173, 176, 177, 181
Mustafa bin Halim 295
Nahas Pasha 65, 68, 70, 93, 105
Narayanganj 314
Newbold, Douglas 105, 106, 108, 109, 111-113, 160, 162, 168
Newdigate, Capt S 140
Nicholson, Nigel 172
Nicola 193, 194, 209, 214
Nolan, Pat 252
Noon, Malik Feroz Khan 288, 298-300, 305-307, 310, 311
Noon, Nur Khan 299
Norman, Gerald 155, 156
Nuttall, Wilfred 306, 316
OETA (Occupied Enemy Territories Administration) 121, 122, 124, 129-134, 136-138
Ogden, Ronnie 310
Osborne, Hope 291, 292
Owen, Colonel R C R 62, 87, 90
Palewski, Gaston 129
Parker, Geoffrey 145
Parr, Martin W 51, 57, 58, 61, 62, 66, 71, 73, 107
Pawson, Guy/Helen 75, 76, 79, 81, 84
Pearson, Maria 249
Pearson, Nanny 90, 91, 95, 96
Perham, Marjorie 136
Perry, Gordon 11, 35
Platnauer, Maurice 14
Platt, General Sir William
Platt, General William
Platt, Lt Gen Sir William, KCB 102, 111-113, 115, 117-123, 129, 134, 135, 137-139, 143-147, 149
Pluto 197, 227, 237
Pochin, Dr 91
Poletti, Col Charles 174, 175, 179, 182, 187-189, 192, 194, 198, 199, 205, 217-219, 222, 224, 236
Pope Pius XII 205, 206, 210, 242
Pope, Stanley 265
Pozieres Ridge 15, 16
Pratt, C L G 279, 280
Prichard, Evans 80
Purves, Donald/Mabel 96-98
Rabinowitch, Rev Major 163
Ramsey, Archbishop 316
Reallon, Monsieur 146
Reid, John 77, 79
Rennell, Lord Francis 145-148, 160, 166, 168, 171-174, 177, 226
Rey, Charles F 28, 34, 35
Richardson, "Whiskers"/Betty 40-43, 45-48, 99, 105, 106, 109-112
Riches 134
Robb, Maj R L 151, 155, 157
Roberts, Frank/Celeste 62, 65, 166, 252, 269, 272
Robertson, General Sir Brian 167, 173, 174, 184, 196, 198, 220, 230, 235

Rommel, Field Marshal Erwin 152, 162
Ross, Bill 106
Ross, Joe 63, 65, 66, 68, 69, 106
Rowlett, Sir Frederick 90
Royal Military Academy (RMA) Woolwich, "The Shop" 12-14, 26, 29
Rucker, Sir Arthur 253, 255, 256, 259, 260, 266, 273
Russell, Claud 32, 33
Russell Pasha 65
Russell, Patricia 184, 196, 220, 224
Ryder, Charles 87
Sandford, Christine 21, 23, 34, 35, 49, 291-293, 306
Sandford, Major/Colonel D A, DSO, "Dan" 13-15, 17-23, 25, 26, 34, 35
Sandford, Brigadier Daniel Arthur, CBE, DSO, "Dan"/Christine 39, 44, 49, 50, 61, 64, 65, 78, 94, 95, 102, 105, 107, 111-115, 117-119, 121, 130, 135-138
Sandford, Lieut Richard, VC, "Dick" 14, 18, 21
Sarell, Sir Roderick/Lady Pamela 96, 233-236, 240, 241, 265, 287
Saville, Charles 288, 289, 294
Scobie, General Ronald 168
Scully, Maj Tim 175, 242
Seapham, Brigadier 124
Searight 261
Shanti Seldon 299
Shaw, Bill 160
Shea, B S M, BC, DCM 59, 60, 88, 89
Shippe, Guy 128, 179, 208, 211, 220, 254
Shoucair Pasha 65
Simpson Jones, Lt Cdr 144, 146, 241
Skeet, Anne (see also Lindsell) 294-297, 302, 304, 305, 314, 315
Skeet, Hasler 123
Skeet, Ian 294
Skinners Company 10-12
Smallwood, General 125, 131, 146
Smithers, Marjorie (see also Lush, Marjorie) 7, 9
Smuts, General 139, 140, 142-145, 207, 234, 235, 254
Snow, Julian 176, 177, 190, 212, 217, 224, 231, 236
Somme 14-17, 19, 22
Spalding, Lee 103, 105, 106
Spears, Sir Ronald/Lady 160
Spellman, Archbishop 160
Spofford, General Chuck 173, 178
Stack, General Sir Lee 22, 39, 41, 49, 65, 70, 87, 93
Stafford, Frank 129, 131
Stansgate, Lord 181, 207, 232
Steer, George 119, 120, 131, 133
Stephens 289, 293, 306
Stephens, David 250, 257
Stevenson, K T 98
Stewart, Col Arthur 157, 184, 196, 208, 213, 236
Stewart, Hylton 9-11
Stokes, Dick, MP 228, 229, 231, 233
Stokes, Geoffrey 280
Stone, Admiral Ellery 179, 193, 200, 201, 207, 209, 212-214, 224, 237
Stork, Operation 226, 227
Storrs, Ronald 160, 167
Sturgess, Maj Gen R G, "Bob" 140-145
Suhrawaddy, Hussain Shaheed, PM 299, 305-307, 310, 313
Syfret, Rear Admiral E N 140, 142, 143
Sylvia 39, 81, 91, 95, 100, 111, 240, 245, 265, 273, 312-315
Symes, Sir Stewart/Lady Viola 39, 85, 87, 92-94, 103, 108, 111, 241, 242, 261
Symon, Sir Alec/Lady Dorothy 305, 312, 316

Tafari, Ras 25, 27-33, 35
Taffara Ato 137
Tait, Geoffrey 280, 306, 314-316
Talbot, Evan 179, 196, 200, 208, 211, 220
tanks 16, 17
Tasfai 32, 49, 50, 53, 57, 60, 78, 134, 136
Temnomeroff 243, 244
Temple, Archbishop William 68, 97
Theron, Frank/Adrey 224, 234, 261
Thesiger, Wilfred 22, 25, 31
Thomas, Bertram 259
Thomas, Eddie 285
Thorne, Colonel 172, 175
Thorold, Commander 142
Titherington, Geoffrey/Winifred 97, 99, 140
Tomlin, Col Julian 221, 222, 226, 229, 230
Tripoli, surrender of 153
Tynemouth 13, 14
Tyszkiewicz, Mish 250, 258, 259
Umberto, Prince of Piedmont 181, 185, 187, 192, 193, 201, 215, 229, 233
UNRRA (United Nations Relief and Rehabilitation Administration) 239-241, 243, 245-250
Upjohn, Lord Gerald 179, 181, 205, 213, 219, 220, 223
Vesuvius, eruption 177, 182-184, 187-191
Victor Emmanuel III, HM King 173, 176
Vidler, Canon 279, 280
Villa Carradoro, Posilipo 176, 180, 184, 194, 231
Villa Volpi 156, 160, 164, 167, 169, 261
Villa Zenardo 242
Villers Bretonneux 19, 20
Volpi, Count Giuseppi 156
Vyshinski 181
Waizara Mennen, Empress 31, 78, 136
Wajid Ali 298, 300, 305
Ward, Barrington 167
Ward Perkins, John/Margaret 231, 242, 291
Warren, Admiral 181, 234
Watt, Miss 280
Wavell, General Sir Archibald 117-124, 126, 127, 130, 137, 138
Weir, Sir Michael 285, 286
Werk, Ato Tafara 31
Wetherall, Maj Gen Charles 125-128, 132, 133
Whitaker, Capt Geoffrey RN 293
Wilbrandt, Dr Hans 250, 252, 259, 276
Willis, Charles Armine, "Chunky"/Clare 38-40
Wilson, General Jumbo 173, 177, 202, 207, 210, 220
Wingate, Erskine 120-122, 130, 133
Wingate, Sir Reginald 87
Winter, R K 57, 58, 60, 62, 67, 81, 89, 96, 100, 103, 115
Wisdom, Colonel 162
Wood, General Walter 243, 246
Wood, General John 240, 241, 243-247
Wreford Brown, Col Peter 282, 292
Wylie, Colonel Doughty 33
Ypres 19
Yule, Noel 295, 296
Zaphiro, Philip 26, 28
Zauditu, Empress 29, 30, 32, 33